Directory
A–Z

THIS EDITION WRITTEN AND RESEARCHED BY

Paula Hardy

Alison Bing, Abigail Blasi, Cristian Bonetto, Kerry Christiani, Gregor Clark,
Joe Fullman, Duncan Garwood, Robert Landon, Vesna Maric, Virginia Maxwell,
Olivia Pozzan, Brendan Sainsbury, Donna Wheeler, Nicola Williams

welcome to Italy

Bella Vita

In few places do art and life intermingle so effortlessly. This may be the land of Dante, Michelangelo, da Vinci and Botticelli but it's also the home of Salvatore Ferragamo, Giorgio Armani and Gualtiero Marchesi. Food, fashion, art and architecture – you'll quickly learn that the root of Italian pathology is an unswerving dedication to living life well. A surprising number of Italians care deeply about the floral aftertastes of sheep cheese, the correct way to cut marble and the nuances of a Vivaldi concerto. Lurking behind the *disinvoltura* – the appearance of effortlessness – is a passionate attention to life's fine print. So slow down, start taking note of life's details and enjoy your own *bella vita*.

Bon Appetito

Then there's the food. Italy is quite literally a feast of endless courses, but no matter how much you gorge yourself, you'll always feel as though you haven't made it past the antipasti. Even the simplest snack can turn into a revelation, whether you're downing a slice of Slow Food pizza, a paper cone of *fritto misto* (fried seafood) or pistachio-flavoured gelato. The secret is an intense, even savage, attention to top-notch ingredients and fresh, seasonal produce. Although the origins of Italian food are earthy and rustic, and the Slow Food Movement aims to protect those artisanal roots, the modern Italian kitchen is also endlessly inventive. Get creative in Eataly's Slow Food super-

Despite incessant praise, Italy continues to surprise and delight. If you get it right, travelling in the bel paese *(beautiful country) is one of those rare experiences in life that cannot be overrated.*

(left) View of Malcesine across Lago di Garda (p267)
(below) Duomo, Milan (p229)

market, sample top-class wines at Rome's International Wine Academy and tour vineyards and olive groves to learn the latest production techniques that go into making that award-winning wine and olive oil sitting on your dining table.

Bel Paese

As if in homage to its people's love of fashion, Italy's outline – a 'boot' – makes it one of the most recognisable countries in the world. It is long and elegant – *c'e bella* – and is flanked on three sides by four Mediterranean seas (the Adriatic, Ionian, Ligurian and Tyrrhenian). The northern wall of the Alps and the Dolomites frostily encircle the north, fringed by sparkling glacial lakes, while fiery volcanoes – Vesuvius, Etna and Stromboli – simmer in the south. Beyond the stereotypical image of art cities and museums, Italy is a place for doing as well as seeing. What can top descending the vertical chasm of the Gola Su Gorropu gorge or riding cowboy-style across the marshes of the Maremma and diving sun-split waters full of coral and barracuda? So, just when you think every nook and cranny of this amazing country has been explored, experienced and exhausted, flick through a few pages of this book and discover that some of Italy's best-kept secrets lie right beneath your nose.

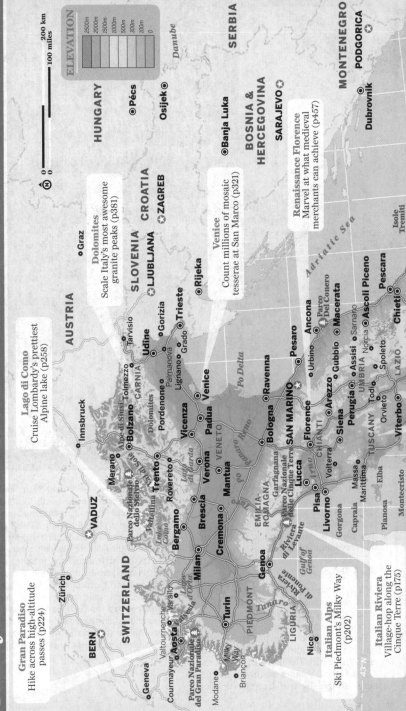

Gran Paradiso
Hike across high-altitude passes (p224)

Lago di Como
Cruise Lombardy's prettiest Alpine lake (p258)

Dolomites
Scale Italy's most awesome granite peaks (p381)

Venice
Count millions of mosaic tesserae at San Marco (p321)

Renaissance Florence
Marvel at what medieval merchants can achieve (p457)

Italian Alps
Ski Piedmont's Milky Way (p202)

Italian Riviera
Village-hop along the Cinque Terre (p175)

ELEVATION

2500m
2000m
1500m
1000m
500m
300m
100m
0

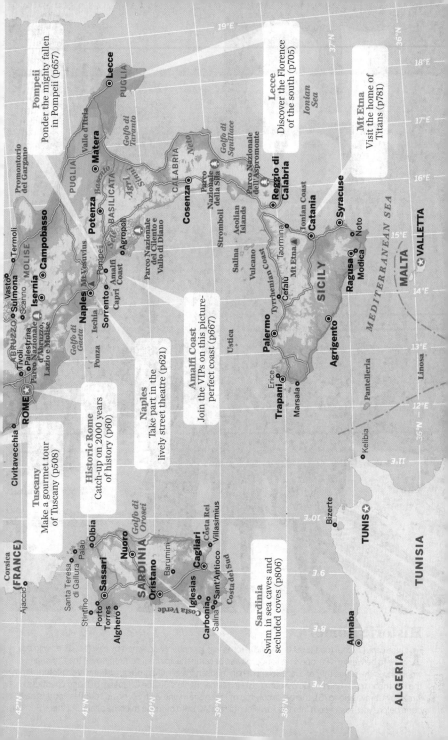

Tuscany
Make a gourmet tour of Tuscany (p508)

Historic Rome
Catch-up on 2000 years of history (p60)

Naples
Take part in the lively street theatre (p621)

Amalfi Coast
Join the VIPs on this picture-perfect coast (p667)

Sardinia
Swim in sea caves and secluded coves (p806)

Pompeii
Ponder the mighty fallen in Pompeii (p657)

Lecce
Discover the Florence of the south (p705)

Mt Etna
Visit the home of Titans (p781)

Corsica (FRANCE)
Ajaccio

Santa Teresa di Gallura
Stintino
Porto Torres
Alghero
SARDINIA
Sassari
Nuoro
Oristano
Barumini
Iglesias
Carbonia
Sant'Antioco
Costa del Sud
Costa Verde
Salina
Cagliari
Villasimius
Costa Rei
Golfo di Orosei
Olbia
Palau

ROME
Civitavecchia
Tivoli
Palestrina
Parco Nazionale d'Abruzzo, Lazio e Molise
Sulmona
Scanno
Vasto
Termoli
Campobasso
Isernia
MOLISE
ABRUZZO
Promontorio del Gargano
PUGLIA
Lecce
Matera
BASILICATA
Potenza
Golfo di Taranto
Valle d'Itria
Golfo di Squillace
Neto
CALABRIA
Cosenza
Parco Nazionale del Pollino
Parco Nazionale della Sila
Agri
Sinni
Basento
Parco Nazionale dell'Aspromonte
Reggio di Calabria
Ionian Coast
Catania
Syracuse
Noto
Taormina
Mt Etna
SICILY
Ragusa
Modica
Agrigento
Palermo
Cefalù
Tyrrhenian Coast
Vulcano
Salina
Stromboli
Aeolian Islands
Ustica
Erice
Trapani
Marsala

Golfo di Gaeta
Ponza
Ischia
Sorrento
Capri
Naples
Mt Vesuvius
Pompeii
Amalfi Coast
Agropoli
Parco Nazionale del Cilento e Vallo di Diano

Ionian Sea

MEDITERRANEAN SEA

MALTA
VALLETTA

Pantelleria
Linosa
Kelibia
Bizerte
TUNIS
TUNISIA
Annaba
ALGERIA

18 TOP EXPERIENCES

Historic Rome

1 Once *caput mundi* (capital of the world), Rome was legendarily spawned by a wolf-suckled wild boy, grew to be Western Europe's first superpower, became the spiritual centrepiece of the Christian world and is the repository of over two and a half thousand years of European art and architecture. From the Pantheon (p73) and the Colosseum (p61) to Michelangelo's Sistine Chapel (p110) and countless works by Caravaggio (p78), there's simply too much to see in one visit. So, do as countless others have done before you: toss a coin into the Trevi Fountain (p140) and promise to come again. St Peter's Basilica

Virtuoso Venice

2 Stepping through the portals of Basilica di San Marco (p321), try to imagine what it might have been like for an illiterate, burlap-clad, medieval peasant glimpsing those shimmering gold mosaic domes for the first time. It's not such a stretch – once you see those millions of tiny gilt tesserae (hand-cut glazed tiles) cohere into a singular heavenly vision, every leap of the human imagination since the 12th century seems comparatively minor.

Ruins of Pompeii

4 Nothing piques human curiosity quite like a mass catastrophe and few can beat the ruins of Pompeii (p657), a once thriving Roman town frozen 2000 years ago in its death throes. Wander the Roman streets, exploring the column-lined forum, the city brothel, the 5000-seat theatre and the frescoed Villa dei Misteri, and ponder Pliny the Younger's terrifying account of the tragedy: 'Darkness came on again, again ashes, thick and heavy. We got up repeatedly to shake these off; otherwise we would have been buried and crushed by the weight'.

Renaissance Florence

3 From Brunelleschi's red-tiled dazzler, the Duomo (p458), to Michelangelo's greatest hits, *David* (p469) and Botticelli's *The Birth of Venus* (p463), Florence, according to Unesco, contains 'the greatest concentration of universally renowned works of art in the world'. Whereas Rome and Milan have torn themselves down and been rebuilt many times, central Florence looks much as it did in 1550, with stone towers and cypress-lined gardens. The effect is rather like a Renaissance painting, which makes perfect sense when you think about it.

RICHARD I'ANSON / LONELY PLANET IMAGES ©

Amalfi Coast

5 With its scented lemon groves, flower-strewn cliffsides, bobbing fishing boats and tumbling, sherbet-hued towns, the Amalfi Coast still claims the crown as the prettiest coast on the peninsula. Others may argue that the title belongs to Liguria's Cinque Terre or Calabria's Costa Viola, but the Hollywood divas and starry-eyed day trippers agree. The stretch from Sorrento (p662) to Positano (p667) is the least developed and most beautiful. Positano

Museum Madness

6 A browse through your art history textbook will no doubt highlight seminal movements such as classical, Renaissance, mannerist, baroque, futurist and metaphysical – all of which were forged in Italy by artists including Giotto, da Vinci, Michelangelo, Botticelli, Bernini, Caravaggio, Carracci, Boccioni, Balla and de Chirico. Find the best of them in Rome's Museo e Galleria Borghese (p111) and swish new MAXXI gallery (p113), Florence's Uffizi (p463), Venice's Galleria dell'Accademia (p335), Bergamo's Accademia Carrara (p275) and Milan's Museo del Novecento (p232). Uffizi Gallery

JEAN-PIERRE LESCOURRET / LONELY PLANET IMAGES ©

The Dolomites

7 Scour the globe and you'll find plenty of taller, bigger and more geologically volatile mountains, but few can match the romance of the pink-hued, granite Dolomites (p301). Maybe it's their harsh, jagged summits, dressed in spring with vibrant skirts of wildflowers, or the rich cache of Ladin legends that line their valleys – or perhaps it's just the notion that this tiny pocket of northern Italy has produced some of the most daring mountaineers on the planet.

GLENN VAN DER KNIJFF / LONELY PLANET IMAGES ©

Neapolitan Street Life

8 There's nothing like waking up to the sound of the Porta Nolana market (p628): what a feast for the senses! It's as much akin to a North African bazaar as to a European market – fruit vendors raucously hawk their wares in Neapolitan dialect, swordfish heads seem to cast sidelong glances at you across piles of sardines on ice, then there's the irresistible perfume of lemons and oranges and the just-baked aroma of *sfogliatelle* (sweetened ricotta pastries).

9 Often regarded as just plain 'dark', the Italian Middle Ages had an artistic brilliance that's hard to ignore. Perhaps it was the sparkling hand-cut mosaic of Ravenna's Byzantine basilicas (p445) that provided the guiding light, but something inspired Giotto di Bondone to leap out of the darkness with his daring naturalistic frescoes in Padua's Scrovegni Chapel (p366) and the Basilica di San Francesco in Assisi (p562). With them he gave the world a new artistic language and from then it was just a short step to Masaccio's *Trinity* (p468) and the dawning light of the Renaissance. Basilica di Sant'Apollinare Nuovo, Ravenna

Lovely Lake Como

10 Formed at the end of the last ice age, dazzling Lake Como, nestled in the shadow of the Rhaetian Alps, is the most spectacular of the Lombard lakes, its grand Liberty-style villas home to movie moguls and Arab sheikhs. Surrounded on all sides by luxuriant greenery, the lake's siren calls include the landscaped gardens of Villa Melzi d'Eril (p262), Villa Carlotta (p264) and Villa Balbianello (p263), which blush pink with camellias, azaleas and rhododendrons in April and May.

Italian Riviera

11 For the sinful inhabitants of the Cinque Terre's (p175) five villages – Monterosso, Vernazza, Corniglia, Manarola and Riomaggiore – penance involved a lengthy and arduous hike up the vertiginous cliffside to the local village sanctuary to appeal for forgiveness. Scale the same sanctuary trails today, through terraced vineyards and hillsides covered in *macchia* (shrubbery), and it's hard to think of a more benign punishment as the heavenly views unfurl. Riomaggiore

Coastal Landscapes

12 The English language doesn't contain sufficient adjectives to describe the varied blue, green and, in the deepest shadows, purple hues of Sardinia's seas. Picture-perfect they may be, but Sardinia is still a wild, raw place with rugged coastal scenery from the tumbledown boulders of Santa Teresa di Gallura (p835) and the wind-chiselled cliff face of the Golfo di Orosei (p844) to the celebrity-crammed Costa Smeralda (p834) and the windswept beauty of the Costa Verde's dune-backed beaches (p821). Spiaggia Scivu

13 Break bread with celebrity restaurateur Fabbio Picchi at members club Teatro del Sale (p483) and sample simple, heart-warming, belly-filling Tuscan cooking. The secret ingredient in Tuscan cuisine is, well, the ingredients. In a land of legendary flavours, from San Miniato truffles (p508) to wild-boar sausages and hunks of bluish *bistecca alla fiorentina* (T-bone steak), Tuscan farmers still tend to their pigs, cows, olives and grapes with the pride of artisans. Sample the very best at Il Santo Bevitore (p484) and Osteria di Passignano (p528). Central Market, Florence

Savoy Palaces

14 Equivalent to the Medicis in Florence and the Borgheses in Rome, Turin's Savoy princes had a penchant for extravagant royal palaces. While Turin's Palazzo Madama (p195) and Palazzo Reale (p195) are impressive enough, they barely hold a candle to Italy's mini-Versailles the Reggia de Venaria Reale (p196). The none-too-modest hunting lodge of Duke Carlo Emanuele II is one of the largest royal residences in Europe and its mammoth €200-million restoration involved the preservation of 11,000 sq ft of frescoes and 1.5 million sq ft of stucco and plasterwork. Reggia de Venaria Reale

Parco Nazionale del Gran Paradiso

15 Italy's 'Grand Paradise' was the country's first national park, bequeathed by Vittorio Emanuele II when he donated his hunting reserve to the state in 1922. Part of the Graian Alps, it encompasses 724km of marked trails and mule tracks, 57 glaciers, Alpine pastures awash with wild pansies, gentians and Alpenroses, and a healthy population of Alpine ibex for whose protection the park was originally established. The eponymous Gran Paradiso mountain (4061m) is the only mountain in the park, which is accessed from quiet Cogne (p224).

Italian Alps

16 What the Valle d'Aosta (p219) lacks in size (it is Italy's smallest, least populous region) it more than makes up for in height, for this narrow valley is ringed by the icy peaks of some of Europe's highest mountains including Mont Blanc, the Matterhorn, Monte Rosa and Gran Paradiso. Equipped with some of the best skiing facilities on the continent you can descend hair-raisingly into France, Switzerland or Piedmont from the prestigious resorts of Courmayeur, Cervinia and Monterosa.

Baroque Lecce

17 The extravagant architectural character of many Puglian towns is down to the local style of *barocco leccese* (Lecce baroque). The local stone was so soft, art historian Cesare Brandi boasted it could be carved with a pen-knife. Craftsmen vied for ever greater heights of creativity, crowding facades with swirling veg-etal designs, gargoyles and strange zoomorphic figures. Lecce's Basilica di Santa Croce (p705) is the high point of the style, so outrageously busy the Marchese Grimaldi said it made him think a lunatic was having a nightmare.

Mount Etna

18 Known to the Greeks as the 'column that holds up the sky', Mt Etna (p781) is Europe's largest volcano and one of the world's most active. The ancients believed the giant Tifone (Typhoon) lived in its crater and lit up the sky with regular, spectacular pyrotechnics. At 3329m it literally tow-ers above Sicily's Ionian Coast, and since 1987 its slopes have been part of the Parco dell'Etna, an area that encompasses both alpine forests and the forbiddingly black summit.

GREG ELMS / LONELY PLANET IMAGES ©

MICHAEL GEBICKI / LONELY PLANET IMAGES ©

need to know

Currency
» Euro (€)

Language
» Italian

When to Go

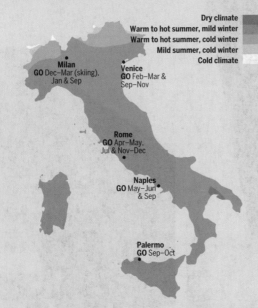

Dry climate
Warm to hot summer, mild winter
Warm to hot summer, cold winter
Mild summer, cold winter
Cold climate

Milan
GO Dec–Mar (skiing),
Jan & Sep

Venice
GO Feb–Mar &
Sep–Nov

Rome
GO Apr–May,
Jul & Nov–Dec

Naples
GO May–Jun
& Sep

Palermo
GO Sep–Oct

High Season
(Jul–Aug)

» Queues at big
sights and on the
road, especially in
August.

» Prices rocket for
Christmas, New Year
and Easter.

» Late December to
March is high season
in the Alps and
Dolomites.

Shoulder
(Apr–Jun & Sep–Oct)

» Good deals on
accommodation,
especially in the
south.

» Spring is best for
festivals, flowers and
local produce.

» Autumn provides
warm weather and
the grape harvest.

Low Season
(Nov–Mar)

» Prices at their
lowest – up to 30%
less than in high
season.

» Many sights
and hotels closed
in coastal and
mountainous areas.

» A good period for
cultural events in
large cities.

Your Daily Budget

Budget less than
€100

» Dorm bed: €15–25

» Double room in a
budget hotel: €50–100

» Pizza or pasta:
€8–12

» Excellent markets
and delis for
self-catering

Midrange
€100–200

» Double room in a
hotel: €80–180

» Lunch and dinner
in local restaurants:
€25–45

Top end over
€200

» Double room in a
four- or five-star hotel:
€200–450

» Top restaurant
dinner: €50–150

Money

» ATMs at every airport, most train stations and widely available in towns and cities. Credit cards accepted in most hotels and restaurants.

Visas

» Generally not required for stays of up to 90 days (or at all for EU nationals); some nationalities need a Schengen visa (p918).

Mobile Phones

» European and Australian phones work; other phones should be set to roaming. Use a local SIM card for cheaper rates on local calls.

Driving

» Drive on the right; the steering wheel is on the left side of the car. Be aware that headlights are legally required on all motorways (even during the day).

Websites

» **Lonely Planet** (www.lonelyplanet. com/italy) Destination information, hotel bookings, travellers forum and more.

» **Trenitalia** (www. trenitalia.com) Italian railways website.

» **Agriturismi** (www. agriturismi.it) Guide to farm accommodation.

» **Slow Food** (www. slowfood.com) For the best local producers, restaurants and markets.

» **Enit Italia** (www. italiantourism.com) Official Italian-government tourism website.

Exchange Rates

Australia	A$1	€0.72
Canada	C$1	€0.71
Japan	¥100	€0.98
NZ	NZ$1	€0.57
Switzerland	Sfr1	€0.82
UK	UK£1	€1.16
US	US$1	€0.75

For current exchange rates see www.xe.com.

Important Numbers

To dial listings in this book from outside Italy, dial your international access code (00), Italy's country code (39) then the number (including the '0').

Italy's country code	☑ +39
International access code	☑ +00
Ambulance	☑ +118
Police	☑ +113
Fire	☑ +115

Arriving in Italy

» **Fiumicino airport**
Trains & Buses: every 30 minutes, 6am to 11pm
Night Bus: hourly, 12.30am to 5am
Taxis: €40 set fare; 45 minutes

» **Malpensa airport**
Malpensa Express & Shuttle: every 30 minutes, 5am to 10.30pm
Night Bus: limited services, 11pm to 5am
Taxi : €79 set fare; 50 minutes

» **Capodichino airport**
Airport Shuttle: every 20 minutes, 6.30am to 11.40pm
Taxi: €19 set fare; 30 minutes

In Italy to Shop!

Ever wondered how every Italian seems to own a stash of fine merino wool Prada knitwear, a Ferragamo bag and a whole host of designer footwear and eyewear? How do they afford it?

What you lack, but what every style-conscious Italian knows, is exactly when and where to shop for bargains. Time your trip right and pick up designer fashion for a snip of the usual price at the annual sales (saldi) in January and July. Discounts start at 30% and increase to 50% as the sale goes on, but get there early if you don't want to be left with the oversized, ill-fitting, odd-coloured items that have been rejected by the rest of the shopping fraternity. At other times of the year score at the big city flea markets or head for the discount outlets in Lombardy and Piedmont (see p250).

first time

Everyone needs a helping hand when they visit a country for the first time. There are phrases to learn, customs to get used to and etiquette to understand. The following section will help demystify Italy so your first trip goes as smoothly as your fifth.

Language

Unlike many other European countries, English is not widely spoken in Italy. Of course, in the main tourist centres you can get by, but in the countryside and south of Rome you'll need to master a few basic phrases. This will improve your experience no end, especially when ordering in restaurants, some of which have no written menu. See the language section of this book (p931) for all the phrases you'll need to get by.

Booking Ahead

Reserving a room is essential during high season and key events (such as the furniture and fashion fairs in Milan) when demand is extremely high. Big-name restaurants and experiences (such as an evening at the opera) also need to be booked ahead.

Hello.	Buongiorno.
I would like to book...	Vorrei prenotare...
a single room	una camera singola
a double room	una camera doppia con letto matrimoniale
in the name of...	in nome di...
from... to... (date)	dal... al...
How much is it...?	Quanto costa...?
per night/per person	per la notte/per persona
Thank you very much.	Grazie (mille).

What to Wear

Appearances matter in Italy. The concept of *la bella figura* (literally 'making a good impression') encapsulates the Italian obsession with beauty, gallantry and looking good. Milan, the fashion capital of the country, is rigidly chic. Rome and Florence are marginally less formal, but with big fashion houses in town sloppy attire just won't do. In the city, suitable wear for men is generally trousers (pants) and shirts or polo shirts, and for women skirts, trousers or dresses. Shorts, T-shirts and sandals are fine in summer and at the beach, but long sleeves are required for dining out. For evening wear, smart casual is the norm. A light sweater or waterproof jacket is useful in spring and autumn, and sturdy shoes are a good idea when visiting archaeological sites.

What to Pack

» Passport
» Credit card
» Drivers licence
» Phrasebook
» Travel plug
» Mobile (cell) phone charger
» Sunscreen
» Waterproof jacket
» Camera
» Money belt
» Walking boots or sandals
» Beach bag or backpack
» Smart-casual clothes
» Universal adaptor
» Earplugs
» Hat and sunglasses
» Sweater, fleece or light jacket

Checklist

» Check the validity of your passport

» Check your airline's baggage restrictions

» Organise travel insurance (see p913)

» Make bookings (for big, popular sights and museums, opera and accommodation)

» Inform your credit/ debit card company of your travel plans

» Check if you can use your mobile (cell) phone (p916)

» Find out what you need to do to hire a car (see p925)

Etiquette

Italy is a surprisingly formal society; the following tips will help you avoid any awkward moments.

» Greetings

Shake hands and say *buongiorno* (good day) or *buona sera* (good evening) to strangers; kiss both cheeks and say *come stai* (how are you) to friends. Use *lei* (you) in polite company; use *tu* (you) with friends and children. Only use first names if invited.

» Asking for help

Say *mi scusi* (excuse me) to attract attention; and use *permesso* (permission) when you want to pass someone in a crowded space.

» Religion

Dress modestly (cover shoulders, torsos and thighs) and be quiet and respectful when visiting religious sites.

» Eating & Drinking

When dining in an Italian home, bring a small gift of sweets *(dolci)* or wine and dress well. Let your host lead when sitting and starting the meal. Take a small amount first so you can be cajoled into accepting a second helping. If you do not want more wine, leave your glass full. When dining out summon the waiter by saying *per favore* (please?).

Tipping

» When to Tip

Tipping is customary in restaurants, but optional elsewhere.

» Taxis

Optional, but most people round up to the nearest euro.

» Restaurants

Most restaurants have a cover charge *(coperto)*, usually €1 to €2, and a service charge *(servizio)* of 10% to 15%. If service isn't included a small tip is appropriate.

» Bars

There is no need to tip for drinks at a bar, although some people may leave small change; if drinks are brought to your table, tip as you would in a restaurant.

Money

Credit and debit cards can be used almost everywhere with the exception of some rural towns and villages. Visa and MasterCard are among the most widely recognised, but others like Cirrus and Maestro are also well covered. American Express is only accepted by some major chains and big hotels, and few places take Diners Club. Ask if bars and restaurants take cards before you order. Chip-and-pin is the norm for card transactions. ATMs are everywhere, but be aware of transaction fees. Some ATMs in Italy reject foreign cards. If this happens, try a few before assuming the problem is with your card. In theory you can change travellers cheques at banks and post offices, but some readers have reported problems and hefty commissions, even on cheques made out in euros. To avoid per-cheque charges get your cheques in large denominations.

what's new

For this new edition of Italy, our authors have hunted down the fresh, the transformed, the hot and the happening. These are some of our favourites. For up-to-the-minute recommendations, see lonelyplanet.com/italy.

MAXXI, Rome

1 Winner of the 2010 Stirling Prize for architecture, Rome's new MAXXI gallery, designed by Zaha Hadid, curves and coils like Kubrick's *Space Odyssey* interiors (p113).

Cinque Terre Trails

2 New national park bike trails (complete with bike rental) have opened along the Cinque Terre. Most trails head out from the Santuario della Madonna di Montenero (p223).

Sicilian Flights

3 Sicily's Trapani airport is busy expanding. Ryanair has added 13 new routes, including flights from Scandinavia and Eastern Europe (p803).

Museo del Vino a Barolo

4 Barolo's new interactive wine museum was designed by François Confino (the guy behind Turin's fab film museum). There's a different wine tasting every day (p210).

Venissa, Mazzorbo

5 Dine on rising star Paola Budel's inspired lagoon cuisine at Venissa. If you're lucky you may get to sample the estate's new vintage of the heritage Dorona grape (p358).

Sella Nevea, Giulie Alps

6 Looking for a bling-free ski base? Then try Sella Nevea. This resort has opened new ski lifts that link it to Bovec in Slovenia, making for a satisfying 30km of slopes (p408).

La Maddalena Hotel & Yacht Club

7 The US Navy's NATO barracks in the Maddalena archipelago has had one of the best facelifts of the year from star-chitects Zaha Hadid, William Sawaya and Dominique Perrault (p837).

Happy 150th Birthday

8 Turin's Museo Nazionale del Risorgimento Italiano opened just in time to celebrate the 150th anniversary of Italian unification. Take Italy's most interesting history lesson here (p194).

Pop-up Wine Shops, Carso

9 *Osmize* (private wine cellars) predate the pop-up phenomena by a few centuries, as 18th-century Carso farmers had the right to sell their surpluses once a year, tax-free. Now they're in fashion once again (p400).

Pur Südtirol, Merano

10 An inspired new concept shop showcasing top-notch farm produce and specially commissioned wood, glass and textiles, alongside a wine bar hosting regular tasting and cultural events (p308).

Family Apartments, Tuscany

11 Available on a nightly basis, Kristin and Kaare's family-friendly 2italia apartments fill a big gap in Tuscany's accommodation market. The pair also organises tours and cooking courses (p505).

Palazzo Grimani, Venice

12 Venice's Palazzo Grimani has reopened to the public after nearly 30 years. It houses Doge Antonio Grimani's Graeco-Roman antiquities and high-calibre temporary exhibitions (p343).

if you like...

Fabulous Food

Italy's bucolic hills, fertile valleys and terraced hillsides are a giant natural pantry, tended by farmers with pride. Bra's Slow Food Movement protects and promotes traditional producers and products – look out for its symbol, a well-fed snail.

Bologna Nicknamed *la grassa* (literally 'the fat'), Bologna straddles Italian food lines between the butter-led north and the tomato-based cuisine of the south (p420).

Truffles Go to Piedmont (p206), Tuscany (p508) and Umbria (p579).

Seafood So fresh you can eat it raw in Venice (p353), Sardinia (p806), Sicily (p743) and Puglia (p685).

Parmesan Parma's cheese (p429) is simply the most famous. Try the *burrata* (cheese made from mozzarella and cream) and the Taleggio, too.

Il Frantoio Its eight-course lunches are the definition of Slow Food (p703).

Pizza Italy's most famous export, but who makes the best: Naples (p637) or Rome (p123)?

Medieval Hill Towns

There's no simpler pleasure than wandering around the alleys of Italy's medieval villages. Hand-laid cobbles snake up hillsides to sculpted fountains, shuttered windows shade families sitting down to lunch and washing hangs like holiday bunting.

Asolo Perched mountainside, Asolo's nickname is 'the town of 100 vistas' (p377).

Umbria Medieval hill towns galore: start with Spello (p569), Spoleto (p576) and Macerata (p595).

Montalcino This medieval hill town is lined with wine bars where you can sample its celebrated Brunello wines (p536).

Cefalù Sun, sea, cobbled alleys and one of Sicily's finest mosaic-clad cathedrals (p760.

Il Castello Cagliari's *castello* (castle) contains a perfectly preserved medieval town (p810).

Maratea A 13th-century *borgo* (medieval town) with pint-sized piazzas, winding alleys and startling views across the Gulf of Policastro (p728).

Puglia From the Valle d'Itria (p699) to the sierras of the Salento (p705), Puglia is dotted with biscuit-coloured hilltop towns.

Wine Tasting

From Etna's elegant whites to Barolo's complex reds, Italian wines are as varied as the country's terrain. Sample them in cellars, over long, lazy lunches or dedicate yourself to a full-blown tour.

Wine routes Discover why chianti isn't just a cheap table wine left over from the 1970s on this delightful tour (p524).

Festa dell'Uva e del Vino In early October the wine town of Bardolino is taken over by wine and food stalls (p273).

VinItaly Sample exceptional, rarely exported blends at Italy's largest annual wine expo (p378).

Museo del Vino a Barolo Explore the history of wine through art and film at Barolo's new wine museum (p210).

Al Sorriso Expert food and wine pairings in one of Italy's finest restaurants (p258).

Valpolicella & Soave Wine tastings in these two Veneto regions are free and fabulous (p380).

Cantine Aperte Private wine cellars throughout the country open their doors to the public on the last Sunday in May.

» Palazzo Reale (p644), Caserta

Modern Art

Weighed down with over 2000 years of history, it sometimes seems as though Italy has entirely missed out on the era of modern art. Not so. Although often overshadowed by its illustrious past, there are some exciting modern developments, if you know where to look.

Biennale World-class, avant-garde art and architecture exhibitions take place annually in Venice on alternate years (p350).

MAXXI Rome's new contemporary art museum designed by architect of the moment Zaha Hadid (p113).

Museo del Novecento A first-class 20th-century art museum in modernist Milan (p232).

Palazzo Grassi The exceptional contemporary collection of French billionaire François Pinault is showcased against Tadao Ando interior sets (p334).

MADRE Don't miss Naples' big-name contemporary art collection (p628).

Museion Bolzano's contemporary collection highlights the ongoing dialogue between Trento, Austria and Germany (p301).

Arte Povera Castello di Rivoli is home to exhibits of Turin's radical, anti-establishment art movement of the 1960s (p195).

Villas & Palaces

From the residences of Roman emperors and Renaissance princes to the palatial homes of aristocratic dynasties, take a peek inside some of Italy's most extravagant homes and reconsider the concept that 'less is more'.

Rome Don't miss Palazzo e Galleria Doria Pamphilj (p77), Palazzo Farnese (p78) and Palazzo della Civiltà del Lavoro (p98).

Palazzi dei Rolli A collection of 42 Unesco-protected lodging palaces (p163).

Caserta One of the greatest achievements of Italian baroque architecture, Palazzo Reale was even worthy of a role in *Star Wars* (p644).

Palazzo Ducale The doge's palace complete with golden staircase and interrogation rooms (p321).

Villa Maser Andrea Palladio and Paolo Veronese conspired to create the Veneto's finest country mansion (p377).

Villa Romana del Casale See where the home decor obsession began with this Roman villa's 3500-sq-metre mosaic floor (p793).

Il Vittoriale degli Italiani Gabriele d'Annunzio's bombastic estate would put a Roman emperor to shame (p270).

Markets

Art nouveau arcades, star-chitect designed fairgrounds, stall-packed bazaars – Italy has a market to suit all tastes. Get there early and muscle in for the best buys.

Milan Italy's market city, Milan is furnished with world-class fairgrounds and a 'golden quad' of fabulous fashion (p229).

Porta Nolana Elbow your way past sing-song fishermen, fragrant bakeries and bootleg CD stalls for a slice of Neapolitan street theatre (p628).

Pescaria Shop for lagoon specialities in Venice's 600-year-old fish market (p357).

Catania Fruit, fish, meat and veg stalls packed down cobbled alleys beneath striped awnings, Catania's market is more African bazaar than Mediterranean market (p775).

Porta Portese A modern *commedia dell'arte* takes place every Sunday between vendors and bargain hunters at Rome's mile-long flea market (p139).

Arezzo On the first weekend of every month, Arezzo hosts Italy's oldest and biggest antiques market (p540).

Porta Palazzo The largest outdoor food market in Europe (p198).

If you like... surprises, take a tour of Naples' *sottosuolo* (underground) and explore Greek-era grottoes, Palaeo Christian burial chambers, royal Bourbon escape routes and WWII air-raid shelters.

Islands & Beaches

Counting all its offshore islands and squiggly indentations, Italy's coastline stretches 7600km from the sheer cliffs of the Cinque Terre, down through Rimini's brash resorts to the bijou islands in the Bay of Naples and Puglia's sandy shores.

Puglia Italy's best sandy beaches, including the gorgeous Baia dei Turchi (p715) and the cliff-backed beaches of the Gargano (p694).

Aeolian Islands Sicily's seven volcanic islands sport hillsides of silver-grey pumice, black lava beaches and lush green vineyards (p762).

The Lido Glamorous beach-going just 15 minutes by *vaporetti* (small passenger ferry) from Venice (p347).

Sardinia Take your pick of our favourite beaches (p821), including the Aga Khan's personal fave, Spiaggia del Principe (p833).

Procida Pastel-hued Procida is still a fishing village through and through (p653).

Rimini Swap high culture for raves on the beach in Rimini (p452).

Elba This island sits at the heart of the Parco Nazionale Arcipelago Toscano, Europe's largest marine park (p512).

Frescoes

Practised in ancient Egypt and Crete, India and Mexico, the art of *buon fresco* – painting pigment on lime mortar or plaster – has been around for millennia, but few examples boast the vivid narrative drama as seen in those of the Italian masters.

Sistine Chapel Michelangelo's show-stealing ceiling fresco (p110).

Pompeii The *Dionysiac Frieze* in the dining room of the Villa dei Misteri is one of the world's largest ancient frescoes (p657).

Giotto Masterly works in the Scrovegni Chapel (p366) and the Basilica di San Francesco (p562).

Matera Ancient cave churches, including the Crypt of Original Sin, are adorned with Old Testament scenes and saints (p723).

Chiesa di San Giovanni Evangelista Correggio's magnificent mannerist dome is quite literally a heavenly vision (p430).

Mantua For Mantegna's Camera degli Sposi (p278) and Camera dei Giganti (p278).

Pinturicchio Perugia (p549) and Spello (p569) showcase the work of Umbria's home-grown talent, Pinturicchio.

Gardens

First they fixed the drawing room and then they started on the garden; Italy's penchant for the 'outdoor room' has been going strong since Roman emperors landscaped their holiday villas. Renaissance princes refined the practice, but it was 19th-century aristocrats who really went to town.

Reggia de Venaria Reale Take a botanical, cultural or gastronomic tour to explore the 10 hectares of the Venaria's gardens (p196).

The Italian Lakes Fringed with fabulous gardens such as those at Isola Madre (p254), Villa Balbianello (p263) and Villa Taranto (p255).

Villa d'Este Tivoli's superlative High Renaissance garden dotted with fantastical fountains and cypress-lined avenues (p146).

Ravello View the Amalfi Coast from the Belvedere of Infinity (p675) and listen to classical music concerts in romantic 19th-century gardens (p675).

La Mortella A tropical paradise inspired by the gardens of Granada's Alhambra (p651).

Giardini Pubblici Venice's first green space and the home of the celebrated Biennale with its avant-garde pavilions (p343).

month by month

January

Following hot on the heels of New Year is Epiphany. In the Alps and Dolomites it's ski season, while in the Mediterranean south winters are mild and crowd-free, although many resort towns are firmly shut.

Regata della Befana

Witches in Venice don't ride brooms: they row boats. Venice celebrates Epiphany on 6 January with a fleet of brawny men dressed up as witches (*befane*).

Ski Italia

Italy's top ski resorts are in the northern Alps and the Dolomites, but you'll also find resorts in the Apennines, Le Marche and even Sicily. The best months of the season are January and February. See our pick of the pistes, p41.

February

'Short' and 'accursed', is how Italians describe February. In the mountains the ski season hits its peak in line with school holidays. Further south it's chilly, but almond trees blossom and herald the carnival season.

Carnevale

In the period leading up to Ash Wednesday, many Italian towns stage pre-Lenten carnivals. Venice's Carnevale (p350; www.carnevale.venezia.it) is the most famous. The largest is in Viareggio (p507).

Mostra Mercato del Tartufo Nero

An early-spring taste of truffles from the gastronomic Umbrian town of Norcia. Thousands of visitors sift through booths tasting all things truffle alongside other speciality produce (p580).

March

The weather in March is capricious: sunny, rainy and windy all at once. The official start of spring is 21 March, but the main holiday season starts with Easter week.

Settimana Santa

On Good Friday, the pope leads a candlelit procession to the Colosseum and on Easter Sunday he gives his blessing in St Peter's Square, while in Florence, a cartful of fireworks explodes in Piazza del Duomo (p477). Other notable processions take place in Taranto (Puglia; p719) and Trapani (Sicily; p802).

April

Spring has sprung and April sees the Italian peninsula bloom. The mountains of Sicily and Calabria are carpeted with wildflowers, while the gardens of the Italian north show off their tulips and early camellias.

Settimana del Tulipano

Tulips erupt in bloom in the grounds of Villa Taranto on Lake Maggiore; the dahlia path is also in bloom, as is the dogwood, in what is considered one of Europe's finest botanical gardens (p255).

VinItaly

Sandwiched between the Valpolicella and Soave wine regions, Verona hosts the world's largest wine fair, VinItaly (p378; www.vinitaly.com). Over five days 4000 international exhibitors turn your head with wine tastings, lectures and seminars.

May

The month of roses and early summer produce makes May a perfect time to travel, especially for walkers. The weather is warm but not too hot and prices throughout Italy are good value. It's also patron-saint season.

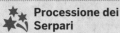 Processione dei Serpari

The strangest patron-saint day is held in Cocullo (p608). A statue of St Dominic is draped with live snakes and carried in the Snake Charmers' Procession.

Festa di San Gennaro

As patron-saint days go, Naples' Festa di San Gennaro has a lot riding on it: securing the city from volcanic and other disasters. The faithful gather in the cathedral to see San Gennaro's blood liquefy. If it does, the city is safe. Repeat performances take place on 19 September and 16 December (p634).

Ciclo di Rappresenta-zioni Classiche

Classical intrigue in an evocative setting, the Festival of Greek Theatre, held from mid-May to mid-June, brings Syracuse's 5th-century-BC amphitheatre to life with performances from Italy's acting greats (p786; www.indafondazione.org).

June

The summer season kicks off in June. The temperature cranks up quickly, beach lidos start to open in earnest and some of the big summer festivals commence. Republic Day, on 2 June, is a national holiday.

La Biennale di Venezia

Held in odd-numbered years, the Venice Biennale (p350; www.labiennale.org) is one of the art world's most prestigious events. Exhibitions are held in venues around the city from June to October.

Festival dei Due Mondi

Held in the Umbrian hill town of Spoleto from late June to mid-July, the Festival of Two Worlds (p577; www.spoletofestival.it) is an international arts event, featuring music, theatre, dance and art.

July

School is out and Italians everywhere are heading away from cities and to mountains or beaches for their summer holidays. Prices and temperatures rise. While the beach is in full swing, many cities host summer art festivals.

Il Palio

Daredevils in tights thrill the crowds with this chaotic bareback horse race (p520) around the piazza in Siena. Preceding the race is a parade in medieval costume. Held on 2 July and 16 August.

Taormina Arte

Ancient ruins and languid summer nights in July and August set a seductive scene for Taormina's arts festival (p772; www.taormina-arte.com). It features films, theatre and concerts.

Estate Romana

Between June and September Rome puts on a summer calendar of events that turn the city into an outdoor stage. The program encompasses music, dance, literature and film, and events are staged in some of Rome's most attractive venues (p115).

August

August in Italy is hot, expensive and crowded. Everyone is on holiday and, while not everything is shut, many businesses and restaurants do close for part of the month.

Ferragosto

After Christmas and Easter, Ferragosto, on 15 August, is Italy's biggest holiday. It marks the Feast of the Assumption, but even before Christianity the Romans honoured their gods on Feriae Augusti. Naples celebrates with particular fervour.

Mostra del Cinema di Venezia

The Venice Film Festival (p350) is held at the Lido and attracts the international film glitterati with its red-carpet premieres and paparazzi glamour.

September

This is a glorious month to travel in Italy. Summer waxes into autumn and the start of the harvest season sees lots of local *sagre* (food festivals) spring up. September is also the start of the grape harvest.

Festival delle Sagre

On the second Sunday of September over 40 communes in the province of Asti put their wines and local gastronomic products on display (www.festival dellesagre.it).

Regata Storica

On the first Sunday in September, gondoliers in period dress work those biceps in this regatta, where period boats are followed by gondola and other boat races along the Grand Canal in Venice (p350).

October

October is a fabulous time to visit the south, when the days still radiate with late-summer warmth and the *lidos* (beaches) are emptying out. Further north the temperature starts to drop and festival season comes to an end.

Salone Internazionale del Gusto

Hosted by the home-grown Slow Food Movement, this biennial food expo is held

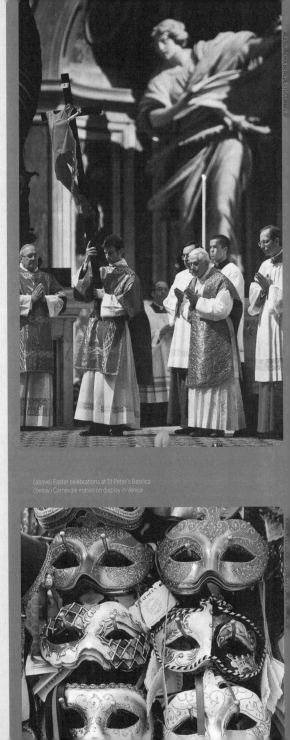

(above) Easter celebrations at St Peter's Basilica
(below) Carnevale masks on display in Venice

in Turin in even-numbered years (p197).

November

The advent of winter creeps down the peninsula in November, but there's plenty going on. Most notably, this is truffle season. It's also the time for the chestnut harvest, mushroom picking and All Saints' Day.

Ognissanti
Celebrated all over Italy as a national holiday, All Saints' Day on 1 November commemorates the Saint Martyrs, while All Souls' Day, on 2 November, is set aside to honour the deceased.

Truffle Season
From Alba (www.fieradeltartufo.org) and Asti in the north to Tuscany's San Miniato (www.san-miniato.com), November is prime truffle time.

Opera Season
Italy is home to four of the world's great opera houses: La Scala in Milan (p240), La Fenice in Venice (p360), Teatro San Carlo in Naples (p633) and Teatro Massimo in Palermo (p751). The season traditionally runs from mid-October to March, although La Scala opens later on St Ambrose Day, 7 December.

December

The days of alfresco living are firmly at an end. December is cold and Alpine resorts start to open for the early ski season, although looming Christmas festivities warm things up.

Natale
The weeks preceding Christmas are studded with religious events. Many churches set up nativity scenes known as *presepe*. Naples (p622) is especially famous for these. On Christmas Eve the pope gives midnight mass in St Peter's Square (p103).

itineraries

Whether you've got six days or 60, these itineraries provide a starting point for the trip of a lifetime. Want more inspiration? Head online to lonelyplanet.com/thorntree to chat with other travellers.

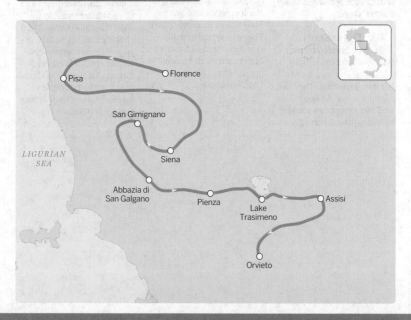

Two Weeks
Classic Art Cities

> The centre of the Renaissance and home to Michelangelo and Dante, Tuscany and Umbria's treasury of architectural styles and artistic expression have made them justifiably world-famous. Start this two-week exploration with three days in **Florence**, where the entire scooter-crammed centre is a World Heritage Site and the Uffizi Gallery houses Italy's finest collection of Renaissance art. Decamp to **Pisa** to see the architectural ensemble that makes up the Piazza dei Miracoli and then swap Renaissance for Gothic in **Siena**, spending at least two days before heading on to the fairy-tale medieval towers of **San Gimignano**; arrive late in the day so you can enjoy the tiny hill town without the strain of crowds. On day eight make a slow procession to **Pienza**, stopping at the **Abbazia di San Galgano** on the way. From Pienza, skirt the southern shore of **Lake Trasimeno** to reach **Assisi**, where you can admire those Giotto frescoes that caused such a stir in the Middle Ages. You'll want at least two days to do them justice before heading southeast to end with **Orvieto**'s lavish, mosaic-clad cathedral.

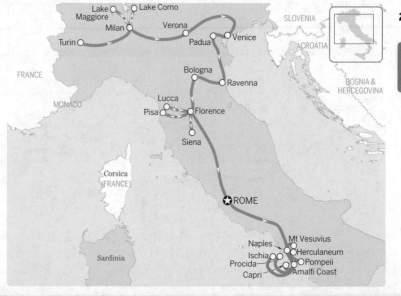

The Grand Tour

> Originally the preserve of aristocratic young men – part scholar's pilgrimage, part rite of passage – the grand tour is now for anyone with enough time on their hands to travel the length of the Italian peninsula from north to south (or vice versa). The itinerary traditionally started in **Turin** (and, less often, **Milan**). In Turin your cultural guide might show you the Savoy palaces, in particular the Venaria Reale, Italy's mini-Versailles, and in Milan, Leonardo da Vinci's *The Last Supper*. Short excursions to **Lake Maggiore** or **Lake Como** might also be in order to enjoy the landscaped lake gardens of Villa Taranto and Villa Carlotta respectively. Board the train for **Venice**, stopping in **Verona** for a night or two along the way to catch some opera in the Roman Arena. At least four days are needed to enjoy the architectural masterpiece that is Venice – the 'locus of decadent Italianate allure'.

During week two start your journey south by taking in Giotto's ground-breaking frescoes in **Padua**'s Scrovegni Chapel, **Ravenna**'s dazzling Byzantine mosaics and **Bologna**'s culinary delights before pausing in **Florence** for a few days. Here grand tour days were filled with extensive museum visits admiring the monuments and art works of the Renaissance alongside Roman sculptures in the archaeological museum. Day trips to Romanesque **Lucca**, Renaissance **Pisa** or Gothic **Siena** might also feature, time permitting.

By week three you will have arrived in **Rome** to study the ruins of the ancient world and the exhaustive art collections at the Vatican, Villa Borghese and Capitoline Hill. Don't try to do it all! Select a few highlights to enjoy and allow plenty of time for coffee in Piazza Navona or dinner in some of Rome's more avant-garde restaurants. Then, head straight to **Naples** for opera at the Teatro San Carlo and archaeological day trips to **Herculaneum** and **Pompeii**. Consider also exploring the city's catacombs or scaling **Mt Vesuvius**. Then end your month-long tour along the romantic **Amalfi Coast** from where you can day trip to the offshore islands of **Capri**, **Ischia** or **Procida**.

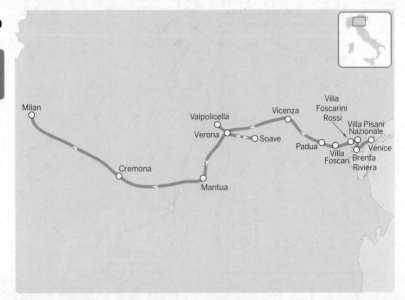

Two Weeks
Venice to Milan

In the 16th century the Venetian summer began early in June, when every household loaded onto barges for a summer sojourn along the **Brenta Riviera**. You too can make like a Venetian on a boat trip along the Riviera after spending a few days in **Venice**. Marvel at the Tiepolo frescoes of **Villa Pisani Nazionale**, drop in to the Shoemakers' Museum at **Villa Foscarini Rossi** and stop in at Palladio's **Villa Foscari**.

Boat trips end in **Padua** where you can overnight overlooking the Basilica di Sant'Antonio. Don't miss the small wonders next door in honour of St George: the frescoed Oratorio di San Giorgio and the Titian-filled Scoletta del Santo. With advance booking, you can see Padua's crowning glory: Giotto's frescoed Scrovegni Chapel, or head for the historic centre to linger at a cafe in Padua's arcaded twin piazzas.

On day six hop on the train to **Vicenza**. Spend the afternoon watching sunlight ripple across the soaring facades of Palladio's *palazzi* (mansions) and illuminate the story-book Villa Valmarana 'ai Nani', covered floor-to-ceiling with frescoes by Giambattista and Giandomenico Tiepolo, before heading on to **Verona** for three or four days. Here mornings can be spent viewing Mantegnas at Basilica di San Zeno Maggiore, while afternoons call for window-shopping on Via Mazzini. Then listen to opera in the Roman Arena and wander Verona's balconied backstreets where Romeo wooed Juliet.

From Verona, day trip northwest to **Valpolicella**, where you can sample the highly prized Amarone by appointment at Montecariano Cellars, or back east to **Soave** for a sampling of its namesake DOC white wine at Azienda Agricola Coffele.

On day 11 dip southwest to regal **Mantua** for an impressive display of dynastic power and patronage at the Gonzagas' fortified family pad, the Palazzo Ducale. Or for something altogether more dramatic witness the giants trying to storm Mt Olympus in Giulio Romano's fresco in the Camera dei Giganti at Palazzo Te.

Finally, wind up with a two-day stop in **Cremona** where you can chat with artisans in one of the 100 or so violin-making shops around Piazza del Comune before hearing them in action at the Teatro Amilcare Ponchielli and then heading on to end your tour in **Milan**.

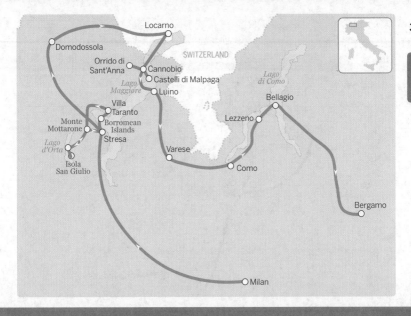

Two Weeks
A Lakes Tour

A short drive northwest of **Milan**'s Malpensa airport and you're on the edge of one of Italy's most serene scenes, Lago Maggiore. Like grandees before you, this tour takes you up the west flank of the lake into Switzerland (keep an ID or passport with you) via belle époque **Stresa**.

Spend three nights in Stresa and visit the lavish villas and gardens of the **Borromean Islands**: Isola Madre for its romantic gardens and wisteria-clad Staircase of the Dead; and Isola Bella for its priceless art collection, vast ballrooms and shell-encrusted grotto. Picnic amid the tulips and rhododendrons of **Villa Taranto** and take the funicular up to **Monte Mottarone**. Day trip to **Lago d'Orta** and the bijou **Isola San Giulio**.

On day four head north from Stresa via the Lago Maggiore Express to **Domodossola**, cutting back east on the quaint Centovalli, or 'Hundred Valleys', railway, which whisks you along a vertigo-inducing track above swooping valleys to swanky **Locarno** in Switzerland. In Locarno wander ancient piazzas and admire the Lombard architecture, before joining market-goers on the ferry back to **Cannobio** in Italy. Nestled at the foot of the Val Cannobino, Cannobio makes a good base for a few days of walking, cycling or sailing. A tour up the valley affords fabulous views from the narrow gorge **Orrido di Sant'Anna**, while boat trips bob around the ruined **Castelli della Malpaga**.

Finally, on day eight skip across the lake to **Luino** on the eastern shore and straight on to celebrity haunt **Como**, via **Varese**. Amble the flower-laden lakeside to view art exhibits at Villa Olmo before finding a shady sunlounger poolside at the Lido di Villa Olmo. You could spend days playing in Como, hiring out seaplanes and boats, or hiking the mountainous hinterland of the Triangolo Lariano. If you're ambitious you can walk all the way to chic **Bellagio**. Otherwise take the lake road on day 10 and lunch on perch in **Lezzeno**.

Try not to be seduced by Bellagio's beauty and save two days at the end of your trip for patrician **Bergamo**. Here you can finish your tour in style with the extraordinary Carrara art collection and some of the finest Lombard-Renaissance architecture in the region.

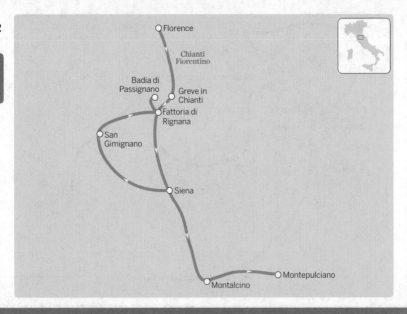

One Week
Tuscan Wine Routes

With its beautifully crafted landscapes of olive groves, vineyards and cypresses, central Italy is more than a catalogue of grand-slam sites. Start this wine tour with a big *cin-cin* in **Florence**, wining and dining in top Tuscan style at wine cellar–bakery Cantinetta dei Verrazzano, where you can sip prized vintages while munching on salty radicchio-topped focaccia. Other key wine addresses include Francesco Vini, Il Santino and Le Volpi e l'Uva. Or perhaps take a preparatory one-day wine course at the Food & Wine Academy before you set off? Versed in the ways of a true oenophile, head south out of town to Chianti Fiorentino.

Tour the new wine museum at **Greve in Chianti** to get a better understanding of Chianti's long and illustrious history as a wine making region, then taste top-class regional wines at Le Cantine di Greve in Chianti. While in Chianti, spend a couple of nights on a farm at **Fattoria di Rignana**. And what a farm: 120 acres of vineyards, woodland and olive groves, growing Sangiovese, merlot, Malvasia, Trebbiano Bianco and the precious Canaiolo Nero grape, which forms the base ingredient of vintage Chianti Classico. While there, day trip to the historic wine cellars at **Badia di Passignano** and dine at the Antinori Estate's Osteria di Passignano.

From here you have a choice: continue south via **Siena** to **Montalcino**, home of Tuscany's finest wine, Brunello, or after stopping in Siena loop back northwest towards Florence and pick up the Strada del Vino Vernaccia di San Gimignano, where you can arrange a Vernaccia vineyard tour and overnight in the medieval city of **San Gimignano**.

If you decide to head south to Montalcino you can join the town in celebrating its new vintage in February at Benvenuto Brunello; otherwise, make the pilgrimage to Ristorante di Poggio Antico for a tour of its award-winning vineyard followed by a meal and tasting. End in rival wine-town **Montepulciano**, where you can tour the cellars of Cantine Contucci and Cantina del Redi, and take a raft of wine tours offered by the association of the Strada del Vino Nobile di Montepulciano. In June you can enjoy it all along with classical concerts in Palazzo Ricci.

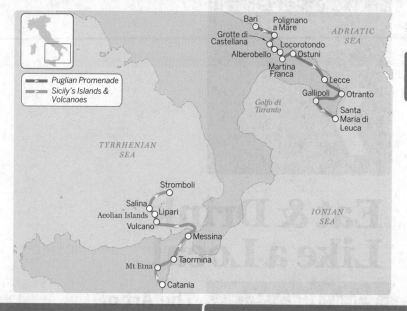

Map legend:
- Puglian Promenade
- Sicily's Islands & Volcanoes

Locations shown: Bari, Polignano a Mare, Grotte di Castellana, Locorotondo, Alberobello, Ostuni, Martina Franca, Lecce, Gallipoli, Otranto, Santa Maria di Leuca, ADRIATIC SEA, Golfo di Taranto, TYRRHENIAN SEA, IONIAN SEA, Stromboli, Salina, Aeolian Islands, Lipari, Vulcano, Messina, Taormina, Mt Etna, Catania

Two Weeks
Puglian Promenade

For the majority of visitors to Italy, a trip 'south' means Naples and the Amalfi Coast: what a shame! Puglia, which forms the heel of Lo Stivale (The Boot), is one of the country's most underrated regions. Fly in to **Bari**, where you find the relics of Father Christmas in the Romanesque cathedral. Strike out south, via **Polignano a Mare**, to the famous **Grotte di Castellana**. From here a two- to three-day drive south will take you through some of the finest Valle d'Itria towns, including **Alberobello**, with its hobbit-like, conical *trulli* houses, wine-producing **Locorotondo**, beautiful baroque **Martina Franca** and chic, whitewashed **Ostuni**. In Martina Franca you get just a small taste of what is awaiting you in **Lecce**, otherwise known as the 'Florence of the south' for its operatic architectural ensembles and scholarly bent. Hire a bike and spend at least three or four days there before striking out to the fortified ports of **Otranto** in the southeast or **Gallipoli** in the southwest, with their sandy blue-flag accredited beaches. If you don't get caught up gulping raw sea urchins and octopuses, push south to **Santa Maria di Leuca**, the very tip of the Italian stiletto.

10 Days
Sicily's Islands & Volcanoes

It's well known that Italy is the country with the most World Heritage Sites, but it's less well known that those sites sit in Europe's most volcanically active country. In fact, Italy is home to mainland Europe's only active volcanoes – Mt Vesuvius, Stromboli and Etna. Fly in to **Catania**, and spend a day or two admiring a city built almost entirely from black lava rock. Then head straight up to the crater rim of **Mt Etna** either under your own steam or on a guided tour of grottoes and lava tunnels. On day four move on to picturesque **Taormina** to view Etna framed by the crumbling Roman backdrop of the amphitheatre, before heading to the port at **Messina** to catch the hydrofoil for the **Aeolian Islands**. For the next six days island-hop along this volcanic ridge, enjoying natural volcanic mudbaths on **Vulcano**, exploring pumice mines on **Lipari**, trekking the twin peaks of **Salina**'s extinct craters and watching **Stromboli**'s constant pyrotechnics against a still night sky.

Eat & Drink Like a Local

When to Go

While *sagre* (local food festivals) go into overdrive in autumn, there's never a bad time to raise your fork in Italy. For specific details on food events, see p24.

Spring (Mar–May)

Asparagus, artichokes and Easter specialities, plus a handful of festivals like Turin's Cioccolatò (p197) and Ascoli Piceno's Fritto Misto all'Italiana (p598).

Summer (Jun–Aug)

Time for eggplants, peppers, berries and seafood by the sea. Beat the heat with gelato and Sicilian *granita*.

Autumn (Sep–Nov)

Food festivals galore and gems like chestnuts, mushrooms and game. Truffle hunters head to Piedmont, Tuscany and Umbria while wine connoisseurs hit Elba's wine harvest and Merano's wine festival.

Winter (Dec–Feb)

Time for Christmas and Carnevale treats. Fishermen serve up sea urchins and mussels on Sardinia's Poetto beach, while Umbria celebrates the black truffle with the Mostra Mercato del Tartufo Nero (p580).

The Art of Eating Well

A bulging boot of enviable produce and culinary know-how, Italy is a paradise for taste buds. Locals are fiercely proud of their regions' specialities, and tucking into them is an essential part of any Italian sojourn. Whet your appetite with the following food-trip essentials; to dig deeper see (p898).

Food Experiences

So much produce, so many specialities, so little time! Fine-tune your culinary radar with the following edible musts.

Meals of a Lifetime

» **Pizzarium, Rome** (p129) Superlative dough and toppings make for unforgettable *pizza al taglio* (pizza by the slice).

» **All'Arco, Venice** (p354) Top-of-the-class *cicheti* (Venetian tapas) in new- and old-school flavours.

» **La Locanda di Pietracupa** (p528) Elegant, modern takes on classic Tuscan dishes in the vino-versed Chianti region.

» **Il Cigno, Mantua, Lombardy** (p281) Superbly executed Lombard specialities in a 15th-century abode.

» **L'Antico Forziere, Casaline, Umbria** (p559) Gorgeous, inventive dishes and a dessert sampler to die for.

» (above) Vegetable stall, Florence
» (left) Cheese

WHAT TO BOOK

Generally, all high-end and popular restaurants should be booked ahead, especially for Friday and Saturday evenings and Sunday lunch. In major tourist cities and towns, always book restaurants in the summer high season and during Easter and Christmas. Cooking courses, such as Milan's La Cucina Italiana (p241), Bologna's La Vecchia Scuola Bolognese (p418), the Cinque Terre's Arbaspàa (p196) and Lecce's Awaiting Table (p707), should also be booked ahead.

» **Il Frantoio, Puglia** (p703) Legendary eight-course feasts at an olive grove–fringed *masseria* (working farm).

» **Ristorante Gallura, Olbia, Sardinia** (p833) Fresh, seasonal produce gets a workout in dishes like sea anemones fried in yoghurt.

Cheap Treats

» **Pizza al taglio** 'Pizza by the slice' is the perfect piazza-side nibble.

» **Arancini** Deep-fried rice balls stuffed with *ragù* (meat sauce), tomato and vegetables.

» **Pecorino** A nutty, crumbly sheep's-milk cheese perfect in fresh, crunchy *pane* (bread).

» **Prosciutto crudo** Sweet-smelling and satisfyingly salty, air-dried ham is another perfect *panino* filler.

» **Porchetta rolls** Warm sliced pork (roasted whole with fennel, garlic and pepper) in a crispy roll; a market staple in Umbria.

» **Pane e panelle** Palermo chickpea fritters on a sesame roll.

» **Gelato** The best Italian gelato uses seasonal ingredients and natural colours (no bright-green pistachio!).

Dare to Try

» **Pajata** A creamy Roman pasta dish made with calves' entrails containing the mothers' congealed milk.

» **Missoltini** A boldly flavoured Como speciality of sun-dried fish cured in salt and bay leaves.

» **Uove di seppie (cuttlefish eggs)** A Venetian treat, poached in salted water and sometimes spiked with *anice stellato* (star anise) in honour of Venice's spice-trading past.

» **Lardo di Colonnata** Tuscany's luscious cured pig lard keeps cardiologists in the black.

» **Pani ca meusa** Push the boundaries with this classic Palermo sandwich of beef spleen and lungs dipped in boiling lard.

» **Zurrette** Sardinian black pudding made of sheep's blood, cooked in a sheep's stomach with herbs and fennel.

Local Specialities

The Italian term for 'pride of place' is *campanilismo* but a more accurate word would be *formaggismo:* loyalty to the local cheese. Clashes among medieval city-states involving castle sieges and boiling oil have been replaced by competition in speciality foods and wines. So leave your compass at home: subtle flavour variations will pinpoint your location like a gastronomic GPS.

Piedmont

Piedmont's culinary offerings are nothing short of rich, warming and decadent. Birthplace of the Slow Food Movement, this is the place to warm up with *lumache* (snails), prized truffles, eggy pasta, lavish chocolate and pedigreed red wines such as Barolo, Barbaresco and Barbera. Prepare to indulge.

» **Alba** Famed for white truffles, hazelnuts, Ferrero chocolate and award-winning Barolo and Barbaresco reds.

» **Turin** Birthplace of Lavazza coffee and vermouth, with top-notch chocolate and nougat, a buzzing *aperitivo* scene and Slow Food emporium Eataly.

» **Cherasco** Lauded for *lumache* and hazelnut-laced *Baci di Cherasco* (Cherasco Kisses) chocolates.

Lombardy

Italy's wealthiest, most populated region is less about pasta and more about risotto and *burro* (butter). Its capital, Milan, is home to the classic *risotto alla milanese* (saffron and bone marrow risotto), *panettone* (a yeast-risen sweet bread), and some of Italy's most uberfashionable restaurants. Other regional musts include gorgonzola cheese and artisanal *salumi* (cured meats).

» **Mantua** Boasts the region's highest concentration of fine-dining and Slow Food restaurants. Signature dishes include *risotto alla pilota* (pork and sausage risotto) and *mostarda di mele* or *mantovana* (sweet-and-sour apple or pear mustard).

» **Milan** Designer restaurants, luxe food emporium Peck and trendy *aperitivo* bars. Don't miss *risotto alla milanese* and Yuletide *panettone*.

» **Valtellina** An Alpine valley famed for Sforzato red, Bitto cheese, *bresaola* (air-cured beef) and *pizzoccheri della Valtellina* (buckwheat pasta ribbons with wilted cabbage, potatoes and mountain cheese).

Venice & the Veneto

Not all bubbly *prosecco* (type of sparkling wine) and fiery grappa, Italy's northeast peddles perfect seafood, polenta and the odd foreign spice – think *sarde in soar* (grilled sardines in a sweet-and-sour sauce), *risotto alle seppie* (cuttlefish-ink risotto) and *polenta con le quaglie* (polenta with quails).

» **Venice** Sail in for *cicheti* and fresh Rialto Market produce like lagoon seafood (look for tags reading 'nostrano', meaning 'ours'), *radicchio di Treviso* (red, bitter chicory) and Bassano del Grappa asparagus. Eat lagoon specialities on Burano and look out for *castraure di Sant'Erasmo* (purple baby artichokes), grown only on Sant'Erasmo island.

» **Valpollicella** A prime wine region, well known for Amarone, Valpollicella Superiore, Ripasso, Recioto and inspired renegade IGT red blends from sought-after winemakers like Giuseppe Quintarelli.

Tuscany

A gastronomic giant, celebrated for its golden olive oils, smoky porcini mushrooms, luscious *cinghiale* (wild boar) and full-blooded red wines.

» **Castelnuovo di Garfagnana** Fresh autumnal porcini, chestnuts and local farm-grown *farro* (spelt).

» **San Miniato** Hunt for delicate white truffles from October to December and celebrate their mystique at the white-truffle fair (Sagra del Tartufo), held over three weekends in November.

» **Il Chianti** Rolling hills speckled with world-famous vineyards and top-notch modern Tuscan eateries.

» **Montepulciano** Home of Vino Nobile red and its equally quaffable second-string Rosso di Montepulciano. Savour local *cinta senese* (indigenous Tuscan pig) and Terre di Siena extra-virgin olive oil.

» **Montalcino** Famed for the red wine Brunello and the consistently good Rosso di Montalcino, prized extra-virgin olive oils, *pecorino* cheese, porcini mushrooms, truffles and *cinta senese*.

» **The Valdichiana** *The* valley for world-famous Chianina beef (used in *bistecca alla fiorentina*, T-bone steak), *pici* (a type of hand-rolled pasta) and *ravaggiolo* (sheep's-milk cheese wrapped in fern fronds).

Emilia-Romagna

A culinary powerhouse and creator of some of Italy's most iconic edibles, from lasagne with *ragù* to the planet's most grated cheese, *parmigiano reggiano* (Parmesan).

» **Bologna** Home of *pasta alla bolognese* (pasta with white wine, tomato, oregano, beef and belly pork), meat-stuffed tortellini and the deli-packed streets of the Quadrilatero.

» **Modena** Shop for Modena aged balsamic vinegar, tuck into *zampone* (stuffed pig's trotters) and *cotechino* (boiled pork sausage), and wash it all down with a glass or three of sparkling red Lambrusco.

» **Parma** Nibble on the town's most famous trio, *parmigiano reggiano*, *prosciutto di Parma* (cured ham) and *mortadella* (pork cold cut).

Umbria

Gourmets revere Umbria, known for its wild asparagus, mushrooms and hearty boar sausages. Uncork a bottle of mighty *sagrantino di Montefalco* red and grate a black Norcia truffle over fresh *tagliatelle* (ribbon pasta).

» **Torgiano** On the Strada dei Vini del Canto wine trail, Torgiano reveres its wine and olives with two dedicated museums.

» **Lago Trasimeno** Lake fish shine in dishes like *regina alla porchetta* (roasted carp stuffed with garlic, fennel and herbs) and *tegemacchio* (fish stew made with garlic, onions, tomatoes and a medley of underwater critters).

» **Norcia** Italy's capital of pork, packed with famous *norcinerie* (butcher shops) filled with hung hams and stuffed boar's heads and shops selling dried meats from acorn-fed pigs.

BRUCE BI / LONELY PLANET IMAGES ©

» (above) Beef carpaccio salad
» (left) Pizza

RICHARD I'ANSON / LONELY PLANET IMAGES ©

Rome & Lazio

Food fit for a pope, from thin-crust pizza and spaghetti carbonara, to *supplì* (risotto balls) and espresso-soaked tiramisu.

» **Rome** Head to Testaccio for nose-to-tail staples like *trippa alla romana* (tripe cooked with potatoes, tomato, mint and *pecorino* cheese) and the Ghetto for kosher classics including deep-fried *carciofi* (artichokes) and *pizza ebraica* (dense cake made with raisins, almonds, pine nuts and candied fruit).

» **Frascati** Tour the vineyards and sniff, swill and sip the area's delicate white wine.

Naples & Campania

Explosions of flavour come with the territory in Campania, where hot *peperoncino* (chilli pepper), tomatoes and citrus thrive in volcanic soil and retro bars serve thick, rich espresso. Procida lemons get cheeky in *limoncello* (icy lemon liqueur) while the region's vines shine in drops like intense red Taurasi and the dry white Fiano di Avellino.

» **Naples & surrounds** Tuck into Italy's best pizza and *mozzarella di bufala* (buffalo mozzarella), on-the-go snacks like *crocchè* (potato croquettes), and al dente gems like *spaghetti alle vongole* (spaghetti with clams) and *pasta cacio e pepe* (pasta with caciocavallo cheese and pepper). Make room for *sfogliatella* (sweetened ricotta pastry) and runny *babà* (rum-soaked sponge cake).

» **Cetara** Sample Italy's best anchovies in a tiny Amalfi Coast town. Savour the flavour with *spaghetti con alici e finocchietto selavatrice* (spaghetti with anchovies and wild fennel).

Puglia

Like the Wild West with better food: head southeast for peppery olive oil, crunchy *pane*, and honest *cucina povera* (poor man's cuisine). Breadcrumbs lace everything from *strascinati con la mollica* (pasta with breadcrumbs and anchovies) and *tiella di verdure* (baked vegetable casserole), while carbolicious snacks include *puccia* (bread with olives) and ring-shaped *taralli* (pretzel-like biscuits).

» **Salento** Linger over lunch at a *masseria* and make a toast with hearty reds like Salice Salentino and Primitivo di Manduria.

Sicily

Expect cuisine with kick, from the wild-caught tuna and sardines to *fiori di zucca ripieni* (cheese-stuffed squash blossoms). Channel ancient Arab influences with fragrant fish couscous and spectacular sweets like *cannoli* (pastry shells filled with sweet ricotta), and praise Sicilian culinary skill with a bottle of devilish red Nero d'Avola.

» **Palermo** Snack on fried eggplant with lemon or *sfincione* (spongy, oily pizza topped with onions and *caciocavallo* cheese), and sit down to *pasta con le sarde* (pasta with sardines, pine nuts, raisins and wild fennel) and *involtini di pesce spada* (thinly sliced swordfish fillets rolled up and filled with breadcrumbs, capers, tomatoes and olives).

» **Catania** Pay tribute to Sicily's Norman invaders with *pasta alla Norma* (pasta with basil, eggplant, ricotta and tomato).

TABLE MANNERS

While Italian diners will usually forgive any foreign faux pas, following a few tips should impress the toughest of gastrosnobs. On the coffee front, milky options like caffe latte and cappuccino are usually morning drinks, with espresso and macchiato the preferred post-lunch options. Coffee with dessert is fine, but ordering one with your main meal is a culinary travesty. Make eye contact when toasting, and eat spaghetti with a fork, not a spoon. Eating bread with your pasta is considered *un pò strano* (a bit strange), though using it to wipe any remaining sauce from your plate (affectionately called *fare la scarpetta*) is fine. Feel free to give your *complimenti allo chef* (compliments to the chef), and in the right circumstances, a hearty handshake and cheek kisses may be in order. On the subject of *il conto* (the bill), whoever invites usually pays. Splitting the bill is common enough, though itemising it is *molto vulgare* (very vulgar). If there is no *servizio* (service charge), consider leaving a 10% to 15% tip. In bars, Italians usually tip the barista €0.10 or €0.20. And if you're lucky enough to be invited to someone's home for a meal, never go empty handed – wine, chocolates or flowers will ensure you make *la bella figura* (good impression).

» **Noto, Modica & Ragusa** Celebrate earthy flavours with *lolli con le fave* (hand-rolled pasta with fava beans), *macco di fave* (fava bean purée with wild fennel) and *ravioli di ricotta al sugo di maiale* (ricotta ravioli served with a pork-meat sauce) and savour Modica's spiced chocolate creations.

How to Eat & Drink Like a Local

Now that your appetite is piqued, it's time for the technicalities of eating *all'italiana*.

When to Eat

» **Colazione (Breakfast)** A continental affair, often little more than a pre-work espresso, accompanied by a *cornetto* (Italian croissant) or brioche.

» **Pranzo (Lunch)** Traditionally the main meal of the day, with many businesses closing for *la pausa* (afternoon break). Standard restaurant times are noon to 2.30pm, though most locals don't lunch before 1pm.

» **Aperitivo** Particularly popular in northern cities, post-work drinks usually take place between 5pm and 8pm, when the price of your drink includes a buffet of tasty morsels.

» **Cena (Dinner)** Traditionally a little lighter than lunch, though still a main meal. Standard restaurant times are 7.30pm to around 11pm (sometimes even later in the summer and in the south).

Choosing a Restaurant

» **Ristorante (Restaurant)** Crisp linen, formal service and refined dishes make restaurants the obvious choice for special occasions.

» **Trattoria** A family-owned version of a restaurant, with cheaper prices, more-relaxed service, and classic regional specialities. Avoid places offering a 'tourist menu'.

» **Osteria** Historically a tavern focused on wine, the modern version is usually an intimate, relaxed trattoria or wine bar offering a handful of dishes from a verbal menu.

» **Enoteca** Perfect for a little *vino* downtime, wine bars often serve snacks to accompany your tipple.

» **Agriturismo** A working farmhouse offering accommodation, as well as food made with farm-grown produce. Some allow guests to participate in farm activities.

» **Pizzeria** A top place for a cheap feed, cold beer and a buzzing, convivial vibe. The best pizzerias are often crowded: be patient.

» **Tavola calda** Literally a 'hot table', these cafeteria-style options peddle cheap premade food like self-service pasta, roast meats and *pizza al taglio*.

Menu Lowdown

» **Menù a la carte** Choose whatever you like from the menu.

» **Menù di degustazione** Degustation menu, usually consisting of six to eight 'tasting size' courses.

» **Menù turistico** The dreaded 'tourist menu' usually signals mediocre fare for gullible tourists – steer clear!

» **Piatto del giorno** Dish of the day.

» **Antipasto** A hot or cold appetiser. For a tasting plate of different appetisers, request an *antipasto misto* (mixed antipasto).

» **Primo** First course, usually a substantial pasta, rice or *zuppa* (soup) dish.

» **Secondo** Second course, often *carne* (meat) or *pesce* (fish).

» **Contorno** Side dish, usually *verdura* (vegetable).

» **Dolce** Dessert; including *torta* (cake).

» **Frutta** Fruit; usually the epilogue to a meal.

» **Nostra produzione** Made in-house; used to describe anything from bread and pasta to *liquori* (liqueurs).

» **Surgelato** Frozen; usually used to denote fish or seafood that has not been freshly caught.

For information on eating price ranges in this book, see p912.

Outdoor Experiences

Best Experiences

Hiking The Dolomites, Piedmont's Gran Paradiso, Trentino's Stelvio and Calabria's Pollino parks, Umbria's Piano Grande and the coastal tracks of the Cinque Terre, the Amalfi Coast, Sicily and Sardinia are all super.

Cycling The Po Delta and Bolzano offer good networks, as do the wine regions of Franciacorta, Barolo, Barbaresco and Chianti. Urban options include Rome's Via Appia, Ferrara, Lucca, Bologna and Lecce.

Skiing Cross-border into Slovenia at Sella Nevea; skiing and snowboarding in Courmayeur; downhill and cross-country in Cortina d'Ampezzo, the Valle d'Aosta and Sella Ronda.

Diving Marine parks abound. The best are off the Cinque Terre, the Gargano Promontory, Elba, the Sorrento Peninsula, the Aeolian Islands, Ustica and Sardinia.

Best Times to Go

April to June Walk among wildflowers.

July & September Water sports and warm-water diving without the August crowds.

December, February & March The best ski months for atmosphere (Christmas), snow and value.

Blessed with hills, mountains, lakes and 7600km of coastline, Italy offers much more than Roman ruins and Renaissance art. Adrenalin addicts can get their fix in any number of ways: there's mountain biking, climbing and skiing in the Alps; hard-core hiking in the Dolomites; horse riding in the Apennines; you can climb active volcanoes in Sicily; and shoot white-water rapids in Calabria. Less daunting, Lombardy and Tuscany's rolling landscape offers scenic cycling.

On the coast, sport goes beyond posing on packed beaches. The precipitous peaks of the Amalfi Coast harbour a network of ancient shepherd paths, while Sardinia's cobalt waters and Sicily's Aeolian Islands boast some of Italy's best diving. Windsurfers flock to Sardinia, Sicily and the northern lakes to pit themselves against fierce local winds.

Hiking & Walking

Italy is a walker's paradise. Thousands of kilometres of *sentieri* (marked trails) crisscross the peninsula, ranging from tough mountain treks to gentle lakeside ambles. In season (the end of June to September), the jagged peaks of the Dolomites provide superb walking and spectacular scenery.

The Alps

One of the great mountain ranges of Europe, the Alps stretch from Slovenia in the east, via the southern borders of Austria and Switzerland to France in the west. For hikers, they offer heady mountain vistas, swooping forested valleys and views over large glacial lakes such as Garda, Como and Maggiore.

To the east in Friuli Venezia you'll find the Giulie and Carnic Alps, where you can hike in pursuit of lynx, marmots and eagles amid curious Tyrolean villages. Heading west, the white ridges pass through Trento's Parco Nazionale dello Stelvio, northern Italy's (and the Alps') largest national park, spilling into next-door Lombardy. Lombardy's great lakes – encompassing Garda, Como, Iseo, Maggiore and Orta – are prime hiking territory mixing mountain and lake vistas. Particularly scenic is the crumpled ridge of mountains in Como's Triangolo Lariano, and Garda's impressive Monte Baldo.

Finally, in the far west, dropping into Piedmont and Liguria, are the Graian, Maritime and Ligurian Alps, which take in the Valle d'Aosta, the vast Gran Paradiso park and the lesser-known Parco Naturale delle Alpi Marittime, before making a sharp and dramatic descent to the Cinque Terre and Portofino park on the Ligurian coastline.

Accommodation in the mountains is in huts *(rifugi)* or chalets, which should be booked ahead in high season. For serious hiking you'll need to bring appropriate equipment and detailed trail maps. Tourist offices and visitor centres provide some information, resources and basic maps for easier tourist routes.

The Dolomites

Soaring across the borders of the Veneto, Trentino and Alto-Adige, the Dolomites are a stunning mountain range. Unesco thought so too, and declared the mountains and their unique ecosystem a World Heritage Site in 2009. Equally well known for their skiing and cycling, the Dolomites offer some of Italy's most scenic (and vertiginous) walking trails, which are sprinkled with wildflowers in spring.

Top Trails

» **Alpi di Siusi, Alto-Adige** (p311) Europe's largest plateau ends dramatically at the base of the Sciliar Mountains. Average stamina will get you to Rifugio Bolzano, one of the Alps' oldest mountain huts. The more challenging peaks of the Catinaccio group and the Sassolungo are nearby.

» **Val Pusteria, Alto-Adige** (p314) This narrow Tyrolean valley runs from Bressanone to San Candido. At the far end of the valley are the Sesto Dolomites, which are criss-crossed with spectacular walking trails, including moderate trails around the iconic Tre Cime di Lavaredo (Three Peaks).

» **Val Gardena, Alto-Adige** (p314) One of only five valleys where the Ladin heritage is still preserved. Located amid the peaks of the Gruppo del Sella and Sassolungo there are challenging *alte vie* (high-altitude) trails and easier nature walks such as the Naturonda at Passo di Sella (2244m).

» **Brenta Dolomites, Trentino** (p295) The Brenta group is well known to mountaineers for its sheer cliffs and tricky ascents, which are home to some of Italy's most famous *vie ferrate* (trails with permanent steel cables and ladders), including the Via Ferrata delle Bocchette.

» **Parco Nazionale delle Dolomiti Bellunesi, Veneto** (p382) A Unesco Heritage park offering trails amid wildflowers. This park also harbours the high-altitude Alte Vie delle Dolomiti trails, which are accessible between June and September.

Central Italy

In central Italy, Abruzzo's national parks are among Italy's least explored. Here, you can climb Corno Grande (p603), the Apennines' highest peak, and explore vast, silent valleys. Likewise, Umbria's Monti Sibillini and Piano Grande are well off the typically trodden path, and both burst into a blooming carpet of wildflowers in spring.

Tuscany's only significant park with good walking trails is in the southern Maremma, where you can sign up for walks of medium difficulty. For most people though, an easy amble through picturesque Chianti will suit them just fine.

The South

Backed by the spiky ridge of the southern Apennines, Campania, Basilicata and Calabria have some stunning coastal hikes. For spectacular sea views head to the Amalfi Coast and Sorrento Peninsula, where age-old paths such as the Sentiero degli Dei (Path of the Gods; p674) disappear into wooded mountains and ancient lemon groves.

Further south, crossing the border between Calabria and Basilicata is the Parco Nazionale del Pollino (p733), Italy's largest national park. It acts like a rocky curtain

ITALY'S BEST PARKS & RESERVES

PARK	FEATURES	ACTIVITIES	BEST TIME TO VISIT	PAGE
Abruzzo, Lazio e Molise	granite peaks, beech woods, bears, wolves	hiking, horse riding	May–Oct	p610
Appennino Tosco-Emiliano	mountains, forests, lakes	skiing, cycling, hiking, horse riding	Feb–Oct	p432
Arcipelago di La Maddalena	rocky islets, beaches, translucent sea	sailing, diving, snorkelling	Jun–Sep	p836
Asinara	albino donkeys, former prison	cycling, boat tours, snorkelling	Jun–Sep	p831
Aspromonte	coniferous forests, high plains, vertiginous villages	hiking	May–Oct	p737
Cilento e Vallo di Diano	Greek temples, dramatic coastline, caves	hiking, swimming, birdwatching	May–Oct	p681
Cinque Terre	Unesco World Heritage Site, colourful fishing villages, terraced hillsides	hiking, diving	Apr–Oct	p175
Delta del Po	marshes, wetlands	cycling, birdwatching	May–Oct	p442
Dolomiti Bellunesi	Unesco World Heritage Site, rock spires, highland meadows, chamois	skiing, hiking, mountain biking	Dec–Oct	p382
Dolomiti di Sesto	jagged mountains, Tre Cime di Lavaredo (Three Peaks)	hiking, mountain biking, rock climbing	Jun–Sep	p315
Etna	active volcano, black lava fields, forests	hiking, horse riding	May–Oct	p781
Gargano	ancient forests, limestone cliffs, grottoes	diving, hiking, cycling, snorkelling	Jun–Sep	p694
Golfo di Orosei e del Gennargentu	sheer cliffs, granite peaks, prehistoric ruins	hiking, sailing, rock climbing, canyoning	May–Sep	p839
Gran Paradiso	Alpine villages, mountains, meadows, ibex	skiing, snowboarding, hiking, climbing, mountain biking	Dec–Oct	p224
Gran Sasso e Monti della Laga	ragged peaks, birds of prey, wolves	skiing, hiking, climbing	Dec–Mar	p603
Madonie	Sicily's highest peaks, wooded slopes, wolves, wildflowers	hiking, horse riding	May–Jun, Sep–Oct	p761
Majella	mountains, deep gorges, bears	hiking, cycling	Jun–Sep	p608
Maremma	reclaimed marshes, beaches	hiking, horse riding, birdwatching	May–Oct	p540
Monti Sibillini	ancient hamlets, mountains, eagles	hiking, mountain biking, paragliding	May–Oct	p599
Pollino	mountains, canyons, forest, Larico pines, rare orchids	rafting, canyoning, hiking	Jun–Sep	p733
Prigionette	forest paths, albino donkeys, Giara horses, wild boar	hiking, cycling	May–Oct	p830
Sciliar-Catinaccio	pasture lands, valleys, villages	hiking, cycling	Jun–Sep	p311
Sila	wooded hills, lakes, remote villages, mushrooms	skiing, hiking, canyoning, horse riding	Dec–Mar, May–Oct	p735
Stelvio	Alpine peaks, glaciers, forests	year-round skiing, hiking, cycling, mountain biking	Dec–Sep	p309
Vesuvio	active volcano, black lava fields, woods	hiking	Apr–Oct	p656

separating Calabria from the rest of Italy and has the richest repository of flora and fauna in the south. Walkers in the park can enjoy varied landscapes, from deep river canyons to alpine meadows. Calabria's other national parks – the Sila and Aspromonte – offer similarly dramatic hiking, particularly the area around Sersale in the Sila, where there are myriad waterfalls and you can trek through the Valli Cupe canyon (p735).

Sicily & Sardinia

Surprisingly, Italy's diverse offshore islands offer some of the best walking in the country. Most people may think of Capri and Ischia as playboy summer spots, but they both offer fantastic walking trails that enable you to enjoy the islands away from the beach crowds.

Likewise, Sicily and Sardinia with their unique topographies provide wonderful walking opportunities. Take your pick of volcano hikes in Sicily: the mother of them all is Mt Etna, but there's a whole host of lesser volcanoes on the Aeolian Islands from extinct Vulcano, where you can descend to the crater floor, to a three-hour climb to the summit of Stromboli to see it exploding against the night sky. From Etna you can also trek across into the Madonie park, or, on Sicily's east coast, you can track the shoreline in the Riserva Naturale dello Zingaro (p804).

By contrast, Sardinia's granite peaks offer more-challenging hikes. The Golfo di Orosei e del Gennargentu park offers a network of old shepherd tracks on the Supramonte plateau and incorporates the prehistoric site of Tiscali and the Gola Su Gorropu canyon, which requires a guide and involves some rock climbing.

Rock Climbing

The huge rock walls of the Dolomites set testing challenges for rock climbers of all levels, with everything from simple, single-pitch routes to long, multipitch ascents, many of which are easily accessible by road. To combine rock climbing with high-level hiking, you can clip onto the *vie ferrate* in the Brenta Dolomites.

For hard-core mountaineering, alpinists can pit themselves against Europe's highest peaks in the Valle d'Aosta. Courmayeur and Cogne, a renowned ice-climbing centre, make good bases.

To the south, the Gran Sasso massif is a favourite. Of its three peaks, Corno Grande (2912m) is the highest and Corno Piccolo (2655m) the easiest to get to.

Other hot spots include Monte Pellegrino outside Palermo in Sicily, and Domusnovas and the Supramonte in Sardinia.

The best source of climbing information is the **Club Alpino Italiano** (CAI; www.cai.it).

Skiing

Most of Italy's top ski resorts are in the northern Alps. Sestriere hosted the downhill events at the 2006 Winter Olympics, and names like Cortina d'Ampezzo, Madonna di Campiglio and Courmayeur will be familiar to serious ski buffs. But skiing is not limited to the north: travel down the peninsula and you'll find smaller resorts throughout the Apennines, in Lazio, Le Marche and Abruzzo.

Facilities at the bigger centres are generally world-class, with pistes ranging from nursery slopes to tough black runs. As well as *sci alpino* (downhill skiing), resorts might offer *sci di fondo* (cross-country skiing) and *sci alpinismo* (ski mountaineering).

SELVAGGIO BLU – THE ULTIMATE TREK

Reckoned by many to be the toughest trek in Italy, Sardinia's seven-day Selvaggio Blu (Savage Blue) is not for the faint-hearted. Stretching 45km along the Golfo di Orosei, the trek traverses wooded ravines, chasms, gorges and cliffs and passes many caves. It's not well signposted (a deliberate decision to keep it natural) and there's no water en route. Furthermore, it involves rock climbs of up to UIAA grade IV+ (challenging), and abseils of up to 45m.

For information, Italian speakers can consult www.selvaggioblu.it, a website with descriptions of each day's walk, advice on what to take and when to go (namely in spring or autumn).

» (above) Kitesurfing, Lago di Garda
» (left) Hikers on the Tour du Mont Blanc in Valle d'Aosta, Piedmont

The ski season runs from December to late March, although there is year-round skiing in Trentino Alto-Adige and on Mont Blanc (Monte Bianco) and the Matterhorn in the Valle d'Aosta. As a general rule, January and February are the best, busiest and most expensive months. For better value look further afield to the Friuli's expanding Sella Nevea runs or Tarvisio, one of the coldest spots in the Alps, where the season is often extended into April.

The best bargain of the ski year is the *settimana bianca* (literally 'white week') package covering accommodation, food and ski passes.

Snowboarding

Ski purists might lament the fact, but snowboarding has arrived in Italy. Two hot spots are Madonna di Campiglio in Trentino and Breuil-Cervinia in Valle d'Aosta. Madonna's facilities are among the best in the country and include a snowboard park with descents for all levels and a dedicated boarder-cross zone. Breuil-Cervinia, situated at 2050m in the shadow of the Matterhorn, is better suited to intermediate and advanced levels.

Cycling

Whether you want a gentle ride between trattorias, a 100km road race or a teeth-rattling mountain descent, you'll find a route to suit in Italy. Tourist offices can usually provide details on trails and guided rides, and bike hire is available in most cities and key activity spots.

Tuscany's famously rolling countryside is a favourite with cyclists, particularly the wine-producing Chianti area south of Florence. In Umbria, the Valnerina and Piano

---

TOP SKI RESORTS

Friuli Venezia Giulia

» **Tarvisio** (www.tarvisiano.org) 60km of cross-country tracks and great freeriding.

» **Sella Nevea** (www.sellanevea.net) 30km of slopes linking to Bovec in Slovenia.

» **Forni di Sopra** (www.fornidisopra.com) Family-friendly, offering skiing, ice-skating and sledging.

Valle d'Aosta

» **Via Lattea** (Milky Way; www.vialattea.it) 400km of pistes linking five ski resorts, including one of Europe's most glamorous, Sestriere.

Piedmont

» **Limone Piemonte** (www.limonepiemonte.it) 80km of runs, including some for Nordic skiing.

» **Courmayeur** (www.courmayeur.com) Dominated by spectacular Mont Blanc, Courmayeur allows access to legendary runs such as the Vallee Blanche.

» **Cervinia** (www.cervinia.it) In the shadow of the Matterhorn and within skiing distance of Zermatt; good for late-season snow and family facilities.

» **Monte Rosa** (www.monterosa-ski.com) Comprised of three valleys – Val d'Ayas, Val d'Gressoney and Alagna Valsesia – Monte Rosa is characterised by Walser villages and white-knuckle off-piste skiing and heli-skiing.

Trentino Alto-Adige

» **Sella Ronda** (www.sella-ronda.info) A 40km circumnavigation of the Gruppo di Sella range (3151m, at Piz Boé) is one of the Alps' iconic ski routes.

» **Alta Badia** (www.altabadia.org) 130km of slopes including the legendary Gran Risa.

Veneto

» **Cortina d'Ampezzo** (www.infodolomiti.it) Downhill and cross-country skiing with runs ranging from bunny slopes to the legendary Staunies black mogul run.

BIKE TOURS

» **Darwin Cooperative** (www.cooperativadarwin.it) Organises tours in English, French, German and Spanish along Rome's scenic Via Appia Antica.

» **I Bike Tuscany** (www.ibiketuscany.com) Year-round one-day tours for riders of every skill level. Transport to Chianti and a support vehicle are provided.

» **Iseobike** (www.iseobike.com) Tours around the Franciacorta wine region, with wine tastings.

» **Mountainbike Ogliastra** (www.mountainbikeogliastra.it) Organises scenic road cycling itineraries in Sardinia as well as challenging downhill routes on old mule tracks.

» **Colpo di Pedale** (www.colpodipedale.it) Trips for all levels on racers, mountain bikes and city bikes around Piedmont's Langhe wine region.

» **Ciclovagando** (www.ciclovagando.com) Organises full-day tours of 20km, departing from various Puglian towns including Ostuni and Brindisi.

Grande at Monte Vettore have beautiful trails and quiet country roads to explore. Further north, the flatlands of Emilia-Romagna and the terraced vineyards of Barolo, Barbaresco and Franciacorta are also ideally suited for bike touring. In the south, Puglia's flat rolling countryside and coastal paths are another good spot.

In summer many Alpine ski resorts offer seriously good cycling. Mountain bikers will be spoilt for choice in the peaks around Lago di Garda, Lake Maggiore and the Dolomites in Trentino Alto-Adige. Another challenging area is the tough, granite landscape of the Supramonte in eastern Sardinia.

The best time for cycling is spring, when it's not too hot and the countryside is looking its best. If cycling is a focus of your trip, get hold of a copy of Lonely Planet's *Cycling Italy*.

Diving

Diving is one of Italy's most popular summer pursuits, and there are hundreds of schools offering courses, dives for all levels and equipment hire.

Most diving schools open seasonally, typically from about June to October. If possible, avoid August, when the Italian coast is besieged by holidaymakers and prices are at their highest.

Information is available from local tourist offices and online at **DiveItaly** (www.diveitaly.com, in Italian).

Top Dive Sites

» **Aeolian Islands, Sicily** A volcanic ridge with warm, volcanic waters encompassing the islands of Vulcano, Lipari, Salina, Panarea, Stromboli, Alicudi and Filicudi. Dive in sea grottoes around the remains of old volcanoes.

» **Capri, Ischia & Procida, Campania** These three islands in the Bay of Naples offer exceptional diving (and underwater photo opportunities) amid sun-struck sea grottoes.

» **Cinque Terre Marine Reserve, Liguria** One of the few places to dive in the north of the country. Dives head out of Riomaggiore and Santa Margherita.

» **Capo Caccia, Sardinia** The dive site for Sardinia's coral divers, Capo Caccia also features the largest underwater grotto in the Mediterranean.

» **Isole Tremiti, Puglia** These wind-eroded islands off Puglia's Gargano Promontory are part of a marine park and are pock-marked with huge sea grottoes.

» **Pantelleria, Sicily** A spectacular volcanic seabed surrounds the black lava island of Pantelleria.

» **Parco Nazionale dell'Arcipelago di La Maddalena, Sardinia** The Maddalena marine park boasts translucent waters and diving around 60 islets.

» **Parco Nazionale Arcipelago Toscano, Tuscany** Europe's largest marine park encompasses the Tuscan archipelago and the island of Elba.

» **Punta Campanella Marine Reserve, Campania** Vivid marine life flourishing among underwater grottoes and ancient ruins. Dives head out from Marina del Cantone, including outings to the stunning Bay of Ieranto.

» **Ustica, Sicily** Italy's first marine reserve, this volcanic island is rich with underwater flora and fauna and hosts the International Festival of Underwater Activities in July.

» (above) Sailing, Mediterranean Sea
» (left) Cycling, Dolomites

Sailing

Italy, virtually surrounded by water, has a proud maritime tradition and you can hire a paddle boat or sleek sailing yacht almost anywhere in the country. Sailors of all levels are catered for: experienced skippers can island-hop around Sicily and Sardinia, or along the Amalfi, Tuscan, Ligurian or Triestino coasts on chartered yachts; weekend boaters can explore hidden coves in rented dinghies around Puglia, in the Tuscan archipelago and around the Sorrento Peninsula; and speed freaks can take to the Lombard lakes in all manner of sporty speedboats.

Down south, on the Amalfi Coast, prime swimming spots are often only accessible by boat. It's a similar story on the Cilento coast south of Naples and the islands of Elba, Capri, Ischia and Procida.

Sardinia and Sicily also provide superb sailing. In Sardinia, the Golfo di Orosei, Santa Teresa di Gallura and the Maddalena archipelago are the top sailing spots; in Sicily, the Aeolian Islands' cobalt waters are perfect for idle island-hopping.

Italy's most prestigious sailing regattas are Lago di Garda's September Centomiglia (www.centomiglia.it), which sails just south of Gargnano, and the Barcolana Regatta (www.barcolana.it) held in Trieste in October. The Barcolana is the Med's largest regatta and attracts some 20,000 sailors. Sardinia hosts the World Championships in Cagliari in September. The island's main sailing portal is www.sailingsardinia.it (in Italian).

White-water Sports

A mecca for water rats, the Sesia river in northern Piedmont is Italy's top white-water destination. At its best between April and September, it runs from the slopes of Monte Rosa down through the spectacular scenery of the Valsesia. Operators in Varallo offer various solutions to the rapids: there's canoeing, kayaking, white-water rafting, canyoning, hydrospeed and tubing.

In Alto-Adige, the Val di Sole is another white-water destination, as is Monti Sibillini in Umbria.

At the southern end of the peninsula, the Lao river rapids in Calabria's Parco Nazionale del Pollino provide exhilarating rafting, as well as canoeing and canyoning. Trips can be arranged in Scalea.

Windsurfing

Considered one of Europe's prime windsurfing spots, Lago di Garda enjoys excellent wind conditions: the northerly *peler* blows in early on sunny mornings, while the southerly *ora* sweeps down in the early afternoon as regular as clockwork. The two main centres are Torbole, home of the World Windsurf Championship, and Malcesine, 15km south.

For windsurfing on the sea, Sardinia is a hot spot. In the north, Porto Pollo, also known as Portu Puddu, is good for beginners and experts – the bay provides protected waters for learners, while experts can enjoy the high winds as they funnel through the channel between Sardinia and Corsica. Competitions such as the Chia Classic are held off the southwest coast, while the Kitesurf World Cup is held off the beaches between Vignola and Santa Teresa di Gallura. To the northeast, there's good windsurfing on the island of Elba, off the Tuscan coast.

Equipment hire is available at all the places mentioned here.

regions at a glance

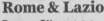

Rome & Lazio

Roman Sites ✓✓✓
Food ✓✓✓
Museums & Galleries ✓✓✓

Ancient Icons
Rome's ancient centre is history in 3D. Here Romulus killed Remus on the Palatine Hill, Christians were fed to lions in the Colosseum and emperors took to the spa at the Terme di Caracalla. Ponder the remains of the great and the good in the catacombs along the Via Appia Antica.

Food
The Roman palate favours earthy old-school flavours such as pig's cheek, offal, salt cod and *bucatini all'amatriciana* (pasta with tomato, pancetta and chilli-peppers), but that's not to say that dining out is provincial. The Italo-fusion fare of new-school chefs lends stalwart staples a contemporary twist.

Museums & Galleries
The breadth of cultural treasures housed in Rome's countless museums and galleries is, quite frankly, embarrassing. If you plan on hitting several of them, it's worth considering one of the various discount cards available.

p56

Turin, Piedmont & the Italian Riviera

Walking ✓✓✓
Villages ✓✓
Food ✓✓✓

Hiking & Skiing
From the slopes of the Milky Way and the Valle d'Aosta to wild coastal hikes along the Cinque Terre, this north-west corner of the country is an outdoor paradise. The Gran Paradiso park is aptly named.

Unspoilt Villages
With chic medieval fishing villages along the Cinque Terre; quaint, wine-growing villages on Langhe hilltops; and secretive Walser villages in the Valle d'Aosta, you're spoilt for choice.

Gourmet Paradise
Home to the Slow Food Movement, Piedmont has an embarrassment of culinary riches, from the truffles of Alba and Asti to the renowned wines of the Langhe region.

p156

Milan & the Lakes

Shopping ✓✓✓
Gardens ✓✓✓
Food ✓✓✓

Fashion Capital
Every fashion addict worth their slate-grey, cashmere cardigan knows that Milan takes fashion and design as seriously as others take biotech or engineering. Top-notch discount outlets mean that everyone can make a *bella figura* (good impression) here.

Villas & Gardens
Framed by gazebos, blushing bushes of camellias, artfully tumbling terraces and world-class statuary, Lombardy's lakeside villas knock the socks off the 'luxury getaway' concept.

Culture & Cuisine
Bergamo, Brescia, Cremona and Mantua, the cultured cities of the Po Plain combine wonderful art and architecture with a slew of sophisticated, regional restaurants.

p228

Trento & the Dolomites

Activities ✓✓✓
Wellness ✓✓
Food ✓✓✓

Adrenalin Rush
Ski, hike, ice-climb, sledge-ride or Nordic walk in the Sella Ronda and the remote Stelvio park. Real adrenalin junkies will want to scale the WWI-era *vie ferrate* (literally 'roads of iron').

Thermal Spas
Attend to your wellness in the thermal baths at Terme Merano or Vigilius, then stock up on tisanes and cosmetics incorporating Alpine herbs, grapes, apples and Mountain Pine.

Austrian Accents
Bolzano beer halls, strudels, Sachertorte, sourdough breads and buckwheat cakes are just some of the region's Austro-Italian specialities. Combine with regional wines such as Gewürztraminer, riesling and award-winning Sylvaner.

p284

Venice & the Veneto

Art ✓✓✓
Architecture ✓✓✓
Wine ✓✓✓

Moving Pictures
Action-packed paintings by Titian, Veronese and Tintoretto illuminate the way to the modern art on view at Venice's Biennale. The Church repeatedly tried and failed to censor these artists, who were avant-garde for their time.

Reflected Glories
Story-book castles, gracious country villas and an entire city of palaces on the water, the Veneto's architectural landmarks admire their own reflections in the snaking canals.

Inspired Wine Pairings
Wine aficionados throng VinItaly booths to try collector-favourite Veneto DOC Amarone, Valpolicella, Soave and *prosecco* (sparkling wine) – plus dozens of innovative blends and cult wines seldom tasted outside the Veneto.

p316

Friuli Venezia Giulia

History ✓✓
Wilderness ✓✓✓
Food & Wine ✓✓✓

Archaeological Sites
Aquileia offers up a whole Roman town for exploration, while Cividale del Friuli and Grado retain some rare, early-Christian churches.

Rural Retreats
The forests of the Carnic and Giulian Alps are wild and verdant, the Laghi di Fusine are still populated by lynx and deer and the Forni di Sopra are spread thick with wild Alpine flowers.

Culinary Adventure
Friuli's crossroads cuisine incorporates smoked trout and DOC prosciutto from San Daniele, spicy brioche, gamey Mittel dishes and traditional sauerkraut. There's also some very exciting wine coming out of the Carso and the Colli Orientali.

p384

Emilia-Romagna & San Marino

Cycling ✓✓
Architecture ✓
Food ✓✓✓

Urban Cycling
Reggio Emilia was recently voted Italy's best cycling city. During the week Bologna's cobbled streets look like Oxford, and Parma is largely pedestrianised. Best of all, circumnavigate the 9 kilometres of Ferrara's old city walls.

Holy Architecture
Tour the churches for a quick art history lesson from Ravenna's dazzling Byzantine mosaics and Modena's Romanesque cathedral to Bologna's Gothic-Renaissance Basilica di San Petronio.

Famous Flavours
Come with an empty stomach and try the most famous dishes: Modena's balsamic, Parma's ham and cheese, and Bologna's *bolognese ragù* (bolognese sauce) and *mortadella* (pork cold cut).

p410

Florence & Tuscany

Art ✓✓✓
Food ✓✓✓
Wine ✓✓✓

Fabulous Frescoes

Read the story of the evolving Renaissance in the vibrant frescoes in Florence, Siena, Arezzo and San Gimignano by greats Piero della Francesca, Giotto, Masaccio, Ghirlandaio and Fra Angelico.

Autumnal Treats

Truffles and olive oil are two quintessential Tuscan flavours. Autumn heralds many more, such as wild porcini mushrooms and gamey wild boar.

Vineyard Trails

Nothing quite fulfils the Tuscan dream like a tour of Chianti's gentle, terraced hills. Explore further afield to sample Montepulciano's Vino Nobile and Montalcino's heavyweight Brunello, which vies for top wine slot with Piedmont's Barolo.

p454

Umbria & Le Marche

Villages ✓✓✓
Scenery ✓✓
Food ✓✓

Step Back in Time

Perched snugly on their peaks like so many storks on chimneys, Umbria's hill towns – Perugia, Assisi, Gubbio, Urbino – are the proud protectors of local traditions, not to mention postcard pretty.

Spectacular Views

Mountainous and wild, views come at you from all angles in Umbria and Le Marche. Shoot up the *funivia* (cable car) in Gubbio for stunning views or soar above Monti Sibillini and the Piano Grande in your own hang-glider.

Forest Fare

Richly forested and deeply rural, the Umbrian larder is stocked with hearty flavours from wild boar and pigeon to Norcia's *cinta senese* (Tuscan pig) salami and black truffles.

p545

Abruzzo & Molise

Scenery ✓✓
Hiking ✓✓
Wilderness ✓✓✓

Road Less Taken

Discover 'old' Italy in the isolated mountain villages of Pescocostanzo, Scanno, Chieti and Sulmona. Enroute from Sulmona to Scanno, pass through the dramatically wild scenery of the Gole di Sagittario gorge.

Mighty Mountains

From Corno Grande (2912m) to Monte Amaro (2793m), Abruzzo's parks offer free-from-the-crowds hiking and skiing. The most popular route is the ascent of Corno Grande.

Back to Nature

This is an area of outstanding natural beauty and rural, back-country charm. Encompassing three national parks, the ancient forests still harbour bears, chamois and wolves and have walking trails.

p602

Naples & Campania

Coastline ✓✓✓
Roman Sites ✓✓✓
Food ✓✓✓

Cliffs & Coves

From the citrus-fringed panoramas of the Amalfi Coast to Ischia's tropical gardens and Capri's dramatic cliffs, the views from this coastline are as famous as the celebrities who holiday here.

Volcanoes

Sitting beneath Mt Vesuvius, the Neapolitans abide by the motto *carpe diem* (literally 'seize the day'). And why not? All around them, at Pompeii, Ercolano, Cuma and the Phlegraean Fields, are reminders that life is short.

Pizza & Pasta

Vying hard for Italy's culinary crown, Campania produces coffee, pizza, tomato pasta, *sfogliatelle* (sweetened ricotta pastries) and an incredible panoply of seafood, eaten every which way you can.

p618

Puglia, Basilicata & Calabria

Beaches ✓✓✓
Activities ✓✓
Food ✓✓✓

Sicily

Food ✓✓✓
History ✓✓✓
Activities ✓✓✓

Sardinia

Beaches ✓✓✓
Activities ✓✓✓
Prehistory ✓✓

Seaside Savvy

Lounge beneath white cliffs in the Gargano, gaze on violet sunsets in Tropea and spend summer on the golden beaches of Otranto and Gallipoli.

Wild Places

With its crush of spiky mountains, Basilicata and Calabria are where the wild things are. Burst through the clouds in mountaintop Pietrapertosa, pick bergamot in the Aspromonte and take time to swap pleasantries with the locals.

Culture & Cuisine

Puglia has turned its poverty into a fine art: check out the renovated cave dwellings in Matera and then feast on creamy *burrata* (cheese made from mozzarella and cream) and turnip greens in Ostuni and Lecce.

p683

Seafood & Sweets

Sicilian cuisine will dazzle seafood lovers and set sweet teeth on edge. Tuna, sardines, swordfish and shellfish come grilled, fried or seasoned with mint or wild fennel. Desserts are laden with citrus, ricotta, almonds and pistachios.

Cultural Hybrid

A Mediterranean crossroads for centuries, Sicily spoils history buffs with Greek temples, Roman and Byzantine mosaics, Phoenician statues, Norman-Romanesque castles and art nouveau villas.

Volcanoes & Islands

Outdoors enthusiasts can swim and dive in volcanic waters, hike the Aeolian Islands' dramatic coastlines or watch the thrilling fireworks of Stromboli and Etna.

p743

Sun, Sand & Surf

Famous for its fjord-like coves, crystalline waters and windswept sand dunes. Surfers, kitesurfers, sailors and divers flock to the Costa Smeralda, Porto Pollo, the Golfo di Orosei and the Maddalena archipelago.

Moving Mountains

Sardinia's awe-inspiring mountains provide a massive playground for hikers and free-climbers. Climbs afford stunning sea views, while Supramonte hikes traverse old shepherd routes.

Prehistoric Rocks

With its landscape of grey granite rocks, Sardinia is littered with strange prehistoric dolmens, menhirs, wells and *nuraghi* (huge, mysterious stone towers built by the island's earliest inhabitants).

p806

Look out for these icons:

 TOP CHOICE Our author's recommendation

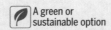 A green or sustainable option

FREE No payment required

On the Road

Rome & Lazio

Best Places to Eat

» Casa Coppelle (p123)

» L'Asino d'Oro (p127)

» Glass Hosteria (p128)

» Pizzarium (p129)

» Gelarmony (p129)

Best Places to Stay

» Hotel Sant'Anselmo (p121)

» Hotel Campo de' Fiori (p118)

» Donna Camilla Savelli (p121)

» Arco del Lauro (p122)

» Villa Spalletti Trivelli (p119)

Why Go?

Even in Italy, a country of exquisite cities, Rome is special. Pulsating, seductive and utterly disarming, the Italian capital is an epic, monumental metropolis that will steal your heart and haunt your soul. There are just too many reasons to fall in love with it: its artistic and architectural masterpieces, its operatic piazzas, its romantic corners and cobbled lanes. History reverberates all around yet modern life is lived to the full – priests in designer shades walk through the Vatican talking into mobile phones, scooters scream through medieval alleyways and stylish drinkers sip at tables on baroque piazzas. Rome also boasts a busy cultural calendar with arts festivals and a surprisingly alternative underground scene.

To visit Rome is to begin a love affair, but to ensure it lasts, find time to explore the hills of Lazio and enjoy the region's extraordinary riches, from the ancient Roman port of Ostia Antica to azure volcanic lakes.

When to Go
Rome

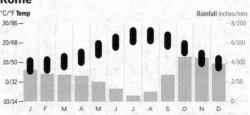

| **Apr** Lovely sunny weather, fervent Easter celebrations, Settimana della Cultura and Rome's birthday. | **May–Jul** Rome's festival calendar gets into full swing as summer temperatures soar. | **Sep–Oct** It's still warm but the crowds die down and Romaeuropa music festival comes to town. |

Top Roman Sights

With so many world-class monuments, galleries and museums in Rome, it can be difficult to decide which to visit. To help you, here's our selection of must-see sights. The Colosseum is an obvious choice, as are the Vatican Museums – one of the world's great museum complexes and home to the Sistine Chapel. Adjacent to the museums, St Peter's Basilica is the most important church in the Catholic world and a treasure trove of Renaissance and baroque art. If you like baroque art, you'll love the Museo e Galleria Borghese and Piazza Navona. Not far from the piazza, the Pantheon is the best preserved of Rome's ancient monuments. For the city's finest ancient art check out the Museo Nazionale Romano: Palazzo Massimo alle Terme and the Capitoline Museums on the sublime Piazza del Campidoglio. Not far away, ancient ruins lie littered across the atmospheric Palatino (Palatine Hill).

And, of course, to ensure that you return to Rome, be sure to throw a coin into the Trevi Fountain.

DAY TRIPS FROM ROME

It can be difficult to drag yourself away from Rome, but the surrounding Lazio region harbours some exceptional sights, most within easy day-trip distance of the capital. Nearest of all are the beautifully preserved ruins of **Ostia Antica**, ancient Rome's main port town. To the east of Rome, and easily accessible by bus or car, Tivoli is home to **Villa Adriana**, the vast summer residence of the emperor Hadrian, and **Villa d'Este**, famed for its fabulous fountains. Slightly further afield, Lazio's Etruscan treasures are quite special. The easiest to get to are in **Cerveteri**, but push on up to **Tarquinia** and you'll be rewarded with some truly amazing frescoed tombs.

Outstanding Works of Art

» Michelangelo's frescoes in the Sistine Chapel (p110) are among the world's most famous works of art.

» Raphael's great masterpiece *La Scuola d'Atene* (The School of Athens) hangs in the Stanze di Raffaello (Raphael Rooms; p110) in the Vatican Museums.

» Gian Lorenzo Bernini's sculptures at the Museo e Galleria Borghese (p111) show a genius at the top of his game.

» Caravaggio's St Matthew cycle in the Chiesa di San Luigi dei Francesi (p78) features his signature chiaroscuro style.

CATACOMBS

Visit the creepy catacombs on Via Appia Antica to see where Rome's pioneering Christians buried their dead. Hundreds of thousands of tombs line the pitch-black tunnels.

Best Viewpoints

» Il Vittoriano (p72)

» Dome of St Peter's Basilica (p103)

» Priori dei Cavalieri di Malta (boxed text, p79)

» Gianicolo Hill (p99)

» Castel Sant'Angelo (p140)

Top Pizzerias

» Pizzarium (p129)

» Pizzeria da Baffetto (p123)

» Forno di Campo de' Fiori (p123)

» Da Michele (p126)

Resources

» 060608 (www.060608. it) is Rome's official tourist website.

» Pierreci (www.pierreci.it) has information and ticket booking for Rome's monuments.

» Vatican (www.vatican.va) is the place to book tickets for the Vatican Museums.

» Auditorium (www.audi torium.com) has concert listings for the Auditorium Parco della Musica.

Rome & Lazio Highlights

1 Imagine the crowd's roar at the Vatican's **Colosseum** (p61)

2 Gaze heavenwards in the Vatican's **Sistine Chapel** (p110)

3 Admire the audacious dome at the **Pantheon** (p73)

4 Gape at the grandeur of **St Peter's Basilica** (p102)

5 Revel in ravishing baroque sculpture at the **Museo e Galleria Borghese** (p111)

6 Check out ancient interior design at the **Museo Nazionale Romano: Palazzo Massimo alle Terme** (p90)

7 Explore the haunting ruins of the palatial **Palatino** (p65)

8 Go underground at the **Basilica di San Clemente** (p92)

9 Delve into frescoed Etruscan tombs in **Tarquinia** (p147)

10 Walk in ancient footsteps at the preserved port town of **Ostia Antica** (p143)

To Palestrina (39km)

Via Prenestina

Via Casilina

To Frascati (16km)

Colli Albani

Ponte Lungo

Furio Camillo

Via Appia Nuova

To Castel Gandolfo (18km)

Marrana della Caffarella

See Appia Antica Map (p98)

SAN LORENZO

Via La Spezia

TUSCOLANO

Re di Roma

Via Appia Antica (Appian Way)

APPIO-LATINO

Manzoni

Piazza Vittorio Emanuele II

San Giovanni

See Celio Hill & Lateran Map (p94)

Cavour

Colosseo

Basilica di San Clemente

Colosseum

Parco San Sebastiano

See Trevi Map (p86)

See Ancient Rome Map (p62)

Palatino

Terme di Caracalla

Campidoglio (Capitoline Hill)

See Centro Storico Map (p74)

Circo Massimo

Viale Aventino

Aventine Hill

Stazione Roma-Ostiense

Circonvallazione Ostiense

See Trastevere & Gianicolo Map (p100)

See Aventino & Testaccio Map (p96)

Via del Porto Fluviale

Via Ostiense

OSTIENSE

Garbatella

To EUR (4km)

Via Cristoforo Colombo

Stazione San Pietro

Gianicolo (Janiculum)

Villa Doria Pamphilj

TRASTEVERE

Via Portuense

Stazione Trastevere

Basilica di San Paolo Fuori le Mura

San Paolo

Via Ostiense

Viale Guglielmo Marconi

MONTEVERDE

Circonvallazione Gianicolense

GIANICOLENSE

PORTUENSE

To Ostia Antica (25km); Sabaudia (95km)

ROME

POP 2.74 MILLION

History

According to myth, Rome was founded on the Palatino (Palatine Hill) by Romulus and Remus, the twin sons of Vestal Virgin Rhea Silva and the God of War, Mars. Historians proffer a more prosaic version of events, involving Romulus becoming the first king of Rome on 21 April 753 BC and the city comprising Etruscan, Latin and Sabine settlements on the Palatine, Esquiline and Quirinale Hills.

Following the fall of Tarquin the Proud, the last of Rome's seven Etruscan kings, the Roman Republic was founded in 509 BC. From modest beginnings, it spread to become the dominant Western superpower until internal rivalries led to civil war. Julius Caesar, the last of the Republic's consuls, was assassinated in 44 BC, leaving Mark Antony and Octavian to fight for the top job. Octavian prevailed and, with the blessing of the Senate, became Augustus, the first Roman emperor.

Augustus ruled well, and the city enjoyed a period of political stability and unparalleled artistic achievement – a golden age for which the Romans yearned as they endured the depravities of Augustus' successors Tiberius, Caligula and Nero. A huge fire in AD 64 then reduced Rome to tatters. But the city bounced back and by AD 100 it had a population of 1.5 million and was the undisputed *caput mundi* (capital of the world). It couldn't last, though, and when Constantine moved his power base to Byzantium in 330, Rome's glory days were numbered. In 455 it was routed by the Vandals and in 476 the last emperor of the Western Roman Empire, Romulus Augustulus, was deposed.

By the 6th century, Rome's population had sunk to a measly 80,000; the city was in a bad way and in desperate need of a leader. Into the breach stepped the Church. Christianity had been spreading since the 1st century AD thanks to the underground efforts of apostles Peter and Paul, and under Constantine it received official recognition. In the late 6th century Pope Gregory I did much to strengthen the Church's grip over the city, laying the foundations for its later role as capital of the Catholic world.

The medieval period was a dark age, marked by almost continuous fighting; the city was reduced to a semi-deserted battlefield as the powerful Colonna and Orsini families battled for supremacy and the bedraggled population trembled in the face of plague, famine and flooding (the Tiber regularly broke its banks).

But out of the ruins grew the Rome of the Renaissance. At the behest of the city's great papal dynasties – the Barberini, Farnese and Pamphilj, among others – the leading artists of the 15th and 16th centuries were summoned to work on projects such as the Sistine Chapel and St Peter's Basilica. But the enemy was never far away, and in 1527 the Spanish forces of Holy Roman Emperor Charles V ransacked Rome.

Another rebuild was in order, and it was to the 17th-century baroque masters Bernini and Borromini that Rome's patrons turned. Exuberant churches, fountains and *palazzi* (mansions) sprouted all over the city, as these two bitter rivals competed to produce ever-more virtuosic masterpieces.

The next makeover followed the unification of Italy and the declaration of Rome as its capital. Mussolini, believing himself a modern-day Augustus, left an indelible stamp, bulldozing new imperial roads and commissioning ambitious building projects such as the monumental suburb of EUR.

Post-Fascism, the 1950s and '60s saw the glittering era of *la dolce vita* and hasty urban expansion, resulting in Rome's sometimes wretched suburbs. A clean-up in 2000 had the city in its best shape for decades, and in recent years some dramatic modernist building projects have given the Eternal City some edge, such as Richard Meier's Museo dell'Ara Pacis and Massimiliano Fuksas' ongoing Centro Congressi in EUR.

WATCH YOUR VALUABLES

Rome is a relatively safe city, but petty crime is rife. Pickpockets follow the tourists, so watch out around the Colosseum, Piazza di Spagna, Piazza San Pietro and Stazione Termini. Be particularly vigilant around the bus stops on Via Marsala, where thieves prey on disoriented travellers fresh in from Ciampino Airport. Crowded public transport is another hot spot – the 64 Vatican bus is notorious. If travelling on the metro, try to use the end carriages, which are usually less crowded.

ROME IN...

Two Days

Get to grips with ancient Rome at the **Colosseum**, the **Roman Forum** and **Palatino** (Palatine Hill). Spend the afternoon exploring the **Capitoline Museums** before an evening in **Trastevere**. On day two, hit the Vatican. Marvel at **St Peter's Basilica** and the **Sistine Chapel** in the vast **Vatican Museums**. Afterwards ditch your guidebook and get happily lost in the animated streets around **Piazza Navona** and the **Pantheon**.

Four Days

On day three, check out the **Trevi Fountain**, the **Spanish Steps** and the outstanding **Museo e Galleria Borghese**. At night, head to **Campo de' Fiori** for a drink, eat somewhere in the centre and then finish up with a drink in the charming **Monti** district. Next day, visit the **Palazzo e Galleria Doria Pamphilj** or the **Museo Nazionale Romano: Palazzo Massimo alle Terme** before exploring the **Jewish Ghetto** and bijou backstreets such as **Via del Governo Vecchio** or **Via dei Coronari**. Round the day off with the student drinkers and fashionable diners in **San Lorenzo**.

A Week

Venture out to **Via Appia Antica**, home of the **catacombs**, and take a day trip: choose between **Ostia Antica** or the Etruscan treasures of **Cerveteri** or **Tarquinia**.

◉ Sights

They say that a lifetime's not enough for Rome *(Roma, non basta una vita!)*. There's simply too much to see. So the best plan is to choose selectively, and leave the rest for next time.

Rome is a sprawling city, but the centre is relatively compact and most sights are concentrated in the area between Stazione Termini, the city's main transport hub, and the Vatican. Halfway between the two, the Pantheon and Piazza Navona lie at the heart of the *centro storico* (historic centre), while to the south, the Colosseum lords it over the city's great ancient ruins: the Roman Forum and Palatino. On the west bank of the Tiber, St Peter's Basilica trumpets the presence of the Vatican.

ANCIENT ROME

Colosseum   MONUMENT
(Map p62; ☑06 3996 7700; Piazza del Colosseo; adult/reduced incl Roman Forum & Palatino €12/7.50, audioguide €5.50; ☺8.30am-1hr before sunset) A monument to raw, merciless power, the Colosseum (Colosseo) is the most thrilling of Rome's ancient sights. It's not just the amazing completeness of the place, or its size, but the sense of violent history that resonates: it was here that gladiators met in mortal combat and condemned prisoners fought off wild beasts in front of baying, bloodthirsty crowds. Two thousand years

later it's Italy's top tourist attraction, pulling in between 16,000 and 19,000 people on an average day.

Built by the emperor Vespasian (r AD 69–79) in the grounds of Nero's palatial Domus Aurea, the Colosseum was inaugurated in AD 80. To mark the occasion, Vespasian's son and successor Titus (r 79–81) held games that lasted 100 days and nights, during which some 5000 animals were slaughtered. Trajan (r 98–117) later topped this, holding a marathon 117-day killing spree involving 9000 gladiators and 10,000 animals.

Originally known as the Flavian Amphitheatre, the 50,000-capacity stadium may have been ancient Rome's most fearful arena, but it wasn't the biggest – the Circo Massimo could hold up to 200,000 people. The name Colosseum, when introduced in medieval times, was not a reference to its size but to the Colosso di Nerone, a giant statue of Nero that stood nearby.

The outer walls have three levels of arches, articulated by columns topped by capitals of the Ionic (at the bottom), Doric and Corinthian (at the top) orders. The external walls were originally covered in travertine, and marble statues once filled the niches on the 2nd and 3rd storeys. The upper level, punctuated with windows and slender Corinthian pilasters, had supports for 240 masts that held up a canvas awning over the arena, shielding the spectators from sun and rain.

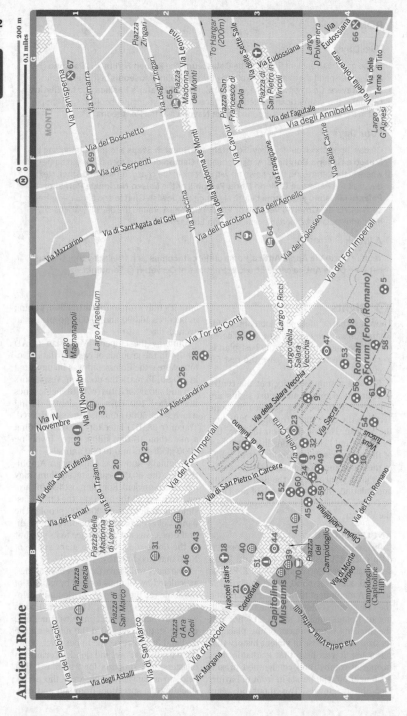

Ancient Rome

ROME & LAZIO ROME

MONTI

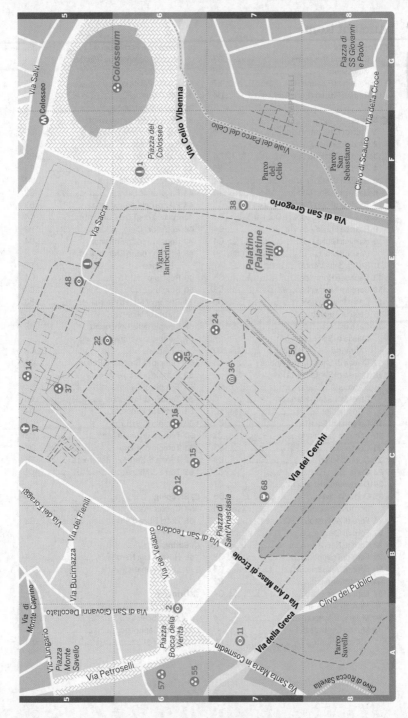

Ancient Rome

The 80 entrance arches, known as *vomitoria,* allowed the spectators to enter and be seated in a matter of minutes.

The Colosseum's interior was divided into three parts: the arena, *cavea* and podium. The arena had a wooden floor covered in sand to prevent the combatants from slipping and to soak up the blood. Trapdoors led down to the underground chambers and passageways beneath the arena floor – the hypogeum. Animals in cages and sets for the various battles were hoisted onto the arena by a complicated system of pulleys. The *cavea,* for spectator seating, was divided into three tiers: knights sat in the lowest tier, wealthy citizens in the middle and the plebs in the highest tier. The podium, a broad terrace in front of the tiers of seats, was reserved for emperors, senators and VIPs.

With the fall of the empire in the 6th century, the Colosseum was abandoned. In the Middle Ages, it became a fortress occupied by two of the city's warrior families: the Frangipani and the Annibaldi.

Damaged several times by earthquakes, it was later used as a quarry for travertine and marble for Palazzo Venezia, Palazzo Barberini and Palazzo Cancelleria among other buildings. Pollution and vibrations caused by traffic and the metro have also taken their toll.

The top tier and hypogeum have recently been opened to the public. Visits, which cost €8 on top of the normal Colosseum ticket and are by guided tour only, require advance booking.

Arco di Costantino   MONUMENT
(Map p62) On the western side of the Colosseum, this triumphal arch was built in 312 to honour the emperor Constantine's victory over rival Maxentius at the battle of Ponte Milvio (Milvian Bridge).

Palatino (Palatine Hill)   ARCHAEOLOGICAL SITE
(Map p62; ☎06 3996 7700; www.pierreci.it; Via di San Gregorio 30; adult/reduced incl Colosseum & Roman Forum €12/7.50, audioguide €5; ☉8.30am-1hr before sunset) Sandwiched between the Roman Forum and the Circo Massimo, the Palatino (Palatine Hill) is an atmospheric area of towering pine trees, majestic ruins and memorable views. According to legend, this is where Romulus killed his twin and founded Rome in 753 BC. Archaeological evidence cannot prove the legend, but it has dated human habitation here to the 8th century BC.

COLOSSEUM TIPS

Some useful tips to beat the Colosseum queues:

» Buy your ticket from the Palatino entrance (about 250m away at Via di San Gregorio 30) or the Roman Forum entrance (Largo della Salara Vecchia).

» Get the Roma Pass, which is valid for three days and a whole host of sites.

» Book your ticket online at www. pierreci.it (plus booking fee of €1.50).

» Join an official English-language tour – €4 on top of the regular Colosseum ticket price.

» Visit in the late afternoon rather than mid-morning

» Outside the Colosseum, you'll almost certainly be hailed by centurions offering to pose for a photo. They are not doing this for love and will expect payment. There's no set rate but €5 is more than enough – and that's €5 period, not €5 per person.

As the most central of Rome's seven hills (and because it was both close to and above the Roman Forum) the Palatino was ancient Rome's poshest neighbourhood. The emperor Augustus lived here all his life and successive emperors built increasingly opulent palaces. However, after Rome's decline it fell into disrepair, and in the Middle Ages churches and castles were built over the ruins. During the Renaissance, members of wealthy families established gardens on the hill.

Most of the Palatino as it appears today is covered by the ruins of Emperor Domitian's vast complex, which served as the main imperial palace for 300 years. Divided into the Domus Flavia (imperial palace), Domus Augustana (the emperor's private residence) and a *stadio* (stadium), it was built in the 1st century AD.

On entering the complex from Via di San Gregorio, head uphill until you come to the first recognisable construction, the stadio, probably used by the emperors for private games and events. Adjoining the stadium are the remains of the complex built by Septimius Severus, comprising baths (the Terme di Settimio Severo) and a palace (the Domus Severiana).

On the other side of the *stadio* are the ruins of the huge Domus Augustana, the emperor's private residence. It was built on two levels, with rooms leading off a *peristilio* (peristyle or garden courtyard) on each floor. You can't get down to the lower level, but from above you can see the basin of a fountain and beyond it rooms that were paved with coloured marble. In 2007 a mosaic-covered vaulted cavern was discovered more than 15m beneath the Domus. Some believe this to be the Lupercale, a cave believed by ancient Romans to be where Romulus and Remus were suckled by a wolf.

The grey building near the Domus Augustana houses the Museo Palatino and its collection of archaeological artefacts. Highlights include a beautiful 1st-century bronze, the *Erma di Canefora,* and a wonderful bust of Giovane Principessa, daughter of Nero's successor Marcus Aurelius.

North of the museum is the Domus Flavia, the public part of the palace complex. This was centred on a grand columned peristyle – the grassy area you see with the base of an octagonal fountain – off which the main halls led. To the north was the emperor's throne room; to the west, a second big hall that the emperor used to meet his advisors; and to the south, a large banqueting hall, the *triclinium*.

Among the best-preserved buildings on the Palatino is the Casa di Livia, northwest of the Domus Flavia. Home to Augustus' wife Livia, it was built around an atrium leading onto what were once reception rooms, decorated with frescoes of mythological scenes, landscapes, fruits and flowers. In front is the Casa di Augusto (entry in groups of 5; ⊘11am-4.30pm Mon, Wed, Sat & Sun), Augustus' separate residence, which contains superb frescoes in vivid reds, yellows and blues.

Behind the Casa di Augusto are the Capanne Romulee (Romulean Huts), where it is thought Romulus and Remus were brought up after their discovery by the shepherd Faustulus.

Northeast of the Casa di Livia lies the criptoportico, a 128m tunnel where Caligula was thought to have been murdered, and which Nero later used to connect his Domus Aurea with the Palatino. Lit by a series of windows, it was once decorated by elaborate stucco. Nowadays it's used to stage temporary exhibitions.

The area west of this was once Tiberius' palace, the Domus Tiberiana, but is now the site of the 16th-century Orti Farnesiani, one of Europe's earliest botanical gardens. Twin pavilions stand at the northern point of the garden, commanding breathtaking views over the Roman Forum.

Roman Forum
(Foro Romano)   ARCHAEOLOGICAL SITE
(Map p62; ☑06 3996 7700; www.pierreci.it; Largo della Salara Vecchia; adult/reduced incl Colosseum & Palatino €12/7.50, audioguide €5; ⊘8.30am-1hr

---

MAKING THE MOST OF YOUR EURO

Several discount cards are available for those planning on some serious museum-going. You can buy the cards at any of the monuments or museums listed (or online at www.pierreci.it) and the Roma Pass is also available at Comune di Roma tourist information points.

Note that EU citizens between the ages of 18 and 24 and over the age of 65 are entitled to significant discounts at most museums and galleries in Rome. Unfortunately student discounts don't usually apply for citizens of non-EU countries.

» Appia Antica Card (adult/reduced €7.50/4.50, valid 7 days) For the Terme di Caracalla, Mausoleo di Cecilia Metella and Villa Quintili.

» Archaeologia Card (adult/reduced €23/13, valid 7 days) For entrance to the Colosseum, Palatino, Roman Forum, Terme di Caracalla, Palazzo Altemps, Palazzo Massimo alle Terme, Terme di Diocleziano, Crypta Balbi, Mausoleo di Cecilia Metella and Villa Quintili.

» Roma Pass (www.romapass.it; €25, valid 3 days) Includes free admission to two museums or sites (choose from a list of 38) as well as reduced entry to extra sites, unlimited public transport within Rome, and reduced entry to other exhibitions and events. If you use this for more-expensive sights such as the Capitoline Museums and the Colosseum you'll save money.

BARBARA NAZZARO: ARCHITECT

Technical Director at the Colosseum, Barbara Nazzaro, explains what went on in the hypogeum, the underground complex of corridors, cages and lifts beneath the amphitheatre's main arena.

'The hypogeum was on two levels and about 1000 people worked down there. The gladiators entered through an underground corridor which led directly in from the nearby Ludus Magnus (gladiator school). This corridor was later cut through by a drain, but you can still see the original floor. In side corridors, which stand over a natural spring, boats were kept. When they wanted these boats up in the arena they would let the spring water in and flood the tunnels. Later these side passages were used for winch mechanisms, all of which were controlled by a single pulley system. There were about 80 lifts going up to the arena as well as cages where wild animals were kept. You can still see the spaces where these were.

'The hypogeum was used until about 508, when it was virtually buried by the effects of blocked drains and a big earthquake which caused parts to fall from the upper layers of the Colosseum.'

before sunset) Today an impressive, if rather confusing, sprawl of ruins, the Roman Forum was once a gleaming complex of marble-clad temples, proud basilicas and vibrant public spaces: the gleaming heart of an ancient city.

Originally an Etruscan burial ground, it was first developed in the 7th century BC and expanded over subsequent centuries. Its importance declined after the 4th century until eventually it was used as pasture land. In the Middle Ages it was known as the Campo Vaccino (literally 'Cow Field') and extensively plundered for its stone and marble. The area was systematically excavated in the 18th and 19th centuries, and excavations continue to this day.

Entering from Largo della Salara Vecchia (you can also enter directly from the Palatino) you'll see the Tempio di Antonino e Faustina, ahead to your left. Erected in AD 141 by the Senate and dedicated to the empress Faustina and later to the emperor Antoninus Pius, it was transformed into a church in the 8th century, so the soaring columns now frame the Chiesa di San Lorenzo in Miranda. To your right the Basilica Fulvia Aemilia, built in 179 BC, was a 100m-long public hall, with a two-storey porticoed facade lined by shops. Opposite the basilica stands the Tempio di Giulio Cesare (Temple of Julius Caesar) built by Augustus in 29 BC.

At the end of the short path you come to the Via Sacra, which traverses the Forum from northwest to southeast. Head right up Via Sacra and you reach the Curia, the meeting place of the Roman Senate, which was rebuilt by Julius Caesar, Augustus, Domitian and Diocletian, before being converted into a church in the Middle Ages. What you see today is a 1937 reconstruction of Diocletian's Curia. The bronze doors are copies – the originals were used by Borromini for the Basilica di San Giovanni in Laterano.

In front of the Curia, and hidden by scaffolding, is the Lapis Niger, a large piece of black marble that covered a sacred area said to be the tomb of Romulus.

At the end of Via Sacra stands the 23m-high Arco di Settimio Severo (Arch of Septimius Severus). Dedicated to the eponymous emperor and his two sons, Caracalla and Geta, it was built in AD 203 to celebrate the Roman victory over the Parthians. Nearby, at the foot of the Tempio di Saturno, is the Millarium Aureum, which marked the centre of ancient Rome, from where distances to the city were measured.

On your left are the remains of the Rostrum, an elaborate podium where Shakespeare had Mark Antony make his famous 'Friends, Romans, countrymen...' speech. In front of this, the Colonna di Foca (Column of Phocus) marks the centre of the Piazza del Foro, the Forum's main market and meeting place. The last monument erected in the Roman Forum, it was built in honour of the Eastern Roman Emperor Phocus.

Roman Forum

In ancient times, a forum was a market place, civic centre and religious complex all rolled into one, and the greatest of all was the Roman Forum (Foro Romano). Situated between the Palatino (Palatine Hill), ancient Rome's most exclusive neighbourhood, and the Campidoglio (Capitoline Hill), it was the city's busy, bustling centre. On any given day it teemed with activity. Senators debated affairs of state in the **Curia 1**, shoppers thronged the squares and traffic-free streets, crowds gathered under the **Colonna di Foca 2** to listen to politicians holding forth from the **Rostrum 2**. Elsewhere, lawyers worked the courts in basilicas including the **Basilica di Massenzio 3**, while the Vestal Virgins quietly went about their business in the **Casa delle Vestali 4**. Special occasions were also celebrated in the Forum: religious holidays were marked with ceremonies at temples such as the **Tempio di Saturno 5** and the **Tempio di Castore e Polluce 6**, and military victories were honoured with dramatic processions up Via Sacra and the building of monumental arches like the **Arco di Settimio Severo 7** and the **Arco di Tito 8**.

The ruins you see today are impressive but they can be confusing without a clear picture of what the Forum once looked like. This spread shows the Forum in its heyday, complete with temples, civic buildings and towering monuments to heroes of the Roman Empire.

TOP TIPS

» Get grandstand views of the Forum from the Palatino and Campidoglio.

» Visit first thing in the morning or late afternoon; crowds are worst between 11am and 2pm.

» In summer it gets hot in the Forum and there's little shade, so take a hat and plenty of water.

Colonna di Foca & Rostrum
The free-standing, 13.5m-high Column of Phocus is the Forum's youngest monument, dating to AD 608. Behind it, the Rostrum provided a suitably grandiose platform for pontificating public speakers.

Campidoglio (Capitoline Hill)

Admission
Although valid for two days, admission tickets only allow for one entry into the Forum, Colosseum and Palatino.

Tempio di Saturno
Ancient Rome's Fort Knox, the Temple of Saturn was the city treasury. In Caesar's day it housed 13 tonnes of gold, 114 tonnes of silver and 30 million *sestertii* worth of silver coins.

JONATHAN SMITH / LONELY PLANET IMAGES ©

GEOFF STRINGER / LONELY PLANET IMAGES ©

Tempio di Castore e Polluce
Only three columns of the Temple of Castor and Pollux remain. The temple was dedicated to the Heavenly Twins after they supposedly led the Romans to victory over the Etruscans.

Arco di Settimio Severo

One of the Forum's signature monuments, this imposing triumphal arch commemorates the military victories of Septimius Severus. Relief panels depict his campaigns against the Parthians.

Curia

This big barnlike building was the official seat of the Roman Senate. Most of what you see is a reconstruction, but the interior marble floor dates to the 3rd-century reign of Diocletian.

Basilica di Massenzio

Marvel at the scale of this vast 4th-century basilica. In its original form the central hall was divided into enormous naves; now only part of the northern nave survives.

Julius Caesar RIP

Julius Caesar was cremated on the site where the Tempio di Giulio Cesare now stands.

Via Sacra

Tempio di Giulio Cesare

Casa delle Vestali

White statues line the grassy atrium of what was once the luxurious 50-room home of the Vestal Virgins. The virgins played an important role in Roman religion, serving the goddess Vesta.

Arco di Tito

Said to be the inspiration for the Arc de Triomphe in Paris, the well-preserved Arch of Titus was built by the emperor Domitian to honour his elder brother Titus.

The eight granite columns that rise up behind the Colonna are all that remain of the 5th-century Tempio di Saturno (Temple of Saturn), one of Rome's most important temples and home to the state treasury. Behind the temple, backing onto the Capitoline Hill, are (north to south) the ruins of Tempio della Concordia (Temple of Concord), the remaining columns of Tempio di Vespasiano (Temple of Vespasian and Titus) and the Portico degli Dei Consenti.

Passing over to the path that runs parallel to Via Sacra, you'll see the stubby ruins of the Basilica Giulia, which was begun by Julius Caesar and finished by Augustus. At the end of the basilica are the three Corinthian columns of the Tempio di Castore e Polluce (Temple of Castor and Pollux), built at the beginning of the 5th century BC to mark the defeat of the Etruscan Tarquins in 489 BC. South of the temple is the Chiesa di Santa Maria Antiqua, the oldest Christian church in the Forum.

Back towards Via Sacra is the Casa delle Vestali (House of the Vestal Virgins), home of the virgins who tended the sacred flame in the adjoining Tempio di Vesta. The six priestesses were selected from patrician families when aged between six and 10 to serve in the temple for 30 years. If the flame in the temple went out the priestess responsible would be flogged, and if she lost her virginity she would be buried alive, since her blood couldn't be spilled. The offending man would be flogged to death.

Continuing up Via Sacra, past the Tempio di Romolo (Temple of Romulus), you come to the Basilica di Massenzio, the largest building on the forum. Started by the Emperor Maxentius and finished by Constantine in 315 (it's also known as the Basilica di Costantino), it originally covered an area of approximately 100m by 65m. A colossal statue of Constantine, pieces of which are on display at the Capitoline Museums, was unearthed at the site in 1487.

Beyond the basilica, you come to the Arco di Tito (Arch of Titus), built in AD 81 to celebrate Vespasian and Titus' victories against Jerusalem. In the past, Roman Jews would avoid passing under this arch, the historical symbol of the beginning of the Diaspora.

Basilica di SS Cosma e Damiano   CHURCH
(Map p62; Via dei Fori Imperiali; ⊗9am-1pm & 3-7pm) Backing onto the Roman Forum, this 6th-century basilica incorporates parts of the Foro di Vespasiano and Tempio di Romolo,

with the latter visible through the glass wall at the end of the nave. But the real reason to visit are the vibrant 6th-century apse mosaics, depicting Christ's Second Coming. Also worth a glance, off the tranquil 17th-century cloisters, is a lavish Neapolitan presepe (nativity scene; admission €1; ⊗10am-1pm & 3-6pm Fri-Sun) dating from the 18th century.

Carcere Mamertino   HISTORICAL SITE
(Mamertine Prison; Map p62; Clivo Argentario 1; admission €10; ⊗9.30am-7pm summer, to 5pm winter, last admission 40min before close) At the foot of the Campidoglio, the Mamertine Prison was ancient Rome's maximum-security prison. Visitors are escorted into the depths of the jail, beneath the ground-level church, to see where St Peter was supposedly imprisoned. According to legend the apostle converted his jailers and created a miraculous stream of water to baptise them.

Imperial Forums   ARCHAEOLOGICAL SITE
(Map p62) The ruins over the road from the Roman Forum are known collectively as the Imperial Forums (Fori Imperiali). Constructed between 42 BC and AD 112 by successive emperors, they were largely buried in 1933 when Mussolini built Via dei Fori Imperiali. Excavations have since unearthed much of them, but work continues and visits are limited to the Mercati di Traiano (Trajan's Markets), accessible through the Museo dei Fori Imperiali.

Little that's recognisable remains of the Foro di Traiano (Trajan's Forum), except for some pillars from the Basilica Ulpia and the Colonna di Traiano (Trajan's Column), whose minutely detailed reliefs celebrate Trajan's military victories over the Dacians (from modern-day Romania).

To the southeast, three temple columns arise from the ruins of the Foro di Augusto (Augustus' Forum), now mostly under Via dei Fori Imperiali. The 30m-high wall behind the forum was built to protect it from the fires that frequently swept the area.

The Foro di Nerva (Nerva's Forum) was also buried by Mussolini's road-building, although part of a temple dedicated to Minerva still stands. Originally, it would have connected the Foro di Augusto to the 1st-century Foro di Vespasiano (Vespasian's Forum), also known as the Forum of Peace.

On the other side of the road, three columns on a raised platform are the most visible remains of the Foro di Cesare (Caesar's Forum).

Museo dei Fori Imperiali   MUSEUM

(Map p62; ✆06 06 08; www.mercatiditraiano.it; Via IV Novembre 94; adult/reduced €11/9; ⊙9am-7pm Tue-Sun, last admission 6pm) Housed in Trajan's 2nd-century market complex, this striking museum provides a fascinating introduction to the Imperial Forums with detailed explanatory panels and a smattering of archaeological artefacts. From the main hallway, a lift whisks you up to the Torre delle Milizie (Militia Tower), a 13th-century redbrick tower, and the upper levels of the Mercati di Traiano (Trajan's Markets). These markets, housed in a three-storey semicircular construction, hosted hundreds of traders selling everything from oil and vegetables to flowers, silks and spices.

Piazza del Campidoglio   PIAZZA

(Map p62) This elegant piazza, designed by Michelangelo in 1538, is the centrepiece of the Campidoglio (Capitoline Hill), one of the seven hills on which Rome was founded. In ancient times, Rome's two most important temples stood here: one dedicated to Jupiter Capitolinus and the other (which housed Rome's mint) to Juno Moneta. More than 2000 years on, the hill is still a political powerhouse as the seat of Rome's municipal government.

You can reach the piazza from the Roman Forum, but the most dramatic approach is via the Cordonata, the graceful staircase that leads up from Piazza d'Ara Coeli. At the top, the piazza is bordered by three *palazzi:* Palazzo Nuovo to the left, Palazzo Senatorio straight ahead, and Palazzo dei Conservatori on the right. Together, Palazzo Nuovo and Palazzo dei Conservatori house the Capitoline Museums, while Palazzo Senatorio is home to Rome's city council.

In the centre, the bronze equestrian statue of Marcus Aurelius is a copy. The original, which dates from the 2nd century AD, is in the Capitoline Museums.

Capitoline Museums   ART GALLERY

(Musei Capitolini; Map p62; ✆06 06 08; www.musei capitolini.org; Piazza del Campidoglio 1; adult/reduced €12/10, audioguide €5; ⊙9am-8pm Tue-Sun, last admission 7pm) The world's oldest national museums were founded in 1471 when Pope Sixtus IV donated a few bronze sculptures to the city, forming the nucleus of what is now one of Italy's finest collections of classical art.

The entrance is in Palazzo dei Conservatori, where you'll find the original core of the sculptural collection on the 1st

SILVIA PROSPERI: TOUR GUIDE

A tour guide since 2005, Silvia Prosperi knows Rome's great sights inside out. Here she advises on some of the city's lesser-known hits.

Favourite sights

I love too many sights. The Colonna di Traiano is a masterpiece that is sometimes neglected. The archaeological museum at Palazzo Massimo alle Terme is another underrated attraction. I also love the atmosphere of the Etruscan museum at Villa Giulia and the view from the terrace of Castel Sant'Angelo.

Most underrated sights

As to underrated sights, the Mercati di Traiano are really interesting, as is Bramante's Tempietto on the Gianicolo.

floor. On the 2nd floor is a masterpiece-packed art gallery.

Before you head upstairs, take a moment to admire the ancient masonry littered around the ground-floor courtyard, most notably a mammoth head, hand and foot. These all come from a 12m-high statue of Constantine that originally stood in the Basilica di Massenzio in the Roman Forum.

Of the sculpture on the 1st floor, the Etruscan *Lupa Capitolina* (Capitoline Wolf) is the most famous. Donated to the Roman people by Pope Sixtus IV, the 5th-century-BC bronze wolf stands over her suckling wards Romulus and Remus, who were added in 1471. Other crowd-pleasers include the *Spinario,* a delicate 1st-century-BC bronze of a boy removing a thorn from his foot, and Gian Lorenzo Bernini's *Medusa.* Also on this floor, in the modern Exedra of Marcus Aurelius, is the original of the equestrian statue that you see in the piazza.

Upstairs, the Pinacoteca contains paintings by Titian, Tintoretto, Reni, Van Dyck and Rubens. The Sala Santa Petronella boasts two important works by Caravaggio: *La buona ventura* (The Fortune Teller; 1595), which shows a gypsy pretending to read a young man's hand but stealing his ring; and *San Giovanni Battista* (St John the Baptist; 1602), a sensual and unusual depiction of the New Testament saint.

A tunnel links Palazzo dei Conservatori to Palazzo Nuovo on the other side of the square via the Tabularium, ancient Rome's central archive, beneath Palazzo Senatorio.

Palazzo Nuovo contains some real show-stoppers. Chief among them is the *Galata morente* (Dying Gaul), a Roman copy of a 3rd-century-BC Greek original that movingly depicts the anguish of a dying Frenchman. Another superb figurative piece, although of a very different nature, is the *Venere Capitolina* (Capitoline Venus), a sensual yet demure portrayal of the nude goddess.

Chiesa di Santa Maria in Aracoeli   CHURCH

(Map p62; Piazza Santa Maria in Aracoeli; ⊙9am-12.30pm & 3-6.30pm) Marking the highest point of the Campidoglio, this 6th-century church sits on the site of the Roman temple to Juno Moneta. According to legend it was here that the Tiburtine Sybil told Augustus of the coming birth of Christ, and the church still has a strong association with the nativity. Features include an impressive Cosmatesque floor and an important 15th-century fresco by Pinturicchio. Local football hero Francesco Totti got married here.

Il Vittoriano   MONUMENT

(Map p62; Piazza Venezia; admission free; ⊙ 9.30am-5.30pm summer, to 4.30pm winter) Known also as the Altare della Patria (Altar of the Fatherland), this massive mountain of white marble towers over Piazza Venezia. Begun in 1885 to commemorate Italian unification and honour Victor Emmanuel II, it incorporates the Tomb of the Unknown Soldier, as well as the Museo Centrale del Risorgimento (Via di San Pietro in Carcere; admission free; ⊙9.30am-6pm) documenting Italian unification.

For Rome's best 360-degree views, take the Roma dal Cielo (adult/reduced €7/3.50; ⊙9.30am-6.30pm Mon-Thu, to 7.30pm Fri-Sun) lift from the side of the building up to the very top of the monument.

Palazzo Venezia   PALAZZO

(Map p62; Piazza Venezia) On the western side of Piazza Venezia, this was the first of Rome's great Renaissance palaces. For centuries it served as the embassy of the Venetian Republic, although its best-known resident was Mussolini, who famously made speeches from the balcony overlooking the square.

To see inside, visit the sprawling, under-visited Museo Nazionale del Palazzo Venezia (☎06 678 01 31; Via del Plebiscito 118; adult/reduced €4/2; ⊙8.30am-7.30pm Tue-Sun) with its superb Byzantine and early-Renaissance paintings and an eclectic collection of jewellery, tapestries, ceramics, bronze figurines, arms and armour.

ROMULUS & REMUS, ROME'S LEGENDARY TWINS

The most famous of all Roman legends is the story of Romulus and Remus, the mythical twins who are said to have founded Rome on 21 April 753 BC.

Romulus and Remus were born to the Vestal Virgin Rhea Silva after she'd been seduced by Mars. At their birth they were immediately sentenced to death by their great-uncle Amulius, who had stolen the throne of Alba Longa from his brother, and Rhea Silva's father, Numitor. But the sentence was never carried out, and the twins were abandoned in a basket on the banks of the Tiber. Following a flood, the basket ended up on the Palatino (Palatine Hill), where the babies were saved by a she-wolf and later brought up by a shepherd, Faustulus.

Years later, and after numerous heroic adventures, the twins decided to found a city on the site where they'd originally been saved. But they didn't know where this was, so they consulted the omens. Remus, on the Aventine Hill, saw six vultures, but his brother, over on the Palatino, saw 12. The meaning was clear and Romulus began building, much to the fury of his brother. The two subsequently argued and Romulus killed his twin.

Romulus continued building and soon had a city. To populate it he created a refuge on the Campidoglio, Aventine, Celian and Quirinale Hills, to which a ragtag population of criminals, ex-slaves and outlaws soon decamped. However, the city still needed women. Romulus's solution to this problem was to invite everyone in the surrounding country to celebrate the Festival of Consus (21 August). As the spectators watched the festival games, Romulus and his men pounced and abducted all the women, an action known as the Rape of the Sabine Women.

Basilica di San Marco
CHURCH

(Map p62; Piazza di San Marco; ⊙8.30am-noon & 4-6.30pm Mon-Sat, 9am-1pm & 4-8pm Sun) This 4th-century basilica stands over the house where St Mark the Evangelist is said to have stayed while in Rome. Its main attraction is a shimmering 9th-century apse mosaic, depicting Christ with saints and Pope Gregory IV.

Bocca della Verità
MONUMENT

(Map p62; Piazza della Bocca della Verità 18; donation €0.50; ⊙9.30am-4.50pm) A round piece of marble once used as an ancient manhole cover, the Bocca della Verità (Mouth of Truth) is one of Rome's great curiosities. Legend holds that if you put your hand in the carved mouth and tell a lie, it will bite your hand off.

The mouth lives in the portico of the beautiful, medieval Chiesa di Santa Maria in Cosmedin. Originally built in the 8th century, the church was given a major revamp in the 12th century, when the seven-storey bell tower and portico were added and the floor was decorated with Cosmati inlaid marble. Opposite the church are two small Roman temples: the round Tempio di Ercole Vincitore and the Tempio di Portunus. Just off the piazza, the Arco di Giano (Arch of Janus) is a four-sided Roman arch that once covered a crossroads.

CENTRO STORICO

FREE Pantheon
MONUMENT

(Map p74; Piazza della Rotonda; audioguide €5; ⊙8.30am-7.30pm Mon-Sat, 9am-6pm Sun) Along with the Colosseum, the Pantheon is one of Rome's iconic sights. A striking 2000-year-old temple (now a church), it is the city's best-preserved ancient monument and one of the most influential buildings in the Western world. The greying, pock-marked exterior might look its age, but inside it's a different story and it's an exhilarating experience to pass through its towering bronze doors and have your vision directed upwards to the world's largest unreinforced concrete dome.

Its current form dates from around AD 120, when Emperor Hadrian built over Marcus Agrippa's original temple (27 BC) – you can still see Agrippa's name inscribed on the pediment. Hadrian's temple was dedicated to the classical gods – hence the name Pantheon, a derivation of the Greek words *pan* (all) and *theos* (god) – but in AD 608 it was consecrated as a Christian church. During the Renaissance it was much studied (Brunelleschi used it as inspiration for

his Duomo in Florence) and became an important burial chamber. Today you'll find the tomb of Raphael, alongside those of kings Vittorio Emanuele II and Umberto I.

However, the real fascination of the Pantheon lies in its massive dimensions and extraordinary dome. Considered the Romans' most important architectural achievement, it was the largest dome in the world until the 15th century and is still the largest unreinforced concrete dome ever built. Its harmonious appearance is due to a precisely calibrated symmetry – its diameter is exactly equal to the Pantheon's interior height of 43.3m. Light enters through the oculus, an 8.7m opening in the dome that also served as a symbolic connection between the temple and the gods. Rainwater enters but drains away through 22 almost-invisible holes in the sloping marble floor.

Somewhat the worse for wear, the exterior is still imposing, with 16 Corinthian columns (each a single block of stone) supporting a triangular pediment. Rivets and holes in the brickwork indicate where the original marble-veneer panels were removed.

Thanks to its consecration as a church in the 7th century, the building was spared the Christian neglect that left other structures to crumble, although it wasn't entirely safe from plundering hands. The gilded-bronze roof tiles were removed and Bernini used bronze from the portico for the baldachin at St Peter's Basilica. Thankfully, the original Roman bronze doors remain.

Chiesa di Santa Maria Sopra Minerva
CHURCH

(Map p74; Piazza della Minerva; ⊙8am-7pm Mon-Fri, 8am-1pm & 3.30-7pm Sat & Sun) Bernini's much-loved Elefantino sculpture trumpets the presence of the Dominican Chiesa di Santa Maria Sopra Minerva, Rome's only Gothic church. Built on the site of an ancient temple to Minerva, it has been much altered over the centuries and little remains of the original 13th-century design.

Inside, in the Cappella Carafa (also called the Cappella della Annunciazione), you'll find two superb 15th-century frescoes by Filippino Lippi and the majestic tomb of Pope Paul IV. Left of the high altar is one of Michelangelo's lesser-known sculptures, *Cristo Risorto* (Christ Bearing the Cross; 1520). An altarpiece of the Madonna and Child in the second chapel in the northern transept is attributed to Dominican friar and painter Fra Angelico, who is also buried in the church.

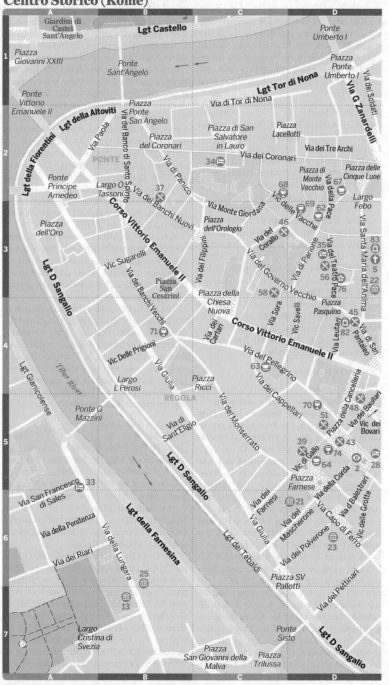

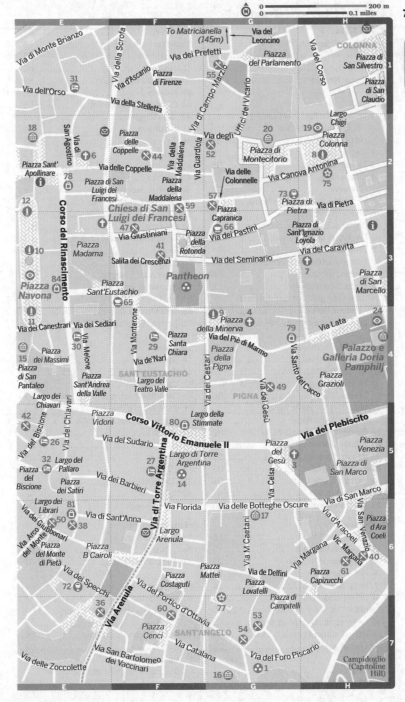

ART & POLITICS ON VIA DEL CORSO

On Via del Corso, the arrow-straight road that links Piazza Venezia to Piazza del Popolo, you'll find one of Rome's finest private art galleries. You wouldn't know it from the grimy exterior but the Palazzo e Galleria Doria Pamphilj (Map p74; ☑06 679 73 23; www. dopart.it; Via del Corso 305; adult/reduced €10.50/7.50; ☺10am-5pm, last admission 4.15pm) houses an extraordinary collection of works by Raphael, Tintoretto, Brueghel, Titian, Caravaggio, Bernini and Velázquez.

The *palazzo* dates from the mid-15th century, but the lavish interior is the work of the Doria Pamphilj family, who acquired it in the 18th century. Masterpieces abound, but look out for Titian's powerful *Salomè con la testa del Battista* (Salome with the Head of John the Baptist) and two early works by Caravaggio: *Riposso durante la fuga in Egitto* (Rest During the Flight into Egypt) and *Maddalene Penitente* (Penitent Magdalen). The collection's undisputed star is the Velázquez portrait of Pope Innocent X, who grumbled that the depiction was 'too real'. In the same room, the *Gabinetto di Velázquez* is Bernini's interpretation of the same subject.

A short walk to the north of the gallery, the 30m-high Colonna di Marco Aurelio heralds the presence of Palazzo Chigi (Map p74; www.governo.it, in Italian; Piazza Colonna 370; admission free; ☺guided visits 9am-2pm Sat Sep-Jun, booking obligatory), the official residence of the Italian prime minister. Next door, on Piazza di Montecitorio, the Bernini-designed Palazzo di Montecitorio (Map p74; ☑800 012955; www.camera.it; Piazza di Montecitorio; admission free; ☺guided visits 10am-5.30pm, 1st Sun of month) is home to Italy's Chamber of Deputies.

The body of St Catherine of Siena, minus her head (which is in Siena), lies under the high altar, and the tombs of two Medici popes, Leo X and Clement VII, are in the apse.

Chiesa di Sant'Agostino   CHURCH

(Map p74; Piazza di Sant'Agostino; ☺7.45am-noon & 4-7.30pm) This early-Renaissance church contains two outstanding works of art: Raphael's 1512 fresco *Isaiah* and Caravaggio's *Madonna dei Pellegrini* (Madonna of the Pilgrims; 1604), which caused uproar when it was unveiled in 1604, due to its depiction of Mary as barefoot and her two devoted pilgrims as filthy beggars.

Museo Nazionale Romano:
Palazzo Altemps   MUSEUM

(Map p74; ☑06 683 35 66; www.pierreci.it; Piazza Sant'Apollinare 44; adult/reduced €7/3.50; ☺9am-7.45pm Tue-Sun, last admission 7pm) This gem of a museum houses the best of the Museo Nazionale Romano's formidable collection of classical sculpture. Many pieces come from the celebrated Ludovisi collection, amassed by Cardinal Ludovico Ludovisi in the 17th century. Prize exhibits include the 5th-century *Trono Ludovisi* (Ludovisi Throne), a carved marble throne depicting Aphrodite being plucked from the sea as a newborn babe. It shares a room with two colossal heads, one of which is the goddess Juno and dates from around 600 BC. The wall frieze (about half of which remains) depicts the 10 plagues of Egypt and the Exodus.

The building's baroque frescoes provide an exquisite decorative backdrop. The walls of the Sala delle Prospettive Dipinte are decorated with landscapes and hunting scenes seen through trompe l'œil windows. These frescoes were painted for Cardinal Altemps, the rich nephew of Pope Pius IV (r 1560–65) who bought the *palazzo* in the late 16th century. Note that there is sometimes a €3 exhibition supplement.

Piazza Navona   PIAZZA

(Map p74) With its baroque *palazzi* and extravagant fountains, pavement cafes, hawkers and surging crowds, stadium-sized Piazza Navona is Rome's most iconic public square. Laid out on the ruins of an arena built by Domitian in AD 86, it was paved over in the 15th century and for almost 300 years hosted the city's main market.

Of the piazza's three fountains, Bernini's high-camp Fontana dei Quattro Fiumi (Fountain of the Four Rivers) dominates. Depicting personifications of the Nile, Ganges, Danube and Plate rivers, it's festooned with a palm tree, lion and horse and topped

CHIESA DI SAN LUIGI DEI FRANCESI

(Map p74; Piazza di San Luigi dei Francesi; ☉10am-12.30pm & 4-7pm, closed Thu afternoon) Church of Rome's French community since 1589, this baroque treasure trove boasts three canvases by Caravaggio: *La Vocazione di San Matteo* (The Calling of Saint Matthew), *Il Martiro di San Matteo* (The Martyrdom of Saint Matthew) and *San Matteo e l'Angelo* (Saint Matthew and the Angel), together known as the St Matthew cycle. These are among Caravaggio's earliest religious works, but are inescapably by his hand, with their down-to-earth realism and stunning use of chiaroscuro.

by an obelisk. Legend has it that the figure of the Nile is shielding his eyes from the Chiesa di Sant'Agnese in Agone (www.santagneseinagone.org; ☉9.30am-12.30pm & 3.30-7pm Tue-Sat, 9am-1pm & 4-8pm Sun), designed by Bernini's bitter rival, Borromini. The truth, more boringly, is that Bernini completed his fountain two years before his contemporary started work on the facade and the gesture indicates that the source of the Nile was unknown at the time.

At the northern end of the piazza is the 19th-century Fontana del Nettuno, while the Fontana del Moro to the south was designed in 1576. Bernini added the Moor holding a dolphin in the mid-17th century, and the surrounding Tritons are 19th-century copies. Piazza Navona's largest building is the 17th-century Palazzo Pamphilj, built for Pope Innocent X and now home to the Brazilian Embassy.

Museo di Roma
MUSEUM

(Map p74; ☏06 8205 9127; www.museodiroma.it; Piazza di San Pantaleo 10; adult/reduced €9/7; ☉9am-7pm Tue-Sun, last admission 6pm) The baroque Palazzo Braschi houses the Museo di Roma's eclectic collection of paintings, photographs, etchings, clothes and furniture, charting the history of Rome from the Middle Ages to the early 20th century. The *palazzo* itself contains some beautiful frescoed halls, including the extravagant Sala Cinese and the Egyptian-themed Sala Egiziana.

Campo de' Fiori
PIAZZA

(Map p74) Noisy, colourful 'Il Campo' is a major focus of Roman life: by day it hosts a much-loved market, while at night it morphs into a raucous open-air pub. Towering over the square is the Obi-Wan-like form of Giordano Bruno, a monk who was burned at the stake for heresy in 1600.

FREE Palazzo Farnese
PALAZZO

(Map p74; www.ambafrance-it.org, in Italian & French; Piazza Farnese; 15yr over only; ☉tours 3pm, 4pm & 5pm Mon & Thu, by appointment only) One of Rome's greatest Renaissance *palazzi*, Palazzo Farnese was started in 1514 by Antonio da Sangallo the Younger, continued by Michelangelo and finished by Giacomo della Porta. Nowadays, it's the French Embassy and open only to visitors who've booked a guided tour – make a booking via the website. Visits (in Italian or French) take in the Galleria dei Carracci, home to a series of frescoes by Annibale Carracci, said by some to rival those of the Sistine Chapel.

The twin fountains in the square are enormous granite baths taken from the Terme di Caracalla.

Largo di Torre Argentina
PIAZZA

(Map p74) A busy transport hub, Largo di Torre Argentina is set around the sunken Area Sacra and the remains of four Republican-era temples, all built between the 2nd and 4th centuries BC. On the piazza's western flank is Rome's premier theatre, the Teatro Argentina, built close to the spot where Julius Caesar was murdered on 15 March 44 BC.

Chiesa del Gesù
CHURCH

(Map p74; www.chiesadelgesu.org; Piazza del Gesù; ☉7am-12.30pm & 4-7.45pm) An imposing, much-copied example of late-16th-century Counter-Reformation architecture, this is Rome's most important Jesuit church. The facade by Giacomo della Porta is impressive, but it's the awesome gold and marble interior that is the real attraction. Of the art on display, the most astounding work is the *Trionfo del Nome di Gesù* (Triumph of the Name of Jesus), the swirling, hypnotic vault fresco by Giovanni Battista Gaulli (aka Il Baciccia), who also painted the cupola frescoes and designed the stucco decoration.

Baroque master Andrea Pozzo designed the Cappella di Sant'Ignazio in the northern transept. Here you'll find the tomb of Ignatius Loyola, the Spanish soldier and saint who founded the Jesuits in 1540. The altar-tomb is an opulent marble-and-bronze affair with columns encrusted with lapis lazuli. On top, the terrestrial globe, representing the Trinity, is the largest solid piece of lapis lazuli in the world. On either side are a couple of sculptures whose titles neatly encapsulate the Jesuit ethos: to the left, *Fede che vince l'Idolatria* (Faith Defeats Idolatry); and on the right, *Religione che flagella l'Eresia* (Religion Lashing Heresy).

The Spanish saint lived in the church from 1544 until his death in 1556. His private rooms (⊘4-6pm Mon-Sat, 10am-noon Sun), which contain a masterful trompe l'œil by Andrea del Pozzo, are just to the right of the main church.

Museo Nazionale Romano:
Crypta Balbi   MUSEUM
(Map p74; ☑06 3996 7700; www.pierreci.it; Via delle Botteghe Oscure 31; adult/reduced €7/3.50; ⊘9am-7.45pm Tue-Sun, last admission 7pm) The least known of the Museo Nazionale

Romano's four museums, the Crypta Balbi is built around the ruins of medieval and Renaissance structures, themselves set atop the ancient Teatro di Balbus (13 BC). Duck down into the underground excavations, then examine artefacts taken from the Crypta, as well as items found in the forums and on the Oppio and Celian Hills. Note that there is sometimes a €3 exhibition supplement.

Museo Ebraico di Roma   MUSEUM
(Jewish Museum of Rome; Map p74; ☑06 6840 0661; www.museoebraico.roma.it; Via Catalana; adult/reduced €10/4; ⊘10am-6.15pm Sun-Thu, to 3.15pm Fri summer, 10am-4.15pm Sun-Thu, 9am-1.15pm Fri winter) Rome's Jewish community is one of Europe's oldest, dating from the 2nd century BC. Between 1555 and the late 19th century, and then again during WWII, Rome's Jews were confined to the area known as the Jewish Ghetto, now a lively and atmospheric neighbourhood. The museum, housed in Europe's second-largest synagogue, chronicles the engrossing historical, cultural and artistic heritage of the city's Jewry. You can also book one-hour guided walking tours of the Ghetto (adult/reduced €8/5) at the museum.

ROME'S OPTICAL ILLUSIONS

The 16th-century Palazzo Spada (Map p74; Via Capo di Ferro 13; adult/reduced €5/2; ⊘8.30am-7.30pm Tue-Sun) is home to one of Rome's most famous optical tricks – Borromini's famous perspective. What appears to be a 25m-long corridor lined with columns leading to a hedge and life-sized statue is, in fact, only 10m long. The sculpture, which was a later addition, is actually hip-height and the columns diminish in size not because of distance but because they actually get shorter. And look more closely at that seemingly perfect hedge. Borromini didn't trust the gardeners to clip a real hedge precisely enough so he made one of stone.

Another celebrated illusion is Andrea Pozzo's trompe l'œil ceiling fresco at the Chiesa di Sant'Ignazio di Loyola (Map p74; Piazza di Sant'Ignazio; ⊘7.30am-7pm Mon-Sat, 9am-7pm Sun). To get the best view, stand on the small yellow spot on the nave floor and look up. The ceiling (which, in fact, is absolutely flat) appears to curve upwards. But walk a little further into the church and the deception becomes clear.

The other two optical wonders are both viewpoints. In Aventino, visit the Piazza dei Cavalieri di Malta (Map p96), a small but ornate square designed by the 18th-century Venetian artist Piranesi. There's no obvious view but look through the keyhole of the Priori dei Cavalieri di Malta and you'll see the dome of St Peter's Basilica perfectly aligned at the end of a hedge-lined avenue.

Finally, close to the beautiful park of Villa Doria Pamphilj (Map p58) in western Rome, stop off in Via Piccolomini, where you have a wonderful view of St Peter's dome – in fact, far better than the view from St Peter's Square, where it's hard to see over the facade. Here the dome looms, filling the space at the end of the road, framed by trees. Strangely, though, as you move towards it, the cupola seems to get smaller as the view widens.

Show time on Rome's Piazzas

From the baroque splendour of Piazza Navona to the bawdy clamour of Campo de' Fiori and the all-embracing majesty of St Peter's Square, Rome's showcase piazzas encapsulate much of the city's beauty, history and drama.

Piazza del Popolo

1 Neoclassical Piazza del Popolo (p83), once the city's main northern entrance, is a vast, sweeping space where executions were held. Today crowds gather for political rallies, outdoor concerts or just to hang out.

Campo de' Fiori

2 Campo de' Fiori (p78) is the workaday cousin of the more refined Piazza Navona over the way. While Piazza Navona has street artists and baroque baubles, Campo de' Fiori has market traders, heaving bars, and a noisy, unpretentious atmosphere.

Piazza del Campidoglio

3 The centrepiece of the Campidoglio (Capitoline Hill), the Michelangelo-designed Piazza del Campidoglio (p71) is thought by many to be the city's most beautiful piazza. Surrounded on three sides by stately *palazzi*, it's home to the Capitoline Museums.

St Peter's Square

4 The awe-inspiring approach to St Peter's Basilica, St Peter's Square (p103) is a masterpiece of 17th-century urban design. The work of Gian Lorenzo Bernini, it's centred on a towering Egyptian obelisk and flanked by two grasping colonnaded arms.

Piazza Navona

5 In the heart of the historic centre, Piazza Navona (p140) is the picture-perfect Roman square. Graceful baroque *palazzi* (mansions), flamboyant fountains, packed pavement cafes and cleverly costumed street artists set the scene for a daily invasion of camera-toting tourists.

Clockwise from top left
1. Chiesa di Santa Maria del Popolo, Piazza del Popolo
2. Campo de' Fiori 3. Statue, Piazza del Campidoglio
4. St Peter's Square.

TOP FIVE FILM LOCATIONS

Rome's celebrated monuments have played a starring role in many films over the years.

» **Trevi Fountain** (p140) Scene of Anita Ekberg's sensual dip in *La Dolce Vita*.

» **Bocca della Verità** (p73) Gregory Peck goofs around with Audrey Hepburn in *Roman Holiday*.

» **Piazza Navona** (p140) In *Eat Pray Love* Julia Roberts finds ice-cream solace in front of the Chiesa di Sant'Agnese in Agone.

» **Piazza di Spagna** Drama over drinks at the foot of the Spanish Steps in *The Talented Mr Ripley*.

» **Pantheon** (p73) Tom Hanks checks out Raphael's tomb in *Angels and Demons*.

Other classic Roman films include *Belly of an Architect; Three Coins in a Fountain; Yesterday, Today and Tomorrow; Bicycle Thieves;* and *Rome, Open City*.

Area Archeologica del Teatro di Marcello e del Portico d'Ottavia
ARCHAEOLOGICAL SITE

(Map p74; Via del Teatro di Marcello; ⊙9am-7pm summer, to 6pm winter) To the east of the Ghetto is the archaeological area of the Portico d'Ottavia, the oldest *quadriporto* (four-sided porch) in Rome. The columns and fragmented pediment once formed part of a vast rectangular portico, supported by 300 columns. Erected by a builder called Octavius in 146 BC, it was rebuilt in 23 BC by Augustus, who kept the name in honour of his sister Octavia. From the Middle Ages until the late 19th century, the portico housed the city's fish market.

Beyond the portico is the Teatro di Marcello, akin to a smaller Colosseum with later buildings tacked on top. The 20,000-seat theatre was planned by Julius Caesar and built by Augustus around 13 BC. In the 16th century, a *palazzo* was built onto the original building, which today houses some exclusive apartments.

Isola Tiberina
NEIGHBOURHOOD

(Map p100) To reach the Tiber Island, the world's smallest inhabited island, cross the Ponte Fabricio, which itself is also a record-breaker: it dates from 62 BC and is Rome's oldest standing bridge. The Isola has been associated with healing since the 3rd century BC, when the Romans built a temple to Aesculapius (god of healing) here, and today it is home to the Ospedale Fatebenefratelli. Standing on the site of the Roman temple is the 10th-century Chiesa di San Bartolomeo all'Isola (⊙9am-1pm & 3.30-5.30pm Mon-Sat, 9am-1pm & 7-8pm Sun). It has a Romanesque bell tower and a marble well-head, believed to have been built over the same spring that provided healing waters for the temple.

The Ponte Cestio, built in 46 BC and rebuilt in the late 19th century, connects the island with Trastevere to the south. Also to the south are the remains of Ponte Rotto (Broken Bridge), ancient Rome's first stone bridge, which was all but swept away in a 1598 flood.

TRIDENTE, TREVI & THE QUIRINALE

To the north of the *centro storico,* Tridente has long had a reputation as an upmarket bohemian enclave: Keats and Shelley hung out on Piazza di Spagna, Goethe held court on Via del Corso, and *La Dolce Vita* filmmaker Federico Fellini lived on Via Margutta. Nowadays it's the heart of the city's shopping district, packed with glittering designer boutiques catering to high-rolling shoppers. Encompassing the Spanish Steps, Piazza di Spagna and Piazza del Popolo, the latter marks the convergence of the three roads – Via di Ripetta, Via del Corso and Via del Babuino – forming a trident, hence the name. It's a short walk from here to the famous Trevi Fountain and the presidential palace, the Quirinale.

Piazza di Spagna & the Spanish Steps
PIAZZA, MUSEUM

(Map p84) The Spanish Steps (Scalinata della Trinità dei Monti) provide a perfect auditorium for people-watching, and have been a magnet for visitors since the 18th century. The Piazza di Spagna was named after the Spanish Embassy to the Holy See, and consequently the steps were so-named, although they were designed by the Italian Francesco de Sanctis and built in 1725 with a legacy from the French. They lead to the French Chiesa della Trinità dei Monti, which was commissioned by King Louis XII of France and consecrated in 1585. In addition to the great views from outside, it boasts some wonderful frescoes by Daniele da Volterra. His *Deposizione* (Deposition), in the second chapel on the left, is regarded as a masterpiece of mannerist painting. If you don't fancy climbing the steep steps, there's a lift up from Spagna metro station.

At the foot of the steps, the Barcaccia (the 'sinking boat' fountain) is believed to be by Pietro Bernini, father of the famous Gian Lorenzo.

Keats-Shelley Memorial House   MUSEUM
(Map p84; ☑06 678 42 35; www.keats-shelley-house.org; Piazza di Spagna 26; adult/reduced €4.50/3.50; ☉10am-1pm & 2-6pm Mon-Fri, 11am-2pm & 3-6pm Sat) Overlooking the Spanish Steps, this is where the 25-year-old Keats died of tuberculosis in 1821, after an obviously unsuccessful trip to Rome to improve his health – being quarantined in a boat outside Naples and then treated by his Scottish doctor for problems of the digestive system rather than his real health problem didn't help. The cramped apartments nowadays form an evocative museum dedicated to the ill-fated romantic poets (Shelley drowned off the Tuscan coast, and both he and Keats are buried in the non-Catholic Cemetery close to Piramide), housing poems, letters and memorabilia of Keats, Shelley, Byron and their friends.

Piazza del Popolo &
Around   PIAZZA, CHURCH
(Map p84) For centuries the site of public executions, this elegant ellipse of a piazza is one of Rome's most impressive public spaces. It was laid out in 1538 to provide a suitably grandiose entrance to what was then the main northern gateway into the city.

Guarding its southern end are Carlo Rainaldi's twin 17th-century baroque churches, Chiesa di Santa Maria dei Miracoli and Chiesa di Santa Maria in Montesanto, while over on the northern flank is the Porta del Popolo, created by Bernini in 1655 to celebrate Queen Christina of Sweden's defection to Catholicism. In the centre, the 36m-high obelisk was brought by Augustus from Heliopolis, in ancient Egypt, and moved here from the Circo Massimo in the

mid-16th century. To the east are the Pincio Hill Gardens.

Chiesa di Santa Maria del Popolo   CHURCH
(Map p84; ☑06 361 08 36; Piazza del Popolo; ☉7am-noon & 4-7pm Mon-Sat, 8am-1.30pm & 4.30-7.30pm Sun) Next to the Porta del Popolo is one of Rome's earliest, richest Renaissance churches. The first chapel was built here in 1099 to exorcise the ghost of Nero, who was buried on this spot and whose ghost was said to haunt the area. It was overhauled in 1462, after which Pinturicchio painted his beautiful frescoes. In Raphael's Cappella Chigi (mostly completed by Bernini some 100 years later) you'll find a famous mosaic of a kneeling skeleton. Adding some fierce, exquisitely rendered drama to the Cappella Cerasi, to the left of the altar are two Caravaggio masterpieces: the *Conversion of St Paul* and the *Crucifixion of St Peter* (both 1600–01).

Casa di Goethe   HISTORICAL BUILDING
(Map p84; ☑06 3265 0412; www.casadigoethe.it; Via del Corso 18; adult/reduced €4/3; ☉10am-6pm Tue-Sun) Close to the Piazza del Popolo is the modest, lovingly maintained Casa di Goethe, where the German writer enjoyed his stay (1786–88), but complained about the noisy locals. Its collection includes his drawings and etchings from the period, as well as interesting souvenirs of his stay.

Museo dell'Ara Pacis   MUSEUM
(Map p84; ☑06 8205 9127; www.arapacis.it; Lungotevere in Augusta; adult/reduced €9/7, audioguide €3.50; ☉9am-7pm Tue-Sun) Many Romans detest Richard Meier's minimalist glass-and-marble pavilion (the first modern construction in Rome's historical centre since WWII), but it is no longer likely to be completely pulled down, as Mayor Gianni Alemanno had promised on his election in 2008. However, the wall dividing the busy Lungotevere Augusta from Piazza Augusto Imperatore – which has been criticised for obscuring the baroque facade of the church of San Rocco all'Augusteo – is to be dismantled, according to new plans approved by the architect.

Inside is the less-controversial Ara Pacis Augustae (Altar of Peace), Augustus' great monument to peace. One of the most important works of ancient Roman sculpture, the vast marble altar (it measures 11.6m by 10.6m by 3.6m) was completed in 13 BC and positioned near Piazza San Lorenzo in Lucina, slightly to the southeast of its current site.

ROME & LAZIO ROME

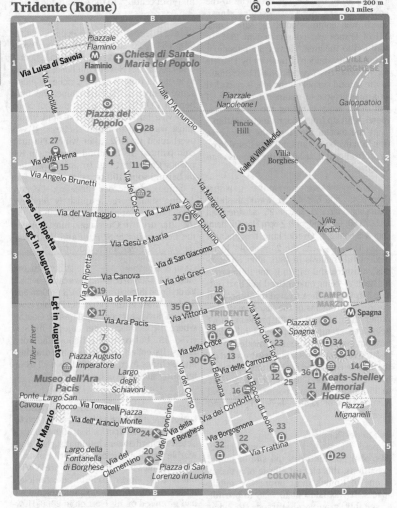

The location was calculated so that on Augustus' birthday the shadow of a huge sundial on Campus Martius would fall directly on it. Over the centuries the altar fell victim to Rome's avid art collectors, and panels ended up in the Medici collection, the Vatican and the Louvre. However, in 1936 Mussolini unearthed the remaining parts and decided to reassemble them in the present location.

Of the reliefs, the most important depicts Augustus at the head of a procession, followed by priests, the general Marcus Agrippa and the entire imperial family.

Mausoleo di Augusto
MAUSOLEUM

(Mausoleum of Augustus; Map p84) What was once one of the most imposing monuments in ancient Rome is now an unkempt mound of earth, overgrown with weeds. Plans for a major revamp by architect Francesco Cellini are afoot, but as yet there's no sign of activity on the ground.

The mausoleum, which was built in 28 BC and originally measured 87m in diameter, is the last resting place of Augustus, who was buried here in AD 14, and his favourite nephew and heir Marcellus. During the Middle Ages the mausoleum served as a fortress and was later used as a vineyard, a private garden and a travertine quarry. Mussolini had it restored in 1936 with an eye to being buried here himself.

Trevi Fountain FOUNTAIN
(Fontana di Trevi; Map p86) This fountain almost fills an entire piazza, and is Rome's most famous fountain, its iconic status sealed when Anita Ekberg splashed here in *La Dolce Vita*. The flamboyant baroque ensemble was designed by Nicola Salvi in 1732 and depicts Neptune's chariot being led by Tritons with sea horses – one wild, one docile – representing the moods of the sea. The water comes from the *aqua virgo*, a 1st-century-BC underground aqueduct, and the name Trevi refers to the *tre vie* (three roads) that converge at the fountain. It's traditional to throw a coin into the fountain to ensure your return to the Eternal City. It's usually very busy around the fountain during the day, so it's worth trying to visit later in the evening when you can appreciate its foaming majesty without the hordes.

Time Elevator CINEMA
(Map p86; ☎06 6992 1823; www.time-elevator.it; Via dei Santissimi Apostoli 20; adult/reduced €12/9; ☉10.30am-7.30pm; 🖈) Just off Via del Corso, this cinema is ideal for armchair sightseers. There are three programs, but the one to see is *Time Elevator Rome*, a 45-minute virtual journey through 3000 years of Roman history. Shows kick off at half-past every hour, and children and adults alike love the panoramic screens, flight-simulator technology and surround-sound system. Note that children under five aren't admitted and anyone who suffers motion sickness should probably give it a miss.

Piazza Barberini PIAZZA
(Map p86) In the centre of traffic-busy Piazza Barberini is Bernini's **Fontana del Tritone** (Fountain of the Triton), created in 1643 for Pope Urban VIII, patriarch of the Barberini family. Bernini also sculpted the **Fontana delle Api** (Fountain of the Bees), in the northeastern corner, for the powerful Barberini family, whose crest features three bees.

ROME & LAZIO ROME

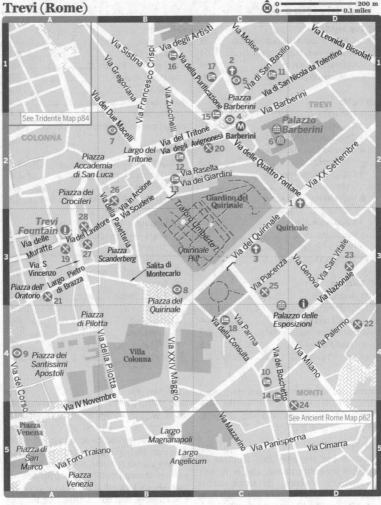

0 — 200 m
0 — 0.1 miles

See Tridente Map p84

See Ancient Rome Map p62

Galleria Nazionale d'Arte Antica: Palazzo Barberini

ART GALLERY

(Map p86; ☎06 2258 2493; www.galleriaborghese.it; Via delle Quattro Fontane 13; adult/reduced €5/2.50; ☺9am-7.30pm Tue-Sun, ticket office closes 7pm) The 17th-century Palazzo Barberini was commissioned by Urban VIII to celebrate the Barberini family's rise to papal power. Many high-profile baroque architects worked on it, including rivals Bernini and Borromini; the former contributed a large squared staircase, the latter a helicoidal one. Today the palace houses part of Galleria Nazionale, a Renaissance and baroque art feast. Besides works

by Raphael, Caravaggio, Guido Reni, Bernini, Filippo Lippi, Holbein, Titian and Tintoretto, there is the captivating ceiling of the main salon, the *Triumph of Divine Providence* (1632–39) by Pietro da Cortona. Don't miss Hans Holbein's famous portrait of a portly Henry VIII (c 1540) and Filippo Lippi's luminous *Annunciazione e due devoti*. Caravaggio masterpieces include *St Francis in Meditation, Narcissus* (c 1571–1610), and the mesmerisingly horrific *Judith Beheading Holophernes* (c 1597–1600), which features some wonderfully realistic facial expressions. Another must-see is Raphael's lovely *La Fornarina* (The Baker's Girl), a portrait of his mistress Margherita Luti, who worked in a bakery on Via di Santa Dorotea in Trastevere. If you have a bag, ensure you have €1 for a locker.

Chiesa di Santa Maria della Concezione   CHURCH

(Map p86; ☎06 487 11 85; Via Vittorio Veneto 27; admission by donation; ◎9am-noon & 3-6pm Fri-Wed) Descend into the Capuchin cemetery below this church and you'll be gobsmacked. Between 1528 and 1870 the Capuchin monks used the bones of 4000 of their departed brothers in a most macabre take on interior decoration. There are vertebrae used as fleurs-de-lis, and femur light fixtures. The message in the last crypt reads: 'What you are now we used to be; what we are now you will be.' Happy holidays!

Palazzo del Quirinale   PALAZZO

(Map p86; ☎06 4 69 91; www.quirinale.it; admission €2.50; ◎8.30am-noon Sun mid-Sep–Jun) At the top of the Quirinal (Quirinale) Hill, this immense palace served as the papal summer residence for almost three centuries until the keys were handed over (begrudgingly, and staring down the barrel of a gun) to Italy's new king in 1870. It was passed on to the president of the republic in 1948. At the end of the Sunday visit, there is a free concert in the chapel.

Chiesa di Sant'Andrea al Quirinale   CHURCH

(Map p86; ☎06 474 08 07; Via del Quirinale 29; ◎8.30am-noon & 3.30-7pm Mon-Sat, 9am-noon & 4-7pm Sun) Along Via del Quirinale are two masterpiece churches, designed by the baroque era's great rivals: Bernini and Borromini. This late-17th-century church was designed by Bernini and is regarded by many as one of his greatest works. Faced with severe space limitations, he managed to produce a sense of grandeur by designing an elliptical floor plan with a series of chapels opening onto the central area. It is said that in his old age the artist liked to come here to enjoy its peaceful atmosphere.

Chiesa di San Carlo alle Quattro Fontane   CHURCH

(Map p86; ☎06 488 31 09; Via del Quirinale 23; ◎10am-1pm & 3-6pm Mon-Fri, 10am-1pm Sat, noon-1pm Sun) This is Borromini's first church and bears all the hallmarks of his genius. The elegant curves of the facade, the play of convex and concave surfaces, the dome illuminated by hidden windows – all combine to transform a minuscule space into a light, airy interior. Nowadays perched on a traffic-choked junction, it is a great place to escape from the busy street.

THE MYSTERIOUS CASE OF THE TREVI COINS

Around €3000 is thrown into the Trevi Fountain on an average day. It's accepted practice that this money is collected daily and goes to the Catholic charity Caritas. However, in 2002, D'Artagnan (real name Roberto Cercelletta, an unemployed 50-year-old man) was discovered to have spent 34 years raiding the fountain for change. He was banned from the fountain, and new security measures were put in place. Despite his ban, D'Artagnan returned a few days' later, shouting to the surrounding crowds and slashing his belly in protest. A year later, a court ruled that the money could not be stolen as it has been discarded.

Eight years later, there was a further scandal when a TV company secretly filmed the fountain, discovering that D'Artagnan and some helpers were still collecting the money, with the apparent complicity of the police. When the reporter asked the police why they were not taking any action, he was pushed into the fountain by the collectors. In the following days, D'Artagnan staged a further belly-slashing protest, clambering onto the rocks surrounding the fountain to display his wounds. The police countered any criticism with the defence that there was no legal basis for arresting the coin-gatherers, but they notably didn't ask the men to abide by the law against entering the fountains of Rome, which is usually strictly enforced (as you'll soon find out if you try to dabble your feet). Rome's mayor, Gianni Alemanno, now plans to pass legislation to make removal of coins from the fountain an offence.

TERMINI, ESQUILINO & SAN LORENZO

The largest of Rome's seven hills, the Esquilino extends from the Colosseum to Stazione Termini, encompassing Via Cavour (a broad traffic-heavy avenue between Termini and Via dei Fori Imperiali), the mosaic-lined Basilica di Santa Maria Maggiore, and the increasingly trendy, boho area of Monti, which is dotted with individual boutiques, restaurants and wine bars. This was one of Rome's oldest areas, notoriously the red-light district at the time of the Republic. Much of Esquilino was covered with vineyards and gardens until the late 19th century, when they were dug up to make way for grandiose apartment blocks.

Chiesa di Santa Maria della Vittoria CHURCH
(Map p90; ☑06 482 61 90; Via XX Settembre 17; ⊗8.30am-noon & 3.30-6pm Mon-Sat, 3.30-6pm Sun) This modest church is home to a magnificent and intriguing work of religious art, Bernini's overtly sexual *Ecstasy of St Theresa*, in which religious fervour is equated with rather more earthly pleasure as the saint swoons in sensual delight, pierced by an arrow by a teasing angel. Watching the whole scene from two side balconies are a number of figures, including Cardinal Federico Cornaro, for whom the chapel was built. It's a stunning work, bathed in soft natural light filtering through a concealed window. Visit in the afternoon for the best effect.

Basilica di Santa Maria Maggiore CHURCH
(Map p90; ☑06 6988 6800; Piazza Santa Maria Maggiore; audioguide €5; ⊗7am-7pm) One of Rome's four patriarchal basilicas (the others being St Peter's, San Giovanni in Laterano and San Paolo Fuori-le-Mura), this one was built on the summit of the Esquiline Hill in the 5th century. Outside, the 18.78m-high column in the Piazza di Santa Maria Maggiore came from the Basilica di Massenzio in the Roman Forum, and the church exterior is decorated with glimmering 13th-century mosaics, protected by a porch with five openings, designed by Ferdinando Fuga.

The great interior retains its original 5th-century structure, despite the basilica having been much altered over the centuries. The nave floor is a fine example of 12th-century Cosmati paving. The 75m belfry, the highest in Rome, is 14th-century Romanesque; Ferdinand Fuga's 1741 facade is baroque, as is much of the sumptuous interior. Particularly spectacular are the 5th-century mosaics in the triumphal arch and nave, depicting Old Testament scenes. Binoculars will come in handy. The central image in the apse, signed by Jacopo Torriti, dates from the 13th century and represents the coronation of the Virgin Mary.

The baldachin over the high altar seethes with gilt cherubs; the altar itself is a porphyry sarcophagus, which is said to contain the relics of St Matthew and other martyrs. A plaque to the right of the altar marks the spot where Gian Lorenzo Bernini and his father Pietro are buried. Steps lead down to the *confessio* (a crypt in which relics are placed), where a statue of Pope Pius IX kneels before a reliquary containing a fragment of Jesus' manger.

The sumptuously decorated Cappella Sistina, last on the right, was built by Domenico Fontana in the 16th century and contains the tombs of Popes Sixtus V and Pius V.

Through the souvenir shop on the right-hand side of the church is a **museum** (adult/child €4/2; ⊙9am-6pm) with a motley collection of religious artefacts. More interesting is the upper **loggia** (☑06 6988 6802; admission €5; ⊙2-5pm), where you'll find some iridescent 13th-century mosaics.

Basilica di San Pietro in Vincoli   CHURCH
(Map p62; ☑06 488 28 65; Piazza di San Pietro in Vincoli 4a; ⊙8am-12.30pm & 3.30-7pm Apr-Sep, 8am-12.30pm & 3-6pm Oct-Mar) Pilgrims and art lovers flock to this basilica for two reasons: to see St Peter's chains and to see Michelangelo's tomb of Pope Julius II. The church was built in the 5th century to house the chains that bound St Peter when he was imprisoned in the Carcere Mamertino. Some time after St Peter's death, the chains were sent to Constantinople for a period before returning to Rome as relics. They arrived in two pieces and legend has it that when they were reunited they miraculously joined together. They are now displayed under the altar.

To the right of the altar is Julius' monumental tomb. At its centre is Michelangelo's buff *Moses,* with two small horns sticking out of his head. Subject of much curiosity, the horns were inspired by a mistranslation of a biblical passage: where the original said that rays of light issued from Moses' face, the translator wrote 'horns'. Michelangelo was aware of the mistake, but gave Moses horns anyway. The statues of Leah and Rachel flanking Moses were probably completed by Michelangelo's students. Despite its imposing scale, the tomb was never finished – Michelangelo planned 40 statues but got sidetracked by the Sistine Chapel, and Pope Julius II was buried in St Peter's Basilica.

If you're planning on really doing the sights, think about buying the Appia Antica Card (see boxed text, p66). Near the start of the road, the **Appia Antica Regional Park Information Point** (off Map p98; ☑06 513 53 16; Via Appia Antica 58-60; ⊙9.30am-1.30pm & 2-5.30pm Mon-Sat, 9.30am-5.30pm Sun, to 4.30pm daily winter) is very informative. You can buy a map of the park here and hire **bikes** (per hr/day €3/10). The park authorities organise a series of free guided tours, on foot and by bike, on Sunday mornings. You can also download a free audioguide to the Caffarella Valley on the website. In addition, **Darwin Cooperative** (www.cooperativadarwin.it) leads group walking or biking tours in English, French, Spanish and German.

Access to the church is via a flight of steps through a low arch that leads up from Via Cavour.

Domus Aurea   HISTORICAL SITE
(Map p94; Via della Domus Aurea 1; ⊙closed for restoration) Over the road from the Colosseum, the Domus Aurea (Golden House) was Nero's great gift to himself, a vast palace spread over the Palatine, Oppio and Celian Hills. Built after the fire of AD 64 and named after the gold that, with mother-of-pearl, covered its facade, it included frescoed banqueting halls, *nymphaeums* (grottoes or caves for recreation and worship), baths and terraces. Its grounds, which covered up to a third of the city, included a large artificial lake. It's estimated only around 20% remains of the original complex. The baths and underlying ruins were abandoned by the 6th century, and it's this area that is currently being excavated. It has formerly been open to the public, but has frequently had to be closed for extensive repairs following flooding and due to collapses in the structure – it was last open in 2010.

Piazza della Repubblica   PIAZZA
(Map p90) Flanked by grand neoclassical colonnades, the landmark Piazza della Repubblica was laid out as part of Rome's post-unification makeover. Around this monumental roundabout are dotted buildings housing most of Museo Nazionale Romano's world-famous archaeological collection.

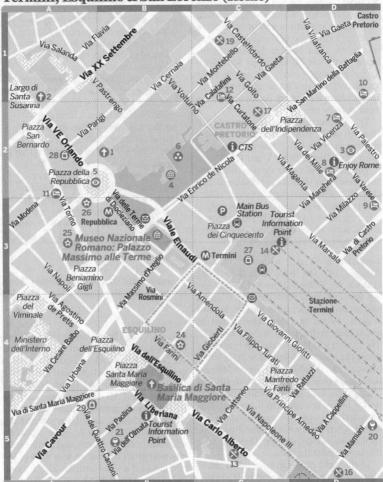

Museo Nazionale Romano: Palazzo
Massimo alle Terme   ART GALLERY
(Map p90; ☎06 3996 7700; www.pierreci.it; Largo
di Villa Peretti 1; adult/reduced €7/3.50, audioguide
€4; ⊙9am-7.45pm Tue-Sun) A treasure trove
of classical art, the light-filled Palazzo Massimo
alle Terme is one of Rome's finest galleries,
but remains almost off the beaten
track in its position a few steps away from
Termini station.

The ground and 1st floors are devoted to
some incredibly fine sculpture, including
the mesmerising *Boxer* that dates from the
1st century BC; upstairs there's an exquisite
crouching Aphrodite from Tivoli's Villa
Adriana, the softly contoured, 2nd-century
BC *Sleeping Hermaphrodite,* and the iconic
vision of perfection that is the *Discus
Thrower.* Yet the sensational mosaics and
frescoes on the 2nd floor blow everything
else away. The layout has been revamped so
that the rooms are arranged how they were
within the villas, and lighting brings out the
rich colours of the frescoes. There are intimate
cubicula (bedrooms), which feature
religious, erotic and theatre subjects, and
delicate landscape paintings from the dark-painted
winter *triclinium* (dining room).

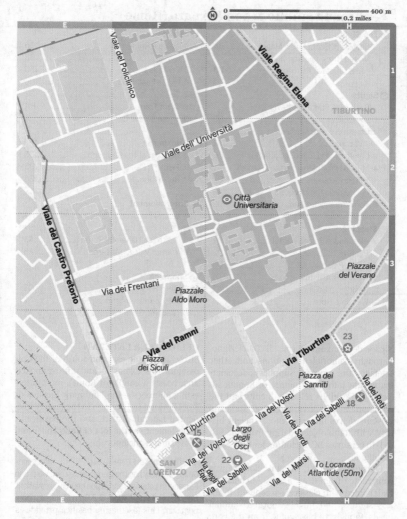

The show-stopping highlight is the frescoes (dating from 30 BC to 20 BC) that once lined Villa Livia, one of the homes of Augustus' wife Livia Drusilla. These, covering an entire room, depict an illusionary, realistic yet paradisiacal garden full of a wild tangle of roses, pomegranates, iris and camomile under a deep-blue sky. These decorated a summer *triclinium*, a large living and dining area built half underground to provide protection from the heat. The new display includes special lighting that mimics the modulation of daylight and highlights the richness of the millennia-old colours.

Museo Nazionale Romano: Terme di Diocleziano   MUSEUM

(Map p90; ☎06 3996 7700; www.pierreci.it; Viale Enrico de Nicola 78; adult/reduced €7/3.50, audio-guide €5; ☺9am-7.45pm Tue-Sun). The Terme di Diocleziano is a complex of baths, libraries, concert halls and gardens that was ancient Rome's largest, covering about 13 hectares and having a capacity for 3000 people. Completed in the early 4th century, it fell into disrepair after the aqueduct that fed the baths was destroyed by invaders in about AD 536. Today the bath complex ruins constitute part of the impressive Museo

ROME & LAZIO ROME

Nazionale Romano: Terme di Diocleziano. Through memorial inscriptions and other artefacts, the museum supplies a fascinating insight into the structure of Roman society, with exhibits relating to cults and the development of Christianity and Judaism. Upstairs delves into even more ancient history, with tomb objects dating from the 9th to 11th centuries BC, including jewellery and amphorae.

Outside, the vast, elegant cloister was constructed from drawings by Michelangelo. It's lined with classical sarcophagi, headless statues, and huge sculptured animal heads, thought to have come from the Foro di Traiano.

Basilica di Santa Maria degli Angeli   CHURCH
(Map p90; ☎06 488 08 12; www.santamaria degliangeliroma.it; Piazza della Repubblica; ⏰7am-8.30pm Mon-Sat, to 7.30pm Sun) This hulking basilica occupies what was once the central hall of Diocletian's baths complex. It was originally designed by Michelangelo, but only the great vaulted ceiling remains from his plans.

CELIO HILL & LATERAN

Stretching to the east and south of the Colosseum, this extensive and oft-overlooked area boasts a couple of Rome's most interesting churches – the landmark Basilica di San Giovanni in Laterano in the largely residential Lateran district, and the Basilica di San Clemente at the foot of Celio Hill – and some superb ancient ruins.

Basilica di San Clemente   CHURCH
(Map p94; www.basilicasanclemente.com; Via di San Giovanni in Laterano; admission church/excavations free/€5; ⏰9am-12.30pm & 3-6pm Mon-Sat, noon-6pm Sun) This fascinating basilica provides a vivid glimpse into Rome's multilayered past: a 12th-century basilica built over a 4th-century church, which stands over a 2nd-century pagan temple and 1st-century Roman house. Beneath everything are foundations dating from the Roman Republic.

The medieval church features a marvellous 12th-century apse mosaic depicting the *Trionfo della Croce* (Triumph of the Cross) and some wonderful Renaissance frescoes in the Chapel of St Catherine, to the left of the entrance. Steps lead down to the 4th-century *basilica inferiore,* mostly destroyed by Norman invaders in 1084, but with some faded 11th-century frescoes illustrating the life of San Clement. Follow the steps down another level and you'll come to a 1st-century Roman house and a dark, 2nd-century temple to Mithras, with an altar showing the god slaying a bull. Beneath it all, you can hear the eerie sound of a subterranean river, running through a Roman Republic–era drain.

Basilica di San Giovanni in Laterano
CHURCH

(Map p94; Piazza di San Giovanni in Laterano 4; audioguide €5; ⊘7am-6.30pm) For a thousand years this monumental cathedral was the most important church in Christendom. Founded by Constantine in AD 324, it was the first Christian basilica built in the city and, until the late 14th century, was the pope's main place of worship. It is still Rome's official cathedral and the pope's seat as the bishop of Rome.

Surmounted by 15 7m-high statues – Christ with St John the Baptist, John the Evangelist and the 12 Apostles – Alessandro Galilei's huge white facade is a mid-18th-century example of late-baroque classicism, designed to convey the infinite authority of the Church. The central bronze doors were moved here from the Curia in the Roman Forum, while to their right is the Holy Door, which is only opened in Jubilee years.

The interior has been revamped on numerous occasions, although it owes much of its present look to Francesco Borromini, who was called in by Pope Innocent X to redecorate it for the 1650 Jubilee. But elements of earlier interiors survive, including the delightful 15th-century mosaic floor and the pointed Gothic baldachin over the papal altar. In front of the altar, a double staircase leads to the *confessio,* which houses the Renaissance tomb of Pope Martin V.

On the first pilaster in the right-hand nave is an original, if incomplete, fresco by Giotto. While admiring it, cock your ear towards the next pilaster, where a monument to Pope Sylvester II (r 999–1003) is said to sweat and creak when the death of a pope is imminent.

To the left of the altar, the beautiful cloister (admission €2; ⊘9am-6pm) was built by the Vassalletto family in the 13th century. The twisted columns were once completely covered with inlaid marble mosaics, remnants of which can still be seen.

Palazzo Laterano
PALAZZO

(Map p94; Piazza San Giovanni in Laterano) Flanking Piazza San Giovanni in Laterano, itself dominated by Rome's oldest and tallest obelisk, is Domenico Fontana's 16th-century Palazzo Laterano. Part of the original 4th-century basilica complex, it was the official papal residence until the popes moved to the Vatican in 1377, and today houses offices of the diocese of Rome.

Just around the corner, the octagonal 4th-century baptistry (⊘7.30am-12.30pm & 4-6.30pm) served as the prototype for later Christian churches and bell towers. Inside, admire decorative mosaics, some of which date back to the 5th century.

Scala Santa & Sancta Sanctorum
CHURCH

(Map p94; Piazza di San Giovanni in Laterano 14; Scala/Sancta free/€3.50; ⊘Scala 6.15am-noon & 3.30-6.45pm summer, 6.15am-noon & 3-6.15pm winter, Sancta 10.30-11.30am & 3-4pm, closed Wed am & Sun year-round) The Scala Santa is said to be the staircase that Jesus walked up in Pontius Pilate's palace in Jerusalem.

SUBTERRANEAN CULT

Mithraism was a cult that was hugely popular with the ancient Roman military. According to its mythology, Mithras, a young, handsome god, was ordered to slay a wild bull by the Sun. As the bull died it gave life, as its blood flow caused wheat and other plants to grow. In Mithraic iconography, a serpent and dog are usually shown attacking the bull to try to prevent this, while a scorpion attacks its testicles.

Mithraic temples are always deep and dark, but the cult's fascination with dank, dark caves doesn't reflect a sinister undercurrent. Rather, its cave-temples represented the cosmos, because it was created from the earth. Here devotees underwent complex processes of initiation, rising through ranks such as 'soldier' and 'raven'. They also ate bread and water as a representation of the body and the blood of the bull. Sound familiar? The early Christians thought so too, and were fervently against the cult, feeling its practices were too close to their own. It's ironic that Rome's best-preserved Mithraic temple lies beneath the beautiful Christian Basilica di San Clemente.

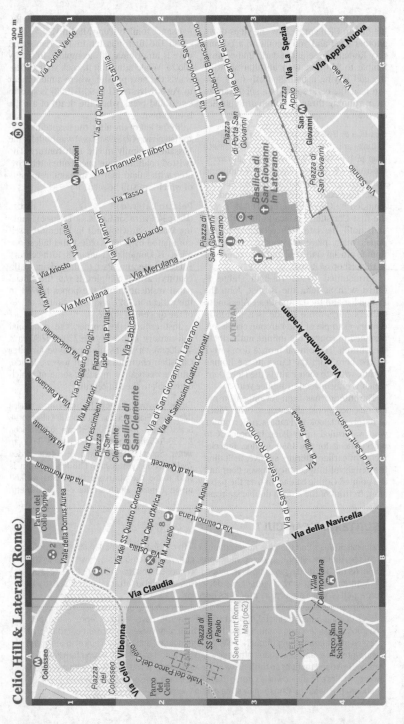

Celio Hill & Lateran (Rome)

0 — 0 — 200 m
0 — 0.1 miles

ROME & LAZIO SIGHTS

Consequently you can only climb it on your knees. At the top of the stairs, the Sancta Sanctorum (Holy of Holies) was the popes' private chapel and contains spectacular 13th-century frescoes.

SOUTHERN ROME

Southern Rome is an extensive and multi-faceted neighbourhood that comprises several distinct areas: Via Appia Antica, famous for its catacombs; San Paolo, home of one of the city's great patriarchal basilicas; trendy Via Ostiense, where most of Rome's coolest clubs are housed in ex-industrial buildings; and EUR, Mussolini's otherworldly building development.

Heading southeast from Porta San Sebastiano, Via Appia Antica (Appian Way) is one of the world's oldest roads and a much-prized Roman address. It's a beautiful part of town, with crumbling ruins set in jewel-green fields and towering umbrella pines lining the horizon. And what lies beneath supplies even more reason for visiting – some 300km of underground tunnels used as burial chambers by the early Christians.

Basilica di San Paolo
Fuori le Mura   CHURCH

(St Paul's Outside the Walls; Map p58; ☑06 6988 0800; Via Ostiense 190; ⊙6.45am-6.30pm) The biggest church in Rome after St Peter's Basilica (and the world's third-largest) stands on the site where the eponymous saint was buried after being decapitated in AD 67. Built by Constantine in the 4th century, it was largely destroyed by fire in 1823 and much of what you see today is a 19th-century reconstruction.

However, many treasures survived the fire, including the 5th-century triumphal arch, with its heavily restored mosaics, and the Gothic marble tabernacle over the high altar. This was designed in about 1285 by Ar-

nolfo di Cambio together with another artist, possibly Pietro Cavallini.

Looking upwards, doom-mongers should check out the papal portraits beneath the nave windows. Every pope since St Peter is represented and legend has it that when there is no room for the next portrait, the world will fall. There are eight places left.

The stunning 13th-century Cosmati mosaic work in the **cloisters** (admission free; ⊙9am-1pm & 3-6pm) of the adjacent Benedictine abbey also survived the 1823 fire.

Via Appia Antica   HISTORICAL SITE

(Appian Way; Map p98; ⛟) Heading southeast from Porta San Sebastiano, Via Appia Antica was known to the Romans as the *regina viarum* (queen of roads). Named after Appius Claudius Caecus, who laid the first 90km section in 312 BC, it was extended in 190 BC to reach Brindisi, some 540km away on the southern Adriatic coast.

Flanked by some of the city's most exclusive private villas, as well as Roman tombs, the long cobbled road is a great place for a walk or cycle. It runs as straight as a die through jewel-green countryside, and is rich in ruins and history – this is where Spartacus and 6000 of his slave rebels were crucified in 71 BC. The road is best known for its catacombs, around 300km of underground tunnels used as burial chambers by the early Christians (see the boxed text, p99). You can't visit all 300km, but three major catacombs (San Callisto, San Sebastiano and Santa Domitilla) are open for exploration, via half-hourly guided tours in English, Italian, French, German and Spanish.

GETTING THERE & AROUND

To get to Via Appia Antica and the catacombs, catch bus 218 from Piazza di San Giovanni in Laterano, bus 660 from the Colli Albani stop on metro A, or bus 118 from the Piramide stop on metro B. Alternatively, if

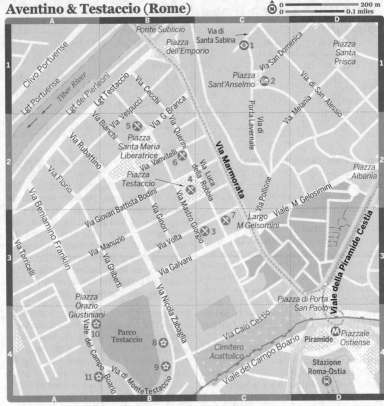

Aventino & Testaccio (Rome)

◎ Sights
1 Piazza dei Cavalieri di Malta C1

🛏 Sleeping
2 Hotel Sant'Anselmo C1

✴ Eating
3 Da Felice C3
4 Piazza Testaccio Market B2

5 Pizzeria Remo.....................................B2
6 Trattoria da Bucatino...........................B2
7 Volpetti Più C3

✴ Entertainment
8 AKAB B4
9 Conte Staccio B4
10 L'Alibi A4
11 Villaggio Globale A4

you're spending the day here and want to see several sights, the hop-on, hop-off **Archeobus** (€12) departs from Termini every hour, followed by a stop at Piazza Venezia and then the Colosseum, before going on to the Terme di Caracalla. Sunday is a good day to visit, when the road is closed to traffic; on other days bear in mind that the first section, from Porta San Sebastian for about three miles, is not particularly pedestrian

friendly. From the area around the Tempio di Romolo to the point where it meets the Via Appia Nuova, it's most atmospheric, and virtually traffic free every day.

Chiesa del Domine Quo Vadis CHURCH
(off Map p98; Via Appia Antica 51; ⊙8am-6pm)
This church is built at the point where St Peter, while fleeing Rome, is said to have met a vision of Jesus. Peter asked: 'Domine, quo

vadis?' ('Lord, where are you going?') When Jesus replied, 'Venio Roman iterum crucifigi' ('I am coming to Rome to be crucified again'), Peter decided to join him and on his return was arrested and executed. In the centre of the church's aisle there are models of Christ's footprints; the originals are up the road in the Basilica di San Sebastiano.

Catacombs of San Callisto CATACOMB
(Map p98; ☏06 5130 1580; Via Appia Antica 110 & 126; www.catacombe.roma.it; adult/reduced €8/4; ⊙8.30am-noon & 2.30-5pm Thu-Tue, to 5.30pm Apr-Sep, closed Feb) Founded at the end of the 2nd century and named after Pope Calixtus I, these catacombs became the official cemetery of the newly established Roman Church. In the 20km of tunnels explored to date, archaeologists have found the tombs of some 500,000 people and seven popes who were martyred in the 3rd century. The patron saint of music, St Cecilia, was also buried here, although her body was later moved to the Basilica di Santa Cecilia in Trastevere. When her body was exhumed in 1599, over 1000 years after her death, it was apparently perfectly preserved.

Catacombs of San Sebastiano CATACOMB
(Map p98; ☏06 785 03 50; www.catacombe.org; Via Appia Antica 136; adult/reduced €8/4; ⊙8.30am-noon & 2-5pm Mon-Sat, to 5.30pm Apr-Sep, closed Nov) These catacombs were a safe haven for the remains of St Peter and St Paul during the reign of Vespasian. Frescoes, stucco work, epigraphs and three immaculate mausoleums can be seen on the 2nd level, as well as fascinating etched graffiti by visiting pilgrims, dating from when the saints' bodies were housed here sometime after 258 AD.

Basilica di San Sebastiano CHURCH
(Map p98; ☏06 780 00 47; Via Appia Antica 136; ⊙8.30am-noon & 2-5pm Mon-Sat, to 5.30pm Apr-Sep, closed Nov) Founded in the 4th century, this basilica preserves one of the arrows allegedly used to kill St Sebastian, and the column to which he was tied. On the other side of the church you'll find a marble slab with the imprints of Jesus' feet.

Catacombs of San Domitilla CATACOMB
(Map p98; ☏06 511 03 42; Via delle Sette Chiese 283; adult/reduced €8/4; ⊙9am-noon & 2-5pm Wed-Mon, closed Jan) Among Rome's largest and oldest, these catacombs stretch for about 17km. Established on the private burial ground of Flavia Domitilla, niece of Emperor Domitian, they contain Christian wall

TERME DI CARACALLA

(Map p58; ☏06 3996 7700; Viale delle Terme di Caracalla 52; adult/reduced incl Mausoleo di Cecilia Metella & Villa dei Quintili €8/4, audioguide €5; ⊙9am-1hr before sunset Tue-Sun, 9am-2pm Mon year-round) Sandwiched between the Celian and Aventine Hills, the remnants of the emperor Caracalla's vast baths complex are among Rome's most awe-inspiring ruins. Spread over 10 hectares, the original leisure centre, which was inaugurated in AD 217 and used until the 6th century, could hold up to 1600 people and included *caldaria* (hot bath), a lukewarm *tepidarium* (tepid bath), a swimming pool, gymnasiums, libraries, shops and gardens. Underground, slaves sweated in 9.5km of tunnels, tending to the complex plumbing systems.

In summer, the ruins provide a spectacular stage for outdoor opera performances.

paintings and the underground Chiesa di SS Nereus e Achilleus, a 4th-century church dedicated to two Roman soldiers who were martyred by Diocletian.

Villa di Massenzio HISTORICAL BUILDING
(Map p98; ☏06 780 13 24; www.villadimassenzio.it; Via Appia Antica 153; adult/reduced €3/2; ⊙9am-1.30pm Tue-Sat) The outstanding feature of this 4th-century villa is the **Circo di Massenzio**, Rome's best-preserved ancient racetrack – you can still make out the starting stalls used for chariot races. The 10,000-seat arena was built by Maxentius around 309, but he died before ever seeing a race here.

Above the arena are the now-weed-covered ruins of Maxentius' imperial residence. Near the racetrack, the **Mausoleo di Romolo** (Tombo di Romolo) was built by Maxentius for his son Romulus. The huge mausoleum was originally crowned with a large dome and surrounded by an imposing colonnade, in part still visible.

Mausoleo di Cecilia Metella MAUSOLEUM
(Map p98; ☏06 3996 7700; Via Appia Antica 161; admission incl Terme di Caracalla & Villa dei Quintili adult/reduced €8/4; ⊙9am-1hr before sunset Tue-Sun) This 1st-century-BC mausoleum encloses a now roofless burial chamber built for the daughter of the consul Quintus

Metellus Creticus. The walls are made of travertine and the sorry-looking interior is decorated with a sculpted frieze featuring Gaelic shields, ox skulls and festoons. In the 14th century it was converted into a fort by the Caetani family, who used to threaten passing traffic into paying a toll.

Villa dei Quintili   HISTORICAL BUILDING
(☎06 3996 7700; www.pierreci.it; Via Appia Nuova 1092; adult/reduced incl Terme di Caracalla & Mausoleo di Cecilia Metella €8/4; ⊙9am-1hr before sunset Tue-Sun) This vast 2nd-century villa was the luxurious abode of two brothers who were consuls under Emperor Marcus Aurelius. Its splendour was the brothers' downfall: in a fit of jealousy, Emperor Commodus had them both killed, taking over the villa for himself. The highlight is the well-preserved baths complex with a pool, *caldarium* (hot bath) and *frigidarium* (cold bath).

EUR

Mussolini's Orwellian quarter of wide boulevards and linear buildings (now largely used by banks and government ministries) merits a visit to see its spectacular rationalist architecture.

One of the few planned developments in Rome's history, EUR was built for an international exhibition in 1942 and, although war intervened and the exhibition never took place, the name stuck – Esposizione Universale di Roma (Roman Universal Exhibition) or EUR.

Most iconic is the area's 'Square Colosseum', the **Palazzo della Civiltà del Lavoro** (Palace of the Workers). A rationalist masterpiece clad in gleaming white trav-

ertine, it was designed by Giovanni Guerrini, Ernesto Bruno La Padula and Mario Romano, and built between 1938 and 1943, consisting of six rows of nine arches rising to a height of 50m. Close by is the Palazzo degli Uffici complex, designed by Gaetano Minnucci. Its most famous building is the **Salone delle Fontane** (Showroom of the Fountains), designed between 1937 and 1939 as the ticket office for the exhibition. The building is home to **Caffè Palombini** (Piazza Adenauer Konrad 12), a popular cafe with original fittings from between 1939 and 1942, and 1960s furniture.

Other buildings of note at EUR are the brutalist **post office** dating from 1940 and designed by Studio BBPR; Arnaldo Foschini's monumental **Chiesa Santi Pietro e Paolo**, built from 1938 to 1955; and Nervi and Vitellozzi's futuristic **Palazzetto dello Sport**, built in 1958 and now functioning as the PalaLottomatica, a venue for concerts and sport. The wonderful **Palazzo dei Congressi** was built between 1938 and 1954 and designed by Adalberto Libera. It's another must-see, and in summer occasionally hosts club nights on the terrace.

The **Centro Congressi 'Nuvola'** ('Cloud' Congress Centre), designed by superstar Roman architect Massimiliano Fuksas, will soon be another feature on EUR's curious landscape. Inspired by a cloud-gazing daydream, a steel and Teflon cloud will be suspended by steel cables in a glass box.

To get to EUR, take metro B to EUR Palasport.

TRASTEVERE & GIANICOLO

With its network of cobbled lanes, flapping washing hung between 17th-century ivy-draped facades, and crumbling ochre buildings, Trastevere is bewitchingly pretty, and gets packed on summer evenings. It also has a powerful local character, rivalling Monti as Rome's oldest district. Its working-class roots are still strong, despite colonisation by wealthy foreigners. It's over the river from the *centro storico,* hence the name *tras tevere* – across the Tiber.

Rising up behind Trastevere, the summit of Gianicolo (Janiculum; Map p100) offers incredible bird's-eye views of Rome.

Basilica di Santa Cecilia in Trastevere
CHURCH

(Map p100; ☑06 589 92 89; Piazza di Santa Cecilia 22; basilica free, Cavallini fresco & crypt each €2.50; ⊙basilica & crypt 9.30am-12.30pm & 4-6.30pm, Cavallini fresco 10am-12.30pm Mon-Sat) The last resting place of Saint Cecilia (the patron saint of music) features a stunning 13th-century fresco by Pietro Cavallini in the nuns' choir – the door is to the left of the church as you face it. Inside the church itself, below the altar, Stefano Moderno's mysterious, breathtaking sculpture is a delicate rendition of exactly how Saint Cecilia's miraculously preserved body was

apparently found when it was unearthed in the Catacombs of San Callisto in 1599. Beneath the church you can visit the excavations of a maze of Roman houses, one of which is thought to have been that of the young Cecilia.

Chiesa di San Francesco d'Assisi a Ripa
CHURCH

(Map p100; ☑06 581 90 20; Piazza San Francesco d'Assisi 88; ⊙7am-noon & 4-7pm Mon-Sat, 7am-1pm & 4-7.30pm Sun) This church is home to Bernini's *Blessed Ludovica Albertoni,* in which her religious ecstasy ripples with sexuality. St Francis of Assisi is said to have stayed in the church for a period in the 13th century and you can still see the rock that he used as a pillow.

Basilica di Santa Maria in Trastevere
CHURCH

(Map p100; ☑06 581 48 02; Piazza Santa Maria in Trastevere; ⊙7.30am-9pm) Trastevere's glittering heart is the beautiful Piazza Santa Maria in Trastevere, which features what is said to be the oldest church dedicated to the Virgin Mary in Rome. Begun in AD 337, a major overhaul in 1138 saw the addition of the Romanesque bell tower and glittering facade. The portico came later, added by Carlo Fontana in 1702.

TOMBS & CATACOMBS

Rome's persecuted Christian community built an extensive network of communal subterranean burial grounds outside the city walls, as the laws of the time decreed.

During periods of persecution, martyrs were often buried in catacombs beside the fathers of the Church and the first popes. However, because space was limited and became increasingly sought-after, a trade in tomb real estate developed, becoming increasingly cut-throat until Pope Gregory I abolished the sale of graves in AD 597. However, Christians had already started to abandon the catacombs as early as 313, when Constantine issued the Milan decree of religious tolerance.

Following the decree, Christians opted to bury their dead in catacombs near the churches and basilicas that were being built within the city walls (often above pagan temples). This became common practice under Theodosius, who made Christianity the state religion in 394.

In about 800, after frequent incursions by invaders, the bodies of the martyrs and first popes were transferred to the basilicas inside the city walls. The catacombs were abandoned and eventually many were forgotten. In the Middle Ages only three catacombs were known. Those of San Sebastiano were the most frequented as a place of pilgrimage, since they had earlier been the burial place of St Peter and St Paul.

In the mid-19th century, scholars of Christian archaeology began a program of scientific research, and so far more than 30 catacombs in the Rome area have since been uncovered. Many have graves with touching inscriptions such as one in the Catacombs of Domitilla, erected by Aurelius Ampliatus and his son Gordianus to their wife and mother, Aurelia: 'An incomparable spouse, a truly chaste woman who lived 25 years, two months, three days and six hours.'

Trastevere & Gianicolo (Rome)

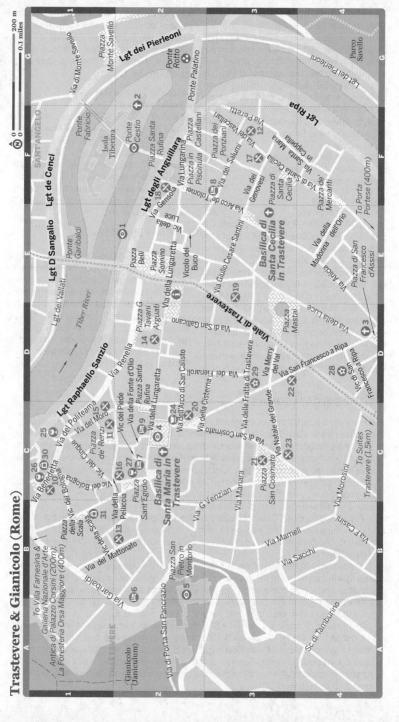

Inside, the 12th-century mosaics star. In the apse, look out for Christ and his mother flanked by various saints and, on the far left, Pope Innocent II holding a model of the church. Beneath this are six mosaics by Pietro Cavallini illustrating the life of the Virgin (c 1291). The building itself incorporates 21 ancient Roman columns, some from the Terme di Caracalla, and its wooden ceiling dates from the 17th century.

Villa Farnesina   HISTORICAL BUILDING
(Map p74; ☎06 6802 7268; Via della Lungara 230; adult/reduced €5/4; ☺9am-1pm Mon-Sat) This gorgeous 16th-century villa features some awe-inspiring frescoes by Sebastiano del Piombo, Raphael and the villa's original architect, Baldassare Peruzzi. The most famous frescoes are in the Loggia of Cupid and Psyche on the ground floor, which are attributed to Raphael, who also painted the *Trionfo di Galatea* (Triumph of Galatea) in the room of the same name. On the 1st floor, Peruzzi's dazzling frescoes in the Salone delle Prospettive are a superb illusionary perspective of a colonnade and panorama of 16th-century Rome.

Galleria Nazionale d'Arte Antica di Palazzo Corsini   ART GALLERY
(Map p74; ☎06 6880 2323; www.galleria borghese.it; Via della Lungara 10; adult/reduced €4/2; ☺8.30am-7.30pm Tue-Sun) This frescoed palace houses part of Italy's national art collection, the highlight of which is Caravaggio's mesmerising *San Giovanni Battista* (St John the Baptist).

Tempietto di Bramante   HISTORICAL BUILDING
(Map p100; ☎06 581 39 40; www.sanpietroin montorio.it; Piazza San Pietro in Montorio 2; ☺tempietto 9.30am-12.30pm & 4-6pm Tue-Sun Apr-Sep, 9.30am-12.30pm & 2-4pm Tue-Sun Oct-Mar, church 8.30am-noon & 3-4pm Mon-Fri) Considered to be the first great building of the High Renaissance, Bramante's sublime *tempietto* is built in the courtyard of the Chiesa di San Pietro in Montorio: the very spot on which St Peter is supposed to have been crucified. More than a century later, in 1628, Bernini added a staircase, and also contributed a chapel to the adjacent church. It's quite a climb uphill, but you're rewarded by the views. To cheat, take bus 870 from Via Paola just off Corso Vittorio Emanuele II near the Tiber.

QUEUE JUMPING AT THE VATICAN MUSEUMS

Here's how to jump the ticket queue – although we can't help with lines for the security checks.

» Book tickets at the museums' online ticket office (http://biglietteriamusei. vatican.va/musei/tickets). On payment, you'll receive email confirmation that you should print and present, along with a valid ID card or passport, at the museum entrance. Note that tickets bought online incur a €4 booking fee. You can also book guided tours (adult/reduced €31/24) online.

» Time your visit: Wednesday mornings are a good bet as everyone is at the pope's weekly audience at St Peter's; afternoon is better than the morning; avoid Mondays, when many other museums are shut.

» Book a tour with a reputable guide.

VATICAN CITY, BORGO & PRATI

The Vatican, the world's smallest sovereign state (a mere 0.44 sq km), sits atop the low-lying Vatican hill just a few hundred metres west of the Tiber. Centred on the domed bulk of St Peter's Basilica, it is the capital of the Catholic world and jealous guardian of one of the world's great artistic patrimonies.

Established under the terms of the 1929 Lateran Treaty, the Vatican is the modern vestige of the Papal States, the papal fiefdom that ruled Rome and much of central Italy until Italian unification in 1861. As part of the agreement, signed by Mussolini and Pope Pius XI, the Holy See was also given extraterritorial authority over a further 28 sites in and around Rome, including the basilicas of San Giovanni in Laterano, Santa Maria Maggiore and San Paolo Fuori le Mura.

As an independent state, the Vatican has its own postal service, newspaper, radio station and army. The nattily dressed, po-faced Swiss Guards, all practising Catholics from Switzerland, were first used by Julius II in 1506 and are still responsible for the pope's personal security.

The Vatican's current look is the culmination of more than 1000 years of chipping and chopping. The Leonine walls date from 846 when Leo IV had them put up after a series of Saracen raids, while the Vatican palace, now home to the Vatican Museums, was originally constructed by Eugenius III in the 12th century. Subsequent popes extended it, fortified it and decorated it according to their political and artistic needs.

Between the Vatican and the river lies the cobbled, medieval district of the Borgo, while to the north Prati is a graceful residential area.

FREE St Peter's Basilica   CHURCH
(Map p104; www.vatican.va; Piazza San Pietro; audioguide €5; ⊙7am-7pm summer, to 6pm winter) In this city of outstanding churches, St Peter's Basilica (Basilica San Pietro) outdazzles them all. Rome's largest, richest and most spectacular church is a magnificent monument to artistic genius, as well as a major tourist attraction, and on a busy day around 20,000 visitors pass through. If you want to be one of them, remember to dress appropriately – no shorts, miniskirts or bare shoulders.

The original basilica was built by Constantine in the 4th century. Standing on the site of Nero's stadium, the Ager Vaticanus, where St Peter is said to have been buried between AD 64 and 67, it was consecrated in AD 326. Like many early churches, it eventually fell into disrepair, and it wasn't until the mid-15th century that efforts were made to restore it, first by Pope Nicholas V and then, rather more successfully, by Julius II.

PAPAL AUDIENCES

At 11am on Wednesday, the pope addresses his flock at the Vatican (in July and August in Castel Gandolfo near Rome). For free tickets, download the request form from the Vatican website (www.vatican.va) and fax it to the Prefettura della Casa Pontificia (☑06 6988 5863). Pick them up at the office through the bronze doors under the colonnade to the right of St Peter's.

When he is in Rome, the pope blesses the crowd in St Peter's Square on Sunday at noon. No tickets are required.

In 1506 Bramante came up with a design for a basilica based on a Greek-cross plan, with a central dome and four smaller domes.

It took more than 150 years to complete the new basilica, now the second biggest in the world (the largest is in Yamoussoukro in Côte d'Ivoire). Bramante, Raphael, Antonio da Sangallo, Giacomo della Porta and Carlo Maderno all contributed, but it is generally held that St Peter's owes most to Michelangelo, who took over the project in 1547 at the age of 72 and was responsible for the design of the dome.

The facade and portico were designed by Maderno, who inherited the project after Michelangelo's death. He was also instructed to lengthen the nave towards the piazza, effectively altering Bramante's original Greek cross plan to a Latin cross.

Free English-language tours of the basilica are run from the Vatican tourist office, the Centro Servizi Pellegrini e Turisti, at 9.45am on Tuesday and Thursday and at 2.15pm every afternoon between Monday and Friday.

Interior

The cavernous 187m-long interior covers more than 15,000 sq metres and contains many spectacular works of art, including Michelangelo's hauntingly beautiful *Pietá* at the head of the right nave. Sculpted when he was only 25, it is the only work he ever signed – his signature is etched into the sash across the Madonna's breast.

Nearby, the red porphyry disc just inside the main door marks the spot where Charlemagne and later Holy Roman Emperors were crowned by the pope.

Dominating the centre of the basilica is Bernini's 29m-high baldachin. Supported by four spiral columns and made with bronze taken from the Pantheon, it stands over the high altar, which itself sits on the site of St Peter's grave. The pope is the only priest permitted to serve at the high altar.

Above, Michelangelo's dome soars to a height of 119m. Based on Brunelleschi's design for the Duomo in Florence, the towering cupola is supported by four solid stone piers, named after the saints whose statues adorn their Bernini-designed niches – Longinus, Helena, Veronica and Andrew.

At the base of the Pier of St Longinus, to the right as you face the high altar, is a famous bronze statue of St Peter, believed to be a 13th-century work by Arnolfo di Cambio. It's a much-loved piece and its right

foot has been worn down by centuries of pilgrims' kisses and caresses.

Dome

To climb the **dome** (with/without lift €7/5; ⊙8am-5.45pm summer, to 4.45pm winter), the entrance is to the right of the basilica. A small lift takes you halfway up, but it's still a long climb to the top (320 steps). Press on, however, and you're rewarded with stunning views. It's well worth the effort, but bear in mind that it's steep, long and narrow: not recommended for those who suffer from claustrophobia or vertigo.

Museo Storico Artistico

Accessed from the left nave, the **Museo Storico Artistico** (Treasury; adult/reduced €6/4; ⊙9am-6.15pm summer, to 5.15pm winter) sparkles with sacred relics and priceless artefacts, including a tabernacle by Donatello and the 6th-century Crux Vaticana, a cross studded with jewels that was a gift of the emperor Justinian II.

Vatican Grottoes

The **Vatican Grottoes** (admission free; ⊙9am-6pm summer, to 5pm winter) contain the tombs of numerous popes, including John Paul II, whose simple sepulchre contrasts starkly with many of the flamboyant monuments in the basilica above. You can also see several huge columns from the original 4th-century basilica. The entrance is through the right side of the portico.

Tomb of St Peter

Excavations beneath the basilica have uncovered part of the original church and what the Vatican believes is the **Tomb of St Peter** (admission €10, over 15yr only). In 1942 the bones of an elderly, strongly built man were found in a box hidden behind a wall covered by pilgrims' graffiti. After more than 30 years of forensic examination, in 1976 Pope Paul VI declared the bones to be those of St Peter.

The excavations can only be visited on a 90-minute guided tour. To book a spot email the **Ufficio Scavi** (Excavations Office; Fabbrica di San Pietro; ⌨06 6988 5318; scavi@fsp.va), as far in advance as possible.

St Peter's Square   PIAZZA
(Map p104) One of the world's great public spaces, Bernini's St Peter's Square (Piazza San Pietro) was laid out between 1656 and 1667 for Pope Alexander VII.

Vatican City, Borgo & Prati (Rome)

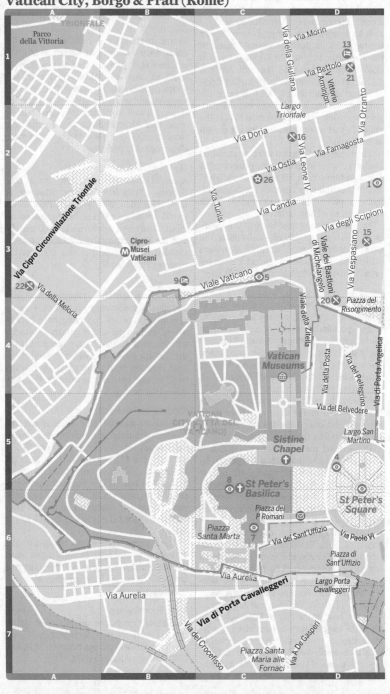

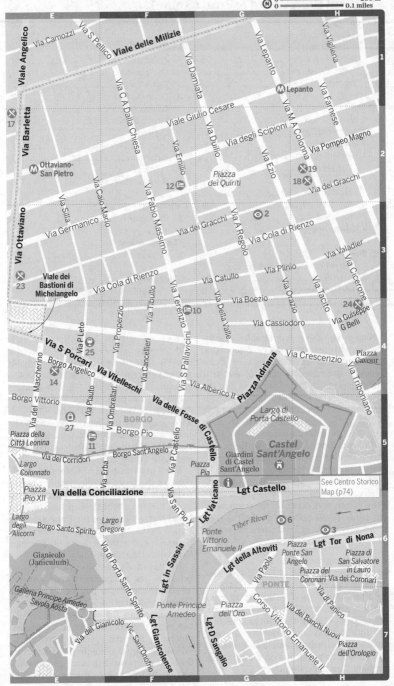

Viale Angelico

Via Camozzi

Via S Pellico

Viale delle Milizie

Via Damiata

Via Lepanto

Via Vigliena

1

Via Barletta

17 ⊗

Via C A Dalla Chiesa

Viale Giulio Cesare

Via Duilio

Via degli Scipioni

Via M A Colonna

M Lepanto

Via Farnese

Via Pompeo Magno

2

M Ottaviano-San Pietro

Via Caio Mario

Via Fabio Massimo

Via Emilio

Piazza dei Quiriti

12 🏛

Via Ezio

⊗ 19

18 ⊗

Via dei Gracchi

Via Silla

Via Germanico

Via dei Gracchi

Via A Regolo

⊙ 2

Via Cola di Rienzo

3

Via Ottaviano

Via Cola di Rienzo

Via Tibullo

Via Catullo

Via Plinio

Via Valadier

Viale dei Bastioni di Michelangelo

23 ⊗

Via Properzio

Via Terenzio

Via Della Valle

Via Boezio

Via Orazio

Via Cicerone

Via Tacito

⊙ 10

Via Cassiodoro

24 ⊗

Via Guiseppe G Belli

4

Via S Porcari

Via P Leto

🍷 25

Via Cancellieri

Via S Pallavicini

Via Crescenzio

Piazza Cavour

Via Triboniano

Mascherino

Borgo Angelico

Via Vitelleschi

Via S Alberico II

Piazza Adriana

14 ⊗

Via Plauto

Via delle Fosse di Castello

Largo di Porta Castello

Borgo Vittorio

Via del

🔒 27

Via Ombrellari

BORGO

Borgo Pio

11 🏛

Castel Sant'Angelo

5

Piazza della Città Leonina

Via dei Corridori

Via Erba

Via P Castello

Borgo Sant'Angelo

Piazza Pia

Giardini di Castel Sant'Angelo

Largo Colonnato

Piazza Pio XII

Via della Conciliazione

Via San Pio X

Lgt Vaticano

ⓘ

Lgt Castello

See Centro Storico Map (p74)

Largo degli Alicorni

Borgo Santo Spirito

Largo I Gregore

Ponte Vittorio Emanuele II

Tiber River

⊙ 6

⊙ 3

6

Gianicolo (Janiculum)

Via di Porta Santo Spirito

Lgt in Sassia

Lgt della Altoviti

Piazza Ponte San Angelo

Via Paola

Lgt Tor di Nona

Piazza di San Salvatore in Lauro

Piazza del Coronari

Via dei Coronari

Galleria Principe Amedeo Savola Aosta

Via del Gianicolo

Vic Sant'Onofrio

Lgt Gianicolense

Ponte Principe Amedeo

Lgt D Sangallo

Piazza dell'Oro

PONTE

Corso Vittorio Emanuele II

Via dei Banchi Nuovi

Via di Panico

Piazza dell'Orologio

7

E F G H

Vatican City, Borgo & Prati (Rome)

Seen from above, it resembles a giant keyhole with two semicircular colonnades, each consisting of four rows of Doric columns, encircling a giant ellipse that straightens out to funnel believers into the basilica. The effect was deliberate – Bernini described the colonnades as representing 'the motherly arms of the church'. The 25m obelisk in the centre was brought to Rome by Caligula from Heliopolis in Egypt and later used by Nero as a turning post for the chariot races in his circus.

The scale of the piazza is dazzling: at its largest it measures 340m by 240m; there are 284 columns and, on top of the colonnades, 140 saints. In the midst of all this the pope seems very small as he delivers his weekly address at noon on Sunday.

Vatican Museums MUSEUM
(Musei Vaticani; Map p104; ☎06 6988 4676; www. vatican.va; Viale Vaticano; adult/reduced €14/8, last Sun of month free; ⊙9am-6pm Mon-Sat, last admission 4pm, 9am-2pm last Sun of month, last admission 12.30pm) Visiting the Vatican Museums is a thrilling and unforgettable experience, but one that requires stamina and patience. Queues are the norm, and once inside there are some 7km of exhibitions.

Founded by Pope Julius II in the early 16th century and enlarged by successive pontiffs, the museums are housed in what is known collectively as the Palazzo Apostolico Vaticano. This massive 5.5-hectare complex consists of two palaces – the Vatican palace (nearer to St Peter's) and the Belvedere Palace – joined by two long galleries. On the inside are three courtyards: the Cortile della Pigna, the Cortile della Biblioteca and, to the south, the Cortile del Belvedere.

You'll never manage to explore the whole complex in one go, so selectivity is the way to go. Each gallery contains priceless treasures, but for a whistle-stop tour (see the boxed text, p107) get to the Pinacoteca, the Museo Pio-Clementino, Galleria delle Carte Geografiche, Stanze di Raffaello (Raphael Rooms) and the Sistine Chapel.

On the whole, exhibits are not well labelled, so you might find it useful to hire an audioguide (€7) or buy the *Guide to the Vatican Museums and City* (€12).

The museums are well equipped for visitors with disabilities: there are suggested itineraries, lifts and specially fitted toilets. Wheelchairs are available free of charge from the Special Permits desk in the entrance hall and can be reserved in advance by emailing accoglienza.musei@scv.va. Parents with toddlers can take prams into the museums.

Pinacoteca

Often overlooked by visitors, the papal picture gallery boasts Raphael's last work, *La Trasfigurazione* (1517–20), and paintings by Giotto, Bellini, Caravaggio, Fra Angelico, Filippo Lippi, Guido Reni, Van Dyck, Pietro da Cortona and Leonardo da Vinci, whose *San Gerolamo* (St Jerome; c 1480) was never finished.

Museo Gregoriano Egizio (Egyptian Museum)

Founded by Gregory XVI in 1839, this museum contains pieces taken from Egypt in Roman times. The collection is small but there are fascinating exhibits including the *Trono di Rameses II,* part of a statue of the seated king, vividly painted sarcophagi dating from around 1000 BC, and some macabre mummies.

Museo Chiaromonti & Braccio Nuovo

The Museo Chiaromonti is effectively the long corridor that runs down the lower east side of the Belvedere Palace. Its walls are lined with thousands of statues representing everything from immortal gods to playful cherubs and ugly Roman patricians. Near the end of the hall, off to the right, is the Braccio Nuovo (New Wing), which contains a famous sculpture of Augustus and a statue depicting the Nile as a reclining god

covered by 16 babies (supposedly representing the number of cubits the Nile rises when it floods).

Museo Pio-Clementino

Housed in the Belvedere Palace, this stunning museum showcases some spectacular classical statuary, including the peerless *Apollo Belvedere* and the 1st-century *Laocoön and His Sons,* both in the **Cortile Ottagono** (Octagonal Courtyard). Before you go into the courtyard take a moment to admire the 1st-century *Apoxyomenos,* near the entrance in a room where Leonardo da Vinci once slept. This sculpture of an athlete scraping himself down is an early example of the sculptural technique known as *contrapposto* and one of the earliest known sculptures to depict a figure with a raised arm.

To the left as you enter the courtyard, the *Apollo Belvedere* is a 2nd-century Roman copy of a 4th-century-BC Greek bronze. A beautifully proportioned representation of the sun god Apollo, it's considered one of the great masterpieces of classical sculpture. Nearby, the *Laocoön* depicts a muscular Trojan priest and his two sons in mortal struggle with two sea serpents. When the statue was unearthed on the Esquiline Hill in 1506, Michelangelo and Giuliano da Sangallo confirmed that it was the same sculpture that

VATICAN MUSEUMS – THE 'BEST OF' TOUR

Duration: Three hours

Home to one of the world's richest art collections, the Vatican Museums are vast – it's said that if you spent one minute on every exhibit it would take you 12 years to see everything. This tour takes in the museums' greatest hits, culminating in the Sistine Chapel.

Once you've passed through the entrance complex, head up the escalator beside the modern spiral staircase. At the top, signs indicate left for the Sistine Chapel and Raphael Rooms. Before following these, nip out to the terrace for views over St Peter's dome and the Vatican Gardens. Re-enter and follow onto the Cortile della Pigna, home to a huge Augustan-era bronze pine cone. Cross the courtyard and enter a long corridor – the Museo Chiaromonti. Don't stop here but continue left, up the stairs, to the Museo Pio-Clementino. Follow the flow of people through the Cortile Ottagono and onto the Sala Croce Greca (Greek Cross Room), from where stairs lead up to the Galleria dei Candelabri (Gallery of the Candelabra), the first of three galleries along a lengthy corridor. It gets very crowded up here as you are funnelled through the Galleria degli Arazzi (Tapestry Gallery) and onto the Galleria delle Carte Geografiche (Map Gallery). At the end of the corridor, carry on through the Sala Sobieski to the Sala di Costantino, the first of the four Stanze di Raffaello (Raphael Rooms). From the last Raphael Room, the one-way system routes you past a section of modern art onto the Sistine Chapel. Once in the chapel, head over to the far wall to get the best views of the frescoes. Another good tip is to bring a pocket mirror to get good close-ups of the ceiling.

1. Colosseum, Rome (p61)
Ancient Rome's most fearful arena was built by the emperor Vespasian and inaugurated in AD 80.

2. Emperor Constantine statue, Rome (p71)
The foot in the Capitoline Museums' courtyard comes from a statue that originally stood in the Roman Forum.

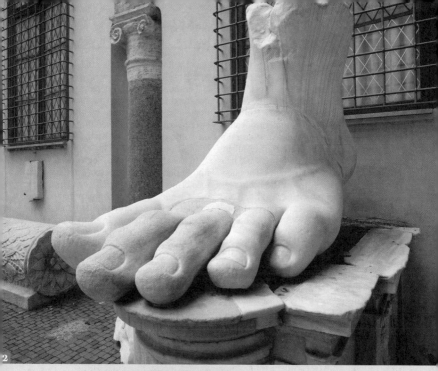

3. Statue, Vatican Museums, Rome (p106)
A rich art collection is showcased in this massive complex of museums, galleries and courtyards.

4. Pantheon, Rome (p73)
This striking 2000-year-old temple features the world's largest unreinforced concrete dome.

5. St Peter's Basilica, Rome (p102)
Rome's largest, richest and most spectacular church attracts up to 20,000 visitors on a busy day.

had been cited by Pliny the Elder some 1500 years earlier.

In the **Sala delle Muse** (Room of Muses) the highlight is the fantastic *Torso Belvedere*, a Greek sculpture from the 1st century BC, which Michelangelo used as inspiration for his nude figures *(ignudi)* in the Sistine Chapel. Continuing on, the **Sala Rotonda** (Round Room) contains a number of colossal statues, including the gilded-bronze figure of Ercole (Hercules), and an exquisite floor mosaic featuring sea monsters and battles between Greeks and centaurs. The enormous basin in the centre of the room was found in Nero's Domus Aurea and is made out of a single piece of red porphyry stone.

Museo Gregoriano Etrusco

On the upper level of the Belvedere (off the 18th-century Simonetti staircase), the Museo Gregoriano Etrusco contains artefacts unearthed in the Etruscan tombs of southern Etruria (now northern Lazio), as well as a collection of Greek vases and Roman antiquities. Of particular interest is the *Marte di Todi* (Mars of Todi), a full-length bronze statue of a warrior dating from the 4th century BC, in the Sala dei Bronzi.

Galleria delle Carte Geografiche (Map Gallery)

The last of three galleries – the other two are the Galleria dei Candelabri (Gallery of the Candelabra) and the Galleria degli Arazzi (Tapestry Gallery) – this 120m-long corridor is hung with 40 16th-century topographical maps of Italy.

Stanze di Raffaello (Raphael Rooms)

The four Raphael Rooms were the private apartments of Pope Julius II. Raphael himself painted the Stanza della Segnatura (1508–11) and the Stanza d'Eliodoro (1512–14), while both the Stanza dell'Incendio (1514–17) and the Stanza di Costantino (1517–24) were decorated by students following his designs.

The first room you come to is the **Stanza di Costantino**, which features a huge fresco depicting Constantine's defeat of Maxentius at the battle of Milvian Bridge. The next, the **Stanza d'Eliodoro**, which was used for private audiences, is decorated with frescoes illustrating God's protection of the church. The most famous, the *Cacciata d'Eliodoro* (Expulsion of Heliodorus from the Temple) symbolises Julius' military victory over foreign powers. To the left is *Mass of Bolsena*, showing Julius II paying homage to a relic

from a 13th-century miracle in the lakeside town of Bolsena. Next is *Leone X ferma l'invasione di Attila* (Leo X Repulsing Attila) by Raphael and his students. On the fourth wall, the *Liberazione di San Pietro* (Liberation of St Peter) depicts the saint being freed from prison. The masterly depiction of light in this fresco was Raphael's answer to critics who claimed that he had won the contract to paint the rooms thanks to his connections rather than his ability.

In the **Stanza della Segnatura**, you'll find Raphael's earliest frescoes and his great masterpiece, *La Scuola d'Atene* (The School of Athens), featuring philosophers and scholars gathered around Plato and Aristotle. The lone figure in front of the steps is believed to be Michelangelo, while the figure of Plato is said to be a portrait of Leonardo da Vinci, and Euclide (in the lower right) is Bramante. Raphael also included a self-portrait in the lower right corner (he's the second figure from the right).

Sistine Chapel (Capella Sistina)

This is the one place in the Vatican Museums that not one of the 12,000 daily visitors wants to miss. Home to two of the world's most famous works of art – Michelangelo's ceiling frescoes and the *Giudizio Universale* (Last Judgment) on the west wall – this 15th-century chapel is where the papal conclave is locked to elect the pope.

The chapel was originally built in 1484 for Pope Sixtus IV, after whom it is named, but it was Julius II who commissioned Michelangelo to decorate it in 1508. The great artist was initially reluctant to take on the job – he considered himself a sculptor not a painter – but Julius prevailed and over the next four years Michelangelo painted the entire 800-sq-metre ceiling. To do so he designed a curved scaffolding system that allowed him to work in an awkward backward-leaning position, and employed a steady stream of assistants to help with the plasterwork (producing frescoes involves painting directly onto wet plaster).

The ceiling frescoes, which are best viewed from the chapel's main entrance (at the opposite end from the visitor's entrance), represent nine scenes from the book of Genesis: *God Separating Light from Darkness; Creation of the Sun, Moon and Planets; Separation of Land from Sea; Creation of Adam; Creation of Eve; Temptation and Expulsion of Adam and Eve from the Gar-*

den of Eden; Noah's Sacrifice; The Flood; and the *Drunkenness of Noah.*

The most famous scene is the *Creation of Adam,* which shows a bearded God pointing his index figure at Adam, thus bringing him to life. In the *Temptation and Expulsion of Adam and Eve from the Garden of Eden,* Adam and Eve are sent packing after accepting the forbidden fruit from Satan, represented by a snake with the body of a woman coiled around a tree.

The main scenes are framed by pulsating, muscular *ignudi* (athletic male nudes).

Covering the chapel's 200-sq-metre west wall, and portraying some 391 characters, Michelangelo's highly charged *Giudizio Universale* depicts the souls of the dead being torn from their graves to face the wrath of God. The subject was chosen by Pope Paul III as a warning to Catholics to toe the line during the Reformation, which was then sweeping Europe. When it was unveiled in 1541, its dramatic, swirling mass of predominantly naked bodies caused controversy, and Pope Pius IV later had Daniele da Volterra, one of Michelangelo's students, add blush-sparing fig leaves and loincloths.

The 15th-century wall frescoes, which depict scenes from the lives of Moses (on the south wall) and Christ (on the north wall), were painted by a team of Renaissance artists that included Botticelli, Domenico Ghirlandaio, Pinturicchio and Luca Signorelli. Highlights include Botticelli's *Temptations of Christ* (the second fresco on the right) and Perugino's superbly composed *Christ Giving the Keys to St Peter* (the fifth fresco on the right).

Castel Sant'Angelo   MUSEUM
(Map p104; ✆06 681 91 11; Lungotevere Castello 50; adult/reduced €5/2.50; ⊘9am-7.30pm, last admission 6.30pm Tue-Sun) With its chunky round keep, this castle is an instantly recognisable landmark. Built as a mausoleum for the emperor Hadrian, it was converted into a papal fortress in the 6th century and named after an angelic vision that Pope Gregory the Great had in 590. Thanks to a secret 13th-century passageway to the Vatican palaces, the Passetta di Borgo, it provided sanctuary to many popes in times of danger, including Clemente VI, who holed up here during the 1527 sack of Rome.

Its upper floors are filled with lavishly decorated Renaissance interiors, including, on the 4th floor, the beautifully frescoed Sala Paolina. Two stories further up, the ter-

race, immortalised by Puccini in his opera *Tosca,* offers great views over Rome.

Ponte Sant'Angelo   BRIDGE
(Map p104) Opposite the castle, this ancient bridge was built by Hadrian in AD 134 to provide an approach to his mausoleum. In the 17th century, Bernini and his pupils sculpted the figures of angels that line the pedestrian walkway, supplying intense drama.

VILLA BORGHESE & NORTHERN ROME

Museo e Galleria Borghese   ART GALLERY
(Map p112; ✆06 3 28 10; www.galleriaborghese. it; Piazzale del Museo Borghese 5; adult/reduced €8.50/5.25, audioguide €5; ⊘9am-7pm Tue-Sun, pre-booking necessary) If you only have time (or inclination) for one art gallery in Rome, make it this one. Not only is it exquisite, but it provides the perfect introduction to Renaissance and baroque art without being overwhelming. To limit numbers, visitors are admitted at two-hourly intervals, so you'll need to call to pre-book, and enter at an allotted entry time – but trust us, it's worth it.

The collection, which includes works by Caravaggio, Bernini, Botticelli, Rubens, Raphael and Titian, was formed by Cardinal Scipione Borghese (1579–1633), the most knowledgeable and ruthless art collector of his day. It's housed in the Casino Borghese, whose neoclassical look is the result of a 17th-century revamp of Scipione's original villa.

The villa is divided into two parts: the ground-floor gallery, with its superb sculptures, intricate Roman floor mosaics and over-the-top frescoes; and the upstairs picture gallery.

Things get off to a cracking start in the **entrance hall**, decorated with 4th-century floor mosaics of fighting gladiators and a gravity-defying bas-relief, *Marco Curzio a Cavallo,* of a horse and rider falling into the void, by Pietro Bernini (Gian Lorenzo's father).

Sala I is centred on Antonio Canova's daring depiction of Napoleon's sister, Paolina Bonaparte Borghese, reclining topless as *Venere vincitrice* (Conquering Venus; 1805–08). Yet it's Gian Lorenzo Bernini's spectacular sculptures – flamboyant depictions of pagan myths – that really steal the show. Just look at Daphne's hands morphing into leaves in the swirling *Apollo e Dafne* (1622–25) in **Sala III**, or Pluto's hand pressing into the seemingly soft flesh of Persephone's thigh in the *Ratto di Proserpina* (Rape of Persephone; 1621–22) in Sala IV.

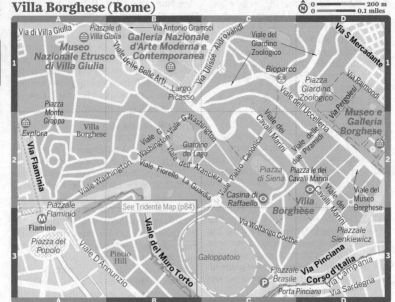

Caravaggio dominates **Sala VIII**. There's a dissipated-looking *Bacchus* (1592–95), the strangely beautiful *La Madonna dei Palafenieri* (Madonna with Serpent; 1605–06) and *San Giovanni Battista* (St John the Baptist; 1609–10), probably Caravaggio's last work. Then there's the much-loved *Ragazzo col Canestro di Frutta* (Boy with a Basket of Fruit; 1593–95) and the dramatic *Davide con la Testa di Golia* (David with the Head of Goliath; 1609–10) – Goliath's severed head is said to be a self-portrait.

Upstairs, the pinacoteca offers a wonderful snapshot of European Renaissance art. Don't miss Raphael's extraordinary *La Deposizione di Cristo* (The Deposition; 1507) in **Sala IX**, and his *Dama con Liocorno* (Lady with a Unicorn; 1506). In the same room is the superb *Adorazione del Bambino* (Adoration of the Christ Child; 1495) by Fra Bartolomeo and Perugino's *Madonna con Bambino* (Madonna and Child; first quarter of the 16th century).

Other highlights include Correggio's erotic *Danae* (1530–31) in **Sala X**, Bernini's self-portraits in **Sala XIV** and Titian's early masterpiece, *Amor Sacro e Amor Profano* (Sacred and Profane Love; 1514) in **Sala XX**.

Villa Borghese PARK

Locals, lovers, tourists, joggers – no one can help heeding the call of this ravishing baroque park just north of the *centro storico*. Cardinal Scipione Borghese, top dog in one of Rome's most powerful families, created these grounds in the 17th century, and they're perfect for sun-dappled picnics, a pastoral hiatus and a chance for kids to run about and shout.

You can enter from Piazzale Flaminio, from the top of Pincio Hill above the Spanish Steps or from the top of Via Vittorio Veneto. Bike hire is available at various points, including Via delle Belle Arti, for about €5/15 per hour/day.

Galleria Nazionale d'Arte Moderna e Contemporanea ART GALLERY

(Map p112; ☎06 3229 8221; www.gnam.beni culturali.it; Viale delle Belle Arti 131; adult/reduced €8/4; ☺8.30am-7.30pm, last admission 6.45pm Tue-Sun) This oft-overlooked gallery of modern and contemporary art is definitely worth a visit. Set in a vast belle époque palace are works by some of the most important exponents of modern Italian art. There are canvases by the Macchiaioli (the Italian Impressionists) and futurists Boccioni and Balla, as well as several impressive sculptures by Canova and major works by Modigliani and De Chirico. International artists are also represented, with works by Degas, Cezanne, Kandinsky, Klimt, Mondrian, Pollock and Moore. The gallery's charming terrace cafe is the perfect place for a languorous breather.

Museo Nazionale Etrusco di Villa Giulia
MUSEUM

(Map p112; ☑06 322 65 71; www.ticketeria.it; Piazzale di Villa Giulia 9; adult/reduced €4/2; ☺8.30am-7.30pm, last admission 6.30pm Tue-Sun) Italy's finest collection of pre-Roman Etruscan treasures is considerately presented in Villa Giulia, Pope Julius III's 16th-century pleasure palace. Exhibits, many of which came from burial tombs in the surrounding Lazio region, range from bronze figurines and black *bucchero* tableware to temple decorations, terracotta vases and a dazzling display of sophisticated jewellery.

Must-sees include a polychrome terracotta statue of Apollo, the 6th-century-BC *Sarcofago degli Sposi* (Sarcophagus of the Betrothed) and the Euphronios Krater, a celebrated Greek vase that was returned to Italy in 2008 after a 30-year tug of war between the Italian government and New York's Metropolitan Museum of Art.

Museo Nazionale delle Arti del XXI Secolo (MAXXI)
ART GALLERY

(☑06 321 01 81; www.fondazionemaxxi.it; Via Guido Reni 2f; adult/reduced €11/7; ☺11am-7pm Tue, Wed, Fri & Sun, to 10pm Thu & Sat) More than the exhibitions of contemporary art and architecture, the real attraction here is the building itself. Anglo-Iraqi architect Zaha Hadid has remodelled a former barracks into a light-filled showroom of snaking white walkways, staircases, and acres of glass, cement and steel. The gallery, which is just off Via Flaminia, is easily reached by tram from Piazzale Flaminio, above Flaminio metro station.

Courses

Cooking & Wine Tasting

Roman Kitchen
COOKING

(Map p74; ☑06 678 5759; www.italiangourmet.com) Cookery writer Diane Seed (*The Top One Hundred Pasta Sauces)* runs cooking courses from her kitchen in Palazzo Doria Pamphilj. There are one-day, two-day, three-day and week-long courses costing €200 per day and €1000 per week.

International Wine Academy of Roma
WINE TASTING

(Map p84; ☑06 699 08 78; www.wineacademyroma.com; Vicolo del Bottino 8) Learn about Italy's wine regions and hone your tasting skills at Rome's prestigious academy. For more, see the boxed text, p902.

Città del Gusto
COOKING

(☑06 551 11 21; www.gamberorosso.it, in Italian; Via Fermi 161) For details of the demonstrations, workshops, lessons and courses held at this foodie complex see the boxed text, p902.

Language

There are hundreds of schools offering individual and group language courses in Rome. Costs vary enormously, but bank on €300 to €390 for a two-week group course or about €40 to €45 for individual lessons. Some schools also offer accommodation packages for shorter courses. Reputable schools include the following:

Arco di Druso
LANGUAGE

(Map p104; ☑06 3975 0984; www.arcodidruso.com; Via Otranto 12)

Centro Linguistico Italiano Dante Alighieri
LANGUAGE

(Map p58; ☑06 4423 1400; www.clidante.it; Piazza Bologna 1)

Divulgazione Lingua Italiana Soc
LANGUAGE

(DILIT; Map p90; ☑06 446 25 93; www.dilit.it; Via Marghera 22)

Italiaidea
LANGUAGE

(Map p86; ☑06 6994 1314; www.italiaidea.com; 1st fl, Via dei Due Macelli 47)

Torre di Babele Centro di Lingua e Cultura Italiana
LANGUAGE

(Map p58; ☑06 4425 2578; www.torredibabele.com; Via Cosenza 7)

Arts & Crafts

Art Studio Café
MOSAICS

(Map p104; ☑06 3260 9104; www.artstudiocafe.it; Via dei Gracchi 187a) This cafe, exhibition space and mosaic school offers a range of classes. Learn how to cut and glaze enamel tesserae, how to mix colours and how best to mount your final composition. One-day sessions start at €50.

Tours

A Friend in Rome
WALKING

(☑06 6614 0987; www.afriendinrome.it) Your friend in Rome is Silvia Prosperi, who organises tailor-made tours (on foot, by bike or

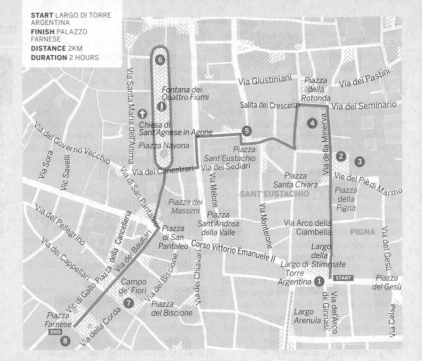

START LARGO DI TORRE
ARGENTINA
FINISH PALAZZO
FARNESE
DISTANCE 2KM
DURATION 2 HOURS

Via Santa Maria dell'Anima
Via Giustiniani
Piazza della Rotonda
Via dei Pastini
Fontana dei Quattro Fiumi
Salita dei Crescenzi
Via del Seminario
Via del Governo Vecchio
Chiesa di Sant'Agnese in Agone
Piazza Navona
Via della Minerva
Via Sora
Vic Savelli
Via di San Pantaleo
Via dei Canestrari
Piazza Sant'Eustachio
Via dei Sediari
Piazza Santa Chiara
Via dei Piè di Marmo
Via del Pellegrino
Piazza dei Massimi
Via Melone
Piazza Sant'Andrea della Valle
SANT'EUSTACHIO
Piazza della Pigna
Via dei Cappellari
Piazza di San Pantaleo
Corso Vittorio Emanuele II
Via Monterone
Via Arco della Ciambella
PIGNA
Via del Gesù
Vic di Gallo
Piazza della Cancelleria
Via dei Baullari
Via del Biscione
Via Chiavari
Largo della Stimmate
Largo di Torre Argentina
Via del Gesù
Campo de' Fiori
Piazza del Biscione
START
Piazza del Gesù
Piazza Farnese
END
Via della Corda
Largo Arenula
Via dell'Arco de Ginnasi
Via Celsa

Walking Tour
Centro Storico

❭ Rome's tightly packed historical centre is ideal for leisurely strolling. There's loads to see and even without trying you'll come across some of the city's best-known sights. This tour takes you through the heart of the area.

Start off in ① **Largo di Torre Argentina**, a busy square set around the ruins of four Republic-era temples and the site of Julius Caesar's assassination in 44 BC. From here it's a short walk up Via dei Cestari, past Bernini's much-loved ② **Elefantino**, to the 13th-century ③ **Chiesa di Santa Maria Sopra Minerva**, Rome's only Gothic church. Continue past the church and you get to the ④ **Pantheon**, ancient Rome's best-preserved monument. Built in 27 BC, modified by Hadrian in the 2nd century AD and consecrated as a Christian church in 608, it's an architectural masterpiece capped by the largest unreinforced concrete dome ever built. From the Pantheon, follow signs towards Piazza Navona, stopping off en route for a coffee at ⑤ **Caffè Sant'Eustachio**,

reckoned by many to be the capital's best. A short hop away, ⑥ **Piazza Navona** is central Rome's showpiece square. Here, among the street artists, tourists, touts and pigeons, you can compare the two giants of Roman baroque: Bernini, creator of the Fontana dei Quattro Fiumi, and Borromini, responsible for the Chiesa di Sant'Agnese in Agone. On the other side of Corso Vittorio Emanuel II, the busy road that bisects the *centro storico,* life centres on ⑦ **Campo de' Fiori**. By day this noisy square stages a colourful market but at night it transforms into a raucous open-air pub, beloved of foreign students and lusty Romans. Just beyond, Piazza Farnese is a refined square overlooked by the Renaissance ⑧ **Palazzo Farnese**. This magnificent *palazzo* (mansion), now home to the French Embassy, boasts some superb frescoes, said by some to rival those of the Sistine Chapel. To see them, though, you'll need to book well in advance.

by scooter) to suit your interests. She covers the Vatican and main historical centre as well as neighbourhoods such as Aventino, Trastevere, Celio and Monti. Rates are €50 per hour, with a minimum of three hours for most tours. She can also arrange mosaic lessons, cooking classes and coastal cruises.

Battelli di Roma
BOAT
(Map p104, Map p100; ☑06 9774 5498; www.battelli diroma.it; adult/reduced €16/12) Runs hour-long hop-on, hop-off cruises along the Tiber between Ponte Sant'Angelo and Ponte Nenni. Trips depart at 10am from Ponte Sant'Angelo, 10.10pm from Isola Tiberina, and then hourly until 6.30pm.

Trambus 110open
BUS
(☑800 281281; www.trambusopen.com; family/adult/reduced €50/20/18; ☻every 15min 8.30am-8.30pm) This open-top, double-decker bus departs from Piazza dei Cinquecento in front of Termini station, and stops at the Colosseum, Bocca della Verità, Piazza Venezia, St Peter's, Ara Pacis and Trevi Fountain. The entire tour lasts two hours but the tickets are valid for 48 hours and allow you to hop on and off as you please. Get tickets online, on board, from the info boxes on Piazza dei Cinquecento or the Colosseum, or from authorised Trambus Open dealers.

Trambus Archeobus
BUS
(☑800 281281; www.trambusopen.com; family/adult €40/12; ☻half-hourly 9am-4.30pm) This is a stop-and-go bus that takes sightseers down Via Appia Antica, stopping at points of archaeological interest along the way. It departs from Piazza dei Cinquecento and tickets, valid for 48 hours, can be bought online, on board, from the info boxes on Piazza dei Cinquecento or the Colosseum, or from authorised Trambus Open dealers.

Roma Cristiana
BUS, WALKING
(☑06 6989 6380; www.operaromanapellegrinaggi.org) The Vatican-sponsored Opera Romana Pellegrinaggi runs the hop-on, hop-off Open Bus Roma Cristiana (24hr/one circuit €18/13; ☻every 20min 8.40am-7pm) departing from Via della Conciliazione and Termini. It also operates a range of walking tours, including tours of the Vatican Museums (adult/reduced €26/19; ☻10am, 11am, noon & 2pm Mon-Sat). Tickets are available on board the bus, online, or at the meeting point just off Piazza San Pietro.

Bici & Baci
BIKE, SCOOTER
(☑06 482 84 43; www.bicibaci.com; Via del Viminale 5; tours €35; ☻10am, 3pm & 7pm Mar-Oct, on request Nov-Feb) Bici & Baci runs daily bike tours of central Rome, taking in the historical centre, Campidoglio and the Colosseum, as well as tours on vintage Vespas and in classic Fiat 500 cars. For the Vespa and Fiat 500 tours you'll need to book 24 hours ahead. Routes and prices vary according to your requests.

Enjoy Rome
WALKING
(☑06 445 18 43; www.enjoyrome.com; Via Marghera 8a) Offers three-hour walking tours of the Vatican (under/over 26 years €25/30) and Ancient & Old Rome (€25/30) as well as various other packages – see the website for further details. Note that tour prices do not cover admission charges to the Vatican Museums or Colosseum.

⚜ Festivals & Events

Settimana della Cultura
CULTURAL
For a week in April public museums and galleries open free of charge (www.beniculturali.it, in Italian).

Easter
RELIGIOUS
On Good Friday, the pope leads a candlelit procession around the Colosseum. At noon on Easter Sunday he blesses the crowds in St Peter's Square.

Mostra delle Azalee
CULTURAL
From mid-April to early May, the Spanish Steps are decorated with 600 vases of blooming azaleas in the Exhibition of Azaleas.

Natale di Roma
CULTURAL
Rome celebrates its birthday on 21 April with music, historical recreations, fireworks and free entry to many museums.

Primo Maggio
MUSIC
Rome's May Day rock concert attracts huge crowds and international performers to the Piazza di San Giovanni in Laterano.

Festa dei Santi Pietro e Paolo
RELIGIOUS
Romans celebrate the feast of patron saints Peter and Paul on 29 June. Festivities are centred on St Peter's Basilica and Via Ostiense.

Estate Romana
CULTURAL
(www.romeguide.it/estate_romana) From June to October Rome's big summer festival includes hundreds of cultural events and activities across the capital.

ROME FOR CHILDREN

Romans love children, and even if there are few child-friendly facilities in town, your little 'uns will be welcome just about everywhere.

» Restaurants are very laid-back when it comes to accommodating children and will happily serve a *mezza porzione* (child's portion) and provide *seggioloni* (highchairs). Some hotels can supply a *culla* (cot) on request.

» Children under 10 years old travel free on all public transport.

» You can buy baby formula and sterilising solutions at all pharmacies. Disposable nappies (diapers; *pannolini* in Italian) are available from supermarkets and pharmacies.

» In Villa Borghese, Casina di Raffaello (Map p112; ☎06 4288 8888; www.casinadiraffaello. it; Viale della Casina di Raffaello) is a well-equipped day-care centre with a nice little playground, a small library and a soft play area. Accessing the facilities costs €5 per child.

» On the downside, cobbled streets and badly parked cars can make getting around with a pram or pushchair difficult, as can tiny lifts in older buildings.

» Useful websites include http://piccolituristi.turismoroma.it, which has loads of practical information and provides a three-day child-friendly itinerary.

Sights

Rome's museums and galleries are not ideal for rampaging toddlers, but many of the bigger ones now offer educational services and children's workshops. Some even host kid-friendly events. Museums, galleries and archaeological sites are generally free for EU citizens under 18. Suggested sights for kids:

Colosseum (p61)

Villa Borghese (p142)

Bioparco (Map p112; ☎06 360 82 11; www.bioparco.it; Viale del Giardino Zoologico 1; adult €12.50, child over 1m & under 12yr €10.50, child under 1m free; ☉9.30am-6pm Apr-Oct, to 5pm Nov-Mar) Rome's zoo.

Explora (Map p112; ☎06 361 37 76; www.mdbr.it; Via Flaminia 82; adult/child over 3yr/child 1-3yr/child under 1yr €7/7/3/free; ☉9.30am-7.30pm Tue-Sun Sep-Jul, 11.30am-7pm Tue-Sun Aug) Museum dedicated to kids under 12. Visits by guided tour only. Bookings advised and essential at weekends. Outside there's a free play park open to all.

Time Elevator (p85) Not for the under-fives.

Appia Antica and the catacombs (p95) The catacombs are best for children over about 12.

Ostia Antica (p143)

Villa d'Este (p146)

Villa Adriana (p145)

Cerveteri (p146)

Tarquinia (p147)

Festa de'Noantri CULTURAL
Trastevere's annual party, held in the third week of July, involves plenty of food, wine, prayer and dancing.

Festa della Madonna della Neve RELIGIOUS
On 5 August, rose petals are showered on celebrants in the Basilica di Santa Maria Maggiore to commemorate a miraculous 4th-century snowfall.

RomaEuropa CULTURAL
(www.romaeuropa.net, in Italian) From September to November, top international artists take to the stage for Rome's autumn festival of theatre, opera and dance.

Festival Internazionale del Film di Roma FILM
(www.romacinemafest.it) Held at the Auditorium Parco della Musica in late October,

Rome's film festival rolls out the red carpet for big-screen big shots.

🛏 Sleeping

While there's plenty of choice, accommodation in Rome is expensive. The nicest place to stay is the *centro storico,* where you'll have everything on your doorstep. Mid-range choices abound, but there's only a smattering of good budget options. There's also a lot to be said for bunking down in peaceful Prati, which harbours some excellent restaurants, is near the Vatican and on metro line A. Trastevere is drop-dead gorgeous and a great place to spend summer evenings, but can be noisy, especially in high season.

If you're on a tight budget, the cheapest places are around Stazione Termini. This area, although not as bad as it's sometimes made out to be, is not Rome's nicest, and some of the streets to the west of the station, particularly Via Giolitti, can be unsafe at night. Women in particular should be careful. That said, it is still possible to walk into the *centro storico* from Termini, and most other sights are only a convenient metro ride away.

You'll find a full list of accommodation options (with prices) at www.060608.it.

Although Rome doesn't have a low season as such, the majority of hotels offer discounts from November to March (excluding the Christmas and New Year period) and some also in August. Expect to pay top whack in spring and autumn and over the main holiday periods (Christmas, New Year and Easter).

Always try to book ahead. If you arrive without a reservation, there's a hotel reservation service (☑06 699 10 00; booking fee €3; ☺7am-10pm) next to the tourist office at Stazione Termini.

Accommodation Options

Alongside *alberghi* (traditional hotels) and *pensioni* (cheap family-run hotels often housed in converted apartments), there are hundreds of B&Bs, hostels and religious institutions. For longer stays consider renting an apartment.

Often excellent value for money, B&Bs cover the gamut from modest family lodgings to upmarket boutique-style accommodation at midrange to top-end prices. The following agencies all offer online booking services.

Bed & Breakfast Association of Rome (www.b-b.rm.it) Lists B&Bs and short-term apartment rentals.

Bed & Breakfast Italia (www.bbitalia.com) Rome's longest-established B&B network.

Cross Pollinate (www.cross-pollinate.com) Has B&Bs, private apartments and guesthouses.

Sleeping Rome (www.sleepingrome.com) Offers B&B and has good short-term apartment rentals.

Private hostels no longer cater solely to backpackers and many now offer decent hotel-style rooms as well as traditional dorms. For information on Rome's (and Italy's) official HI hostels, contact the Italian Youth Hostel Association (Associazione Italiana Alberghi per la Gioventù; ☑06 487 11 52; www.aighostels.com; Via Cavour 44).

Religious institutions tend to offer basic, no-frills facilities, but are cheap, clean and often quiet. Many impose strict curfews. It's always wise to book well in advance. For a list of institutions, check out www.santasusanna.org/comingtorome.

For longer stays, renting an apartment might well work out cheaper than an extended hotel sojourn. You can usually find a studio flat or one-bedroom apartment near

---

HOTEL TAX

Everyone staying overnight in Rome has to pay a room occupancy tax on top of their regular accommodation bill. Since January 2011, this has amounted to the following:

» €1 per person per night for a maximum of five days in camping grounds

» €2 per person per night for a maximum of 10 days in *agriturismi* (farm stay accommodation), B&Bs, guesthouses, and one-, two- and three-star hotels

» €3 per person per night for a maximum of 10 days in four- and five-star hotels.

The tax is applicable to anyone who is not a resident in Rome. Note that prices quoted in this chapter do not include the tax.

the centre of Rome for around €900 per month. Useful rental resources:

Accommodations Rome (www.accomodationsrome.com)

Flat in Rome (www.flatinrome.it)

Flats in Italy (www.flatsinitaly.com)

Italy Accom (www.italy-accom.com)

Leisure in Rome (www.leisureinrome.com)

Rental in Rome (www.rentalinrome.com)

Sleep in Italy (www.sleepinitaly.com)

ANCIENT ROME

Caesar House   HOTEL €€€
(Map p62; ☑06 679 26 74; www.caesarhouse.com; Via Cavour 310; s €150-230, d €170-270; ✱🛜) Quiet and friendly, yet in the thick of it on busy thoroughfare Via Cavour, this is a refined apartment hotel. Its smart public areas are polished and modern, while rooms reveal a warm, peachy decor, four-poster beds and small bathrooms. The suite has a view over the forum.

Hotel Duca d'Alba   HOTEL €€
(Map p62; ☑06 48 44 71; www.hotelducadalba.com; Via Leonina 14; s €90-190, d €100-240; ✱@🛜) An appealing four-star hotel in the Monti district, this has small, but charming rooms. Most have fabric-covered or hand-painted walls, wood-beamed ceilings, big flat-screen TVs and sleek button-studded headboards; and many have big showers with modern square shower heads.

CENTRO STORICO

Hotel Campo de' Fiori   BOUTIQUE HOTEL €€€
(Map p74; ☑06 687 48 86; www.hotelcampodefiori.com; Via del Biscione 6; s €170-220, d €200-270, 2-person apt €130-150, 4-person apt €180; ✱@🛜🛗) This rakish four-star has the lot – sexy decor, an enviable location just off Campo de' Fiori, attentive staff and a panoramic roof terrace. It even serves scrambled eggs and bacon for breakfast. The 23 rooms are individually decorated but the overall feel is contemporary decadence with boldly coloured flock walls, gilt mirrors and restored bric-a-brac. The hotel also offers 11 apartments in the vicinity, ideal for families.

Teatropace 33   HOTEL €€
(Map p74; ☑06 687 90 75; www.hotelteatropace.com; Via del Teatro Pace 33; s €69-150, d €110-240; ✱) This friendly three-star, which is wonderfully central in a lane near Piazza Navona, is a class choice. In a former cardinal's residence, it has 23 beautifully appointed rooms decorated with parquet flooring, damask curtains and exposed-wood beams. There's no lift, just a monumental 17th-century stone staircase and a porter to carry your bags.

Relais Palazzo Taverna   BOUTIQUE HOTEL €€
(Map p74; ☑06 2039 8064; www.relaispalazzotaverna.com; Via dei Gabrielli 92; s €70-140, d €100-210; ✱@) Housed in a 15th-century *palazzo* deep in the heart of the historical centre, this contemporary boutique hotel sets its bold, modern aesthetic against a lovely historical setting. Amenities such as plasma-screen satellite TVs, and tea- and coffee-making facilities ice the cake.

Hotel Teatro di Pompeo   HOTEL €€
(Map p74; ☑06 687 28 12; www.hotelteatrodipompeo.it; Largo del Pallaro 8; s €140-160, d €180-210; ✱@🛜) Built on top of a theatre that Pompey constructed in 55 BC (now the breakfast room), this charming hotel is tucked away behind Campo de' Fiori. Rooms boast a classic old-fashioned feel with polished wood bedsteads and terracotta-coloured floor tiles. The best, on the 3rd floor, also have sloping wood-beamed ceilings.

Hotel Navona   HOTEL €€
(Map p74; ☑06 6821 1392; www.hotelnavona.com; Via dei Sediari 8; s €120-140, d €160-200; ✱🛜) This family-run hotel occupies several floors of a 15th-century *palazzo* near Piazza Navona. Rooms on the reception floor are fairly small, with traditional gilt-framed decor and antique furniture, while those upstairs are completely different, boasting medieval ceilings and a contemporary silver-grey colour scheme. No lifts.

Argentina Residenza   BOUTIQUE HOTEL €€
(Map p74; ☑06 6819 3267; www.argentinaresidenza.com; Via di Torre Argentina 47; r €120-200; ✱🛜) This quiet boutique hotel is hidden on the 3rd floor of a building on Largo di Torre Argentina. All the bustle of the piazza will seem a very long way away as you slip into your jacuzzi and relax in your tastefully modern wood-beamed room.

Hotel Mimosa   PENSIONE €
(Map p74; ☑06 6880 1753; www.hotelmimosa.net; Via di Santa Chiara 61, 2nd fl; s €55-85, d €70-118, tr €90-160, without bathroom s €45-70, d €50-98; ✱@) This long-standing *pensione* is one of the few budget options in the historical centre. It's all fairly basic but rooms have

Rome's gay scene remains much smaller than in other European capitals. Rome is essentially conservative: the merest mention of same-sex unions would have most politicians spluttering into their cappuccino, and intolerance seems to have become worryingly more prevalent in recent years. However, the Gay Pride march (which takes place every June), the annual summer Gay Village and regular gay nights at local clubs are signals of a thriving, if underground, scene.

Rome's main cultural and political gay organisation is the **Circolo Mario Mieli di Cultura Omosessuale** (✆06 541 39 85; www.mariomieli.it, in Italian; Via Efeso 2a), off Via Ostiense near the Basilica di San Paolo Fuori le Mura. It organises social and political events, including Rome Pride, which takes place every year in June.

The national organisation for lesbians is **Coordinamento Lesbiche Italiano** (✆06 686 42 01; www.clrbp.it, in Italian; Via San Francesco di Sales 1b). The centre has a women-only hostel, La Foresteria Orsa Maggiore (p122).

Useful listings guides include the free monthly *AUT*, *Clubbing* and *Guide Magazine*, and the international gay guide, *Spartacus*, available at gay and lesbian organisations and in bookshops. Also check www.azgay.it, which produces a gay-friendly guide to Rome, available at tourist booths. In summer there is a **Gay Village** (www.gayvillage.it) festival, with various clubs and special events – the location changes annually, but it's usually in EUR.

The city has a small gay and lesbian nightclub and bar scene, though numerous nightclubs have gay nights (see p135). Also check out the following:

» **Coming Out** (Map p94; www.comingout.it; Via di San Giovanni in Laterano 8; ◷10.30am-2am) Spot this easygoing bar in the shadow of the Colosseum by the rainbow sign and the mixed, convivial crowds spilling out into the street. There are regular drag acts, DJs and live acts.

» **Taverna Edoardo II** (Map p74; ✆06 6994 2419; www.edoardosecondo.com; Vicolo Margana 13-14; ◷8pm-1am Wed-Sun) Restaurant-bar that feels like a private members' club.

» **Hangar** (off Map p62; ✆06 4881 3971; Via in Selci 69a; ◷10.30pm-2.30am, closed Tue & 3 weeks Aug) Veteran men-only club. Porn-night Mondays and Striptease Thursdays are popular.

» **L'Alibi** (Map p96; ✆06 574 34 48; www.lalibi.it; Via di Monte Testaccio 44; ◷midnight-5am Thu-Sun) Sultry, cavernous gay club playing soulful house.

---

recently been made over and they now come with laminated parquet floors and a clean cream and brown colour scheme. Payment in cash only.

Albergo del Sole PENSIONE €€
(Map p74; ✆06 687 94 46; www.solealbiscione.it; Via del Biscione 76; s €100, d €125-160; P✳☎) Dating from 1462, this is said to be the oldest hotel in Rome. There's nothing special about the functional rooms, but there's a pleasant 2nd-floor roof terrace, wi-fi is available (€1.50) and the location near Campo de' Fiori is a lively spot. Air-con is only available in some rooms. No credit cards and no breakfast.

Hotel Portoghesi HOTEL €€
(Map p74; ✆06 686 42 31; www.hotelportoghesi roma.com; Via dei Portoghesi 1; s €130-160, d €160-200; ✳@☎) This cosy, low-key hotel is on a picturesque street near Piazza Navona. Rooms are comfortable enough, if rather bland, although some (particularly the singles) are pretty small. Staff are pleasant and the peaceful roof terrace is a bonus.

TRIDENTE, TREVI & THE QUIRINALE

TOP CHOICE / **Villa Spalletti Trivelli** HOTEL €€€
(Map p86; ✆06 4890 7934; www.villaspalletti. it; Via Piacenza 4; r €330-345; P✳@☎) With 12 rooms in a glorious mansion in central Rome, Villa Spalletti Trivelli has upped the ante for luxurious stays in the capital. Rooms are soberly and elegantly decorated, overlooking the gardens of the Quirinale or the estate's own Italian garden. The overall feel is that of staying in the stately home of some aristocratic friends.

TOP CHOICE **Hotel Panda** HOTEL €

(Map p84; ☑06 678 01 79; www.hotelpanda.it; Via della Croce 35; s with/without bathroom €80/68, d with/without bathroom €108/78; ☎) Only 50m from the Spanish Steps, in an area where a bargain is a Bulgari watch bought in the sales, the friendly, efficient Panda is an anomaly: a budget hotel, and a splendid one. The clean rooms are smallish but nicely furnished, and there are several triples with a bed on a cosy mezzanine. Air-con costs €6 extra per night. A few streets to the north, sister establishment **Okapi Rooms** (Via della Penna 57) offers accommodation of a similar price and standard.

TOP CHOICE **La Piccola Maison** B&B €

(Map p86; ☑06 4201 6331; www.lapiccolamaison. com; Via dei Cappuccini 30; s €50-140, d €70-200; ☀☎) The excellent Piccola Maison has a great location close to Piazza Barberini, pleasingly plain rooms decorated with contemporary flair, and thoughtful staff. It's a great deal.

Portrait Suites BOUTIQUE HOTEL €€€

(Map p84; ☑06 6938 0742; www.portraitsuites. com; Via Bocca di Leone 23; r €410-670; P☀☎) Owned by the Ferragamo family, this is a discreet, exclusive residence, designed by Florentine wonder-architect Michele Bonan. There are 14 exquisitely styled suites and studios across six floors in a town house overlooking Via Condotti, plus a dreamy 360-degree roof terrace and made-in-heaven staff. There's no restaurant, but you can have meals delivered. Breakfast is served in your room or on the terrace.

Babuino 181 BOUTIQUE HOTEL €€€

(Map p84; ☑06 3229 5295; www.romeluxurysuites. com/babuino; Via del Babuino 181; r €180-250; ☀☎) A beautifully renovated old *palazzo* in the heart of the shopping district, Babuino offers discreet luxury, with gorgeous rooms with touches such as a Nespresso machine and fluffy bathrobes. Breakfast is great, too (including fresh juice, toasted sandwiches and good pastries).

Hotel Barocco HOTEL €€

(Map p86; ☑06 487 2001; www.hotelbarocco.com; Piazza Barberini 9; d €160-330; ☀@☎) In a superbly convenient location, this well-run, welcoming 41-room hotel overlooking Piazza Barberini (the pricier rooms have views) has a classic feel, with rooms featuring oil paintings, gleaming linen, gentle colour schemes and fabric-covered walls; breakfast is ample and served in a wood-panelled room.

Daphne B&B B&B €€

(Map p86; ☑06 8745 0086; www.daphne-rome. com; Via di San Basilio 55; d with bathroom €140-235, without bathroom €100-150; ☀@☎) Boutique B&B Daphne is a gem. Run by an American-Italian couple, it has chic, sleek, comfortable rooms, helpful English-speaking staff, top-notch breakfasts and the loan of a mobile phone for your stay. There are rooms in two locations – the one off Via Veneto is the pick, but there's a second at Via degli Avignonesi 20. Book months ahead.

Hotel Modigliani HOTEL €€

(Map p86; ☑06 4281 5226; Via della Purificazione 42; s €100-168, d €115-202; ☀☎) Run by an artistic couple, the Modigliani is all about attention to detail and customer service. The 23 dove-grey rooms are spacious and light, with red and gold bedspreads, and the best have views and balconies – either outside or over the quiet internal courtyard garden that's a lovely place for a drink.

Hotel Scalinata di Spagna HOTEL €€

(Map p84; ☑06 6994 0896; www.hotelscalinata. com; Piazza della Trinità dei Monti 17; d €150-190; ☀☎) Given its location – perched alongside the Spanish Steps – the Scalinata is surprisingly modestly priced. An informal and friendly place, it's something of a warren, with a great roof terrace, and low corridors leading off to smallish, old-fashioned, yet romantic rooms (think plush furnishings and gilt-edged mirrors), the best coming with balconies. Book early for a room with a view.

Crossing Condotti GUESTHOUSE €€€

(Map p84; ☑06 6992 0633; www.crossingcondotti. com; Via Mario de' Fiori 28; r €180-300; ☀☎) A five-room place, this is one of Rome's new breed of upmarket guesthouses, where all the fittings, linen and comforts are top-notch, and the pretty (though not large) rooms have lots of character and antique furnishings. Smack bang in designer heaven, Crossing Condotti doesn't serve breakfast, but has a well-stocked kitchen with drinks and a Nespresso machine.

Fellini B&B B&B €€

(Map p86; ☑06 4274 2732; www.fellinibnb.com; Via Rasella 55; s €70-150, d €90-170, apt €210-370; ☀) A multistorey warren, cheery, efficient Fellini has light, well-furnished spick-and-span rooms with parquet floors and comfortable beds. The standout option is the top-floor four-person apartment, which has a huge terrace with a view.

Apollo Hotel
HOTEL €€

(Map p86; ☎06 488 5889; www.albergoapollo.it; Via dei Serpenti 109; s €110-140, d €120-185; ❄️@🛜) Well run and appointed, the Apollo is an excellent choice in the upmarket bohemian district of Monti.

Hotel Artorius
HOTEL €€

(Map p90; ☎06 482 1196; www.hotelartoriusrome. com; Via dei Boschetto 13; d €160-185; ❄️🛜) The art deco flavoured lobby looks promising, and the rest also delivers in this small Monti hotel, with simple, plain rooms and a family-run feel. Rooms are not large but perfectly comfortable, and one (room 109) has a terrace.

TERMINI, ESQUILINO & SAN LORENZO

Residenza Cellini
HOTEL €€

(Map p90; ☎06 4782 5204; www.residenzacellini.it; Via Modena 5; d €145-240; ❄️🛜) With grown-up furnishings featuring potted palms, polished wood, pale yellow walls, oil paintings and a hint of chintz, this charming, family-run hotel on a quiet road offers spacious, elegant rooms, all with satellite TV and jacuzzi or hydro-massage showers. There's a sunny flower-surrounded terrace for summer breakfasts.

🌿 Beehive
HOSTEL €

(Map p90; ☎06 4470 4553; www.the-beehive.com; Via Marghera 8; dm €20-25, d without bathroom €70-80; 🛜) More boutique chic than backpacker crash pad, the Beehive is one of the best hostels in town. Run by a southern Californian couple, it's an oasis of style with original art works on the walls, funky modular furniture and a vegetarian cafe (prices don't include breakfast). Beds are in a spotless, eight-person mixed dorm or in one of six private double rooms, all with fans. Book ahead.

Welrome Hotel
HOTEL €

(Map p90; ☎06 4782 4343; www.welrome.it; Via Calatafimi 15-19; s €80-100, d €90-110; ❄️🛜♨️) The owners of the Welrome have a personal mission to look after their guests: not only do Mary and Carlos take huge pride in their small, spotless hotel but they will also enthusiastically point out the cheapest places to eat, tell you where not to waste your time and point you to what's good to do. Families

should go for the huge room named after Piazza di Spagna; a cot is provided at no extra charge.

Hotel des Artistes
HOSTEL, HOTEL €

(Map p90; ☎06 445 43 65; www.hoteldesartistes. com; Via Villafranca 20; dm €14-52; r without bathroom €69-95, r with bathroom €105-119; ❄️@) The wide range of rooms here are decked out in wood and gold with faux-antique furniture and rich reds, gilt lamps and terracotta or tiled floors, and have decent bathrooms. Offers discounts for longer stays and/or cash payment.

Funny Palace
HOSTEL €

(Map p90; ☎06 4470 3523; www.hostelfunny.com; Via Varese 31, 5th fl; dm €15-25, s without bathroom €30-70, d without bathroom €55-100; @🛜) Run by a friendly international crew, with the Splashnet Laundry as its office-laundry-internet cafe, this great little backpacker hostel has doubles, triples and quads, with a comfortable, homey feel. No credit cards. It also runs the similar Amazing Place around the corner.

Alessandro Palace Hostel
HOSTEL €

(Map p90; ☎06 446 19 58; www.hostelalessandro. com; Via Vicenza 42; dm €18-35, d €70-110; ❄️@🛜) This long-standing favourite appeals to both budgeting families and backpackers, and offers spick-and-span, terracotta-floored doubles, triples and quads, as well as dorms sleeping from four to eight, all with cheery bedspreads. Every room has its own bathroom plus hairdryer. In some you can only open the windows a fraction.

AVENTINO & TESTACCIO

TOP CHOICE Hotel Sant'Anselmo
HOTEL €€€

(Map p96; ☎06 57 00 57; www.aventinohotels. com; Piazza Sant'Anselmo 2; s €130-265, d €150-290; ❄️@) Set amid the terracotta walls and umbrella pines of the peaceful Aventino district, this is a delightful romantic hideaway. Its rooms are not always the biggest but they are stylish, marrying carved beds, heavy brocades and dripping chandeliers with modern touches and contemporary colours. A few also have terraces offering dreamy views.

TRASTEVERE & GIANICOLO

TOP CHOICE Donna Camilla Savelli
HOTEL €€€

(Map p100; ☎06 58 88 61; www.hotelsavelli.com; Via Garibaldi 27; r €230-450; 🅿️❄️@🛜) If you have the cash, stay in this converted convent that was originally designed by great baroque architect Borromini. It's been beautifully updated, with furnishing in muted colours that complement the serene concave and convex curves of the architecture, and service is excellent. The priciest of the 78 rooms overlook the cloister garden or have views of Rome and are decorated with antiques, but the cheaper ones are still lovely.

TOP CHOICE Arco del Lauro B&B €€

(Map p100; ☑9am-2pm 06 9784 0350, 346 2443212; Via Arco de' Tolomei 27; s €75-125, d €95-145; ❉☎) Through a large stone arch and on a narrow cobbled street, this fab six-room B&B in an ancient *palazzo* is a find, offering gleaming white rooms that combine rustic charm with minimalist simplicity. The largest room has a high wood-beamed ceiling. Beds are comfortable, showers are powerful and the owners are eager to please. Book well ahead.

Suites Trastevere B&B €€

(Map p100; ☑347 0744086; www.trastevere.bb suites.com; Viale Trastevere 248; s €70-105, d €80-160; ❉☎) On the 4th floor of a honey-hued *palazzo* on the wide main drag and tramway running from Trastevere, this friendly, popular B&B has dramatically frescoed rooms, each themed after local sights, such as the Colosseum and the Pantheon.

Villa della Fonte B&B €€

(Map p100; ☑06 580 37 97; www.villafonte.com; Via della Fonte dell'Olio 8; s €110-145, d €135-170; ❉☎) A lovely terracotta-hued, ivy-shrouded gem, Villa della Fonte occupies a 17th-century building in a street off Piazza Santa Maria in Trastevere. It only has five rooms, all of which are simply decorated but have pretty outlooks, good bathrooms and comfortable beds covered with lovely linen. The sunny garden terrace (for breakfast in warm weather) is a plus.

Residenza Arco de' Tolomei B&B €€

(Map p100; ☑06 5832 0819; www.bbarcodei tolomei.com; Via Arco de' Tolomei 27; d €145-220; ❉☎) Next to Arco del Lauro, this gorgeous place is decorated with polished antiques and rich contrasting chintzes that make the interiors feel like a country cottage. It's also a lovely place to stay, and the owners are friendly and helpful.

Hotel Santa Maria HOTEL €€

(Map p100; ☑06 589 46 26; www.hotelsanta maria.info; Vicolo del Piede 2; s €90-190, d €130-260; P❉@☎♿) Walk along the ivy-lined approach and you'll enter a tranquil haven. The rooms surround a spacious modern cloister (a former convent site), shaded by orange trees. Rooms are cool and comfortable, with slightly fussy decor and terracotta floors. There are some much larger family rooms. Staff are helpful and professional, and it's wheelchair friendly. Nearby is the more intimate, prettily rustic Residenza Santa Maria, under the same management.

La Foresteria Orsa Maggiore HOSTEL €

(Map p74; ☑06 689 37 53; www.casainternazionale delledonne.org, in Italian; Via San Francesco di Sales 1a, 2nd fl; dm €26, s/d without bathroom €52/72, s/d with bathroom €75/110; @) This lesbian-friendly, predominantly women-only guesthouse (boys aged 12 or younger are welcome) is housed in a restored 16th-century convent. It is run by the Casa Internazionale delle Donne (International Women's House) and offers safe and well-priced accommodation in a quiet corner of Trastevere. The 13 simple rooms sleep two, four, five or eight, and some have views onto the attractive internal garden. There's a 3am curfew. Wheelchair accessible.

VATICAN CITY, BORGO & PRATI

Hotel San Pietrino HOTEL €€

(Map p104; ☑06 370 01 32; www.sanpietrino.it; Via Bettolo 43; s €45-75, d €65-112, s without bathroom €35-55, d without bathroom €55-85; ❉@☎) In Prati, not far from Ottaviano metro station, San Pietrino is a lovely little hotel. Its rooms are characterful and prettily decorated, with terracotta floors, some with statuary, and carvings in the hallways. Added bonuses are the comfortable beds, wi-fi and helpful staff.

Hotel Bramante HOTEL €€€

(Map p104; ☑06 6880 6426; www.hotelbramante. com; Vicolo delle Palline 24-25; s €100-160, d €150-220; ❉☎) In the atmospheric Borgo, Hotel Bramante feels like a country house in the city, full of rustic elegance, oriental rugs, beams and antiques. It's housed in the 16th-century building that was home to architect Domenico Fontana before Pope Sixtus V banished him from Rome, and has just 16 characterful rooms.

Colors Hotel HOTEL €

(Map p104; ☑06 687 40 30; www.colorshotel.com; Via Boezio 31; s/d from €30/40; ❉@) Popular with young travellers, this is a friendly, laid-back hotel with 23 brightly painted rooms spread over three floors (no lift, though).

There are also cheaper rooms with shared bathrooms and, in July and August, six-bed dorms (€18 to €30 per person).

Hotel Lady
PENSIONE €

(Map p104; ☎06 324 21 12; www.hotelladyroma. it; Via Germanico 198, 4th fl; d €70-100, s without bathroom €45-75, d without bathroom €55-85; ☎) A homey old-school *pensione,* the Hotel Lady is a quiet and inviting place. The eight rooms are snug, comfortable and spotless, and rooms 4 and 6 have wood-beamed ceilings. Breakfast, which is optional but costs €5 to €10 extra, is served in the attractive salon.

Casa di Accoglienza Paolo VI
RELIGIOUS ACCOMMODATION €

(Map p104; ☎06 390 91 41; www.ospitiamocon cuore.it; Viale Vaticano 92; s/d/tr/q €35/65/83/95; ✺) This is a lovely, palm-shaded convent, right opposite the entrance to the Vatican Museums, where the welcoming sisters offer small, sunny rooms, which are so clean they gleam. Book way ahead. No breakfast.

 Eating

Rome bulges with trattorias, *ristoranti,* pizzerias and *enoteche* (wine bars serving food). Excellent places dot the *centro storico,* Trastevere, Prati, Testaccio (the heartland of Roman cuisine, featuring lots of offal) and San Lorenzo. Be warned that the area around Termini has quite a few substandard restaurants, and also choose carefully around the Vatican, which is packed with tourist traps. Many restaurants close down for several weeks during the traditional summer holiday month of August.

ANCIENT ROME

Hostaria da Nerone
TRATTORIA €€

(Map p62; ☎06 481 79 52; Via delle Terme di Tito; meals €35; ☺Mon-Sat) This old-school, family-run trattoria is not the place for a romantic dinner or a special-occasion splurge, but if you're after a filling meal after exploring the Colosseum, it does the job. Tourists tuck into classic Roman pasta and salads on the few outside tables, while in the yellowing, woody interior visiting businessmen cut deals over saltimbocca and tiramisu.

CENTRO STORICO

TOP CHOICE **Casa Coppelle**
MODERN ITALIAN €€

(Map p74; ☎06 6889 1707; www.casacoppelle.it; Piazza delle Coppelle 49; meals €35) Intimate and elegant with wonderful French-inspired food and a warm, attractive buzz, this is a great find. Brick walls, books, flowers and subdued lighting set the romantic scene for simple yet delicious food. The steaks, in particular, are superb, especially if served with the delicious thinly sliced potato crisps. There's a thoughtful wine list and service is attentive.

Pizzeria da Baffetto
PIZZERIA €

(Map p74; ☎06 686 16 17; Via del Governo Vecchio 114; pizzas €6-9; ☺6.30pm-1am) For the full-on Roman pizza experience, get down to this local institution. Meals are raucous, chaotic and fast, but the thin-crust pizzas are spot on and the vibe is fun. To partake, join the queue and wait to be squeezed in wherever there's room. There's also **Baffetto 2** (Map p74; Piazza del Teatro di Pompeo 18; ☺6.30pm-12.30am Mon-Fri, 12.30-3.30pm & 6.30pm-12.30am Sat & Sun) near Campo de' Fiori.

Forno di Campo de' Fiori
PIZZA BY SLICE €

(Map p74; Campo de' Fiori 22; pizza slices about €3; ☺7.30am-2.30pm & 4.45-8pm Mon-Sat) This is one of Rome's best takeaway joints, serving bread, *panini* and delicious straight-from-the-oven *pizza al taglio* (by the slice). Aficionados say to go for the pizza *bianca* (white pizza with olive oil, rosemary and salt), but the *panini* and pizza *rossa* ('red' pizza, with olive oil, tomato and oregano) are just as good.

Cul de Sac
WINE BAR €€

(Map p74; ☎06 6880 1094; www.enotecaculdesac. com; Piazza Pasquino 73; meals €30; ☺noon-4pm & 6pm-12.30am) This is a fabulous little *enoteca* (wine bar), just off Piazza Navona, with a tiny terrace and narrow, pine- and bottle-lined interior. The knowledgeable, swift waiters pass about platters of cold meats, pâtés and cheeses, and moreish mains: try the meatballs with white wine and mash. There's a phone-directory-sized wine list. Book ahead in the evening.

Ditirambo
MODERN ITALIAN €€

(Map p74; ☎06 687 16 26; www.ristoranteditirambo. it; Piazza della Cancelleria 72; meals €35; ☺closed Mon lunch) This hugely popular new-wave trattoria offers a laid-back, unpretentious atmosphere and innovative, organic cooking. Vegetarians are well catered for, with dishes such as *vellutata di ceci con rughetta e riduzione di aceto balsamico* (cream of chickpeas with rocket and a balsamic vinegar reduction). Book ahead.

Lo Zozzone
SANDWICH SHOP €

(Map p74; Via del Teatro Pace 32; panini from €6; ⊙Mon-Sat) With a few inside tables and a mile-long menu of *panini,* the affection-ately named 'dirty one' is a great spot for a cheap lunchtime bite. The filling *panini* are made with *pizza bianca* and combinations of cured meats, cheeses and vegetables.

Antico Forno Roscioli
BAKERY €

(Map p74; Via dei Chiavari 34; pizza slices from €2; ⊙7.30am-8pm Mon-Fri, 7.30am-2.30pm Sat) This is not the renowned delicatessen and wine bar, but its brother bakery around the corner. Join the lunchtime crowds for a slice of pizza (the *pizza bianca* is legendary) or a freshly baked pastry. There's also a counter serving a selection of hot pasta dishes and vegetables.

Ar Galletto
TRADITIONAL ITALIAN €€

(Map p74; ☑06 686 17 14; www.ristoranteargalletto roma.com; Piazza Farnese 102; meals €35-40; ⊙Mon-Sat) You wouldn't expect there to be anywhere reasonably priced on Piazza Farnese, one of Rome's loveliest squares, but this long-running *osteria* (casual tavern or eatery presided over by a host) is the real thing, with good, honest Roman food, a warm local atmosphere and dazzlingly set exterior tables. Roast chicken is the house speciality (*galletto* means little rooster).

Armando al Pantheon
TRATTORIA €€

(Map p74; ☑06 6880 3034; www.armandoal pantheon.it; Salita dei Crescenzi 31; meals €40; ⊙closed Sat dinner) A family-run trattoria, Armando's is wood-panelled, inviting, au-thentic and near the Pantheon. Philosopher Jean-Paul Sartre and footballer Pelé are among the luminaries who have dined on its popular brand of traditional Roman fare. Book ahead.

Giggetto al Portico d'Ottavia
TRADITIONAL ITALIAN €€

(Map p74; ☑06 686 11 05; www.giggettoalportico. it; Via del Portico d'Ottavia 21a; meals €40; ⊙Tue-Sun) An atmospheric setting in the Ghetto, rustic interiors, white-jacketed waiters and *fabuloso* Roman-Jewish cooking – this is a quintessential Roman restaurant. Celebrate all things fried by tucking into the marvellous *carciofi alla giudia* (Jewish-style artichokes), *fiore di zucca* (zucchini or squash flowers) and *baccalá* (cod) and follow on with a *zuppa di pesce* (fish soup) or *rigotoni alla gricia* (pasta with cured pig's cheek).

Giggetto 2
TRADITIONAL ITALIAN €

(Map p74; ☑06 6476 0369; Via Angelo in Pescheria 13-14; meals €20) For those on a budget, this simple cafe sits behind its older and better-known parent, Giggetto al Portico d'Ottavia. It serves no-nonsense pasta and meat dish-es, as well as pizza and very drinkable wine at €8 per bottle.

Enoteca Corsi
OSTERIA €

(Map p74; ☑06 679 08 21; Via del Gesù 88; meals €25; ⊙lunch Mon-Sat) Merrily worse for wear, family-run Corsi is a genuine old-style Ro-man *osteria.* The look is rustic and the at-mosphere one of cheery organised chaos. On offer are homey dishes prepared using good, fresh ingredients, and the menu fol-lows the culinary calendar (so if it's gnocchi, it's a Thursday).

Gino
TRATTORIA €€

(Map p74; ☑06 687 34 34; Vicolo Rosini 4; meals €30; ⊙Mon-Sat) Hidden away down a narrow lane close to parliament, Gino's is perennial-ly packed with gossiping politicians. Join the right honourables for well-executed staples such as *rigotoni alla gricia* and meatballs, served under hanging garlic bulbs and gaud-ily painted vines. No credit cards.

Osteria Sostegno
MODERN ITALIAN €€

(Map p74; ☑06 679 38 42; www.ilsostegno.it; Via delle Colonnelle 5; meals €35-40; ⊙Tue-Sun) Follow the green neon arrow to find this well-kept secret. An intimate place, it's a fa-vourite of journalists and politicians, with excellent dishes such as *caprese* (tomato and buffalo mozzarella salad) and *ravioli di ricotta e spinaci con limone e zafferano* (ricotta and spinach ravioli with lemon and saffron).

Alfredo e Ada
TRADITIONAL ITALIAN €

(Map p74; ☑06 687 88 42; Via dei Banchi Nuovo 14; meals €20; ⊙Mon-Fri) For a taste of au-thentic Roman cooking, head to this tiny brick-arched and wood-panelled place. It's distinctly no-frills – the wine list consists of two choices, red or white – but the food is filling, warming and just like *nonna* would have cooked it.

Da Francesco
PIZZERIA €

(Map p74; ☑06 686 40 09; Piazza del Fico 29; pizzas €6-9, meals €30; ⊙closed Tue) Gingham paper tablecloths, jovial waiters, groaning plateloads of pasta, tasty pizza: this quintes-sential Roman kitchen has character coming

Ice cream is a natural, delectable part of Roman life, and the city is dotted with superb *gelaterie artigianale* (makers of handmade gelato). If going off-guidebook, a handy tip is to look at the pistachio flavour. Pale olive equals good; bright green is bad. When it gets really hot, from around June to August, every Roman's favourite cooling pursuit is to eat *grattachecca* (crushed ice drowned in fruit syrup) by the river. There are several riverside stands around Rome's central bridges.

Here's our road-tested guide to the best gelatarie in the city:

» **San Crispino** (☎06 679 39 24) Via della Panetteria (Map p86; Via della Panetteria 42; ☺noon-12.30am Mon, Wed, Thu & Sun, noon-1.30am Fri & Sat); Piazza della Maddalena (Map p74; Piazza della Maddalena 3; ☺noon-12.30am Mon, Wed, Thu & Sun, noon-1.30am Fri & Sat) This is possibly the world's best gelato. What! You want a cone? The delicate, strictly natural and seasonal flavours are served only in tubs (cones would detract from the taste).

» **Alberto Pica** (Map p74; ☎06 686 84 05; Via della Seggiola 12; ☺8.30am-2am Mon-Sat year-round, 4pm-2am Sun, closed 2 weeks Aug) The original Mr Pica worked for Giolitti, and this historical Roman gelateria has been open since 1960. In summer, it offers flavours such as *fragolini de bosco* (wild strawberry) and *petali di rosa* (rose petal), but rice flavours are specialities whatever the season.

» **Fior di Luna** (Map p100; ☎06 6456 1314; Via della Lungaretta 96; ☺noon-1am) A small artisanal ice creamery, it only uses fresh, seasonal ingredients, and is the ideal place to stop when you're wandering around Rome's prettiest district after dinner.

» **Gelateria Giolitti** (Map p74; ☎06 699 12 43; Via degli Uffici del Vicario 40; ☺7am-2am) This started as a dairy in 1900 and still keeps the hordes happy with succulent sorbets and creamy chocolates. Gregory Peck and Audrey Hepburn swung by in *Roman Holiday* and it used to deliver marron glacé to Pope John Paul II.

» **Ara Coeli** (Map p74; ☎06 679 50 85; Piazza d'Aracoeli 9; ☺11am-11pm) Close to the base of the Campidoglio, Ara Coeli is handily located and offers more than 40 flavours of excellent organic ice cream, semicold varieties, Sicilian *granita* and yoghurt.

» **Old Bridge** (Map p104; ☎06 3972 3026; Viale dei Bastioni di Michelangelo 5; ☺9am-2am) Conveniently set near the wall of the Vatican, this tiny parlour has been cheerfully dishing up generous portions of homemade ice cream for over 20 years. Try the chocolate or pistachio, and, go on, have a dollop of cream on top.

out of its ears, and tables and chairs spilling out onto the pretty piazza. Rock up early or queue. No credit cards.

Filetti di Baccalà STREET FOOD €
(Map p74; Largo dei Librari 88; meals €20; ☺dinner Mon-Sat) On a pretty, scooter-strewn piazza, this tiny stuck-in-time institution is a classic Roman *friggitoria* (shop selling fried food). The house speciality is battered cod, but you can also have crispy veggies, such as *puntarella* (chicory), and crisp-fried zucchini flowers.

Sora Margherita TRADITIONAL ITALIAN €€
(Map p74; ☎06 687 42 16; Piazza delle Cinque Scole 30; meals €30; ☺closed dinner Mon-Thu & all day Sun) No-frills Sora Margherita started out as a cheap kitchen for hungry locals, but word

has spread and it's now a popular lunchtime haunt. Expect queues, a rowdy atmosphere, and classic Roman-Jewish dishes such as *carciofi alla giudia*. Service is prompt and you're expected to be likewise.

TRIDENTE, TREVI & THE QUIRINALE
Colline Emiliane EMILIA-ROMAGNAN €€€
(Map p86; ☎06 481 75 38; Via degli Avignonesi 22; meals €45; ☺Tue-Sat, Sun lunch, closed Aug) This welcoming, tucked-away trattoria off Piazza Barberini flies the flag for Emilia-Romagna, the well-fed Italian province that has gifted the world Parmesan, balsamic vinegar, bolognese sauce and Parma ham. On offer here are delicious meats, homemade pasta, rich *ragù* (meat and tomato sauce) and desserts worthy of a moment's silence.

Palatium WINE BAR €€
(Map p84; ☑06 6920 2132; Via Frattina 94; meals €40; ⊙11am-11pm Mon-Sat, closed Aug) Conceived as a showcase of Lazio's bounty, this sleek *enoteca* close to the Spanish Steps serves excellent local specialities, such as *porchetta* (pork roasted with herbs), artisan cheese and delicious salami, as well as an impressive array of Lazio wines (try lesser-known drops such as Aleatico). *Aperitivo* is a good bet, too.

Open Colonna MODERN €€€
(Map p86; ☑06 4782 2641; Via Milano 9a; meals €20-80; ⊙noon-midnight Tue-Sat & Sun lunch) Spectacularly set at the back of Palazzo delle Esposizioni, superchef Antonello Colonna's superb, chic restaurant is tucked on a mezzanine floor under an extraordinary glass roof. The cuisine is new Roman: innovative takes on traditional dishes, cooked with wit and flair. The best thing? There's a more basic but still delectable fixed two-course lunch or buffet for €15, and Saturday and Sunday brunch at €28, served in the dramatic, glass-ceilinged hall, with a terrace for sunny days.

Nino TUSCAN €€
(Map p84; ☑06 679 5676; Via Borgognona 11; meals €60; ⊙lunch & dinner Mon-Sat) With a look of wrought-iron chandeliers, polished dark wood and white tablecloths that's surely pretty unchanged since it opened in 1934, Nino is enduringly popular with the rich and famous. Waiters can be brusque if you're not on the A-list, but the food is good hearty fare, including memorable steaks and Tuscan bean soup.

Da Michele PIZZA BY SLICE €
(Map p86; ☑349 252 5347; Via dell'Umiltà 31; pizza slices from €2; ⊙8am-5pm Mon-Fri, to 8pm summer) A handy address in Spagna district: buy your fresh, light and crispy *pizza al taglio* and you'll have a delicious quick bite; there are a few interior bar-style seats.

Vineria Chianti TUSCAN €€
(Map p86; ☑06 678 75 50; Via del Lavatore 81-82; meals €45; ⊙lunch & dinner) Many restaurants around the Trevi Fountain dish up overpriced tourist fare, but this pretty ivy-clad wine bar is one of the exceptions: bottle-lined inside, it has watch-the-world-go-by outside seating in summer. Cuisine is Tuscan, so the beef is particularly good, but it also serves up imaginative salads, plus pizza in the evenings.

Pizzeria al Leoncino PIZZERIA €
(Map p84; ☑06 686 77 57; Via del Leoncino 28; pizzas €6.50-8.50; ⊙Thu-Tue, dinner only Sat & Sun) A boisterous neighbourhood pizzeria with a wood-fired oven, Leoncino has two small rooms, cheerful decor and gruff but efficient waiters who will serve you an excellent Roman-style pizza and ice-cold beer faster than you can say '*delizioso*'.

Matricianella TRATTORIA €€
(Map p84; ☑06 683 21 00; Via del Leone 2; meals €40; ⊙Mon-Sat, closed Aug) Tucked away near Piazza di San Lorenzo in Lucina, this is a chic trattoria with gingham tablecloths, chintzy murals and streetside seating. Romans go crazy for the delectable fried antipasti, the *carciofi alla giudia*, the meatballs and the Jewish-style stew. Bookings essential.

Antico Forno SANDWICH SHOP €
(Map p86; ☑06 679 28 66; Via delle Muratte 8; ⊙7am-9pm) Near the Trevi Fountain, Antico Forno is one of Rome's oldest bakery shops, and its well-stocked deli counter has a grand array of freshly baked *panini,* focaccia and pizza.

La Buca di Ripetta RESTAURANT €€
(Map p84; ☑06 321 93 91; Via di Ripetta 36; meals €50; ⊙daily) Popular with actors and directors from the district, this foodie destination offers robust Roman cuisine. Try the *zuppa rustica con crostini di pane aromatizzati* (country-style soup with rosemary-scented bread) or the *matolino di latte al forno alle erbe con patate* (baked suckling pork with potatoes) and you'll be fuelled for either more sightseeing or a serious snooze.

Pastificio FAST FOOD €
(Map p84; Via delle Croce; pasta dishes €4; ⊙1-3pm Mon-Sat) A great find in this pricey 'hood, Pasticcio is a pasta shop that serves up two choices of pasta at lunchtime. It's fast food, Italian style – great fresh pasta with tasty sauces.

'Gusto PIZZERIA €
(Map p84; ☑06 322 62 73; Piazza Augusto Imperatore 9; pizzas €6-9.50) Once a mould-breaking warehouse-style gastronomic complex – all exposed-brickwork and industrial chic – 'Gusto is still buzzing after all these years. It's a great place to sit on the terrace and eat Neapolitan-style pizzas (rather than the upmarket restaurant fare, which receives mixed reports). There's live music on Tuesday and Thursday evenings.

TOP CHOICE L'Asino d'Oro
MODERN ITALIAN €€

(Map p62; ☎06 4891 3832; Via del Boschetto 73; meals €40) This fabulous restaurant has been transplanted from Orvieto and its Umbrian origins resonate in Lucio Sforza's delicious cooking. It's unfussy yet innovative, with dishes featuring lots of flavourful contrasts, such as slow-roasted rabbit in a rich berry sauce and desserts that linger in the memory. For such excellent food, this intimate, informal yet classy place is one of Rome's best deals, especially for the set lunch.

Panella l'Arte del Pane
FAST FOOD €

(☎06 487 24 35; Via Merulana 54; ⊙8am-11pm Mon-Thu, to midnight Fri & Sat, 8.30am-4pm Sun) With a sumptuous array of *pizza al taglio*, *supplì* (fried rice balls), focaccia, and fried croquettes, this is a sublime fast lunch stop, where you can sip a glass of chilled *prosecco* (type of sparking wine) while eying up gastronomic souvenirs from the deli.

Roscioli
FAST FOOD €

(Via Buonarroti 48; pizzas €2-3; ⊙7am-8.15pm Mon-Sat) This off-the-track branch of this splendid deli-bakery-pizzeria, in a road leading off Piazza Vittorio Emanuele, has delish *pizza al taglio*, pasta dishes and so on that make it ideal for a swift lunch or picnic stock-up.

Agata e Romeo
MODERN ITALIAN €€€

(Map p90; ☎06 446 61 15; Via Carlo Alberto 45; meals €120; ⊙Mon-Fri) This elegant, restrained place was one of Rome's gastronomic pioneers, and still holds its own as one of the city's most gourmet takes on Roman cuisine. Chef Agata Parisella designs and cooks menus, offering creative uses of Roman traditions, while husband Romeo curates the wine cellar and daughter Maria Antonietta chooses the cheeses. Bookings essential.

Da Danilo
TRATTORIA €€

(☎06 482 5176; Via Petrarca 13; meals €50; ⊙Tue-Sat lunch, Mon-Sat dinner) On a street leading off Piazza Vittorio Emanuele II, Da Danilo is ideal if you're looking for a fine robust meal a short walk from Termini. A classic neighbourhood place, it offers icons of Roman cooking in a rustic, eternal-Roman-trattoria atmosphere. Good for digging into a dish of *cacio e pepe* or carbonara, which are reliable favourites.

La Carbonara
TRATTORIA €€

(Map p62; ☎06 482 5176; Via Panisperna 214; meals €35; ⊙Mon-Sat) On the go since 1906, this busy restaurant was favoured by the infamous Ragazzi di Panisperna, a group of young physicists, including Enrico Fermi, who constructed the first atomic bomb. The waiters are brusque, it crackles with energy and the interior is covered in graffiti – tradition dictates that diners should leave their mark in a message on the wall. The speciality is the eponymous carbonara.

Formula 1
PIZZERIA €

(Map p90; ☎06 445 38 66; Via degli Equi 13; pizzas from €6; ⊙6.30pm-1.30am Mon-Sat) As adrenalin-fuelled as its name, at this basic, historical San Lorenzo pizzeria, waiters zoom around under whirring fans delivering tomato-loaded bruschetta, fried zucchini flowers, *supplì al telefono* and bubbling thin-crust pizza to eternal crowds of feasting students.

Tram Tram
TRATTORIA €€

(Map p90; ☎06 49 04 16; Via dei Reti 44; meals €45; ⊙Tue-Sun) This trendy, yet old-style, lace-curtained trattoria takes its name from the trams that rattle past outside. It offers tasty traditional dishes, such as *involtini di pesce spada con patate* (rolls of swordfish with potato). Book ahead.

Indian Fast Food
INDIAN €

(Map p90; ☎06 446 07 92; Via Mamiani 11; curries €5.50-7.50; ⊙11am-10.30pm) Basic, formica tables, Hindi hits, neon lights, chapatti and naan, lip-smacking samosas and bhajis, and a choice of main curry dishes: you could almost imagine yourself in India in this authentic joint.

Trimani Wine Bar
WINE BAR €€

(Map p90; ☎06 446 96 30; Via Cernaia 37b; meals €40; ⊙Mon-Sat, closed 2 weeks Aug) This is a top-of-the-range wine bar, with a delectable range of dishes – from oysters to lentil soup to salami and cheeses served with mustard and jam – plus a choice of over 4500 international wines (be steered by the seriously knowledgeable waiters), and delicious bread and olive oil.

Da Ricci
PIZZERIA €

(Map p86; ☎06 488 11 07; Via Genova 32; pizzas €8; ⊙7pm-midnight Tue-Sun) In a tranquil, cobbled cul-de-sac a step away from smoggy Via Nazionale, Rome's oldest pizzeria started life as an *enoteca* in 1905, and its wood-panelled interior feels like it hasn't changed much since. The sign says Est! Est!! Est!!! – Da Ricci's other name – named after its white wine from the north of Lazio. Pizzas are thick-based Neapolitan-style (though you can get thin-based if you like), and work best with lots of toppings.

CELIO HILL & LATERAN

Il Bocconcino
TRATTORIA €€

(Map p94; ☑06 770 791 75; www.ilbocconcino.com; Via Ostilia 23; meals €30-35; ⊙Thu-Tue, closed Aug) Visited the Colosseum and *need* lunch in a local trattoria? Try 'the little mouthful' in the area heading up towards San Giovanni. A cut above many of the eateries in this touristy neighbourhood, it serves excellent pasta and imaginative meat and fish mains such as *rombo in impanatura di agrumi* (turbot with citrus fruit coating).

AVENTINO & TESTACCIO

Da Felice
TRADITIONAL ITALIAN €€

(Map p96; ☑06 574 68 00; Via Mastro Giorgio 29; meals €40; ⊙Mon-Sat) Locals and foodies swear by this Testaccio institution, famous for its classic Roman cuisine. The decor might be post-industrial chic – exposed-brick walls, chequered marble floor, hanging lamps – but the menu is stolidly traditional. Highlights include glorious *tonnarelli cacio e pepe* (square-shaped pasta with *pecorino* Romano cheese and black pepper) and wonderful roast lamb.

Trattoria da Bucatino
TRATTORIA €€

(Map p96; ☑06 574 68 86; Via Luca della Robbia 84; meals €30; ⊙Tue-Sun) This laid-back neighbourhood trattoria is hugely popular. Ask for a table upstairs (with wood panels, Chianti bottles and a mounted boar's head) and dig into huge portions of Roman soul food. The *bucatini all'amatriciana* is a must and meaty *secondi* (second courses) are also excellent, but do try to save room for a home-cooked dessert.

Pizzeria Remo
PIZZERIA €

(Map p96; ☑06 574 62 70; Piazza Santa Maria Liberatrice 44; pizzas from €6; ⊙7pm-1am Mon-Sat) Pizzeria Remo is one of the city's most popular pizzerias, always full of noisy young Romans. The pizzas are thin Roman classics with toppings loaded onto the crisp, charred base. Place your order by ticking your choices on a sheet of paper slapped down by an overstretched waiter. Expect to queue.

Volpetti Più
TRADITIONAL ITALIAN €

(Map p96; Via Volta 8; meals under €15; ⊙10.30am-3.30pm & 5.30-9.30pm Mon-Sat) One of the few places in town where you can sit down and eat well for less than €15, Volpetti Più is a sumptuous *tavola calda,* offering an opulent choice of pizza, pasta, soup, meat, vegetables and fried nibbles.

TRASTEVERE & GIANICOLO

TOP CHOICE Glass Hosteria
CREATIVE ITALIAN €€

(Map p100; ☑06 5833 5903; Vic del Cinque 58; meals €70; ⊙dinner Tue-Sun) Trastevere's foremost foodie address, the Glass Hosteria is a breath of fresh air in the neighbourhood, a modernist-styled, sophisticated setting with cooking to match. Chef Cristina creates inventive, delicate dishes that combine with fresh ingredients and traditional elements to delight and surprise the palate.

Osteria della Gensola
TRATTORIA €€

(Map p100; ☑06 581 63 12; Piazza della Gensola 15; meals €50; ⊙closed Sun mid-Jun–mid-Sep) Tucked away in Trastevere, this tranquil, classy, yet unpretentious trattoria thrills foodies with delicious food that has a Sicilian slant and emphasis on seafood, including an excellent tuna tartare, linguine with fresh anchovies and divine *zuccherini* (tiny fish) with fresh mint. The set menu costs €41.

Paris
TRADITIONAL ITALIAN €€

(Map p100; ☑06 581 53 78; Piazza San Calisto 7a; meals €45; ⊙Tue-Sat, lunch Sun, closed 3 weeks Aug) An old-school Roman restaurant set in a 17th-century building, Paris is a great, traditional and upmarket place to while away an evening, plus the best place outside the Ghetto to sample Roman-Jewish cuisine, such as delicate *fritto misto con baccalà* (deep-fried vegetables with salt cod) and *carciofi alla giudia.* There's a sunshaded terrace.

Da Augusto
TRATTORIA €

(Map p100; ☑06 580 37 98; Piazza de' Renzi 15; meals €25; ⊙lunch & dinner Fri-Wed) For a true Trastevere feast, plonk yourself at one of Augusto's rickety tables and prepare to enjoy some mamma-style cooking. The hardworking waiters dish out hearty platefuls of *rigatoni all'amatriciana* and *stracciatella* (clear broth with egg and Parmesan) among a host of Roman classics.

Da Lucia
TRATTORIA €

(Map p100; ☎06 580 36 01; Vicolo del Mattonato 2; meals €30; ☺Tue-Sun) Eat beneath the fluttering knickers of the neighbourhood at this terrific trattoria, frequented by hungry locals and tourists, and packed with locals for Sunday lunch. On a cobbled backstreet that is classic Trastevere, it serves up a cavalcade of Roman specialities including *trippa all romana* (tripe with tomato sauce) and *pollo con peperoni* (chicken with peppers), as well as bountiful antipasti and possibly Rome's best tiramisu. Cash only.

Le Mani in Pasta
RESTAURANT €€€

(Map p100; ☎06 581 60 17; Via dei Genovesi 37; meals €50; ☺Tue-Sun) Popular and lively, this rustic, snug place has arched ceilings and an open kitchen that serves up delicious fresh pasta dishes such as *fettucine con ricotta e pancetta*. The grilled meats are great, too.

Da Enzo
TRATTORIA €€

(Map p100; ☎06 581 83 55; Via dei Vascellari 29; meals €25; ☺Mon-Sat) This snug dining room with rough yellow walls and lots of character serves up great, seasonally based Roman meals, such as spaghetti with clams and mussels or grilled lamb cutlets. There's a tiny terrace on the quintessential Trastevere cobbled street.

Sisini
FAST FOOD €

(Map p100; Via di San Francesco a Ripa 137; pizza slices & pastas from €2; ☺9am-10.30pm Mon-Sat, closed Aug) Locals love this fast food joint (the sign outside says 'Supplì'), serving up fresh *pizza al taglio* and different pasta and risotto dishes served in plastic boxes – there's one small table where you can eat standing up, or you can take away. It's also worth sampling the *supplì* and roast chicken.

Forno la Renella
PIZZA BY SLICE €

(Map p100; ☎06 581 72 65; Via del Moro 15-16; ☺9am-9pm) The wood-fired ovens at this historical Trastevere bakery have been going for decades, producing a delicious daily batch of pizza, bread and biscuits. Piled-high toppings (and fillings) vary seasonally. It's popular with everyone from skinheads with big dogs to elderly ladies with little dogs.

Panattoni
PIZZERIA €

(Map p100; ☎06 580 09 19; Viale di Trastevere 53; pizzas €6.50-9; ☺6.30pm-1am Thu-Tue) Panattoni is nicknamed *l'obitorio* (the morgue) because of its marble-slab tabletops, but thankfully the similarity stops there. This is one of

Trastevere's liveliest pizzerias, with paper-thin pizzas, a clattering buzz, testy waiters, streetside seating and fine fried starters (specialities are *supplì* and *baccalá*).

Beer & Fud
PIZZERIA €

(Map p100; ☎06 589 40 16; Via Benedetta 23; meals €25; ☺6.30pm-1am Tue-Sun, closed Aug) This buzzing, vaulted pizzeria wins plaudits for its small menu of organic pizzas, crostini and delicious fried things (potato, pumpkin etc) and has a microbrewery on site. Save room for dessert. Book ahead.

VATICAN CITY, BORGO & PRATI

TOP CHOICE Gelarmony
GELATERIA €

(Map p104; Via Marcantonio Colonna 34; ice creams from €1.50; ☺10am-late) Once you've had a pyramid-sized *arancino* (deep-fried rice ball) at Mondo Arancina, head next door to this superb gelateria for dessert. Alongside delicious ice cream, there's a devilish selection of creamy Sicilian sweets, including the best *cannoli* (pastry tubes filled with sweetened ricotta and chocolate pieces) this side of Palermo.

Mondo Arancina
SICILIAN €

(Map p104; Via Marcantonio Colonna 38; arancine from €2) All sunny yellow ceramics, cheerful crowds and tantalising deep-fried snacks, this bustling takeaway brings a little corner of Sicily to Rome. Star of the show is the classic fist-sized *arancino,* a fried rice ball stuffed with *ragù* and peas. Pay first at the till and then take your receipt to the food counter.

Pizzarium
PIZZA BY SLICE €

(Map p104; Via della Meloria 43; pizza slices €2-3) It's worth searching out this unassuming takeaway near the Cipro-Musei Vaticani metro stop for superb fried snacks and *pizza a taglio*. Pizza toppings are original and intensely flavoursome and the pizza base manages to be both fluffy and crisp. Eat standing up, and wash it down with a chilled beer.

Angeli a Borgo
TRADITIONAL ITALIAN €€

(Map p104; ☎06 686 96 74; www.angeliaborgo. com; Borgo Angelico 28; pizzas from €5.50, meals €25-30) It is possible to escape the crowds and eat well near St Peter's. Just a few blocks back from the basilica, this is a laid-back restaurant-pizzeria with a high brick ceiling, yellow walls and an ample menu. There are wood-fired pizzas and focaccia, abundant pasta and interesting main courses. If all else fails, the tiramisu is exceptional.

APERITIVO, ANYONE?

Young Romans love the *aperitivo* (happy hour). A fashion that started in Milan, it sees bars offering a snack buffet from around 6pm to 9pm – usually with a special charge for a drink and food of around €7 to €10. If the buffet is lavish enough, sometimes the city's bright young things can skip dinner altogether. Great places to drink up and chow down include Freni e Frizoni (p134), Femme (p132) and Il Pentagrappolo (see p133).

Hostaria Dino e Tony   TRATTORIA €€
(Map p104; ✆06 3973 3284; Via Leone IV; meals €30-35; ⊘Mon-Sat) Something of a rarity, Dino e Tony is an authentic trattoria in the Vatican area. Kick off with the monumental antipasto, a minor meal in its own right, before plunging into its signature dish, *rigatoni all'amatriciana*. Finish up with a *granita di caffè*, a crushed ice coffee served with a full inch of whipped cream. No credit cards.

Cacio e Pepe   TRATTORIA €
(✆06 321 72 68; Via Avezzana 11; meals €25; ⊘closed Sat dinner & Sun) North of Lepanto metro station, this humble trattoria is as authentic as it gets. Romans flock here in droves, squeezing into the stamp-sized interior or hunkering down at the gingham-clad pavement tables, for simple, no-nonsense home cooking. Keep it simple with the signature dish, *cacio e pepe* – fresh *bucatini* slicked with buttery cheese and pepper – followed by *pollo alla cacciatora* (hunter's chicken).

Settembrini Café   MODERN ITALIAN €
(Via Settembrini 25; meals €15) A favourite lunchtime haunt of media execs from the nearby RAI TV offices, this trendy cafe near Piazza Mazzini does a roaring trade in tasty bar snacks and fresh pasta. Next door, the main restaurant (✆06 323 26 17; Via Settembrini 25; meals €60; ⊘closed Sat lunch & Sun) is highly regarded by Roman foodies for its modern cuisine and exemplary wine list.

Osteria dell'Angelo   TRATTORIA €€
(Map p104; ✆06 372 94 70; Via Bettolo 24; set menus €25 & €30; ⊘closed Mon & Sat lunch & all day Sun) Former rugby player Angelo presides over this, his hugely popular neighbourhood trattoria (reservations are a must). The set menu features a mixed antipasti, a robust Roman-style pasta and a choice of hearty mains with a side dish. To finish, you're offered lightly spiced biscuits to dunk in sweet dessert wine.

Dal Toscano   TUSCAN €€
(Map p104; ✆06 3972 5717; www.ristorantedaltoscano.it; Via Germanico 58-60; meals €40; ⊘Tue-Sun) Carnivores will adore Dal Toscano, an old-fashioned *ristorante* that serves top-notch Tuscan food, with an emphasis on superb meat. Start with the hand-cut Tuscan prosciutto, then try the colossal char-grilled *bistecca alla fiorentina* (T-bone steak). You'll need to book.

Ristorante l'Arcangelo   MODERN ITALIAN €€
(Map p104; ✆06 321 09 92; Via Belli 59-61; meals €60; ⊘closed lunch Sat & Sun) Frequented by politicians and local celebs, this upmarket restaurant serves traditional Roman staples alongside more innovative creations – think tripe with mint and *pecorino* (sheep's-milk cheese) or spicy pigeon with apples and mustard.

Pizzeria Amalfi   PIZZERIA €
(Map p104; ✆06 3973 3165; Via dei Gracchi 12; pizzas from €6) While Roman pizzas are thin and crispy, Neapolitan pizzas are thicker and more doughy. And that's what you get at this bustling Naples-themed pizzeria just off the main road from Ottavian metro stop to St Peter's.

Dolce Maniera   BAKERY €
(Map p104; Via Barletta 27; ⊘24hr) This 24-hour basement bakery supplies much of the neighbourhood with breakfast. Head here for cheap-as-chips *cornetti* (croissants), slabs of pizza, *panini* and an indulgent array of cakes.

VILLA BORGHESE & NORTHERN ROME

Bar Pompi   PASTRIES & CAKES €
(Via Cassia 8; tiramisu €3; ⊘Tue-Sun) Just behind happening Piazzale Ponte Milvio on the northern side of the Tiber, this small bar is famous for its tiramisu. And rightly so – it's fabulous. It comes in four forms: classic, strawberry, pistachio, and banana and nutella. And after much painstaking research, the prize goes to the pistachio.

SELF-CATERING

For fresh fruit and vegetables, there are many outdoor markets, open from 7.30am to 1pm Monday to Saturday:

Campo de' Fiori (Map p74) In the Centro Storico.

Piazza San Cosimato Market (Map p100) In Trastevere.

Piazza Testaccio Market (Map p96) In Testaccio.

Piazza Vittorio Emanuele II Market Near Stazione Termini.

Via del Lavatore Market (Map p86) Near Trevi Fountain.

You can also stock up at the small supermarkets dotted around town.

Conad (Map p90; Stazione Termini) At the train station.

DeSpar Via Nazionale (Map p86; Via Nazionale 212-213); Via Giustiniani (Map p74; Via Giustiniani 18b-21) Near Palazzo Barberini and the Pantheon, respectively.

Di per Di (Map p84; Via Vittoria) Near the Spanish Steps.

Sir (Map p90; Piazza dell'Indipendenza 28) Near Museo Nazionale Romano: Palazzo Massimo alle Terme.

Todis (Map p100; Via Natale del Grande 24) Near Basilica di Santa Maria Trastevere.

🍷 Drinking

Bars and cafes are an essential part of Roman life. Most Romans breakfast in a cafe (a slurp of a cappuccino and a sugary bun) and pop back at least once for a pick-me-up espresso later in the afternoon. For drinks other than coffee, there are traditional *enoteche*, a few pubs (trendy by virtue of their novelty), some super-sleek designer bars and some alternative counter-culture hang-outs. A growing trend in Rome is the microbrewery, with artisanal beers becoming increasingly popular as brewing takes off across Italy.

Much of the action is in the *centro storico*. Campo de' Fiori is popular with a younger crowd – and it is fun, though can be a bit rowdy and trashy. For a more up-market scene, check out the bars in the alleyways around Piazza Navona. Trastevere is another bar-filled area where locals and tourists mingle merrily. San Lorenzo is the student area and is another great place to

bar-crawl. Dotted with bars and clubs, it's packed, grungy, a little more crazy than the centre, and offers cheaper drinks. Pigneto is the other fashionable, artsy nightlife zone, and a great place to bar-hop on a summer's night.

Recent clampdowns on taking drinks outside licensed premises have cooled the city-centre scene somewhat.

ANCIENT ROME

Cavour 313   WINE BAR €

(Map p62; ☑06 678 54 96; www.cavour313.it; Via Cavour 313; dishes €7-14; ☺10am-3.30pm & 7pm-midnight, closed Aug) Close to the Colosseum and Forum, wood-panelled, intimate wine bar Cavour 313 attracts everyone from actors and politicians to tourists. Sink into its pub-like cosiness and while away hours over sensational wine (over 1200 labels), cold cuts, cheeses and daily specials.

Caffè Capitolino   CAFE

(Map p62; Capitoline Museums, Piazzale Caffarelli 4; ☺Tue-Sun) Hidden behind the Capitoline Museums, this stylish rooftop cafe commands memorable views. It's a good place to take a museum time-out and relax with a drink or snack (*panini*, salads and pizza), although you don't need a ticket to drink here – it's accessible via an entrance behind Palazzo dei Conservatori.

0,75   BAR

(Map p62; www.075roma.com; Via dei Cerchi 65; ☺11am-2am) A funky bar on the Circo Massimo, it's good for a lingering drink, weekend brunch (11am to 3pm), *aperitivo* or a light lunch. It's a friendly place with a laid-back vibe, an extensive wine list, a cool exposed-brick look and mellow tunes. Free wi-fi.

CENTRO STORICO

Caffè Sant'Eustachio   CAFE

(Map p74; Piazza Sant'Eustachio 82; ☺8.30-1am Sun-Thu, to 1.30am Fri, to 2am Sat) This small unassuming cafe, generally three-deep at the bar, serves Rome's best coffee. The famous *gran caffè* is created by beating the first drops of espresso and several teaspoons of sugar into a frothy paste, then adding the rest of the coffee on top. It's superbly smooth and guaranteed to put some zing into your sightseeing. Specify if you want it *amaro* (bitter) or *poco zucchero* (with a little sugar).

Etablì
BAR

(Map p74; ☑06 9761 6694; www.etabli.it; Vicolo delle Vacche 9a; ☺bar 6pm-2am Tue-Sun, restaurant 7.30pm-midnight) Etablì is a fab rustic-chic bar-cum-restaurant where Roman lovelies float in to have a drink, read the paper, indulge in *aperitivo* and use the wi-fi. It's laid-back and good-looking, with an eclectic soundtrack and original French country decor. Restaurant meals average about €35.

Open Baladin
BAR

(Map p74; www.openbaladin.com; Via degli Specchi 6; ☺12.30pm-2am) A designer beer bar near Campo de' Fiori, Open Baladin is leading the way in Rome's recent discovery of all things beery. It's a slick, stylish place with more than 40 brews on tap and up to 100 bottled beers, mainly produced by Italian artisanal breweries. There's also a food menu with *panini,* burgers and daily specials.

Salotto 42
BAR

(Map p74; www.salotto42.it; Piazza di Pietra 42; ☺10am-2am Tue-Sat, to midnight Sun & Mon) On a picturesque piazza, facing the columns of the Temple of Hadrian, this is a hip, glamorous lounge bar, complete with vintage armchairs, sleek sofas and a collection of two-tonne design books. Run by an Italian-Swedish couple, it has an excellent *aperitivo* spread and serves a Sunday brunch (€15).

Barnum Cafe
CAFE

(Map p74; www.barnumcafe.com; Via del Pellegrino 87; ☺9.30am-midnight) This is a relaxed spot to check your email over a freshly squeezed orange juice (€3) or while away an hour reading a newspaper on one of the tatty old armchairs dotted around the white-brick interior. Light lunches are served and *aperitivo* hour starts at 7.30pm.

Chiostro del Bramante Caffè
CAFE

(Map p74; www.chiostrodelbramante.it; Via della Pace; ☺10am-11pm) This is a well-kept secret: a footfall from Piazza Navona, you can have a drink, a snack or a light lunch (€10), all the while making use of the free wi-fi in the peaceful Renaissance splendour of Bramante's cloister. *Aperitivo* from 7pm.

Caffè Tazza d'Oro
CAFE

(Map p74; Via degli Orfani 84; ☺Mon-Sat) A busy, stand-up bar, it has burnished fittings and some of the capital's best coffee. Its espresso hits the mark perfectly and there's a range of delicious coffee concoctions, such as *granita di caffè* and *parfait di caffè,* a €3 coffee mousse.

Circus
BAR

(Map p74; Via della Vetrina 15; ☺10am-2am Tue-Sun) A great little cafe-bar, tucked around the corner from Piazza Navona, this is a funky, informal place to lounge and chat, with DJs on Fridays, art exhibitions and lots of books to browse through. Free wi-fi.

Femme
BAR

(Map p74; Via del Pellegrino 14; ☺6pm-2am Tue-Sun) Entering this bar, with its funky sounds and modernist look, is like wandering into a Calvin Klein advert, with ubercool stunners everywhere you look. The cocktails are the business and the splendid *aperitivo* is almost worth losing one's cool over.

Caffè Farnese
CAFE

(Map p74; Via dei Baullari 106) We're with Goethe, who thought Piazza Farnese one of the world's most beautiful squares. Judge for yourself from the vantage point of this unassuming cafe. On a street between Campo de' Fiori and Piazza Farnese, it's ideally placed for whiling away the early afternoon hours. Try the *caffè alla casa* (house coffee) – made to a secret recipe.

Il Goccetto
WINE BAR

(Map p74; Via dei Banchi Vecchi 14; ☺11.30am-2pm & 6.30pm-midnight Mon-Sat) Join the cast of regulars at this old-style *vino e olio* shop for delicious wine by the glass, accompanied by a tasty assortment of snacks (cheeses, salamis, crostini etc) and large helpings of neighbourhood banter.

Bar della Pace
CAFE

(Map p74; Via della Pace 5; ☺9am-3am Tue-Sun, 4pm-3am Mon) The quintessential *dolce vita* cafe, inside it's gilded baroque and mismatched wooden tables; outside locals and tourists strike poses over their Campari against a backdrop of ivy. The perfect people-watching spot.

Vineria Reggio
WINE BAR

(Map p74; Campo de' Fiori 15; ☺8.30am-2.30am) The pick of the bars and cafes on Campo de' Fiori, this has a small, bottle-lined, cosy interior and outside tables. Busy from lunchtime onwards, it attracts tourists and *fighi* (cool) Romans like bees to a honeypot. Wine by the glass from €4.

TRIDENTE, TREVI & THE QUIRINALE

TOP CHOICE Salotto BAR

(Map p84; Via della Penna 22; ☺noon-3am) Sister to city-centre venue Salotto 42 and summer-only Salotto Gianicolo, this attracts a similar mix of fashionistas and stylish Romans. As part of the art deco Hotel Locarno, it has a lovely Agatha Christie–era feel, and a green-ery-shaded outdoor terrace in summer. Cocktails cost a chichi €16, proving that you do have to suffer for beauty.

Stravinskij Bar – Hotel de Russie BAR

(Map p84; ☏06 328 88 70; Via del Babuino 9) Can't afford to stay at Picasso's old haunt the Ho-tel de Russie? Then splash out on a drink in its enchanting bar, set in the courtyard with sunshaded tables overlooked by ter-raced gardens. It's impossibly romantic in the best kind of 19th-century-traveller, *dolce vita* way.

L'Antica Enoteca WINE BAR

(Map p84; ☏06 679 08 96; Via della Croce 76; meals €35; ☺11am-1am) Locals and tourists alike prop up the 19th-century wooden bar (or nab an outside table or one in the back room) to sample wines by the glass, snack on antipasti and order well-priced soul food such as pasta or polenta.

Caffè Greco CAFE

(Map p84; ☏06 679 17 00; Via dei Condotti 86; ☺9am-8pm) Keats and Casanova were among the early regulars at this historical gilt-and-velvet-lined cafe. It opened in 1760 and al-though still going strong, it's of more inter-est for its history than anything it serves. To sample the bygone atmosphere, do as the locals do and take a coffee at the bar.

TERMINI, ESQUILINO & SAN LORENZO

Ai Tre Scalini WINE BAR

(Map p62; ☏06 4890 7495; Via Panisperna 251; ☺noon-1am & 6pm-1am) 'The Three Steps' is always packed, with crowds (mostly local, with a smattering of tourists) spilling out onto the street. As well as a tasty choice of wines, it sells the damn fine Menabrea beer, brewed in northern Italy. You can also tuck into a heart-warming array of cheeses, sa-lami and dishes such as *porchetta di Aric-cia con patate al forno* (roasted Ariccia pork with roast potatoes).

Solea Club BAR

(Map p90; ☏328 9252925; Via dei Latini 51; ☺9pm-2am) With lots of vintage sofas, chairs, and cushions on the floor, this has the look of a chill-out room in a decadent baroque man-sion. It's full of San Lorenzo hipsters loung-ing all over the floor, drinking the so-mean-they-snarl mojitos. Fun.

Bar Zest at the Radisson BAR

(Map p90; ☏06 44 48 41; Via Filippo Turati 171; ☺10.30am-1am) The Radisson hotel is not ideally located as a base, but to pop by for a cocktail (€16) at the 7th-floor bar is another matter. Waiters are cute, chairs are by Jasper Morrison, views are through plate-glass, and there's a sexy rooftop pool.

Fiddler's Elbow PUB

(Map p90; ☏06 487 21 10; Via dell'Olmata 43; ☺5pm-2am) Near the Basilica di Santa Maria Maggiore, the granddaddy of Rome's Irish pubs sticks to the formula that has served it well over the last 25 years: Guinness, darts, crisps, football and rugby, attracting a mix of Romans, expats and tourists.

CELIO HILL & LATERAN

Il Pentagrappolo WINE BAR

(Map p94; Via Celimontana 21b; ☺noon-3pm & 6pm-1am Tue-Sun) A few blocks from the Col-osseum, these attractive star-vaulted rooms offer 250 labels to choose from and about 15 wines by the glass. There's live jazz or soul on Thursday, Friday and Saturday nights and a daily *aperitivo* (6pm to 8.30pm).

TRASTEVERE & GIANICOLO

TOP CHOICE Bar San Calisto BAR

(Map p100; ☏06 589 56 78; Piazza San Calisto 3-5; ☺6-2am Mon-Sat) Those in the know head to the down-at-heel 'Sanca' for its basic, stuck-in-time atmosphere and cheap prices (a beer costs €1.50). It attracts everyone from drug dealers, intellectuals and pseudo-intellectu-als to keeping-it-real Romans, alcoholics and American students. It's famous for its choco-late – drunk hot with cream in winter, eaten as ice cream in summer. Try the Sambuca con la Mosca ('with flies' – raw coffee beans).

Ma Che Siete Venuti a Fà PUB

(Map p100; Via Benedetta 25; ☺3pm-2am) Also known as the Football Pub, the name means 'What did you come here for?' (it's a football chant), but the answer, rather than anything to do with the beautiful game, could be at-mosphere and beer. It's a pint-sized place, but packs a huge number of artisanal beers into its interior, with delicious caramel-like tipples such as Italiano Bibock (by Birrificio Italiano).

Freni e Frizioni BAR

(Map p100; ☑06 5833 4210; Via del Politeama 4-6; ◔6.30pm-2am) All the young dudes' favourite cool Trastevere bar was a garage in a former life, hence its name ('brakes and clutches'). The arty crowd flocks here to slurp well-priced drinks (especially mojitos), feast on the good-value *aperitivo* and spill into the piazza out the front.

Ombre Rosse BAR

(Map p100; ☑06 588 41 55; Piazza Sant'Egidio 12; ◔8am-2am Mon-Sat, 11am-2am Sun) This is another seminal Trastevere hang-out; grab a table on the terrace and watch the world go by. The cosmopolitan clientele ranges from elderly Italian wide boys to chic city slickers. Tunes are slinky and there's live music (jazz, blues and world) on Tuesday and Thursday evenings and Sunday lunchtimes from October to May.

VATICAN CITY, BORGO & PRATI

Art Studio Café CAFE

(Map p104; www.artstudiocafe.it; Via dei Gracchi 187a) A cafe, exhibition space and craft school all in one, this bright and breezy spot serves one of Prati's most popular *aperitivi*. It's also good for a light lunch, something like chicken couscous or fresh salad, or a restorative mid-afternoon tea.

Passaguai WINE BAR

(Map p104; www.passaguai.it; Via Leto 1; ◔10am-2am Mon-Sat) A cavelike basement wine bar, Passaguai has a few outdoor tables and feels pleasingly off the beaten track. There's a good wine list and range of artisanal beers, and the food – such as cheeses and cold cuts – is tasty, too. Free wi-fi.

☆ Entertainment

Entertainment in Rome can be simply parking yourself at a streetside table and watching the world go by. But there's a substantial cultural scene here too, particularly in summer when the Estate Romana (Roman Summer) festival sponsors hundreds of theatre, cinema, opera and music events. Many performances take place in parks, gardens and church courtyards, with classical ruins and Renaissance villas providing atmospheric backdrops. Autumn is also full of cultural activity, with specialised festivals dedicated to dance, drama and jazz.

Romac'è (www.romace.it, in Italian; €1) is Rome's most comprehensive listings guide, and comes complete with a small English-language section; it's published every Wednesday. Another useful guide is *Trova Roma,* which comes as a free insert with *La Repubblica* every Thursday. The English-language magazine Wanted in Rome (www.wantedinrome.com; €1) also contains listings of festivals, exhibitions, dance shows, classical music events, operas and cinema releases. It's published every second Wednesday. Useful websites include www.romaturismo.it and www.comune.roma.it.

Classical Music

An abundance of spectacular settings makes Rome a superb place to catch a classical music concert. The city's cultural and musical hub is the Auditorium Parco della Musica, but free concerts are often held in churches, especially at Easter and around Christmas and New Year. Seats are available on a first-come, first-served basis and the programs are generally excellent. Check newspapers and listings for programs.

Auditorium Parco della Musica CULTURAL CENTRE

(Map p58; ☑06 8024 1281; www.auditorium.com; Viale Pietro de Coubertin 30) Rome's premier concert venue, and one of Europe's most popular arts centres, this state-of-the-art modernist complex combines architectural innovation with perfect acoustics. Designed by Renzo Piano, its three concert halls and 3000-seater open-air arena stage everything from classical music concerts to tango exhibitions, book readings and film screenings. The auditorium is also home to Rome's top orchestra, the world-class Orchestra dell' Accademia Nazionale di Santa Cecilia (www.santacecilia.it). To get to the auditorium, take tram 2 from Piazzale Flaminio or bus M from Stazione Termini, which departs every 15 minutes between 5pm and the end of the last performance.

Teatro Olimpico THEATRE

(Map p58; ☑06 326 59 91; www.teatroolimpico.it, in Italian; Piazza Gentile da Fabriano 17) This is home to the Accademia Filarmonica Romana (www.filarmonicaromana.org, in Italian), one of Rome's most important classical music organisations. The theatre's program features everything from classical soloists to opera performances, multimedia events and regular ballet.

Opera

Rome's indoor opera season runs from December to June, then moves outside in summer, to the spectacular setting of the Terme di Caracalla.

Teatro dell'Opera di Roma   OPERA

(Map p90; ✆06 4807 8400; www.operaroma. it; Piazza Beniamino Gigli; ⏰box office 9am-5pm Mon-Sat, 9am-1.30pm Sun) After seeing the functional and Fascist-era exterior, the interior of Rome's premier opera house – all plush red and gilt – is a stunning surprise. This theatre has an impressive history: it premiered Puccini's *Tosca*, and Maria Callas sang here. Built in 1880, it was given a Fascist makeover in the 1920s. Contemporary productions don't always match the splendour of the setting, but you may get lucky. Tickets for the ballet cost anywhere between €12 and €80; for the opera you'll be forking out between €23 and €150.

Nightclubs

Rome is no nightlife nirvana, though there's plenty of late-night fun to be had if you seek it out. An evening out here starts late and goes on till early morning, with a good night finishing with a cappuccino and *cornetto* in one of the many early-opening cafes. Concerts are typically listed for 10pm, but don't kick off till around 11pm, and clubs usually don't warm up until well after 1am.

Some of the more popular clubs can be tricky to get into: men will often find themselves turned away. Drinks can also be expensive and of indifferent quality, whether mojito or beer; €10 per drink is usual, but many places charge €15. Ostiense, the postindustrial area spreading south of Piramide, is where serious clubbers head. It has an eclectic range of warehouse venues catering to tastes from tango to electrobeat.

Alternatively, get down to Testaccio at midnight and saunter to the end of Via Galvani – you'll find more clubs than at a Captain Caveman fancy-dress ball. Some of these are loud, boozy meat markets, but there's an undeniable buzz about it all, and there are a few havens of hip serving up cutting-edge tunes.

Circolo degli Artisti   LIVE MUSIC

(✆06 7030 5684; www.circoloartisti.it; Via Casilina Vecchia 42; ⏰7pm-2am Tue-Thu, to 4.30am Fri-Sun) One of Rome's nightlife venues that hits the spot, Circolo is *the* place for alternative music gigs. Friday night cracks open the electronica and house for gay night – Omogenic – and Saturday sees the fun-packed Screamadelica (punk-funk, ska and new

wave), usually also featuring a live band. There's even a cool garden bar and admission is either free or a snip.

Goa   NIGHTCLUB

(✆06 574 82 77; Via Libetta 13; ⏰11pm-4.30am Tue-Sun Oct-May) Goa is Rome's serious super-club, with international names (recent guests include 2ManyDJs), a fashion-forward crowd, podium dancers and heavies on the door. The night to head here, though, is Thursday, when top Italian DJ Claudio Coccoluto showcases the best of Europe's electronic music DJs. Lesbian night, Venus Rising (www.venusrising.it), hits Goa on the last Sunday of the month.

Micca Club   LIVE MUSIC

(✆06 8744 0079; www.miccaclub.com; Via Pietra Micca 7a; ⏰10pm-2am Mon, Tue & Thu, 10pm-4am Fri & Sat, 6pm-1am Sun Sep-Apr, Fri & Sat only May) At eclectic Micca, pop art and jelly-bright lighting fills ancient arched cellars. The program features everything from burlesque and the Italian Torture Garden to glam rock and swing, with loads of live gigs. There's an admission fee if a gig's on and at the weekend. Register online for discounts.

Villaggio Globale
LIVE MUSIC

(Map p96; www.ecn.org/villaggioglobale/joomla; Lungotevere Testaccio 1) For a warehouse-party vibe, head to Rome's best-known *centro sociale* (social centre), housed in the city's graffiti-sprayed ex-slaughterhouse. Entrance is usually around €5, beer is cheap, and the music focuses on dancehall, reggae, dubstep and drum 'n' bass.

Alexanderplatz
LIVE MUSIC

(Map p104; ☎06 3974 2171; www.alexanderplatz.it; Via Ostia 9; ☺7am-2pm Sep-Jun) Rome's top jazz joint attracts international performers and a passionate, knowledgeable crowd. You'll need to book a table if you want dinner, and the music starts around 10pm. In July and August the club ups sticks and transfers to the grounds of Villa Celimontana.

Conte Staccio
NIGHTCLUB

(Map p96; www.myspace.com\contestaccio; Via di Monte Testaccio 65b; ☺8pm-5am) With an under-the-stars terrace and arched interior, Conte Staccio is one of the most popular venues on the Testaccio clubbing strip, serving up a regular menu of DJs and live gigs. Admission is usually free during the week and cocktails are around €8.

Lettere Caffè
LIVE MUSIC

(Map p100; ☎06 9727 0991; www.letterecaffe.org; Via di San Francesco a Ripa 100-01; ☺7pm-2am, closed mid-Aug–mid-Sep) Like books? Poetry? Blues and jazz? Then you'll love this place – a clutter of barstools and books, where there are regular live gigs, poetry slams, comedy and gay nights, followed by DJ sets playing indie and new wave.

Locanda Atlantide
NIGHTCLUB

(Map p90; ☎06 4470 4540; www.locandatlantide.it; Via dei Lucani 22b; ☺usually 9pm-2am, Oct-Jun) Enter this backstreet, graffiti-covered door to tickle Rome's grungy underbelly: you'll descend into a cavernous place decked with retro junk to see poetry, alternative music, experimental theatre and performance art. It's good to know that punk is not dead.

Rialtosantambrogio
CULTURAL CENTRE

(Map p74; ☎06 6813 3640; www.rialto.roma.it; Via di San'Ambrogio 4) In the Ghetto, this ancient courtyard-centred building is Rome's most central *centro sociale*, with an art-school vibe. Its edgy program is open to all, with gigs, central Rome's best club nights, exhibitions and art-house cinema.

Big Mama
LIVE MUSIC

(Map p100; ☎06 581 25 51; www.bigmama.it; Vicolo di San Francesco a Ripa 18; annual membership €14; ☺9pm-1.30am, show 10.30pm Thu-Sat, closed Jun-Sep) To wallow in the Eternal City blues, there's only one place to go – this cramped Trastevere basement, which also hosts jazz, funk, soul and R&B.

AKAB
NIGHTCLUB

(Map p96; www.akabcave.com; Via di Monte Testaccio 68-69) This eclectic former workshop has an underground cellar, an upper floor, a garden and a whimsical door policy. On Tuesdays it's electronica L'Etrika, while it goes hip hop and R&B on Thursday. Expect local live (often cover) bands on Friday, R&B and house on Saturday. Entrance is €15, including a complimentary drink.

Dimmidisí
NIGHTCLUB

(Map p90; ☎06 446 18 55; www.dimmidisiroma.it; Via dei Volsci 126b) This intimate, small-scale, white-walled loft of a club is devoted to new music, including jazz, soul, dub, electronica and breakbeat. There are regular DJs and it's a good place to see live bands.

Rising Love
NIGHTCLUB

(☎06 8952 0643; www.risinglove.it; Via delle Conce 14; ☺11pm-4am Tue-Sun Oct-May) For those who like their electro, techno, funky groove and an underground vibe, this white, industrial, arty cultural association will tick all the boxes. Guest DJs as well as local talent get the crowd rocking, and there are regular special nights.

Qube
NIGHTCLUB

(☎06 438 54 45; www.qubedisco.com; Via di Portonaccio 212; ☺10.30pm-5.30am Thu-Sat Oct-May) In Rome's eastern suburbs, the city's hugest disco offers Radio Rock night on Thursday and the superb gay night Muccassassina (www.muccassassina.com) on Friday, which attracts a mixed crowd. Saturday is Fruit Party, with regular international guest DJs.

Alpheus
NIGHTCLUB

(☎06 574 78 26; www.alpheus.it, in Italian; Via del Commercio 36; ☺Tue-Sun Oct-May) Alpheus hosts an eclectic array of sounds in its four rooms, including Argentine tango (plus lessons), hard rock and house, with plenty of live gigs. Saturday is the popular 'Gorgeous, I am' gay night, with lots of go-go dancers and guest DJs.

La Maison
NIGHTCLUB

(Map p74; www.lamaisonroma.it; Vicolo dei Granari 3) Join Rome's glossy see-and-be-seen crowd to flirt and frolic over poppy tunes and commercial house. La Maison is smooth, mainstream and exclusive, yet more fun than you might expect. That is, if you can get past the door-police.

Cinemas

Of Rome's 80-odd cinemas only a handful show films in the original language (marked VO or *versione originale* in listings). Expect to pay around €8, with many cinemas offering discounts on Wednesdays.

Warner Village Moderno
CINEMA

(Map p90; ✆892 111; Piazza della Repubblica 45) Film premieres are often held at this multiplex, which screens Hollywood blockbusters (both in English and Italian) and major-release Italian films.

Sport

Watching a football game at the impressive 70,000 seater **Stadio Olimpico** (Map p58; Foro Italico, Viale dei Gladiatori 2) is an unforgettable experience. Throughout the season (September to May) there's a game most Sundays involving one of the city's two teams: AS Roma, known as the *giallorossi* (yellow and reds; www.asroma.it), or Lazio, the *biancazzuri* (white and blues; www.sslazio.it, in Italian). Ticket prices start at €10 and can be bought at Lottomatica (lottery centres), the stadium, ticket agencies, www.listicket.it or one of the many Roma or Lazio shops around the city. Try the **AS Roma Store** (Map p74; Piazza Colonna 360) or **Lazio Point** (Map p90; Via Farini 34).

To get to the stadium take metro line A to Ottaviano and then bus 32.

🔒 Shopping

Tridente (Map p84) is where you'll find all the big designer names. Prada, Gucci, Salvatore Ferragamo, Dolce & Gabbana, Missoni, Moschino, Valentino, Emporio Armani and Versace are all dotted on and around the grid of streets stretching south of Piazza di Spagna, with Via Condotti as the area's beautifully clad backbone.

Vintage shops and smaller designer boutiques dot the wonderful Via del Governo Vecchio (Map p74). If you're looking for antiques or unusual gifts, try Via dei Coronari (Map p74) or Via dei Banchi Vecchi (Map p74). Via Margutta (Map p84) is lined with upmarket art galleries and antique shops.

Time your visit to coincide with the *saldi* (sales) and you'll pick up some great bargains, although you'll need to be up for some bare-knuckle shopping. Winter sales run from early January to mid-February and summer sales from July to early September.

Armando Rioda
ARTISANAL

(Map p84; Via Belsiana 90) Looking longingly at the accessory shops of Via Condotti, but can't afford an exquisitely made big-name handbag? Climb the well-worn stairs to this workshop, choose from a swatch of the softest leathers, and you can shortly be the proud owner of a handmade, designer-style bag, wallet, belt or briefcase. If you have a bag specially made, you're looking at around €200 to €250.

Confetteria Moriondo & Gariglio
SWEETS & PASTRIES

(Map p74; Via del Piè di Marmo 21-22) We're with Roman poet Trilussa, who dedicated several sonnets to this place. It's no ordinary sweetshop but a bygone temple of bonbons. Rows of handmade chocolates and sweets (more than 80 varieties, many made to historical recipes) lie in ceremonial splendour in old-fashioned glass cabinets.

Bottega di Marmoraro
ARTISANAL

(Map p84; Via Margutta 53b) This particularly charismatic hole-in-the-wall shop is lined with marble carvings, where you can get marble tablets engraved with any inscription you like (€15). Peer inside at lunchtime and you might see the *marmoraro* (marble artisan) cooking a pot of tripe for his lunch on the open log fire.

Sermoneta
ACCESSORIES

(Map p84; ✆06 679 19 60; Piazza di Spagna 61; ⏰9.30am-8pm Mon-Sat, 10.30am-7pm Sun) Buying leather gloves in Rome is a rite of passage for some, and this is *the* shop to do it. At Rome's most famous glove-seller, choose from a kaleidoscopic range of top-quality leather and suede gloves from €29. Expert assistants will size up your hand in a glance. Just don't expect them to smile.

Luna & L'Altra
FASHION

(Map p74; Piazza Pasquino 76) One of a number of independent fashion boutiques on and around Via del Governo Vecchio, this reverential gallery-like space stocks clothes and accessories by hip designers Issey Miyake, Dries Van Noten, Rick Owen and Yohji Yamamoto.

Danielle
SHOES

(Map p84; ☏06 6792467; Via Frattina 85a) If you're female and in need of an Italian-made shoe fix, this is an essential stop on your itinerary, for both classic and fashionable styles – including foxy heels, boots and ballet pumps – made in soft leather, in myriad colours and at extremely reasonable prices.

TAD
DEPARTMENT STORE

(Map p84; ☏06 3269 5131; Via del Babuino 155a) TAD is a conceptual store that sells an entire lifestyle. Here you can get kitted out in Chloe or Balenciaga, have a haircut, buy scent and flowers, and furnish your apartment with wooden daybeds and perspex dining chairs. Don't forget to pick up hip soundtracks to your perfect life from the CD rack. The serene Italian-Asian cafe is the perfect ladies-who-lunch pit stop.

Borsalino
ACCESSORIES

(Map p84; ☏06 3265 0838; Piazza del Popolo 20; ⊙10am-7.30pm Mon-Sat, 10.30am-7.30pm Sun) Romans really cut a dash in a hat, but don't fret – you can learn. Borsalino is *the* Italian hatmaker, favoured by 1920s criminal Al Capone, Japanese Emperor Hirohito and Humphrey Bogart. Think fedoras, pork-pie styles, felt cloches and woven straw caps.

Mario Pelle
ARTISANAL

(Map p84; Via Vittoria 15; ⊙Mon-Fri) Ring the bell at this unassuming doorway and hurry up flights of stairs to a family-run leather workshop that feels like it hasn't changed for decades. The elderly artisans create belts (€70 to €100), watch straps (€40 to €90), bags, picture frames, travel cases and other such elegant stuff. You can take along a buckle or watch to which you want a belt or strap fitted.

Fausto Santini
SHOES

(Map p84; ☏06 678 41 14; Via Frattina 120; ⊙11am-7.30pm Mon, 10am-7.30pm Tue-Sat, 11am-2pm & 3-7pm Sun) Style mavens adore Roman designer Fausto Santini for his simple, architectural shoe designs. Colours are beautiful and the quality impeccable. For bargains, check out the outlet shop, Giacomo Santini (Map p90; Via Cavour 106), where stock from previous seasons is discounted up to half-price. Both shops sell bags, too.

Ibiz – Artigianato in Cuoio
ACCESSORIES

(Map p74; Via dei Chiavari 39) In this pint-sized workshop, Elisa Nepi and her father craft exquisite, well-priced leather goods – including wallets, bags, belts and sandals – in simple designs and rainbow colours. With €40 you can pick up a wallet, purse or pair of sandals.

Nardecchia
ART

(Map p74; Piazza Navona 25) This historical Piazza Navona shop specialises in antique prints, ranging from 18th-century etchings of Rome by Giovanni Battista Piranesi to more-affordable 19th-century prints. Reckon on about €120 for a small framed print.

Feltrinelli
BOOKSTORE

(Map p74; www.lafeltrinelli.it, in Italian; Largo di Torre Argentina 11; ⊙9am-8pm Mon-Fri, 9am-10pm Sat, 10am-9pm Sun) Italy's most famous bookseller (and publisher) has shops across the capital. This one has a wide range of books (in Italian) on art, photography, cinema and history, as well as an extensive selection of Italian literature and travel guides in various languages, including English. You'll also find CDs, DVDs and a range of stationery products.

Officina della Carta
ARTISANAL

(Map p100; ☏06 589 55 57; Via Benedetta 26b; ⊙10am-1pm & 3.30-7.30pm Mon-Sat) This tiny workshop produces delicately hand-painted, paper-bound boxes, photo albums, recipe books, notepads, photo frames and diaries, as well as charming marionette theatres.

Ai Monasteri
COSMETICS

(Map p74; www.monasteri.it; Corso del Rinascimento 72) This apothecary-like shop stocks all-natural cosmetics, sweets, honeys, jams and wines, all made by monks. Stock up on sage toothpaste, rose shampoo, cherry brandy and a mysterious-sounding elixir of love.

Vertecchi
ART

(Map p84; Via del Croce 70; ⊙3.30am-7.30pm Mon, 10am-7.30pm Tue-Sat) Ideal for last-minute gift buying, this large paperware and art shop has beautiful printed paper, and an amazing choice of notebooks, art stuff and trinkets.

Officina Profumo Farmaceutica di Santa Maria Novella
COSMETICS

(Map p74; Corso del Rinascimento 47) This historical perfumery was established in Florence by Dominican friars in 1221 and has been concocting seductive scents and unguents ever since. Like Ai Monasteri, it sells all-natural perfumes, cosmetics, herbal infusions, teas and potpourri.

Furla
ACCESSORIES

(Map p84; ☑06 6920 0363; Piazza di Spagna 22)
Popular local chain Furla offers well-priced,
well-made bags, wallets, umbrellas and belts
in candy-bright colours. Other branches are
dotted all over town.

Porta Portese Flea Market
MARKET

(Piazza Porta Portese) To see another side of
Rome, head to this mammoth flea market.
With thousands of stalls selling everything
from rare books and spare bike parts to Pe-
ruvian shawls and MP3 players, it's crazily
busy and a lot of fun. Keep your valuables
safe and wear your haggling hat.

Scala Quattordici
FASHION

(Map p100; ☑06 588 35 80; Via della Scala 13-14)
Make yourself over à la Audrey Hepburn
with these classically tailored clothes in
beautiful fabrics – either bespoke or off the
peg. It's pricey (a frock will set you back
€600 or so) but oh so worth it.

Centro Russia Ecumenica
Il Messaggio dell'Icona
ART, SOUVENIRS

(Map p104; Borgo Pio 141) Nuns and priests
from around the world pop into this serene
shop to buy religious-themed prints and
postcards, prayer cards and original painted
icons, some glinting with real gold leaf.

Feltrinelli International
BOOKSTORE

(Map p90; ☑06 482 78 78; Via Orlando 84-86;
☺9am-8pm Mon-Sat, 10.30am-1pm & 4-8pm
Sun) Mainly English-language stock, with a
smattering of French, Spanish etc.

Anglo-American Book Co
BOOKSTORE

(Map p84; ☑06 679 52 22; www.aab.it; Via della
Vite 102; ☺10am-7.30pm Tue-Sat, 3.30-7.30pm
Mon) Literature, travel guides and reference
books in English. Also has a kids' section.

Borri Books
BOOKSTORE

(Map p90; ☑06 482 84 22; Stazione Termini;
☺7am-11pm Mon-Sat, 8am-10pm Sun) There's a
good selection of English-language books
(including kids' and travel books) in this
Stazione Termini shop.

❶ Information

Emergency
Ambulance (☑118)
Police (☑113/112)
Main police station (Questura; ☑06 46 86;
Via San Vitale 11)

Internet Access
Costs are usually between €4 and €6 per hour.

INFO BY PHONE

The Comune di Roma (city council) runs
a free multilingual **tourist information
line** (☑06 06 08; www.060608.it; ☺9am-
9pm), providing information on culture,
shows, hotels and transport. You can
also book theatre, concert, exhibition
and museum tickets on this number.
If you need information, the city's free
☑06 06 08 number is useful. By calling it you reach a Comune di Roma call
centre staffed 24 hours, with English-,
French-, Arabic-, German-, Spanish-,
Italian- and Chinese-speaking staff
available from 4pm to 7pm. The Comune also publishes the useful monthly
L'Evento (What's On) pamphlet, as well
as *Un Ospite a Roma* (A Guest in Rome;
www.unospitearoma.it, www.aguestinrome.
com). These, and other information
(including maps), can be picked up at
tourist information points.

Internet Point (Via dei Serpenti 89; per hr €4;
☺8am-10pm) Close to Via Nazionale.

Media
The following are all published in English, apart
from *Roma C'è*, which has an English section.

Osservatore Romano (www.vatican.va) Weekly
editions of the Vatican's official daily newspaper
online.

Roma C'è (www.romace.it) Comprehensive
listings magazine with an English section (€1);
published on Wednesday and sold at newsstands.

Wanted in Rome (www.wantedinrome.com) A
free online version of this useful expat magazine
(€1) is updated every second Wednesday and
features classified ads, listings and reviews.

Medical Services
Rather than go to a *pronto soccorso* (Accident
and Emergency) department, you can try calling
the **Guardia Medica** (☑06 570600). You can
also call a private doctor to come to your hotel
or apartment. Call-out/treatment fee will probably be around €130, but worth it if you have
insurance. Try **Roma Medica** (☑338 622 4832;
☺24 hr). Night pharmacies are listed in daily
newspapers and in pharmacy windows.

Ospedale di Odontoiatria G Eastman (☑06
84 48 31; Viale Regina Elena 287b) For emergency dental treatment.

Ospedale San Giacomo (☑06 3 62 61; Via A
Canova 29)

Ospedale Santo Spirito (☎06 6 83 51; Lungotevere in Sassia 1)

Pharmacy Piazza Cinquecento (☎06 488 00 19; Piazza Cinquecento 51; ⏰24hr); Stazione Termini (⏰7.30am-10pm)

Policlinico Umberto I (☎06 4 99 71, first aid 06 4997 9501; Viale del Policlinico 155) Near Stazione Termini.

Money

There are ATMs and exchange booths at Stazione Termini (Map p90), Fiumicino Airport and Ciampino Airport. In town, there are loads of ATMs and exchange booths, including: **American Express** (☎06 6 76 41; Piazza di Spagna 38; ⏰9am-5.30pm Mon-Fri, 9am-12.30pm Sat).

Post

There are post office branches at Via delle Terme di Diocleziane 30 (Map p90), Via della Scrofa 61/63 (Map p74), Stazione Termini (Map p90; next to platform 24) and Via Arenula (Map p86).

Main post office (Piazza di San Silvestro 20; ⏰8.30am-6.30pm Mon-Fri, 8.30am-1pm Sat) Collect poste restante mail here.

Tourist Information

Enjoy Rome (Map p90; ☎06 445 18 43; www.enjoyrome.com; Via Marghera 8a; ⏰9am-5.30pm Mon-Fri, 8.30am-2pm Sat) An excellent private tourist office that runs tours and publishes the free and useful *Enjoy Rome* city guide.

Rome Tourist Board (APT; ☎06 06 08; www.romaturismo.it; ⏰9am-6pm) Has an office at Fiumicino Airport in Terminal B, International Arrivals.

There are tourist information points dotted around town, including the following:

Castel Sant'Angelo (Map p104; Piazza Pia; ⏰9.30am-7pm)

Ciampino Airport (International Arrivals, baggage reclaim area; ⏰9am-6.30pm)

Fiumicino Airport (Terminal C, International Arrivals; ⏰9am-6.30pm)

Piazza Navona (Map p74; ⏰9.30am-7pm)

Piazza Santa Maria Maggiore (Map p90; Via dell'Olmata; ⏰9.30am-7pm)

Piazza Sonnino (Map p100; ⏰9.30am-7pm)

Stazione Termini (Map p90; ⏰8am-8.30pm) Next to platform 24.

Trevi Fountain (Map p86; Via Marco Minghetti; ⏰9.30am-7pm) This tourist point is nearer to Via del Corso than the fountain.

Via Nazionale (Map p86; ⏰9.30am-7pm)

Travel Agencies

CTS (www.cts.it, in Italian) Corso Vittorio Emanuele II (☎06 687 26 72; Corso Vittorio Emanuele II 297); Via degli Ausoni (☎06 445 01 41; Via degli Ausoni 5); Via Solferino (☎06 462 0431; Via Solferino 6a) Italy's official student travel service offers discounted air, rail and bus tickets to students and travellers aged under 30, as long as you have a EURO<26 Youth Card or an International Student Identity Card (ISICs, which CTS also issue). Otherwise you need a CTS card, which costs €30 (€15 for students over 12) and is valid for 14 months.

Websites

Enjoy Rome (www.enjoyrome.com) Useful advice from an independent tourist agency.

In Rome Now (www.inromenow.com) Savvy internet magazine compiled by two American expats.

Parla Food (www.parlafood.com) Lippy American food blog with excellent blog links.

Roma Turismo (www.romaturismo.it) Rome Tourist Board's comprehensive website. Lists all official accommodation options, upcoming events and more.

❶ Getting There & Away

Air

Rome's main international airport **Leonardo da Vinci** (☎06 6 59 51; www.adr.it), better known as Fiumicino, is on the coast 30km west of the city. The much smaller **Ciampino Airport** (☎06 6 59 51; www.adr.it), 15km southeast of the city centre, is the hub for low-cost carriers such as **Ryanair** (www.ryanair.com) and **easyJet** (www.easyjet.com). **Left-luggage** (International Arrivals, Terminal 3; per 24hr €6; ⏰6.30am-11.30pm) is available at Fiumicino.

Boat

Rome's port is at Civitavecchia, about 80km north of Rome. Main ferry companies:

Sardinia Ferries (☎199 400500; www.corsica-ferries.it) To/from Golfo Aranci (Sardinia).

Grimaldi Lines (☎081 464444; www.grimaldi-lines.com) To/from Catania (Sicily), Trapani (Sicily), Porto Torres (Sardinia), Barcelona (Spain), Malta and Tunis (Tunisia).

SNAV (☎081 4285555; www.snav.it) To/from Palermo (Sicily) and Olbia (Sardinia).

Tirrenia (☎892 123; www.tirrenia.it) To/from Arbatax, Cagliari and Olbia (all Sardinia).

Bookings can be made at the Termini-based **Agenzia 365** (⏰7am-9pm), at travel agents or online at www.traghettiweb.it. You can also buy directly at the port.

Half-hourly trains depart from Roma Termini to Civitavecchia (€4.50 to €12.50, one hour). On arrival, it's about 700m to the port (to your right) as you exit the station.

From Stazione Termini you can catch trains to the following cities and many others. All fares quoted are 2nd class.

TO	SERVICE TYPE	FARE (€)	DURATION (HR)
Florence	fast	45	1½
	slow	17.05	4
Milan	fast	91	3½
	medium	49.50	6¾
Naples	fast	45	1½
	slow	10.50	2¾
Palermo	day	65.50-98.50	11-13½
	night	56.50-92.50	11-13½
Venice	fast	76	3¾
	medium	45.50	5½

Bus

Long-distance national and international buses use the **Autostazione Tiburtina** (Piazzale Tiburtina) in front of Stazione Tiburtina, east of the city centre. Take metro line B from Termini to Tiburtina. You can get tickets at the bus terminus or at travel agencies. Bus operators:

Interbus (☑091 34 25 25; www.interbus.it, in Italian) To/from Sicily.

Marozzi (☑080 579 01 11; www.marozzivt.it, in Italian) To/from Sorrento, Bari, Matera and Lecce.

SENA (☑0861 199 19 00; www.senabus.it) To/from Siena and Tuscany.

Sulga (☑800 099661; www.sulga.it, in Italian) To/from Perugia, Assisi and Ravenna.

For destinations in the Lazio region, **Cotral** (☑800 174471; www.cotralspa.it) buses depart from numerous points throughout the city. The company is linked with Rome's public transport system, which means that you can buy tickets that cover city buses, trams, metro and train lines, as well as regional buses and trains.

Car & Motorcycle

Driving into central Rome is a challenge, involving traffic restrictions, one-way systems, a shortage of street parking, and aggressive drivers.

Rome is circled by the Grande Raccordo Anulare (GRA) to which all autostradas (motorways) connect, including the main A1 north–south artery (the Autostrada del Sole) and the A12, which connects Rome to Civitavecchia and Fiumicino Airport.

Car hire is available at both airports and Stazione Termini from the following:

Avis (☑06 481 43 73; www.avisautonoleggio.it)

Europcar (☑06 488 28 54; www.europcar.com)

Hertz (☑06 474 03 89; www.hertz.com)

Maggiore National (☑06 488 00 49; www.maggiore.com)

Train

Almost all trains arrive at and depart from **Stazione Termini** (Map p90), Rome's principal station. There are regular connections to other European countries, all major Italian cities, and many smaller towns.

Train information is available from the **train information office** (☉6am-midnight) next to platform 1, online at www.ferroviedellostato.it, or (if you speak Italian) by calling ☑89 20 21. **Left luggage** (1st 5hr €4, 6-12hr per hr €0.60, 13hr & over per hr €0.20; ☉6am-11.50pm) is on the lower-ground floor under platform 24. Rome's other principal train stations are Stazione Tiburtina, Stazione Roma-Ostiense and Stazione Trastevere.

❶ Getting Around

To/From the Airport

FIUMICINO The easiest way to get to/from the airport is by train, but there are also bus services if you need transport in the wee hours. By taxi, the set fare to/from the city centre is €40, which is valid for up to four passengers with luggage. Note that taxis registered in Fiumicino charge a set fare of €60, so make sure you catch a Comune di Roma taxi.

Leonardo Express train (adult/child €14/free) Runs to/from platforms 27 and 28 at Stazione Termini. Departures from Termini every 30 minutes between 5.52am and 10.52pm; from the airport between 6.36am and 11.36pm. Journey time is 30 minutes.

FR1 train (one way €8) Connects the airport to Trastevere, Ostiense and Tiburtina stations. Departures from the airport every 15 minutes (hourly on Sunday and public holidays) between 5.57am and 11.27pm; from Tiburtina between 5.05am and 10.33pm.

Airport Shuttle (☑06 4201 3469; www.air portshuttle.it) Transfers to/from your hotel for €25 for one person, then €6 for each additional passenger up to a maximum of eight.

Cotral bus (www.cotralspa.it; one way €4.50 or €7 if bought on bus) Runs to/from Stazione Tiburtina via Stazione Termini. Night departures from Tiburtina at 12.30am, 1.15am, 2.30am and 3.45am and from the airport at 1.15am, 2.15am, 3.30am and 5am. Journey time is one hour.

CIAMPINO The best option is to take one of the regular bus services into the city centre. You can also take a bus to Ciampino train station and then pick up a train to Stazione Termini. By taxi, the set rate to/from the airport is €30.

Airport Shuttle (☑06 4201 3469; www.air portshuttle.it) Transfers to/from your hotel for €25 for one person, then €5 for each additional passenger up to a maximum of eight.

Terravision bus (www.terravision.eu; one way/return €4/8) Twice-hourly departures to/from Via Marsala outside Stazione Termini. From the airport services are between 8.15am and 12.15am; from Via Marsala between 4.30am and 9.20pm. Buy tickets at Terracafè in front of the Via Marsala bus stop. Journey time is 40 minutes.

Cotral bus (www.cotralspa.it; one way/return €3.90/6.90) Runs 15 daily services to/from Via Giolitti near Stazione Termini. Also buses to/from Anagnina metro station (€1.20) and Ciampino train station (€1.20), where you can connect with trains to Stazione Termini (€1.30).

Car & Motorcycle

ACCESS & PARKING Most of the historical centre is closed to normal traffic from 6.30am to 6pm Monday to Friday, from 2pm to 6pm Saturday, and from 11pm to 3am Friday to Sunday. Restrictions also apply in Trastevere (6.30am-10am Mon-Sat, 11pm-3am Fri-Sun), San Lorenzo (9pm-3am Fri-Sun), Monti (11pm-3am Fri-Sun) and Testaccio (11pm-3am Fri-Sun).

All streets accessing the 'Limited Traffic Zone' (ZTL) have been equipped with electronic-access detection devices. If you're staying in this zone, contact your hotel, which will fax the authorities with your number plate, thus saving you a fine. For details, check www.agenziamo-bilita.roma.it or call ☑06 57 003.

Blue lines denote pay-and-display parking spaces with tickets available from meters (coins only) and *tabaccaio* (tobacconist's shop). Expect to pay up to €1.20 per hour between 8am and 8pm (11pm in some places). After 8pm (or 11pm) parking is free until 8am the next morning. If your car gets towed away, check with the **traffic police** (☑06 6 76 91). Car parks:

Piazzale dei Partigiani (per hr/day €0.77/5; ⊘24hr)

Stazione Termini (Piazza dei Cinquecento; per hr/day €2/18; ⊘6am-1am)

Stazione Tiburtina (Via Pietro l'Eremita; weekday/Sun per hr €2/free; ⊘6am-10pm)

Villa Borghese (Viale del Galoppatoio 33; per hr/day €2/20; ⊘24hr)

SCOOTER HIRE To hire a scooter you'll need a credit card and photo ID. You may also have to leave a cash deposit. Reliable operators:

Bici e Baci (☑06 482 84 43; www.bicibaci.com; Via del Viminale 5; per day scooters €19-80)

BUSES FROM TERMINI

From Piazza dei Cinquecento outside Stazione Termini buses run to all corners of the city.

DESTINATION	BUS NO
Campo de' Fiori	40/64
Colosseum	75
Pantheon	40/64
Piazza Navona	40/64
Piazza Venezia	40/64
St Peter's Square	40
Terme di Caracalla	714
Trastevere	H
Villa Borghese	910

Eco Move Rent (📞06 4470 4518; www.ecomoverent.com; Via Varese 48-50; per day scooters €45-95)

Public Transport

Rome's public transport system includes buses, trams, metro and a suburban train network.

TICKETS These are valid for all forms of transport and come in various forms:

Single (BIT; €1) Valid for 75 minutes, during which time you can use as many buses or trams as you like, but can only go once on the metro.

Daily (BIG; €4) Unlimited travel until midnight of the day of purchase.

Three-day (BTI; €11) Unlimited travel for three days.

Weekly (CIS; €16) Unlimited travel for seven days.

Children under 10 travel free. Note also that tickets do not include routes to Fiumicino Airport. Buy tickets at *tabacchi*, newsstands and from vending machines at main bus stops and metro stations. They must be purchased before you start your journey and validated in the yellow machines on buses, at the entrance gates to the metro or at train stations. Ticketless riders risk an on-the-spot €50 fine.

The **Roma Pass** (see the boxed text, p66) comes with a three-day travel pass valid within the city boundaries. The **Vatican and Rome card** (1/2/3 days €19/21/25) provides unlimited travel on all public transport within the city and on the Open buses operated by Roma Cristiana (p115). Buy them online at www.operaromanapellegrinaggi.org (click on the Roma Cristiana Experience/Open Bus links) or at the Roma Cristiana meeting point near Piazza San Pietro.

BUS & TRAM Both buses and trams are run by **ATAC** (📞06 57 003; www.atac.roma.it). The **main bus station** (Map p90; Piazza dei Cinquecento) is in front of Stazione Termini, where there's an **information booth** (⏱7.30am-8pm). Largo di Torre Argentina, Piazza Venezia and Piazza San Silvestro are also important hubs. Buses generally run from about 5.30am until midnight, with limited services throughout the night.

Night buses operate on more than 20 lines, most of which pass Termini and/or Piazza Venezia. Buses are marked with an N after the number. Night-bus stops have a blue owl symbol. Departures usually occur every 30 minutes, but can be much slower.

METRO Rome has two metro lines, A (orange) and B (blue), which cross at Termini, the only point at which you can change from one line to the other. Take line A for the Trevi Fountain (Barberini), Spanish Steps (Spagna), and St Peter's (Ottaviano-San Pietro); and line B for the Colosseum (Colosseo).

Trains run between 5.30am and 11.30pm (to 1.30am on Friday and Saturday). However, until April 2012 line A is closing at 9pm every day except Saturday for construction work on a third line. To replace it there are two temporary bus lines: MA1 from Battistini to Arco di Travertino and MA2 from Piazzale Flaminio to Anagnina.

All the metro stations on line B have wheelchair access except for Circo Massimo, Colosseo and Cavour (direction Laurentina), while on line A Cipro-Musei Vaticani station is one of the few stations equipped with lifts.

OVERGROUND RAIL NETWORK Rome's overground rail network is useful only if you are heading out of town to the Castelli Romani, the beaches at Lido di Ostia or the ruins at Ostia Antica.

Taxi

Official licensed taxis are white with the symbol of Rome on the doors. Always go with the metered fare, never an arranged price (the set fares to and from the airports are exceptions). In town (within the ring road) flag fall is €2.80 between 7am and 10pm on weekdays, rising to €4 on Sundays and holidays, and €5.80 between 10pm and 7am. Then it's €0.92 per km. Official rates are posted in taxis and on www.viviromaintaxi.eu.

You can book a taxi by phoning the Comune di Roma's automated **taxi line** (📞06 06 09) or calling a taxi company direct. Note that when you call for a cab, the meter is switched on immediately and you pay for the cost of the journey from wherever the driver receives the call.

La Capitale (📞06 49 94)

Pronto Taxi (📞06 66 45)

Radio Taxi (📞06 35 70)

Samarcanda (📞06 55 51)

Tevere (📞06 41 57)

LAZIO

With a capital like Rome, it's unsurprising that the rest of Lazio gets overlooked. But when Rome starts to feel like the Eternal City for all the wrong reasons, do as the Romans do and leave the city behind. You'll discover a region that's not only beautiful – verdant and hilly in the north, parched and rugged in the south – but also a historical and cultural feast.

Ostia Antica

With preservation in places matching that of Pompeii, the ancient Roman port of Ostia Antica is an extraordinary site, where

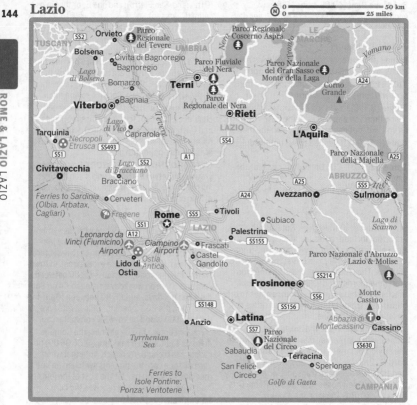

you can wander through complete Roman streets, gape at Roman toilets and see a Roman menu in situ.

Founded in the 4th century BC, Ostia (referring to the mouth or *ostium* of the Tiber) became a great port and later a strategic centre for defence and trade. Decline arrived in the 5th century AD when barbarian invasions and the outbreak of malaria led to the abandonment of the city, and then its slow burial – up to 2nd-floor level – in river silt, hence its survival. Pope Gregory IV re-established the town in the 9th century.

⊙ Sights

Scavi Archeologici di Ostia Antica   RUINS
(☑06 5635 2830; www.ostiantica.info, in Italian; Viale dei Romagnoli 717; adult/child €6.5/free, car park €2.50; ⊙8.30am-7pm Tue-Sun Apr-Oct, to 6pm Mar, to 5pm Nov-Feb, last admission 1hr before close) Providing a vivid picture of everyday Roman life, these ruins are spread out and

you'll need a few hours to do them justice. You can buy a handy map of the site from the ticket office for €2.

Ostia was a busy port until 42 AD, and the town is made up of restaurants, laundries, shops, houses and public meeting places, giving a good impression of what life here must have been like. The main thoroughfare, the **Decumanus Maximus**, runs over 1km from the city's entrance (the Porta Romana) to the Porta Marina, which originally led to the sea.

At one stage, Ostia had 20 bath complexes. The huge **Terme di Nettuno**, which occupied a whole block and dates from Hadrian's renovation of the port, has the most impressive mosaics, which you can view from a raised platform. They include a stunning one of Neptune driving his seahorse chariot, surrounded by sea monsters, mermaids and mermen. In the centre of the complex you'll find the remains of a large arcaded courtyard called the Palaestra, in which athletes used to train. There's an impressive mosaic here of four athletes engaged in boxing and wrestling.

Next to the baths is a good-sized amphitheatre, built by Agrippa and later enlarged to hold 3000 people. Stucco is still discernable in the entrance hall. Behind the amphitheatre is the Piazzale delle Corporazioni (Forum of the Corporations), the offices of Ostia's merchant guilds, which sport well-preserved mosaics depicting the different interests of each business.

Further towards the Porta Marina is one of the highlights of the site: the Thermopolium (the equivalent in contemporary Rome is the *tavola calda* – 'hot table'), an ancient cafe that's breathtakingly similar to our modern-day versions. There's a bar counter, a kitchen to the right and a small courtyard at the rear, where customers would have sat next to the fountain and relaxed over a drink. Above the bar is a fresco advertising the bill of fare. Across the road from here are some spectacularly well-preserved latrines, set in a sociable crescent, part of the Terme di Foro complex.

The site also has a more modern cafeteria/bar where you can buy *panini* and pasta dishes (but packing a picnic is a good idea), toilets, gift shop and museum, which houses statues and sarcophagi excavated on site.

Castello di Giulio II   CASTLE
(☑06 5635 8013; Piazza della Rocca; ⊘free guided tours 10am & noon Tue-Sun, plus 3pm Tue & Thu, max 30 people) Near the entrance to the excavations is this imposing castle, an impressive example of 15th-century military architecture, which lost its purpose when a freak flood changed the course of the river, making the location less accessible.

ⓘ Getting There & Away

From Rome, take metro line B to Piramide, then the Ostia Lido train from Stazione Porta San Paolo (next to the metro station), getting off at Ostia Antica. Trains leave about every half-hour and the trip takes approximately 25 minutes. It is covered by the standard BIT tickets (see p143). On arrival, exit Ostia Antica station and walk over the pedestrian bridge. Go straight ahead and you'll see the castle to your right and the ruins straight ahead.

The ruins are also easy to reach by car. Take Via del Mare, which runs parallel to Via Ostiense, or the A12 in the direction of Fiumicino, and follow the signs for the *scavi* (ruins).

Tivoli

POP 56,275 / ELEV 225M

For millennia, the hilltop town of Tivoli has been a summer escape for rich Romans, a status amply demonstrated by its two Unesco World Heritage Sites, Villa Adriana and Villa d'Este – holiday homes that are sumptuous hedonistic playgrounds.

More like a town than a villa, Villa Adriana was the country estate of Emperor Hadrian, while the 16th-century Villa d'Este is a wonder of the High Renaissance. You can visit both in a day, though you'll have to start early.

Information is available from the tourist information point (☑07 7431 3536; ⊘9am-5.30pm) on Piazza Garibaldi, where the bus arrives.

⊙ Sights

Villa Adriana   ARCHAEOLOGICAL SITE
(☑06 3996 7900; adult/reduced €8/4 parking €2; ⊘9am-7pm, last admission 5.30pm; ⊕) Emperor Hadrian's summer residence Villa Adriana, 5km outside Tivoli, set new standards of luxury when it was built between AD 118 and 134 – a remarkable feat given the excesses of the Roman Empire. A model near the entrance gives you an idea of the scale of the original complex, which you'll need several hours to explore. Consider hiring an audioguide (€5), which gives a helpful overview. There's a small cafeteria next to the ticket office, but a nicer option is to bring a picnic lunch or eat in Tivoli.

A great traveller and enthusiastic architect, Hadrian personally designed much of the complex, taking inspiration from buildings he'd seen around the world. The pecile, a large porticoed pool area where the emperor used to stroll after lunch, was a reproduction of a building in Athens. Similarly, the canopo is a copy of the sanctuary of Serapis near Alexandria, with a long canal of water, originally surrounded by Egyptian statues, representing the Nile.

To the east of the *pecile* is one of the highlights, Hadrian's private retreat, the Teatro Marittimo. Built on an island in an artificial pool, it was originally a mini-villa accessible only by swing bridges, which the emperor would have raised when he felt like a dip. Nearby, the fish pond is encircled by an underground gallery where Hadrian liked to wander. There are also nymphaeums, temples and barracks, and a museum with the latest discoveries from ongoing excavations (often closed).

Villa d'Este PALAZZO

(☎199 766 166, 0445 230310; www.villadestetivoli.info; Piazza Trento; adult/reduced €8/4; ⏲8.30am-1hr before sunset Tue-Sun; ♿) In Tivoli's hilltop centre, the steeply terraced gardens of Villa d'Este are a superlative example of the High Renaissance garden, dotted by fantastical fountains all powered by gravity alone. The villa was once a Benedictine convent, converted by Lucrezia Borgia's son, Cardinal Ippolito d'Este, into a pleasure palace in 1550. From 1865 to 1886 it was home to Franz Liszt and inspired his compositions *To the Cypresses of the Villa d'Este* and *The Fountains of the Villa d'Este*.

The rich mannerist frescoes of the villa interior merit a glance, but it's the garden that you're here for: water-spouting gargoyles and elaborate avenues lined with deep-green, knotty cypresses. One fountain (designed by Gian Lorenzo Bernini) used its water pressure to play an organ concealed in the top part of its structure, and this plays regularly throughout the day. Another highlight is the 130m-long path of the Hundred Fountains, which joins the Fountain of Tivoli to the Fountain of Rome.

The villa is a two-minute walk north from Largo Garibaldi. Picnics are forbidden, but there's a stylish cafe, or numerous restaurants in town, including **Trattoria del Falcone** (☎07 7431 2358; Via del Trevio 34; meals €30; ⏲Wed-Mon), a lively trattoria with exposed-stone walls that's been serving up classic pasta dishes since 1918.

ℹ Getting There & Around

Tivoli is 30km east of Rome and is accessible by Cotral bus from outside the Ponte Mammolo station on metro line B (€1.60, every 15 minutes, 50 minutes). However, it's best to buy a Zone 3 BIRG ticket (€6), which will cover you for the whole day.

The easiest way to visit both sites is to visit the Villa D'Este first, as it is close to Tivoli town centre. Then take the Cotral bus back towards Ponte Mammolo (€1) from Largo Garibaldi, asking the driver to stop close to Villa Adriana. After visiting the villa, you can then take the same bus (€2, 50 minutes) back to Ponte Mammolo.

By car you can either take Via Tiburtina or, to save yourself some time, the Rome–L'Aquila autostrada (A24).

Cerveteri

POP 35,700 / ELEV 81M

The highly cultured ancient Etruscans had some of their most powerful strongholds in the north of Lazio. Dating from around 800 BC, the Etruscans used sophisticated architectural and artistic techniques that the Romans later adapted and claimed as their own. They were a major thorn in Roman flanks until the 3rd and 4th centuries BC, when successive waves of legionnaires swept aside the last Etruscan defences. Cerveteri and Tarquinia were two of the major city-states in the Etruscan League; together they form a Unesco World Heritage Site.

Cerveteri, or Kysry to the Etruscans and Caere to Latin-speakers, was one of the most important commercial centres in the Mediterranean from the 7th to the 5th centuries BC. As Roman power grew, however, so Cerveteri's fortunes faded, and in 358 BC the city was annexed by Rome.

The first half of the 19th century saw the first tentative archaeological explorations in the area, and in 1911 systematic excavations began in earnest.

For information about the site, visit the helpful **tourist information point** (☎06 9955 2637; Piazza Aldo Moro; ⏲9.30am-1.30pm).

Necropoli di Banditaccia NECROPOLIS

(☎06 3996 7150; Via del Necropoli; admission/reduced €6/3, incl museum €8/4; ⏲8.30am-1hr before sunset; ♿) This 10-hectare necropolis is laid out as an afterlife townscape, with streets, squares and terraces of tombs. The most common type of construction is the tumulus, a circular structure cut into the earth and topped by a cumulus – a topping of turf. Signs indicate the path to follow and some of the major tombs, including the 6th-century-BC **Tomba dei Rilievi**, are decorated with painted reliefs of figures from the underworld, cooking implements and other household items.

Museo Nazionale di Cerveteri MUSEUM

(Piazza Santa Maria; admission €6/3, incl necropolis €8/4; ⏲8.30am-7.30pm Tue-Sun) In Cerveteri's medieval town centre is this splendid museum, where treasures taken from the tombs help to bring the dead to life – figuratively, at least.

Antica Locanda
le Ginestre
TRADITIONAL ITALIAN €€

(☑06 994 06 72; Piazza Santa Maria 5; meals €35; ☺Tue-Sun) This highly recommended, top-notch family-run restaurant has delicious food prepared with organically grown local produce and is served in the elegant dining room or flower-filled courtyard garden. Book ahead.

❶ Getting There & Around

Cerveteri is easily accessible from Rome by regular Cotral bus (€3.50, 55 minutes, hourly) from outside the Cornelia metro stop on metro line A. When you arrive at Cornelia, go up the escalators and onto the main road – the stop is on the same side of the street a little way from the metro entrance (look for the Cotral sign). Buses leave Cerveteri for Rome from the main square, at the bottom of the staircase coming from the museum.

From the information point, take an hourly shuttle bus to the the tomb complex 2km out of town. The bus leaves seven to nine times per day starting at 8.30am and finishing at 5pm (earlier in winter; €0.70). The trip takes five minutes and costs €1. Alternatively, follow the well-signposted road – it's a pleasant 15-minute walk.

By car, take either Via Aurelia (SS1) or the Civitavecchia autostrada (A12) and exit at Cerveteri-Ladispoli.

Tarquinia

POP 16,560 / ELEV 169M

Tarquinia is another fascinating Unesco World Heritage Site, with a necropolis of around 6000 tombs. The town alone, with its well-preserved medieval centre, is worth a visit in its own right, especially as it has a fantastic Etruscan museum housed in a beautiful medieval *palazzo*. Legend suggests that the town was founded towards the end of the Bronze Age in the 12th century BC. Later home to the Tarquin kings of Rome before the creation of the Roman Republic, it reached its prime in the 4th century BC, before a century of struggle ended with surrender to Rome in 204 BC.

For information about the town and its sights, pop into the **tourist office** (☑0766 84 92 82; info@tarquinia@apt.it; Piazza Cavour 1; ☺9am-1pm & 4.30-7.30pm), which is on your left as you walk through the town's medieval gate (Barriera San Giusto).

Museo Nazionale Tarquiniese   MUSEUM
(☑06 3996 7150; Piazza Cavour; adult/child €6/3, incl necropolis €8/4; ☺8.30am-7.30pm Tue-Sun)

Just beyond the tourist office is the exquisite 15th-century Palazzo Vitelleschi, a courtyard-centred house that contains this fine museum. Highlights of its collection are a breathtaking terracotta frieze of winged horses (the Cavalli Alati) and several complete frescoed tombs on the upper floors, full of incredibly vibrant paintings.

Tarquina Necropolis   NECROPOLIS
(☑06 3996 7150; adult/child €6/3, incl museum adult/child €8/4; ☺8.30am-1hr before sunset Tue-Sun; ♿) To see the famous painted tombs in situ, head to this necropolis, 2km from town. There are around 6000 tombs in this area, of which around 200 are painted. The first digs began here in 1489. Now protected by Unesco, the tombs have suffered centuries of exposure and are maintained at constant temperatures, and are visible through glass partitions. There are some beautiful hunting and fishing scenes in the Tomba della Caccia e della Pesca; scenes featuring dancers, she-lions and dolphins in the Tomba delle Leonesse; and a surprising S&M scene of a man whipping a woman in the Tomba della Fustigazione (Tomb of the Flogging).

To get to the necropolis from the tourist office, walk up Corso Vittorio Emanuele and turn right at Piazza Nazionale into Via di Porta Tarquinia. Continue past the Chiesa di San Francesco and then down Via Ripagretta until you see the necropolis on your left. Alternatively, a shuttle bus leaves from outside the tourist office (free, every 20 minutes 9am to 1pm and 4pm to 7pm Monday to Saturday), returning to town five minutes after it arrives at the necropolis. Alternatively, the local bus serving the necropolis also runs regularly and costs €0.70.

Il Cavatappi   TRADITIONAL ITALIAN €€
(☑07 6684 2303; Via dei Granari 19; meals €30; ☺Fri-Sun) The town has various decent lunch spots, including this one that's tucked away in the old town. It specialises in dishes made with local products and has a small streetside terrace; otherwise grab a picnic and head up to the town viewpoint at the top of Via Alberata Dante Alighieri.

❶ Getting There & Away

The best way to reach Tarquinia is by train; catch the train from Termini (€6.20, one hour and 20 minutes, half-hourly). Buy a return ticket, as the ticket office in Tarquinia only operates in the morning. After getting off at Tarquinia station, you'll need to catch the line BC shuttle bus to the centre of town.

By car, take the autostrada for Civitavecchia and then the Via Aurelia (SS1). Tarquinia is about 90km northwest of Rome.

Civitavecchia

POP 52,200

There's no compelling reason to come to Civitavecchia, other than to take a ferry to Sardinia, though you could make a stop long enough to eat at one of the good fish restaurants in this pleasant town. Established by Emperor Trajan in AD 106, it was later conquered by the Saracens, but regained importance as a papal stronghold in the 16th century. The medieval town was almost completely destroyed by bombing during WWII.

The port is about a 400m walk from the train station. As you leave the station, turn right into Viale Garibaldi and follow the road along the seafront. If you're stopping for a meal, try upmarket La Scaletta (0766 2 43 34; Lungoporto Gramsci Antonio 65).

ℹ️ Getting There & Away

BOAT For information on ferries to/from Sardinia, see the boxed text, p810.

BUS Cotral buses from Rome to Civitavecchia leave from outside the Cornelia station on metro line A (€4.50, 1½ hours, hourly). When you arrive at Cornelia, go up the escalators and onto the main road – the stop is on the same side of the street, a little way from the metro entrance (look for the Cotral sign). The bus stop in Civitavecchia is on Viale Guido Baccelli. Civitavecchia is covered by a Zone 5 BIRG ticket (€9).

TRAIN Regional services run regularly between Stazione Termini in Rome and Civitavecchia (€4.50, 1¼ hours), with fewer services on Sunday. Intercity services take 40 minutes, but cost €13.50. Civitavecchia station is close to the port.

Viterbo

POP 62,800 / ELEV 327M

Viterbo is a medieval gem with a beautiful and interesting city centre, despite having sustained WWII bomb damage. It makes a good base for exploring Lazio's rugged north, or can be visited on a day trip from Rome.

Founded by the Etruscans and eventually taken over by Rome, Viterbo developed into an important medieval centre, and in the 13th century became the residence of the popes. Papal elections were held in the Gothic Palazzo dei Papi where, in 1271, the entire college of cardinals was briefly imprisoned. The story goes that after three years of deliberation the cardinals still hadn't elected a new pope. Mad with frustration, the Viterbesi locked the dithering priests in a turreted hall and starved them into electing Pope Gregory X.

In addition to its historical appeal, Viterbo is famous for its therapeutic hot springs.

◉ Sights

FREE **Palazzo dei Priori**　　　PALAZZO
(Piazza del Plebiscito; ⊙9am-1pm & 3-7pm) The elegant Renaissance Piazza del Plebiscito is dominated by this imposing palace. Now home to the town council, it's worth venturing inside for the 16th-century frescoes that colourfully depict Viterbo's ancient origins – the finest are in the Sala Regia on the 1st floor. Outside, the elegant courtyard and fountain were added two centuries after the *palazzo* was built in 1460.

Cattedrale di San Lorenzo　　　CHURCH
(Piazza San Lorenzo) For an idea of how rich Viterbo once was, head to Piazza San Lorenzo, the religious heart of the medieval city. It was here that the cardinals came to vote for their popes and pray in the 12th century. Built originally to a simple Romanesque design, this cathedral owes its current Gothic look to a 14th-century makeover; later damage by Allied bombs meant the roof and nave had to be rebuilt.

Museo del Colle del Duomo　　　MUSEUM
(Piazza San Lorenzo; adult/reduced incl guided visit to Palazzo dei Papi, Sala del Conclave & Loggia €7/5; ⊙10am-1pm & 3-8pm Tue-Sun, to 6pm winter) Next door to the cathedral, this museum displays a small collection of religious artefacts, including a reliquary said to contain the chin(!) of John the Baptist.

Palazzo dei Papi　　　PALAZZO
(Piazza San Lorenzo; 0761 34 17 16) On the northern side of the square, this 13th-century *palazzo* was built to entice the papacy away from Rome. Head up the stairs to the graceful Gothic loggia (colonnade) to peer into the Sala del Conclave, the hall where five popes were elected.

Chiesa di Santa Maria Nuova
CHURCH

(Piazza Santa Maria Nuova; ⊙10am-1pm & 3-5pm) This 11th-century Romanesque church, the oldest in Viterbo, was restored to its original form after bomb damage in WWII. The cloisters are particularly lovely, and are believed to date from an earlier period.

Museo Nazionale Etrusco
MUSEUM

(⌛0761 32 59 29; Piazza della Rocca; admission €6; ⊙8.30am-7.30pm Tue-Sun) For a shot of Etruscan culture head to this museum, which has an interesting collection of local artefacts housed in an attractive *palazzo* by the town's northern entrance.

Chiesa di San Francesco
CHURCH

(⌛0761 34 16 96; Piazza San Francesco; ⊙8am-6.30pm) A short walk away from Museo Nazionale Etrusco is this Gothic church, which contains the tombs of two popes: Clement IV (d 1268) and Adrian V (d 1276). Both are attractively decorated, particularly that of Adrian, which features Cosmati work (multicoloured marble and glass mosaics set into stone and white marble).

Museo Civico
MUSEUM

(⌛0761 34 82 75; Piazza Crispi; admission €3.10; ⊙9am-7pm Tue-Sun summer, to 6pm winter) On the other side of town, this museum features more Etruscan goodies, as well as curious fake antiquities created in the 15th century by Annius of Viterbo, a monk and forger trying to give Viterbo extra kudos. There's also a small art gallery, the highlight of which is Sebastiano del Piombo's *Pietà*.

🛏 Sleeping & Eating

Tuscia Hotel
HOTEL €

(⌛0761 34 44 00; www.tusciahotel.com; Via Cairoli 41; s €44-50, d €68-76; 🅿 ❀) The best of the city's midrange options, this central, spick-and-span three-star place is leagues ahead of the competition in cleanliness and comfort. The rooms here are large, light and kitted out with satellite TV; nine rooms have aircon. There's a sunny roof terrace.

Agriturismo Antica Sosta
AGRITURISMO €

(⌛0761 25 13 69; SS Cassia Nord; s/d €40/70) Set in pea-green countryside 5km from Viterbo, this mansion has spacious, simple rooms. There's also a delicious restaurant (meals €35), serving scrumptious dishes such as *strozzapreti con salsiccia, porcini e pancetta* ('priest-strangler' pasta with sausage, porcini mushrooms and cured ham).

Ristorante Enoteca La Torre
WINE BAR €€€

(⌛0761 22 64 67; Via della Torre 5; meals €65; ⊙lunch Thu-Tue, dinner Thu-Wed) This is Viterbo's best restaurant: the Japanese chef combines precision and delicacy of presentation with innovative uses of fresh seasonal produce.

Ristorante Tre Re
TRATTORIA €€

(⌛0761 30 46 19; Via Gattesco 3; meals €35; ⊙Fri-Wed) This historical trattoria dishes up steaming plates of tasty local specialities and seasonally driven dishes. None is more typical than the *pollo alla viterbese*, excellent roast chicken stuffed with spiced potato and green olives.

Gran Caffè Schenardi
CAFE €

(⌛0761 34 58 60; Corso Italia 11-13) The Schenardi has been operating since 1818, and the wonderfully ornate interior looks like it hasn't changed much since, though the coffee and cakes are nothing out of the ordinary.

ℹ Information

Post office (Via Filippo Ascenzi) Opposite the tourist office.

Tourist office (⌛0761 32 59 92; www.provincia.vt.it, in Italian; Via Filippo Ascenzi; ⊙10am-1pm & 3-6pm Tue-Sun)

ℹ Getting There & Away

BUS From Rome, Cotral buses (€4.80, 1½ hours, every 30 minutes) depart from the Saxa Rubra station on the Ferrovia Roma-Nord train line. Catch the train (standard BIT) to Saxa Rubra from Piazzale Flaminio (just north of Piazza del Popolo). Viterbo is covered by a Zone 5 BIRG ticket (€9).

In Viterbo, ensure you get off at Porta Romana, not the intercity bus station at Riello, which is a few kilometres northwest of the town. If this happens, you can catch a bus into town (€1). Returning to Rome, take the bus from the Porta Romana or Piazzale Gramsci stops.

CAR & MOTORCYCLE Viterbo is about a 1½-hour drive up Via Cassia (SS2). Enter the old town through the Porta Romana onto Via Giuseppe Garibaldi, which becomes Via Cavour. The best bet for parking is either Piazza Martiri d'Ungheria or Piazza della Rocca.

TRAIN Services depart hourly from Monday to Saturday and every two hours on Sunday from Rome's Ostiense station (get off at Viterbo Porta Romana). The journey takes nearly two hours and costs €4.50 one way.

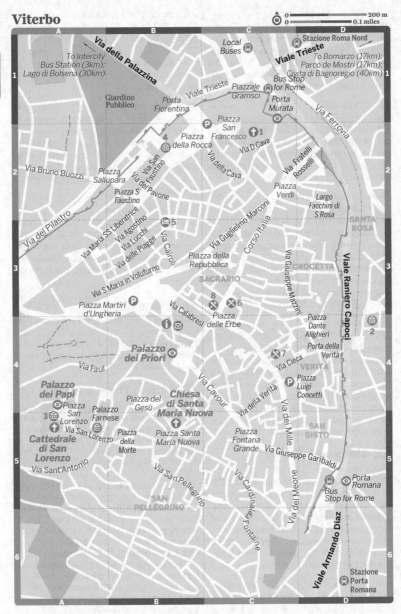

Around Viterbo

The main reason Romans go to Viterbo is for the thermal springs, about 3km west of town. The easiest to get to are the **Terme dei Papi** (☏0761 35 01; www.termedeipapi.it; Strada Bagni 12; pool €12, Sun €25; ☺9am-7pm Wed-Mon, plus 9.30pm-1am Sat), where you can take a dip in the sulphurous pool, have an invigorating massage (from €65 for 50 minutes) or treat yourself to a gloopy mudbath (from €15). Take the bus from Viterbo's Viale Trento (€1).

Viterbo

For less mud and more High Renaissance spectacle, head to the wonderful Villa Lante, 4km northeast of Viterbo at Bagnaia. This mannerist drama of a garden, with terraces, water cascades and gaily waving statues, forms part of the large, bucolic park (☑0761 28 80 08; admission €2; ⊗8.30am-1hr before sunset Tue-Sun) that surrounds the 16th-century villa. To get to Bagnaia from Viterbo, take the bus from Viale Trieste (€1).

Nearby, another Renaissance wonder is the pentagonal Palazzo Farnese (☑0761 64 60 52; admission €5; ⊗8.30am-6.45pm Tue-Sun), with its internal circular courtyard. It's at Caprarola, 20km southeast of Viterbo. The walls were started by a great military engineer, Antonio da Sangallo the Younger, then adapted by Vignal. The extraordinary interior contains paintings by some of the finest mannerist artists of the day. Don't miss the frescoes by Taddeo and Federico Zuccari in the Sala del Concilio di Trento. Regular buses leave from the Riello bus station just outside Viterbo for Caprarola (€2, 40 minutes).

At Bomarzo, 17km northeast of Viterbo, is a 16th-century curiosity that will entertain children and adults alike, the Parco dei Mostri (Monster Park; ☑0761 92 40 29; www.parcodeimostri.com; admission/reduced €10/8; ⊗8am-sunset). The gardens of the Palazzo Orsini are peopled by ancient gigantic sculptures, including an ogre, giant and a dragon. From Viterbo, catch the Cotral bus from Piazzale Giordano Bruno to Bomarzo (€0.60, 40 minutes), then follow the signs to Palazzo Orsini.

Around 32km north of Viterbo, in beautiful, emerald-green countryside, lies handsome Bagnoregio, from where you can visit *il paese che muore* (the dying town) of the Civita di Bagnoregio that it has replaced. This dramatically scenic hilltop town is accessible via a long bridge. Already on the decline, its fate was sealed by a serious 17th-century earthquake. Set on a piece of volcanic tuff that is slowly crumbling, its buildings are gradually collapsing around the edges. The permanent population numbers around 12, though it multiplies in summer. For info, check www.civitadibagnoregio.it. Bagnoregio is accessible via regular Cotral buses from Viterbo (€2.50, 35 minutes), then the old town is around a 2km walk.

Castelli Romani

About 20km south of Rome, the Colli Albani (Alban Hills) and their 13 towns are collectively known as the Castelli Romani. Since early Roman days they've provided a green refuge from the city and today Romans still flock to the area on hot summer weekends. The most famous towns are Castel Gandolfo, where the pope has his summer residence, and Frascati, famous for its delicate white wine.

FRASCATI

An easy bus or train ride from Rome, pretty Frascati makes for a refreshing day trip, with hazy views over Rome, and delicious food and wine.

At Frascati Point (☑06 9401 5378; Piazza G Marconi; ⊗8am-8pm), you can access information about local wines, vineyards and *cantinas* (wine cellars). The building is the former stables of the Villa Aldobrandini, recently renovated by Italy's hippest architect, Massimiliano Fuksas, and including Museo Tuscolano (☑06 941 71 95; ⊗10am-6pm Tue-Fri, 10am-7pm Sat), with artfully lit Republican and imperial artefacts and interesting models of Tuscolo villas.

The imposing villa that rises from gardens above the square is the 16th-century Villa Aldobrandini, designed by Giacomo della Porta and built by Carlo Maderno; it's closed to the public, but you can visit the gardens (⊗8am-2pm & 3-6pm Mon-Fri).

If you have a car, head up to the ruins of ancient Tusculum. All that remains of this once imposing town is a small amphitheatre, a crumbling villa and a small stretch of road leading up to the city. The grassy hilltop, however, is a popular spot to do some walking and it commands some fine views.

However, the reasons people really come to Frascati are to eat and drink, and for a breath of fresh air in the dog days of summer (it's a few degrees cooler up here). The area is famous for its white wine and there are plenty of places where you can try it and other local varieties.

The town's best restaurant is Cacciani (✆06 942 03 78; Via Al Diaz; meals €55; ☉Tue-Sat), with fine food and a graceful terrace, but most fun are the town's famous rough-and-ready *cantinas,* which usually sell *porchetta,* olives, salami and cheeses, to go with jugs of the fresh young white wine. You can also pick up a *porchetta panini* from one of the stands that do a brisk weekend trade around Piazza del Mercato.

To try a typical *fraschette* (*osteria* that traditionally served only *porchetta* and wine) head to Hosteria San Rocco (✆06 9428 2786; Via Cadorna 1; ☉lunch & dinner). Called 'Da Trinco' by locals, it serves up traditional pasta dishes such as *spaghetti alla gricia* or saltimbocca, and a fine array of antipasti.

CASTEL GANDOLFO & AROUND

A short drive away in elegant Grottaferrata there's a 15th-century abbey (✆06 945 93 09; Viale San Nilo; ☉7am-12.30pm & 3.30pm-1hr before sunset), founded in 1004. It's now home to a congregation of Greek monks who sport tall black hats, and has a decidedly mystic atmosphere, the elaborate interior thick with incense. To eat in the town, try the recommended Da Franchino (✆06 945 91 72; Via Principe Amadeo).

Continuing southwest brings you to Castel Gandolfo, a smart hilltop *borgo* (medieval town). Dominating the town is the pope's summer residence, a 17th-century confection, where he holds audiences in July and August.

The town overlooks the great azure expanse of Lago di Albano, where you can swim, and there are places to rent sun loungers and pedalos around its banks, as well as cafes. The lake makes a great escape from Rome on a hot day.

The smaller of the two volcanic lakes in the Castelli Romani, Lago di Nemi was the centre of a cult to the goddess Diana in ancient times, and favourite holiday spot of the emperor Caligula. The Museo delle Navi Romani (✆06 939 80 40; Via Diana 15; admission €3; ☉9am-7pm Mon-Sat, to 1pm Sun) on the shore of the lake was built by Mussolini to house two Roman boats salvaged from the lake in 1932. These dated from Caligula's time but were tragically destroyed by fire in 1944 – what you see now are scale models of the originals. You can grab a bite to eat at the clifftop Trattoria la Sirena del Lago (✆06 936 80 20; Via del Plebiscito 26; meals €30), where the local game and trout are excellent and the local wine refreshing. Nemi is also famous for its wild strawberries – sprinkled over almost everything (especially ice cream) in season.

❶ Getting There & Around

There are buses to Frascati, but the best way to reach the city is by train from Stazione Termini (€1.90, 30 minutes, about hourly Monday to Saturday, every two hours Sunday).

To get from Frascati to Grottaferrata (€1, 10 minutes, every 30 to 40 minutes), catch a Cotral bus from Piazza Marconi. Buses also leave from here to Genzano di Roma (€1, 45 minutes, about hourly), from where you can catch another bus to Nemi (€1, 10 minutes, about hourly). There are buses to Castel Gandolfo, but it's far easier to reach by train from Rome's Stazione Termini (€1.90, 40 minutes); it's not possible to catch a train between Frascati and Castel Gandolfo, but there are buses from Piazza Marconi (€1, 30 minutes).

Palestrina

POP 21,340

The pretty town of Palestrina stands on the slopes of Monte Ginestro, one of the foothills of the Apennines. In imperial times it was an important getaway, favoured by wealthy Romans during the stifling summer.

It was dominated by the Santuario della Fortuna Primigenia, a massive sanctuary dating from the 2nd century BC, which had six terraced levels and was dedicated to the goddess of fortune. It would have covered much of what is now the town's *centro storico,* but was largely built over. In the 17th century the Palazzo Colonna Barberini was built on its uppermost terrace, and today houses the fantastic Museo Archeologico Nazionale di Palestrina

(☎06 953 81 00; Piazza della Cortina; admission €5; ⊙9am-8pm, ticket office closes at 7pm). Highlights of its collection include the wonderful 'Capitoline Triad', a marble sculpture of Jupiter, Juno and Minerva; and a spectacular 2nd-century-BC mosaic showing the flooding of the Nile, an incredibly rich depiction of daily life in ancient Egypt. The cryptoportico once surrounded the highest terrace of the sanctuary and has been incorporated into the palace.

The best spot for lunch is **Ristorante Stella** (☎06 953 81 72; Piazza della Liberazione 3; meals €30) in the 1960s hotel of the same name just down from the cathedral. It serves delicious dishes such as *pappardelle alla lepre* (egg-noodle pasta with hare and tomato sauce) and *risotto al tartufo* (risotto with truffles).

Take a Cotral bus from Ponte Mammolo Metro stop in Rome (€2.50, one hour, half-hourly). It is covered by a Zone 3 BIRG ticket (€6). When you arrive in Palestrina, get off at the second stop along the main street and walk up the *very* steep stairs and narrow roads to reach the museum, which is high on the hill above the cathedral.

By car it's a straightforward 39km along Via Prenestina (SS155).

Along the Coast

Fregene and the Lido di Ostia, the two beaches nearest Rome, are all about Roman socialising in summer (when many clubs move out here), but they are afflicted by traffic jams and polluted water. For a serener, cleaner experience, head for the coast further south.

SABAUDIA

Developed on reclaimed land by sun-worshipping Fascists, Sabaudia, 120km southeast of Rome, is a stark 1930s curiosity and the centre of the lovely **Parco Nazionale del Circeo** (www.parcocirceo.it; Via Carlo Alberto 104; ⊙9am-1pm & 2.30-5pm), an 800-hectare area of sand dunes, rocky coastline, forest and wetlands. The **visitor centre** (☎07 7351 1385) can provide details on activities available in the area including fishing, birdwatching, walking and cycling.

Cotral buses leave from outside the Laurentina station on metro line B heading for Terracina and pass by Sabaudia en route (€5.50, two to three hours depending on traffic).

SPERLONGA

Fashionable coastal town Sperlonga is all about tourism. Its whitewashed *centro storico* is a buzzing spot (in summer, at least) and there are two inviting, sandy beaches either side of a rocky promontory.

Other than the beach, the town's main attraction is the **Museo Archeologico di Sperlonga** (☎07 7154 8028; Via Flacca, km1.6; admission/reduced €4/2; ⊙9am-7pm), home to sculptures and masks dating from the 2nd century BC, and a cave with a circular pool used by the emperor Tiberius. The remains of his villa are in front of the cave.

Hotel Mayor (☎07 7154 9245; Via 1 Romita 4; www.hotelmayor.it; s €65-140, d €90-150; P ❄), just off the main seafront road into town, has plain but fairly smart and clean rooms, some with balconies.

To treat yourself to seafood so fresh it virtually wriggles off the plate, head to rustic **Gli Archi** (☎07 7154 83 00; Via Ottaviano 17; meals €40) up in the medieval quarter. Signature dishes include a tantalising *linguine agli scampi* (long pasta with scampi) and *zuppa di cozze* (mussel soup). It's worth eating buffalo mozzarella while you're here – it's superfresh because there are many producers in the area.

To get to Sperlonga from Rome, take a regional train from Stazione Termini to Fondi-Sperlonga (€6.20, 1¼ hours, about 20 daily). From the Fondi train station, you can catch the connecting **Piazzoli** (www.piazzoli.com) bus to Sperlonga (€1, 10 minutes, hourly). Returning from Sperlonga, the bus to Fondi leaves from the main road in the lower town.

Sperlonga is 120km from Rome by car. Take the Via Pontina (SS148) and follow signs to Terracina and then Sperlonga.

Isole Pontine

This group of small islands between Rome and Naples serves as an Italian Hamptons. Roman weekenders descend in droves to eat shellfish at little terrace restaurants, swim in emerald coves and take boat trips round the craggy coast. Be warned that Ponza and Ventotene – the only two inhabited islands – get packed out during holiday periods, and they're not cheap. It's best to visit in spring or autumn.

They've long been a favoured getaway – Homer refers to Ponza in the *Odyssey*. But as the Roman Empire declined, the islands

ST BENEDICT, CAVEMAN

St Benedict is generally regarded as the father of Western monasticism. Fleeing the vice that had so disgusted him as a student in Rome, he sought the gloom of the grotto at Subiaco to meditate and pray. During this time he attracted a large local following that eventually provoked the ire of his fellow friars and forced him onto the road.

Remote-feeling and dramatic, Subiaco is well worth the trip to see its wonderful monasteries and impressive abbey, with breathtaking views. The **Monastery of St Benedict** (☏07 748 50 39; ⓧ9am-12.15pm & 3.30-6.15pm via guided visit) is carved into the rock over the saint's former cave. Apart from its stunning setting, described by Petrarch as 'the edge of Paradise', it's adorned with rich 13th- to 15th-century frescoes.

Halfway down the hill from St Benedict is the **Monastery of St Scholastica** (☏07 748 55 69; ⓧ9am-12.30pm & 3-6.30pm, 3.30-7pm Jun-Aug), the only one of the 13 monasteries built by St Benedict still standing in the Valley of the Amiene. It has a restaurant offering set menus for €18 and €26. If you decide to stay the night, its **Foresteria** (☏07 748 55 69; www.benedettini-subiaco.org; per person full board €58) is a great place to spend a comfortable and contemplative night. But book ahead, as Benedictine clergy from around the world often make the pilgrimage here to work in the monastery's famous **library** and **archive**.

From Subiaco, St Benedict headed south until, it's said, three ravens led him to the top of Monte Cassino. Here, in 529 AD, he founded the abbey that was to be his home until he died in 547. One of the medieval world's most important Christian centres, the monumental **Abbey of Monte Cassino** (☏07 7631 1529; ⓧ8.30am-12.30pm & 3.30-5pm, to 6pm Jul & Aug) has been destroyed and rebuilt several times throughout its history, most recently in 1953. During WWII the abbey was central to German efforts to stop the Allied push north. After almost six months of bitter fighting, the Allies finally bombed the abbey in May 1944 in a desperate attempt to break through. In Cassino, there's a helpful **tourist office** (☏07 762 12 92; Via Di Biasio; www.apt.frosinone.it; ⓧ8.30am-1.30pm & 4-6pm Mon-Fri, 8.30am-1.30pm Sat).

To get to the monasteries in Subiaco from Rome by public transport, take a Cotral bus to Piazza Falcone, Subiaco (€6.30, 1¼ hours, every 15 to 30 minutes Monday to Friday, less frequently at weekends) from Ponte Mammolo on metro line B. The shorter trip takes the A24; the longer trip is via Tivoli. The bus stops a little way from the Monastery of St Scholastica – it's a 3km scenic, if demanding, uphill walk.

For Cassino, take one of the regular trains from Stazione Termini (€7.40, 80 minutes to two hours); some are faster than others. There are regular buses from Piazza San Benedetto up to the abbey. If you walk, it'll take around two hours to get up the hill and 1½ hours to walk back down!

---

were left vulnerable to violent attacks by the Saracens and by groups from mainland Italy and the nearby Aeolian Islands. During this period the island's main visitors were exiled outcasts from society.

A golden age came in the 18th century, but commerce flourished at the expense of the natural habitat. Today Ponza is ecologically still in poor shape: there's a lot of erosion caused by terraced farming, and migrating birds would do better to find a different route between Europe and Africa, as hunting is hugely popular. Fortunately, the islands are now under national park protection.

🛏 Sleeping

Many of the locals rent out individual rooms to tourists; you'll find them touting at the port. Otherwise, the **Pro Loco tourist office** (☏0771 800 31; www.prolocodiponza.it) will help you out. The following places are on Ponza.

Villa Ersilia   RENTAL ROOMS €
(☏0771 800 97; www.villaersilia.it) This company rents out a variety of simple rooms, studios and apartments. Prices range from €35 to €100 per person per night.

Villa Laetitia BOUTIQUE GUESTHOUSE €€
(☎0771 985 10 03; www.villalaetitia.com; Salita Scotti; d €230) Book ahead for this haven of chic. A residence owned by the Fendi family, it has just three rooms that are exquisitely decorated with fabulous artefacts, with amazing sea views.

❶ Getting There & Around

Ponza and Ventotene are accessible by car ferry or hydrofoil from Anzio, Terracina, Naples and Formia. Some services run year-round but others run only from late June to the start of September. The major companies are **SNAP** (www.snapnavigazione.it, in Italian), **Caremar** (www.caremar.it, in Italian) and **Vetor** (www. vetor.it). Timetable information is available from the websites, from most travel agents and, in summer, from the Rome section of *Il Messaggero* and *Il Tempo* newspapers. Prices vary according to the point of departure and whether you're on a hydrofoil or ferry (journey time varies from 80 minutes to 2½ hours) – from Terracina to Ponza the 2½-hour daily ferry crossing costs from €20 (return).

Cars and large motorbikes are forbidden on Ponza in summer, but there's a good local bus service (tickets €1). Otherwise, you can rent a scooter or even a golf buggy to get around.

Turin, Piedmont & the Italian Riviera

Includes »

Best Places to Eat

» Osteria dei Sognatori (p207)
» Sfashion (p198)
» Ombre Rosse (p168)
» Delle Antiche Contrade (p204)

Best Places to Stay

» Hotel Cairoli (p167)
» Hotel Langhe (p207)
» Hotel Residence Torino Centro (p197)
» Hotel Barolo (p210)

Why Go?

The beauty of northwestern Italy is its density. You only have to take a short train ride out of Turin and everything changes: food, culture, scenery – even the language.

The seduction starts in Liguria, a thin, precipitous coastal strip famous for its food (pesto and focaccia), swanky resorts and the once-powerful independent trading empire of Genoa. Piedmont is a flat, fertile medallion of land trapped between the Alps and the Mediterranean, an economic and political powerhouse that provided the nation with its first capital (Turin), a popular car (Fiat) and – more recently – Slow Food and fine wine. Mountainous Aosta, meanwhile, is a semi-autonomous Alpine region with a different history, its own language, and ample skiing and hiking terrain, all guarded by Europe's highest mountains.

If the three regions share anything in common it's their Savoia connections and proud sense of history. Italy, in the modern sense, was invented right here.

When to Go
Turin

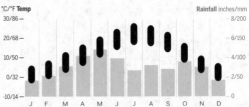

Jan–Mar Most reliable snow cover for skiing in the Alps.

Apr Fewer crowds and better hiking on the Ligurian coast.

Sep & Oct Late-season hiking in the Alps and autumn food festivals in Turin and Alba.

Northwest Culinary Inventions

» **Pesto** Pasta sauce originating in Genoa made from ground basil, pine nuts, olive oil, garlic and hard cheese

» **Focaccia** A flat oven-baked bread topped with herbs that hails from Liguria

» **Breadsticks** The thin crunchy sticks known as *grissini* were allegedly invented in Turin province in 1679

» **Nutella** Hazelnut spread first concocted by the Ferrero chocolate dynasty in Alba in 1963

» **Fontina** Pungent, earthy cheese that has been produced in the Valle d'Aosta since the 12th century

» **Arborio** Short-grain creamy rice used in risotto from the eponymous town in northern Piedmont

SLOW FOOD

Slow Food was the 1980s brainchild of a group of disenchanted Italian journalists from the Piemontese town of Bra. United by their taste buds, they ignited a global crusade against the fast-food juggernaut whose plastic tentacles were threatening to engulf Italy's centuries-old gastronomic heritage. Their mantra was pleasure over speed and taste over convenience in a manifesto that promoted sustainability, local production and the protection of long-standing epicurean traditions. Paradoxically, Slow Food grew quickly after its 1987 inauguration and by the early 2000s it was sponsoring more restaurants in Piedmont than McDonald's. In 2004 its founder Carlo Petrini opened up a University of Gastronomic Sciences in Pollenzo as a way of passing the baton onto future generations. The mindset worked. Today Slow Food counts 100,000 members in 150 countries and has attracted big-name affiliates such as Turin-founded supermarket company Eataly and popular ice-cream manufacturer Grom, as well as dozens of characterful and refreshingly slow restaurants – all of them defiantly individualistic.

Best Places for Walking

» **Parco Nazionale del Gran Paradiso** One of Italy's few true wilderness areas is packed with trails, wildlife and solitude.

» **Courmayeur** The meeting point of three of Italy's great long-distance paths: Aosta's Alte Vie 1 and 2, and the 165km Tour du Mont Blanc.

» **Cinque Terre** Cliffside hikes through terraced farmland and soporific fishing villages little changed since the Middle Ages.

» **Barbaresco** Walks and wine tastings in the undulating vine-striped hills of Piedmont's Langhe region.

» **Portofino** A priceless pocket of coastal wilderness sandwiched in between Italy's poshest resorts.

» **Maritime Alps** The Alps' western extremity has majestic hiking possibilities flush up against the border with France.

Unesco World Heritage Sites

» **Cinque Terre** Medieval fishing villages and landscaped cliffsides on the Ligurian coast.

» **Residences of the Royal House of Turin** A collection of baroque pleasure palaces in and around Turin including Palazzo Madama, Reale and Venaria Reale.

» **Sacri Monti** Nine sacred mountains in Piedmont and Lombardy with chapels and pilgrims' paths dedicated to the Christian faith.

» **Palazzi dei Rolli** Forty-two Renaissance and baroque palaces in Genoa.

Best Wines

» Barolo
» Barbaresco
» Barbera d'Asti
» Dolcetto d'Alba
» Sciacchetrà
» Asti Spumante

Turin, Piedmont & the Italian Riviera Highlights

1 Recline beneath the regal furnishings with a *bicerin* in a fin-de-siècle cafe in **Turin** (p199)

2 Discover the art and architecture of a once-great maritime empire in Genoa's amazing **Palazzi dei Rolli** (p163)

3 Discuss *terroir*, tannins and taste with the wine-quaffers of the **Barolo region** (p210)

4 Hike the blue trail, the red trail, the sanctuary trails – in fact, any trails on the stunning cliffsides of **Cinque Terre** (p175)

5 Work out who's French, Italian and Swiss-Walser in the multicultural **Valle d'Aosta** (p216)

6 Escape the clamorous Valle d'Aosta on foot with an excursion into the **Parco Nazionale del Gran Paradiso** (p225)

7 Descend on Alba in October to see white truffles sell for big prices in the annual **Truffle Festival** (p207)

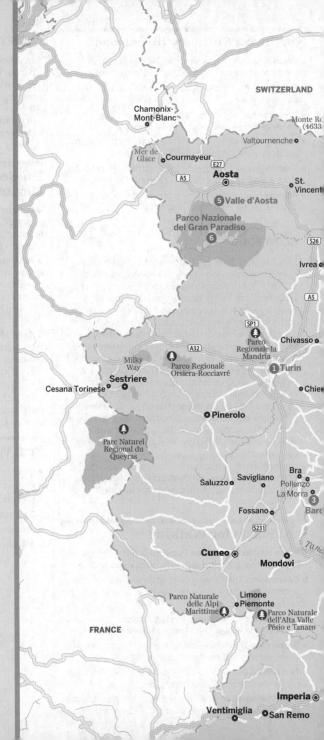

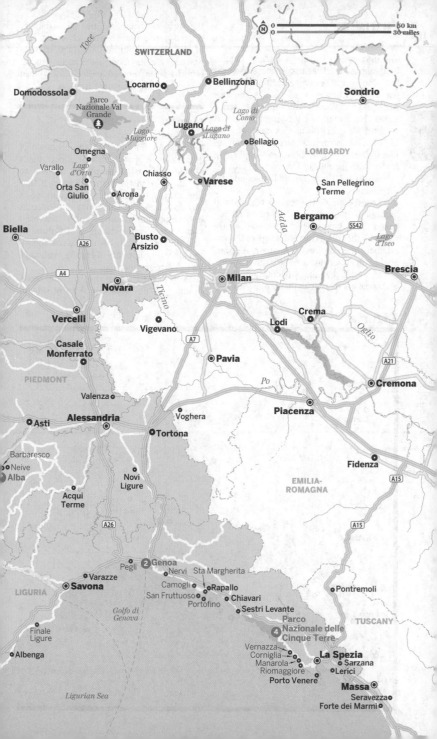

LIGURIA

POP 1.61 MILLION

The first thing to strike you about Liguria is its almost total lack of flatness. Wedged in a sinuous arc between Piedmont and the sea, this is where the Alps and Apennines cascade precipitously into the Mediterranean. The demanding topography has had an indelible effect on almost every facet of Ligurian life. Farming is carried out on ingeniously terraced cliff faces, and impossibly stacked fishing villages have long plundered the sea to both make their livings and fill their menus.

Anchored beside the region's best natural harbour is noble Genoa. Known as *La Superba* (The Superb One) to biased locals, it's a city that once ruled over one of the finest maritime empires in medieval Europe. Spread on either side are the swanky resorts of the so-called Italian Riviera, punctuated with pockets of timelessness, most notably the Portofino peninsula and the legendary Cinque Terre. Surprisingly, given its lack of obvious agricultural land, Liguria is renowned for its food: anchovies, lemons, crunchy focaccia bread and an earthy green sauce known to the world as pesto.

Genoa

POP 609,746

Contrasting sharply with the elegance of Turin, Genoa is a big crawling port that's almost Dickensian in places, thanks to its narrow, twisting lanes *(caruggi)* that are more reminiscent of the clamour of Morocco than the splendour of Venice. A once-important trading centre that bred such historic game-changers as Columbus and Mazzini, the city breathes a cosmopolitan air, with remnants of empire evident in its weighty art heritage.

Deep in the maze of the gritty old town, beauty and the beast sit side by side in

Liguria

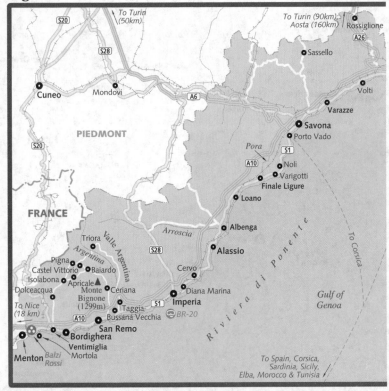

streets that glimmer like a film noir movie set. Old men smoke languidly outside noisy bars and prostitutes stand like sentries in dark doorways, while on the periphery memories of the great years echo through the gold-leaf halls of the Unesco-sponsored Palazzi dei Rolli – a myriad collection of 16th- and 17th-century 'lodging palaces'.

The Most Serene Republic of Genoa ruled the Mediterranean waves during the 12th to the 13th centuries before deferring to the superior power of Piedmont. Its crusading noblemen once established colonies in the Middle East and North Africa, and its emblematic flag, the red cross of St George, was greedily hijacked by the English.

Since hosting Expo 1992 and being championed as 2004's European City of Culture, Genoa has undergone some radical renovations, with its once-tatty port area now hosting Europe's largest aquarium and one of its best maritime museums.

History

Genoa's name is thought to come from the Latin *ianua,* meaning 'door'. Founded in the 4th century BC, it was an important Roman port and was later occupied by Franks, Saracens and the Milanese. The first ring of Genoa's defensive walls was constructed in the 12th century. (The only remaining section of these walls, Porta Soprana, was built in 1155, although what you see today is a restored version.)

A victory over Venice in 1298 led to a period of growth, but bickering between the Grimaldis, Dorias, Spinolas and other dynasties caused internal chaos. The Grimaldis headed west, establishing the principality of Monaco – hence the similarity of Monaco's language, Monegasque, to the Genoese dialect.

In the 16th century, under the rule of Imperial Admiral Andrea Doria, Genoa benefited

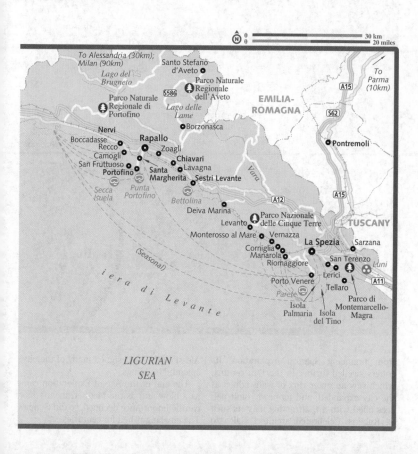

TURIN, PIEDMONT & THE ITALIAN RIVIERA LIGURIA

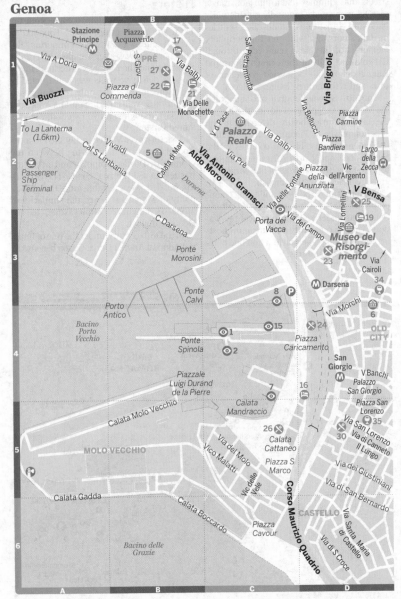

from financing Spanish exploration. Its coffers swelled further in the 17th century, which saw an outer ring of walls added as the city expanded, and its newly built palaces filled with art, attracting masters such as Rubens. Celebrated architect Galeazzo

Alessi (1512–72) designed many of the city's splendid buildings.

The end of the Age of Exploration came as a blow and as the Mediterranean's mercantile importance declined, so did Genoa's. The city languished for centuries.

Christopher Columbus is Genoa's most famous son. In 1992 the 500th anniversary of his seminal voyage to America transformed Genoa's ancient harbour from a decaying backwater into a showpiece for the city. Renzo Piano orchestrated the overhaul, adding a number of striking permanent attractions. Two years later, Genoa was named a European City of Culture, spurring further renovations and additions to the cityscape, including several new museums and a much-needed metro system.

◉ Sights

Aside from its Ligurian cuisine, Genoa's tour de force is its Palazzi dei Rolli. Forty-two of these plush 'lodging palaces' – built between 1576 and 1664 to host visiting European gentry – were placed on the Unesco World Heritage list in 2006. They are mostly located on or around Via Garibaldi and Via Balbi.

Musei di Strada Nuova   ART GALLERY
(combined ticket adult/reduced €8/6; ⊙9am-7pm Tue-Fri, 10am-7pm Sat & Sun) Skirting the northern edge of what was once the city limits, pedestrianised Via Garibaldi (formerly called the Strada Nuova) was planned by Galeazzo Alessi in the 16th century. It quickly became the city's most sought-after quarter, lined with the palaces of Genoa's wealthiest citizens. Three of these *palazzi* (mansions) – Rosso, Bianco and Doria-Tursi – comprise the Musei di Strada Nuova. Between them, they hold the city's finest collection of old masters.

Tickets must be purchased at the bookshop inside Palazzo Doria-Tursi (Via Garibaldi 9). This palace's highlight is the Sala Paganiniana, which showcases a small but absorbing collection of legendary violinist Niccolò Paganini's personal effects. Pride of place goes to his 'Canone' violin, made in Cremona in 1743. One lucky musician gets to play the maestro's violin during October's Paganiniana festival. Other artefacts on show include letters, musical scores and his travelling chess set. Elsewhere the collections are centred on ceramics and coins.

Lavishly frescoed rooms in Palazzo Rosso (www.museopalazzorosso.it; Via Garibaldi 18) are the backdrop for several Van Dyck portraits of the local Brignole-Sale family. Other standouts include Guido Reni's *San Sebastiano* and Guercino's *La morte di Cleopatra,* as well as works by Veronese, Dürer and Bernardo Strozzi.

Genoa was the first northern city to rise against Nazi occupation and the Italian Fascists during WWII, liberating itself before Allied troops arrived. After the war the city developed rapidly, although by the 1970s decline had set in as industries folded.

Flemish, Spanish and Italian artists feature at **Palazzo Bianco** (www.museopalazzobianco.it; Via Garibaldi 11). Rubens' *Venere e Marte* and Van Dyck's *Vertumna e Pomona* are among the highlights, which also include works by Hans Memling, Filippino Lippi and Spanish masters Murillo and Zurbarán.

Palazzo Ducale MUSEUM
(www.palazzoducale.genova.it; Piazza Giacomo Matteotti 9; admission €5-10; ☉exhibitions 9am-9pm Tue-Sun) Once the seat of an independent republic, this grand palace was built in the mannerist style in the 1590s and largely refurbished after a fire in the 1770s. Today it hosts high-profile temporary art exhibitions (an excellent Monet and Matisse show was running at last visit). There are several smaller museums inside, including the **Museo del Jazz** (www.italianjazzinstitute.com, in Italian; admission free; ☉4-7pm Mon-Sat by reservation), with a collection of original recordings. The *palazzo* also has a bookshop, and the fine M-Cafe (p169).

Cattedrale di San Lorenzo CHURCH
(Piazza San Lorenzo; ☉9am-12.30pm & 3.30-7pm) Impressive even by Italian standards, Genoa's black-and-white-striped Gothic-Romanesque cathedral owes its continued existence to the poor quality of a British WWII bomb that failed to ignite here in 1941. Fronted by twisting columns and crouching lions, it was first consecrated in 1118. The two bell towers and cupola were added in the 16th century.

Inside, above the central doorway, there's a great lunette with a painting of the Last Judgment, the work of an anonymous Byzantine painter of the early 14th century. In the sacristy, the **Museo del Tesoro** (adult/child €5.50/4.50; ☉tours 9am-noon & 3-6pm Mon-Sat) preserves various dubious holy relics, including the medieval Sacro Catino, a glass vessel once thought to be the Holy Grail. Other artefacts include the polished quartz platter upon which Salome is said to have received John the Baptist's head, and a fragment of the True Cross.

DON'T MISS

CORSO ITALIA

When you've had your fill of the rats and pungent alleys of the old city, decamp (as locals do) to the oceanside promenade known as Corso Italia, which lies approximately 3km east of the city centre. This broad 2.5km-long pavement is where Genovese Romeos pledge undying love to their Juliets, and joggers justify last night's gelati. The beach here is pebble, but the Corso displays some lovely Liberty facades and ends in unexpectedly cute Boccadasse, a once separate fishing village that appears like a sawn-off part of Cinque Terre out of the surrounding urbanity.

TOP CHOICE **Palazzo Reale**   PALAZZO, MUSEUM
(www.palazzorealegenova.it; Via Balbi 10; adult/child €4/2; ☉9am-7pm Thu-Sun, to 1.30pm Tue & Wed) If you only get the chance to visit one of the Palazzi dei Rolli, make it this one – a veritable Versailles with terraced gardens, exquisite furnishings and a fine collection of Renaissance art. The gilded 'Hall of Mirrors' is worth the entry fee alone. Add in frescoes, stuccos and numerous other artefacts collected by its two illustrious Genovese owners, the Balbis and the Durazzos, and you'll be blinking gold for hours afterwards. Complimentary guided tours enhance the experience.

Museo del Risorgimento   MUSEUM
(www.istitutomazziniano.it; Via Lomellini 11; adult/reduced €4/2.80; ☉9am-7pm Tue-Fri, 10am-7pm Sat) One of numerous Risorgimento (reunification period) museums in Italy, Genoa's has extra significance: it is housed in the residence where Italian patriot and activist Giuseppe Mazzini was born in 1805. Occupying rooms that once sheltered the so-called 'soul of Italy' are flags, personal possessions and well-laid-out and succinct explanations (some of them in English) of the complicated process of Italy's unification.

Chiesa del Gesù   CHURCH
(Piazza Giacomo Matteotti; ☉4.30-7pm) Half-hidden behind the cathedral, but emulating it in its ecclesial brilliance, this former Jesuit church dating from 1597 has an intricate and lavish interior. The wonderfully frescoed walls and ceiling are anchored by two works by the great Dutch artist Rubens. *Circoncisione* hangs over the main altar, and *Miracoli di San Ignazio* is displayed in a side chapel.

Casa della Famiglia Colombo   MUSEUM
(Piazza Dante; admission €4; ☉9am-noon & 2-6pm Sat & Sun) Not the only house claiming to be the birthplace of the navigator Christopher Columbus (Calvi in Corsica is another contender), this one probably has the most merit, as various documents inside testify. Curiously it stands just outside the old city walls in the shadow of the Porta Soprana gate built in 1155. Columbus allegedly lived here from 1455 until 1470, when he was between the ages of four and 19.

Piazza de Ferrari   PIAZZA
After the asphyxiation of the *caruggi,* this fountain-embellished main piazza ringed by magnificent buildings feels as if you've just come up for air. Showcase architecture includes the art nouveau Palazzo della Borsa (closed to the public), which was once the country's stock exchange; the neoclassical Teatro Carlo Felice (see p170); and the impressive central fountain.

Museo d'Arte Orientale   MUSEUM
(Piazzale Mazzini 1; adult/reduced €4/2.80; ☉9am-1pm Tue-Fri, 10am-7pm Sat & Sun) Just east of Via Garibaldi, a path from Piazza Corvetto twists through terraced gardens to one of Europe's largest collections of Japanese art, bringing together some 20,000 items, including porcelain, bronzes, costumes and musical instruments.

Old City   NEIGHBOURHOOD
The heart of medieval Genoa – bounded by Porta dei Vacca, the streets of Via Cairoli, Via Garibaldi and Via XXV Aprile, and the Porta Soprana – is famed for its *caruggi.* As evidenced by the washing pegged on lines strung outside the buildings, these dark, almost cave-like laneways and dank, odoriferous blind alleys are largely residential, with a sprinkling of bars, shops and cafes. Particularly after dark, parts of the *caruggi* can feel somewhat unnerving. Although it's not overly dangerous (especially compared with a decade ago), take care in the zone west of Via San Luca and south to Piazza Banchi, where most of the old city's lowlife

MAKING THE MOST OF YOUR EURO

Serial museum-goers should pick up the **Card Musei** (Museum Card; www.museigenova. it; 24/48hr €12/16). The card gives free admission to around 20 of Genoa's museums and discounted access to several more. You can buy it at various museums, information booths or online at www.happyticket.it.

(prostitution, drugs and so on) concentrates. East of the piazza is Via Orefici, where you'll find market stalls.

Galleria Nazionale ART GALLERY

(www.palazzospinola.it; Piazza Superiore di Pellicceria 1; adult/reduced €5/3; ☺9am-8pm Tue-Sat, 2-8pm Sun) This gallery's paintings are wonderfully displayed over four floors of the 16th-century Palazzo Spinola, once owned by the Spinola family, one of the Republic's most formidable dynasties. The main focus is Italian and Flemish Renaissance art of the so-called 'Ligurian school' (look out for Van Dyck, Rubens and Strozzi), but it's also worth visiting to gape at the decorative architecture.

Museo delle Culture del Mondo MUSEUM

(Museum of World Cultures; www.castellodalbertis genova.it; Corso Dogali 18; adult/reduced €6/4.50; ☺10am-6pm) Towering over the western end of town, **Castello D'Albertis** houses an eclectic museum showcasing artefacts collecting by its globetrotting owner. The neo-Gothic edifice was built in 1892 on the ruins of a much older castle for the Capitano Enrico D'Albertis, who hauled back all manner of 'curiosities' from his extensive sea voyages. Where else could you find a stuffed platypus, a fragment of the Great Wall of China and a handful of sand from San Salvador (Columbus' first disembarkation point) in the same cabinet? If you don't fancy the climb up to Corso Dogali, there's a lift from Via Balbi (€0.70) to the castle gates.

Porto Antico NEIGHBOURHOOD

(www.portoantico.it) The port that once controlled a small empire has reaffirmed itself as one of the best places to enjoy a *passeggiata* (evening stroll) since a decade-long facelift in the late 1990s and early 2000s. Young nightlife searchers and kids are particularly well catered for.

Acquario AQUARIUM

(www.acquariodigenova.it; Ponte Spinola; adult/ child €18/12; ☺9.30am-7.30pm; 🖎) No glorified fish tank, Genoa's bright-blue aquarium is one of the largest in Europe, with more than 5000 sea creatures, including sharks, swimming in six million litres of water. The adjoining floating barge takes visitors on a voyage through the Age of Discovery and into a Madagascan rainforest. The aquarium has disabled access. Opening hours are lengthened in high summer and at weekends.

Biosfera BIOSPHERE DOME

(Ponte Spinola; adult/reduced €5/3.50; ☺10am-sunset Tue-Sun) A giant glass ball housing a humid mini-ecosystem with tropical plants, butterflies and birds, the Biosphere is an interesting and innovative addition to the port, although its assorted greenery probably won't delay you more than 15 minutes. The ambient temperature inside is controlled by computers.

Il Bigo LOOKOUT

(Calata Cattaneo; adult/reduced €4/3; ☺2-6pm Mon, 10am-6pm Tue-Sun) The port's most eye-catching and futuristic structure is this giant spider-like contraption that hoists a cylindrical viewing cabin 200m into the air for mediocre city views that struggle to justify the price tag. The lift has access for visitors with disabilities.

Galata Museo del Mare MUSEUM

(www.galatamuseodelmare.it, in Italian; Calata di Mari 1; admission €11; ☺10am-7.30pm, closed Mon Nov-Feb) Rivalled only by Barcelona and Venice as a medieval/Renaissance maritime power, it stands to reason that Genoa's 'museum of the sea' is one of its most relevant and interesting. Hi-tech exhibits tracing the history of seafaring from earliest times through the ages of sail and steam justify the rather steep entry fee.

Il Galeone Neptune PIRATE SHIP

(Mole Ponte Calvi; adult/reduced €5/3; ☺10am-6pm; 🖎) This full-sized replica pirate ship was built in 1986 as a prop in the Roman Polanski movie *Pirates*. Moored permanently in the port, it is now a favourite playground for kids re-enacting scenes from *Peter Pan* and *Pirates of the Caribbean* with their beleaguered parents.

Genoa–Casella Railway
NARROW-GAUGE RAILWAY

Spectacular views of Genoa's forts can be seen from the 1929 narrow-gauge railway, which snakes 25km north from the Stazione Genova (www.ferroviagenovacasella.it, in Italian; Via alla Stazione per Casella 15) to the village of Casella (one way/return €2/3.20, one hour, eight to 12 daily) in the Scrivia valley. Stazione Genova is 1.3km north of Stazione Brignole: it's 15 minutes by foot or you can catch bus 33.

La Lanterna
HISTORICAL SITE, MUSEUM

(Via Alla Lanterna; admission €6; ⊙10am-7pm Sat & Sun) The port may have changed radically since its '90s rebirth, but its omnipresent sentinel hasn't moved an inch since 1543. Genoa's emblematic lighthouse is one of the world's oldest and tallest – and it still works, beaming its light over 50km to warn ships and tankers. Visitors can climb 172 steps and ponder exhibits in an adjacent museum of lamps, lenses and related history. The Lanterna is best accessed via a special 800m walking trail that starts at the ferry terminal. It's surrounded by a fine park.

⌕ Tours

Information and tickets for boat trips round the port and destinations further afield are available from the ticket booths (Ponte Spinola; ⊙9.30am-6.30pm Sep-Jun, 9am-8pm Jul & Aug) beside the aquarium at Porto Antico.

Whale Watch Liguria
WHALE-WATCHING

(www.whalewatchliguria.it; tickets €33; ⊙1pm Sat Apr-Oct) These five-hour spring/summer tours are run in consultation with the World Wide Fund for Nature and include fascinating background on the world's largest mammals provided by an onboard biologist.

Genova Tours
BUS

(adult/child €15/7.50) Runs three or four open-topped bus tours daily, with headphone commentary in five languages. It's best to confirm the departure point for your specific trip; tourist offices can provide departure details. Tickets are sold on the bus.

✦ Festivals & Events

Slow Fish
FOOD

(www.slowfish.it) Every odd-numbered year in early May, this festival celebrates seafood with a fish market and tastings. Affiliated with the Slow Food Movement, it also runs free workshops focusing on water pollution, good fishing practices and aquaculture.

Palio delle Quattro Antiche Repubbliche Marinare
SAILING

(Regatta of the Four Ancient Maritime Republics) In June, Genoa is one of four historical maritime cities (along with Pisa, Amalfi and Venice) that race in this regatta. The next event in Genoa is in 2012.

Premio Paganini
MUSIC

In homage to Genoese violinist Niccolò Paganini (1782–1849), this is an international violin competition held in September.

🛏 Sleeping

Dozens of hotels are spread round town. The greatest concentration is near Stazione Principe on and around Via Balbi.

TOP CHOICE Hotel Cairoli
HOTEL €

(☑010 246 14 54; www.hotelcairoligenova.com; Via Cairoli 14/4; s €55-90, d €65-105; ✲@🖘) Window-shoppers wouldn't know it, but Mondrian lurks three flights up in this Genoa *palazzo*. Themed on various modern artists, the rooms at the cleverly put-together Cairoli exhibit the personalities and works of various famous artists. Add in a communal library, chill-out area, internet room, fully equipped gym, free newspapers, terrace and informative maps on the wall and you have five stars in a three-star wrapping. It's multilingual and friendly, too.

B&B Palazzo Morali
B&B €

(☑010 246 70 27; www.palazzomorali.com; Piazza della Raibetta; s €50-70, d €70-100; P✲🖘) Your instant reaction on entering the rarefied world of Palazzo Morali is: I've stumbled upon a secret Palazzo Rolli that Unesco forgot to list. When you come to your senses, you'll realise that 'B&B' is a misnomer at this exquisite place situated on the top two floors of a lofty building overlooking Genoa's port. Palatial rooms (some with shared bathroom) are embellished with gold-leafed four-poster beds and Genovese art, and breakfast feels more like a banquet than an early-morning snack.

Hotel Bristol Palace
HOTEL €€€

(☑010 59 25 41; www.hotelbristolpalace.com; Via XX Settembre 35; s €147-350, d €166-470; P✲@🖘) Under the huge portals of Via XX Settembre lies one of Genoa's fanciest pads, a belle époque masterpiece exhibiting atmospheric, airy rooms with geometric parquet flooring and original antiques (as well as mod cons). Enter the domain via a sweeping staircase with an ornamental glass roof visible at the top.

Hostel Genova
HOSTEL €

(☏010 242 24 57; hostelge@iol.it; Via G Costanzi 120; dm/s/d incl breakfast from €16/23.50/44; ⏰reception 9am-3.30pm & midnight-7am Feb–mid-Dec; ℗) A steep 2km north of the centre, Genoa's only hostel has rules that won't endear it to free-spirited backpackers: its eight-bed dorms are single-sex, there's a lockout from 9am to 3.30pm, a 1am curfew, and Hostelling International (HI) cards are mandatory. Catch bus 40 from Stazione Brignole to the end of the line. Has access for guests with disabilities.

Hotel Acquaverde
HOTEL €

(☏010 26 54 27; www.hotelacquaverde.it; Via Balbi 29; s €40-45, d €55-65; ❄️🛜) On the top three floors of a restored 17th-century town house (accessed by a lift), the Acquaverde's rooms are simple but comfortable. If you're self-catering, four rooms have their own kitchen facilities (€80 to €130). There's also access for travellers with disabilities.

Hotel della Posta Nuova
HOTEL €€

(☏010 25 29 29; www.albergopostagenova.com; Via Balbi 24; s €40-115, d €60-130; ℗❄️) No real surprises at this journeyman hotel 150m from Stazione Principe, though it's clean, safe and relatively friendly for such a transient quarter. Rooms are smallish and simple but admit plenty of natural light. The ones on the top floor have a terrace overlooking Via Balbi.

Hotel Cristoforo Colombo
HOTEL €€

(☏010 251 36 43; www.hotelcolombo.it; Via di Porta Soprana 27; s €88-160, d €110-170) A rather charming family-run hotel ideally situated near the San Lorenzo cathedral with 18 colour-accented rooms with postmodern furnishings. Breakfast is served on an inviting 6th-floor rooftop terrace.

Albergo Carola
HOTEL €

(☏010 839 13 40; Via Groppallo 4; s/d from €28/50, with bathroom from €35/60) Albergo Carola's nine well-kept rooms are on the 3rd floor of a lovely old building near Stazione Brignole. It's clean, central and charming. And look at the price!

Hotel Europa
HOTEL €

(☏010 25 69 55; www.hoteleuropagenova.it; Via delle Monachette 8; s/d €72/105; ℗❄️@🛜) Tucked down a little laneway a few footsteps from Stazione Principe, Europa's small rooms come with elegant peach-toned decor and amenities such as flat-screen satellite TV and minibar.

✕ Eating

It's practically impossible to leave town without tasting *pesto genovese* (the famous sauce that appears on menus everywhere). Ubiquitous local specialities focaccia (especially topped with cheese) and *farinata* (a thin pancake made from chickpea flour) make cheap takeaway snacks. Nail a place with a visible oven and dive in when you see the baker stocking his display cases with a fresh round. *Torta pasqualina* (spinach, ricotta cheese and egg tart), *pansotti* (spinach-filled ravioli with a thick, creamy hazelnut sauce) and freshly caught seafood are also good.

🅣🅞🅟 Ombre Rosse
TRADITIONAL ITALIAN €€€

(☏010 27 57 608; Vico Indoratori 20; meals €35-35) Encased in one of the oldest medieval houses in the city, dating from the early 13th century, Ombre Rosse offers another dose of urban serendipity. First there's the dark but romantic interior, full of books, posters and interesting nooks. Second is the alfresco seating in a delightful small park (one of the few in Genoa's dense urban grid). Third and most importantly is the 100% Ligurian food – *trofie al pesto*, pasta with *salsa de noci* and fine *verdure torta* (vegetable quiche) with a side salad.

Trattoria della Raibetta
TRATTORIA €€

(www.trattoriadellaraibetta.it; Vico Caprettari 10-12; meals €20-30; ⏰lunch & dinner Tue-Sun) The most authentic Genoese food can be procured in the family-run joints hidden in the warren of streets near the cathedral. The Raibetta's menu is unfussy and fish-biased. Try the seafood with *riso venere* (a local black rice) or the signature homemade *trofiette al pesto*. The octopus salad makes a good overture, while the wine is a toss-up between 200 different vintages.

Lupo
TRADITIONAL ITALIAN €€

(www.lupoanticatrattoria.it; Via delle Monachette 20; meals €25-30; ⏰12.30-3pm & 7.30pm-midnight) Inviting aromas of home cooking – cuttlefish in tomato sauce, ravioli in walnut sauce, and homemade desserts – greet you at the door, as do owners who welcome you like a lost Columbus. Lupo's wine list is outstanding, and its antiques and *objets d'art* – such as cast-iron candelabras, a grandfather clock and black-and-white photographs suspended on wire strings – create a refined yet relaxed ambience.

Da Gaia
TRADITIONAL ITALIAN €€€

(Vico dell'Argento 13r; meals €30-50; ⊘closed Sun) Don't let the dark, Dickensian alley put you off. Gaia is a ray of light in murky surroundings, and regularly voted the best restaurant in town by those who should know (ie the locals). It's famous for its fish, so try the antipasto vegetable plate before diving into prawns, sea bass or tuna. It also does all the Genovese staples (pesto, *noci*) and a good stewed rabbit.

I Tre Merli
MODERN ITALIAN €

(Palazzina Millo, Porto Antico; snacks €7-12, meals €20-25) Grander than some of its portside counterparts, this well-positioned restaurant is flanked by towering black-and-white-striped columns. Excellent Ligurian cuisine includes salted cod fritters, and veal stuffed with porcini mushrooms and potatoes. Otherwise, you can just have a glass of wine with wood-fired snacks such as *focaccia col formaggio* (Liguria's answer to cheese on toast).

Antica Trattoria del Porto Maria
TRATTORIA €€

(Piazza Caricamento 22; meals €20-30; ⊘lunch Tue-Sun, dinner Fri & Sat) Classic Genoese cuisine such as scampi in brandy is dished up at this atmospheric little old-port trattoria with green-and-white chequered tables down a flight of steps in an old storeroom.

M-Cafe
SANDWICH SHOP, CAFE €

(Palazzo Rosso, Via Garibaldi 18; ⊘) You'll need this neat little haven of modernity in Genoa's 'museum street' for a quick panini and espresso to refresh your brain in between spells of art gawping.

Al Veliero
SEAFOOD €€

(☏010 246 57 73; Via Ponte Calvi 10r; meals €30-40; ⊘Tue-Sun) On the steps of the port, Al Veliero is seafood central, where the fish is served simply but delicately to much local acclaim.

🍷 Drinking

The revamped Porto Antico has captured much of the youthful night-time scene, but never underestimate the lure of the *caruggi*. You'll also find sophisticated new drinking spots intermingled with old-time favourites throughout the city, particularly in the streets just northwest of Piazza de Ferrari. Piazza della Erbe is clad with cafe terraces where you can linger over a coffee or something stronger.

TOP CHOICE La Nouvelle Vague
WINE BAR

(www.nouvelle-vague.it; Vico de Gradi 4r; ⊘to 1am Sun-Thu, to 2am Fri & Sat) The *carrugi* pull many surprises, but few are as sweet as this enclave of cool underground intellectualism beneath the clammy confusion of Genoa's medieval streets. Nouvelle Vague is a French-themed bookshop and bar where you can sip Italian wine while leafing through the works of Genet and Proust. Photos of a gamine Jean Seaberg adorn the walls and the top-drawer aperitif snacks that accompany all drink orders have led to numerous dinner cancellations.

Fratelli Klainguti
CAFE €

(Via di Soziglia) Pre-dating cappuccinos and Lavazza coffee, Klainguti presumably found other ways to pull in the clientele when it opened in 1828. These days, caffeine and pastries do the trick for most people who are happy to pay over the odds to get served by a waiter in a bowtie under an ostentatious chandelier. Simple *primi* (first courses) start at a more reasonable €5.

Café degli Specchi
CAFE

(Via Salita Pollaiuoli 43r; mains €7-10; ⊘Mon-Sat) A bit of Turin disconnected and relocated 150km to the south, this roaring-'20s, tiled, art deco showpiece was (and is) a favourite hang-out of the literati. You can sink your espresso at street level or disappear upstairs amid the velvet seats and mirrors for coffee, cake and an *aperitivo* (happy hour) buffet.

Café di Barbarossa
BAR, CAFE

(Piano di Sant'Andrea 21-3r; ⊘7am-4pm Mon, to 2.30am Tue-Fri, 5pm-2.30am Sat & Sun) A life-sized statue of Elvis outside the entrance kitschily disguises a good-time bar-cafe set in a medieval red-brick cellar below the towering 12th-century Porta Soprana. Outside there's a leafy deck.

La Madeleine Café Teatro
BAR

(☏010 246 53 12; Via della Maddalena 103) Live bands blast till 10pm most nights at this energetic cafe-theatre-music bar.

☆ Entertainment

At the western end of the Porto Antico, the Magazzini del Cotone (one-time cotton warehouses) have been converted into an entertainment area with a multiplex cinema, games arcade and shops.

Teatro Carlo Felice   THEATRE
(www.carlofelice.it, in Italian; Passo Eugenio Montale 4) Take in a play or opera at Genoa's stunning four-stage opera house.

Teatro della Tosse   THEATRE
(www.teatrodellatosse.it, in Italian; Piazza Renato Negri 4) Casanova trod the boards of the city's oldest theatre, which dates from 1702.

🔒 Shopping

Heading southwest, elegant Via Roma, with its art nouveau boutiques and adjacent glass-covered Galleria Mazzini, is Genoa's most exclusive designer-shopping street. It links Piazza Corvetto with Piazza de Ferrari.

ℹ Information

Internet Cafe (Via Balbi 110; per hr €1; ⊗9am-8pm Mon-Fri, 2-8pm Sat) Near Stazione Principe.

Ospedale San Martino (☎010 55 51; Largo Rosanna Benci 10) Hospital.

Police station (☎010 5 36 61; Via Armando Diaz 2)

Post office Main post office (Via Dante; ⊗8am-6.30pm Mon-Sat); Stazione Principe (⊗8am-6.30pm Mon-Fri, to 12.30pm Sat)

Tourist offices Airport (⊗9am-1pm, 1.30-5.30pm); Via Garibaldi (⊗9am-6.30pm); Piazza Ferrari (next to Teatro Carlo Felice; ⊗9am-1pm, 2.30-6.30pm)

ℹ Getting There & Away

Air

Regular domestic and international services, including easyJet flights, use **Christopher Columbus airport** (Aeroporto Internazionale di Cristoforo Colombo; www.airport.genova.it), 6km west of the city in Sestri Ponente.

Boat

Ferries sail to/from Spain, Sicily, Sardinia, Corsica and Tunisia from the **international passenger terminal** (terminal traghetti; www. porto.genova.it; Via Milano 51). Only cruise ships use the 1930s passenger ship terminal on Ponte dei Mille.

Fares listed following are for one-way, low-/high-season deck-class tickets. Ferry operators based at the international passenger terminal include the following:

Grandi Navi Veloci (www.gnv.it) Ferries to Sardinia (Porto Torres, €88, year-round; Olbia, €81, June to September) and Sicily (Palermo, €50, year-round). Also ferries to Barcelona, Tunis and Tangier (Morocco).

Moby Lines (www.mobylines.it) Ferries year-round to Corsica (Bastia, €39) and Sardinia (Olbia, €67).

From June to September, **Cooperativa Battellieri del Golfo Paradiso** (www.golfoparadiso. it) operates boats from Porto Antico to Camogli (one way/return €10/15), Portofino (€12/20) and Porto Venere (€18/33).

Consorzio Liguria Via Mare (www.liguriaviamare.it) runs a range of seasonal trips to Camogli, San Fruttuoso and Portofino, Monterosso in the Cinque Terre, and Porto Venere.

Bus

Buses to international cities depart from Piazza della Vittoria, as do buses to/from Milan's Malpensa airport (€16, two hours, 6am and 3pm) and other interregional services. Tickets are sold at **Geotravels** (Piazza della Vittoria 30r) and **Pesci Viaggi e Turismo** (Piazza della Vittoria 94r).

Train

Genoa's Stazione Principe and Stazione Brignole are linked by train to the following destinations.

TO	FARE (€)	DURATION (HR)	FREQUENCY
Milan	13.70	1½	up to 8 daily
Pisa	17	2	up to 8 daily
Rome	37.50	5¼	6 daily
Turin	9.10	1¾	7-10 daily

Stazione Principe tends to have more trains, particularly going west to San Remo (€14.50, two hours, five daily) and Ventimiglia (€11.60, 2¼ hours, six daily).

ℹ Getting Around

To/From the Airport

AMT (www.amt.genova.it) line 100 runs between Stazione Principe and the airport at least every hour from 5.30am to 11pm (€4, 30 minutes). Tickets can be bought from the driver.

A taxi to or from the airport will cost around €15.

Public Transport

AMT (www.amt.genova.it) operates buses throughout the city and there is an **AMT information office** (Via d'Annunzio; ⊗7.15am-6pm Mon-Fri, 7am-7pm Sat & Sun) at the bus terminal. Bus line 383 links Stazione Brignole with Piazza de Ferrari and Stazione Principe. A ticket valid for 90 minutes costs €1.50. Tickets can be used on main-line trains within the city limits, as

well as on the currently expanding **metro** (www.
genovametro.com), which has numerous stations across the city.

Around Genoa

NERVI

A former fishing village engulfed by Genoa's
urban sprawl, modern Nervi classifies itself
as a 'resort' – though with plenty of ritzier
Riviera competition, it's rarely top of anyone's holiday list. Its saving graces are its
bounty of museums and galleries, and the
2km cliffside promenade, the Passeggiata
Anita Garibaldi.

◉ Sights

All four of Nervi's museums and galleries
can be accessed in a combined ticket (€10)
or they're included on the Genoa Museum
Card (see the boxed text, p166).

Galleria d'Arte Moderna   ART GALLERY
(Via Capolungo 3; adult/reduced €6/5; ⊙10am-7pm
Tue-Sun) This museum – the most celebrated
of the four – displays works by 19th- and
20th-century artists such as Filippo De Pisis,
Arturo Martini and Rubaldo Merello.

Raccolte Frugone   ART GALLERY
(Via Capolungo 9; adult/reduced €4/2.80; ⊙9am-
7pm Tue-Fri, 10am-7pm Sat & Sun) More 19th-
and early-20th-century Italian art, including Eduardo Rubino's sensual marble nude,
Il Risveglio, is displayed here in the Villa
Grimaldi Fassio, overlooking the leafy, squir-
rel-filled Parchi di Nervi.

Wolfsoniana   MUSEUM
(www.wolfsoniana.it; Via Serra Gropallo 4; adult/re-
duced €5/4; ⊙10am-7pm Tue-Sun) Some 18,000
items from the period 1880–1945 are displayed at the Wolfsoniana. On show are
items documenting this turbulent time in
Italy's history, including advertising and propaganda posters, along with architectural
drawings, paintings and furnishings.

Museo Giannettino Luxoro   MUSEUM
(Via Mafalda di Savoia 3; adult/reduced €4/2.80;
⊙9am-1pm Tue-Fri, 10am-1pm Sat) Going back
earlier in time, this place has a rich collection of 18th-century clocks, silverware, ceramics and furniture, displayed in a splendidly restored villa. The entrance fee also
includes entry to Raccolte Frugone.

✗ Eating

Chandra Bar   INTERNATIONAL €
(Passeggiata Garibaldi 26r; meals €18-25; ⊙3pm-
2am Tue-Sat, 11.30am-2am Sun) Situated on the
seafront promenade, the Chandra serves up
pasta and daily specials of freshly caught
fish occasionally spiced up with Thai and
Brazilian inflections. Also live music.

❶ Getting There & Away

Nervi is 7km east of Genoa and best reached
by frequent trains from Stazione Brignole and
Stazione Principe (€1.20, 20 to 25 minutes).

PEGLI

Roughly 9km west of Genoa's centre, flower-filled parks make Pegli a peaceful spot
to retreat from the urban tumult. Like
Nervi, this former seafront village now lies
within the city boundaries of Genoa; and,
again like Nervi, it has yet more museums.
A combined ticket for all of the following
sights costs €8.

◉ Sights

Museo di Archeologia Ligure   MUSEUM
(www.museoarcheologicogenova.it; Via Pallavicini
11; admission €4; ⊙9am-7pm Tue-Fri, 10am-7pm
Sat & Sun) This museum in the striking Villa
Pallavicini, holds displays of locally excavated artefacts from the prehistoric through to
the Roman period, as well as a collection of
Egyptian antiquities.

Museo Navale   MUSEUM
(www.museonavale.it; Villa Doria, Piazza Bonavino
7; admission €4; ⊙9am-1pm Tue-Fri, 10am-7pm
Sat & Sun) Maritime matters are covered in
a former residence of the Doria clan with an
exhibition of models, photographs and other
reminders of the days when Genoa sported
a significant sea force from the 15th to 19th
centuries.

Parco Villa Pallavicini   PARK
(Via Pallavicini; admission €3.50; ⊙9am-7pm Apr-
Sep, to 5pm Oct-Mar) Pallavacini is a manicured park with formal lawns, lakes and
glasshouse that is an epitome of the lush
Italian Riviera landscape. The neighbouring
Giardino Botanico (admission €3.50; ⊙9am-
12.30pm Tue-Sun) is home to a small collection
of exotic plants.

❶ Getting There & Away

Frequent trains from Genoa's Stazione Brignole
and Stazione Principe (€1.20, 20 to 25 minutes)
travel to Pegli.

Riviera di Levante

Running claustrophobically from Genoa's eastern sprawl, you're quickly apprehended by the deep blue waters of the Mediterranean fringed by some of Italy's most elite resorts, including jet-set favourite Portofino. Anything but off the beaten track, this glittering stretch of coast is hugely popular but never tacky. Heading further east, swanky resorts battle bravely with increasingly precipitous topography.

CAMOGLI
POP 5621

This still-authentic fishing village, 25km east of Genoa, has trompe l'œil decorating its alleys and cobbled streets, beneath a canopy of umbrella pines and voluptuous olive groves.

Camogli's name means 'house of wives', hailing from the days when the women ran the village while their husbands were at sea. Fishing traditions continue here, especially during the second weekend in May when fishermen celebrate the **Sagra del Pesce** (Fish Festival) with a big fry-up – hundreds of fish are cooked in 3m-wide pans along the busy waterfront.

⊙ Sights & Activities

From the main esplanade, Via Garibaldi, boats sail to the **Punta Chiappa**, a rocky outcrop on the Portofino promontory where you can swim and sunbathe like an Italian.

A trail from the train station leads along Via Nicolò Cuneo and up countless steps to the church of **San Rocco di Camogli** (follow the two red dots). From here the path continues 3km to the clifftop **batterie**, a WW2 German anti-aircraft gun emplacement.

🛏 Sleeping

Delve down the lanes away from the water to escape the lunchtime crowd and search for some of the town's extra-crunchy focaccia.

Hotel Cenobio dei Dogi HOTEL €€€
(☏0185 72 41; www.cenobio.com; Via Cuneo 34; s €120-160, d €160-230; [P][❄][☎][⚲]) Welcome to Riviera luxury. The Cenobio's name means 'gathering place of the doges', and yes, the Genovese dukes used to holiday here eons ago – sensible souls! Choose from one of 105 refined rooms that still manage to feel intimate.

❶ Information

Tourist office (www.camogli.it, in Italian; Via XX Settembre 33; ⊙9am-12.30pm & 3.30-6pm Mon-Sat, 9am-1pm Sun) Has a list of diving schools and boat-rental operators.

❶ Getting There & Away

Camogli is on the Genoa–La Spezia train line with regular connections to Santa Margherita (€1.80, five minutes) and Rapallo (€1.80, 10 minutes).

The **Cooperativa Battellieri del Golfo Paradiso** (www.golfoparadiso.it) runs boats year-round to Punta Chiappa (one way/return €5/8) and San Fruttuoso (€8/11). Between June and September there are services to Genoa's Porto Antico (€10/15), Portofino (€10/16) and the Cinque Terre (€20/27.50).

SAN FRUTTUOSO

The yin to Portofino's yang, San Fruttuoso is a slice of ancient tranquillity preserved amid some of Italy's ritziest coastal resorts. There are no roads here – thank heavens! Access is either by boat or on foot.

⊙ Sights

Abbazia di San Fruttuoso di Capodimonte CHURCH
(adult/child €4/2.50; ⊙10am-6pm May-Sep, to 4pm Mar, Apr & Oct, also to 4pm public holidays & day prior to public holidays Dec-Feb) The hamlet's extraordinary Benedictine abbey was built as a final resting place for Bishop St Fructuosus of Tarragona (martyred in Spain in AD 259). It was rebuilt in the mid-13th century with the assistance of the Doria family. The abbey fell into decay with the decline of the religious community, and in the 19th century it was divided into small living quarters by local fishermen.

In 1954 a bronze **statue** of Christ was lowered 15m to the seabed, offshore from the abbey, to bless the waters. Dive to see it or view it from a boat if the waters are calm – the Cooperativa Battellieri del Golfo Paradiso can provide details. Replicas were lowered in St George's harbour, Grenada, in 1961, and off Key Largo in Florida in 1966.

❶ Getting There & Away

San Fruttuoso's isolation is maintained by its lack of road access. You can walk in on foot from Camogli (a tricky, rocky hike with metal hand supports) or Portofino, a steep but easier 5km cliffside walk. Both hikes take about 2½ hours one way. Alternatively, you can catch a boat from Camogli (one way/return €8/11) or Punta Chiappa (€5/8).

PORTOFINO
POP 493

Even the trees are handsome in Portofino, a small but perfectly coiffured coastal village that sits on its own peninsula like a Milanese model glued to the catwalk. Spending the night here might be beyond the wallet-stretching capabilities of the hoi polloi, but mere mortals should save up to enjoy an expensive cappuccino next to Portofino's yacht-filled harbour logging the ubiquity of Ferrari key-rings and Gucci handbags.

⊙ Sights

Castello Brown
CASTLE

(www.portofinoevents.com; Via alla Penisola 13a; admission €3.50; ⊙vary) From the sublime harbour, a flight of stairs signposted 'Salita San Giorgio' leads past the **Chiesa di San Giorgio** to Portofino's unusual castle, a 10-minute walk altogether (confirm the opening times with the tourist office prior to setting out, as the castle often hosts private events). The Genoese-built castle saw action against the Venetians, Savoyards, Sardinians and Austrians, and later fell to Napoleon. In 1867 it was transformed by the British diplomat Montague Yeats Brown into a private mansion. The fabulous tiled staircase is one of the showpieces of the neo-Gothic interior, while there are great views from the garden. For a better outlook, continue for another 300m or so along the same track to the **lighthouse**.

⚡ Activities

If you're feeling flush, chat to the boat-taxi operators in the harbour about snorkelling and sightseeing trips.

🌿 Parco Naturale Regionale di Portofino
HIKING

(www.parks.it/parco.portofino) Unbeknown to the soft-top-sportscar drivers who zoom in via the sinuous road from Santa Margherita, the Portofino peninsula is criss-crossed with 60km of narrow trails, many of them surprisingly remote and all of them free of charge. The tourist office has maps. A good but tough day hike (there are exposed sections) is the 18km coastal route from Camogli to Santa Margherita via San Fruttuoso and Portofino. There are handy train connections at both ends.

🛏 Sleeping

Warning: staying the night can severely damage your credit card!

Eden
BOUTIQUE HOTEL €€€

(☑0185 26 90 91; www.hoteledenportofino.com; Vico Dritto 18; d €140-270; P✳) You've arrived in heaven, so you might as well stay there. Eden is an apt word on the quiet cobbled side streets a stone's throw from Portofino's idyllic harbourfront where this residential-like hotel does a good job at looking posh without being too pretentious.

Hotel Splendido
LUXURY HOTEL €€€

(☑0185 26 78 01; www.hotelsplendido.com; Salita Baratta 16; s/d from €562/975; P✳@🌐🏊) The megarich or those intent on blowing their life's savings check into this bastion of whimsy and wisteria to follow in the footsteps of the Duke of Windsor, Frank Sinatra and countless other zillionaires. Ordinary Joes can freely wander round the columns and cupolas while nurturing fanciful dreams.

✗ Eating & Drinking

Portofino favours Serie A footballers and lottery winners, though the average traveller can usually rustle up sufficient cash (€5) for a harbourside cappuccino.

Pizzeria Il Portico
PIZZERIA €€

(Via Roma 21; meals €20-25; ⊙closed Tue) Wander a block from the harbour and pizza margheritas can be procured for €6. At Il Portici, diners can enjoy dishes such as octopus salad, *vongole* (clams) and Genovese specials on chequered tablecloths outside.

Caffè Excelsior
CAFE €€

(Piazza Martiri dell'Olivetta 54) Standard €1.30 cappuccinos are a pipe dream here, but what you're paying for isn't the coffee but the perch: a lovely cafe with romantic alfresco booths where Greta Garbo used to hide behind dark glasses.

ⓘ Information

Tourist office (www.apttigullio.liguria.it; Via Roma 35; ⊙10am-1pm & 1.30-4.30pm Tue-Sun) Has free trail maps for the Parco Naturale Regionale di Portofino and information on mountain-bike rental, as well as seasonal sail and motorboat rental.

ⓘ Getting There & Around

ATP (www.atp-spa.it) bus 882 runs to Portofino from outside the tourist office in Santa Margherita (€1.50, every 30 minutes), but by far the best way is to walk. A designated path tracks the gorgeous coastline for 3km.

From April to October, **Servizio Marittimo del Tigullio** (www.traghettiportofino.it) runs daily ferries from Portofino to/from San Fruttuoso (€7.50/10.50), Rapallo (€7/10.50) and Santa Margherita (€5.50/8.50).

Motorists must park at the village entrance, with obligatory parking fees starting from €4.50 per hour (cash only).

SANTA MARGHERITA
POP 10.035

After the chaos of Genoa, Santa Margherita materialises like a calm Impressionist painting. You wouldn't want to change a single detail of its picture-perfect seaside promenade, where elegant hotels with Liberty facades overlook million-dollar yachts in this favourite fishing-village-turned-wealthy-retirement-spot. Fortunately, unlike in Portofino, you don't have to be a millionaire to stay here.

Sights & Activities

Santa Margherita's idyllic position in a sheltered bay on the turquoise Golfo di Tigullio makes it a good base for sailing, water-skiing and scuba diving. Those feeling less active can simply stretch out on its popular beach.

FREE **Villa Durazzo**   MUSEUM, GARDEN
(www.villadurazzo.it; Piazzale San Giacomo 3; ⊙9am-1pm & 2.30-6.30pm) Villa Durazzo is Santa Margherita personified: an exquisite mansion and gardens that are linked to a 16th-century castle overlooking the sea. You can take an aromatic stroll among lemon trees, hydrangea and camellia hedges, and other flora typical of the town's hot climate, in the lavish Italian gardens. The house is being made into a museum and is regularly used for weddings. There's a lovely coffee terrace.

Sleeping

Lido Palace Hotel   HOTEL €€
(☎0185 28 58 21; www.lidopalacehotel.com; Via Doria 3; s €110-140, d €140-200; P❋🏠) Right on the waterfront and oozing old-school refinement, this Liberty-style grande dame offers the quintessential Santa Margherita experience. Rooms are generously proportioned and the breakfast buffet is bountiful. The restaurant has an outdoor terrace with elevated views and there are half- and full-board options.

Fasce   HOTEL €€
(☎0185 28 64 35; www.hotelfasce.it; Via Luigi Bozzo 3; s/d €98/108; ❋@) This is one of Santa Margherita's cheaper options, with a rooftop sun deck, 16 decent-sized rooms (though bathrooms are teensy) and a limited breakfast. Parking costs an extra €18.

Eating & Drinking

Trattoria dei Pescatori   SEAFOOD €€
(Via Bottaro 43-44; meals around €35; ⊙Wed-Mon Sep-Jun, daily Jul & Aug) *Moscardini affogati* (spicy stewed baby octopus) is the summertime speciality of Santa Margherita's first-ever restaurant, opened in 1910. Autumn brings wild mushrooms to the table, while year-round Pescatori serves a delicious regional fish soup, oven-baked fish with olives and pine nuts, and handmade pasta in all shapes and sizes.

Bar Colombo   CAFE, BAR €€
(Via Pescino 13; ⊙to late Tue-Sun) A celebration of art nouveau, this resplendent coffee bar-restaurant on the seafront is the former hang-out of silver-screen stars such as Burton and Taylor.

Information

Tourist office (www.apttigullio.liguria.it; Piazza Vittorio Veneto; ⊙9.30am-12.30pm & 2.30-5.30pm Mon-Sat) Has a raft of information about water sports along the gulf.

Parco Naturale Regionale di Portofino (www.parks.it/parco.portofino; Viale Rainusso 1) Maps and information on hiking.

Getting There & Around

ATP Tigullio Trasporti (www.tigullio trasporti.it, in Italian) runs buses to/from Portofino (every 20 minutes) and Camogli (every 30 minutes).

By train, there are hourly services to/from Genoa (€3, 35 minutes) and La Spezia (€5.50, 1½ hours).

Servizio Marittimo del Tigullio (www.traghettiportofino.it; Via Palestro 8/1b) runs seasonal ferries to/from Cinque Terre (one way/return €17/24.50), Porto Venere (€21/32), San Fruttuoso (€9.50/14.50), Portofino (€5.50/8.50) and Rapallo (€3.50/4.50).

RAPALLO
POP 30.571

WB Yeats, Max Beerbohm and Ezra Pound all garnered inspiration in Rapallo and it's not difficult to see why. With its bright-blue changing cabins, palm-fringed beach and diminutive 16th-century castle perched above the sea (hosting temporary art exhibitions), the town has a refined and nostalgic air. That's not to say it isn't friendly. Rapallo's compactness gives it a less elite atmosphere than its jet-set neighbours. It's at its busiest on Thursdays, when market stalls fill central Piazza Cile.

Sights

Rapallo's seafront promenade – Lungomare Vittorio Veneto – is an unwitting street theatre of the beautiful and the damned. It's worth checking inside the picturesque impossible-to-miss castle where temporary exhibitions are sometimes held.

Cable Car

(Piazzale Solari 2; one way/return €5.50/8; ⊙9am-12.30pm & 2-6pm) When you've had your fill of the promenade poseurs, rise above them in a 1934-vintage cable car up to Santuario Basilica di Montallegro (612m), a sanctuary built on the spot where, on 2 July 1557, the Virgin Mary was reportedly sighted. Walkers and mountain bikers can follow an old mule track (5km, 1½ hours) to the hilltop site.

🛏 Sleeping

Hotel Miro   HOTEL €€

(☎0185 23 41 00; www.hotelmiro.net; Lungomare Vittorio Veneto 32; s €70-125, d €90-145; P❄) Right on the seafront, this charming boutique hotel with an occluded entrance behind a promenade cafe has retained much of its historical character, with canopied beds and floral-print wallpaper.

Hotel L'Approdo   HOTEL €€

(☎0185 23 45 45; www.approdohotel.it; Via San Michele di Pagana 160; d €98-156; ❄) Set on the hillside, L'Approdo has some great sea views, but if you're willing to forgo them and look out onto the garden instead, you can negotiate a lower rate. Rooms are shiny and modern, and some are wheelchair accessible. Parking (€10 per day) needs to be booked ahead.

🍴 Eating

Behind rows of parked scooters, the waterfront has plenty of places to eat, drink and snack.

Antica Cucina Genovese TRADITIONAL ITALIAN €€

(Via Santa Maria del Campo 133; meals €18-30; ⊙Tue-Sun) Handmade pasta dishes include a huge variety of vegetarian options such as chestnut ravioli with pesto, as well as vegan fare such as potato and mushroom stew. The open kitchen also prepares meat and fish dishes, and there's a great range of Ligurian wines.

Biancaneve   CAFE €

(Lungomare Vittorio Veneto 37) Old dames in heavy jewellery mix with the nouveau riche under the awning of this seafront cafe. There are stashes of *Vogue*-like magazines to flick through inside and some impressive signed photos on the wall (Mick Jagger included).

ℹ Information

Tourist office (www.apttigullio.liguria.it; Lungo Vittorio Veneto 7; ⊙9.30am-12.30pm & 2.30-5.30pm Mon-Sat) Details of walks in the area plus maps.

ℹ Getting There & Away

Trains run along the coast to Genoa (€3, 40 minutes) and La Spezia (€5.50, one hour).

Servizio Marittimo del Tigullio (www.trag hettiportofino.it) runs boats to/from Santa Margherita (one way/return €3.50/4.50), Portofino (€7/10.50), San Fruttuoso (€10/15.50), Genoa (€13.50/19), the Cinque Terre (€17/24.50) and Porto Venere (€21/32). Not all operate daily, and many are seasonal – the website posts updated schedules.

Cinque Terre

If you ever get tired of life, bypass the therapist and decamp immediately to Cinque Terre. Here five crazily constructed fishing villages, set amid some of the most dramatic coastal scenery on the planet, ought to provide enough ammunition to bolster the most jaded of spirits. A Unesco World Heritage Site since 1997, Cinque Terre isn't the undiscovered Eden it was 30 years ago, but frankly – who cares? Sinuous paths tempt the antisocial to traverse seemingly impregnable cliffsides, while a 19th-century railway line cut through a series of coastal tunnels ferries the less brave from village to village. Thankfully cars – those most ubiquitous of modern interferences – were banned over a decade ago.

Rooted in antiquity, Cinque Terre's five towns date from the early medieval period. Monterosso, the oldest, was founded in AD 643 when beleaguered hill dwellers moved down to the coast to escape from invading barbarians. Riomaggiore came next, purportedly established in the 8th century by Greek settlers fleeing persecution in Byzantium. The others are Vernazza, Corniglia and Manarola. Much of what remains in the towns today dates from the late High Middle Ages, including several castles and a quintet of illustrious parish churches.

Buildings aside, Cinque Terre's unique historical feature is the steeply terraced cliffs bisected by a complicated system of fields and gardens that has been hacked, chiselled, shaped and layered over the course of nearly two millennia. So marked are these artificial contours that some scholars have compared the extensive *muretti* (low stone walls) to the Great Wall of China in their grandeur and scope.

1. Riomaggiore (p181)
Women in Riomaggiore, the Cinque Terre's easternmost and largest village.

2. Manarola (p180)
Colourful houses in the village of Manarola, famous for its sweet Sciacchetrà wine.

3. Corniglia (p180)
Vineyard-surrounded Corniglia sits atop a 100m-high rocky promontory and has no direct sea access.

4. **Cinque Terre National Park (p178)**
Hiking past vineyards between Manarola and Corniglia.

5. **Vernazza (p179)**
This village boasts the only secure landing point on the Cinque Terre coast.

⚡ Activities

WALKING

Coming to Cinque Terre and not hiking is like sitting down for dinner in an Italian restaurant and eschewing the wine. The blue-riband hike is the 12km Sentiero Azzurro (Blue Trail; marked No 2 on maps), a one-time mule path that links all five oceanside villages by foot. The trail dates back to the early days of the Republic of Genoa in the 12th and 13th centuries and, until the opening of the railway line in 1874, it was the only practical means of getting from village to village. To walk the Blue Trail you must first purchase a Cinque Terre card for €5. Far from flat, the Azzurro is a narrow, precipitous hike, though people of all shapes and sizes complete it every day. The most popular direction of traffic is east–west, beginning in Riomaggiore and finishing in Monterosso, starting on the famed Via dell'Amore. If you're not up to going the full distance, try walking as far as the middle village, Corniglia, and getting a train back.

Just a few kilometres shy of a full-blown marathon, the 38km Sentiero Rosso (Red trail; marked No 1 on maps) – which runs from Porto Venere to Levanto – dangles a tempting challenge to experienced walkers who aim to complete it in nine to 12 hours. For every 100 people you see on the Sentiero Azzurro, there are less than a dozen up here plying their way along a route that is mainly flat, tree-covered and punctuated with plenty of shortcuts. An early start is assured by an efficient train and bus connection to Porto Venere (via La Spezia), while refreshments en route are possible in a liberal smattering of welcoming bars and restaurants.

MOUNTAIN BIKING

Since 2009 the national park has allowed mountain bikes on some of its paths. The starting point of most of the paths is the Santuario della Madonna di Montenero, accessible by road or *sentiero* No 3 above Riomaggiore

🎓 Courses

Arbaspàa   COOKING

(📞0187 76 00 83; www.arbaspaa.com; courses €109-129) Prepare Ligurian specialities in a farmhouse near the town of Levanto. Cooking lessons are available on Monday and Tuesday from March to October.

ⓘ Information

Online information is available at www.cinque terre.it and www.cinqueterre.com.

Parco Nazionale (www.parconazionale5terre. it; ⊙7am-8pm) Offices in the train stations of all five villages and also in La Spezia station.

ⓘ Getting There & Around

BOAT In summer Cooperativa Battellieri del Golfo Paradiso (www.golfoparadiso.it) runs boats to the Cinque Terre from Genoa (one way/ return €18/33). Seasonal boat services to/from Santa Margherita (€17/24.50) are handled by Servizio Marittimo del Tigullio (www.traghet tiportofino.it).

From late March to October, La Spezia–based Consorzio Marittimo Turistico Cinque Terre Golfo dei Poeti (www.navigazionegolfodeipoeti. it) runs daily shuttle boats between all of the Cinque Terre villages (except Corniglia), costing €18 one way including all stops, €23 return on weekdays and €25 on weekends.

CAR & MOTORCYCLE Private vehicles are not allowed beyond village entrances. If you're arriving by car or motorcycle, you'll need to pay to park in designated car parks. In some villages, minibus shuttles depart from the car parks (one way/return €1.50/2.50) – park offices have seasonal schedules.

TRAIN Between 6.30am and 10pm, one to three trains an hour trundle along the coast between Genoa and La Spezia, stopping at each of the Cinque Terre's villages. Unlimited 2nd-class rail travel between Levanto and La Spezia is covered by the Cinque Terre card (see the boxed text, p182).

MONTEROSSO

POP 1527

The most accessible village by car and the only Cinque Terre settlement to sport a tourist beach, Monterosso is the furthest west and least quintessential of the quintet (it was briefly ditched from the group in the 1940s). Noted for its lemon trees and anchovies, the village is split into two parts (old and new) linked by an underground tunnel that burrows beneath the blustery San Cristoforo promontory.

◉ Sights

Convento dei Cappuccini   CHURCH

Monterosso's most interesting church and convent complex is set on the hill that divides the old town from the newer Fegina quarter. The striped church, the Chiesa di San Francesco, dates from 1623 and has a painting attributed to Van Dyck (*Crocifissione*) to the left of the altar. Nearby, the ruins of an old castle have been converted into a cemetery.

🛏 Sleeping

Unlike the other four towns, Monterosso has a credible stash of hotels to choose from.

Each of Cinque Terre's villages is associated with a sanctuary perched high on the cliff-sides above the azure Mediterranean. Reaching these religious retreats used to be part of a hefty Catholic penance, but these days the walks through terraced vineyards and across view-splayed cliffs are a lot less onerous.

Monterosso to Santuario della Madonna di Soviore From Via Roma in the village, follow trail 9 up through forest and past the ruins of an old hexagonal chapel to an ancient paved mule path that leads to Liguria's oldest sanctuary. Here you'll find a bar, restaurant and views as far as Corsica on a clear day.

Vernazza to Santuario della Madonna di Reggio From underneath Vernazza's railway bridge, follow trail 8 up numerous flights of steps and past 14 sculpted Stations of the Cross to this 11th-century chapel with a Romanesque facade.

Corniglia to Santuario della Madonna delle Grazie This sanctuary can be approached from either Corniglia (on trail 7b) or Vernazza (trail 7), though the latter is better. Branch off the Sentiero Azzurro and ascend the spectacular Salla di Comeneco to the village of San Bernardino where you'll find the church with its adored image of Madonna and child above the altar.

Manarola to Santuario della Madonna delle Salute The pick of all the sanctuary walks is this breathtaking traverse (trail 6) through Cinque Terre's finest vineyards to a diminutive Romanesque-meets-Gothic chapel in the tiny village of Volastra.

Riomaggiore to Santuario della Madonna di Montenero Trail 3 ascends from the top of the village, up steps and past walled gardens to a restored 18th-century chapel with a frescoed ceiling that sits atop an astounding lookout next to the park's new cycling centre.

La Poesia   B&B €€
(☏0187 81 72 83; www.lapoesia-cinqueterre.com; Via Genova 4; d €90-180) Shoehorned up a backstreet in the older part of town, La Poesia's three rooms (named Clizia, Annetta and Aspasia for the women to which Nobel Prize–winning poet Eugenio Montale dedicated his poems) occupy an early-17th-century house. Breakfast is served on a terrace surrounded by lemon trees and the house has a regal quality missing elsewhere in Cinque Terre.

Hotel Palme   HOTEL €€
(☏0187 82 90 13; www.hotelpalme.it; Via IV Novembre 18; s €60-120, d €80-160; ☺Apr-Oct; P ❄) True to its name, Palme has lazy palm-filled gardens, refurbished rooms and a handy location in the newer part of the village.

Hotel Baia   HOTEL €€
(☏0187 81 75 12; www.baiahotel.it; Via Fegina 88; s €100-150, d €120-180; ❄☎) Big beds and basic rooms with killer seafront views characterise Baia, which sits next to the railway station right on the beach. There's a three-night minimum stay.

✗ Eating

Along the seafront, restaurants dish up local anchovies straight out of the sea, served fried, raw (with lemon juice), pickled in brine or in a *tian* (baked with potatoes and tomatoes). To wash them down, stop in at one of several wine bars throughout the village.

Focacceria Enoteca Antonia   SNACKS €
(Via Fegina 124; focaccia slice €2-3; ☺9am-8pm Fri-Wed Mar-Oct) To pack an authentic Ligurian beach picnic, head to where Paola and her husband Giuseppe make 15 kinds of piping-hot focaccia from scratch and also stock well-priced local wines.

La Cantina del Pescatore   SNACKS €
(Via V Emanuele 19; snacks €4-9; ☎) You can also buy local food and wine at this newly opened restaurant, including excellent jam, spreads and *lemoncino* liquor, making it worthwhile for a snack lunch. Try the pesto on toast, salads, hot dogs (for kids) and local wine. There's free wi-fi.

VERNAZZA
POP 987

Guarding the only secure landing point on the Cinque Terre coast, Vernazza's small quintessential Mediterranean harbour guards what is perhaps the quaintest of the five villages. Lined with little cafes, Vernazza's main cobbled street, Via Roma, links seaside Piazza Marconi with the train station. Side streets lead to the village's trademark Genoa-style *caruggi* (narrow lanes).

◉ Sights

Piazza Matteotti and the harbour are a delight. There's a tiny sandy beach here and swimming is possible.

Chiesa di Santa Margherita d'Antiochia
CHURCH

(Piazza Matteotti) The waterfront is framed by a small Gothic-Ligurian church built in 1318 after a murky legend about the bones of St Margaret being found in a wooden box on a nearby beach. It is notable for its 40m-tall octagonal tower.

Castello Doria
CASTLE

(admission €1.50; ◉10am-7pm) The oldest surviving fortification in Cinque Terre dates from around 1000. Today it is a collection of ruins with some astounding views. Climb up through the winding *caruggi* to the entrance.

◉ Sleeping & Eating

Gianni Franzi
SEAFOOD, GUESTHOUSE €€

(✆0187 82 10 03; www.giannifranzi.it; Piazza Matteotti 5; meals €22-30, s/d €70/100; ◉mid-Mar–early Jan) Traditional Cinque Terre seafood (mussels, seafood, ravioli and lemon anchovies) has been served up in this harbourside trattoria since the 1960s. More recently they've been renting rooms with views, all of which share a communal terrace. Cheaper single rooms with a shared bathroom go for €45.

Gambero Rosso
SEAFOOD €€

(www.ristorantegamberorosso.net; Piazza Marconi 7; meals €30-35) If you've subsisted on focaccia, splash out here on Gambero's house special for dinner: *Tegame di Venazza* (anchovies with baked potatoes and tomatoes).

Batti Batti
SNACKS €

(Via Roma 3) The bastion of that cheap Cinque Terre trademark – focaccia – Batti Batti knocks out the best slices in the village (some would say in the whole Cinque Terre). There's pizza slices too.

CORNIGLIA
POP 600

Corniglia is the 'quiet' middle village that sits atop a 100m-high rocky promontory surrounded by vineyards. It is the only Cinque Terre settlement with no direct sea access (steep steps lead down to a rocky cove). Narrow alleys and colourfully painted four-storey houses characterise the ancient

core, a timeless streetscape that was name-checked in Boccaccio's *Decameron*. To reach the village proper from the railway station you must first tackle the 377-step **Lardarina**.

◉ Sights

Centrally located Corniglia is the only place where you can see all five settlements in the same panorama.

La Torre
LOOKOUT

This medieval lookout is reached by a stairway that leads up from the diminutive main square (Piazza Taragio).

Belvedere Santa Maria
LOOKOUT

Follow Via Fieschi through the heart of the village and you'll eventually dead-end at this heart-stopping lookout with sweeping sea views.

Guvano Beach
BEACH

This hard-to-find, clothing-optional beach is situated between Cornigla and Vernazza. Getting there involves walking through an abandoned railway tunnel – ask a local for directions.

◉ Sleeping & Eating

As elsewhere in the Cinque Terre, fish is the mainstay of Corniglia's restaurants – you can't go wrong by asking for whatever's fresh.

Ostello di Corniglia
HOSTEL €

(✆0187 81 25 59; www.ostellocorniglia.com; dm/d €24/60; ◉) Cinque Terre's newest hostel is perched at the top of the village and has two eight-bed dorms and four doubles (with private bathroom). Prices are negotiable. There's a lockout from 1pm to 3pm.

Case di Corniglia
RENTAL ROOMS €

(✆0187 81 23 42; www.casedicorniglia.com; Via alla Stazione 19) These recently refurbished rent-a-rooms are spread over two buildings in the village's main street. Good for families or groups.

Caffe Matteo
CAFE €

(Piazza Taragio) While the rest of Corniglia siestas, the Matteo stays open all day with its chairs spilling into the tiny main square. Don't leave without trying the pesto lasagne.

MANAROLA
POP 850

Bequeathed with more grapevines than any other Cinque Terre village, Manarola is famous for its sweet Sciacchetrà wine. It's also awash with priceless medieval relics, supporting claims that it is the oldest of the five.

Due to its proximity to Riomaggiore (852m away), the village is heavily trafficked, especially by Italian school parties. The spirited locals speak an esoteric local dialect known as Manarolese.

Sights

Piazzale Papa Innocenzo IV
PIAZZA

At the northern end of Via Discovolo, you'll come upon this small piazza, dominated by a bell tower used as a defensive lookout. Opposite, the Chiesa di San Lorenzo dates from 1338 and houses a 15th-century polyptych. If you're geared up for a steep walk, from nearby Via Rollandi you can follow a path that leads through vineyards to the top of the mountain.

Punta Buonfiglio
LOOKOUT

Manarola's prized viewpoint is on a rocky promontory on the path out of town (Sentiero Azzurro) towards Corniglia where walkers stop for classic photos of the village. A rest area has been constructed here. Nearby are the ruins of an old chapel once used as a shelter by local farmers.

Museo dello Sciacchetrá
MUSEUM

(Via Discovolo 225) Sporadic opening hours haunt this tiny museum where you can quiz whoever's around about traditional vine-growing methods.

Sleeping & Eating

Ostello 5 Terre
HOSTEL €

(☑0187 92 02 15; www.cinqueterre.net/ostello; Via Riccobaldi 21; dm €20-23, d €55-65; ☉Mar-Dec; @) This hostel rents out mountain bikes, kayaks, Nordic-walking poles and snorkelling gear. Its single-sex, six-bed dorms come with their own bathrooms, and there's English-language satellite TV, Playstation and a book exchange. Lockout times are 10am to 4pm (or 5pm June to August).

Marina Piccola
SEAFOOD, GUESTHOUSE €

(☑0187 92 01 03; www.hotelmarinapiccola.com; Via Lo Scalo 16; meals €22-30, s/d €90/120) A shoal of fish dishes and the house speciality *zuppa di datteri* (date soup) are served up here along with sea views. If you want to stay, the 'little marina' has good deals for half- and full-board.

Cinque Terre Gelataria & Creperia
GELATERIA €

(Via Discovolo) It's all subjective, but if you did a snap survey of Cinque Terre's best ice-cream joints, this would be the likely winner.

Cinque Terre's easternmost village, Riomaggiore is the largest of the five and acts as its unofficial HQ (the main park office is based here). Its peeling pastel buildings tumble like faded chocolate boxes down a steep ravine to a tiny harbour – the region's favourite postcard view – and glow romantically at sunset. The famous Sentiero Azzurro coastal path (p178) starts here. The first hideously busy section to Manarola is called the Via dell'Amore.

Sights & Activities

Outside the train station near the water's edge, murals depict the backbreaking work of Cinque Terre farmers who, over the centuries, built the Cinque Terre with their bare hands. The village also has a couple of small churches and a ruined castle on a headland overlooking the settlement.

Torre Guardiola
NATURE RESERVE

(admission €1.50; ☉9am-1pm Aug, 9am-1pm & 4-7pm Feb-Jul, Sep & Oct) Birdlife and local flora can be seen from a nature observation and bird-watching centre located on a promontory of land just east of Riomaggiore. The building was a former naval installation in WWII, known as La Batteria Racchia. Today there's a small bar and panels explaining the surrounding flora. The Torre is reachable via a trail that starts just west of Fossola Beach.

Fossola Beach
BEACH

This small pebbly beach is located immediately southeast of Riomaggiore marina. It's rugged but secluded. Swimmers should be wary of rocks and currents.

Cooperative Sub 5 Terre
DIVE CENTRE

(☑0187 92 00 11; www.5terrediving.it; Via San Giacomo; ☉vary seasonally) To dive or snorkel in the translucent waters of the protected marine park, contact this outfit in the subway at the bottom of Via Colombo. It also rents out canoes and kayaks.

Sleeping

B&Bs and a handful of hotels are situated in the village, but the town's forte is room- and apartment-rental agencies.

Hotel Zorza
HOTEL €

(www.hotelzorza.com; Via Colombo 231; d from €90; ❋☜) One of the few hotels in the five villages, the Zorza is a little sleepier than your average big-town affair. The reception shuts down at 7pm-ish, but opens in the morning for a decent breakfast. Well-kept middle-ranking rooms are spread across the sinuous 17th-century house of a former wine-grower.

Edi
RENTAL ROOMS €€

(☏0187 92 03 25; Via Colombo 111; r €60-180) This rental agency on the main drag has five rooms and seven two- to four-bed apartments for rent, many with sea views. It also operates the village laundry next door.

La Casa di Venere
RENTAL ROOMS €€

(☏349 075 31 40; www.lacasadivenere.com; Via Colombo 194; d €50-120, tr €80-150) This agency offers some of the cheapest harbourside rooms. All are clean, bright and modern, and some have to-die-for views.

✗ Eating

Riomaggiore has the best selection of restaurants in the five villages.

TOP CHOICE Dau Cila
MODERN ITALIAN €€

(www.ristorantedaucila.com; Via San Giacomo 65; meals €25-30; ☺8am-2am Mar-Oct) Perched within pebble-lobbing distance of Riomaggiore's snug harbour (which is crammed with fishing nets and overturned boats), Dau Cila is an obvious place to tuck into the local seafood. It also has the best wine cellar in town. You can pair the best local stuff with cold plates such as smoked tuna with apples and lemon, or lemon-marinaded anchovies with pears and Parmesan.

La Lampara
MODERN ITALIAN €€

(Via Malborghetto 2; meals €25; ☺7am-midnight) There's always lots of tourists here, but you won't feel like one as the service is so genuinely personable. Fish dishes predominate, though the pizza and pasta *al pesto* are also formidable.

Around Cinque Terre

LA SPEZIA
POP 95,641

It's an understandable oversight. Situated minutes to the east of Cinque Terre by train, the hard-working port town of La Spezia is routinely overlooked. If you happen to get delayed, give it a once-over: it's home to Italy's largest naval base, where echoes of Genoa ring through the narrow winding streets of the Old Town. Not surprisingly, La Spezia has some cosy trattorias showcasing the standard Ligurian delicacies of wine, bread and pesto sauce.

La Spezia's bustle peaks on 19 March, the feast day of the city's patron saint, San Giuseppe (St Joseph). Celebrations see a giant market fill the port and surrounding streets, and the naval base (off limits the rest of the year) open to the public.

◉ Sights

Museo Amedeo Lia
MUSEUM

(www.castagna.it/mal; Via Prione 234; adult/reduced €6.50/4; ☺10am-6pm Tue-Sun) This fine-arts museum in a restored 17th-century friary is La Spezia's star attraction. The collection covers the 13th to 18th centuries and includes paintings by masters such as Tintoretto, Montagna, Titian and Pietro Lorenzetti. Also on show are Roman bronzes and ecclesiastical treasures such as Limoges crucifixes and illuminated musical manuscripts.

Castello di San Giorgio
CASTLE

(www.castagna.it/sangiorgio; Via XXVII Marzo; adult/reduced €5/4; ☺9.30am-12.30pm & 3-6pm Wed-Mon) An assortment of local archaeological artefacts from prehistoric to medieval times is on display at this lofty castle.

🛏 Sleeping & Eating

There are several cheap hotels around the train station, but they tend to be scruffy. The waterfront has plenty of relaxed places to wine and dine.

MAKING THE MOST OF YOUR EURO

Easily the best way to get around the Cinque Terre is with a Cinque Terre card.

Two versions of the card are available: with or without train travel. Both include unlimited use of walking paths and electric village buses, as well as cultural exhibitions. Without train travel, a basic one-/two-/three-/seven-day card for those aged over four years costs €5/8/10/20. A card that also includes unlimited train trips between the towns costs €8.50/14.70/19.50/36.50.

Both versions of the card are sold at all Cinque Terre park information offices.

Albergo Birillo
HOTEL €

(☎0187 73 26 66; Via Dei Mille 11/13; s €30-50, d €65-75) This homey haven has rather tight-fitting rooms, which are made up for by the ultrafriendly owners, who'll fill you in on the town's hidden attractions. Situated a few blocks from Via Prione and near plenty of good eateries, it makes an economical alternative to digs in Cinque Terre.

Vicolo Intherno
MODERN ITALIAN €€

(Via della Canonica 22; meals around €25; ⏰Tue-Sat) Take a seat around chunky wooden tables beneath beamed ceilings at this Slow Food–affiliated restaurant and wash down the *torte di verdure* (Ligurian vegetable pie) or stockfish with local vintages.

❶ Information

Cinque Terre Park Office (☎0187 74 35 00; internet access per 10min €0.80; ⏰7am-8pm) Inside La Spezia's train station. See p201 for other park offices.

Tourist office (www.aptcinqueterre.sp.it; Viale Giuseppe Mazzini 47; ⏰9am-1pm & 2.30-5.30pm Mon-Sat, 9am-1pm Sun)

❶ Getting There & Away

Buses run by **Azienda Trasporti Consortile** (ATC; www.atclaspezia.it, in Italian) are the only way to reach Porto Venere (€1.45, approximately every 30 minutes) and Lerici (€1.45, approximately every 15 minutes).

La Spezia is on the Genoa–Rome railway line and is also connected to Milan (€23.50, three hours, four daily), Turin (€27, 3½ hours, several daily) and Pisa (€5.20, 50 minutes, almost hourly). The Cinque Terre and other coastal towns are easily accessible by train (see p226) and boat (p184).

PORTO VENERE
POP 3942

If Cinque Terre were ever to pick up an honorary sixth member, Porto Venere would surely be it. Perched on the Gulf of Poets' western promontory, the village's sinuous seven- and eight-storey harbourfront houses form an almost impregnable citadel around the muscular Castello Doria. The Romans built Portus Veneris as a base en route from Gaul to Spain, and in later years Byzantines, Lombards, the Genovese and Napoleon all passed through here. Cinque Terre's marathon-length Sentiero Rosso trail to Levanto (p223) starts here, just behind the castle. Hikers, take a deep breath...

☉ Sights

Outside the hectic summer season, Porto Venere is something of a ghost town – and all the more alluring for it.

Castello Doria
CASTLE

(admission €2.20; ⏰10.30am-1.30pm & 2.30-6pm) A formidable example of the Genoese military architecture, no one knows when the original castle was built though the current structure dates from the 16th century. A highly strategic citadel in its time, it once stood on the front line with Genoa's maritime feud with Pisa. There are magnificent views from its ornate terraced gardens.

Chiesa di San Pietro
CHURCH

This wind- and wave-lashed church, built in 1198 in Gothic style, stands on the ruins of a 5th-century palaeo-Christian church. Before that it was a Roman temple dedicated to the goddess Venus (born from the foam of the sea), from whom Porto Venere takes its name.

Grotta Arpaia
GROTTO

At the end of the quay, a Cinque Terre panorama unfolds from the rocky terraces of Grotta Arpaia, a former haunt of Byron, who once swam across the gulf from Porto Venere to Lerici to visit his mate, Shelley. Traces of a pagan temple have been uncovered on the quay, inside the black-and-white-marble Chiesa di San Pietro, which was built in 1277. Just off the promontory lie the tiny islands of Palmaria, Tino and Tinetto.

⌂ Sleeping & Eating

A half-dozen or so restaurants line Calata Doria, by the sea. A block inland, Porto Venere's main old-town street, Via Cappellini, has several tasty choices.

Albergo Genio
HOTEL €€

(☎0187 79 06 11; www.hotelgenioportovenere.com; Piazza Bastreri 8; s €80-95, d €100-125; ⏰mid-Feb–mid-Jan; 🅿🌣) From Piazza Bastreri, scale the spiral stairs in the round tower to reach this charming seven-room hotel. In summer breakfast is served alfresco beneath the vines, and some rooms are equipped with air-conditioning.

La Lanterna
B&B €

(☎0187 79 22 91; www.lalanterna-portovenere.it; Via Capellini 109; d €75-85; 🌣) Down by Porto Venere's picturesque harbourfront, this little guesthouse has just two airy rooms (there's also an option of a four-person apartment on request). Breakfast isn't included, but can be arranged; otherwise stroll to a nearby cafe.

ℹ️ Information

Tourist office (www.portovenere.it; Piazza Bastreri 7; ⏰10am-noon & 3-8pm Jun-Aug, 10am-noon & 3-6pm Thu-Tue Sep-May) Sells a couple of useful maps and walking guides in English.

ℹ️ Getting There & Away

Porto Venere is served by daily buses from La Spezia (see p183).

From late March to October, **Consorzio Maritimo Turistico Cinque Terre Golfo dei Poeti** (www.navigazionegolfodeipoeti.it) sails from Porto Venere to/from Cinque Terre villages (one way with all stops €15, return €20 to €22) and runs boat excursions to the islands of Palmaria, Tino and Tinetto (€9), as well as services to La Spezia and Lerici (call for seasonal information).

LERICI & AROUND
POP 10,447

Magnolia, yew and cedar trees grow in the 1930s public gardens at Lerici, an exclusive retreat of pool-equipped villas clinging to the cliffs along its beach. In another age Byron and Shelley sought inspiration here.

👁️ Sights & Activities

From Lerici a scenic 3km coastal stroll leads northwest to San Terenzo, a seaside village with a sandy beach and Genoese castle. The Shelleys stayed at the waterfront Villa Magni (closed to visitors) in the early 1820s and Percy drowned here when his boat sank off the coast in 1822 on a return trip from Livorno.

Another coastal stroll, 4km southeast, takes you past magnificent little bays to Tellaro, a fishing hamlet with pink-and-orange houses cluttered about narrow lanes and tiny squares. Sit on the rocks at the Chiesa San Giorgio and imagine an octopus ringing the church bells – which, according to legend, it did to warn the villagers of a Saracen attack.

Castello di Lerici   CASTLE, MUSEUM
(Piazza San Giorgio 1) For outstanding views make your way on foot or by public lift to Lerici's symbolic 12th-century castle, once taken by the Pisans but today given over to a rather bizarre collection of dinosaurs in its Museo di Palaeontologia (fossils have been found near here).

🍽️ Sleeping & Eating

Locanda Miranda   INN, GASTRONOMIC €€€
(📞0187 96 40 12; Via Fiascherina 92; d €120, d with half-board €180, set menus €40-60; 🅿️) Tellaro is home to this gourmet hideaway, an exquisite seven-room inn with art- and antiques-decorated rooms, and a Michelin-starred restaurant specialising exclusively in seafood (not for vegetarians or carnivores!).

ℹ️ Information

Tourist office (Via Biaggini 6; ⏰9am-1pm & 2.30-5.30pm Mon-Sat, 9am-1pm Sun) Can advise on walking and cycling in the area, as well as accommodation.

Riviera di Ponente

Curving west from Genoa to the French border, the Ponente stretch of the Ligurian coast is more down-to-earth than the flashy Rivieria di Levante. As a result it shelters some unlikely escape hatches, particularly along the stretch of coast from Noli to Finale Ligure.

SAVONA
POP 62,494

Behind Savona's sprawling port facilities, the city's unexpectedly graceful medieval centre is well worth getting off the train to check out. Among the old-town treasures to survive destruction by Genoese forces in the 16th century are the baroque Cattedrale di Nostra Signora Assunta (Piazza Cattedrale) and the lumbering Fortezza del Priamàr (Piazza Priamar). This imposing fortress guards a couple of sculpture museums and the Civico Museo Storico Archeologico (Piazza Priamar; admission €2.50; ⏰10am-noon & 3-5pm Tue-Sat, 3-5pm Sun), which displays archaeological finds.

Art aficionados won't want to miss the Pinacoteca Civica Savona (Piazza Chabrol 1/2; admission €4; ⏰8.30am-1pm & 2-7pm Mon, Tue & Thu, 2-9pm Wed & Fri, 8.30am-1pm & 8-11pm Sat & Sun), which has an important collection of religious paintings, including a Madonna and child by Taddeo di Bartolo, dating from the 14th to 15th centuries, and two Picassos.

Six- to seven-hour whale-watching trips (www.whalewatchliguria.it; tickets €35) depart Savona at 10am from July to September.

🍽️ Sleeping & Eating

The tourist office can help book accommodation, both in the city and the coastal towns to the west.

Villa de' Franceschini
HOSTEL €

(☑019 26 32 22; www.ostellionline.org; Via alla Strà 'Conca Verde' 29; dm/d €13/32; ⊙mid-Mar–Oct; P@) Savona has one of Liguria's few hostels; it's 3km from the train station in a sprawling park.

Albergo Savona
HOTEL €

(☑019 82 18 20; Piazza del Popolo 53; s €30-40, d €45-62) A no-frills cheap sleep wedged between the train station and the old town, and handy for both.

Vino e Farinata
TRADITIONAL ITALIAN €

(Via Pia 15; meals €17-20; ⊙Tue-Sat) To enter this place in the cobbled centre, you'll have to walk past the two ancient chefs: one shovelling fish into a wood-fired oven and the other mixing up batter in a barrel-sized whisking machine. The result: Ligurian *farinata* (flat bread), the menu staple in this very local restaurant that also hordes some excellent wines.

❶ Information

Tourist office (Corso Italia 157r; ⊙9am-12.30pm & 3-6pm Mon-Sat, 9am-12.30pm Sun) A short stroll from Savona's sandy beach.

❶ Getting There & Around

SAR (☑0182 2 15 44) and **ACTS** (www.tpllinea.it) buses, departing from Piazza del Popolo and the train station, are the best options for reaching points inland.

Trains run along the coast to Genoa's Stazione Brignole (€3.30, 45 minutes, almost hourly) and San Remo (€5.70, 1¾ hours, eight daily).

Corsica Ferries (www.corsicaferries.com) runs up to three boats daily between Savona's Porto Vado and Corsica.

FINALE LIGURE
POP 11.669

Set amid lush Mediterranean vegetation, this township actually comprises several districts. Finale Ligure has a wide, fine-sand beach; the walled medieval centre, known as Finalborgo, is a knot of twisting alleys set 1km back from the coast on the Pora river. Finale Marina sits on the waterfront, while the more residential Finale Pia runs along the Sciusa river in the direction of Genoa.

Each year in March, Finalborgo's cloisters are home to the Salone dell'Agroalimentare Ligure, where local farmers and artisan producers display delicacies and vintages.

🛏 Sleeping & Eating

The promenade along Via San Pietro and Via Concezione is crammed with eateries.

Hotel Florenz
HOTEL €€

(☑019 69 56 67; www.florenz.it; Via Celesia 1; s €52-75, d €74-120; ⊙closed Nov & Feb; P@≋) This rambling 18th-century former convent just outside Finalborgo's village walls (800m from the sea) is one of the area's most atmospheric spots to sleep.

HI – Finale Ligure
HOSTEL $

(☑019 69 05 15; Via Generale Caviglia 46; dm/d €15.50/44) Offering the Florenz stiff competition is this youth hostel in a castle (Castello Vuillermin) no less, with stunning views from its terrace. It's 1km from the station and up 300-plus steps. It accepts nonmembers for a small supplement.

Osteria ai Cuattru Canti
OSTERIA €

(Via Torcelli 22; set menus €20; ⊙Tue-Sun) Delicious Ligurian cuisine is cooked up at this rustic place in Finalborgo's historic centre.

❶ Information

Tourist office (Via San Pietro 14; ⊙9am-12.30pm & 3-6.30pm Mon-Sat & 9am-noon Sun Jul & Aug) From the train station on Piazza Vittorio Veneto, at Finale Marina's western end, walk down Via Saccone to the sea and this office.

❶ Getting There & Away

SAR (☑0182 2 15 44) buses yo-yo every 30 minutes to/from Finale Ligure and Savona (€2.20, 50 minutes), stopping en route in Finalborgo (€1, five minutes) and Noli (€1.30, 20 minutes).

SAN REMO
POP 56.879

Fifty kilometres east of Europe's premier gambling capital lies San Remo, Italy's wannabe Monte Carlo, a sun-dappled Mediterranean resort with a casino, a clutch of ostentatious villas and lashings of Riviera-style grandeur. Known colloquially as the City of Flowers for its colourful summer blooms, San Remo also stages an annual music festival (the supposed inspiration for the Eurovision Song Contest) and the world's longest professional one-day cycling race, the 298km Milan–San Remo classic.

During the mid-19th century the city became a magnet for regal European exiles such as Empress Elizabeth of Austria and Tsar Nicola of Russia, who favoured the town's balmy winters. Swedish inventor Alfred Nobel maintained a villa here and an onion-domed Russian Orthodox church reminiscent of Moscow's St Basil's Cathedral still turns heads down by the seafront.

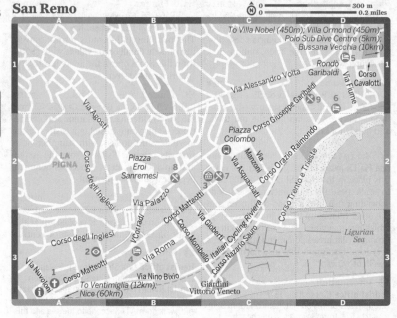

Beyond the manicured lawns and belle époque hotels, San Remo hides a little-visited old town, a labyrinth of twisting lanes that cascade down the Ligurian hillside. Curling around the base is a new 25km bike and walking path that tracks the coast as far as Imperia, following the course of a former railway line and passing through the town's two character-filled harbours.

◎ Sights

Chiesa Russa Ortodossia   CHURCH

(Via Nuvoloni 2; admission €1; ⊙9.30am-noon & 3-6pm) Non-Catholic churches are rare in Italy, so make the most of this multicoloured classic built for the Russian community that followed Tsarina Maria to San Remo in 1906. The Russian Orthodox church – with its onion domes and pale-blue interior – was designed by Alexei Shchusev, who later planned Lenin's mausoleum in Moscow. These days it's used as an exhibition space for Russian icons.

Il Casinò Municipale   CASINO

(www.casinosanremo.it; Corso degli Inglesi) San Remo's belle époque casino (one of only four in Italy) was dealing cards when Vegas was still a waterhole in the desert. The building dates from 1905 and was designed by Parisian architect, Eugenio Ferret. Slot machines (there are over 400 of them) open at 10am; other games (roulette, blackjack, poker etc) kick off at 2.30pm. Dress smart-casual and bring ID.

FREE **Museo Civico**   MUSEUM

(Corso Matteotti 143; ⊙9am-noon & 3-6pm Tue-Sat) Housed in the 15th-century Palazzo

Borea d'Olmo, several rooms in this museum, some with fine frescoed ceilings, display local prehistoric and Roman archaeological finds, paintings and temporary exhibitions. Highlights include Maurizio Carrega's *Gloria di San Napoleone* (painted in 1808 as a sycophantic homage to the Corsican despot of the same name) and bronze statues by Franco Bargiggia.

FREE Villas   MUSEUM, GARDEN

A short stroll east of town, elegant villas include the Moorish Villa Nobel (Corso Felice Cavallotti 112; ⊙11am-12.30pm Tue-Fri), housing a museum dedicated to Swedish inventor Alfred Nobel, who established the Nobel Prize while living here; and the peaceful Japanese gardens of Villa Ormond (Corso Felice Cavallotti 51; ⊙gardens 8am-7pm).

Bussana Vecchia   HISTORICAL SITE

Ten kilometres northeast of San Remo lies an intriguing artists colony. On Ash Wednesday 1887, an earthquake destroyed the village of Bussana Vecchia and survivors were eventually forced to abandon it. It remained a ghost town until the 1960s, when artists moved in and began rebuilding the ruins using the original stones from the rubble. After successfully standing up to authorities who wanted to remove them, a thriving community of international artists remains in residence today.

🕴 Activities

In a spirit befitting a city that hosts professional cycling's greatest Spring Classic, San Remo has recently completed a 25km walking and cycling path known as the Italian Cycling Riviera. The path – which runs along the route of a former railway line – connects Ospedaletti to San Lorenzo al Mare via San Remo and eight other seaside towns. Bike hire is offered; enquire at the tourist office.

The Polo Sub Dive Centre (Via Lungomare, Arma di Taggia) offers diving for €35 per immersion from the Darsena Porto in Taggia, 5km to the east.

🎎 Festivals & Events

Corso Fiorito   FLOWER

This colourful parade, held over the last weekend in January, kicks off the town's annual festivities.

Festival di San Remo   MUSIC

(www.festivaldisanremo.com, in Italian) Celebrating Italian music, this has been going since

1951, and attracts top Italian and international talent each March.

Rally Storico   CAR

(www.sanremorally.it) In April, San Remo's famous car rally revs up for cars made between 1931 and 1981.

🛏 Sleeping

San Remo has no shortage of hotels, although summer and festival times can be busy and a few places shut from September until just before Christmas.

Hotel Eletto   HOTEL €€

(☎0184 53 15 48; www.elettohotel.it; Corso G Matteotti 44; s €80-95, d €90-135; P❄) Let the Parisian art nouveau entrance canopy lure you to a friendly reception desk where they'll direct you upstairs to clean, refurbished soundproofed rooms in a central location.

Hotel Liberty   HOTEL €

(☎0184 50 99 52; www.hotellibertysanremo.com; Rondò Garibaldi 2; s €50-60, d €70-100; ❄P) Equipped with new, young owners and a new name, this 10-room hotel is set in a Liberty-style villa off a small traffic circle about 100m from the train station. The small but clean rooms are quiet and infused with faded elegance, while most sights of note are only footsteps away.

Hotel Marinella   HOTEL €€

(☎0184 50 59 00; www.hotelmarinella.it; Via Ruffini 21; s/d €78/105; ❄P) Across the road from the waterfront, most of Marinella's sunsplashed, tiled rooms have balconies, and all are spotless and spacious. The hotel's attached glass restaurant (mains around €15) is a bit like dining in a goldfish bowl, but the sea views are worth it.

🍴 Eating & Drinking

Cheap trattorias fill the old-town alleys around Piazza Eroi Sanremesi and open-air snack bars stud the length of Corso Nazario Sauro, the promenade overlooking the old port.

TOP Cantine CHOICE

Sanremesi   TRADITIONAL ITALIAN €

(Via Palazzo 7; meals €20; ⊙Tue-Sun) Meet the locals at this time-worn tavern over *trofie al pesto* or a delicious *stoccafisso alla sanremasa* (stockfish with tomato and potatoes).

Cuvea   TRADITIONAL ITALIAN €

(Corso Giuseppe Garibaldi 110; set menus €15-20, mains €8-9) This cosy, brightly lit place lined with wine bottles overflows with locals tucking into its homemade traditional dishes such as pesto-doused pasta.

Caffè Ducale   CAFE €
(Corso Matteotti 145; lunch menus €18-22; ⊘7.30am-midnight) Italian panache with an added dash of San Remo swankiness make this elegant cafe-*enoteca-salon de thé* one of the most refined joints east of the Côte d'Azur. Enjoy a few *aperitivi* under the weighty chandeliers before heading off to the casino to blow what's left of your holiday budget.

❶ Information
Tourist office (www.rivieradeifiori.org; Largo Nuvoloni 1; ⊘8am-7pm Mon-Sat, 9am-1pm Sun)

❶ Getting There & Away
Riviera Trasporti (Piazza Colombo 42) buses leave regularly from the bus station for the French border, east along the coast and inland destinations.

From San Remo's underground train station there are trains to/from Genoa (€10.10, three hours, hourly), Ventimiglia (€2.40, 15 minutes, hourly) and stations in between.

VENTIMIGLIA
POP 25.693

Long before the French–Italian border bore any significance, Ventimiglia harboured a stoic Roman town known as Albintimulium that survived until the 5th century AD when it was besieged by the Goths.

◉ Sights
On a hill on the western bank of the Roia river, Ventimiglia's medieval town is crowned with a 12th-century **cathedral** (Via del Capo). The town itself is largely residential.

FREE Area Archeologica   ARCHAEOLOGICAL SITE
(⊘3-5.30pm Sat & Sun) Sandwiched between the road and the railway line on the eastern edge of town, these Roman ruins bear testimony to Ventimiglia's Roman romance and include the remains of an amphitheatre and baths dating from the 2nd and 3rd centuries AD.

Market   MARKET
(⊘8am-3pm or 4pm) These days Ventimiglia is better known as a border town, with a huge Friday market when hundreds of stalls sell food, clothes, homewares, baskets and everything else under the sun. The market is concentrated on Piazza della Liberta, near the river, and is popular with French day trippers.

✏ Giardini Botanici
Hanbury   BOTANICAL GARDEN
(Corso Montecarlo 43, La Mortola; adult/child €7.50/4; ⊘9.30am-6pm) Established in 1867 by English businessman Sir Thomas Hanbury, the 18-hectare Villa Hanbury estate is planted with 5800 botanical species from five continents, including cacti, palm groves and citrus orchards. Today it's a protected area, under the care of the University of Genoa. Take bus 1a from Via Cavour in Ventimiglia; the bus continues on to the Ponte San Lodovico frontier post, from where you can walk down to the Balzi Rossi on the French border.

🛏 Sleeping & Eating
Cheap, cheerful eateries congregate around Via Cavour.

Hotel Seagull   HOTEL €
(☎0184 35 17 26; www.seagullhotel.it; Passeggiata Marconi 24; s/d from €55/75; P ✱ ☎) A 10-minute stroll along the seafront from Ventimiglia's town centre, this family-run hotel has simple but appealing sky-blue-and-white rooms, a fragrant garden and a breezy terrace. Both half- and full-board options are available.

❶ Information
Tourist office (Via T Hanbury 3a; ⊘9am-12.30pm & 3.30-7pm Mon-Sat Jul & Aug, 9am-12.30pm & 3-6.30pm Mon-Sat Sep-Jun) Just steps from the train station.

❶ Getting There & Away
From the **train station** (Via della Stazione), Corso della Repubblica leads to the beach. Trains connect Ventimiglia with Genoa (€11.60, two to 3½ hours, hourly), Nice (50 minutes, hourly) and other destinations in France.

PIEDMONT

POP 4.47 MILLION

Italy's second-largest region arguably is its most elegant; a purveyor of Slow Food and fine wine, regal *palazzi* and an atmosphere that is superficially more *francais* than *Italiano*. But dig deeper and you'll discover that Piedmont has 'Made in Italy' stamped all over it. Emerging from the chaos of the Austrian wars, the unification movement first exploded here in the 1850s when the noble House of Savoy provided the nascent nation with its first prime minister and its dynastic royal family.

Most Piedmont journeys start in grandiose Turin, famous for football and Fiats. But beyond the car factories, Piedmont is also notable for its food – everything from arborio rice to white truffles – and pastoral landscapes not unlike nearby Tuscany.

The region's smaller towns were once feuding fiefdoms that bickered over trade and religion. Today the biggest skirmishes are more likely to be over cheese recipes and wine vintages. Traditionally, Asti and Alba stand tallest in the culinary stakes, while understated Cuneo uses its long-standing chocolate obsession to help fuel outdoor adventures in the nearby Maritime Alps.

Turin

POP 909,538 / ELEV 240M

There's a whiff of Paris in Turin's elegant tree-lined boulevards and echoes of Vienna in its stately art nouveau cafes, but make no mistake – this city is anything but a copycat. The innovative Torinese gave the world it first saleable hard chocolate, perpetuated one of its greatest mysteries (the Holy Shroud), popularised a best-selling car (the Fiat) and inspired the black-and-white stripes of one of the planet's most iconic football teams (Juventus).

But more important than any of this is Turin's role as instigator of the modern Italian state. Piedmont, with its wily Torinese president, the Count of Cavour, was the engine room of the Risorgimento (literally 'the Resurgence', referring to Italian unification). Turin also briefly served as Italy's first capital and donated its monarchy – the venerable House of Savoy – to the newly unified Italian nation in 1861.

More recently, the 2006 Winter Olympics sparked an urban revival in the city, which has spread to its culture and (most deliciously) cuisine.

History

Whether the ancient city of Taurisia began as a Celtic or Ligurian settlement is unknown: it was destroyed by Hannibal in 218 BC. The Roman colony of Augusta Taurinorum was established here almost two centuries later. In succeeding years, Goths, Lombards and Franks tramped through the city. In 1563 the Savoys abandoned their old capital of Chambéry (now in France) to set up court in Turin, which shared the dynasty's fortunes thereafter. The Savoys annexed Sardinia in

1720, but Napoleon virtually put an end to their power when he occupied Turin in 1798. Turin was occupied by Austria and Russia before Vittorio Emanuele I restored the House of Savoy and re-entered Turin in 1814. Nevertheless, Austria remained the true power throughout northern Italy until the Risorgimento in 1861, when Turin became the nation's inaugural capital. Its capital status lasted only until 1864, and the parliament had already moved to Florence by the time full-sized chambers were completed.

Turin adapted quickly to its loss of political significance, becoming a centre for industrial production during the early 20th century. Giants such as Fiat lured hundreds of thousands of impoverished southern Italians to Turin and housed them in vast company-built and -owned suburbs. Fiat's owners, the Agnelli family (who also happen to own the Juventus football club, Turin's local newspaper and a large chunk of the national daily *Corriere della Sera*), remain one of Italy's most powerful establishment forces. Fiat's fortunes declined later in the 20th century, however, and only revived around a decade ago.

The highly successful 2006 Winter Olympics were a turning point for the city. The Olympics not only ushered in a building boom, including a brand-new metro system, but also transformed Turin from a staid industrial centre into a vibrant metropolis. Turin was European Capital of Design in 2008, hosting conferences and exhibitions, and the national focus of celebrations of the 150th anniversary of the Risorgimento in 2011.

⊙ Sights

Got a week? You might need it to see all the sights Turin has to offer. The time-poor can concentrate on a trio of highlights: the Museo Egizio, the Mole Antonelliana and the Museo della Sindone.

TOP CHOICE **Mole Antonelliana** LANDMARK, MUSEUM
(Via Montebello 20) The symbol of Turin, this 167m tower with its distinctive aluminium spire appears on the Italian two-cent coin. It was originally intended as a synagogue when construction began in 1862, but was never used as a place of worship. In the mid-1990s, the tower became home to the multifloored **Museo Nazionale del Cinema** (www.museonazionaledelcinema.org; adult/reduced €7/5; ⊙9am-8pm Tue-Fri & Sun, to 11pm Sat), which takes you on a fantastic tour

Piedmont

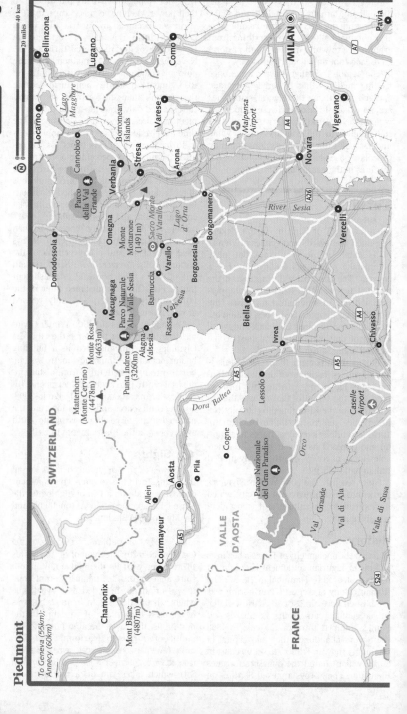

40 km
20 miles

*To Geneva (55km);
Annecy (60km)*

Bellinzona
Locarno
Lugano
Como
MILAN
Pavia

Lago Maggiore

Cannobio
Verbania
Stresa
Varese
Vigevano

Borromean Islands
Arona
Malpensa Airport
Novara

Parco della Val Grande

Omegna
Monte Mottarone (1491m)
Sacro Monte di Varallo
Borgomanero

Lago d' Orta

River Sesia

Vercelli

Domodossola
Varallo
Borgosesia

Macugnaga
Parco Naturale Alta Valle Sesia
Balmuccia
Valsesia
Rassa

Monte Rosa (4633m)
Alagna Valsesia

Biella

Matterhorn (Monte Cervino) (4478m)
Punta Indren (3260m)

Ivrea
Chivasso

SWITZERLAND

Dora Baltea

Lessolo
Caselle Airport

Cogne

Aosta
Pila

Parco Nazionale del Gran Paradiso

Orco

Allein

VALLE D'AOSTA

Courmayeur

Val Grande
Val di Ala
Valle di Susa

Chamonix
Mont Blanc (4807m)

FRANCE

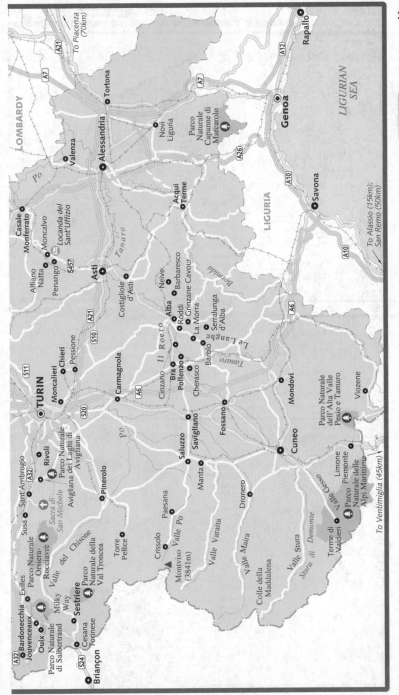

Turin

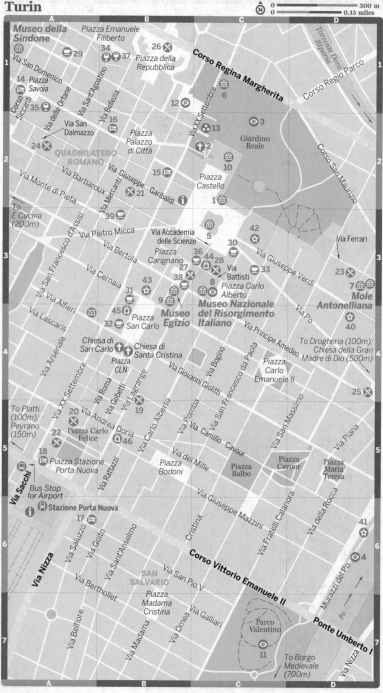

0 — 300 m
0 — 0.15 miles

- Museo della Sindone
- Piazza Emanuele Filiberto
- 29
- 34
- 37
- 26
- Piazza della Repubblica
- Corso Regina Margherita
- Torrente Dora Riparia
- Corso Regio Parco
- Via San Domenico
- 14 Piazza Savoia
- 35
- Corso Siccardi
- Via delle Orfane
- Via Sant'Agostino
- Via San Dalmazzo
- 16
- Via Bellezia
- 6
- 12
- 13
- 3
- Giardino Reale
- 24
- QUADRILATERO ROMANO
- Via Barbaroux
- Via Giuseppe Garibaldi
- 15
- 21
- 2
- 10
- Piazza Palazzo di Città
- Piazza Castello
- Corso San Maurizio
- Via Monte di Pietà
- To È Cucina (200m)
- Via Mercanti
- 39
- 1
- Via Pietro Micca
- Via San Francesco d'Assisi
- Via Bertola
- Via Accademia delle Scienze
- 5
- 30
- 42
- Via Ferrari
- Via Cernaia
- Piazza Carignano
- 36
- 44
- 28
- 27
- 38
- 8
- 33
- Via Giuseppe Verdi
- 23
- Via Battisti
- Piazza Carlo Alberto
- 7
- Mole Antonelliana
- 31
- 43
- 9
- Museo Egizio
- Museo Nazionale del Risorgimento Italiano
- 40
- Via Alfieri
- Via Lascaris
- 45
- 32
- Piazza San Carlo
- Via Po
- Via Principe Amedeo
- To Drogheria (100m); Chiesa della Gran Madre di Dio (500m)
- Chiesa di San Carlo
- Chiesa di Santa Cristina
- Piazza CLN
- Via Giovanni Giolitti
- Via Bogino
- Piazza Carlo Emanuele II
- 25
- Via Arsenale
- Via XX Settembre
- Via Roma
- Via Gobetti
- Via Lagrange
- 19
- Via Carlo Alberto
- Via Pomba
- Via San Francesco da Paola
- Via San Massimo
- To Platti (100m); Peyrano (150m)
- 20
- Via Andrea Doria
- 22
- Piazza Carlo Felice
- 46
- Via Camillo Cavour
- Piazza Cavour
- Piazza Maria Teresa
- Via Piana
- 18
- Piazza Stazione Porta Nuova
- Via Ratazzi
- Via dei Mille
- Piazza Bodoni
- Piazza Balbo
- Via della Rocca
- Via Sacchi
- Bus Stop for Airport
- Stazione Porta Nuova
- 17
- Via Saluzzo
- Via Goito
- Via Sant'Anselmo
- Cristina
- Via Giuseppe Mazzini
- Via Fratelli Calandra
- 41
- Corso Vittorio Emanuele II
- 4
- Via Nizza
- Via Belfiore
- Via Berthollet
- Via Madama
- Via San Pio V
- SAN SALVARIO
- Piazza Madama Cristina
- Via Galliari
- Ponte Umberto I
- Via Omea
- Parco Valentino
- 11
- To Borgo Medievale (700m)
- Murazzi del Po
- Po

through cinematic history, from the earliest magic lanterns, stereoscopes and other optical toys to the present day. Movie memorabilia on display includes Marilyn Monroe's black lace bustiere, Peter O'Toole's robe from *Lawrence of Arabia* and the coffin used by Bela Lugosi's Dracula. At the heart of the museum, the vast Temple Hall is surrounded by 10 interactive 'chapels' devoted to various film genres.

The Mole's glass **panoramic lift** (lift & museum ticket €9) whisks you 85m up through the centre of the museum to the Mole's roof terrace in 59 seconds. Fair warning if you're even slightly prone to vertigo: it's suspended only by cables, so when you look out it's as if you're free-floating in space. The 360-degree

views from the outdoor viewing deck are dazzling by day or night.

Museo della Sindone   MUSEUM
(Via Santo Domenico 28; www.sindone.org; adult/reduced €6/5; ⊙9am-noon & 3-7pm) Encased in the crypt of the Santo Sudario church, this fascinating museum documents one of the most studied objects in human history: the Holy Shroud. Whatever your position on the shroud's authenticity, its story unfolds like a gripping suspense mystery, with countless plots, subplots and revelations. Of particular interest is the story of the shroud post-1898, when camera technology allowed people to see much clearer photographic negatives of the cloth for the first time.

TURIN IN...

Two Days

Two-day tourists will want to start early with a wake-up coffee at a historic coffeehouse – pint-sized **Caffè Mulassano** is a good bet. Flip a euro to decide which museum to visit first – the **Museo Nazionale del Cinema** or the **Museo Egizio**. Check out Slow Food–affiliated baker **Andrea Perino** for lunch and walk it off with a *passeggiata* (stroll) in **Parco Valentino** beside the Po River. On day two visit whichever museum you missed yesterday before grabbing an aperitif and buffet snacks in **I Tre Galli**.

Four Days

If you have two more days, there are a couple more prestigious museums you should add to your itinerary: the **Museo della Sindone**, outlining the history of the Holy Shroud, and the recently refurbished **Museo Nazionale del Risorgimento Italiano**. Be sure to stop afterwards for coffee in **Fiorio** and chocolate in **Al Bicerin**.

One Week

A week will enable you to get out to the outlying sights such as the **Basilica di Superga** and the massive **Reggia de Venaria Reale**. Be sure to also visit **Lingotto** and its Eataly supermarket and that quintessential Italian night-time treat – the opera, at the **Teatro Regio Torino**.

Museo Nazionale del Risorgimento Italiano   MUSEUM
(www.museorisorgimentotorino.it; Via Accademia delle Scienze 5; adult/reduced €7/5; ☺9am-7pm Tue-Sun) If only school history lessons had been this interesting. After extensive renovations, this legendary museum has re-opened with an astounding 30-room trajectory covering the background and details of Italian unification in the very building (the baroque Palazzo Carignano) where many of the key events happened. Not only was this the birthplace of Carlo Alberto and Vittorio Emanuele II, but it was also the seat of united Italy's first parliament from 1861 to 1864. Unmissable!

Museo Egizio   MUSEUM
(Egyptian Museum; www.museoegizio.org; Via Accademia delle Scienze 6; adult/reduced €7.50/3.50; ☺8.30am-7.30pm Tue-Sun) 'The road through Memphis and Thebes passes through Turin' trumpeted French hieroglyphic decoder, Jean-François Champollion in the early 19th century, and he wasn't far wrong. Opened in 1824, this legendary museum in the Palazzo dell'Accademia delle Scienze houses the most important collection of Egyptian treasure outside Cairo. Two of many highlights include a statue of Ramesses II (one of the world's most important pieces of Egyptian art) and over 500 items found in the tomb of Kha and Merit (from 1400 BC) in 1906.

Though it remains open, the museum is undergoing a five-year refurbishment due for completion in 2013.

Galleria Sabauda   ART GALLERY
(adult/reduced €4/2; ☺8.30am-2pm Tue, Fri, Sat & Sun, 2-7.30pm Wed & Thu) As if 3000 years of Egyptology wasn't enough, the Accademia delle Scienze building also houses the incredible collection of art amassed by the Savoy royal family since 1832. Exhibits include works by Van Dyck, Rembrandt, Poussin, Bellini and Titian. A combination ticket for both museums costs €8 for adults (free for children).

Duomo di San Giovanni   CHURCH
(Piazza San Giovanni) Turin's cathedral was built between 1491 and 1498 on the site of three 14th-century basilicas and, before that, a Roman theatre. Most ignore the fairly plain interior and focus on a far bigger myth: the church is home to the famous **Shroud of Turin** (alleged to be the burial cloth in which Jesus' body was wrapped). A copy of the cloth is on permanent display to the left of the cathedral altar, but to get the full story you'll need to visit the Museo della Sindone.

The separate Romanesque-style bell tower looks older than it really is; it was designed by Juvarra and built in 1723. Just to the north lie the remains of a 1st-century Roman amphitheatre, while a little further to the northwest lies Porta Palatina, the red-brick remains of a Roman-era gate.

Piazza Castello
PIAZZA

Turin's central square shelters a wealth of museums, theatres and cafes. Essentially baroque, the grand piazza was laid out from the 14th century to serve as the seat of dynastic power for the House of Savoy.

Museo Civico d'Arte Antica
MUSEUM

(Piazza Castello; www.palazzomadamatorino.it; adult/reduced €7.50/6; ⊙10am-6pm Tue-Sat, to 8pm Sun) The piazza is dominated by Palazzo Madama, a part-medieval, part-baroque castle built in the 13th century on the site of the old Roman gate. It was named after Madama Reale Maria Cristina, the widow of Vittorio Amedeo I, who lived here in the 17th century. Today, part of the palace houses this expansive museum containing four floors of works that document the city's artistic movements post–Italian unification.

Palazzo Reale
PALAZZO

(Piazza Castello; adult/reduced €6.50/3.25; ⊙8.30am-7.30pm Tue-Sun) Statues of the mythical twins Castor and Pollux guard the entrance to this eye-drawing palace and, according to local legend, also watch over the border between the sacred ('white magic') and diabolical ('black magic') halves of the city. Built for Carlo Emanuele II around 1646, its lavishly decorated rooms house an assortment of furnishings, porcelain and other knick-knacks. The surrounding Giardino Reale (Royal Garden; admission free; ⊙9am-1hr before sunset), north and east of the palace, was designed in 1697 by André le Nôtre, who also created the gardens at Versailles.

Armeria Reale
MUSEUM

(Royal Armoury; www.artito.arti.beniculturali.it; Piazza Castello; adult/reduced €4/2; ⊙9am-2pm Tue-Fri, 1-7pm Sat & Sun) If you've had your fill of art, relocate under the porticoes just to the right of the Palazzo Reale gates to see one of Europe's best collections of armaments.

Museo d'Antichità
MUSEUM

(Museum of Antiquity; Via XX Settembre 88c; admission €4; ⊙8.30am-7.30pm Tue-Sun) Across the square from the *duomo*, this museum displays antiquities amassed by the Savoy dynasty, including Etruscan urns, Roman bronzes and Greek vases, alongside assorted locally excavated archaeological finds.

Galleria Civica d'Arte Moderna e Contemporanea
ART GALLERY

(GAM; www.gamtorino.it; Via Magenta 31; adult/reduced €7.50/6; ⊙10am-6pm Tue-Sun) Italy can sometimes feel strangely light on modern art, until you come to Turin. GAM has an astounding 45,000 works in its vaults dedicated to 19th- and 20th-century artists, including De Chirico, Otto Dix and Klee. It cleverly hires art experts to reconfigure its permanent displays on a regular basis. You never know what you're going to get.

Museo d'Arte Contemporanea
ART GALLERY

(www.castellodirivoli.org; Piazza Mafalda di Savoia, Rivoli; adult/reduced €6.50/4.50; ⊙10am-5pm Tue-Fri, 10am-7pm Sat & Sun) Works by Franz Ackermann, Gilbert and George, and Frank Gehry would have been beyond the wildest imagination of the Savoy family, who once resided in the 17th-century Castello di Rivoli where the cutting edge of Turin's contemporary art scene has been housed since 1984. The castle is west of central Turin in the town of Rivoli (not to be confused with the city's metro station named Rivoli). Take the metro to Paradiso station and then bus 36 to Rivoli bus station. Journey time is about one hour. Otherwise, take the metro to the Fermi stop, from where there's a free daily shuttle – see website for shuttle schedules.

ARTE POVERA

Turin is famed for its ground-breaking contemporary art. According to Valentina Marocco of the Museo d'Arte Contemporanea, its origins come from Turin's role as 'the home town of the Arte Povera, a revolutionary art movement that developed at the end of the 1960s.' Adherents to this 'poor art' movement used simple materials to trigger memories and associations through sculpture and installations. One of the school's most famous works was Michelangelo Pistoletto's *Venere degli Stracci* (Venus of the Rags), a classical marble statue facing a huge heap of old clothes and rags. The movement had an enormous impact on an international level through artists like Pistoletto, Mario Merz, Gilberto Zorio and Giuseppe Penone.

Parco Valentino
PARK

(⊘24hr; 🖼) Opened in 1856, this 550,000-sq-metre, French-style park kisses the banks of the Po and and is filled with joggers, promenaders and lovers night and day. Walking southwest along the river brings you to **Castello del Valentino** (closed to the public), a mock chateau built in the 17th century.

Borgo Medievale
HISTORIC PARK

(Parco Valentino; admission free; ⊘9am-8pm Apr-Sep; 🖼) One of Parco Valentino's more esoteric sights is this faux medieval village, built for the Italian General Exhibition in 1884. Its centrepiece is the **Rocca** (Viale Virgilio 107; adult/reduced €5/4; ⊘9am-5pm Tue-Sat, to 6pm Sun), a mock scaled-down castle. Real historians might want to spare their change for the real thing (there's no shortage of medieval villages in Italy), though kids might enjoy the kitsch.

Chiesa della Gran Madre di Dio
CHURCH

(Piazza Vittorio Veneto) Framing the exquisite view southeast over Piazza Vittorio Veneto towards the Po river, this church was built in the style of a mini Pantheon from 1818 to 1831 to commemorate the return of Vittorio Emanuele I from exile. It's small and rounded inside; some claim it's yet another secret repository for the Holy Grail. In 1969 the church was memorably featured in the film *The Italian Job* when Michael Caine and his gang drove their Mini Coopers down the front staircase.

Lingotto
LANDMARK

(www.lingottofiere.it; Via Nizza 294) Around 3km south of the city centre is the **Lingotto Fiere**, Turin's former Fiat factory, which was redesigned by architect Renzo Piano into a congress and exhibition centre. In addition to two striking Le Meridien hotels (see p197), it houses the Eataly supermarket, congress facilities and the precariously perched 'treasure chest' rooftop gallery **Pinacoteca Giovanni e Marella Agnelli** (Via Nizza 230; admission €4; ⊘10am-7pm Tue-Sun), with masterpieces by Canaletto, Renoir, Manet, Matisse and Picasso, among others.

Lingotto is on Turin's new metro line and easily accessible from the city centre.

FREE Basilica di Superga
BASILICA

(www.basilicadisuperga.com; Strada della Basilica di Superga 73) In 1706 Vittorio Amedeo II promised to build a basilica to honour the Virgin Mary if Turin was saved from besieging French and Spanish armies. Like a religious epiphany, the city was saved and architect Filippo Juvarra built the church on a hill across the Po river. Basilica di Superga became the final resting place of the Savoy family, whose lavish tombs make for interesting viewing, as does the dome here. In 1949 the basilica gained a less welcome fame when a plane carrying the entire Turin football team crashed into the church in thick fog, killing all on board. Their tomb rests at the rear of the church.

To get here take tram 15 from Piazza Vittorio Veneto to the Sassi-Superga stop on Corso Casale, then walk 20m to **Stazione Sassi** (Strada Comunale di Superga 4), from where an original 1934 **tram** (one way €4-6, return €6-9; ⊘from Sassi 9am-noon & 2-8pm Mon & Wed-Fri, 9.30am-12.30pm & 2.30-8.30pm Sat & Sun, 30min later from Superga) rattles the 3.1km up the hillside in 18 minutes every day except Tuesday.

Reggia de Venaria Reale
PALAZZO, MUSEUM

(Piazza della Repubblica; www.lavenaria.it; adult/reduced €12/8, gardens €4/3; ⊘9am-6pm Tue-Fri, 9am-9.30pm Sat, 9am-8pm Sun) Welcome to Turin's Versailles, a Unesco-listed palace complex built as a glorified hunting lodge by the frivolous Duke of Savoy Carlo Emanuele II in 1675. It is one of the biggest royal residences in the world and lengthy restoration works were concluded in late 2010. Among the slew of things to see are a huge garden complex, the Fontana del Cervo (stag fountain), the stunning Galeria Grande (Grand Gallery), the Capella di Sant'Uberto and the Juvarra stables. The last three were all designed by the great Sicilian architect Filippo Juvarra in the 1720s. The full trajectory is 2km long and a lot to take in. Check the website for the numerous temporary exhibitions. There are also a cafe and restaurant on site. You can reach the palace complex on bus 11 from Porta Nuova station.

Courses

🍴 Eataly
COOKING

(www.eatalytorino.it; in Italian; from €20) Food sampling, tasting, becoming a chef, sommelier secrets and cookery workshops are held at Turin's famous Slow Food supermarket.

☞ Tours

Turismo Bus Torino
BUS

(1-day ticket adult/child €15/7.50; ⊘10am-6pm) This hop-on, hop-off bus service has on-board staff providing information that

MAKING THE MOST OF YOUR EURO

Serious sightseers will save a bundle with a **Torino + Piemonte Card** (2/5/7 days €22/33/37, junior 2 days €11). It covers admission to most of Turin's monuments and museums, a ride up the Mole Antonelliana panoramic lift, a return trip on the Sassi–Superga cable car, and all public transport costs, including GTT boats on the Po river and the Turismo Bus Torino. It also offers discounts for some guided tours and theatres. You can buy the card at the tourist office.

serves over a dozen different points around central Turin. Tickets are sold on board; information is available from **Gruppo Torinese Trasporti** (GTT; www.gtt.to.it, in Italian; Stazione Porta Nuova; ☺7am-9pm).

Navigazione sul Po BOAT
(return fare €4) Turin transport operates boat trips on the Po. Boats to the Borgo Medievale in Parco Valentino and on to Moncalieri depart from **Imbarco Murazzi** (Murazzi del Po 65) four to seven times daily except Mondays.

Somewhere WALK
(www.somewhere.it) Turin's 'black and white magic' is illuminated on quirky walking tours with 'Somewhere'. The company also runs other tours on lesser-known aspects of the city, such as 'Underground Turin'. Tours cost around €25; confirm departure points when booking.

🎎 Festivals & Events

The tourist office has details of these and other events.

Salone Internazionale del Gusto FOOD
(www.salonedelgusto.it) Every October in even-numbered years, foodies roll into town for this festival organised by Slow Food, with traditional producers from around the world showcasing their wares in a huge market at Lingotto Fiere. A day's entry costs €20, after which tastings cost between €1 and €5.

Cioccolatò FOOD
(www.cioccola-to.it) Turin's famous chocolate is the focus of celebrations during March

Salone Internazionale del Libro di Torino BOOK
(http://en.salonelibro.it) Held every May, Turin's book fair is one of the most important in Europe.

Turino Film Festival FILM
(www.torinofilmfest.org) Currently headed up by Palme d'Or winner Nanni Moretti, it takes place in November.

🛏 Sleeping

Hotel Residence Torino Centro HOTEL €
(☏011 433 82 23; www.hoteltorinocentro.it; Corso Inghilterra 33; d/tr €77/90; P❄✿) The best new player in the field by a good stretch is this chic upgraded convent right behind the Porta Susa train station. Smart modern furnishings combine with old mosaic floors in huge rooms with all mod cons. Service is professional and efficient and there's a funky coffee bar (Coffee Lab Inghiliterra) downstairs in which to enjoy a complimentary breakfast. Best bargain in Turin!

Ai Savoia BOUTIQUE HOTEL €€
(☏339 1257711; www.aisavoia.it; Via del Carmine 1b; r €95-125; P) Occupying an 18th-century town house, this little treasure seems like something out of a small town rather than a big city. The classical decor of each of its three rooms is ornate without being overwrought, and staff are friendly and obliging.

Le Meridien Lingotto & Le Meridien Art + Tech LUXURY HOTEL €€€
(☏011 664 20 00; www.lemeridienlingotto.it; Via Nizza 262; Le Meridien Lingotto d €270-300, Le Meridien Art + Tech d €390-410; P❄✿) These twin hotels are both situated within the historic Fiat car factory, which was built in the 1920s and renovated by Renzo Piano in the late 1980s. The factory's original full-length windows have been retained, allowing light to flood the large, luxurious four-star rooms of Le Meridien Lingotto and those of its five-star annex, Le Meridien Art + Tech. Guests can jog around the former car-testing circuit on the roof, which was featured in the classic 1969 film *The Italian Job*.

Hotel Dogana Vecchia HOTEL €€
(☎011 436 67 52; www.hoteldoganavecchia.com; Via Corte d'Appello 4; s/d €90/110; P) Mozart, Verdi and Napoleon are among those who have stayed at this historic three-star inn. Recent renovations have fortunately preserved its old-world charm, and its location in the Quadrilatero Romano is hard to beat.

Ostello Torino HOSTEL €
(☎011 660 29 39; www.ostellotorino.it; Via Alby 1; dm/s/tw without bathroom €15/22/42; ⌚mid-Jan–mid-Dec; ❄@) Turin's 76-bed HI hostel, 1.8km from Stazione Porta Nuova, can be reached by bus 52 (bus 64 on Sunday) from the train station. Facilities are good (including online computers, wi-fi, and dinner Monday to Saturday for €10) and breakfast's included, but there's an afternoon lockout.

Hotel Due Mondi HOTEL €
(☎011 650 50 84; www.hotelduemondi.it; Via Saluzzo 3; s/d €55/69; ❄@🛜) A close-to-the-station bargain, the Due Mondi equips its small rooms with bright laminated floors, comfortable furnishings and ingenious shower-sauna cubicles. Most rooms have wi-fi, there's a cosy sitting area downstairs and a classy restaurant next door lures you in with tasty-looking food trolleys. With such elegant diversions, the slightly seedy surroundings barely register.

Hotel Roma e Rocca Cavour HOTEL €€
(☎011 561 27 72; www.romarocca.it; Piazza Carlo Felice 60; s €62.50-95.50, d €91-124; P❄) If you've stayed in too many cramped hotel rooms, you'll love this c 1854 hotel opposite the Porta Nuova train station. Hallways are wide, ceilings are high and antique-furnished rooms are sumptuously proportioned, especially the flowing 'comfort' rooms.

Hotel Chelsea HOTEL €€
(☎011 436 01 00; www.hotelchelsea.it; Via XX Settembre 79e; s €85-120, d €110-160; P@) A stone's throw from Turin's main square, Piazza Castello, the Chelsea has modern, softly lit rooms with coordinated bedspreads and drapes. The romantic downstairs restaurant, La Campana, serves Pugliese cuisine.

Hotel Montevecchio HOTEL €
(☎011 562 00 23; www.hotelmontevecchio.com; Via Montevecchio 13; s €40-85, d €60-100; @) In a quiet residential area yet just 300m from Stazione Porta Nuova, this two-star hotel has colourful, stencilled rooms in sunset shades, an above-average buffet breakfast and a guest laundry.

Eating

Turin's cuisine has been influenced by everyone from the French to the Sicilians, but the bulk of the inspiration comes from its own hinterland – Piedmont. Specialities include *risotto alla piemontese* (risotto with butter and cheese), *finanziera* (sweetbreads, mushrooms and chicken livers in a creamy sauce) and panna cotta (like an Italian crème caramel).

The San Salvario neighbourhood, in the southeastern part of the city, has a host of multicultural eateries, particularly around Piazza Madama Cristina, as well as some of the city's best pizzerias and pubs.

TOP CHOICE **Sfashion** PIZZERIA €
(Via Cesare Battisti 13; set menus €21, mains €7.50-14.50) Best pizza in Turin? Mention Sfashion and you'll get more than a few takers. Naples-thick and with wonderfully rustic ingredients (and not too much cheese), they fly like hot bullets from the ovens of comic Torinese TV presenter Piero Chiamretti, whose funky postmodern city-centre set-up pitches retro toys amid an outlandish interior. The other in-house classic is mussels in tomato sauce.

È Cucina FUSION €€
(www.cesaremarretti.com; Via Bertola 27a; meals €20-30) Here's an interesting new Torinese culinary concept: haute cuisine at everyman prices. The meals at this sleek restaurant are courtesy of Bolognese chef Cesare Marretti and his creative scope is breathtaking. There is no printed menu; waitstaff will merely tell you it's a *sorpesa* (surprise). You pay for the number of courses you consume. It's impossible to list or rank the pot-luck dishes. Bank on artichokes with prawns, eggplants overlaid with avocado cream, pears atop salmon, and plenty more.

Kuoki FUSION €
(☎011 839 78 65; Via Gaudenzio Ferrari 2h; set menus €9-25, mains €6-10; ⌚11am-3pm & 6.30-11pm Mon-Sat) Head round the corner from the Mole Antonelliana to this intriguing spot run by Giorgio Armani's former personal chef, Toni Vitiello. At high communal tables, you can dine on Italian blackboard specials, or sushi bar twists such as a Kuoki roll (salmon or tuna with ricotta, olive oil and basil). Toni's other fusion creations include chicken in Coca-Cola with orange peel.

Porta di Savona

TRATTORIA €€

(Piazza Vittoria Veneto 2; meals €25; ⊘lunch & dinner Wed-Sun, dinner only Tue) An economical, unpretentious trattoria, it has a deserved reputation for superb *agnolotti al sugo arrosto* (Piemontese ravioli in a meat gravy), and *gnocchi di patate al gorgonzola*. The mains – including *bollito misto alla piemontese* (boiled meat and vegetable stew) – are equally memorable. Be patient: the food takes a while to arrive, probably because it's 100% homemade and 100% Piemontese.

Ristorante del Cambio

GASTRONOMIC €€€

(⌨011 54 66 90; Piazza Carignano 2; set menus from €60; ⊘Mon-Sat) Crimson velvet, glittering chandeliers, baroque mirrors and a timeless air greet you at this grande dame of the Turin dining scene, regularly patronised by Count Cavour in his day. It first opened its doors in 1757, and classic Piedmont cuisine still dominates the menu. Bookings and smart dress are advised.

Brek

BUFFET €

(www.brek.com; Piazza Carlo Felice 18; buffets from €10; ⊘8.30am-11pm) Only Italians could take 'fast food' and make it both credible *and* edible. Brek is a small self-service restaurant chain where you can pick up fresh pasta, pizza, sausages, salads and desserts. Inside, the ambience is far from plastic. Indeed you might even be inclined to linger awhile in the plant-bedecked outdoor courtyard.

Eataly

CAFE, DELI €

(www.eatalytorino.it; Via Nizza 230; ⊘10am-8pm Tue-Sun) Adjacent to the Lingotto congress centre is the Slow Food Movement's 'supermarket'. Set in a vast converted factory, it houses a staggering array of sustainable food and beverages, with a separate area for each, including cheeses, breads, meats, fish, pasta, chocolate and much more. The best time to visit is around 12.30pm to 2.30pm, when each area has its own little restaurant serving lunch. There's also a high-end restaurant here, for which you'll need to book ahead.

Grom

GELATERIA €

(www.grom.it; Piazza Paleocapa 1d; ⊘noon-midnight Mon-Thu, to 1am Fri & Sat, 11am-11pm Sun) Spot a queue in Turin and you know you're probably in the vicinity of a Grom gelateria. The Slow Food–affiliated ice-cream maker now has 37 outlets (including ones in New York, Tokyo and Paris), but the first-ever

Grom started right here in 2003. Come for a host of organic flavours made from fruit grown on Grom's own Piedmont farm.

Andrea Perino

BAKERY €

(Via Cavour 10; snacks from €4) Ligurians missing their daily bread fix needn't worry. The fresh focaccia has followed you to Turin courtesy of cult Slow Food Torinese baker Andrea Perino, who knocks out generous portions of tasty snacks at this bakery-cum-cafe.

Gofri Piemontéisa

SNACKS €

(www.gofriemiassepiemontesi.it; Via San Tommaso 4a; ⊘11.30-7.30) *Gofri* are thin waffles made from flour, water and yeast, then cooked in hot irons. This traditional dish from the mountainous regions of northern Piedmont has been reinvented as tasty fast food by a local chef. Try the house *gofre* with ham, soft cheese and rocket or one of the equally delicious corn-based *miasse*.

Pappa & Ciccia

MODERN ITALIAN €€

(Via San Dalmazzo 1; meals €30) Easy to miss off Via Garibaldi, this stylish but down-to-earth place has dishes like *agnolotti arrosto sugo*, a fine communal antipasto plate, and a Russian salad *di nonna* (grandma's).

Porta Palazzo

MARKET €

(Piazza della Repubblica; ⊘8.30am-1.30pm Mon-Fri, to 6.30pm Sat) Europe's largest open-air food market has literally hundreds of food stalls. Pick up a picnic.

Drinking

In Turin, drinking can also mean eating. *Aperitivi* is a Turinese institution. As in Milan, if you're on a tight budget, you can fill up on a generous buffet of bar snacks for the cost of a drink. The main drinking spots are the riverside area around Piazza Vittoria Veneto, and the Quadrilatero Romano district.

Turin's historical cafes have their rivals – Trieste and Rome to name but two – but it's splitting hairs really. These are evocative places full of literary legend, architectural excellence, aromatic coffee and the city's best gossip – and gossipers. Then there's the chocolate, either liquid or solid, a speciality unto itself.

TOP CHOICE Caffè San Carlo

CAFE

(Piazza San Carlo 156; ⊘8am-1am) Perhaps the most gilded of the gilded, this glittery cafe dates from 1822. You'll get neckache admiring the weighty chandelier and heartache contemplating your bill (a hefty €4.50 for a cappuccino).

Caffè Mulassano
CAFE

(Piazza Castello 15; ⊘7.30am-10.30pm) With dozens of customers and only five dwarf-sized tables, the art nouveau Mulassano is where regulars sink white-hot espresso *a piedi* while discussing Juventus' current form with the knowledgeable bowtied barista.

Fiorio
CAFE

(Via Po 8; ⊘8.30am-1am Tue-Sun) Garner literary inspiration in Mark Twain's old window seat as you contemplate the gilded interior of a cafe where 19th-century students once plotted revolutions and the Count of Cavour deftly played whist. The bittersweet hot chocolate ain't bad either.

Al Bicerin
CAFE, CHOCOLATE

(Piazza della Consolata 5; ⊘8.30am-7.30pm Mon, Tue, Thu & Fri, to 1pm & 3.30-7.30pm Sat & Sun) Established in 1763 beneath a 14th-century bell tower, the cafe takes its name from *bicerin*, a caffeine-charged hot drink of chocolate, coffee and cream. It also serves snacks such as chocolate on toast.

I Tre Galli
WINE BAR

(www.3galli.com; Via Sant'Agostino 25; ⊘noon-midnight) Spacious and rustic, this is a fabulous spot for a drink at any time, but most people come for the gourmet *aperitivi* snacks served on a buzzing pavement terrace. Meals cost about €15.

Mood
CAFE

(www.moodlibri.it; Via Battisti 3e; ⊘cafe 8am-9pm Mon-Sat, bookshop 10am-9pm Mon-Sat) Are you bluesy, deflated, in dire need of a caffeine injection? Any mood suits this coffee shop/cocktail bar/bookshop combo, as long as you can find room among the wilting shoppers and students flicking through Dante. The interior's slavishly hip, all polished concrete and shiny laminate.

Pastis
WINE BAR

(Piazza Emanuele Filiberto 9; ⊘9am-3.30pm & 6pm-2am) This boldly painted cafe-bar is where Torinese office workers go for a two-hour lunch break – spicy meatballs with an obligatory glass of wine.

La Drogheria
BAR

(Piazza Vittorio Veneto 18; ⊘11am-2am) Occupying the space of an old pharmacy, La Drogheria's sofas are coveted by a studenty crowd who enjoy cheap drinks and *aperitivi* fare before hitting the Murazzi nightlife.

Lobelix
BAR

(Via Corte d'Appello 15f; ⊘7pm-3am Mon-Sat) Beneath the trees on Piazza Savoia, the terrace here is a favourite place for an *aperitivo* – its buffet banquet is one of Turin's most extravagant.

Caffè Torino
CAFE

(Piazza San Carlo 204; ⊘7.30am-1am) This chandelier-lit showpiece opened in 1903. A brass plaque of the city's emblem, a bull (Torino in Italian means 'little bull'), is embedded in the pavement out the front; rub your shoe across it for good luck.

San Tommaso 10
CAFE

(Via San Tommaso 10; ⊘8am-midnight Mon-Sat) The Lavazza family started roasting coffee here in 1900. Now modernised, the cafe offers a staggering variety of flavours as well as an excellent restaurant. Caffeine fiends can buy espresso machines.

Pepino
CAFE, CHOCOLATE

(Piazza Carignano 8; ⊘8.30am-8pm Sun-Thu, to midnight Fri & Sat, longer hr summer) Chocolate in all its guises is available at Pepino, where ice cream dipped in chocolate on a stick was invented in 1937.

Platti
CAFE

(Corso Vittorio Emanuele II 72; ⊘7.30am-9pm) This sweet-laden coffee, cake and liquor shop has a gilded 1870 interior.

☆ Entertainment

Most clubs open from 9pm to late and cover charges vary depending on the night. Turin's clubbing district centres on Murazzi del Po (also called Lungo Po Murazzi), the arcaded riverside area stretching between Pontes Vittorio Emanuele I and Umberto I – follow the crowds (and the music).

Teatro Regio Torino
THEATRE

(☑011 881 52 41; www.teatroregio.torino.it, in Italian; Piazza Castello 215; ⊘ticket office 10.30am-6pm Tue-Fri, to 4pm Sat & 1hr before performances) Sold-out performances can sometimes be watched free on live TV in the adjoining Teatro Piccolo Regio, where Puccini premiered *La bohème* in 1896. Tickets start at €48.

Hiroshima Mon Amour
NIGHTCLUB

(Via Bossoli 83; admission free–€15) This legendary dance club plays everything from folk and punk to tango and techno.

Phuddhu Bar
NIGHTCLUB

(Murazzi del Po; ☺7pm-3am) Drum and bass music on Friday and Saturday nights with DJs are par for the course in this *Murazzi* club in the river.

Cinema Massimo
CINEMA

(Via Giuseppe Verdi 18; admission €7) Near the Mole Antonelliana, the cinema offers an eclectic mix of films, mainly in English or with subtitles. One of its three screens only shows classic films.

Sport

Any football fan knows Turin has two teams, **Torino Football Club** (www.torinofc.it, in Italian) and the infinitely more famous *Vecchia Signora* (Old Lady), aka **Juventus Football Club** (www.juventus.com). Most Torinese favour the former, while the rest of the world leans heavily towards the latter. Watching either is a quasi-religious experience. They both currently play at the **Stadio Olimpico di Torino** (Corso Sebastopoli 123) on the southwestern edge of town, served by buses on match days. For tickets try the **ticket office** (Galleria San Federico 38; tickets from €11; ☺11am-7.30pm) near Piazza San Carlo.

Shopping

Via Roma's arcaded walkways shelter the city's most expensive fashion boutiques, while those along pedestrianised Via Garibaldi are more affordable. Via Po has some great secondhand record shops and vintage and alternative clothes.

Peyrano
CHOCOLATE

(www.peyrano.com; Corso Vittorio Emanuele II 76) Creator of *Dolci Momenti a Torino* (Sweet Moments in Turin) and *grappini* (chocolates filled with grappa), Peyrano has been in operation since 1912. After changing hands in 2002, it went during the recent economic crisis, but was quickly bought back by its original family owners.

Libreria Luxemburg
BOOKSTORE

(Via Battisti 7) This British bookshop is well stocked with light and heavy lit plus a full stash of Lonely Planet guides. There are also daily British newspapers.

Pastificio Defilippis
FOOD

(Via Lagrange 39; ☺8.30am-1pm & 4-7.30pm Mon-Sat) Nose through the open doorway of this 1872 establishment to watch the family making dozens of varieties of pasta; you can buy it here fresh or dried.

Paissa
FOOD

(www.paissa.it; Piazza San Carlo 196) This wonderful old-fashioned emporium in Piazza San Carlo, complete with ladders and a heavy wooden counter, is where you can buy everything Turin is famous for, including *grissini* (breadsticks), wine and chocolates.

❶ Information

A bank, ATM and exchange booth can all be found within Stazione Porta Nuova; others are dotted throughout the city. A 24-hour automatic banknote-change machine can be found outside **Unicredit Banca** (Piazza CLN).

1PC4YOU (☏011 83 59 08; Via G Verdi 20g; per hr €6; ☺9am-10pm Mon-Sat, noon-10pm Sun) Internet access.

Circolo Culturale Maurice (www.mauriceglbt. org, in Italian; Via della Basilica 3-5) Gay and lesbian information.

Farmacia Boniscontro (☏011 53 82 71; Corso Vittorio Emanuele II 66; ☺3pm-12.30am)

Ospedale Mauriziano Umberto I (☏011 5 08 01; Largo Turati 62) Hospital.

Pharmacy (☏011 518 64 67; Stazione Porta Nuova; ☺7am-7.30pm)

Police station (☏011 5 58 81; Corso Vinzaglio 10)

Post office (Via Alfieri 10; ☺8.30am-7pm Mon-Fri, to 1pm Sat)

Tourist office (☏011 535 181); Stazione Porta Nuova (☺9.30am-7pm); Airport (☺8am-11pm); Piazza Castello (☺9am-7pm) The office at Stazione Porta Nuova offers a free accommodation and restaurant booking service.

❶ Getting There & Away

Air

Turin airport (TRN; www.turin-airport.com), 16km northwest of the city centre in Caselle, has connections to European and national destinations. Budget airline Ryanair operates flights to London Stansted, Madrid, Ibiza and Brussels.

Bus

Most international, national and regional buses terminate at the **bus station** (Corso Castelfidardo), 1km west from Stazione Porta Nuova along Corso Vittorio Emanuele II. You can also get to Milan's Malpensa airport from here.

Train

Regular daily trains connect Turin's **Stazione Porta Nuova** (Piazza Carlo Felice) to the following destinations.

DESTI-NATION	FARE (€)	DURATION (HR)	FREQUENCY
Milan	9.55	1¾	28
Aosta	7.90	2	21
Venice	42	5	17
Genoa	9.10	2	16
Rome	from 51.50	7	11

Most also stop at **Stazione Porta Susa** (Corso Inghilterra), which will gradually take over as the main station in the next few years. Some trains also stop at **Stazione Torino Lingotto** (Via Pannunzio 1), though it's generally more convenient to travel between the city centre and Lingotto by metro.

❶ Getting Around

To/From the Airport

Sadem (www.sadem.it, in Italian) runs buses to the airport from Stazione Porta Nuova (40 minutes), also stopping at Stazione Porta Susa (30 minutes). Buses depart every 30 minutes between 5.15am and 10.30pm (6.30am and 11.30pm from the airport). Single tickets cost €5 from **Confetteria Avvignano** (Piazza Carlo Felice 50), opposite where the bus stops, or €5.50 if bought on the bus.

A taxi between the airport and the city centre will cost around €35 to €40.

Car & Motorcycle

Major car-rental agencies have offices at Stazione Porta Nuova and the airport.

Public Transport

The city boasts a dense network of buses, trams and a cable car run by **Gruppo Torinese Trasporti** (GTT; www.gtt.to.it, in Italian), which has an **information office** (☉7am-9pm) at Stazione Porta Nuova. Buses and trams run from 6am to midnight and tickets cost €1 (€13.50 for a 15-ticket carnet and €3.50 for a one-day pass).

Turin's single-line **metro** (www.metrotorino.it) runs from Fermi to Lingotto. It first opened for the Winter Olympics in February 2006. It was extended to Stazione Porta Nuova in October 2007 and Lingotto in March 2011. Work is still being completed on a separate Porta Susa station and there are plans to extend the line further west and south by 2013.

Taxi

Call **Centrale Radio** (☎011 57 37) or **Radio Taxi** (☎011 57 30).

The Milky Way

Neither a chocolate bar nor a galaxy of stars, Piedmont's Milky Way (Via Lattea) consists of two parallel valleys just west of Turin that offer top-notch skiing facilities. The more northern of the two, Valle di Susa, meanders past a moody abbey, the old Celtic town of Susa and pretty mountain villages. Its southern counterpart, the Valle di Chisone, is pure ski-resort territory. The valleys hosted many events at the 2006 Winter Olympics and the facilities and infrastructure are state of the art.

◉ Sights

Brooding above the road 14km from Turin is the Sacra di San Michele (admission €4; ☉9.30am-12.30pm & 3-6pm Tue-Fri, 9.30am-noon & 2.40-6pm Sat & Sun, to 5pm Oct-Mar), a Gothic-Romanesque abbey that has kept watch atop Monte Pirchiriano (962m) since the 10th century. Look out for the whimsical 'Zodiac door', a 12th-century doorway sculpted with *putti* (cherubs) pulling each other's hair. To get to the abbey get off at Sant'Ambrogio station and hike up a steep path for 1½ hours. Alternatively, there's a special bus from Avigliana train station six times a day from May to September. Concerts are held on Saturday evenings in summer; ask for details at the tourist office in Avigliana (population 10,500), 12km west.

A Druid well remains as testimony to the Celtic origins of Susa (population 6580, elevation 503m) before it fell under the Roman Empire's sway. Susa's Roman ruins make for an interesting stop on the way to the western ski resorts. In addition to the remains of a Roman aqueduct, a still-used amphitheatre and the triumphal Arco d'Augusto (dating from 9 BC), you can visit the town's early-11th-century cathedral.

Also worth a brief stop is the forbidding Forte di Exilles (admission €6; ☉10am-7pm Tue-Sun Apr-Sep, to 2pm Oct-Mar), overlooking the quiet village of Exilles, 15km west of Susa. Its military role only ended in 1943.

🏃 Activities

Skiing

The prestigious Via Lattea (www.vialattea. it) ski domain embraces 400km of pistes and five interlinked ski resorts: Sestriere (2035m), Sauze d'Oulx (1509m), Sansicario (1700m), Cesana Torinese (1350m) and Claviere (1760m) in Italy; and Montgenèvre

(1850m) in neighbouring France. Its enormous range of slopes and generally reliable snow conditions provide for skiers and boarders of all abilities. A single daily ski pass costing €34 covers the entire Milky Way, including the French slopes.

Built in the 1930s by the Agnelli clan of Fiat fame, Sestriere (population 885) ranks among Europe's most glamorous ski resorts due to its enviable location in the eastern realms of the vast Milky Way ski area.

The tourist offices have mountains of information on every conceivable summer and winter sport, including heli-skiing, bobsledding, golfing on Europe's highest golf course, walking, free-climbing and mountain biking.

Cross-country skiing in the area is centred on Bardonecchia (population 3084, elevation 1312m), the last stop in Italy before the Fréjus Tunnel.

Hiking

Avigliana's tourist office has route maps and information on summertime walking and mountain biking, including the protected lakes and marshlands in the Parco Naturale dei Laghi di Avigliana (www.parks.it/parco.laghi.avigliana) on the town's western fringe. From Avigliana, experienced walkers can tackle a strenuous climb or take a 30km circular bike trail to the Sacra di San Michele abbey.

Rafting

Rafting and kayaking trips from Cesana Torinese are organised through OK Adventure (www.okadventure.it; 3hr trips €40-50).

🛌 Sleeping & Eating

Many hotels shut outside winter and summer. The area's tourist offices can make hotel reservations.

Sestriere's central square, Piazza Fraiteve, is loaded with places to eat and drink, including the perennially popular pizzeria Pinky (Piazza Fraiteve 5n; pizzas €4-6) and the trendier Napapijri (Piazza Agnelli 1; meals €17-18).

Casa Cesana   HOTEL €
(📞0122 8 94 62; www.hotelcasacesana.com; Viale Bouvier, Cesana Torinese; d €45-50; 🅿❄) Right across from Cesana's ski lift, this timber chalet was built for the 2006 Olympics. Its rooms are light-filled and spotless, there's a well-patronised restaurant open to non-

guests (set menus around €18), and its bar is one of the area's liveliest.

Hotel Susa & Stazione   HOTEL €
(📞0122 62 22 26; www.hotelsusa.it; Corso Stati Uniti 4/6, Susa; s/d €62/85; 🅿) A handy all-round base for the area and located directly opposite Susa's train station, this cycle-friendly hotel has 12 uniform rooms with private bathrooms, plus a restaurant (set menu €20). Staff hand out maps and itinerary proposals.

ℹ Information

There are numerous tourist offices in the valleys:
Avigliana (📞011 936 60 37; Piazza del Popolo 2; ⊕9am-1pm & 2-6pm Mon-Fri)
Cesana Torinese (Piazza Vittorio Amedeo 3; ⊕9am-12.30pm & 2.30-7pm)
Sestriere (www.sestriere.it; Via Louset; ⊕9am-12.30pm & 2.30-7pm)

ℹ Getting There & Away

The main Italy–France motorway and railway line roar along the Valle di Susa, making the area easily accessible by both public transport and car (though motorists should keep change on hand for the numerous tolls).

Sapav buses (www.sapav.it, in Italian) link Susa with Avigliana (€3, 35 minutes), Oulx (€2.20, 45 minutes), Turin (€3.90, 1¼ hours) and the Milky Way resorts. From Sestriere, buses serve Cesana (€1.70, 25 minutes), Oulx (€2.20, 45 minutes) and Turin (€5.70, two to three hours) up to five times daily.

Southern & Eastern Piedmont

Gourmets on the rebound from an Emilia-Romagna food tour (fattened up with balsamic vinegar and Parmesan) might think it couldn't get any better. But it can and it does. The rolling hills, valleys and townships of southern and eastern Piedmont are northern Italy's specialist pantry, weighed down with sweet hazelnuts, rare white truffles, arborio rice, delicate veal, subtle cheeses and Nebbiolo grapes that metamorphose into Barolo and Barbaresco wines. Out here in the damp Po river basin, they give out Michelin stars like overzealous schoolteachers give out house points, and with good reason. The food is sublime, doused in traditions as old as the towns that fostered them. There's Bra, home of the Slow Food Movement; Pollenzo, host to a University of Gastronomic

Sciences; Asti, replete with truffles and wine; and Alba, home of Barolo wines.

Many trace the gourmet routes in a car, but to compensate for the calorific overload, there are also excellent walking and cycling opportunities.

South of Cuneo, and forgotten by most, are the Maritime Alps, a one-time hunting ground for Savoy kings that's now open to hikers.

CUNEO & AROUND
POP 55,464 / ELEV 543M

Cuneo is a condensed version of Turin without the clamour. There is a raft of reasons why you should drop by here, not least the food, the bike friendliness, the hiking possibilities in the nearby Maritime Alps, and the city's signature rum-filled chocolates.

Sitting on a promontory of land between two rivers, Cuneo enjoys excellent Alpine views framed by the high pyramid-shaped peak of Monte Viso (3841m) in the Cottian Alps.

⊙ Sights
The settlement's Napoleonic avenues give it an almost French air.

Piazza Galimberti   PIAZZA
Arriving in Cuneo's gargantuan main piazza, you'd think you just touched down in a capital city. The outsized square was finished in 1884 and sits aside an older portico-embellished town founded in 1198. Some of the heavier arches date back to the Middle Ages.

Museo Civico di Cuneo   MUSEUM
(Via Santa María 10; admission €2.60; ⊙9am-1pm & 3-5.30pm Tue-Thu, to 7pm Fri & Sat) Cuneo has some wonderfully dark and mysterious churches. The oldest is the deconsecrated San Francisco convent and church, which today hosts this museum tracking the history of the town and province.

🏃 Activities
To the southwest lie the Maritime Alps, a rugged outdoor adventure playground where French and Italian influences mix (see the boxed text, p205).

The best-equipped ski town is Limone Piemonte (www.limonepiemonte.it), 20km south of Cuneo and reachable by regular trains (€2.50, 40 minutes). Limone has been a ski station since 1907 and maintains 15 lifts and 80km of runs, including some put aside for Nordic skiing. The town (popula-

tion 1600) has numerous hotels and ski-hire shops. See the website for details.

🛏 Sleeping

TOP CHOICE Hotel Royal Superga   HOTEL €
(☎0171 69 32 23; www.hotelroyalsuperga.com; Via Pascal 3; s €59-89, d €79-109; P✳@☎) For 'Superga' read 'superb'. This appealing, old-fashioned hotel hidden off a corner of Piazza Galimberti mixes some regal touches with a raft of complimentary items. Bank on free wi-fi, free DVDs to watch in your room, free *aperitivo* if you linger in the lobby between 5pm and 9pm, and free city bikes for guests. Breakfast (included) is a delicious spread made from organic produce.

Hotel Palazzo Loverna   HOTEL €€
(☎0171 69 04 20; www.palazzolovera.com; Via Roma 37; s €95-110, d €120-140; P✳☎) A French king and an Italian pope have stayed here, hinting at the Loverna's stately past. Rooms are comfortable if not lavish, but the value for money comes with rare small-town Italian extras such as a gym, sauna and two affiliated restaurants, one of which (Delle Antiche Contrade) has a deserved Michelin star.

Hotel Ligure   HOTEL €
(☎0171 63 45 45; www.ligurehotel.com; Via Savigliano 11; s €55-65, d €78-98; P✳☎) In the heart of the old town, this two-star hotel has a handful of apartments, each with its own kitchen (minimum seven-night stay). If you're just passing through, its freshly spruced-up hotel rooms (with breakfast) are simple but spotless. Friendly trilingual service adds further kudos.

🍴 Eating & Drinking
Typically for Piedmont, Cuneo has some standout places to wine and dine.

Delle Antiche Contrade   GASTRONOMIC €€€
(☎0171 48 04 88; Via Savigliano 11; meals €60; ⊙lunch Tue-Sun, dinner Tue-Sat) This former 17th-century postal station is the culinary workshop of Ligurian chef Luigi Taglienti, who melds the fish of his home region with the meat and pasta of his adopted one. The result: a Michelin star. Those with bottomless wallets can bag a personal table overlooking the kitchen action for a cool €130 per head.

Osteria della Chiocciola   GASTRONOMIC €€
(☎0171 6 62 77; Via Fossano 1; meals €28-33; ⊙Mon-Sat) The lack of outside signage re-

flects an inner confidence at Chiocciola's, where seasoned cooks perform small miracles. Although the restaurant is Slow Food affiliated, the time-poor can still stop by for a glass of wine with cheese and salami on the ground floor. Upstairs, in a buttercup dining room, dawdlers can choose from the handwritten menu's alchemy of flavours.

Arione
CHOCOLATE €

(www.arione-cuneo.com; Piazza Galimberti 14; 8am-8pm Tue-Sat, to 1pm & 3.30-8pm Sun) This 1920s-vintage chocolatier invented the *Cuneesi al Rhum* – a large, rum-laced praline wrapped in cellophane. The chocolates came to the attention of Hemingway, who made a detour from Milan en route to Nice in 1954 to try them – there's a photograph of his visit in the window.

Locanda La Volpe
TRADITIONAL ITALIAN €€

(Via Chiusa Pesio 6; meals €25; closed Wed) The best bet for traditional local food (ie mountain fare including rabbit) is this foxy place tucked down a cobbled side street in the Old Town.

Bruno
CAFE €

(www.localistorici.it; Via Roma 28) Elbow your way to the bar for a morning cappuccino with the locals in this typically grand Cuneo coffee and chocolate house dating from 1864.

ℹ Information
Tourist office (www.comune.cuneo.it; Via Roma 28; 9.30am-12.30pm & 3-6.30pm Mon-Sat)

ℹ Getting There & Away
Regular trains run from Cuneo's central train station, at Piazzale Libertà, to Saluzzo (€2.70, 35 minutes, up to six daily), Turin (€5.30, 1¼ hours, up to eight daily), San Remo (€6.50, 2¼ hours, three daily) and Ventimiglia (€5.80, two hours, around four daily), as well as Nice (2¾ hours, at least six daily) in France. A second train station for the Cuneo–Gesso line serves the small town of Mondovì, from where there are connections to Savona and Genoa.

HIKING IN THE MARITIME ALPS

Northern Italy, crowded? Not if you bring your hiking boots. Shoehorned between the rice-growing plains of Piedmont and the sparkling coastline of Liguria lie the brooding Maritime Alps – a small pocket of dramatically sculpted mountains that rise like stony-faced border guards along the frontier of Italy and France. Smaller yet no less majestic than their Alpine cousins to the north, the Maritimes are speckled with mirror-like lakes, foraging ibexes and a hybrid cultural heritage that is as much southern French as northern Italian.

Despite their diminutive size, there's a palpable wilderness feel to be found among these glowering peaks. Get out of the populated valleys and onto the imposing central massif and you'll quickly be projected into a high-altitude Shangri La. Whistling marmots scurry under rocky crags doused in mist above a well-marked network of mountain trails where the sight of another hiker – even in peak season – is about as rare as an empty piazza in Rome. This is Italy at its most serene and serendipitous. Not 20km to the south lie the swanky resort towns of Portofino and San Remo, where martini-supping celebrities wouldn't be seen dead without their expensive handbags and private yachts. Yet up here in the high country that straddles the invisible border between Italy and France, all you need is a map, a decent pair of shoes and enough cheese and ciabatta to keep you going until dinnertime.

The main trailheads lie to the south of the city of Cuneo in a couple of recently inaugurated regional parks: the **Parco Naturale delle Alpi Marittime** and the **Parco Naturale dell'Alta Valle Pesio e Tamaro**. The Lago di Valscura Circuit (21km) starts in the airy spa of **Terme di Valdieri** and follows an old military road via the Piano del Valasco to an icy lake near the French border. It loops back past the Rifugio Questa before descending via the same route. For a two-day hike try the Marguareis Circuit (35km) that begins in the small ski centre of Limone Piemonte and tracks up across cols and ridges to the **Rifugio Garelli** (0171 73 80 78; dm €36; Jun-Sep). Day two involves looping back through a small segment of France to your starting point in Limone. For more information on both hikes check out Lonely Planet's *Hiking in Italy* guide or consult the APT offices in either Terme or Limone.

SALUZZO
POP 16,877 / ELEV 395M

Like Asti and Alba, Saluzzo was once a powerful city-state and its historical importance – while now diminished – has left a stirring legacy etched in red terracotta bricks.

The town is divided into 'old' and 'new' quarters, and the two sections are a short walk apart. Once a medieval stronghold, the town maintained its independence until the Savoys won it in a 1601 treaty with France. One of its better-known sons was the Italian writer Silvio Pellico (1788–1854). Imprisoned for his patriotism against the Austrian occupation, he wrote parts of his novel *Le Mie Prigioni* (My Prisons) by cutting himself and using his blood as ink. A second well-known local is General Carlo dalla Chiesa (1920–82), whose implacable pursuit of the Mafia led to his assassination.

⊙ Sights

Torre Civica   LANDMARK
(Via San Giovanni; admission €2, incl Museo Civico di Casa Cavassa €6; ⊙10.30am-12.30pm & 2.30-6.30pm Fri-Sun) The burnt-red-tiled rooftops of Saluzzo's old town make a timeless picture from the loggia beneath the 15th-century belfry, which is reached by a steep flight of steps.

La Castiglia   CASTLE
(Piazza Castello; adult/reduced €5/2.50) Saluzzo's medieval rulers meted out justice from this 13th-century castle atop Saluzzo's old town. It was recently refurbished but is open at weekends only. Enquire at the tourist office about guided tours.

Museo Civico di Casa Cavassa   MUSEUM
(Via San Giovanni 5; adult/child €5/2.50, admission incl Torre Civica €6; ⊙10am-1pm & 2-6pm Thu-Sun) This fine example of a 16th-century noble residence contains a valuable 1499 gold-leaved painting, *Nostra Signora dell Grazie* (Our Lady of Mercy) by Hans Klemer.

🛏 Sleeping & Eating

Albergo Ristorante Persico   HOTEL €
(☑0175 4 12 13; www.albergopersico.net; Vicolo Mercati 10; s/d €43/63; ▣❋@☎) This simple but comfy hotel is tucked just off Piazza Cavour in Saluzzo's new town. Discounted half-board options are available at the restaurant (closed Monday), which has regional menus ranging from €15 to €25 for nonguests. Free wi-fi is available in the lobby.

Perpöin   HOTEL, INTERNATIONAL €
(☑0175 4 23 83; www.hotelsaluzzo.com; Via Spielberg 19-27; s €40-70, d €70-100; ▣) Enjoy hearty home cooking (and fresh-from-the-oven Nutella-filled croissants at breakfast) at this family-run hotel-restaurant (set menus €12-25) in the new town's centre. There is no hotel reception (the building is a maze of corridors), so call ahead to confirm your arrival.

Le Quattro Stagioni   MEDITERRANEAN €€
(Via Volta 21; ⊙lunch & dinner Wed-Mon) As the name implies, the food changes with the season at this bodega-cum-restaurant situated in a street of dark porticoes and obscure arcades. The smell of fruity wine through the doorway provides the initial temptation, but just wait till you get inside for crusty pizza and al dente pasta. There's a pleasant *giardino* (garden) attached.

ℹ Information

Tourist office (www.comune.saluzzo.it; Piazza Risorgimento; ⊙9am-12.30pm & 3-6.30pm Mon-Sat, 9am-noon & 3-7pm Sun)

ℹ Getting There & Away

There are buses from Saluzzo to/from Turin (€3.50, 1½ hours, hourly). Otherwise, take a train to Savigliano (€1.70, 30 minutes, up to six daily), from where there are connections for Turin.

ALBA
POP 31,272 / ELEV 172M

In the gastronomic heaven that is Italy, Alba is a leading player courtesy of its black truffles, dark chocolate and wine – including the incomparable Barolo, the Ferrari of reds. Eschewing the modern penchant for junk food, this once-powerful city-state has redirected its energy into showcasing the fine art of *real* cooking, with ingredients plucked from within spear-throwing distance of your restaurant table. All becomes clearer at the annual truffle fair and the equally ecstatic *vendemia* (grape harvest).

The vine-striped Langhe Hills radiate out from the town like a giant undulating vegetable garden, replete with grapes, hazelnut groves and fine wineries. Exploring Alba's fertile larder on foot or with two wheels is a rare pleasure.

⊙ Sights

A historical heavyweight, Alba enjoyed prosperity that reached its apex in the Middle Ages and lasted until 1628 when Savoy took control. At its peak Alba sported more than 100 towers. A less illustrious four remain.

Cattedrale di San Lorenzo
CHURCH

(Piazza Duomo) There's been a cathedral here since the 12th century, though the current terracotta-brick affair is mostly a result of an almost complete neo-Gothic 19th-century makeover. The intricate choir stalls date from 1512.

FREE Museo Civico Archeologico 'Federico Eusebio'
MUSEUM

(Via Vittorio Emanuele II; ⊘3-6pm Tue-Fri, 10am-5.30pm Sat & Sun) Worth a peek for those keen to sober up between wine-tasting excursions, the city museum was founded in 1887. It has archeological and natural history sections.

Festivals & Events

Truffle Festival
FOOD

The countryside around Alba contains precious white truffles and they change hands for ridiculous amounts of money at this annual festival held every weekend in October.

Tours

Alba's tourist office has a special desk organising excursions to both Langhe and Roero valleys. Some are seasonal, including 3½-hour **winery tours** (€80-100; ⊘Sep-Nov) in an air-con minibus, and two-hour **truffle-hunting excursions** (⊘Sep-Oct), with the price dependent on group size. There are year-round **cooking courses** (half-/full-day course €70/100), **horse riding** (per day €80) in the Upper Langhe, **rafting** (3hr adult/child from €20/12) on the Tanaro river, and – for the ultimate view of the vineyards – a **hot-air balloon flight** (incl transfers, wine & breakfast €220-250). Sunrise balloon flights last one hour, but you'll need to allow four hours in total.

Most activities and tours need to be booked at least two days ahead (tours may be cancelled if there aren't sufficient numbers).

Sleeping

TOP CHOICE Hotel Langhe
HOTEL €

(☑0173 36 69 33; www.hotellanghe.it; Strada Profonda 21; s €64-78, d €84-98; [P][❄][🌐]) Two kilometres from the city centre but worth every step (even if you're walking it), Hotel Langhe sits on the cusp of the vineyards that push up against Alba's suburbs and manages to ignite feelings of bucolic bliss despite its proximity to the urban core. The layout is sublime: a wine conservatory, a bright breakfast area and downstairs rooms with French windows that open onto a sunny forecourt.

Hotel San Lorenzo
HOTEL €€

(☑0173 36 24 06; www.albergo-sanlorenzo.it; Piazza Rossetti 6; s/d/tr €85/100/125; ⊘closed 2 weeks Jan & Aug; [P]) It's very simple. Take 11 rooms in a refurbished 18th-century house, stick it just steps from the cathedral, call it a boutique hotel and add a unique downstairs pastry shop ('Golosi') selling butter-, egg- and dairy-free confectionery. The result is one of those only-in-Alba moments. Enjoy it while you can.

Eating & Drinking

The key to finding out about Alba's fantastic cuisine is not by counting Michelin stars, but by word of mouth. Here lie some of the best grandma-in-the-kitchen places north of Sicily.

TOP CHOICE Osteria dei Sognatori
OSTERIA €

(Via Macrino 8b; meals €12-20; ⊘lunch & dinner Mon-Sat) Menu? What menu? You get whatever's in the pot at this rustic beneath-the-radar place and it's always delicious. Bank on homemade pasta in a nutty pesto-like sauce and the best breadsticks in Italy. Walls are bedecked with football memorabilia and B&W snaps of bearded wartime partisans.

Vincafé
WINE BAR €

(www.vincafe.com; Via Vittorio Emanuele II 12; set menus €10-25) It's hip, but by no means exclusive. Anyone can sup on a glass of wine here, as long as you can squeeze through the door (it's small and popular) and have the time and/or expertise to sift through a list of over 350 varieties. If in doubt, choose Barolo. Downstairs, in a cool vaulted stone cellar, the restaurant serves up huge healthy salads and pasta.

Locanda Cortiletto D'Alba
TRADITIONAL ITALIAN €€

(www.cortilettodalba.com; Corso M Coppino 27; meals €20-30 ⊘closed Wed) The Cortiletto is one of those secluded ring-the-front-doorbell kind of places where you're welcomed like a family friend and served like a Savoy king. Seating is on an upstairs terrace or in a downstairs wine cellar, and menu items never stray far from the Langhe hinterland. Think *plin* (ravioli) sautéed in sage and butter, cheese fondue, or veal cooked in Nebbiolo wine. It has five lovely colour-themed rooms upstairs that are rented out from €80 a double.

The Humble Truffle

One of the world's most mystical, revered foodstuffs, truffles are Italy's gastronomic gold; Roman emperor Nero called them the 'food of the gods', while composer Rossini hailed them as the 'mushrooms of Mozart'.

Hunting them out is a specialist activity. Truffles – subterranean edible fungi similar to mushrooms that colonise the roots of certain species of tree – are notoriously hard to find. The most prized variety is the white truffle from the Alba region in Piedmont. Other slightly less aromatic white truffles are found in Tuscany, while black truffles are most prevalent in Umbria and Le Marche.

White truffles are harvested from early October to December, but black truffles are available throughout winter (November to March). The season is crowned in the Umbrian town of Norcia during late February and early March with a boisterous black truffle festival (p580).

Italy's biggest truffle festival is held in Alba (p207) every weekend in October, while other notable extravaganzas enliven the Tuscan towns of San Miniato and San Giovanni d'Asso near Siena, during the second half of November.

TRUFFLE IMMERSION

Despite the apparent secretiveness of truffle-hunting, curious outsiders can join selective hunts. The tourist office in Alba (p210) organises excursions during the season, or you can pitch in with tour agency I Viaggi del Tartufo (www.viaggideltartufo.com). In southern Tuscany in San Giovanni d'Asso the Assotartufi San Giovanni (www.assotartufi.it) organises hunts year-round and sports a unique Museo del Tartufo (www.museodeltartufo.it). Further north, in San Miniato you can learn how to cook with truffles at local restaurant Pepenero (see boxed text, p508) or you can search for them nearby at Barbialla Nuova (see boxed text, p508).

Clockwise from top left
1. White truffle 2. Hunting for truffles near Alba 3. Black truffle appetiser 4. Truffles for sale, Alba truffle festival.

Piazza Duomo-La Piola GASTRONOMIC €€€

(☎0173 44 28 00; www.piazzaduomoalba.it; Piazza Risorgimento 4; meals €20-30, set menus €60-80; ⊙lunch Tue-Sun, dinner Tue-Sat) The best of both worlds are bivouacked in this two-in-one, suit-all-budgets culinary extravaganza in Alba's main square. Downstairs, La Piola sports local blackboard specials, such as *vitello tonnato,* that change daily and allow diners to create their own plates. Upstairs, the theme goes more international in chef Enrico Crippa's Michelin-starred Piazza Duomo, where you can eat creative food beneath colourful wall frescoes painted by contemporary artist Francesco Clemente.

❶ Information

Tourist office (www.langheroero.it; Piazza Risorgimento 2; ⊙9am-6.30pm Mon-Fri, 10am-6.30pm Sat & Sun) In the town's historic centre, it sells walking maps and has internet access.

❶ Getting There & Around

From the **bus station** (Corso Matteotti 10) there are frequent buses to/from Turin (€4, 1½ hours, up to 10 daily) and infrequent buses to/from Barolo (€1.80, 25 minutes, two daily) and other surrounding villages.

From Alba's **train station** (Piazza Trento e Trieste) there are regular trains to/from Turin (€4.40 via Bra/Asti, 50 minutes, hourly).

Irregularity of buses makes touring the Langhe better by car or bike. For bike hire try super-flexible **Motocicli Destefanis** (www.motocicli destefanis.it; Via Margherita 2; bikes per day €15) just to the south of town off Corso Langhe. It also hires out motor-scooters. Car hire goes from about €35 per day or the tourist office can hook you up with a driver (prices vary).

BAROLO REGION

Wine lovers rejoice! This tiny 1800-hectare parcel of undulating land immediately southwest of Alba knocks out what is arguably (but not by many) the finest *vino* in Italy. Unbiased laymen call it Barolo (after the eponymous village where it is produced), but everyone else hails it as the 'wine of kings' and discusses its velvety truffle-scented flavours with an almost religious reverence.

Barolo

POP 750

A wine village for centuries, Barolo is no uppity New World viticultural wannabe. The settlement dates from the 13th century and references to wine production have been commonplace since the late 1600s.

◉ SIGHTS & ACTIVITIES

TOP CHOICE **Castello Falletti** CASTLE

(www.baroloworld.it; Piazza Falletti) Barolo village is lorded over by a castle once owned by the powerful Falletti banking family. Its origins lie in the 10th century, though most of the current structure dates from the 1600s. Today the castle hosts the Museo del Vino a Barolo and, in its cellars, the **Enoteca Regionale del Barolo** (⊙10am-12.30pm & 3-6.30pm Fri-Wed), organised and run by the region's 11 wine-growing communities. The *enoteca* (wine bar) has three Barolo wines available for tasting each day, costing €2 each or €5 for all three.

Museo del Vino a Barolo MUSEUM

(www.wimubarolo.it; adult/reduced €7/5; ⊙10.30am-7pm Fri-Wed, closed Jan-Feb) Put together by the same guy who designed the cinema museum in Turin's Mole Antonelliana, this flashy new museum spread over three floors inside the Castello Falletti uses multimedia innovations and modern technology to tell the story of wine through history, art, music, film, literature and food. Some traditionalists are riled by the gimmicks, but it has quickly established itself as a popular drawcard.

Museo dei Cavatappi MUSEUM

(adult/reduced €4/3; ⊙10am-1pm & 2pm-6.30pm Fri-Wed) This is a rather expensive way to view the evolution of corkscrews (decorative, miniature, multipurpose etc) throughout history. There's also a display of old (empty) Barolo bottles and an equally pricey shop.

⊨ SLEEPING & EATING

TOP CHOICE **Hotel Barolo** HOTEL €€

(☎0173 5 63 54; www.hotelbarolo.it; Via Lomondo 2; s/d €70/110; P@≋) Overlooked by the famous *enoteca*-castle, Hotel Barolo is the ultimate place to sit back on the terrace with a glass of you know what, contemplating the 18th-century Piemontese architecture that guards its shimmering swimming pool. You don't have to go far for a good meal – the on-site Ristorante Brezza has been serving up truffles and the like for four generations. The family have been making wine since 1885.

La Morra

POP 2668

Atop a hill surrounded by vines with the Alps as a backdrop, La Morra is quieter than Barolo, though no less beguiling. It could

LOCAL KNOWLEDGE

CRISTIANA GRIMALDI: DIRECTOR, ENOTECA BAROLO

Tell us a bit about Barolo's growing area.

Barolo's growing area is small – it is only possible to cultivate Nebbiolo grapes in 1800 hectares scattered round Barolo and 11 other wine-growing villages. Furthermore, at 8000kg per hectare, the grape's yield is low. Sixty-five per cent of the wine we make is exported. It is popular in Germany, the US, China and Japan.

Fill us in on Nebbiolo grapes.

Nebbiolo is a strange grape in that it *needs* the climate of Piedmont. Non-native plantings haven't worked, at least not in the same way. Climate is important. Nebbiolo requires relatively wet, humid autumnal conditions, cool-ish temperatures (25°C to 30°C) in the spring and summer, and some winter snow (80cm to 85cm). The grape needs to sleep!

What are the differences between Barbaresco and Barolo?

The main difference is age. Barbaresco is younger and can be drunk within two years of picking. Barolo requires three years to age. Then there is the soil. Barbaresco's soil is sandy; Barolo's consists of mineral-rich clay. As a result the body and flavour of Barbaresco is lighter, fresher and more delicate. Both wines are top-quality well-known labels and sell for a similar high-ish price. Barolo's ageing qualities are legendary and it can be good at 25- to 30-year maturity. I once tasted a 1923 vintage. It was perfect.

What is Barolo best paired with?

Local Castelmango cheese, game and foods with a strong important taste such as *ragù* (meat and tomato sauce).

What other non-Piedmont wine would you recommend?

Nero d'Avola from the south; it's a young wine and not particularly famous yet, but it's of high quality.

be Tuscany, until you taste the *vino,* which could only be one thing – the wine of kings!

Villa Carita B&B B&B €€
(☑0173 50 96 33; www.villacarita.it; Via Roma 105; s/d/ste €90/120/150; ℙ) When you dream of Italy, the chances are somewhere in that dream is a room with a view across sun-dappled vineyards. This B&B not only has 'blink to be sure you're not still dreaming' daytime views from every room (and its panoramic terrace), but also romantic night-time views of the village lights. Tucked below the main building, one room and one suite are hidden in the hillside with their own private terraces.

Belvedere GASTRONOMIC €€€
(☑0173 5 01 90; Piazza Castello 5; set menus €45; ☺lunch Tue-Sun, dinner Tue-Sat Mar-Dec, closed last week Jul) 'Beautiful view' is no arbitrary name – it's adjacent to La Morra's lookout point. But Gian Bovio's *risotto al Barolo,* Barbera-cooked steak and triple pyramid of chocolate all do their best to distract you from the

vistas; as does the bewildering decision of choosing among more than 1000 wines.

BARBARESCO REGION
Same grape, different flavour! Only a few kilometres separate Barolo from Barbaresco, the home of the renowned wine of the same name, but a rainier microclimate and fewer ageing requirements have made the latter into a softer, more delicate red that plays 'queen' to Barolo's 'king'.

Barbaresco
POP 650
The village of Barbaresco is surrounded by vineyards and characterised by its 30m-high, 11th-century tower visible from miles around. There are over 40 wineries and three *enotecas* in the area.

🏌 **ACTIVITIES**
Enoteca Regionale del Barbaresco WINE TASTING
(Piazza del Municipio 7; ☺9.30am-6pm Thu-Tue) Blasphemous as it may seem, you can wor-

WORTH A TRIP

CHERASCO & ITS SNAILS

Located 23km west of Alba, within the Langhe's lush wine country, Cherasco is actually best known for *lumache* (snails). The town is home to the Istituto Internazionale di Elicoltura (International Institute for Heliciculture; ☎0172 48 92 18; www.lumache-elici.com; Via Vittorio Emanuele 55), which provides technical advice for snail breeders (heliciculture is edible-snail breeding). Snails in this neck of the woods are dished up *nudo* (shell-less). They can be pan-fried, roasted, dressed in an artichoke sauce or minced inside ravioli. Piedmont dishes made with snails include *lumache al barbera* (snails simmered in Barbera red wine and ground nuts) and *lumache alla piemontese* (snails stewed with onions, nuts, anchovies and parsley in a tomato sauce).

Traditional trattorias serving such dishes include Osteria della Rosa Rossa (☎0172 48 81 33; Via San Pietro 31; set menus €30-35; ⊙12.30-2pm & 8-9pm Fri-Tue). Reservations are required.

ship Barbaresco wines at this intimate *enoteca* housed inside a deconsecrated church, with wines lined up where the altar once stood. It costs €1.50 per individual tasting; six Barbaresco wines are available to try each day.

Sentiero dei Barbaresco HIKE
Various trails surround the village, including this 13km loop through the undulating vineyards. The *enoteca* and info centre have maps.

🛏 SLEEPING & EATING

The village has four fine restaurants, one of which – Antinè – has a Michelin star.

Casa Boffa PENSIONE €
(☎0173 63 51 74; www.boffacarlo.it; Via Torino 9a; s/d/tr €65/80/100; 🛜) In a lovely house in the centre of the village, Boffa offers four modern, minimalist rooms and one suite above a stunning terrace with limitless Langhe valley views. There's a bright breakfast room downstairs and also an *enoteca* open for tasting (11am to 6pm daily except Wednesday).

🍴 Ristorante
Rabayà TRADITIONAL ITALIAN €€
(☎0173 63 52 23; Via Rabayà 9; set menus €30-45; ⊙Fri-Wed, closed mid-Feb–early Mar) One in a quartet of Barbaresco restaurants, the Rabayà on the fringe of the village is first rate, with the ambience of dining at a private home. Its antique-furnished dining room has a roaring fire, but when the sun's shining there's no better spot than its terrace set high above the vineyards. Try Rabayà's signature rabbit in Barbaresco, followed by a platter of local cheese.

Neive
POP 2930

Ping-ponged between Alba and Asti during the Middle Ages, Neive is a quieter proposition these days, its hilltop medieval layout earning it a rating as one of Italy's *borghi più belli* (most beautiful towns). Come here to taste the village's four legendary wines – Dolcetto d'Alba, Barbaresco, moscato and Barbera d'Alba – amid sun-dappled squares and purple wisteria.

🏃 ACTIVITIES

The tourist office has a list of six different local day hikes from 12.5km to 20km distance.

🍷 Bottega dei Quattro Vini WINE TASTING
(Piazza Italia 2; ⊙vary) This two-room shop was set up by the local community to showcase the four DOC wines produced on Neive's hills. Inside you can sample wines by the glass (€1.80 to €4.50), accompanied by cold local specialities (€3.50 to €10).

🛏 SLEEPING & EATING
La Contea PENSIONE €
(☎0173 67 12 6; www.la-contea.it; Piazza Cocito 8; s/d €70/100) *Enoteca*, shop, restaurant and small hotel, the family-run La Contea has been part of Neive's fabric for eons. Chefs pluck fresh herbs from their window boxes to embellish dishes such as rabbit, *ravioli al plin*, and *brasato al Barbaresco*. The rooms are traditional and comfortable.

❶ Getting There & Away
Neive is on the train line between Alba and Asti. Trains and buses to Alba (€1.40) run hourly.

BRA & POLLENZO
POP 29,796

Home to some of the best gastronomic alchemy in Italy, Bra is the small, unassuming Piemontese town where the Slow Food Movement first took root in 1986. The brainchild of a group of disenchanted local journalists, the initial manifesto ignited a global crusade against the encroaching fast-food juggernaut whose plastic tentacles were threatening to engulf Italy's centuries-old gastronomic traditions. The backlash worked and Bra happily broadcasts its success. There are no cars and no supermarkets in this refreshingly laid-back town's historic centre, where small, family-run shops (which shut religiously for a 'slowdown' twice a week) are replete with organic sausages, handcrafted chocolates and fresh local farm produce.

◉ Sights

Churches   CHURCH
Bra's sloping main square contains some stately baroque architecture best exemplified in the Chiesa di San Andrea (Piazza Caduti), designed by Bernini. The Santuario della Madonna dei Fiori (Viale Madonna dei Fiori) mixes baroque with neoclassical and is devoted to the Madonna, who supposedly appeared here in 1336, while the elegantly domed Chiesa di Santa Chiara (Via Craveri) is a jewel of Piemontese Rococo.

FREE Museo Civico
Artistico-Storico   MUSEUM
(Palazzo Traversa, Via Parpera 4; ⊙3-6pm Tue-Thu, 10am-noon & 3-6pm Sat & Sun 2nd week of month) Bra's history began long before its 1986 Slow Food epiphany and is exhibited in the Palazzo Traversa. Displays include Roman artefacts, 18th-century paintings and medieval weaponry.

Università di Scienze
Gastronomiche   UNIVERSITY
(University of Gastronomic Sciences; www.unisg.it; Piazza Vittorio Emanuele 9) Another creation of Carlo Petrini, founder of the Slow Food Movement, this university established in the village of Pollenzo (4km southeast of Bra) in 2004 occupies a former royal palace, and offers three-year courses in gastronomy and food management. Also here is the acclaimed Guido Restaurante (☏0172 45 84 22; www.guidoristorante.it; set menus €75; ⊙Tue-Sat, closed Jan & Aug) that people have

been known to cross borders to visit, especially for the veal. Next door is the Albergo Dell'Agenzia (s €155, d €195-240) and the Banca del Vino (www.bancadelvino.it; Piazza Vittorio Emanuele II 13), a wine cellar–'library' of Italian wines. Free guided tastings are available by reservation.

🛏 Sleeping & Eating

TOP CHOICE Albergo Cantine Ascheri   HOTEL €€
(☏0172 43 03 12; www.ascherihotel.it; Via Piumati 25; s/d €100/130; [P] [※] [@]) Built around the Ascheri family's 1880-established winery, incorporating wood, steel mesh and glass, this ultracontemporary hotel includes a mezzanine library, 27 sun-drenched rooms and a vine-lined terrace overlooking the rooftops. From the lobby you can see straight down to the vats in the cellar (guests get a free tour). It's just one block south of Bra's train station.

Osteria del Boccondivino   OSTERIA €€
(☏0172 42 56 74; www.boccondivinoslow.it; Via Mendicità Istruita 14; set menus €26-28; ⊙Tue-Sat) Up on the 1st floor of the recessed courtyard of the Slow Food Movement's headquarters, this homey little eatery lined with wine bottles was the first to be opened by the emerging organisation back in the 1980s. The food is predictably fresh and excellent, and the local Langhe menu changes daily.

ℹ Information

Tourist office (www.comune.bra.cn.it, in Italian; Via Moffa di Lisio 14; ⊙9am-1pm & 3-6pm Mon-Fri, 9am-noon Sat & Sun Mar-Nov) Has information on both towns and the region.

ℹ Getting There & Away

From the train station on Piazza Roma, trains link Bra with Turin (€3.50, one hour), via Carmagnola, while buses connect Bra with Pollenzo (€1, 15 minutes, Monday to Saturday morning).

ASTI
POP 75,910 / ELEV 123M

Just 30km apart, Asti and Alba were fierce rivals in medieval times when they faced off against each other as feisty independent strongholds ruled over by feuding royal families. These days the two towns are united by viticulture rather than divided by factionalism. Asti – by far the bigger town – produces the sparkling white Asti Spumante wine made from white muscat grapes, while Alba concocts Barolo and Barbaresco.

✷ Festivals & Events

Palio d'Asti   HORSE RACING

Held on the third Sunday of September, this bareback horse race commemorates a victorious battle against Alba during the Middle Ages and draws over a quarter of a million spectators from surrounding villages. (Alba answers with a tongue-in-cheek donkey race on the first Sunday in October.)

🍷 Douja d'Or   FOOD

This 10-day festival (a *douja* is a terracotta wine jug unique to Asti), held in early September, is complemented by the Delle Sagre food festival on the second Sunday of September.

◉ Sights & Activities

Asti's largely pedestrianised centre is attractive, though less intimate than Alba's.

FREE Torre Troyana o Dell'Orologio   LANDMARK

(Piazza Medici; ⊙10am-1pm & 4-7pm Apr-Sep, 10am-1pm & 3-6pm Sat & Sun Oct) During the late 13th century the region became one of Italy's wealthiest, with 150-odd towers springing up in Asti alone. Of the 12 that remain, only this one can be climbed. Troyana is a 38m-tall tower that dates from the 12th century. The clock was added in 1420.

Cattedrale di Santa Maria Assunta   CHURCH

(Piazza Cattedrale) Rising above Asti's historic core is the enormous belfry of this 13th-century Romanesque-Gothic cathedral. Its grandly painted interior merits a peek.

FREE Palazzo Mazzetti   MUSEUM

(www.palazzomazzetti.it; Corso Alfieri 357; ⊙10.30am-6.30pm Tue-Sun) This 18th-century residence of the Mazzetti family houses the civic museum and an information office. Downstairs you'll find Roman artefacts and a scale model of the city. Upstairs there are Italian paintings from the 17th to 19th centuries.

Enoteca Boero di Boero Mario   WINE TASTING

(Piazza Astesano 17; ⊙9am-noon & 3-8pm daily, closed Mon morning) Roll up your sleeves and get down to Asti's most pleasurable activity – wine tasting. This small, unassuming *enoteca* lines up the glasses morning and afternoon for free tastings administered with expert evaluations from the owner. Don't miss the Barbera d'Asti and the sparkling moscato.

🛏 Sleeping & Eating

Outside the town centre, there are some lovely spots to sleep in the nearby Monferrato vineyards – see p215 or ask Asti's tourist offices for a list of properties, including *agriturismi*.

Fresh food, clothes and all sorts of household paraphernalia are sold at Asti's Wednesday and Saturday morning markets on Piazza Alfieri and Piazza Campo del Palio.

Hotel Palio   HOTEL €€

(☑0141 3 43 71; www.hotelpalio.com; Via Cavour 106; s/d €85/115; P❄❀@⑧) Wedged between the train station and the old town, the Palio's utilitarian exterior belies plusher facilities inside. Reflecting Asti's juxtaposition of old and new, the hotel broadcasts chic, smart rooms with satellite TVs and wi-fi along with an atmospherically decorated inner sanctum. The owners also run the Ristorante Falcon Vecchia, one of Asti's oldest, which opened in 1607.

Osteria La Vecchia Carrozza   OSTERIA €

(Via Caducci 41; meals €18-25; ⊙Tue-Sun) You could be sharing the room with a quartet of nuns or a birthday party of celebrating college graduates at this local spot bedecked with white tablecloths and polished wine glasses, but characterised by plenty of down-to-earth Piemontese ambience. This being Asti, the food is infused with truffles, Barolo wine and a formidable *agnolotti di astigiana*.

Pompa Magna   INTERNATIONAL €€

(www.pompamagna.it; Via Aliberti 65; set menus €20-30; ⊙Tue-Sun; ❀) This split-level brasserie-style restaurant is a great spot for a bruschetta and glass of very good wine (the Pompa Magna also owns an *enoteca* in town at Corso Alfieri 332). But it's worth coming hungry for its chef-prepared menus and especially its *bônnet* (an elaborate chocolate pudding) for dessert.

❶ Information

Tourist office (www.astiturismo.it; Piazza Alfieri 29; ⊙9am-1pm & 2.30-6.30pm) Has details of September's flurry of wine festivals.

❶ Getting There & Away

Asti is on the Turin–Genoa railway line and is served by hourly trains in both directions. Journey time is 30 to 55 minutes to/from Turin (€3.90), and 1¾ hours to/from Genoa (€6.50), stopping at Alba (€2.70, 40 minutes).

MONFERRATO REGION

Vineyards fan out around Asti, interspersed with castles and celebrated restaurants. Buses run from Asti to many of the villages; Asti's tourist offices can provide schedules.

A land of literary giants (contemporary academic and novelist Umberto Eco and 18th-century dramatist Vittorio Alfieri hail from here) and yet another classic wine (the intense Barbera del Monferrato), the Monferrato area occupies a fertile triangle of terrain between Asti, Alessandria and its historical capital, Casale Monferrato (population 38,500).

◉ Sights

The tiny hamlet of Moncalvo (population 3320), 15km north of Asti along the S457, makes a perfect photo stop, with a lookout above its castle, where you'll also find an information office (Piazza Antico Castello; ⊙ Sat & Sun, specific hours vary) and wine tasting.

Many producers conduct cellar tours; the Consorzio Operatori Turistici Asti e Monferrato (www.terredasti.it; Piazza Alfieri 29) in Asti has a detailed list of tours and can provide directions.

⌂ Sleeping & Eating

⌂ **Tenuta del Barone**   AGRITURISMO €
(☎0141 91 01 61; www.tenutadelbarone.com; Via Barone 18, Penango; s €45-50, d €70-75; P☼) This family farm dating from 1550 has been converted into a cheery B&B, where you can sleep in the old stables and feast on huge amounts of homemade food (dinner including wine €25). Medieval-cooking courses and wine tasting are often available. Penango, 2km from Moncalvo, is signposted from Moncalvo's southern end.

⌂ **Tenuta Castello
di Razzano**   BOUTIQUE HOTEL €€
(☎0141 92 21 24; www.castellodirazzano.it; Frazione Casarello 2, Alfiano Natta; d/ste €130/220; P☼@) You can visit this rambling castle just to tour its working winery, and take part in a personal, seated wine tasting (from €6 for five wines and food snacks). But to soak up the antiques-filled castle's atmosphere – you'll want to stay in one of its rooms (the size of small apartments), roam its historical halls or curl up in its book-lined reading room. The new Museo Artevino Razzano (admission €10) bills itself as a museum of art and wine. Entrance is by appointment only. Alfiano Natta is 6km west of Moncalvo.

Locanda del Sant'Uffizio   LUXURY HOTEL €€€
(☎0141 91 62 92; Strada Sant'Uffizio 1, Cioccaro di Penango; s €130-180, d €180-250; P☼@☼) This knockout, restored 17th-century convent (and sleek wellness centre) is set in 4 hectares of vineyards. Many of the convent's rooms – some with original frescoes – reflect the colour of the flowers after which they are named. Bike rental is free, and a pick-up service from Asti can be arranged. Sant'Uffizio has a small, elegant restaurant (lunch/dinner menus €23/55), which is open to nonguests, though you'll need to book ahead. The Locanda is 3.3km south of Moncalvo.

Varallo & the Valsesia

Situated 66km northwest of Vercelli in northern Piedmont, Varallo guards the amazing Sacro Monte di Varallo (www.sacromontedivarallo.it; admission free; ⊙7.30am-6.30pm), the oldest of Italy's nine Sacri Monti (Sacred Mountains), which were inscribed communally as a Unesco World Heritage Site in 2003. The complex consists of an astounding 45 chapels, with 800 religious statues depicting the Passion of Christ set on a rocky buttress high above Varallo on the slopes of Monte Tre Croci. It was founded in 1491 by a Franciscan friar whose aim was to reproduce a version of Jerusalem as a substitute pilgrimage site for local worshippers. The complex is anchored by a basilica dating from 1614, and the subsequent chapels follow the course of Christ's life told through frescoes and life-sized terracotta statues. The scenes are sometimes macabre. The Monte is accessed via a winding walking path from Piazza Ferrari in town.

Beyond Varallo, the Sesia river heads spectacularly north to the foot of the Monte Rosa massif. Alpine slopes climb sharply, offering numerous walking, cycling and white-water-rafting possibilities. The valley's last village, Alagna Valsesia, is an ancient Swiss-Walser settlement-turned-ski resort, which is part of the Monte Rosa Ski Area (www.monterosa-ski.com). It is well known for its off-piste runs. From the town a cable car climbs to Punta Indren (3260m), from where fit walkers/climbers can strike out for the highest *rifugio* in Europe, the Capanna Regina Margherita (☎0163 9 10 39; dm €80) perched atop Punta Gnifetti on the Swiss–Italian border at an astounding 4554m. The ascent requires glacier travel, but non-experts can hire a guide through Corpo Guide

Alagna (www.guidealagna.com; Piazza Grober 1, Alagna Valsesia). Costs are €100 to €383, depending on group size, for the two-day excursion (June to September).

VALLE D'AOSTA

POP 127,866

While its Dolomite cousins exhibit notable German tendencies, Aosta's nuances are French. The result is a curious hybrid culture known as Valdostan, a historical mix of French-Provençal and northern Italian that has infiltrated the food (polenta, spicy sausages and the famous *fontina* cheese) and ensured the survival of an esoteric local language, Franco-Provençal or Valdôtain, a dialect still used by approximately 55% of the population.

Comprising one large glacial valley running east–west, which is bisected by several smaller valleys, the semi-autonomous Val d'Aosta is overlooked by some of Europe's highest peaks, including Mont Blanc (4807m), the Matterhorn (4478m), Monte Rosa (4633m) and Gran Paradiso (4061m). Not surprisingly the region offers some of the best snow facilities on the continent, with opportunities for skiers to descend

Valle d'Aosta

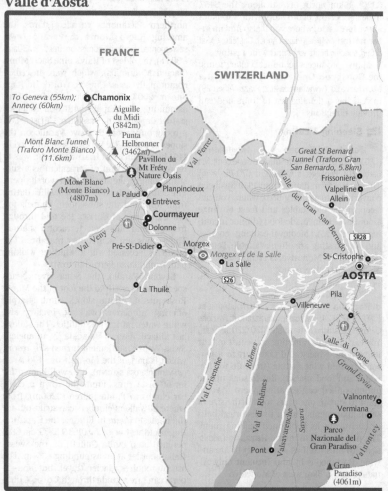

hair-raisingly into France and Switzerland over lofty glaciers or traverse them in equally spectacular cable cars.

When the snow melts, the hiking is even more sublime, with access to the 165km Tour du Mont Blanc, the Gran Paradiso National Park, and Aosta's two blue-riband, high-altitude trails: the Alte Vie 1 and 2.

Aosta's roots are Roman – the eponymous town guards some significant ruins – while annexation by the House of Savoy in the 11th century led to the building of numerous medieval castles. In the 12th and 13th centuries, German-speaking Walsers from Switzerland migrated into the Val di Gressoney and a handful of villages still preserve the vernacular language and architecture.

Aosta

POP 35,078 / ELEV 565M

Jagged Alpine peaks rise like marble cathedrals above the town of Aosta, a once-important Roman settlement that has sprawled rather untidily across the valley floor since the opening of the Mont Blanc tunnel in the 1960s. Bounced around between Burgundy (France) and Savoy (Italy) in the Middle Ages, the modern town remains bilingual

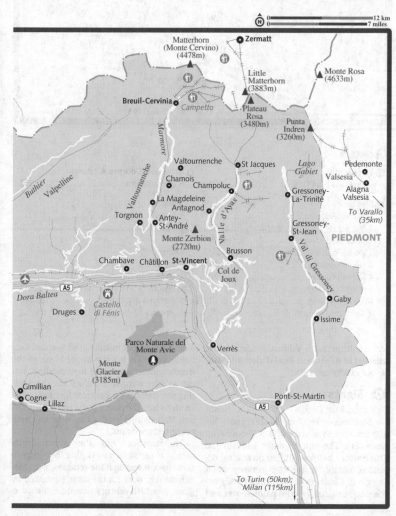

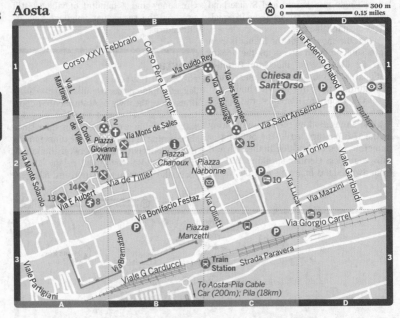

Aosta

◎ Top Sights
Chiesa di Sant'Orso C1

◎ Sights
1 Arco di Augusto D1
2 Cattedrale Santa Maria Assunta B2
Museo del Tesoro .... (see 2)
Porta Praetoria .... (see 15)
3 Roman Bridge D1
4 Roman Forum A2
5 Roman Theatre C1
6 Torre dei Balivi C1
7 Torre dei Fromage C2

◎ Activities, Courses & Tours
8 Meinardi Sport A2

◎ Sleeping
9 Hotel Le Pageot D3
10 Hotel Turin C2

◎ Eating
11 Ad Forum B2
12 Osteria del Calvino A2
13 Ristorante-Pizzeria Ulisse A2
14 Trattoria degli Artisti A2
15 Vecchia Aosta C2

with a culture that is Valdostan, a factor best reflected in its musical local dialect and simple but hearty cuisine.

◎ Sights

Chiesa di Sant'Orso　　　　　　CHURCH
(Via Sant'Orso; ⊙9am-7pm) Aosta's most intriguing church is part of a still-operating monastery. The church dates back to the 10th century but was altered on several occasions, notably in the 15th century when Giorgio di Challant of the ruling family ordered the original frescoes painted over and

a new, lower roof installed. All was not lost: the renovations left the upper levels of the frescoes intact above the new roofline. You can ask the warden to unlock the door, letting you clamber up a narrow flight of wooden steps into the cavity between the original and 15th-century ceilings to view the well-preserved remnants.

The interior and the magnificently carved choir stalls are Gothic, but excavations have unearthed the remains of an earlier church. Beneath the altar, protected by glass, is a 12th-century mosaic, which was only discovered in 1999 when the church's heating system underwent maintenance.

The monastery's beautiful Romanesque cloister, with ornately carved capitals representing biblical scenes, is to the right of the church.

FREE **Roman Ruins**   ARCHAEOLOGICAL SITE
While Aosta's splayed suburbs can be a little hard on the eye, its 2000-year-old central district is awash with Roman ruins. The grand triumphal arch, **Arco di Augusto** (Piazza Arco di Augusto) has been strung with a crucifix in its centre since medieval times. From the arch, head east across the Buthier river bridge to view the cobbled **Roman bridge** – still in use since the 1st century. Backtracking west 300m along Via Sant'Anselmo brings you to **Porta Praetoria**, the main gate to the Roman city.

Heading north along Via di Bailliage and down a dust track brings you to Aosta's **Roman theatre** (Via Porta Praetoria; ⊙9am-7pm Sep-Jun, to 8pm Jul & Aug). Part of its 22m-high facade is still intact. In summer, performances are held in the better-preserved lower section. Further north, the forbidding **Torre dei Balivi**, a former prison, marks one corner of the Roman wall and peers down on the smaller **Torre dei Fromage** (⊙vary depending on exhibition) – named after a family rather than a cheese. It's closed to the public except during temporary art exhibitions

– the tourist office has a program. All that remains of the **Roman forum**, another couple of blocks west, beneath Piazza Giovanni XXIII, is a colonnaded underground walkway known as **Criptoportico**.

Cattedrale Santa Maria Assunta   CHURCH
(Piazza Giovanni XXIII; ⊙6.30am-noon & 3-7pm) The neoclassical facade of Aosta's **cathedral** belies the impressive Gothic interior. Inside, the carved 15th-century walnut-wood choir stalls are particularly beautiful. Two mosaics on the floor, dating from the 12th to the 13th centuries, are also worth studying, as are the religious art treasures displayed in the lovingly attended **Museo del Tesoro** (admission €2.10; ⊙9-11.30am & 3-5.30pm Mon-Sat, 8.30-10am & 10.45-11.30am Sun).

 Activities

Skiing
The nearest skiing to the town of Aosta is the 1800m-high resort of **Pila** (www.pila.it; half-/full-day pass €25/34; ⊙mid-Dec–mid-Apr), accessible by the Aosta–Pila cable car from town or a zigzagging 18km drive south. Its 70km of runs, served by 13 lifts, form one of the valley's largest ski areas. Its highest slope, in the shadow of Gran Paradiso, reaches 2700m and sports an ace snow park with a half-pipe, jump and slide, and freestyle area for boarders and freestyle skiers. The ski station is a village of sorts, but services such as the tourist office, police and

---

SKIING IN THE VALLE D'AOSTA

The Aosta Valley allows access to three of Europe's most prestigious ski areas – Courmayeur, Breuil-Cervinia and Monte Rosa – plus numerous smaller runs.

Courmayeur (www.courmayeur.com) is dominated by spectacular Mont Blanc vistas and allows access to legendary runs such as the Vallée Blanche. Down below, the pretty Alpine town hosts a chilled, non-glitzy après-ski scene. **Breuil-Cervinia** (www.cervinia. it), in the shadow of the Matterhorn, is set at a higher altitude and has more reliable late-season snow. There are good intermediate runs and kids facilities here, but the resort is ugly and rather tacky in places. On the brighter side, you can ski across into Zermatt in Switzerland.

The three valleys to the east are home to the **Monte Rosa ski area** (www.monterosa -ski.com). Champoluc anchors the Val d'Ayas, Gressoney lights up the Val d'Gressoney and Alagna Valsesia is the nexus in the Valsesia. These valleys have a less manic resort scene and harbour some quiet Walser villages. The skiing, however, is white-knuckle, with plenty of off-piste and heli-skiing possibilities particularly in the Valsesia.

The best of the smaller resorts is **Pila** (www.pila.it), easily accessible by cable car from Aosta town, while the pristine **Valle di Cogne**, in Parco Nazionale del Gran Paradiso, is an idyllic place to enjoy cross-country skiing in relative solitude.

A lift pass covering the entire Valle d'Aosta costs €111/241 for three/seven days; add on access to Zermatt and you'll be parting with €171/285. For up-to-date prices and pass variations see www.skivallee.it.

medical services are handled from Aosta. For details on ski passes see the boxed text, p219.

Hiking & Mountain Biking

The lower slopes leading down from Pila into the Dora Baltea valley provide picturesque walks and rides. Mountain bikes can be transported for free on the Aosta–Pila cable car (one way/return €3/5; ⊙8am-12.15pm & 2-5pm or 6pm Jun-Aug) and mountain bikers can buy a one-day pass (transport only; €13), allowing unlimited use of the cable car and chairlifts. The tourist office gives advice on mountain-biking itineraries and walking trails and has lists of Alpine guides and mountain accommodation.

Recommended walking clubs that organise treks and provide guides include the following:

Club Alpino Italiano (CAI; www.caivda.it, in Italian; Corso Battaglione Aosta 81; ⊙6.30-8pm Tue, 8-10pm Fri) West of the city centre.

Meinardi Sport (Via E Aubert; ⊙3-7.30pm Mon, 9am-12.30pm & 3-7.30pm Tue-Sat) A well-stocked sports shop with walking supplies and maps.

Wine & Cheese Tasting

Morgex et de La Salle   WINE TASTING
(www.caveduvinblanc.com; Chemin des Iles 31, La Ruine) The Valle d'Aosta is home to vineyards producing sought-after wines that are rarely available outside the region, including those from Europe's highest vineyard, named for the two villages strung together by its vines. Aosta's tourist office has a free, comprehensive booklet in English with information on cellars you can tour and taste. The vineyard is 25km west of Aosta. Take the A5 before branching off onto SS26.

FREE Valpelline Visitors'
Centre   CHEESE TASTING
(www.fontinacoop.it; Frissonière; ⊙8.30am-12.30pm & 2.30-6.30pm Mon-Fri, 9am-noon & 3-6pm Sat & Sun) In a country where cheese can inspire feuds and debates, if not all-out wars, it's a good idea to get a lowdown on the local curds before you state an opinion; in this case *fontina*. Aosta's signature cheese is made from the full-cream, unpasteurised milk of Valdostan cows that have grazed on pastures up to 2700m above sea level, before being matured for three months in underground rock tunnels. You can learn more about the history, terroir

(the land) and production of *fontina* and other Aostan cheeses at this museum-cum-visitors centre You'll need wheels to get here from Aosta. Follow the SR28 for 7km north to Valpelline, turn east towards Ollomont and after 1.5km turn west along a mountain road to Frissonière.

🎿 Festivals & Events

Fiera di Sant'Orso   WOODCARVING
For over 1000 years the annual winter wood fair has been held on 30 and 31 January around Porta Praetoria, in honour of the town's patron saint who made wooden shoes for the poor (hence you'll see many wooden shoes in craft shops around town). Woodcarvers from all over the valley gather to display their works and present an item to the saint at the Chiesa di Sant'Orso.

🛏 Sleeping

Bar the magnificent (if expensive) Hotel Milleluci, you probably won't be tweeting your mates about the wonders of Aosta's hotel scene. But with hiking and skiing on the agenda, the chances are you won't be spending much time in your room anyway.

TOP CHOICE Hotel Milleluci   LUXURY HOTEL €€€
(☎0165 4 42 74; www.hotelmilleluci.com; Loc Porossan 15; s €110-130, d €130-240; P❄@≋) Old wooden skis, traditionally carved wooden shoes, claw-foot baths, indoor and outdoor pools, a jacuzzi, sauna and gym, and sumptuous skiers' breakfasts make this large, family-run converted farmhouse seem more like a palace. Set on a hillside above town, its balconied rooms look out to the eponymous 'thousand lights' twinkling from Aosta below.

Hotel Turin   HOTEL €
(☎0165 4 45 93; www.hotelturin.it; Via Torino 14; s/d €52/84; P@) A modern, boxy glass-and-steel affair, the Turin is a handy suitcase-drag from the train station and a short distance to carry your skis or snowboard to the cable car.

Hotel Le Pageot   HOTEL €€
(☎0165 3 24 33; www.lepageot.info; Via Carrel 31; s €55-65, d €90-100; P🛜) Next to the bus stop, the no-frills, family-run and clean Le Pageot ought to suit hikers and skiers on a budget even if it doesn't win any architectural/interior design awards.

✕ Eating

Traditional dishes include *seupa valpellinentze* (a thick soup of cabbage, bread, beef broth and *fontina*) and *carbonada con polenta* (soup traditionally made with chamois, though these days usually beef). Open-air cafe terraces spring up on Piazza Chanoux in summer.

TOP CHOICE Trattoria degli Artisti   TRATTORIA €€
(Via Maillet 5-7; meals €18-28; ☺Tue-Sat) Fabulous Valdostan cuisine is dished up at this dark, cosy little trattoria, tucked down an alleyway off Via E Aubert. Antipasti such as puff pastry filled with Valdostan fondue, cured ham and regional salami are followed by dishes such as roe venison with polenta, and beef braised in Morgex et de La Salle white wine.

Ad Forum   MODERN ITALIAN €€
(📞0165 4 00 11; Via Mons de Sales 11; meals €22-30; ☺Tue-Sun; ✱) Another fantastic Aosta restaurant setting, this time in a stylish garden (and interior rooms) built on part of the remains of the Roman forum. Conceptual dishes such as risotto with strawberries and Spumante, or *lasagnetta* with pear and blue cheese, come in generous portions, and you get an equally tasty complimentary aperitif while you wait. The attached *enoteca* has an excellent line-up of wines.

Ristorante-Pizzeria Ulisse   PIZZERIA €
(Via E Aubert 58; meals €15-18; ☺lunch Mon-Sun, dinner Thu-Mon) Ulisse is the sort of place where the food is brought to your table personally by the chef and the cooked-to-perfection €5 *pizza margherita* is, well, perfection.

Vecchia Aosta   TRADITIONAL ITALIAN €€
(📞0165 36 11 86; Piazza Porte Pretoriane 4; set menus €30-35; ☺lunch Tue-Sun, dinner Tue-Sat; ✱) Maybe it's the French influence, but Aosta restaurants such as the Vecchia score consistently highly when it comes to culinary creativity. Grafted onto a section of the old Roman wall, the setting is sublime and the waiters highly knowledgeable. Take their advice and go for the lamb – it's a real holiday highlight.

Osteria del Calvino   PIZZERIA €
(Via Croix de Ville 24; meals $18-25; ☺Tue-Sun) This brand-new three-floor wine bar, restaurant and pizzeria delivers the goods on all fronts thanks to congenial service and good, simple food.

🔒 Shopping

Craft shops in town sell traditional Valdostan objects made by certified local artisans. Unique items to look out for include a *grolla,* a large wooden goblet whose name is derived from the word 'grail' in reference to the Holy Grail, which is said to have passed through the village and been copied by local craftsmen. Another Valdostan tradition is the *coppa dell'amicizia* (friendship cup), a wooden bowl filled with coffee laced with citrus rind and strong grappa and set alight. The 'cup' has anything from two to 15 mouthpieces, out of which friends take turns drinking as it's passed around.

ℹ Information

Banks abound on and around the Piazza Chanoux.
Aosta tourist office (www.regione.vda.it/turismo; Piazza Chanoux 2; ☺9am-6.30pm) Region-wide information including accommodation lists.
Farmacia Centrale (📞0165 26 22 05; Piazza Chanoux 35) Pharmacy.
Hospital (📞0165 30 41; Viale Ginevra 3)
Multimedi@ Service (XXVI Febbraio 15; per 15min €1; ☺9am-8pm) Internet access.
Police station (📞0165 26 21 69; Corso Battaglione Aosta 169) West of the town centre.
Post office (Piazza Narbonne; ☺8.15am-6pm Mon-Fri, to 1pm Sat)

ℹ Getting There & Away

Buses operated by **Savda** (www.savda.it) run to Milan (1½ to 3½ hours, two daily), Turin (two hours, up to 10 daily) and Courmayeur (€3.20, one hour, up to eight daily), as well as French destinations including Chamonix. Services leave from Aosta's **bus station** (Via Giorgio Carrel), virtually opposite the train station. To get to Breuil-Cervinia, take a Turin-bound bus to Châtillon (30 minutes, eight daily), then a connecting bus (one hour, seven daily) to the resort.

Aosta's train station, on Piazza Manzetti, is served by trains from most parts of Italy via Turin (€7.55, two to 2½ hours, more than 10 daily).

Aosta is on the A5, which connects Turin with the Mont Blanc tunnel and France. Another exit road north of the city leads to the Great St Bernard tunnel and on to Switzerland.

Courmayeur

POP 2923 / ELEV 1224M

Flush up against France and linked by a dramatic cable-car ride to its cross-border cousin in Chamonix, Courmayeur is an activity-oriented Aosta village that has grafted up-market ski facilities onto an ancient Roman base. Its pièce de résistance is lofty Mont Blanc, Western Europe's highest mountain – 4807m of solid rock and ice that rises like an impregnable wall above the narrow valleys of northwestern Italy, igniting awe in all who pass.

In winter Courmayeur is a fashion parade of skiers bound for the high slopes above town that glisten with plenty of late-season snow. In summer it wears a distinctly different hat: the Società delle Guide Alpine di Courmayeur is bivouacked here and the town is an important staging post on three iconic long-distance hiking trails: the Tour du Mont Blanc (TMB), Alta Via 1 and Alta Via 2.

◉ Sights

TOP
CHOICE / **Funivie Monte Bianco** CABLE CAR
(www.montebianco.com; return €38; ◷8.30am-12.40pm & 2-4.30pm) Ears pop, eyes widen, mouths gasp. Technically the Mont Blanc cable car might not be the world's highest, but it's surely the most spectacular. You have to admire the ambition of the people who decided to build this astounding piece of human engineering three-quarters of the way up western Europe's highest mountain before heading (over multiple glaciers) into France. The cable car departs every 20 minutes in each direction from the village of **La Palud**, 15 minutes from Courmayeur's main square by a free bus service.

First stop is the 2173m-high midstation **Pavillon du Mt Fréty** (return €16), where there's a restaurant and the Mt Frèty Nature Oasis. At the top of the ridge is **Punta Helbronner** (3462m). Take heavy winter clothes and sunglasses for the blinding snow, and head up early in the morning to avoid the heavy weather that often descends here in the early afternoon. At Punta Helbronner a small, free **museum** displays crystals found in the mountains.

From Punta Helbronner another cable car (from late May to late September, depending on the weather conditions) takes you on a breathtaking 5km transglacial ride across the Italian border deeper into France to the **Aiguille du Midi** (3842m), from where the world's highest cable car transports you down to Chamonix. The total journey from Courmayeur to Chamonix costs €50, and includes a bus back through the Mont Blanc tunnel. It's worth every penny.

⌖ **Pavillon du Mt Fréty**
Nature Oasis NATURE RESERVE
A protected zone of 1200 hectares tucked between glaciers, this nature oasis is accessible from the Pavillon du Mt Fréty at the mid-station of the Funivie Monte Bianco. You can take a walk through the flower-filled Alpine garden, **Giardino Botanico Alpino Saussurea** (admission €2; ◷9.30am-6pm Jul-Sep) in summer (it's blanketed by snow in winter) and enjoy numerous other trails including the **Sentiero Francesco e Giuditta Gatti**, where you have a good chance of spotting ibexes, marmots and deer.

Museo Alpino Duca degli Abruzzi MUSEUM
(Piazza Henry 2; admission €3; ◷9am-noon & 3.30-6.30pm Thu-Tue, 3.30-6.30pm Wed) Courmayeur guiding association's dramatic history unfolds in this small but inspiring museum that tracks the heroic deeds of erstwhile alpinists.

🏃 Activities

Courmayeur is an outdoor-activity heaven. Few come here to idle.

Società delle Guide Alpine di
Courmayeur GUIDED
(www.guidecourmayeur.com; Strada del Villair) Founded in 1859, this is Italy's oldest guiding association. In winter its guides lead adventure seekers off-piste, up frozen waterfalls and on heli-skiing expeditions. In summer, rock climbing, canyoning, canoeing, kayaking and hiking are among its many outdoor activities.

Terme di Pré-Saint-Didier SPA
(☎0165 86 72 72; www.termedipre.it; Allée des Thermes; admission €42-48; ◷9.30am-9pm Sun-Thu, 8.30am-11pm Fri & Sat) Bubbling a natural 37°C from the mountains' depths, the thermal water at Pré-Saint-Didier has been a source of therapeutic treatments since the bath-loving Romans stopped past. A spa opened in 1838, though the present renovated building dates from the 1920s. Admission includes use of a bathrobe, towel and slippers, plus freshly squeezed juices,

CASTELLO DI FÉNIS

Gothic castles are to the Valle d'Aosta what wizards are to Harry Potter. There are over 150 of them and each castle is within view of the next – back in the day, messages were transferred along the valley by flag signals.

If you only have time for one visit, you can't go wrong at the magnificently restored **Castello di Fénis** (adult/reduced €5/3.50; ☉9am-7pm Mar-Sep, 10am-12.30pm & 1.30-5pm Oct-Feb). Owned by the powerful Challant clan from 1242 onwards, it features rich frescoes including an impressive etching of St George slaying a fiery dragon. The castle is laid out in a pentagonal shape with an unusual amalgam of both square and cylindrical towers. It was never really used as a defensive post but served as a plush residence for the Challant family until 1716. The on-site museum allows access to a weaponry display, the kitchens, the battlements, the former residential quarters, and the chapel with its frescoes.

fruit and herbal teas. In addition to saunas, whirlpools and toning waterfalls, there's an indoor-outdoor thermal pool. It's lit by candles and torches on Saturday nights, when it is spectacular amid the snow and stars.

Before leaving the spa, head 50-odd metres beyond the car park in the opposite direction to the village, where a little **Roman bridge** arcs over the trout-filled river.

Skiing

Courmayeur offers some extraordinary skiing in the spectacular shadow of Mont Blanc. The two main ski areas – the Plan Checrouit and Pre de Pascal – are interlinked by various runs (100km worth) and a network of chairlifts. Three lifts leave from the valley floor, one from Courmayeur itself, one from the village of Dolonne and one from nearby Val Veny. They are run by **Funivie Courmayeur Mont Blanc** (www.courmayeur-montblanc.com; Strada Regionale 47). Queues are rarely an issue.

Skiing lessons starting at around €38 an hour are available from the **Scuola di Sci Monte Bianco** (www.scuolascimontebianco.com; Strada Regionale 51), founded in 1922. It also offers cross-country and telemark lessons for similar rates.

Vallee Blanche   SKI DESCENT
This is an exhilarating off-piste descent from Punta Helbronner across the Mer de Glace glacier into Chamonix, France. The route itself is not difficult (anyone of intermediate ability can do it), but an experienced guide is essential to steer you safely round the hidden crevasses. All up, the 24km Vallee Blanche takes around four to five hours, allowing time to stop and take in the view.

Toula Glacier   SKI DESCENT
Only highly experienced, hard-core skiers need apply for this terrifying descent, which also takes off from Punta Helbronner and drops for six sheer kilometres to La Palud. A guide is essential. It's usually easy to join in with a guide-led group.

Walking

In July and August Courmayeur's cable cars whisk walkers and mountain bikers up into the mountains; transporting a bike is free.

Tour du Mont Blanc   WALKING TRAIL
For many walkers (some 30,000 each summer), Courmayeur's trophy hike is the Tour du Mont Blanc (TMB). This 169km trek cuts across Italy, France and Switzerland, stopping at nine villages en route. Snow makes it impassable for much of the year. The average duration is anything from one week to 12 days; smaller sections are also possible. It's possible to undertake the hike without a guide, but if you're unfamiliar with the area, hooking up with a local guide is a good idea as the route traverses glacial landscapes.

Easy day hikes will take you along the TMB as far as the Rifugio Maison Vieille (one hour, 50 minutes) and Rifugio Bertone (two hours). Follow the yellow signposts from the Piazzale Monte Bianco in the centre of Courmayeur.

Mountain Biking

Mountain bikes can be hired for around €15 per day at **Noleggio Courmayeur** (☎0165 84 22 55), in front of the Courmayeur chairlift.

🛏 Sleeping

Ask the tourist office for a list of *rifugi*, usually open from late June to mid-September.

Hotel Bouton d'Or   HOTEL €€

(☎0165 84 67 29; www.hotelboutondor.com; Strada Statale 26/10; s €80-95, d €120-160; [P][❄][@][✿][♨]) Is it a dream? You open your eyes and there before you is the imposing hulk of Mont Blanc. There can't be many hotels where the view is this good, the rooms this clean, or the service this attentive. To top it all, Bouton d'Or is situated in the centre of Courmayeur and sports a sauna, a decent breakfast, a shuttle to the cable car, and a lounge full of interesting Alpine paraphernalia.

Mont Blanc Hotel Village   LUXURY HOTEL €€€

(☎0165 86 41 11; www.hotelmontblanc.it; La Croisette 36; s €173-240, d €198-265; [P][❄][@][✿]) On the hillside of La Salle, 10km east of Courmayeur, this haven of luxury has beautiful stone-and-wood rooms, many with enormous balconies with views across the valley. A series of cave-like nooks conceals spa treatment rooms and steaming saunas. Half-board is available at the hotel's standard restaurant. To truly dine in style, guests and nonguests can head to the hotel's second, gastronomic restaurant.

Hotel Triolet   HOTEL €€

(☎0165 84 68 22; www.hoteltriolet.com; Strada Regionale 63; s €80-100, d €150-190; [P][❄][✿][♨]) Triolet is a tad more elegant than your average ski digs. It's smaller, too, with only 20 rooms, allowing service to remain personal as well as affable. Aside from the usual tick-list, there's a pleasant spa (jacuzzi, steam room, sauna), ski lockers and a vista-laden breakfast room.

🍴 Eating

Quality food shops and restaurants line Via Roma.

La Terraza   INTERNATIONAL €€€

(Via Circonvalazione 73; meals €35-45; ⊙lunch & dinner) This lively, central bar/restaurant/pizzeria has the full gamut of pizzas, steaks and après-ski nosh. True to the local spirit there are also plenty of Valdostan dishes, including polenta, spicy sausage, fondue and pasta with the celebrated *fontina* cheese.

Petit Bistrot   INTERNATIONAL €

(Via Marconi 6) A crêpe window lures you at this cafe-cum-restaurant where Valdostan classics (eg *talgiere di lardo*) mingle with more cross-over snacks (hamburgers with rocket and Parmesan).

Pan Per Focaccia   SNACKS €

(Via dei Giardini 2a) Tucked down a side street is this cosy mountain nook offering cheap crêpes and fresh-from-the-oven focaccia, which you can enjoy perched on a wooden stool inside.

ℹ Information

Ambulance (☎0165 84 46 84)

Centro Traumatologico (☎0165 84 46 84; Strada dell Volpi 3) Medical clinic. The nearest hospital is in Aosta.

Tourist office (www.courmayeur.net, in Italian; Piazzale Monte Bianco 13; ⊙9am-12.30pm & 3-6.30pm)

ℹ Getting There & Away

Three trains a day from Aosta terminate at Pré-St-Didier, with bus connections (20 to 30 minutes, eight to 10 daily) to **Courmayeur bus station** (Piazzale Monte Bianco) outside the tourist office. There are up to eight direct Aosta–Courmayeur buses daily (€3.20, one hour) and long-haul buses serve Milan (€15.50, 4½ hours, three to five daily) and Turin (€9, 3½ to 4½ hours, two to four daily).

Immediately north of Courmayeur, the 11.6km Mont Blanc tunnel leads to Chamonix (France). At the Italian entrance, a plaque commemorates Pierlucio Tinazzi, a security employee who died while saving at least a dozen lives during the 1999 disaster when a freight truck caught fire in the tunnel.

Parco Nazionale del Gran Paradiso

Italy's oldest national park is also one of its most diverse – and aptly named. Gran Paradiso, formed in 1922 after Vittorio Emanuele II gave his hunting reserve to the state (ostensibly to protect the endangered ibex), is a veritable 'grand paradise'. What makes it special is a tangible wilderness feel (rare in Italy). The park's early establishment preceded the rise of the modern ski resort; as a result, the area has (so far) resisted the lucrative lure of the tourist trade with all its chairlifts, dodgy architecture and après-ski clubs.

Gran Paradiso incorporates the valleys around the eponymous 4061m peak (Italy's 7th highest), three of which are in the Valle d'Aosta: the Valsavarenche, Val di Rhêmes and the beautiful Valle di Cogne. On the Piedmont side of the mountain, the park includes the valleys of Soana and Orco.

The main stepping stone into the park is tranquil Cogne (population 1481, elevation 1534m), a refreshing antidote to overdeveloped Breuil-Cervinia on the opposite side of the Val d'Aosta. Aside from its plethora of outdoor opportunities, Cogne is known for its lace-making; you can buy the local fabrics at a charming craft and antique shop, Le Marché Aux Puces (Rue Grand Paradis 4; ⊘closed Wed).

◉ Sights

⬛ Giardino Alpino
Paradisia   BOTANICAL GARDEN
(adult/child €3/1.50; ⊘10am-5.30pm Jun–mid-Sep, to 6.30pm Jul & Aug) The park's amazing biodiversity, including butterflies and Alpine flora, can be seen in summer at this fascinating Alpine botanical garden in the tiny hamlet of Valnontey (1700m), 3km south of Cogne. Guided nature walks from July to September are organised by the Associazione Guide della Nature (Piazza Chanoux 36, Cogne; ⊘9am-noon Mon, Wed & Sat).

🏃 Activities

Gran Paradiso is one of Italy's best walking areas, with over 700km of trails linked by a recuperative network of *rifugi*. The tourist office has free winter and summer trail maps for walker/skiers.

Skiing
Despite a (welcome) dearth of downhill-ski facilities, 80km of well-marked cross-country skiing trails (admission per day €5) line the unspoilt Valle di Cogne. Try trail 23 up to Valnontey and Vermiana, or head east to Lillza. Alas, there is still 9km of downhill slopes. A one-day ski pass covering the use of Cogne's single cable car, chairlift and drag lift costs €23. Skiing lessons are offered by the Scuola Italian Sci Gran Paradiso ski (Piazza Chanoux 38, Cogne). For something more esoteric, try an ice-climbing expedition on the Lillzz waterfall with Società Guide Alpine di Cogne (www.guidealpinecogne.it; Piazza Chanoux 1, Cogne).

Walking
Easy walks around Cogne include the 3km stroll (wheelchair accessible) to the village of Lillaz on trail 23, where there is a geological park and a waterfall that drops 150m in three stages. Trails 22 and 23 will also get you to the village of Valnontey where you can continue up the valley to the hamlet of Vermiana (1½ hours one way). Trail 8 from Cogne leads to another waterfall (Pila) via the village of Gimillian.

A classic, moderately strenuous hike from Valnontey is to the Rifugio Sella (☏0165 7 43 10; www.rifugiosella.com; dm €17), a former hunting lodge of King Vittorio Emanuele II. From the town bridge follow the Alta Via 2 uphill for two to 2½ hours. More-adventurous hikers can continue along the exhilarating Sella–Herbetet Traverse (15km), a seven-hour loop that will drop you back in Valnontey. You'll need a head for heights, and a good map.

Climbing
The main point of departure for the Gran Paradiso peak is Pont in the Valsavarenche. Technically it's no Mont Blanc and can be completed in a day, but you'll need a guide (a two-day ascent for two people starts at €500). Contact the Società Guide Alpine di Cogne (www.guidealpinecogne.it; Piazza Chanoux 1, Cogne).

Horse Riding
Horse riding (per hr €25) and 45-minute horse-and-carriage rides (per carriage of up to 4 people €40) through the mountain meadows are run by Pianta Cavalli (☏333 3147248) in Valnontey.

🛏 Sleeping & Eating

Wilderness camping is forbidden in the park, but there are 11 *rifugi*. The tourist office has a list.

Hotel Bellevue   LUXURY HOTEL €€€
(☏0165 7 48 25; www.hotelbellevue.it; Rue Grand Paradis 22, Cogne; d €170-240, 2-person chalets €250-320; ⊘mid-Dec–mid-Oct; P🐾) Overlooking meadows, this green-shuttered mountain hideaway evokes its 1920s origins with romantic canopied timber 'cabin beds', weighty cowbells strung from old beams and claw-foot baths. There are open fireplaces in some rooms. Afternoon tea is included in the price, as is use of the health spa, and you can also rent mountain bikes and snowshoes. Its four restaurants include a Michelin-starred gourmet affair (closed Wednesday), a cheese restaurant (closed Tuesday) with cheese from the

While the rest of the Valle d'Aosta leans culturally towards France, the three valleys of Ayas, Gressoney and Sesia (the latter is in Piedmont) hide an 800-year-old Walser tradition. The German-descended Walsers migrated from Switzerland's Valais region in the 13th century, and their community has survived intact; many of the people who live in this rugged region still speak German (and Tich dialect) as a mother tongue and inhabit traditional Walser wood-slatted houses built on short stilts.

The main nexus in the Valsesia is Alagna Valsesia (1191m), a small ski resort at the valley head. To reach it you'll need to get a bus from Turin to Varallo (2¼ hours, two daily), where you can connect with buses to Alagna Valsesia.

To the west the Valle d'Ayas harbours its own ski resort, Champoluc (population 500, elevation 1560m), a storybook spot saved from tourism overload by the difficult road twisting from the A5 exit at Verrès around some tortuous hairpin bends. Verrès is on the main Turin–Aosta train line and is the dropping-off point for the Ayas. From here regular buses ply the road to Champoluc (€3, one hour, nine daily).

The main villages in the Val di Gressoney are pretty lakeside Gressoney-St-Jean (population 816, elevation 1385m), and Gressoney-La-Trinité (population 306, elevation 1637m), a few kilometres north – both Walser strongholds.

family's own cellar, a lunchtime terrace restaurant and a brasserie (closed Monday) on the village's main square a few moments' stroll away.

Hotel Sant'Orso
HOTEL €

(☎0165 7 48 21; Via Bourgeois 2, Cogne; s/d €46/92, half-board €71/142; ⊘spring & autumn closures vary; ℗) Cogne personified (ie tranquil, courteous and understated), the Sant'Orso is nonetheless equipped with plenty of hidden extras. Check out the restaurant, small cinema, sauna, kids room and terrace. Further kudos is gained by the fact that you can start your cross-country skiing pretty much from the front door. The owners also run the Hotel du Gran Paradis nearby.

Camping Lo Stambecco
CAMPGROUND €

(☎0165 7 41 52; www.campinglostambecco.com; Valnontey; camping per person/tent/car €7/3/6; ⊘May-Sep; ℗) Pitch up under the pine trees in the heart of the park at this well-run and friendly site. Its sister hotel, La Barme, rents bikes to explore the mountains.

Hotel Ristorante
Petit Dahu
TRADITIONAL ITALIAN €€

(☎0165 7 41 46; www.hotelpetitdahu.com; Valnontey; menus €35, s €36-50, d €72-100; ⊘closed May & Oct; ℗) Straddling two traditional stone-and-wood buildings, this friendly, family-run spot has a wonderful restaurant (also open to nonguests; advance bookings essential) preparing rustic mountain cooking using wild Alpine herbs. It also has rooms

to stay in (singles €36 to €50, doubles €72 to €100).

❶ Information

Consorzio Gran Paradiso Natura (www.gran-paradisonatura.it; Loc Trépont 91, Villeneuve) Also has tourist information.

Tourist office (www.cogne.org; Piazza Chanoux 36; ⊘9am-12.30pm & 2.30-5.30pm Mon-Sat) Has stacks of information on the park and a list of emergency contact numbers.

❶ Getting There & Around

There are up to seven buses daily to/from Cogne and Aosta (50 minutes). Cogne can also be reached by cable car from Pila.

Valley buses (up to 10 daily) link Cogne with Valnontey (€0.90, five minutes) and Lillaz (€0.90, five minutes).

Valtournenche

One of Europe's most dramatic – and deadly – mountains, the Matterhorn (4478m) frames the head of Valtournenche. Byron once stood here and marvelled at 'Europe's noble rock'. Today he'd also get an eyeful of one of the Alps' most architecturally incongruous ski resorts, Breuil-Cervinia. But, ugly or not, Cervinia's ski facilities are second to none; you can hit the snow year-round up here and even zoom across into Zermatt, Switzerland.

⚡ Activities

Plateau Rosa (3480m) and the Little Matterhorn (3883m) in the Breuil-Cervinia ski area offer some of Europe's highest skiing, while the Campetto area has introduced the Valle d'Aosta to night skiing. A couple of dozen cable cars, four of which originate in Breuil-Cervinia, serve 200km of downhill pistes. A one-day ski pass covering Breuil-Cervinia and Valtournenche costs €36.

Contact Breuil-Cervinia's Scuola di Sci del Breuil Cervinia (www.scuolascibreuil. com) or Scuola Sci del Cervino (www.scuola cervino.com) for skiing and snowboarding lessons, and its mountain-guide association Società Guide del Cervino (www.guide delcervino.com; Via J Antoine Carrel 20) to make the most of the Matterhorn's wild off-piste opportunities.

Between July and September several cableways and lifts to Plateau Rosa continue to operate, allowing year-round skiing on the Swiss side of the mountain. A one-day international ski pass costs €50.

❶ Getting There & Away

Savda (📞0165 36 12 44) operates buses from Breuil-Cervinia to Châtillon (one hour, seven daily), from where there are connecting buses to/from Aosta.

Milan & the Lakes

POP 9.83 MILLION / AREA 23,835 SQ KM

Best Places to Eat

» Trattoria Abele la Temperanza (p246)

» Al Sorriso (p258)

» Al Veluu (p264)

» Altavilla (p266)

» Il Cigno (p281)

Best Places to Stay

» Antica Locanda Solferino (p244)

» Hotel Pironi (p256)

» Albergo Silvio (p263)

» Restel de Fer (p271)

» C'A delle Erbe (p279)

Why Go?

Sprawling between the Alps and the Po valley, Lombardy (Lombardia) has a varied landscape: industrious cities, medieval hill towns and lakeside resorts are interspersed with powdered slopes, lemon groves, vineyards and rice paddies.

Dominating it all is Lombardy's capital and Italy's economic powerhouse, Milan. Home to the nation's prime stock exchange, one of Europe's biggest trade-fair grounds and an international fashion hub, it is Italy's second-largest metropolis.

Sparkling, glacial lakes are strung along the north of the region like a glittering necklace. Wedding-cake villas set in tiered gardens adorn elegant towns and coquettish villages along the shores. Further north still, the Valtellina and the Orobie Alps stretch into dramatic national parks, which hide sharp-sided valleys and wildly wooded mountain slopes.

South of the main chain of lakes, cities steeped in history include medieval Bergamo, the age-old violin-making centre of Cremona and the Renaissance city of Mantua.

When to Go
Milan

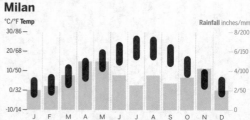

May & Jun Spring flowers, mild weather and concerts in Cremona herald the start of summer.

Sep As many as 350 vessels turn out for the Centomiglia, Lago di Garda's prestigious regatta.

Dec Winter warmers include the Feast of St Ambrogio and opera at La Scala.

MILAN

POP 1.3 MILLION

Milan is Italy's city of the future, a fast-paced metropolis with New World qualities: ambition, aspiration and a highly individualistic, creative culture. In Milan appearances really do matter and materialism requires no apology. The Milanese love beautiful things, luxurious things, and it is for that reason perhaps that Italian fashion and design maintain their global position.

But like the models that stalk the catwalks, many consider Milan to be vain, distant and dull. And it is true the city makes little effort to seduce visitors. But this superficial lack of charm disguises a city of ancient roots and many treasures, that, unlike in the rest of Italy, you'll quite often get to experience without the queues or expectations. A warren of cobbled streets fans out from the Duomo while historic neighbourhoods like Brera and Navigli have character worthy of any tourist brochure. And, although many visitors to the city are likely to know its golden shopping triangle, few realise the varied ways that Milanese buyers select goods in colours, styles and materials seldom seen at outposts any place else.

So while the Milanese may not have time to always play nice, jump in and join them in their intoxicating round of pursuits, be that precision shopping, browsing edgy contemporary galleries or loading up a plate with local delicacies while downing an expertly mixed Negroni at *aperitivo* hour. *Cin-cin!*

History

Celtic tribes settled along the Po river in the 7th century BC, and the area encompassing modern-day Milan has remained inhabited since. In AD 313, Emperor Constantine made his momentous edict granting Christians freedom of worship here. The city had already replaced Rome as the capital of the empire in 286, a role it kept until 402.

A *comune* (town council) was formed by all social classes in the 11th century, and, from the mid-13th century, government passed to a succession of dynasties – the Torrianis, Viscontis and, finally, the Sforzas. It fell under Spanish rule in 1525 and Austrian in 1713. Milan became part of the nascent Kingdom of Italy in 1860.

Benito Mussolini, one-time editor of the socialist newspaper *Avanti!*, founded the Fascist Party in Milan in 1919. He was eventually strung up here by partisans after he sought to escape to Switzerland in 1945. Mussolini had dragged Italy into WWII on Hitler's side in 1940. By early 1945, Allied bombings during WWII had destroyed much of central Milan.

At the vanguard of two 20th-century economic booms, Milan's postwar architect-designers sought to rebuild society, 'from the spoon to the city', as Ernesto Rogers famously put it. As Milan cemented its role as Italy's financial and industrial capital, immigrants poured in from the south and were later joined by others from China, Africa, Latin America, India and Eastern Europe, making for one of the least homogenous cities in Italy. Culturally, the city was the centre of early Italian film production, and in the 1980s and '90s it ruled the world as the capital of design innovation and production. Milan's self-made big shot and media mogul, Silvio Berlusconi, made the move into politics in the 1990s and has since been elected prime minister three times, most recently in 2008.

The city's next big date with destiny is Expo2015, a world exhibition.

◉ Sights

Milan's runway-flat terrain and monumental buildings are defined by concentric ring roads that trace the path of the city's original defensive walls. Although very little remains of the walls, ancient gates – *porta* – act as clear compass points. Almost everything you want to see, do or buy is contained within these city gates.

Duomo CATHEDRAL
(Map p242; www.duomomilano.it; Piazza del Duomo) A vision in pink Candoglia marble, Milan's cathedral aptly reflects the city's creative brio and ambition. Begun by Giangaleazzo Visconti in 1387, its design was originally considered unfeasible. Canals had to be dug to transport the vast quantities of marble to the centre of the city and new technologies were invented to cater for the never-before-attempted scale. There was also that small matter of style. The Gothic lines went out of fashion – *c'e brutta!* (how hideous!)– and were considered 'too French', so it took on several looks as the years, then centuries, dragged on. Its slow construction became the byword for an impossible task (*fabrica del Dom* in the Milanese dialect). Indeed, much of its ornament is 19th-century neo-Gothic, with the final touches only applied in the 1960s.

Milan & the Lakes Highlights

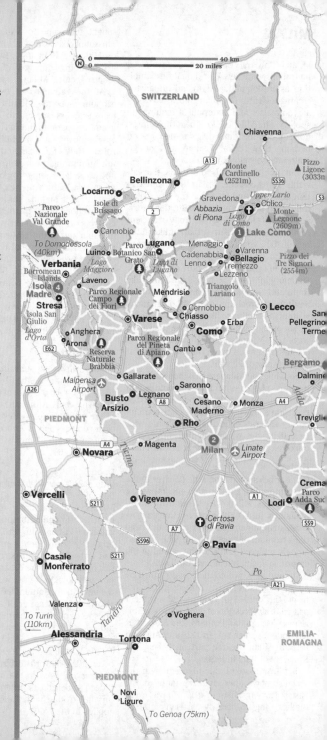

1 Make a tour of **Lago di Como** James Bond–style in your very own cigarette boat (p262)

2 Admire Milanese artistry and inventiveness in the haute couture of the **Quadrilatero d'Oro** (p249) and Leonardo da Vinci's ground-breaking mural, **The Last Supper** (p232)

3 Marvel at one of Italy's finest and least known art collections at Bergamo's **Accademia Carrara** (p275)

4 Stroll among the peacocks in Lago Maggiore's prettiest island garden, **Isola Madre** (p255)

5 Dine on delicately steamed risotto and spicy *mostardo* (mustards) in the gastronomic town of **Mantua** (p281)

6 Take a tutored tasting of Bardolino's best vintages in the kitchen garden of **Guerrieri Rizzardi** (p273)

7 Get right off the beaten path in the Alpine forests and valleys of **Lake Ledro** (p272)

MILAN IN ...

Two Days

Start your day with an early-morning cappuccino and custard-filled brioche at Marchesi before climbing the stairs to the roof of the **Duomo** for a rare bird's-eye view of the city. Have lunch at Giacomo Arengario, the top-floor restaurant of the **Museo del Novecento**, and enjoy eye-popping views of the Duomo's external sculpture, then take a leisurely tour of the exhibits and acquaint yourself with Milan's modernist stars. In the late afternoon join the throngs in the **Galleria Vittorio Emanuele II** before jumping on the metro and heading to **Navigli** for early-evening *aperitivo* and dinner at Grand Hotel Osteria. The next day head to **Corso Magenta** to see Leonardo da Vinci's *Il Cenacolo* (The Last Supper). Grab lunch at Latteria di San Marco and then spend the afternoon wandering the high fashion alleys of the **Quadrilatero d'Oro**. End with suitably high-glamour *aperitivo* at the Bulgari Hotel.

Four Days

With two extra days, you can get to know the city a little better. For art, choose the **Pinacoteca di Brera** or the **Museo Poldi-Pezzoli**. Have a light lunch at Obikà and then book a spa treatment at Angelo Caroli Day Spa. The next day, ride tram 1 for a cheap tour of the city, pack a bag full of goodies from Peck and then chill out in **Parco Sempione**. If you can muster up the energy, finish with a visit to the **Triennale di Milano** design museum and *aperitivo* at Living.

But now its pearly-white facade, rising like the filigree of a fairy-tale tiara, wows the crowds with extravagant detail. A veritable outdoor sculpture museum, its 135 spires showcase 3200 statues. The vast, echoing interior is no less impressive, with 146 stained- glass windows and intricately carved pillars and chapels. Although the ceiling also appears carved, it's a trompe l'œil. High above the altar is a **nail** said to have been the one that impaled Christ's right hand on the cross. Pre-dating the cathedral is the early-Christian baptistry, the Battistero di San Giovanni (admission €4; ☺9.30am-5.15pm Tue-Sun), accessed via a stairwell next to the main entrance. The crypt (admission free) displays the remains of saintly San Carlo Borromeo, who died in 1584, in a glass casket.

By far the most interesting sight, though, is the view from the roof (stairs/lift €5/8; ☺9am-5.30pm), from where you can gaze out over the city towards the Alps through a forest of spires and marble pinnacles. Crowning it all is a gilded copper statue of the **Madonnina** (Little Madonna), the city's traditional protector.

Museo del Novecento   ART GALLERY

(Map p242; ☎02 79 48 89; www.museodel novecento.org; Piazza Duomo 12; adult/reduced €5/3; ☺9.30am-7.30pm Tue-Sun, 2.30-7.30pm Mon) Overlooking the Piazza del Duomo,

with fabulous views of the cathedral from its floor-to-ceiling windows, is Mussolini's **Arengario**, from where he would harangue huge crowds in the glory days of his regime. Now it houses Milan's museum of 20th-century art, surprisingly the city's first modern art museum.

Built around a futuristic spiral ramp (an ode to the Guggenheim), the lower floors of the museum are cramped, but the heady collection, which includes the likes of Boccioni, Campigli, De Chirico, Fontana and Marinetti, is enough to distract. And the space does open up as you progress to the upper floors. The museum also houses some fantastic pieces by Arturo Martini, Italy's most important 20th-century sculptor and author of the carved reliefs on the exterior of the Arengario.

Time your visit before lunch or dinner and end with a meal at the top-floor restaurant, Giacomo Arengario, which is run by the reputable folk from cross-town Da Giacomo.

A smaller portion of the museum's collection is displayed at the Casa Museo Boschi di Stefano (off Map p238; ☎02 2024 0568; www. fondazioneboschidistefano.it; Via Jan 15; admission free; ☺10am-6pm Tue-Sun).

Il Cenacolo Vinciano   MURAL

(Map p238; ☎02 9280 0360; www.cenacolovin ciano.net; adult/reduced €6.50/3.25, plus booking fee €1.50; ☺8.15am-7pm Tue-Sun) Leonardo da Vinci's depiction of Christ and his dinner companions in *The Last Supper* is one of the world's most iconic images.

The restored **mural** is hidden away on one wall of the Cenacolo Vinciano, the refectory adjoining the Chiesa di Santa Maria delle Grazie (Map p238; Corso Magenta; ☺8.15am-7pm Tue-Sun). The mural's restoration, completed in 1999, took more than 22 years. However, despite the painstaking effort, nearly 80% of the original colour has been lost. Da Vinci himself is partly to blame: his experimental mix of oil and tempera was applied on a dry wall between 1495 and 1498, rather than on wet plaster over a week, as is typical of fresco techniques.

Reservations must be booked by phone or online anything from a couple of weeks to two months in advance. Or you can take a city tour that includes a visit. Once booked, you'll be allotted a visiting time and reservation number, which you present 30 minutes before your visit at the refectory ticket desk. If you turn up late, your ticket will be resold. English-language guided tours (€3.25) take place at 9.30am and 3.30pm Tuesday to Sunday – again, you'll need to reserve ahead.

Pinacoteca di Brera
ART GALLERY

(Map p242; ☎02 9280 0361; www.brera.beni culturali.it; Via Brera 28; adult/reduced €9/6.50; ☺8.30am-7.15pm Tue-Sun) Located upstairs from the centuries-old Brera Academy (still one of Italy's most prestigious art schools) this gallery houses Milan's most impressive collection of old masters, much of the bounty 'lifted' from Venice by Napoleon. Rembrandt, Goya and van Dyck all have a place in the collection, but you're here to see the Italians: Titian, Tintoretto, glorious Veronese, a Caravaggio and the Bellini brothers. Much of the work has tremendous emotional clout, most notably Mantegna's brutal and unsentimental *Cristo morto nel Sepolcro e tre Dolenti* (Lamentation over the Dead Christ).

The number of treasures can be overwhelming, so take a break and join the students downstairs for a post-class Peroni. The surrounding neighbourhood of Brera, with its tight cobbled streets and ancient buildings, is a study of boho raffishness dotted with small galleries and artisans' workshops.

Castello Sforzesco
CASTLE, MUSEUM

(Map p242; ☎02 8846 3700; www.milanocas tello.it; Piazza Castello; adult/reduced €7/3.50; ☺9am-5.30pm Tue-Sun) Originally a Visconti fortress, this immense red-brick castle was later home to the mighty Sforza dynasty that ruled Renaissance Milan. The castle's defences were designed by Leonardo da Vinci; Napoleon later drained the moat and removed the drawbridges. Today, it shelters a series of specialised museums, accessible on the same ticket.

Among the standouts are the **Museo d'Arte Antica**, containing Michelangelo's last, unfinished work, *Pietà Rondanini;* the **Pinacoteca e Raccolte d'Arte**, which holds paintings by Bellini, Tiepolo, Mantegna, Titian and van Dyck; the **Museo della Preistoria** for local archaeological finds; and the **Museo degli Strumenti Musicali**, which has priceless early musical instruments.

Parco Sempione
PARK

(Map p242) Sprawling over 47 hectares, Parco Sempione has everything you'd expect from a Milanese park: chic bars, a lovely, Liberty-style aquarium, Acquario Civico, and the Gió Ponti–designed steel tower, Torre Branca (Map p238; ☎02 331 41 20; lift €3; ☺9.30am-midnight Tue-Fri, 10.30am-2pm, 2.30-7.30pm Sat & Sun May–mid-Oct, shorter hr in winter), from the top of which you have a bird's-eye view of the city. Also here is the Triennale di Milano (Map p238; ☎02 72 43 41; www.triennaledesign museum.it; Viale Emilio Alemanga 6; adult/reduced €8/6.50; ☺10.30am-8.30pm Tue-Sun), a permanent museum dedicated to Italian design.

Galleria Vittorio Emanuele II
SHOPPING ARCADE

(Map p242) Directly across from the Duomo sits a precocious feat of engineering framed by an immense archway. So much more than a shopping arcade, the neoclassical Galleria Vittorio Emanuele is a soaring iron-and-glass structure known locally as *il salotto bueno,* the city's fine drawing room. Shaped like a crucifix, it also marks the *passeggiata* (evening stroll) route from Piazza di Duomo to Piazza di Marino and the doors of La Scala.

Giuseppe Mengoni designed the Galleria as a showplace for modern Milan. Tragically, he plummeted to his death from scaffolding just weeks before his 14-year tour de force was completed in 1877. Long-standing Milanese tradition claims you can avoid Mengoni's bad luck by grinding your heel into the testicles of the mosaic bull on the floor.

Fashion

Cobblers, seamstresses, tailors and milliners, Italy's skilled artisans have been shoeing, dressing and adorning Europe's affluent classes with the finest fashions money can buy since the 11th century.

As the Renaissance shone its light on art, music and literature, fashion flourished alongside, promoted by the celebrities of the day, the extravagant Florentine Medicis. In the 17th century Florence lost its gleaming fashion crown to the haute couture houses of Paris, but snatched it back in the 1950s with a modish new concept: fashion soirées. Avant-garde as these soirèes were in the '50s, the Florence fashion scene was rigidly controlled. Shows were held twice a year and only a handful of elite designers were invited.

Breaking with tradition in 1971, fashion and sportswear designer Walter Albini held his first show in Milan. Here, away from the suffocating constraints of the fashion establishment, he was able to experiment in new arenas. For example, instead of specialising in one line such as coats he produced the first prêt-à-porter (ready-to-wear) collection of dresses, shirts, coats, trousers, evening dresses and hats, which could be sold wholesale into shops. In addition he enhanced the role of the designer as creator, which would eventually lead to the huge designer brand names we have today. It was a resounding success and from then on Milan began to eclipse Florence as the fashion capital of Italy.

Milan's rise to global fashion mecca was far from random. No other Italian city, not even Rome, was so well suited to take on this mantle. Firstly, thanks to its geographic position, the city had historically strong links with European markets. It was also Italy's capital of finance, advertising, TV and publishing, with both *Vogue* and *Amica* magazines based there. What's more, Milan had always had a fashion and clothing industry based around the historic textile and silk production of upper Lombardy.

Clockwise from top left
1. Shopper browsing, Milan 2. Valentino shop window, Rome 3. Prada shoes

And, with the city's particular postwar focus on trade fairs and special events, it provided a natural marketplace for the exchange of goods, ideas and information.

As a result, in just over 15 years a new generation of fashion designers – Armani, Versace, Prada, Ferré, Dolce & Gabbana – emerged to conquer the world, transforming clothes, shoes, bags and sunglasses into the new badges of status and wealth. By the early 21st century six of the world's top 10 fashion houses were Italian, and four of those were based in Milan. The Golden Quad, barely 6000 sq metres in area, came to be dominated by over 500 fashion outlets. The pavements themselves were immaculately kept, with carpets, plants and other outdoor decor. Such was the level of display, tourists started to travel to Milan to 'see' the fashion.

If you feel so inclined, just drop into Milan during one of the four fashion weeks (the 'week' is now nine days long) for male and female summer and winter fashions. They are held, respectively, in January and February, and June and September. During these weeks you'll enjoy a carnival atmosphere as over 100,000 models, critics, buyers and producers descend on the city to see more than 350 shows. Book *waaaay* ahead, get a manicure and pack your most fashion-forward threads.

UNDER THE RADAR

» **Cartè, Venice** Handbags, rings and necklaces made out of marbled paper (p360).

» **Fausto Santini, Rome** Simple, architectural shoes in eye-poppingly bright colours (p137).

» **Mariano Rubinacci, Naples** Precisely fitting suits from the patriarch of Neapolitan tailoring (p639).

» **Monica Castiglioni, Milan** Statement jewellery deeply rooted in Milan's modernist traditions (p249).

» **Mrs Macis, Florence** Feminine remakes of elegant 1950s, '60s and '70s clothes and jewellery (p490).

Design

From the cup that holds your morning espresso to the bedside light you click off before you go to sleep, there's a designer responsible – and almost everyone in Milan knows their name. Design here is a way of life.

With the end of WWII, the Milanese authorities were preoccupied with rebuilding their city and housing thousands of citizens who had lost their homes through bomb damage. Luckily for them, during those postwar years the city and surrounding area were characterised by a particular mix of intellectual and professional milieu.

Milan's philosopher-architects and designers – Giò Ponti, Vico Magistretti, Gae Aulenti, Achille Castiglioni, Ettore Sottsass and Piero Fornasetti – were imbued with a modernist sense of optimism. Their postwar mission was not only to rebuild the city but also to redesign the whole urban environment. Italian philosopher Enzo Paci believed that designers sat between 'art and society'. But far from being mere intellectual theorists, this cadre of architect-designers benefitted from a unique proximity to artisanal businesses that spread across the Lombard hinterland north of Milan.

This industrial district, known as Brianza, had grown organically from rural society, retaining many specialist peasant craft skills and hundreds of years of manufacturing experience. For example, from the early days of silkworm farming, where worms were often cultivated in peasant bedrooms, a tradition of family-based textile manufacture evolved; when disease wiped out worms in the early 20th century, families that were practised in woodwork from making instruments required in this industry, turned instead to carpentry. It's no coincidence that the town of Cantù, southeast of Como, which was once dedicated to silkworm farming, is now one of Italy's furniture-making capitals. And so Brianza evolved, giving Milanese designers access to a highly skilled technical workforce who could make their modernist dreams come true.

Clockwise from top left
1. Triennale di Milano design museum, Milan 2. Coffee cups at Spazio Rossana Orlandi, Milan 3. Vespas, Ravello.

Likewise, while these production houses remained true to the craft aspect of their work, they were able to move towards modern sales and production techniques via the central marketplace that was Milan. With the opening of the huge trade-event venue, the Triennale, in 1947, Milan established a formal, creative forum for designers, architects and manufacturers. For the first time design became autonomous from architecture, and courses were launched at the Scuola Politecnica di Design (1954).

Design began to have an impact on everyday objects, such as coffee-makers, lighting and kitchenware.

This direct connection between producer and marketplace meant that Milanese designers remained attuned to the demands of the market and were unashamedly involved in the business of making profits. It was this happy symbiosis between creativity and commercialism that ultimately fine-tuned Italian design to achieve the modernist ideal of creating beautiful but useful objects.

DESIGN CLASSICS

Design in Italy is suffused with emotion: it's expressive, inventive and individual. Consider five of the biggest design names: **Alessi, Piaggio, Cassina, Fiat** and **Zanussi**. Alessi, founded in 1921, transformed our homes with crafted utensils; kettles, toothbrushes and teapots were given star treatment by big-name architect-designers, including Achille Castiglioni, Philippe Starck and Massimiliano Fuksas. Likewise, Zanussi, begun in 1916 by a blacksmith who made wood-burning stoves, launched one of the most successful advertising campaigns of all time with its 'Appliance of Science' campaign. In the realm of furniture, Cassina, launched in 1927, is iconic – the 'Masters' collection even includes pieces by Le Corbusier, Frank Lloyd Wright and Giò Ponti. On the road, the Vespa Piaggio, costing just €65 at its launch in 1946, and the Fiat 500, created in 1957, provided stylish, cheap motorised transport that transformed the lives of urbanites.

Milan

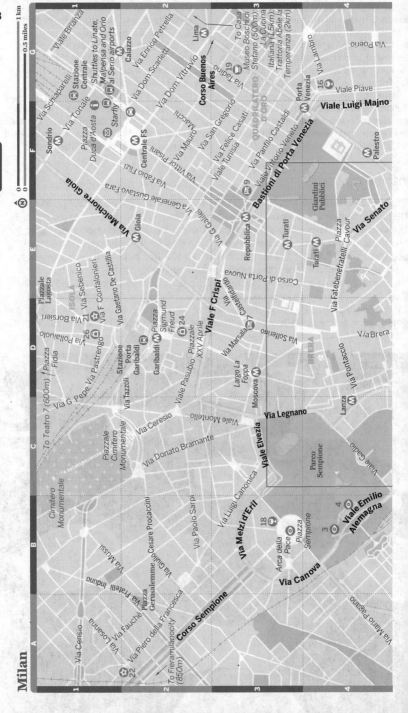

0   0.5 miles
0   1 km

Via Censio
Via Losanna
Via Fratelli Induno
Via Missi
Via Giulio Cesare Procaccini
Via Paolo Sarpi
Via Luigi Canonica
Arca della Pace
Via Melzi d'Eril
Via Canova
Corso Sempione
Piazza Gerusalemme
Via Fauché
Via Piero della Francesca
To Fieramilanocity (850m)
Via Mario Pagano
Via Emilio
Alemagna
Viale Emilio
Alemagna
18
3
4
Piazza Sempione
Parco Sempione
Viale Gadio
Viale Elvezia
Via Legnano
Via Donato Bramante
Via Ceresio
Viale Montello
Piazzale Cimitero Monumentale
Cimitero Monumentale
To Teatro 7 (600m)
Piazza Fidia
Via G Pepe Via Pastrengo
Via Pollaiuolo
26
21
Via F. Contalonieri
Via Sebenico
Via Tazzoli
Stazione Porta Garibaldi
Garibaldi
24
Piazza Sigmund Freud
Piazzale XXV Aprile
Viale Pasubio
Largo La Foppa
Moscova
Via Marsala
Via Castelfidardo
Via Solferino
7
Via Melchiorre Gioia
Gioia
Via Schiaparelli
Via Tonale
Sondrio
Piazza Duca d'Aosta
Stazione Centrale
Shuttles to Linate, Malpensa and Orio al Serio airports
Starfly
Centrale FS
Caiazzo
Via Enrico Petrella
Via Dom Scarletti
Via Dom Vitruvio
Via Vittor Pisani
Via Fabio Filzi
Via Generale Gustavo-Fara
Via Mauro Macchi
Via San Gregorio
Via Felice Casati
Via Tunisia
Corso Buenos Aires
Via Tadino
19
To Casa Museo Boschi di Stefano (500m); La Cucina Italiana (1.5km); Trattoria Abele al la Temperanza (2km)
Lima
QUADRILATERO D'ORO
Via Panfilo Castaldi
Via Vittorio Veneto
9
Bastioni di Porta Venezia
Porta Venezia
Viale Luigi Majno
16
Viale Piave
Via Lambro
Via Poerio
Palestro
Giardini Pubblici
Piazza Cavour
Via Senato
Via Fatebenefratelli
Via Brera
Via Pontaccio
BRERA
Lanza
Turati
Turati
Republica
Corso di Porta Nuova
Viale F Crispi
Piazzale Lagosta
ISOLA
Piazzale Fidia
Via Gaetano De Castillia
Via Galilei

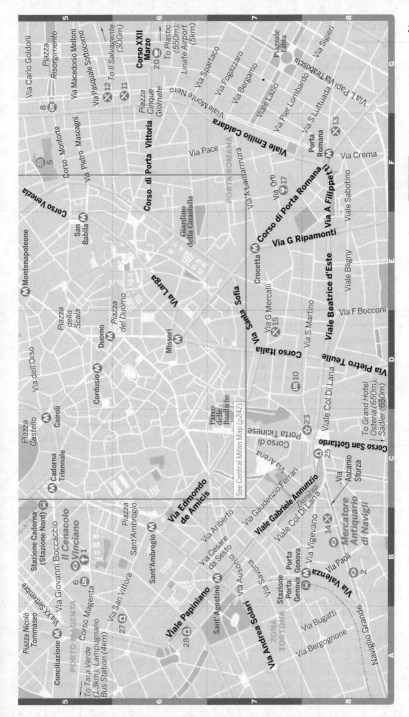

MILAN & THE LAKES SIGHTS

See Central Milan Map (p242)

Teatro alla Scala   OPERA HOUSE
(La Scala; Map p242; www.teatroallascala.org; Via Filodrammatici) Despite technological renovations behind the scenes (superior acoustics and bilingual libretto screens on the backs of seats), the charm of the world's best-known opera house, Teatro alla Scala, remains resolutely of the 18th century.

Six storeys of boxes and galleries are bedecked in gilt and lined in crimson, and, for evening performances at least, audiences are similarly turned out. If you miss out on a show, visit the **Museo Teatrale alla Scala** (La Scala Museum; Map p242; ☎02 4335 3521; Piazza della Scala; adult/child €5/4; ⊗9am-12.30pm & 1.30-5.30pm). Your visit can include a glimpse of the theatre's interior from a box and a backstage tour if you don't clash with rehearsal time.

Museo Poldi-Pezzoli   MUSEUM
(Map p242; ☎02 79 48 89; www.museopoldipezzoli. it; Via Alessandro Manzoni 12; adult/reduced €9/6; ⊗10am-6pm Wed-Mon) Botticelli's *Madonna and Child* is the star attraction at the Poldi-Pezzoli museum, once home to one of Milan's wealthiest aristocratic families and now the city's most important private collection.

Inheriting his vast fortune at the age of 24, Gian Giacomo also inherited his mother's love of art and during extensive European travels he became inspired by the latest art-collecting trends and the 'house museum' that was later to become London's V&A.

As his collection grew, Pezzoli had the idea of transforming his apartments into a series of historically themed rooms. The staircase and the bedroom were baroque in style, the Black Room was inspired by the early Renaissance and the Dante study by the early 14th century. Today the rooms, many of them works of art in themselves, remain much as they were during Pezzoli's lifetime and offer a unique preserved-in-amber insight into the heyday of 19th-century patronage.

Navigli   NEIGHBOURHOOD
South of the city centre, the Navigli neighbourhood is named after the canals from which it got its name. The Naviglio Grande (Big Canal; Map p238) grew from an irrigation ditch to one of the city's busiest thoroughfares, lined with docks, laundries and warehouses, in the 1200s. Canals were the motorways of medieval Milan, transporting salt, oil, cheese, wine and marble for the building of the cathedral to the centre of the city. Later, with the advent of trains and cars, many of them were filled in, leaving the industrial warehouses to form new art studios and galleries.

Nowadays, the area is home to some of Milan's most lively bars. On the last Sunday of every month more than 400 antique and secondhand traders set-up along a 2km stretch of the Naviglio Grande for the **Mercatore Antiquario di Navigli** (www. naviglilive.it), the city's largest antique and flea market.

 Villa Necchi Campiglio VILLA
(Map p238; ☏02 763 40 121; Via Mozart 14; adult/child €8/4; ☉10am-6pm Wed-Sun) On the outside, Milan's urban landscape may seem rigorous and austere, but behind the high walls hide some surprising homes and enchanted gardens. None more so than the restored 1930s Villa Necchi Campiglio designed by Piero Portaluppi for Pavian heiresses Nedda and Gigina Necchi, and Gigina's husband Angelo Campiglio.

Portaluppi's combining of rationalist and art deco styles perfectly symbolises the modernist imaginings of the era – the house had one of the only swimming pools in Milan, as well as revolutionary electronic shuttering. Aside from the gorgeous architectural details, engaging quotidian details include a kitchen cupboard full of pressed linens, monogrammed hairbrushes and silk evening frocks hanging ready for evenings at La Scala.

Pinacoteca Ambrosiana LIBRARY, ART GALLERY
(Map p242; ☏02 80 69 21; www.ambrosiana.it; Piazza Pio XI 2; adult/reduced €10/6.50; ☉9am-7pm Tue-Sun) The **Biblioteca Ambrosiana**, built in 1609 by the dynamic Cardinal Borromeo, was Europe's first public library and now houses over 75,000 volumes and 35,000 manuscripts that include priceless texts such as Leonardo da Vinci's *Atlantic Codex*. Later an art gallery, the Pinacoteca Ambrosiana was added and holds its fair share of Italian heavyweight paintings from the 14th to the 20th century, most famously Caravaggio's *Canestra di frutta* (Basket of Fruit), which launched his career and Italy's ultrarealist traditions.

Activities

As you might expect in a town that regularly plays host to some of the world's most beautiful people, Milan has some luxurious spas.

Bulgari spa SPA
(Map p242; ☏02 805 80 51; www.bulgarihotel. com; Via Privata Fratelli Gabba 7/b) Milan's most

Enjoy your own city tour by hopping on Tram No 1. This retro orange beauty, complete with wooden seats and original fittings, runs along Via Settembrini before cutting through the historic centre along Via Manzoni, through Piazza Cordusio and back up towards Piazza Cairoli and the Castello Sforzesco. A 75-minute ticket (€1.50), which is also valid for the bus and metro, should be purchased from any tobacconist before boarding and stamped in the original *obliteratrice* on the tram.

For something a bit more involved, **Tram ATMosfera** (Map p242; ☏800 808 181; www.atm-mi.it; departs Piazza Castello; meal €65; ☉1pm & 8pm Tue-Sun) has been renovated to incorporate a restaurant where you can eat your way through a five-course menu as you tour the city. The food isn't stunning but the varnished teak walls, glass lanterns and upholstered benches are a treat. Reserve a table at least a day in advance.

luxurious spa, with its gold-mosaic-lined pool, is located in Antonio Cittero's lavishly designed Bulgari Hotel. Treatments from €65.

Spiga 8 Spa at Hotel Baglioni SPA
(Map p242; ☏02 4547 3111; www.baglionihotels. com; Via della Spiga 8) Spiga 8 Spa has a minimalist all-white aesthetic and a menu of treatments that seem good enough to eat, such as the chocolate facial. Treatments from €65.

Courses

Teatro 7 COOKING
(off Map p238; ☏02 8907 3719; www.teatro7.com; Via Thaon di Revel 7) A cutting-edge lab kitchen located in up-and-coming Isola, Teatro 7 hosts culinary events, private dinners and classes for both adults and children. Classes from €65.

La Cucina Italiana COOKING
(off Map p238; ☏02 7064 2242; www.scuolacucina italiana.com; Piazza Aspromonte 15) Cucina Italiana is not just a gourmet magazine, but also a cookery school. Courses include kitchen adventures for children. Lessons from €80.

Central Milan

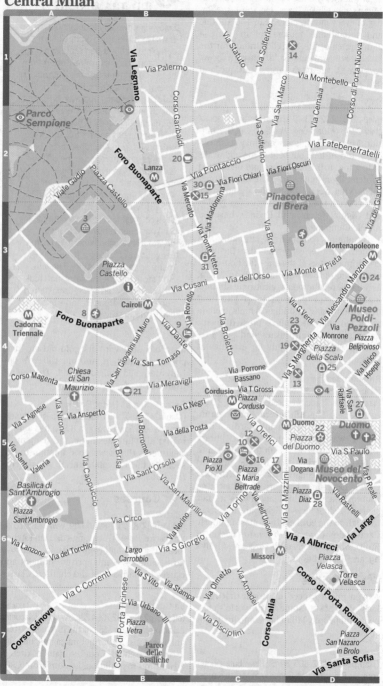

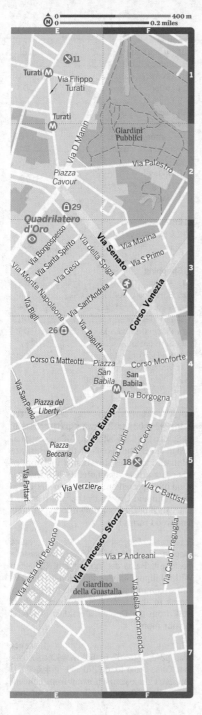

👉 Tours

The tourist office sells tickets for **Autostradale's** (www.autostradale.it; tickets €55) three-hour city bus tours including admission to *The Last Supper,* Castello Sforzesco and La Scala's museum. Although they whizz you through the city's main sights, your entry tickets to the Castello and La Scala are good for the rest of the day, allowing you to go back at your leisure. Tours depart from the taxi rank on the western side of Piazza del Duomo at 9.30am Tuesday to Sunday (except for a couple of weeks during August).

🎊 Festivals & Events

Milan has two linked trade-fair grounds, collectively known as **Fiera Milano** (www.fieramilano.it). The older of the two, **Fieramilanocity** (Map p238), is close to the centre (metro line 2, Lotto Fieramilanocity stop), while the main grounds, **Fieramilano**, are west of town in the satellite town of Rho (metro line 2, Rho Fiera stop). The furniture fair, fashion shows and most large trade fairs take place here.

Other festivals to look out for include the following:

Carnevale Ambrosiano CULTURAL
The world's longest carnival, this event culminates with a procession to the Duomo; held in February.

Cortili Aperti CULTURAL
(www.italiamultimedia.com/cortiliaperti) For one May Sunday, the gates to some of the city's most beautiful private courtyards are opened. Print out a map and make your own itinerary.

Festa del Naviglio CULTURAL
Parades, music and performances take place during the first 10 days of June.

La Bella Estate MUSIC
(www.comune.milano.it) Concerts in and beyond town from June to August. Check the town hall's website.

Festa di Sant'Ambrogio RELIGIOUS
The feast day of Milan's patron saint is celebrated on 7 December with a large Christmas fair, going by the name Obej! Obej! Stalls sell sweets, *panettone* (a yeast-risen sweet bread) and handcrafts. The opening night of La Scala's opera and ballet season is held on the same night.

Central Milan

🛏 Sleeping

Great-value accommodation is hard to come by in Milan and downright impossible during the Salone del Mobile furniture fair, the fashion shows and other large fairs. That said, booking ahead and shopping around on comparison websites can yield some surprisingly good results. The tourist office distributes *Milano Hotels,* which lists over 350 options.

TOP CHOICE Antica Locanda Solferino

GUESTHOUSE €€€

(Map p238; ☑02 657 01 29; www.anticalocanda solferino.it; Via Castelfidardo 2; s €140-270, d €180-400; P❄🛜) This understated Brera beauty is a genuinely charming hideaway, with 11 romantically retro rooms. Decorated with early-20th-century prints, broderie anglais curtains and antique furniture, it attracts a bohemian crowd of artists, writers and musicians. It also lets a two-person apartment kitted out in full 1960s style.

Hotel Spadari Duomo

DESIGN HOTEL €€€

(Map p242; ☑02 7200 2371; www.spadarihotel.com; Via Spadari 11; d €185-345; ❄🛜) Milan's original design hotel, the rooms at the Spadari are miniature galleries showcasing the work of emerging artists. The hotel itself is the creation of respected architect-engineers Urbano Pierini and Ugo La Pietra, who designed every inch of the 'look' down to the sinuous pale-wood furniture.

Foresteria Monforte

B&B €€

(Map p238; ☑02 7631 8516; www.foresteria monforte.it; Piazza del Tricolore 2; d €150-250) With Philippe Starck chairs, flat-screen TVs and a communal kitchen, the three classy rooms in this upmarket B&B are a short walk from the Duomo. Breakfast is served in your room.

3Rooms

B&B €€€

(Map p242; ☑02 62 61 63; www.10corsocomo. com; Corso Como 10; d €270-340; P❄@🛜) If you can't drag yourself away from concept store Corso Como, avail yourself of one of the three keys to its luxurious *palazzo* (mansion) suites. Here you can sleep under Eames bedspreads, sit in Arne Jacobsen chairs and make tea with your Porsche kettle, all of which are for sale on checkout.

Antica Locanda Leonardo GUESTHOUSE €€

(Map p238; ✆02 4801 4197; www.anticalocanda leonardo.com; Corso Magenta 78; s €120, d €165-245; ❊❖) Rooms here exude homey comfort, from the period furniture and parquet floors to the plush drapes. Take breakfast in the quiet, scented interior garden of this 19th-century residence.

Vietnamonamour B&B €€

(✆02 7063 4614; www.vietnamonamour.com; Via Alessandro Pestalozza 7; s €80-100, d €100-120; ❊❖) Beautiful timber floors and Vietnamese furnishings set the tone in this 1903 residence-turned-B&B, with four romantic rooms. Downstairs, the Paris-born Vietnamese owner runs a welcoming Vietnamese restaurant.

Hotel Casa Mia HOTEL €

(Map p238; ✆02 657 52 49; www.hotelcasamia milano.it; Viale Vittorio Veneto 30; s/d €62/85; ❊) Cosying up to Piazza della Repubblica, 'My House' offers straightforward digs handily placed about halfway between Stazione Centrale and the Duomo, just over the road from the Giardini Pubblici. It's recently been renovated, so the rooms currently have an extra gloss to them.

Also recommended:

La Cordata HOSTEL €

(Map p238; ✆02 5831 4675; www.ostellola cordata.com; Via Burigozzo 11; dm/s/d €23/60/80;

❖❖) Spartan but spotless hostel rooms decked out with a dash of design brio.

Tara Verde B&B €€

(off Map p238; ✆02 3653 4959; www.taraverde. it; Via Delleani 22; s €100-110, d €129; ❊❖) Three exotically colourful rooms in a 19th-century *palazzo*.

Alle Meraviglie HOTEL €€€

(Map p242; ✆02 805 10 23; www.allemeraviglie. it; Via San Tomaso 8; d €180-247; ❖❊❖) A boutique hotel with rooms decorated with Milanese fabrics and fresh flowers.

Eating

Milan's dining scene is much like its fashion scene, with new restaurant openings hotly debated and seats at Michelin-starred tables hard to come by. Whether it's dyed-in-tradition or fusion cuisine, you'll eat some of Italy's most innovative and sophisticated food here.

Milan's provincial specialities include polenta and the first course of choice, *risotto alla milanese* (saffron-infused risotto made with bone-marrow stock). Milanese mains include *fritto misto alla milanese* (fried slices of bone marrow, liver and lung), *busecca* (sliced tripe boiled with beans) and *costoletta alla milanese* (breaded veal). Milan is also the home of *panettone* (a yeast-risen sweet bread) and *colomba* (a dry dove-shaped cake, first baked in the 6th century and traditionally accompanied by sweet dessert wine).

Reservations are required for most reputable restaurants and essential for popular and top-end establishments.

MILAN'S BRIGHTEST MICHELIN STARS

Milan's most important contemporary Italian restaurants are equally fashion- and food-oriented:

» **Trussardi alla Scala** (Map p242; ✆02 8068 8201; www.trussardiallascala.com; Piazza della Scala 5; meals €120; ⏱Mon-Fri, dinner Sat) Gualtiero Marchesi alumni Andrea Berton runs the kitchen of this subdued sexy dining room overlooking La Scala. The menu has a pleasing directness, with seasonal dishes such as roast spring lamb with potato, avocado and lime.

» **Cracco-Peck** (Map p242; ✆02 87 67 74; www.ristorantecracco.it; Via Victor Hugo 4; meals €140; ⏱Tue-Fri, dinner Mon, lunch Sat) The gastronomic showcase for Milan's premier delicatessen, Peck. Carlo Cracco conjures up exemplary deconstructive *alta cucina* (haute cuisine) in a formal contemporary environment.

» **Sadler** (off Map p238; ✆02 87 67 30; www.sadler.it; Via Ascanio Sforza 77; meals €120; ⏱Mon-Sat) On the Milanese scene since 1995, Claudio Sadler's culinary wisdom remains undisputed. The trick is to keep flavours simple. Try the pigeon ragout or the black cod with turnip greens, yoghurt and wasabi.

DON'T MISS

PECK EMPORIUM

Forget Leonardo's *Last Supper:* gourmands head to the food and wine emporium **Peck** (Map p242; ☎02 802 31 61; www.peck.it; Via Spadari 7-9; ☺3-7.30pm Mon, 8.45am-7.30pm Tue-Sat). This Milanese institution first opened its doors as a deli in 1883. Since then, it's expanded to a dining room–bar upstairs and an *enoteca* (wine bar). The Aladdin's cave–like food hall is the best in Milan, stocked with some 3200 variations of *parmigiano reggiano* (Parmesan) at its cheese counter, just for starters. Other treats include an exquisite array of chocolates, pralines and pastries; freshly made gelato; seafood; caviar; pâtés; meats; fruit and vegetables; truffle products; olive oils; and balsamic vinegar.

Da Giacomo   SEAFOOD €€
(Map p238; ☎02 760 23 313; Via Pasquale Sottocorno 6; meals €30) This sunny Tuscan restaurant with its custard-coloured walls and mint-green panelling serves an unpretentious menu featuring mainly fish and shellfish. Start with a slice of sardine and caper pizza and follow with the fresh linguine with scampi and zucchini flowers.

TOP CHOICE Trattoria Abele la Temperanza   TRATTORIA €
(off Map p238; ☎02 261 3855; Via Temperanza 5; risotto €9; ☺8pm-1am Tue-Sun; 🐾) This traditional trattoria with its spartan decor, paper table mats and black-and-white photographs has dedicated itself to the pursuit of the perfect risotto. Here you can try over 100 different kinds of risotto alongside other traditional dishes such as *brasato* (braised stew). Go for the 'three rices', a selection of three different risottos, which change daily. Book ahead, don't be late and be prepared to wait 30 minutes for your meal, but rest assured, it's worth it.

Osteria della Lanterna   OSTERIA €€
(Map p238; ☎02 5830 9604; Via Giuseppe Mercalli 14; meals €25-35; ☺Mon-Fri, dinner only Sat) This is one of the few genuine *osterie* (casual taverns or eateries presided over by a host) left in Milan, hosted by the owner-cook, who speaks to customers in Milanese dialect. Despite its unprepossessing appearance, reservations are essential if you want to try the homemade pastas and gnocchi with walnuts and gorgonzola.

Dongiò   CALABRESE €€
(Map p238; ☎02 551 1372; Via Bernardino Corio 3; meals €30-40; ☺Mon-Fri, dinner only Sat; 🐾) One of the best value-for-money restaurants in Milan, this big-hearted Calabrese trattoria serves the spicy flavours of the south on delicious homemade pasta. Starters include bountiful platters of southern salami and piquant cheeses. Reservations recommended.

Grand Hotel Osteria   OSTERIA €€
(off Map p238; ☎02 8951 1586; www.osteriagrandhotel.it; Via Cardinale Ascanio Sforza 75; meals €35-40; ☺dinner Mon-Fri, lunch & dinner Sat & Sun) In summer, dine beneath the flower-laden pergola at this traditional tavern overlooking the Naviglio Pavese. The owner is a wine expert (and an opera enthusiast) and the wine selection is exceptional. He sometimes runs wine, cheese and oil tastings.

Al Bacco   MILANESE €€
(Map p238; ☎02 5412 1637; Via Marcona 1; meals €25-30; ☺dinner Mon-Sat) One-time pupil to the famous chef Claudio Sadler, Andrea now has his own Slow Food–recommended restaurant where he prepares Milanese classics with love. It's an excellent place to sample saffron risotto or veal cutlet. Otherwise, try the homemade pasta with fava beans, pancetta and pecorino or the rabbit with Taggiasche olives.

Trattoria da Pino   MILANESE €€
(Map p242; ☎02 7600 0532; meals €20-25; Via Cerva 14; ☺lunch Mon-Sat) In a city full of models in Michelin-starred restaurants, working-class da Pino's offers the perfect antidote. Sit elbow-to-elbow at long cafeteria-style tables in the rust-red dining room and order up bowls of *bollito misto* (mixed boiled meats), handmade pasta and curried veal nuggets. By 1pm the place is buzzing like a well-oiled machine so arrive early to join the fray.

Latteria di San Marco   TRATTORIA €
(Map p242; ☎02 659 76 53; Via San Marco 24; meals €18-25; ☺Mon-Fri) If you can snare a seat in this tiny and ever-popular restaurant (originally a dairy shop), you'll find old favourites like *spaghetti alla carbonara* mixed in with chef Arturo's own creations, such as *polpettine al limone* (little meatballs with lemon)

or *riso al salto* (risotto fritters) on the ever-changing, mostly organic menu.

El Brellin
ITALIAN, BRUNCH €€€

(Map p238; ☑02 5810 1351; www.brellin.com; cnr Vicolo dei Lavandai 14 & Alzaia Naviglio Grande 14; meals €40-45; ☺Mon-Sat) Housed in a 1700s laundry, El Brellin's candlelit garden is a romantic spot for homemade pasta and specialities like *cazzoeula* (pork rib chops, skin and sausage stew). The Sunday brunch buffet is laden with cured meats, scrambled eggs and whole smoked salmon.

Also recommended:

Bianco Latte
CAFE €

(Map p242; ☑02 5208 6177; www.biancolatte milano.it; Via Filippo Turati 30; gelati €2.50-12) Come here for artisanal ice cream, salads and homemade cakes.

Grom
GELATERIA €

(Map p242; ☑02 8058 1041; www.grom.it; Via Santa Margherita 16; gelati €2-3; ☑) The pistachio is made from nuts sourced in Sicily and the *gianduja* mixes Piemontese hazelnuts with Venezuelan chocolate. Love it or hate it, Grom is good.

Obikà
CHEESE BAR €€

(Map p238; ☑02 8645 0568; www.obika.it; cnr Via Mercato & Via Fiori Chiari; meals €15-25) Choose from sweet to smoked mozzarella balls with an accompaniment of salad or prosciutto. The €8 *aperitivo* is great value.

Princi
BAKERY, PASTRIES

(Map p242; ☑02 87 47 97; www.princi.it; Via Speronari 6; ☺Mon-Sat) Artisanal pastries, bread and pizza.

 Drinking

Milanese bars are generally open until 2am or 3am, and virtually all serve *aperitivi*.

The Navigli canal district, the cobbled backstreets of Brera, and swish Corso Como and its surrounds are all great areas for a drink, Milan-style.

Diana Garden
BAR

(Map p238; ☑02 2058 2081; Viale Piave 42; ☺10pm-1am) Secreted behind a vast leather curtain at the back of the Sheraton, the *aperitivo* at the Diana is one of Milan's most varied. Grab a freshly crushed peach Bellini and lounge around the low-lit garden.

Lacerba
BAR

(Map p238; ☑02 545 54 75; www.lacerba.it; Via Orti 4; ☺noon-3pm & 6.30pm-midnight Mon-Fri, 6.30pm-midnight Sat) An homage to futurism, Lacerba combines dishes from futurist Marinetti's kooky culinary manifesto with innovative cocktail mixes such as basil and honey. Furnished with lipstick-red leather sofas and print wallpapers, it has a sexy low-key ambience.

10 Corso Como
BAR

(Map p238; ☑02 2901 3581; www.10corsocomo. com; Corso Como 10; ☺12.30pm-midnight Mon-Fri, 11.30am-1.30am Sat & Sun) A picture-perfect courtyard, world-class people-watching and an elegant *aperitivo* scene lit at night by a twinkling canopy of fairy lights make Corso Como the best lifestyle concept bar in Milan.

Living
BAR

(Map p242; ☑02 331 00 84; www.livingmilano.com; Piazza Sempione 2; ☺8am-2am Mon-Fri, 9am-2am Sat & Sun) Living has one of the city's prettiest settings, with a corner position and floor-to-ceiling windows overlooking the Arco della Pace. The bounteous *aperitivo* spread and expertly mixed cocktails draw crowds of smart-casual 20- and 30-somethings.

Also recommended:

Botega Caffè Cacao
CAFE

(Map p242; ☑02 8050 6589; www.cafebotega cacao.it; Corso Garibaldi 12; ☺7am-8pm daily) Coffee and pastries in a retro, '50s-style Brera cafe.

Torrefazione Caffè Ambrosiano
CAFE

(Map p238; ☑02 2952 5069; www.torrefazione ambrosiano.it; Corso Buenos Aires 20) No seating, just the best coffee in Milan. There's

---

APERITIVO

Happy hour elsewhere in the world might mean downing cut-price pints, but not in oh-so-stylish Milan. Its nightly *aperitivo* is a two- or three-hour ritual, starting around 6pm, where for €6 to €15, a cocktail, glass of wine, or beer comes with an unlimited buffet of antipasti, bruschetta, cured meats, salads, and even seafood and pasta. (Occasionally you'll pay a cover charge up front that includes a drink and buffet fare, which generally works out the same.) Take a plate and help yourself; snacks are also sometimes brought to your table. Most of the city's bars offer *aperitivi,* including those listed here.

WHAT'S ON

The tourist office stocks several entertainment guides in English: *Milano Mese*, *Hello Milano* (www.hellomilano.it) and *Easy Milano* (www.easymilano.it). The free Italian newspapers distributed on the metro are also handy for what's-on listings.

For club listings, check out *ViviMilano* (http://milano.corriere.it, in Italian), which comes out with the *Corriere della Sera* newspaper on Wednesday; *La Repubblica* (www.repubblica.it, in Italian) is also good on Thursday. Another source of inspiration is *Milano2night* (http://milano.2night.it).

Tickets for concerts, sporting events and the theatre can be booked online through **Ticket One** (☑892101; www.ticketone.it) or **Ticket Web** (☑199 158158; www.ticketweb.it). **Milano Concerti** (☑02 4870 2726; www.milanoconcerti.it) only handles ticketing for international rock concerts.

also a branch on Corso XXII Marzo 18 (Map p238).

Marchesi PASTRIES & CAKES
(Map p242; ☑02 876 730; www.pasticcerriamarchesi.it; Via Santa Maria all Porta 11a; ⊗Mon-Sat) Perfect-every-shot coffee since 1824.

Entertainment

Milan has some of Italy's top clubs and a lavish cultural calendar capped off by La Scala's opera season. The main theatre and concert season opens in October.

Most big names that play Milan do so at major venues outside the city centre, which run shuttle buses for concerts. They include **Mediolanum Forum** (☑199128800; www.forumnet.it) and the **San Siro Stadium** (www.sansiro.net).

Live Music

Le Trottoir LIVE MUSIC
(Map p238; ☑02 837 81 66; www.letrottoir.it; Piazza XXIV Maggio 1; admission €10; ⊗11pm-2am daily) Legendary Le Trottoir is housed in an ex-customs toll gate on the Darsena docks and is a good place to move on to after drinks in Navigli. Drink upstairs in the psychedelic yellow, blue and red Andrea Pinketts lounge or roll out onto the pavement with hundreds of other revellers in summer.

Blue Note JAZZ CLUB
(Map p238; ☑02 6901 6888; www.bluenotemilano.com; Via Borsieri 37; tickets €25-30; ⊗Tue-Sun Sep-Jul) Top-class jazz acts perform here from around the world; get tickets by phone, online or at the door from 7.30pm. It also does a popular easy-listening Sunday brunch (€35 or €55 for two adults and two children).

Nightclubs

Clubs generally stay open until 3am or 4am Tuesday to Sunday; cover charges vary from €10 to upwards of €20. Door policies can be formidable as the night wears on.

Plastic NIGHTCLUB
(off Map p238; ☑02 733 996; www.thisisplastic.com; Viale Umbria 120; ⊗Fri & Sat mid-Sep–Jun) Friday's London Loves takes no prisoners with an edgy, transgressive indie mix and Milan's coolest kids. If you're looking fab, club art director Nicola Guiducci's private Match à Paris on Sunday mashes French pop, indie and avant-garde sounds.

Il Gattopardo Café NIGHTCLUB
(Map p238; ☑02 3453 7699; www.ilgattopardocafe.it; Via Piero della Francesca 47; ⊗Tue-Sat Sep-Jun) This gorgeous champagne-coloured space in a deconsecrated church is filled with flickering candles and baroque-style furniture. Gattopardo's clientele is equally aesthetically blessed. The only way in is with advance booking.

Magazzini Generali NIGHTCLUB
(☑02 539 3948; www.magazzinigenerali.it; Via Pietrasanta 14; ⊗Wed-Sat Oct-May) When this former warehouse is full of people working up a sweat to an international indie act, there's no better place to be in Milan. Most gigs are under €20, and there's free entry on other nights when DJs get the party started.

Opera & Theatre

The opera season runs from November through July, but you can see theatre, ballet and concerts at Teatro alla Scala year-round, with the exception of August.

Teatro alla Scala OPERA HOUSE
(Map p242; box office ☑02 86 07 75; www.teatroallascala.org; Via Filodrammatici 2) You'll need perseverance and luck to secure opera tickets at La Scala (€10 to €180; up to €2000 for opening night). About two months before the first performance, tickets can be bought by telephone and online. One month before the first performance, remaining tickets are sold at the **box office** (Map p242; Galleria del

QUADRILATERO D'ORO

For anyone interested in the fall of a frock or the cut of a jacket, a stroll around the **Quadrilatero d'Oro** (Golden Quad; Map p242), the world's most fabled shopping district, is a must. This quaintly cobbled quadrangle of streets may have always been synonymous with elegance and money (Via Monte Napoleone was where Napoleon's government managed loans), but the Quad's legendary fashion status belongs firmly to Milan's postwar reinvention. During the boom years of the 1950s the city's fashion houses established ateliers in the area bounded by Via Monte Napoleone, Via Sant'Andrea, Via della Spiga and Via Alessandro Manzoni and by the 1960s Milan had outflanked Florence and Rome to become the country's haute couture capital. Nowadays, the world's top designers unveil their women's collections in February/March and September/October, while men's fashion hits the runways in January and June/July.

Sagrato, Piazza del Duomo; ⊘noon-6pm). On performance days, 140 tickets for the gallery are sold two hours before the show (one ticket per customer). Queue early.

Sport

The city's two clubs are the 1899-established AC Milan, owned and presided over by Silvio Berlusconi for the last 25 year,s and the 1908-established FC Internazionale Milano (aka 'Inter'). They play on alternate Sundays during the season at the **San Siro stadium** (Stadio Giuseppe Meazza; ☑02 404 24 32; www.sansirotour.com; Via Piccolomini 5, museum & tours Gate 14; museum adult/reduced €7/5, incl guided tour €12.50/10; ⊘non-match days 10am-6pm). Guided tours of the stadium, built in the 1920s, take you behind the scenes to the players' locker rooms and include a visit to the **Museo Inter e Milan museum**, a shrine of memorabilia, papier-mâché caricatures of players, and film footage.

Take tram 24, bus 95, 49 or 72, or the metro to the Lotto stop, from where a free bus shuttles to the stadium.

🛍 Shopping

Beyond the hallowed streets of the **Golden Quad**, designer outlets and chains can be found along **Corso Buenos Aires** (Ⓜ Corsa Venezia) and **Corso Vercelli** (Ⓜ Conciliazione); younger, hipper labels along **Via Brera** (Ⓜ Montenapoleone) and **Corso Magenta** (Ⓜ Cadorna); while **Corso di Porta Ticinese** and **Navigli** (Ⓜ Porta Genova) are home to the Milan street scene and subculture shops. For cutting-edge talent and great bargains venture down the up-and-coming **Via Tortona** (Ⓜ Porta Genova).

TOP CHOICE **Spazio Rossana Orlandi**   HOME & GARDEN, DESIGN
(Map p238; ☑02 467 44 71; www.rossanaorlandi.com; Via Matteo Bandello 14; ⊘Tue-Sat) Installed in a former tie factory in the Magenta district, finding this iconic interior design studio is a challenge in itself. Once inside though, you'll find it hard to leave this dream-like treasure trove stacked with vintage and contemporary limited-edition pieces from young and upcoming artists.

Monica Castiglioni   JEWELLERY
(Map p238; ☑02 8723 7979; www.monicacastiglioni.com; Via Pastrengo 4; ⊘11am-8pm Thu-Sat) Located in the up-and-coming neighbourhood of Isola, Monica's studio turns out organic and industrial-style jewellery in bronze, silver and gold. Deeply rooted in Milan's modernist traditions, these are statement pieces and well priced for the workmanship.

Il Salvagente   FASHION
(off Map p238; ☑02 7611 0328; www.salvagentemilano.it; Via Fratelli Bronzetti 16; ⊘Tue-Sat, 3-7pm Mon) The grim basement courtyard of Il Salvagente gives scant indication of the big brand names inside. Discounted Prada, Dolce & Gabbana, Versace and Ferretti are just a few of the names on the tightly packed racks. Payment is in cash only.

Borsalino   ACCESSORIES
(Map p242; ☑02 8901 5436; www.borsalino.it; Galleria Vittorio Emanuele II 92; ⊘Tue-Sat) The iconic Alessandrian milliner has worked with design greats like Achille Castiglioni, who once designed a pudding-bowl bowler hat. This outlet in the galleria stocks seasonal favourites. The main showroom is at Corso Venezia 21a.

G Lorenzi
KITCHENWARE, DESIGN

(Map p242; 02 7602 2848; www.lorenzi.it; Via Monte Napoleone 9; Mon-Sat) One of Milan's extant early-20th-century gems, G Lorenzi specialises in the finest-quality grooming and kitchen paraphernalia. There are things here – handcrafted pocket knives set into stag antlers, say – so fine and functional they stand as classic examples of utilitarian design.

Vintage Delirium
VINTAGE

(Map p242; 02 8646 2076; www.vintagedelirium fj.com; Via Sacchi 3; Mon-Fri) Franco Jacassi's multi-level store stocks pristine vintage woollens, 1930s evening wear from Chanel, Dior, Balenciaga and Vionnet, belts, buckles, bags and Neapolitan silk ties from the 1960s.

Sermoneta
ACCESSORIES

(Map p242; 02 7631 7961; www.sermonetagloves. com; Via della Spiga 46) A hole in the wall on chic Via della Spiga, Sermoneta's boutique store sells standards like hand-stitched calfskin gloves alongside more unique styles made of pony skin or peccary hide.

Also recommended:

10 Corso Como
FASHION

(Map p238; 02 2900 2674; www.10corsocomo. com; Corso Como 10; 10.30am-7.30pm Tue, Fri-Sun, to 9pm Wed & Thu, 3.30-7.30pm Mon) Possibly the world's most hyped 'concept shop', with a desirable selection of lifestyle items.

La Rinascente
DEPARTMENT STORE

(Map p242; 02 8 85 21; www.rinascente.it; Piazza Duomo; 10am-midnight) Italy's most prestigious department store doesn't let the fashion capital down.

Art Book Triennale
BOOKSTORE

(02 8901 3403; Viale Emilio Alemagna 6; 10.30am-8.30pm Tue-Sun) This bookshop, located inside the Triennale di Milano, stocks beautifully produced editions as enthralling as the exhibitions themselves.

Alessi
KITCHENWARE

(Map p242; 02 79 57 26; www.alessi.com; Via Manzoni 14-16; Tue-Sun) Alessi's colourful new flagship store, designed by Martí Guixé.

Information

Dangers & Annoyances

Petty theft (pickpocketing for the most part) can be a problem on public transport, around the main train station (Stazione Centrale), as well as in Piazza del Duomo.

Emergency

Foreigners police office (02 6 22 61; Via Montebello 26) For immigration matters.

Police station (02 6 22 61; Via Fatebene-fratelli 11)

Internet Access

Wi-fi is widely available at midrange and top-end hotels (often free, but sometimes for an additional €5) and occasionally in public spaces such as train stations.

Underscore Internetpoint (02 7203 5780; Cairoli metro; per hr €2; 10am-9pm) Located inside the Via Dante entrance of the metro.

Medical Services

Milan Clinic (02 7601 6047; www.milanclinic. com; Via Cerva 25) English-speaking doctors.

Ospedale Maggiore Policlinico (02 5503 3137; www.policlinico.mi.it; Via Francesco Sforza 35)

DESIGNER OUTLETS

To bag real designer discounts, plan a trip to the huge designer outlet malls, which stock most of the global labels at a fraction of the price.

» **Fox Town** (www.foxtown.ch; Via A Maspoli 18, Mendrisio, Switzerland; 11am-7pm) Fifty kilometres north of Milan, this outlet is one of the area's best-kept secrets with over 160 shops running the gamut of brands from Ferragamo to Nike. There's a coach service for shoppers (check the website for details), or catch a train to Chiasso, then Swiss Postbus to the mall.

» **Serravalle Scrivia** (www.mcarthurglen.it/serravalle; Via della Moda 1, Serravalle Scrivia; 10am-8pm) Eighty kilometres south of Milan on the way to Genoa, this Ligurian SoCal-style mall has two-storied streets and over 180 shops, including Frette, Dolce & Gabbana and Petit Bateau. The same coach company that services Fox Town also does Serravalle (www.zaniviaggi.it), or catch a Milan–Genoa train to Arquata Scrivia.

TO MARKET

Markets fill the canalside **Viale Papiniano** in the southwest of the city on Tuesday (Map p238; ☻7.30am-1pm) and Saturday (☻7.30am-5pm). There is an antique market in Brera on **Via Fiori Chiari** (Map p242) and nearby streets every third Sunday of the month. On the second Sunday of every month, an old and antique book fair is held on **Piazza Diaz** (Map p242).

For fresh fruit, vegetables and fish, Milan's main covered market, the **Mercato Comunale** (Map p238; Piazza XXIV Maggio) is open Monday to Saturday. But without a doubt the city's largest market is the antique and collectables market, the **Mercatore Antiquario di Navigli** (Map p238), held on the last Sunday of each month on the Naviglio Grande and Ripa di Porta Ticinese.

Money

There are currency-exchange offices at all the airports and a couple on the western side of Piazza del Duomo.

Banca Cesare Ponti (Piazza del Duomo 19) Good rates and a 24-hour automatic banknote exchange machine.

Banca Intesa San Paolo (Piazza della Scala) A 24-hour booth with currency-exchange machine and ATMs.

Post

Central post office (Map p242; Piazza Cordusio 1)

Tourist Information

Central tourist office (Map p242; ☎02 7740 4343; www.provincia.milano.it/turismo; Piazza Castello 1; ☻9am-6pm Mon-Fri, 9am-1.30pm & 2-6pm Sat, 9am-1pm & 2-5pm Sun)

Welcome Desk Meeting Milano

LINATE AIRPORT (☎02 7020 0443; ☻7.30am-11.30pm)

MALPENSA AIRPORT (☎02 5858 0080; Terminal 1; ☻8am-8pm)

ℹ Getting There & Away

Air

Aeroporto Malpensa (MXP; ☎02 7485 2200; www.sea-aeroportimilano.it) The hub for European and international flights, 50km northwest of the city.

Aeroporto Linate (off Map p238; LIN; ☎02 7485 2200; www.sea-aeroportimilano.it) Seven kilometres east of the city centre, Linate handles some European flights and the majority of domestic flights.

Aeroporto Internazionale di Orio al Serio (BG; ☎035 32 63 23; www.sacbo.it) An increasing number of budget airlines use Bergamo's airport, 55km northeast of Milan.

Bus

Eurolines (☎0861 1991900; www.eurolines.it) Reservations and tickets for international buses to Western and central Europe, Scandinavia and Morocco. Buses depart from the Lampugnano Bus Station.

Lampugnano Bus Station (off Map p238; Via Giulia Natta; Lampugnano metro) Milan's main bus station is west of the city centre next to the Lampugnano metro station. The bulk of national services are run by **Autostradale** (☎02 7200 1304; www.autostradale.it), which has a ticket office at the main tourist office.

Train

Milan has three major train stations. For mainline train information refer to **Trenitalia** (☎199 892021; www.trenitalia.it).

Stazione Centrale (Map p238; Piazza Duca d'Aosta) Milan's Central Station is a masterpiece of rationalist architecture. International high-speed trains serve Switzerland and France, while national and regional trains serve Mantua, Venice, Turin, Rome and Naples.

Stazione Cadorna (Stazione Nord; Map p238; Piazza Luigi Cadorna; www.ferrovienord.it) The private train line Ferrovie Nord Milano connects Milan with northern towns including Como.

Stazione Porta Garibaldi (Map p238; Piazza Sigmund Freud) Operates the bulk of regional services to towns northwest of Milan.

ℹ Getting Around

To/From the Airport

Getting into town on public transport is straightforward and inexpensive. A taxi from Milan to Malpensa airport costs a fixed fee of €85. A taxi to Linate costs between €15 and €20.

Malpensa Express (☎800 500005; www.malpensaexpress.it) This train service departs every 30 minutes to Terminal 1 from **STAZIONE CENTRALE** (adult/child €7/5.50; 45 minutes) and **STAZIONE NORD** (adult/child €11/5.50, 40 minutes). This is the best way to Malpensa, given traffic. However, if you need Terminal 2 the bus or a taxi is preferable due to poor services between the two terminals.

Malpensa & Linate Shuttle (☎02 5858 3185; www.malpensa-shuttle.com; Piazza Luigi di Savoia; ☻ticket office 6am-8.30pm Thu-Tue, to 2pm Wed) Departs every 20 minutes, between 5am and 10.30pm, from outside Stazione Centrale (adult/child €7.50/3.75) and Linate (adult/child €13/6.50). Tickets are sold from the office inside Stazione Centrale or on the bus.

Bus 73 (www.atm-mi.it; Piazza San Babila) Departs every 10 to 15 minutes (€1.50; 20 minutes) between 5.30am and 12.30am. Use regular bus tickets.

Orio Shuttle (☑035 330706; www.orioshuttle. com; Piazza Luigi di Savoia) Every 30 minutes from outside Stazione Centrale (adult/child €7/5; one hour) between 4am and 11.15pm.

Starfly (☑02 5858 7237; www.starfly.net; Piazza Luigi di Savoia) **LINATE** (adult/child €4.50/2.50; 25 minutes) Departs every half-hour between 5.40am and 9.35pm. Tickets are sold on board.

Bicycle

BikeMi (www.bikemi.it) is Milan's public bike network. Daily, weekly or annual passes are available, and you can pick up and drop off at different stations. Get passes online, by phone (ATM; ☑800 808181) or at the ATM info points.

Car & Motorcycle

Street parking costs €1.50 per hour in the city centre (€2 per five hours after 7pm). To pay, buy a SostaMilano card from a tobacconist, scratch off the date and hour, and display it on your dashboard. Underground car parks charge €2.50 for the first half-hour and between €1 and €3 per hour after that, depending on length of stay. Entry to the historic centre is restricted to those who acquire an **Ecopass** (☑02 02 02; www.comune.milano.it/ecopass) in advance. You are better off parking outside the centre and using public transport.

Rental-car companies have offices at Stazione Centrale and both airports.

Public Transport

ATM (☑800 808181; www.atm-mi.it) Runs the metro, buses and trams. The metro is the most convenient way to get around and consists of four underground lines (red MM1, green MM2, yellow MM3 and blue Passante Ferroviario), which run from 6am to midnight.

A ticket costs €1.50 and is valid for one metro ride or up to 90 minutes' travel on ATM buses and trams. You can buy a 10-ride pass for €13.80 or unlimited one-/two-day tickets for bus, tram and metro for €4.50/8.25. Tickets are sold at metro stations, tobacconists and newspaper stands around town. Tickets must be validated on trams and buses.

Taxi

Taxis are only available at designated taxi ranks; you cannot flag them down. Alternatively, call ☑02 40 40, ☑02 69 69 or ☑02 85 85. The average short city ride costs €10.

Around Milan

PAVIA
POP 71,200

First impressions of Pavia are deceptive, as its pretty old town is encircled by an ugly industrial-agricultural belt. However, once you're inside the historic centre, the cobbled streets and piazzas buzz with students attending the ancient university. Half a day is ample time to wander around the grounds and courtyards of the 14th-century university (when it is in term) and visit the extraordinary Carthusian monastery, the Certosa di Pavia.

Plenty of direct trains from Stazione Centrale link Pavia with Milan (€3.40, 25 to 40 minutes).

Certosa di Pavia (Pavia Charterhouse; ☑03 8292 5613; www.certosadipavia.com; Viale Monumento; admission by donation; ☺9-11.30am & 2.30-5.30pm Tue-Sun) is one of the Italian Renaissance's most notable buildings. Giangaleazzo Visconti of Milan founded the monastery, 10km north of Pavia, in 1396 as a private chapel and mausoleum for the Visconti family. Construction proceeded in a stop-start fashion until well into the 16th century, making this a prime example of the transition from Gothic to Renaissance.

While the interior is predominantly Gothic, the exterior is Renaissance. The church is fronted by a spacious courtyard and flanked by a small cloister, which itself leads on to a much grander second cloister, under whose arches are 24 cells, each a self-contained living area for one monk. Several cells are open to the public. In the chapels you'll find frescoes by, among others, Bernardino Luini and the Umbrian master, Il Perugino.

Sila (☑199 153155; www.sila.it) bus 175 (Pavia–Binasco–Milano) runs services from the Pavia bus station (Via Trieste) to the Certosa di Pavia (15 minutes, at least seven daily).

THE LAKES

Writers from Goethe and Stendhal to DH Lawrence and Hemingway have all lavished praise on the Italian lakes, which are dramatically ringed by snow-powdered mountains.

The westernmost of the main lakes, Lago d'Orta, is entirely within Piedmont. The three big ones are, west to east, Lago Maggiore, with its spectacular Borromean Islands; Lago di Como, closed in by densely wooded mountains and sprinkled with opulent villas and exotic gardens; and Lago di Garda, the biggest and the busiest. Its southeast corner (in the Veneto region) has Disney-style family amusement parks, including Italy's largest, Gardaland. The northern reaches of Lago di Garda extend into the Alpine region of Trentino–Alto Adige.

Trains serve many of the lakes' main towns, while passenger and car ferries ply the waters. If you're travelling by car, there are some stunning (but winding) lakeside drives. Heavy traffic and narrow roads make cycling along many stretches of the lakes less than ideal.

Lago Maggiore

By train or by road, travellers traversing the Alps from Switzerland at the Simplon Pass wind down from the mountains and sidle up to the western shore of Lake Maggiore. The star attractions are the Borromean Islands, which, like a fleet of fine vessels, lie at anchor in the Borromean Gulf, an incursion of water between the lake's two main towns, Stresa and Verbania.

More than Como and Garda, Lake Maggiore has retained the belle époque air of its early tourist heyday, when Napoleon first came to town and ordered the building of the Simplon Pass. Attracted by the mild climate and the easy access that the new 1855 railway provided, the European *haute bourgeoisie* flocked to buy and build grand lakeside villas and establish a series of extraordinarily rich gardens.

The northern end of the lake where it narrows between the mountains and enters Switzerland is the prettier, more secluded end. And it's well worth taking the delightful shoreline drive south along the SS34 and SS33.

❶ Getting There & Around

Boat

Navigazione Lago Maggiore (☑ 800 551801; www.navigazionelaghi.it) Operates ferries and hydrofoils around the lake. There are ticket booths in each town next to the embarkation quay; the main office is in Arona. Boats connect Stresa with Arona (40 minutes), Angera (35 minutes) and Verbania Pallanza (35 minutes). Day passes are also available: departing from Stresa, a ticket covering Isola Superiore, Isola Bella and Isola Madre costs €13. Services are drastically reduced in autumn and winter.

The only car ferry connecting the western and eastern shores for motorists sails between Verbania Intra and Laveno. Ferries run every 20 minutes; one-way transport costs between €7 and €11.60 for a car and driver or €4.40 for a bicycle and cyclist.

Bus

Buses leave from the waterfront at Stresa for destinations around the lake and elsewhere, including Milan and Lago d'Orta.

SAF (☑ 0323 55 21 72; www.safduemila.com, in Italian) This daily Verbania Intra-Milan service links Stresa with Arona (20 minutes), Verbania Pallanza (20 minutes), Verbania Intra (25 minutes) and Milan (1½ hours).

Train

Stresa is on the Domodossola–Milan train line. Domodossola, 30 minutes northwest, is on the Swiss border, from where the train line leads to Brig and on to Geneva.

STRESA
POP 5210

Facing due east across the lake, Stresa has a ringside view of the fiery orange sun rising up over the water. Since the 18th century, the town's easy accessibility from Milan has made it a favourite for artists and writers seeking inspiration. Hemingway was one of many; he arrived in Stresa in 1918 to convalesce from a war wound. A couple of pivotal scenes towards the end of his novel *A Farewell to Arms* are set at the Grand Hotel des Iles Borromees, the most palatial of the hotels garlanding the lake.

◉ Sights & Activities

People stream into Stresa to meander along its promenade, explore the hive of cobbled streets in its old centre and visit the Borromean Islands. The pebble beach just west of the main ferry dock is good for a sunbathe.

Funivia Stresa-Mottarone   CABLE CAR
(☑ 0323 3 02 95; www.stresa-mottarone.it; Piazzale della Funivia; adult/child return €17.50/11; ⊙9.30am-5.30pm) Captivating views of the lake unfold during a 20-minute cable-car journey to the top of 1491m-high Monte Mottarone. Cars depart every 20 minutes in summer. On a clear day you can see Lago Maggiore, Lago d'Orta and Monte Rosa, on the Alpine border with Switzerland.

At the Alpino midstation (803m), more than 1000 Alpine and sub-Alpine species flourish in the Giardino Botanico Alpinia (☑ 0323 3 02 95; www.giardinoalpinia.it; adult/child

ⓘ LAGO MAGGIORE EXPRESS

The **Lago Maggiore Express** (www. lagomaggioreexpress.com; adult/child €32/16) is a picturesque day trip you can do under your own steam. It includes train travel from Arona or Stresa to Domodossola, from where you get the charming Centovalli (Hundred Valleys) train to Locarno in Switzerland and a ferry back to Stresa. The two-day version is better value if you have the time, costing €40/20. Tickets are available from the Navigazione Lago Maggiore ticket booths at each port.

€3/2.50; ⊙9.30am-6pm Apr-Oct), a botanical garden dating from 1934.

The mountain itself offers good **biking trails** as well as **walking** opportunities. **Bicicò** (☑0323 3 03 99; www.bicico.it) rents out mountain bikes at the Stresa cable-car station. Rates include a helmet and road book detailing a 25km panoramic descent (about three hours, and accessible to pretty much anyone who can ride a bike) from the top of Mottarone back to Stresa. A one-way trip with a bike on the cable car to Alpino/Mottarone costs €9/12.

Parco della Villa Pallavicino   ANIMAL PARK
(☑0323 3 15 33; www.parcozoopallavicino.it; adult/child €9/6; ⊙9am-6pm Mar-Oct) Barely 1km southeast of Stresa along the SS33, exotic birds and animals roam relatively freely at the child-friendly Villa Pallavicino. It is home to some 40 species of llama, Sardinian donkeys, flamingos and toucans.

🛏 Sleeping & Eating

There are some 40 campgrounds up and down the lake's western shore; the tourist office has a list. Seasonal closings (including hotels) are generally November to February, but this can vary, so it's always best to check ahead.

Villa Aminta   HOTEL €€€
(☑0323 93 38 18; www.villa-aminta.it; Via Sempione Nord 123; d €295-440; P❄🐾🛜) Stay in turn-of-the-century style at fairy-tale Villa Aminta, which offers picture-perfect views of Isola Bella. Rooms decked out with Murano chandeliers, silk curtains, and acres of gilt and velvet resemble the baroque opulence of the Borromeo Palace. The hotel also has its

own private beach, heated pool, fitness centre and a regular shuttle service into Stresa.

Casa Kinka   B&B €
(☑0323 3 24 43; www.casakinka.it; Strada Comunale Lombartino 21, Magognino; s/d €80/100) A lovely B&B set on the hillside above Stresa, about 6km out of town. The friendly owners have two rooms furnished with period pieces, pictures and comfortable beds. The view from the sunloungers over the lake can't be beaten. To get here follow the road to Mottarone and turn off towards Vedasco.

Hotel Elena   HOTEL €
(☑0323 3 10 43; www.hotelelena.com; Piazza Cadorna 15; s/d €55/80; P) Adjoining a cafe, the old-fashioned Elena is situated slap-bang on Stresa's pedestrian central square. All of the comfortable rooms, with parquet floors, have a balcony, many overlooking the square. Wheelchair access is also possible.

La Piemontese   PIEMONTESE €€
(☑0323 3 03 99; Via Mazzini 25; meals €30; ⊙Wed-Mon) This elegant wood-panelled dining room with its wisteria-covered internal courtyard serves Piemontese cuisine, including specialities such as fried snails, duck confit and lake carp with a sweet-and-sour sauce. There's also an excellent cheeseboard serving top-quality gorgonzola, Robiola and Taleggio.

ⓘ Information

Tourist office (☑0323 3 13 08; www.stresa turismo.it; Piazza Marconi 16; ⊙10am-12.30pm & 3-6.30pm mid-Mar–mid-Oct, shorter weekend hr in winter).

BORROMEAN ISLANDS

The Borromean Gulf forms Lago Maggiore's most beautiful corner, and the Borromean Islands can be reached from various points around the lake, although Stresa and Baveno offer the best access.

ISOLA BELLA

Isola Bella took the name of Carlo III's wife, the *bella* Isabella, in the 17th century, when its centrepiece, **Palazzo Borromeo** (☑0323 3 05 56; www.borromeoturismo.it; adult/child €12.50/5.50; ⊙9am-5.30pm Apr–mid-Oct), was built for the Borromeo family. Construction of the villa and gardens was thought out in such a way that the island would have the appearance of a ship, with the villa at the prow and the gardens dripping down 10 tiered terraces at the rear. Well-known guests have included Napoleon and Josephine in 1797 (you can see the bed they slept in), and Prince Charles and Princess Diana in 1985. A separate €4 ticket gives you access to the **Galleria dei Quadri** (Picture Gallery), a series of halls covered from top to bottom with the Borromeo art collection It includes several old masters including Rubens, Titian, Paolo Veronese and Andrea Mantegna. Elsewhere in the villa are other opulent works of art, such as priceless Flemish tapestries and sculptures by Antonio Canova.

Below ground a 3000-year-old fossilised boat is displayed in the palace grottoes, which themselves are studded with pink marble, lava stone and pebbles from the lake bed. Outside, white peacocks strut the gardens, considered one of the finest examples of baroque Italian garden design.

A combined ticket covering admission to the Borromeo and Madre palaces costs €16.50/7.50 per adult/child.

Elvezia (☎0323 3 00 43; Isola Bella; meals €30-35; ☺Tue-Sun Mar-Oct, Fri-Sun Nov-Feb) is the place for authentic family cooking. Booking ahead is essential for dinner in winter.

ISOLA MADRE

All of Isola Madre is taken up by the fabulous 16th- to 18th-century Palazzo Madre (☎0323 3 05 56; adult/child €10.50/5.50; ☺9am-5.30pm Mar-Oct) and its gardens. The latter are more romantic and intimate than those of Palazzo Borromeo, brimming with azaleas, rhododendrons, camellias and hibiscus and home to white peacocks and vibrant-coloured Chinese pheasants. Palace highlights include a neoclassical puppet theatre designed by a scenographer from Milan's La Scala, and a 'horror' theatre with a cast of devilish marionettes.

ISOLA SUPERIORE (PESCATORI)

Lacking any real sights, tiny 'Fishermen's Island' retains much of its original village atmosphere. Apart from an 11th-century apse and a 16th-century fresco in the Chiesa di San Vittore, there isn't anything to see; hence many visitors make it their port of call for lunch. Restaurants cluster around the boat landing, all serving grilled fish fresh from the lake from around €15.

If you want to stay on the island, the Albergo Verbano (☎0323 3 04 08; www.hotelverbano.it; s €100-120, d €150-185; ☺Mar-Dec) has rooms with wrought-iron bedsteads. The hotel will send its own boat out free for guests once the ferries have stopped running.

North of Stresa, Verbania is the biggest town on the lake and is split into three districts. Verbania Pallanza is the most interesting, with a tight web of lanes in its old centre, while Verbania Intra has a pleasant waterfront and handy car ferries to Laveno on the eastern shore.

The city's highlight is the spectacular grounds of the late-19th-century Villa Taranto (☎0323 40 45 55; www.villataranto.it; Via Vittorio Veneto; adult/child €9.50/5.50; ☺8.30am-6pm Mar-Sep, to 5pm Oct). In 1931, royal archer and Scottish captain Neil McEacharn bought the villa from the Savoy family and started to plant some 20,000 species over a 30-year period. With its rolling hillsides of purple rhododendrons and camellias, acres of tulip flowers and hothouses full of equatorial lilies, it is considered one of Europe's finest botanical gardens. During the last week in April, Settimana del Tulipano, tens of thousands of tulips erupt in magnificent multicoloured bloom. You can walk to the gardens along the lakeside from Pallanza (15 minutes) or take the boat to the Villa Taranto landing stage in front of the villa.

Overlooking Pallanza's cute port and the Isolino San Giovanni, the neo-Gothic Ristorante Milano (☎0323 55 68 15; Corso Zanitelli 2; meals €50-60; ☺Wed-Sun, lunch Mon) sits lakeside amid a shady gravel-and-lawn garden. It serves a contemporary menu including lake perch and char with seasonal vegetables. Caffè Bolongaro (☎0323 50 32 54; Piazza Garibaldi 9; pizzas €4.50-8), on the waterfront in Pallanza, serves good pizza.

Verbania's tourist office (☎0323 50 32 49; www.verbania-turismo.it; Corso Zanitello 6-8; ☺9am-1pm & 3-6pm Mon-Fri) is on the waterfront in Verbania Pallanza and has accommodation details. Backpackers will want to make a beeline for the lake's only hostel, Ostello Verbania (☎0323 50 16 48; www.ostelloverbania.com; Via alle Rose 7; dm incl breakfast €21, s €25-28, d €40-56; ☺reception 9am-1pm & 3-7pm; ℗), which is located in a Liberty-style villa high up behind Verbania Pallanza.

CANNOBIO
POP 5150

Sheltered by a high mountain and sitting at the foot of the Cannobino valley, the medieval hamlet of Cannobio, located 5km from the Swiss border, is the prettiest Italian town on the lake. It is a dreamy place;

the elongated Piazza di Vittorio Emanuele III (closed off at the north end by the Bramante-style Santuario della Pietà) has pastel-hued houses that overlook the pedestrianised flagstone square. Although there are no specific sites in the town, its restaurants and hotels are some of the best on the lake. And on Sunday its lakeside market attracts visitors from Switzerland.

The **tourist office** (☎0323 7 12 12; www.procannobio.it; Via Giovanola 25; ⊗9am-noon & 4-7pm Mon-Sat, 9am-noon Sun & holidays) is just inland off the main lakeside road.

🏄 Activities

Cannobio has an active sailing and windsurfing school, **Tomaso Surf & Sail** (☎0323 7 22 14; www.tomaso.com; Via Nazionale 7), next to a gritty beach at the village's northern end. You can also hire small sailing boats here (€120 per day) and make a nice excursion to the ruined **Castelli della Malpaga**, located on two rocky islets to the south of Cannobio, just offshore from Cannero Riviera. In summer, it is a favourite picnic spot.

Alternatively, you can stay landbound and explore the wild beauty of the Val Cannobino on a bike. The route meanders along the scenic SP75, winding its way 28km, following the surging Torrente Cannobino stream, into the heavily wooded hills west of Cannobio to reach Malesco in Valle Vigezzo. Just 2.5km along the valley from Cannobio, in Sant'Anna, the Torrente Cannobino powerfully forces its way through a narrow gorge known as the **Orrido di Sant'Anna**, crossed at its narrowest part by a Romanesque bridge. A further 7km further up the valley, a steep 3km side road consisting of hairpin bends leads up to the central valley's main town, **Falmenta**. Hire mountain bikes in Cannobio from **Cicli Prezan** (☎0323 7 12 30; www.cicliprezan.it; Viale Vittorio Veneto 9; per hr/day €4/14).

🛏 Sleeping & Eating

Hotel Pironi   HOTEL €€
(☎0323 7 06 24; www.pironihotel.it; Via Marconi 35; s €100-120, d €130-180; ℗) Located in a 15th-century monastery, later the home of the Pironi family, this hotel sits at the heart of the historic centre. Behind its thickset walls are beautifully restored rooms filled with antiques, frescoed vaults, exposed-timber beams and an assortment of tastefully decorated bedrooms, some with lake views.

Lo Scalo   MODERN ITALIAN €€€
(☎0323 7 14 80; www.loscalo.com; Piazza Vittorio Emanuele III 32; meals €60; ⊗Wed-Sun, dinner Tue) For an elegant and romantic dinner, it is hard to beat this lakefront high-flyer. The setting is perfect and the cooking is sophisticated and clean, featuring dishes such as ribbon-thin *tagliolini* pasta with cuttlefish, zucchini and tomato and roast guinea fowl from the mountain valleys.

Grotto Sant'Anna   TICINESE €€
(☎0323 7 06 82; Via Sant'Anna 28; meals €30; ⊗Tue-Sun Apr-Jun & Sep-Oct, daily Jul-Aug) Granite tables and benches furnish this Ticino-style grotto overlooking the Orrido di Sant'Anna. Dishes feature mountain specialities such as oven-roasted lamb.

ARONA
POP 14,555

It was in Arona, 20km south of Stresa, that the son of the Count of Arona and Margherita de' Medici, who would go on to be canonised San Carlo Borromeo (1538–84), was born. His birthplace, the Rocca Borromea castle, was later destroyed in 1801; on Napoleon's orders, its stone was reclaimed and used to pave the Via del Sempione. In 1610 San Carlo was declared a saint and his cousin, Federico, ordered the creation of a *sacro monte* (sacred mountain), with 15 chapels lining a path uphill to a church dedicated to the saint. The church and three of the chapels were built, along with a special extra atop the **Sacro Monte di San Carlo** (admission €4; ⊗9am-12.30pm & 2-6.15pm Apr-Sep, Sat & Sun only Oct, to 4.30pm Sat & Sun Mar & Nov-Dec): a hollow 35m bronze-and-copper statue of the saint, commonly known as the Sancarlone (Big St Charles). It can be climbed, affording a spectacular view from the top (children under six years old are not permitted).

To reach the hill, walk or drive 2km west from Piazza del Popolo, Arona's most charming piazza.

Lago d'Orta

Shrouded by thick, dark-green woodlands, little Lago d'Orta measures 13.4km long and just 2.5km wide. It's separated from its bigger and better-known eastern neighbour, Lago Maggiore, by Monte Mottarone.

SANTA CATERINA DEL SASSO

The monastery of Santa Caterina del Sasso (www.santacaterinadelsasso.com; admission free; ⊙8.30am-noon & 2.30-6pm Apr-Oct, closed weekdays Nov-Feb, to 5pm Mar) is spectacularly located at Leggiuno, clinging to the high rocky face of the southeast shore of Lago Maggiore. It is reached by a spiralling staircase, 267 steps from the road above and 80 steps from the lake below (there is also a lift). Father Roberto Comolli, the only Carmelite monk who still lives here, is the spiritual guide of the seven lay oblates of St Benedict who have made it their home.

The complex comprises three separate sections, connected by a stone pathway, which is protected by a parapet from the sheer drop. Enter via a portico to the southern monastery (originally pilgrim accommodation) with its delightful vegetable garden and then on to the small Gothic monastery, which retains a Dance of Death fresco on its upper level. Finally you reach the church of St Catherine, which incorporates a series of 13th- and 14th-century chapels decorated with frescoes, among them Christ Pantocrator in the Cappella di San Nicola. A few ferries from Stresa dock here between March and October (return €6). Otherwise, by car or bus it's 5.6km south of Laveno (watch for the signs for Leggiuno and then a sign for the convent, 1km in off the main road).

⊙ Sights

The focal point of the lake is the medieval village of Orta San Giulio (population 1170), often referred to simply as Orta. Its cream coloured houses are roofed with thick slate tiles, and the central square, Piazza Motta, is overlooked by the Palazotto, a frescoed 16th-century building borne up on stilts above a small loggia. Just across the water sits Isola San Giulio. The island is dominated at its south end by the 12th-century Basilica di San Giulio (⊙9.30am-6.45pm Tue-Sun, 2-5pm Mon Apr-Sep, to 5pm Oct-Mar), full of frescoes that alone make a trip to the island worthwhile. The church, island and mainland town are named after a Greek evangelist, Giulio, who's said to have rid the island of snakes, dragons and assorted monsters in the late 4th century. The footpath encircling the island makes for a peaceful stroll, hence its popular name of Via del Silenzio. You may find the island's only snack restaurant open on busy weekends. Regular ferries (€2.50 return) and private boats (€4 return) make the five-minute crossing.

For more serenity, head up to Sacro Monte, a hillside dotted with some 20 small chapels dedicated to St Francis of Assisi. The parklands here are a great spot for a picnic: pick up picnic fare at Orta San Giulio's Wednesday market.

🛏 Sleeping & Eating

La Contrada dei Monti   BOUTIQUE HOTEL €€
(✆0322 90 51 14; www.orta.net/lacontradadei monti; Orta San Giulio; s €90, d €110-160; 🕸) Hidden down a medieval lane, this 18th-century palazzo has been brought back to life as a boutique hotel. All the rooms are different, some with exposed-stone walls and timber ceilings, others with a more classical style. In summer, breakfast is served in the peaceful rear courtyard.

Piccolo Hotel Olina   HOTEL €
(✆0322 90 56 56; www.ortainfo.com; Via Olina 40, Orta San Giulio; s/d €75/100; 🕸🅿) Artistically decorated with contemporary prints, bright colours and light-wood furniture, this friendly hotel right in Orta San Giulio's medieval heart is a gem. It serves home-baked breakfasts and its excellent avant-garde restaurant, Ristoro Olina (meals €30-35; ⊙Thu-Tue), is open to nonguests.

TOP CHOICE Caffè Jazz   BAR, RESTAURANT €€
(✆333 923 25 22; Via Olina 13; meals €30-35; ⊙Tue-Sun) Located in a medieval building with a pretty flower-filled central courtyard, Caffè Jazz serves simple but well-executed seasonal dishes and salads. A favourite of weekending urbanites from Milan, the food is contemporary in style and the bar serves a good selection of regional wine by the glass.

Agriturismo Il Cucchiaio di Legno   AGRITURISMO €
(✆0322 90 52 80; Via Prisciola 10, Località Legro; set menus €25; ⊙dinner Thu-Fri, lunch & dinner Sat & Sun) An honest-to-goodness *agriturismo* (farm stay accomodation), just 500 metres beyond the train station.

WORTH A TRIP

AL SORRISO

Located in the tiny village of Soriso, 8km south from Orta San Giulio on the road to Gozzano, the unassuming-looking **Al Sorriso** (☑0322 98 32 28; www.alsorriso.com; Via Roma 18, Soriso; tasting menus €140-160; ☺Wed-Sun, closed 2 weeks Jan & 3 weeks Aug), spelt with a double 'r' because *sorriso* means smile, is one of the few restaurants in Italy with three Michelin stars (awarded in 1982, 1989 and 1998).

Head chef Luisa Marelli has created a stellar reputation for herself even though she is entirely self-taught. She describes her culinary style as Piemontese with Mediterranean and international influences, and given Piedmont's geographic proximity to France, dishes are a delectable fusion of the simple and sophisticated. Take the foie gras, for example, balanced with the sweetest red mountain currants, or the reddish-purple prawns sourced in San Remo, which burst with such flavour that they are served simply *crudo* (raw) with an artichoke salad. Mountain mushrooms also feature prominently on the menu, as do Piemontese cheeses. Top-drawer specialities include Piedmont's rare Fassone beef, the equal of any Kobe cut, and the white Alba truffle.

The wine menu is similarly accomplished, featuring vintages and crus spanning 800 labels. Husband and manager, Angelo Valazza, is happy to fine-tune recommendations and quickly puts diners at ease switching effortlessly between five languages.

For those rendered completely inert after their meal, there are a few rooms above the restaurant (doubles from €200).

❶ Getting There & Around

Orta Miasino train station is 3km from the centre of Orta San Giulio. From Milan there are trains from Stazione Centrale (change at Novara; €5.40, two hours).

Navigazione Lago d'Orta (☑0322 84 48 62) Operates ferry boats to numerous lakeside spots from its landing stage on Piazza Motta, including Isola San Giulio (oneway/return €1.80/2.50), Omegna, Pella and Ronco. A day ticket for unlimited travel anywhere on the lake costs €7.30.

Orta San Giulio's **tourist office** (☑0322 90 51 63; www.comune.ortasangiulio.no.it; Via Panoramica; ☺9am-1pm & 2-6pm Wed-Sun Apr-Oct, 8.30am-1.30pm & 2.30-5.30pm Sat & Sun Nov-Mar) has information on the lake. The more convenient **Pro Loco** (☑0322 9 01 55; Via Bossi 10; ☺11am-1pm & 2-6pm Mon & Wed-Fri, 10am-1pm & 2-6pm Sat & Sun) is in the centre of town.

Lago di Como

Set in the shadow of the snow-covered Rhaetian Alps and hemmed in on both sides by steep, wooded hills, Lake Como (also known as Lake Lario) is the most spectacular and least visited of the three major lakes. Shaped like an upside-down letter Y, its winding shoreline is scattered with villages, including delightful Bellagio, which sits at the centre of the two southern branches on a small promontory. Where the southern and western shores converge is the lake's main town, Como.

❶ Getting There & Around

Boat

Navigazione Lago di Como (☑800 551801; www.navigazionelaghi.it) ferries and hydrofoils criss-cross the lake, departing year-round from the jetty at the northern end of Piazza Cavour. One-way fares range from €2 (Como–Cernobbio) to €10.10 (Como–Colico). For sightseeing, consider the one-day central lake ticket, which covers Bellagio, Varenna, Tremezzo and Cadenabbia (€12).

Car ferries link Cadenabbia on the west shore with Varenna on the eastern shore and Bellagio.

Bus

ASF Autolinee (☑031 247247; www.sptlinea.it) operates regular buses around the lake, which depart from the bus station on Piazza Giacomo Matteotti. Key routes include Como–Colico (€5.20, 1½ hours, three to five daily), via all the villages on the western shore, and Como–Bellagio (€2.80, one hour 10 minutes, hourly).

Car

From Milan, take the A9 motorway and turn off at Monte Olimpino for Como. The SP342 leads east to Lecco and west to Varese. The roads around the lake are terribly scenic, but also windy, narrow and busy in summer.

Train

Trains from Milan's Stazione Centrale and Porta Garibaldi station (40 minutes to one hour) operate hourly services to the main Como San Giovanni station; some continue on to Switzerland. Trains from Milan's Stazione Nord use Como's lakeside Stazione FNM (listed on time-tables as Como Nord Lago). Trains from Milan to Lecco continue north along the eastern shore. If you're going to Bellagio, it is better to continue on the train to Varenna and make the short ferry crossing from there.

COMO
POP 84,800

With its charming historic centre, 12th-century city walls and self-confident air, Como is an elegant and prosperous town. Built on the wealth of the silk industry, it remains Europe's most important producer of silk products; you can buy scarves and ties here for a fraction of the cost elsewhere.

◉ Sights & Activities

Como's lakeside location is stunning and flower-laden; lakeside promenades make for pleasant walks to the various sights. The tourist office has walking and cycling information.

Villa Olmo VILLA, MUSEUM
(☑031 576 169; www.grandimostrecomo.it; Via Cantoni 1; adult/reduced €10/8; ⊗9am-8pm Tue-Thu, 9am-10pm Fri-Sun during exhibitions) Set grandly facing the lake, the creamy facade of neoclassical Villa Olmo is one of Como's landmarks. The extravagant structure was built in 1728 by the Odescalchi family, related to Pope Innocent XI. If there is an art exhibition inside, you'll get to admire the sumptuous Liberty-style interiors. Otherwise, you can enjoy the Italianate and English gardens, which are open all day.

Almost as nice as the gardens is the lakeside stroll from Piazza Cavour. Follow **Passeggiata Lino Gelpi** along the water and you'll pass a series of mansions and villas, including Villa Saporiti and the adjacent Villa Gallia, both now owned by the provincial government.

During summer the **Lido di Villa Olmo** (www.lidovillaolmo.it; Via Cernobbio 2; adult/reduced full day €6/4, half-day €4.50/2.50; ⊗9am-7pm mid-May–Sep), an open-air swimming pool and lakeside bar, is open to the public.

Museo della Seta SILK MUSEUM
(Silk Museum; ☑031 30 31 80; www.museosetacomo.com; Via Castelnuovo 9; adult/reduced €10/7; ⊗9am-noon & 3-6pm Tue-Fri) Housed in the ugly 1970s buildings of the Istituto Tecnico Industriale di Setificio textile school, Como's Silk Museum unravels the town's history, with early dyeing and printing equipment on display.

Funicolare Como-Brunate CABLE CAR
(☑031 30 36 08; www.funicolarecomo.it; Piazza de Gasperi 4; oneway/return €2.80/5.10; ⊗6am-midnight mid-Apr–mid-Sep, to 10.30pm mid-Sep–mid-Apr) Northeast along the waterfront, past Piazza Matteotti and the train station, is the Como–Brunate cable car, which was built in 1894. It takes seven minutes to reach hilltop **Brunate** (720m), a quiet village offering splendid views. In **San Maurizio**, a 30-minute, steep walk (mostly along a stony former mule path) from Brunate's funicular stop, scales 143 steps to the top of the lighthouse, built in 1927 to mark the centenary of Alessandro Volta's death. The Como tourist office can provide a map with various suggested walks around Brunate.

TOP CHOICE Aero Club Como SEAPLANE TOURS
(☑031 574 495; www.aeroclubcomo.com; Via Masia 44) For a touch of Hollywood glamour, take one of the seaplane tours from the Aero Club and buzz Bellagio. The 30-minute flight to Bellagio costs €140 for two people. Longer excursions over Lago Maggiore and Lago Lugano are also possible. During summer you'll need to reserve at least three or four days in advance.

FREE Duomo CATHEDRAL
(Piazza del Duomo; ⊗8am-noon & 3-7pm) Although largely Gothic, elements of baroque, Romanesque and Renaissance styles can be seen in Como's fancy, marble-clad cathedral. Built between the 14th and 18th centuries, it is crowned by a high octagonal dome. Next door is the polychromatic **Broletto**, or medieval town hall.

FREE Basilica di Sant'Abbondio BASILICA
(Via Regina; ⊗8am-6pm Apr-Sep, to 4pm Oct-Mar) About 500m south of the city walls and just beyond Viale Innocenzo XI is this remarkable 11th-century Romanesque basilica. Aside from its proud, high structure and impressive apse with beautiful geometric relief decoration around the exterior windows, the highlight is the fresco series inside the apse. Depicting scenes from the life of Christ, from the Annunciation to his burial, they were restored to their former glory in the 1990s. A university occupies what was once the cloister.

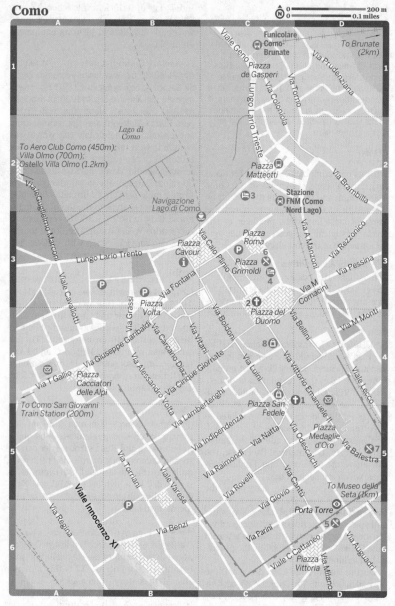

FREE **Basilica di San Fedele** BASILICA
(Piazza San Fedele; ⊙8am-noon & 3.30-7pm)
This 6th-century basilica has been likened
to a clover leaf with its three naves and
three apses. Its 16th-century rose window
and precious 16th- and 17th-century frescoes add to its charm. The facade is a 1914
remake, but the apses are original, featuring some eye-catching sculpture on the east
side.

Como

⊙ Sights

⊨ Sleeping

Albergo Terminus   HOTEL €€€

(☎031 32 91 11; www.hotelterminus-como.it; Lungo Lario Trieste 14; s €145-195, d €150-240; P✲☎) Converted from a 19th-century *palazzo*, the Hotel Terminus retains its turn-of-the-century glamour with art nouveau architectural details, damask upholstery and grand tapestries and swagged curtains. Rooms continue the Liberty theme with soft-hued colours and Como fabrics.

Le Stanze del Lago   APARTMENT €

(☎339 5446515; www.lestanzedellago.com; Via Rodari 6; 2-/4-person apt €80/100; ✲⊞) Five cosy apartments, nicely decked out in a contemporary style with bright colour schemes, make for a good-value deal in the heart of Como. For stays of five days or longer you can use the kitchen too. They all feature double bed, sofa bed, timber ceilings and tiled floor.

Ostello Villa Olmo   HOSTEL €

(☎031 57 38 00; ostellocomo@tin.it; Via di Bellinzona 6; dm incl breakfast €20; ⊙reception 7-10am & 4pm-midnight, closed Dec-Feb; P) In a rambling garden near the lake, Como's HI hostel is two doors up from the heritage-listed villa of the same name. There's a night-time bar (service ceases at 10pm) and meals cost €10. The hostel is 1km from the main train station. Take bus 1, 6 or 11.

✕ Eating

Self-caterers can stock up on fresh fruit and vegetables at Como's **food market**

(⊙8.30am-1pm Tue & Thu, to 7pm Sat) outside Porta Torre.

Trattoria dei Combattenti   TRATTORIA €

(☎031 27 05 74; Via Balestra 5/9; meals €20; ⊙Wed-Mon; ⊞) Housed in the building of the Italian Retired Servicemen's association, this popular trattoria offers indoor seating at communal tables or outdoor seating in a sunny gravel yard. The cooking is simple and tasty, including grilled meats, salad and chunky seafood pasta. The €14 set lunch is good value.

Ristorante Sociale   TRADITIONAL ITALIAN €€

(☎031 26 40 42; www.ristorantesociale.it; Via Rodari 6; meals €25-30; ⊙Wed-Mon) Once attached to the nearby theatre, the Sociale is a local institution. Dine either downstairs in a brick-lined room or upstairs in the dining room with its outsized baroque fireplace and elaborate frescoes. In addition to the menu, which features favourites such as risotto with chicory, there are seasonal dishes of the day.

Crotto del Sergente   TRATTORIA €€

(☎031 28 39 11; www.crottodelsergente.it; Via Crotto del Sergente 13; meals €35; ⊙Thu-Tue, closed Sat lunch) Slow Food–recommended restaurant serving typical Larian dishes in a barrel-vaulted brick dining room not far from the Silk Museum.

ⓐ Shopping

A craft and antiques market fills the piazza in front of the Basilica di San Fedele from 9am to 7pm every Saturday.

A Picci   SILK SHOP

(☎031 26 13 69; Via Vittorio Emanuele II 54; ⊙3-7.30pm Mon, 9am-12.30pm & 3-7.30pm Tue-Sat) Open since 1919, this is the last remaining silk shop in town dedicated to selling Como-designed-and-made silk products such as ties, scarves, throws and sarongs. Products are grouped in price category (starting at €15 for a tie) reflecting the skill and workmanship involved in each piece. Sales assistants are happy to advise on colours and styles. If it's a gift, they'll also wrap it for you.

⊙ Information

Ospedale Sant'Anna (☎031 58 51; Via Napoleona 60) Hospital.

Police station (☎031 31 71; Viale Roosevelt 7)

Post office (Via T Gallio 6; ⊙8.30am-7pm Mon-Fri, 8.30am-12.30pm Sat)

COMO SILK

The art of silk weaving, long a guarded secret in China, only reached Italy in the 13th century. By the 14th century a handful of silk weavers had established themselves on the shores of Lake Como, and the Duchy of Milan promoted the planting of mulberry trees throughout the Po Valley and in the Brianza region. The industry was seasonal and involved the use of farm labour. Women and children would look after the worms day and night, feeding them mulberry leaves from April to October.

When Pietro Boldoni set up the first silk-spinning mills in the early 1500s, Como already had a name for itself as a centre of wool production. When Como was eclipsed by the Maggiore wool mills in the 16th century, Como weavers turned their hand more seriously to silk production. But it wasn't until 1751, when Empress Maria Theresa (1717–80) declared all textiles produced on the lake tax free that the industry really took off.

In 1856 a disease called *pebrina* struck. The disaster virtually wiped out the Italian moth species and raw silk had to be imported from Japan. The subsequent development of synthetic materials in the 1940s coupled with postwar depression (which wiped out key European competitors in Lyon and Krefeld) and the arrival of cheap Chinese imports in world markets put an end to serious silk production in Como.

What remained was Como's skill at refining raw silk, along with artisanal design and printing skills. By the 1950s, Como silk had become the silk of choice for international fashion designers, and today the industry remains dedicated to producing top-quality silk on a small scale.

Out of literally hundreds of silk houses only three big firms remain in Como: Seteria Ratti, Mantero and Canepa. They still employ one-third of the Como population and nowhere in the world is there such a concentration of textile design studios. Italy's only technical textile institute, Como's Istituto Tecnico Industriale di Setificio, founded in 1869, continues to turn out designers, printers and chemical-dyeing experts.

Despite the intense international pressure that the Italian silk industry faces, Moritz Mantero, president of Mantero, is guardedly optimistic about the future: 'The Chinese character for *crisis* has two meanings: risk and opportunity. Manufacturing in the West will increasingly be in high-performance sectors. Companies able to renew themselves constantly in order to be able to meet changes in the market will do well. Como will keep the flag flying through innovation and flexibility'.

Tourist office (☎031 26 97 12; www.lakecomo.org; Piazza Cavour 17; ☺9am-1pm & 2.30-6pm Mon-Sat, 9.30am-1pm Sun Jun-Sep)

BELLAGIO
POP 3050

It's impossible not to be charmed by Bellagio's waterfront of bobbing boats, its maze of steep stone staircases, red-roofed and green-shuttered buildings, dark cypress groves and showy rhododendron-filled gardens. Although summers and weekends teem with visitors, if you turn up on a weekday outside high season, you'll have the little village almost to yourself.

The lavish gardens of Villa Serbelloni (☎031 95 15 55; Via Garibaldi 8; adult/child €8.50/4.50; ☺tours 11.30am & 3.30pm Tue-Sun Apr-Oct), which extend over 20 hectares, cover much of the promontory on which Bellagio sits. Garden visits are by guided tour only; tickets are sold 10 minutes in advance at PromoBellagio.

Garden enthusiasts can also stroll the grounds of neoclassical Villa Melzi D'Eril (☎339 4573838; www.giardinidivillamelzi.it; Lungo Lario Manzoni; adult/child €6/4; ☺9.30am-6.30pm Mar-Nov), built in 1808 for one of Napoleon's associates and coloured by flowering azaleas and rhododendrons in spring. The gardens, which run right down to the lakeside and are adorned with classical statues, were the first English-style park on Lake Como.

For a touch of George Clooney glamour, consider taking a tour in one of Barindelli's (☎338 2110337; www.barindellitaxiboats.com; Piazza Mazzini) slick, mahogany cigarette boats. They offer hour-long sunset tours around the Bellagio headland, which are well worth the €130 for groups of up to 12 people. If you have your own ideas they can also tailor make outings around the lake, or consider making a night of it and using it as a taxi service for a top-class dinner date (€70).

Bellagio's tourist office (☏031 95 02 04; Piazza Mazzini; ⏰9am-12.30pm & 1.30-6pm Mon-Sat, 10am-2pm Sun, shorter afternoon hr in winter), next to the boat landing stage, has information on water sports, mountain biking and other lake activities. Otherwise, PromoBellagio (☏031 95 15 55; www.bellagiolakecomo.com; Piazza della Chiesa 14; ⏰9.30am-1pm Mon, 9.30am-12.30pm & 1.30-4pm Wed-Fri), in the basement of an 11th-century watchtower, also has information.

🛏 Sleeping & Eating

For such a prime spot, there are a surprising number of affordable places to sleep and eat.

TOP CHOICE Albergo Silvio   HOTEL, RESTAURANT €€

(☏031 95 03 22; www.bellagiosilvio.com; Via Carcano 12; d €80-160; ⏰Mar–mid-Nov & Christmas week; P❄🅿🛜🏊) Located above the small fishing hamlet of Loppia, a short walk from the centre of Bellagio through the gorgeous Villa Melzi gardens, this family-run hotel is Bellagio's best-value accommodation. From the contemporary lakefront rooms you look out over the 10th-century church of Santa Maria, the gardens of Villa Melzi and across to Villa Carlotta on the western shore. The hotel restaurant with its outdoor terrace is also wellregarded locally (meals €25 to €40). The hotel has also recently obtained the lease for Bellagio's public *lido* (beach) so hotel guests have free use of the pool, complete with diving board over the lake.

Residence La Limonera   APARTMENT €

(☏031 95 21 24; www.residencelalimonera.com; Via Bellosio 2; studios €70-100, 4-person apt €85-130; @🖥) Located in the upper part of town, this elegant villa in an old lemon grove has been divided into 11 spacious self-catering apartments. Apartments range from studios to larger four-person apartments and all are furnished with tiled floors and wrought-iron beds.

TOP CHOICE Ittiturismo Da Abate   FISH €€

(☏338 584 3814; www.ittiturismodaabate.it; Frazione Villa 4, Lezzeno; meals €25-35; ⏰dinner Tue-Sun, lunch Sun; 🖥) Da Abate is located just 8km south of Bellagio in the hamlet of Lezzeno. Run by Claudio and Giuseppe, it is one of the few fish farms left on the lake and is Slow Food recommended. Sample traditional fish specialities such as *lavarello* in balsamic vinegar, linguine with perch and black olives and the robust-flavoured *missoltino* (fish dried in salt and bay leaves).

Also recommended:

Hotel Florence   HOTEL €€

(☏031 95 03 42; www.hotelflorencebellagio.it; Piazza Mazzini 46; s €120, d €140-200; ⏰Apr-Oct; @) A luxurious Liberty-style hotel in the centre of the village.

Bar Rossi   CAFE, BAR €

(Piazza Mazzini 22-24; snacks €2-5) Have at least one coffee in art nouveau Bar Rossi.

AROUND BELLAGIO

The mountainous territory between Como and Lecco in the south and Bellagio in the north is called the Triangolo Lariano, or the Lake Lario Triangle. Lakeside villages Torno, Careno and Lezzeno line the Como–Bellagio road and hiking trails abound.

The classic trail is known as the Dorsale (Ridge) and zigzags for 31km across the interior of the 'triangle' from the Brunate funicular station in Como to Bellagio. The standard trail, which follows old mule tracks, takes about 12 hours and is usually done in two stages. It passes along rivers and around mountain peaks, skirting towns until you reach San Giovanni, a fraction southwest of Bellagio. A more challenging route is the Dorsale Creste trail, which follows a series of mountain crests. Several *rifugi* (mountain huts) are dotted along the way and you'll find a couple of accommodation options at Pian del Tivano, roughly halfway along the trail.

Another option is to walk the 32km Strada Regia (Royal Way), a partly stone-paved path that links Como to Bellagio by way of several villages such as Torno and Lezzeno. The easiest stretch connects Torno and Pognana Lario (about five hours), while the stage from Pognana to Lezzeno via Nesso branches into mountainous backcountry. Ask at the Como tourist office for the fine *Carta dei Sentieri* (Trail Map, 1:25,000).

WESTERN SHORE

The western shore gets the most sunshine on the lake. For this reason it's lined with lavish villas, where high-fliers from football players to Arab sheiks and film stars reside. The shore stretches 75km from Como north to Sorico; from here you can continue north into Switzerland or east into Trentino–Alto Adige.

CERNOBBIO TO LENNO

Ocean's 11 may have been shot at Bellagio's Vegas namesake, but scenes from *Ocean's 12* were filmed in the Lago di Como village of Cernobbio, at the 19th-century Villa

Erba (Largo Luchino Visconti; closed to the public). Cernobbio is also home to the lake's most magnificent hotel, Villa d'Este (www.villadeste.it). But if you don't have a cool €800 to €950 to spend a night you won't get a glimpse of its palatial interiors.

If you're driving, follow the lower lakeside road (Via Regina Vecchia) north from Cernobbio, which skirts the lake shore past a fabulous row of 19th-century villas (all private) around Moltrasio. A few kilometres north is the villa-lined hamlet of Laglio, home to *Ocean's* star George Clooney (he owns Villa Oleandra). In both places you can stop and wander down the cobbled lanes to the lake.

Finally, in Lenno, Villa Balbianello (☎0344 5 61 10; www.fondoambiente.it; Via Comoedia 5, Località Balbianello; villa & gardens adult/child €12/7, gardens only adult/child €6/3; ☺10am-6pm Tue & Thu-Sun mid-Mar–mid-Nov) takes the prize for the lake's most dramatically situated gardens, dripping down the sides of the high promontory like sauce off a melting ice cream. Scenes from *Star Wars: Episode II* and 2006's James Bond remake, *Casino Royale*, were shot here. The villa itself was built by Cardinal Angelo Durini in 1787. Now it houses a curious collector's museum of all sorts. If you want to see inside, you must join a guided tour (generally in Italian) by 4.15pm. Visitors are only allowed to walk the 1km from the Lenno landing stage to the estate on Tuesday and at weekends; other days, you have to take a taxi boat (☎333 4103854; return €6) from Lenno.

TREMEZZO
POP 1290

Tremezzo is high on everyone's list for a visit to the 17th-century Villa Carlotta (☎0344 4 04 05; www.villacarlotta.it; Riva Garibaldi; adult/reduced €8.50/4.50; ☺9am-6pm Easter-Sep, 10am-4pm mid-Mar–Easter & Oct–mid-Nov), whose botanic gardens are filled with orange trees knitted into pergolas, and some of Europe's finest rhododendrons, azaleas and camellias. The villa, which is strung with paintings and fine alabaster-white sculptures (especially those by Antonio Canova) and tapestries, takes its name from the Prussian princess who was given the palace in 1847 as a wedding present from her mother.

Tremezzo's tourist office (☎0344 4 04 93; Via Statale Regina; ☺9am-noon & 3.30-6.30pm Wed-Mon Apr-Oct) adjoins the boat jetty.

TOP CHOICE
Al Veluu   RESTAURANT, HOTEL €€€

(☎0344 4 05 10; alveluu.com; Via Rogaro 11; meals €50-70; ☺Wed-Mon; 🏊) The other highlight of Tremezzo is this excellent restaurant, situated on the steep hillside above the lake with panoramic views from its terrace. The home-cooked dishes are prepared with great pride and reflect the seasonal produce of both the mountains and the lake. Expect butter-soft, milk-fed kid with rosemary at Easter or wild asparagus and polenta. The terrace is a great place to view the Ferragosto fireworks on 15 August and in winter the log fire is lit in the dining room. Upstairs there are two equally comfortable suites (€130 to €200) each sleeping up to four people. The hotel offers a pick-up from the dock.

CADENABBIA & MENAGGIO

North of Tremezzo, Cadenabbia is a key transport hub and car ferries depart from here to the eastern shore. Given its lack of sights it offers some good-value accommodation, such as the unpretentious Alberghetto della Marianna (☎0344 4 30 95; www.la-marianna.com; Via Regina 57, Cadenabbia di Griante; s €65, €80-95; ☺Wed-Mon; ❄), which has homely rooms with brass beds, parquet floors and small balconies. The attached restaurant, La Cucina di Marianna (☎0344 4 31 11; menus €30-45; ☺Wed-Sun), is also a good place to eat.

A further 3km north, Menaggio (population 3260) has a cute cobbled centre and a central square lined with cafes, which is perfect for lake-gazing. Menaggio is the jumping-off point for Lago di Piano in the Val Menaggio, a remote valley connecting Lago di Como with Lago di Lugano, which straddles the Italian–Swiss border to the west.

Just 100m uphill from Menaggio's ferry wharf, its hostel, Ostello La Primula (☎0344 3 23 56; www.lakecomohostel.com; Via IV Novembre 106; dm incl breakfast €17; ☺reception 8-10am & 4pm-midnight mid-Mar–early Nov; @), has lake views and a restaurant (mains €14). You can also rent bikes and kayaks (€14.50 per day).

Menaggio's tourist office (☎0344 3 29 24; www.menaggio.com; Piazza Garibaldi 3; ☺9am-12.30pm & 2.30-6pm Apr-Oct, closed Wed & Sun Nov-Mar) has brochures on walking and biking.

ALTO LARIO

Beyond Menaggio, the northern stretch of the lake is known as the Alto Lario (Upper Lario). It is far less touristed than the southern shores of the lake and is wonderfully scenic. At Rezzonico, an extension of Santa Maria, is a quiet pebble beach lined with wooden fishingfolk's seats.

The last significant town on the western shore of the Alto Lario is Gravedona (population 2750). Along with Domaso and Dongo further north, it is popular with water sports enthusiasts. Comolakeboats (☑333 4014995; www.comolakeboats.it; Via Antica Regina 26, Domaso) hires out zodiacs (€80 for two hours) and organises waterskiing and wakeboarding.

EASTERN SHORE

Lake Como's eastern shore has a wilder feel to it, but being the less sunny side of the lake it is little touristed. The main town is Lecco (pop 47,800), with a shady, winding waterfront, but little of specific interest; otherwise the key attraction is pretty Varenna situated a short hop across the water from Bellagio. If driving, skip the motorway and meander along the SS36 from Colico south to Lecco.

ABBAZIA DI PIONA

At the northern end of the lake, 3km south of Colico, a side road leads 2km from the SP72 to the Cistercian abbey of Piona (☑0341 94 03 31; www.cistercensi.info/piona; ⊙7am-7pm), set scenically on a promontory stretching out into the lake. The present church is Romanesque, but the highlight (apart from the setting) is the 13th-century cloister.

VARENNA
POP 825

Villa-studded Varenna sits across the lake from Bellagio and vies with its better-known neighbour for the title of prettiest village on the lake. Its pastel-coloured houses rise steeply up the hillside and its gardens and walkways burst with flowers and birdsong. A series of lanes-cum-stairways slither down the hill to the water's edge. About halfway down is Varenna's main street, the pedesterianised Via XX Settembre. Higher up, the SP72 passes the town's two most luxurious villas and the cobbled main square, Piazza San Giorgio, before skooting on north.

Those arriving by ferry land at Piazzale Martiri della Libertà. From here, a 15- to 20-minute stroll follows a flower-laden shoreline pathway up to Piazza San Giovanni and the town's two main attractions, the gardens of Villa Cipressi (☑0341 83 01 13; www.hotelvillacipressi.it; Via IV Novembre 22; adult/child €3/1.50; ⊙9am-7pm Mar-Oct), surround-

ing a luxury hotel (singles €110 to €140, doubles €140 to €190), and, 100m further south, Villa Monastero (☑0341 29 54 50; www.villamonastero.eu; Via IV Novembre; adult/reduced €4/2; ⊙gardens 9am-7pm Mon-Thu, 9am-2pm Fri, house & gardens 2-7pm Fri, 9am-7pm Sat & Sun), a former convent turned into a vast residence by the Mornico family in the 17th century. In both cases, you can stroll through the verdant gardens admiring magnolias, camellias and exotic yuccas. At Villa Monastero you can also wander around the palatial rooms.

From the north end of Varenna (Olivedo), you can make a steep half-hour hike up an old mule path (or drive 3km on the SP65) to the hillside hamlet of Vezio. It is dominated by the 13th-century Castello di Vezio (www.castellodivezio.it; admission €4; ⊙10am-6pm), once part of a chain of early-warning medieval watchtowers. From here you can gaze down on the terracotta rooftops of Varenna and at 4.30pm they host a falconry display.

The top sleeping option in Varenna is Albergo del Sole (☑0341 81 52 18; www.albergodelsole.lc.it; Piazza San Giorgio 21; s €70-85, d €105-120, tr €124-40; ❈✿), a blue-shuttered guesthouse offering half-a-dozen whitewashed rooms with polished wooden floors inspired by the lake's steamboats. There's also a good on-site restaurant.

Other eating choices include Cavallino (☑0341 81 52 19; www.cavallino-varenna.it; Piazza Martiri della Libertà; meals €25-35; ⊙Thu-Tue), where you can sit on Varenna's attractive quayside watching the ferries dock while enjoying fresh seafood dishes, caught by fisherman-owner Giordano Valentini. *Primi* (first courses) consist of succulent lake perch, *lavarello* pâté and homemade *missoltini*. Also homemade is the creamy *risotto mantecato* (mixed with cheese to create the 'creamy' effect). With advance booking you can take a short fishing trip with the owner before coming back to eat your catch.

Also recommended is Vecchia Varenna (☑0341 83 07 93; www.vecchiavarenna.it; Contrada Scoscesa 10; meals €40-45; ⊙Tue-Sun Feb-Dec), which serves faintly nouvelle cuisine on a lakeside terrace.

Varenna's tourist office (☑0341 814 009; www.varennaitaly.com; Via per Esino 3; ⊙10am-12.30pm & 3-5.30pm Mon-Fri, 10am-12.30pm Sat), managed by I Viaggi del Tivano, offers information on the lake's entire eastern shore.

VALTELLINA

From the north end of Lake Como, the Valtellina region cuts a broad swath along the course of the Adda river, between the Swiss mountain frontier to the north and the Alps Orobie to the south. Much of the steep, northern flank is carpeted with vineyards, mostly of the Nebbiolo grape variety, that produce such coveted wines as Sforzato (Sfurzat). Two points of reference are Ponte in Valtellina, 8km east of Sondrio, and Teglio, 8km further east.

The prettiest town along the valley floor is Tirano, terminus for trains arriving from Milan (two hours) via Lake Como and others arriving from Switzerland. At its east end is the quiet old town, with winding lanes next to the gushing Adda.

Located in the heart of the Valtellina's finest vineyards in Bianzone, just north of Teglio, is Altavilla (☑0342 72 03 55; www.altavilla.info; Via ai Monti 46, Bianzone; meals €30; ☺Tue-Sun, daily Aug; Ⓟ), Anna Bertola's charming Alpine chalet and restaurant, one of the gastronomic treats of the region. Expect expert wine recommendations to accompany traditional mountain dishes such as *sciàtt* (buckwheat pancakes stuffed with Bitto cheese) and *pizzocheri* buckwheat pasta. The artisanal salami, mountain venison and aged Bitto cheese are particular highlights, as is the 500-label wine list. Reserve a room (singles €25 to €42, doubles €42 to €68) for the night so you can sleep it off afterwards.

Another highly recommended eatery is Osteria del Crotto (☑0342 61 48 00; www.osteriadelcrotto.it; Via Pedemontana 22, Morbegno; meals €25-35), which serves a whole slew of Slow Food–authenticated products such as *violino di capra della Valchiavenna* (literally 'violin goat of the Valchiavenna'), a traditional salami made from the shank, which is sliced by resting it on the shoulder and shaving it as a violin player moves his bow.

If you're lucky enough to be here on the last weekend in May, you can tour the major wine producers who open their doors for the Cantine Aperte (Open House). The main tourist office (☑0342 21 59 21; www.valtellina.it; Corso Vittorio Veneto 28, Sondrio; ☺9am-12.30 & 2.30-6pm Mon-Fri, 9am-12.30pm Sat) in the transport hub of Sondrio has details of participants.

Lago d'Iseo

Cradled in a deep glacial valley, less than 50km from both Bergamo and Brescia, Lake Iseo (aka Sebino) is one of the least known of the Lombard lakes. Shut in by soaring mountains, it is a magnificent sight. To the lake's north stretches the Valle Camonica, renown for its Stone Age rock carvings. To the south stretches the rolling Franciacorta wine country, and to the west the picture-book-pretty Lake Endine.

With the exception of the south shore, the road closely hugs the water on its circuit around the lake and is especially dramatic south of Lovere.

☉ Sights & Activities

At the lake's southwest edge, the sun sets directly in front of the lakefront promenade in Iseo (population 9200). It's a pleasant spot with a string of squares just behind the waterfront and a public beach where you can hire canoes and pedalo. Iseobike (☑340 3962095; www.iseobike.com;

Via Colombera 2; ☺9.30am-12.15pm & 2.30-7pm May-Aug, Fri-Sun Sep-Apr) can put together tailor-made cycling tours.

Directly west of Iseo is Sarnico (pop 6540), with its lovely Liberty villas, many of which were designed by Giuseppe Sommaruga. Among them, his lakeside Villa Faccanoni (Via Veneto) is the most outstanding. The heart of the old town, known as La Contrada, straggles back from the Oglio river. It is perfect for a wander along the riverside after a morning coffee.

North of Iseo, rising out of the lake, Monte Isola (population 1800), Europe's largest lake island at 4.28 sq km, is easily the lake's most striking feature. Francesco Sforza granted the islanders special fishing rights in the 15th century and the island is still dotted with fishing villages. From Carzano, in the northeast (where boats land; €4 from Sale Marasino), you can climb rough stairs to the summit (599m). A 15km trail allows you to walk or cycle around the island (no cars are permitted).

On the northwest tip of the lake, the port town of **Lovere** (population 5470) is a working harbour with a higgledy-piggledy old centre and a wealth of walking trails in the hills behind it. At the waterfront you'll find the **Accademia Tadini** (☎035 96 27 80; www. accademiatadini.it; Via Tadini 40; adult/reduced €7/5; ⏰3-7pm Tue-Sat, 10am-noon & 3-7pm Sun & holidays), home to a considerable art collection with works by Jacopo Bellini, Giambattista Tiepolo and Antonio Canova. Short drives out of Lovere to nearby villages like **Bossico** and **Esmate** bring you to marvellous lookout points high above the lake.

🛏 Sleeping

Hotel Milano   HOTEL €
(☎030 98 04 49; www.hotelmilano.info; Lungolargo Marconi 4, Iseo; s €44-50, d €70-90; ❄@🛜) This sunny yellow waterfront hotel is one of only two hotels in the centre of Iseo. Make sure to reserve a lake-view room, giving yourself a front-row seat for sunset behind the mountains.

Ostello del Porto   HOSTEL €
(☎035 98 35 29; http://digilander.libero.it/ostellodelporto/; Via Paglia 70; dm/s/d €18/35/50; ⏰mid-Mar-Oct; P@) Lovere's hostel.

Campeggio Monte Isola   CAMPGROUND €
(☎030 982 52 21; Via Croce 144; camping per person & tent €10) Monte Isola's campground is open year-round.

ℹ Information

Iseo Tourist Office (☎030 98 02 09; www. agenzialagoiseofranciacorta.it; Lungolago Marconi 2; ⏰10am-12.30pm & 3.30-6.30pm Easter-Sep, 10am-12.30pm & 3-6pm Mon-Fri, 10am-12.30pm Sat Oct-Easter) Has information on hiking and a list of campgrounds.

Sarnico Pro Loco (☎035 4 20 80; www.prolocosarnico.it; Via Lantieri 6; ⏰9.30am-12.30pm & 3-6.30pm Tue-Sat, 9.30am-12.30pm Sun)

Monte Isola (www.monteisola.com)

ℹ Getting There & Around

SAB (☎035 28 90 00; www.sab-autoservizi. it, in Italian) Runs buses between Sarnico and Bergamo (€2.90, 50 minutes).

Iseo Train Station Links Iseo with Brescia (€2.80, 30 minutes, hourly), where you can connect to Bergamo.

Navigazione sul Lago d'Iseo (☎035 97 14 83; www.navigazionelagoiseo.it) Operates up to eight ferries daily between Sarnico, Iseo, Monte Isola, Lovere and Pisogne. Single fares range from €2 to €5.80. In winter there are reduced services.

Lago di Garda

Poets and politicians, divas and dictators, they've all been drawn to Lake Garda. At 370 sq km it is the largest of the Italian lakes, straddling the border between Lombardy and the Veneto, with soaring mountains to the north and softer hills to the south.

WINE ROADS

South of Lago d'Iseo and stretching towards Brescia are the flourishing vineyards of the **Franciacorta wine region** (www.stradadelfranciacorta.it). It is perfect cycling country, with no high-rises and plenty of villages to explore. In the Middle Ages, monks living in the area were granted privileges to work the land. These 'franchises', or *franchae curtes*, were exempt from taxes, from whence originated the name. The Iseo and Brescia tourist offices can provide brochures and help book visits to wineries (essential on weekdays).

You can pick up the wine route at **Paràtico**, which lies at the region's northwestern tip. The quaint villages of **Nigoline Bonomelli**, **Colombaro**, **Timoline** and **Borgonato** form the heart of the comune of Corte Franca and are home to most of the prestigious winemakers in the area. Just to the north of them is **Provaglio d'Iseo**, the location of the 11th-century **Monastero San Pietro in Lamosa** (www.sanpietroinlamosa.org), which was founded by the Cluniac monks who first started to cultivate the region.

If you're driving through the region, book yourself in to the **Ristorante Gualtiero Marchesi** (www.marchesi.it; meals €150-200; ⏰Tue-Sat, lunch Sun), set in the luxurious country estate of the L'Albereta Hotel in Erbusco, and presided over by Gualtiero Marchesi, one of the best-known names in contemporary Italian dining.

The route ends at **Rodengo-Saiano** where you'll find another impressive monastic complex, the **Abbazia di San Nicola** (www.benedettiniabbaziaolivetana.org).

Vineyards, olive groves and citrus orchards range up the slopes, while villages sit around a string of natural harbours. In the south-west corner, Desenzano del Garda is known as the *porta del lago* (gateway to the lake), with good transport connections.

Garda is the most developed of the lakes and, despite a plethora of accommodation, booking ahead is advised.

ℹ Getting There & Around

Boat

Navigazione sul Lago di Garda (☏800 551801; www.navigazionelaghi.it, in Italian; Piazza Matteotti 2, Desenzano del Garda) Operates passenger ferries year-round. A one-day ticket allowing unlimited travel costs €26.40/13.50 (adult/child).

Motorists can cross the lake using the car ferry between Toscolano-Maderno and Torri del Benaco, or seasonally between Limone and Malcesine.

Bus

APTV (☏045 805 78 11; www.aptv.it) Connects Desenzano del Garda train station with Riva del Garda (two hours, up to six daily). Peschiera del Garda train station is on the Riva del Garda–Malcesine–Garda–Verona APTV bus route, with hourly buses to both Riva (€3.90, one hour 40 minutes) and Verona (€2.90, 30 minutes).

Società Italiana Autoservizi (SIA; ☏030 377 42 37; www.sia-autoservizi.it) Connects Riva del Garda with Brescia (€5.50, two hours) and Milan (3¾ hours, three daily).

Trentino Trasporti (☏0461 821 000; www.ttesercizio.it) Connects Riva del Garda with Trento (€4, 1¾ hours).

Car

Lake Garda's ferry network and region-wide rail links mean you can go car-free, only getting behind the wheel for forays into the hills. In summer the lake's perimeter road is best avoided due to heavy traffic.

Train

The two train stations serving the lake, Desenzano del Garda and Peschiera del Garda, are on the Milan–Venice train line.

SIRMIONE

POP 8050

Sitting on an impossibly narrow peninsula on the southern shore, Sirmione is Garda's most picturesque village. Over the centuries it has attracted the likes of Roman poet Catullus and Maria Callas, and today thousands follow in their footsteps.

The **tourist office** (☏030 91 61 14; Viale Marconi 6; ☉9am-8pm Easter-Oct, 9am-12.30pm & 3-6pm Mon-Fri, 9am-12.30pm Sat Nov-Easter) adjoins the bus station. Motorised vehicles are banned beyond this point, except for those with a hotel booking.

◉ Sights & Activities

From the jetty near the castle, all sorts of vessels will make any manner of trip around the lake – at a price – and an array of water activities can be arranged.

Grotte di Catullo　　　　　ROMAN VILLA
(☏030 91 61 57; adult/reduced €4/2; ☉8.30am-7.30pm Tue-Sat, 9am-2pm Sun Mar-Oct, 8.30am-2pm Tue-Sun Nov-Mar, museum open to 7.30pm Tue-Sat) Occupying a 2-hectare chunk of Sirmione's northern tip, this ruined Roman villa is a picturesque complex of teetering stone arches and tumbledown walls. It's the largest domestic villa unearthed in northern Italy and wandering the olive groves on its terraced hillside opens up appealing views. The villa dates from the Augustan era (late 1st century BC) and despite the name there is no evidence that Catullus actually lived here.

Terme di Sirmione　　　　　THERMAL SPA
(☏030 916 09 44; www.termedisirmione.com; Piazza Don Angelo Piatti; pools €19-49, treatments from €30; ☉2-10pm Mon, 10am-10pm Tue-Sun Mar-Dec) Sirmione is blessed with a series of off-shore thermal springs that pump out water at a natural 37°C. They were discovered in the late 1800s. At the Aquaria spa you can indulge in an array of treatments, from remineralising mud sessions (€50) to ayurvedic massages (€80). Or opt for five hours wallowing in the two thermal pools – the outdoor one is set right beside the lake. Treatments have to be booked in advance but for the pools just turn up with your swimsuit (towels provided).

🍴 Sleeping & Eating

An inordinate number of hotels are crammed into Sirmione, many of which close from the end of October to March. Four campgrounds lie near the town and the tourist office can advise on others around the lake.

Hotel Pace　　　　　HOTEL €€
(☏030 990 58 77; www.pacesirmione.it; Piazza Porto Valentino 5; d €100-125; P@✳) Located lakeside, the baby-pink Hotel Pace has been run by the Barelli family for the last 25 years. James Joyce and Ezra Pound stayed

LAKE GARDA'S AMUSEMENT PARKS

The lake's lower eastern shore is home to larger-than-life dinosaurs, pirate ships, roller coasters and a dolphinarium at the kid-oriented **Gardaland** (☑045 644 97 77; www.gardaland.it; adult/child €36/29; ☉9am-11pm mid-Jun–mid-Sep, 10am-6pm Apr–mid-Jun & last 2 weeks Sep, 10am-6pm Sat & Sun Oct, late Dec & early Jan).

To the north, **CanevaWorld** (☑045 696 99 00; www.canevaworld.it; Via Fossalta 1) has two theme parks. **Aquaparadise** (adult/child €24/19; ☉10am-7pm Jul & Aug, 10am-6pm mid-May–Jun & Sep) has lots of exhilarating water slides, while **Movieland** (adult/child €24/19; ☉10am-6pm Easter-Jun, Sep & weekends Oct, 10am-7pm Jul & Aug) has stunt-packed action shows. Exact opening times may vary slightly throughout the year, so check the website for details.

Free buses shuttle visitors the 2km to both parks to/from the Peschiera del Garda train station.

here during the '30s and the hotel retains its English-country style with buff leather armchairs, art nouveau decor and country garden. The restaurant is Slow Food recommended and features a deck that juts out over the water.

Hotel Marconi
HOTEL €€

(☑030 91 60 07; www.hotelmarconi.net; Via Vittorio Emanuele II 51; s €45-75, d €75-125; [P][@][✱]) Even if you're someone who takes nothing more than coffee for breakfast, the incredible spread of homemade cakes, tarts and pies at this elegant family-run hotel is a feast for the eyes. The restrained rooms are all subtle peach shades and crisp fabrics and there's a lakeside deck complete with blue-and-white-striped umbrellas.

Ristorante La Rucola
TRADITIONAL ITALIAN €€€

(☑030 91 63 26; www.ristorantelarucola.it; Vicolo Strentelle 7; meals €60-75; ☉Fri-Wed) Sirmione's most elegant restaurant combines a 1970s nightclub vibe (upholstered, low-backed lounge chairs) with farmhouse chic. The food, however, is classic lake cooking featuring sea bass, prawns and numerous seasonal risottos.

Also recommended:

Camping Sirmione
CAMPGROUND €

(☑030 91 90 45; www.camping-sirmione.com; Via Sirmioncino 9, Colombane; camping 2 people, car & tent €36; ☉Mar-Oct; [P][⛵]) A well-kept campground at the base of the peninsula.

La Fiasca
TRATTORIA €€

(☑030 990 61 11; Via Santa Maria Maggiore; meals €30; ☉Thu-Tue) An authentic trattoria serving dishes with gusty flavours such as pappardelle with boar *ragù* (meat and tomato sauce).

DESENZANO DEL GARDA
POP 26,900

An easygoing commuter town 9km southwest of Sirmione, Desenzano del Garda is known as the 'gateway to the lake'. It's not as pretty as some of its counterparts, but its ancient harbour, broad promenades and vibrant Piazza Matteotti make for pleasant wanderings. It is also a hub for nightlife in the high summer.

Desenzano's best-known site is its remarkably well-preserved Roman mosaics at the **Roman Villa** (☑030 914 3547; Via Crocifisso 2; adult/reduced €2/1; ☉8.30am-7pm Mar-Oct, to 5pm Oct-Feb). Built 2000 years ago, the villa was remodelled in the 2nd century, with most of the mosaics being added in the 4th century. Wooden walkways lead directly over vivid scenes of chariot-riding, grape-gathering cherubs. Stroll through the remains of the luxurious *triclinium* (dining room), past semicircular baths to a *cubiculum* (bedroom), before ending at a vestibule that opened towards the lake.

For more information on the town, consult the main **tourist office** (☑030 914 15 10; Via Porto Vecchio 34; ☉9am-12pm & 3-6pm Mon-Sat).

SALÒ
POP 10,700

Wedged between the lake and precipitous mountains, Salò exudes an air of grandeur. Its long waterfront promenade is lined with ornate buildings and palm trees, while the graceful bell tower of its 15th-century cathedral overlooks atmospheric lanes.

In 1943 Salò was named the capital of the Social Republic of Italy as part of Mussolini and Hitler's last-ditch efforts to organise Italian Fascism in the face of advancing allied forces. This episode, known as the Republic of Salò, saw more than 16 public and private

TASTING OLIVE OIL

Lake Garda's microclimate resembles the Mediterranean's, ensuring ideal olive-growing conditions. The lake's banks produce a tiny 1% of Italy's olive oil, but the product is renowned for being light, soft and sweet. Some 15 varieties of olive are grown here; the local black fruit produces subtler tasting oil, while the green olives are spicier.

Frantoio Montecroce (☏030 991 15 04; www.frantoiomontecroce.it; Viale Ettore Andreis 84; admission free; ☉8am-noon & 3-7pm Mon-Sat), set in the hills above Desenzano, is the perfect place for a tutored tasting in the lake's oil. The same family has been harvesting olives for four generations and their oils have won numerous prestigious prices. The mill's granite wheels, gleaming machines and stainless steel vats give a real insight into the modern production process, while family members provide tasting tips.

buildings in the town commandeered and turned into Mussolini's ministeries and offices. Strolling between the sites is a surreal tour of the dictator's doomed ministate. The tourist office has an English-language map and booklet featuring significant locations.

It's not often that you get to explore a private island in the company of its aristocratic owners, but you can at the tiny, comma-shaped Isola del Garda (☏328 384 92 26; www.isoladelgarda.com; tour incl boat ride €24-30; ☉Apr-Oct) just off Salò. The sumptuous neo-Gothic Venetian villa is owned by Contessa Cavazza, and your visit is likely to be guided by a member of her family. The two-hour tour takes in a clutch of opulent rooms, some with a disarming real-life family feel. At the end of the trip you can sample oil, wine and cheese from the family estates.

Boats depart from Salò, Gardone Riviera, Garda and Sirmione, but they only leave each location once or twice a week.

GARDONE RIVIERA
POP 2725

Gardone's glory days were in the late 19th and early 20th centuries, and today the resort's opulent villas and ornate architecture make it one of the lake's most elegant holiday spots. About 12km north of Gardone is Gargnano (population 3050), a tiny harbour that fills with million-dollar yachts come September when sailing fans gather for the Centomiglia, the lake's most prestigious sailing regatta.

The tourist office (☏0365 374 87 36; Corso della Repubblica 8; ☉9am-12.30pm & 2.30-6pm Mon-Sat) stocks information on activities.

⊙ Sights

Il Vittoriale degli Italiani   MUSEUM
(☏0365 29 65 11; www.vittoriale.it; Piazza Vittoriale; gardens & museums adult/reduced €16/12;

⊙grounds 8.30am-8pm Apr-Sep, to 5pm Oct-Mar, museums to 7pm Apr-Sep, 9am-1pm & 2-5pm Oct-Mar) Poet, soldier, hypochondriac and proto-Fascist, Gabriele d'Annunzio (1863–1938) defies easy definition, as does his estate, Il Vittoriale. Bombastic, extravagant and unsettling, it's home to every architectural and decorative excess and the decor certainly sheds light on the man.

He retreated to Gardone in 1922, claiming that he wanted to escape the world that made him sick. In his main house, the **Prioria**, black velvet drapes line cluttered, gloomy rooms (he was allergic to sunlight) crammed with classical figurines, leopard skins, leather-bound books and masses of cushions and china. Highlights include the bronze tortoise (cast from one that died from overeating) and d'Annunzio's study with its very low lintel – designed so visitors would have to bow as they entered. Visits are by guided tour only (in Italian).

Giardino Botanico Fondazione
André Heller   SCULPTURE PARK
(☏336 410877; www.hellergarden.com; Via Roma 2; adult/child €9/5; ☉9am-7pm Mar-Oct) This compact flower-filled oasis is a delight for plant lovers and art enthusiasts alike. Laid out in 1900, the gardens were redesigned in the late 1990s by multimedia artist André Heller. Tiny paths wind through different climate zones, from central American plains to African savannah. Hidden among the greenery are 30 pieces of contemporary sculpture.

🛏 Sleeping & Eating

Locanda Agli Angeli   HOTEL €€
(☏0365 2 09 91; www.agliangeli.com; Via Dosso 7; s €45-70, d €80-180; P ☀) A delightful renovation has produced an 18th-century *locanda* (inn) of old polished wood, gauzy curtain fabrics and bursts of lime, orange and

aquamarine. The terrace has a compact pool and views across rooftops and the lake beyond. The restaurant is also good, serving classic Lake Garda cooking.

RIVA DEL GARDA
POP 15,990

Even on a lake blessed with dramatic scenery, Riva del Garda still comes out on top. Encircled by towering rock faces and a looping strip of beach, its appealing centre is a medley of grand architecture, maze-like streets and wide squares. Riva lies across the border from Lombardy in the Alpine region of Trentino–Alto Adige; for centuries the town's strategic position saw it fought over by the competing powers of the bishops of Trento, the republic of Venice, Milan's Viscontis and Verona's Della Scala families. It remained part of Austria until 1919, subsequently saw fierce fighting in the Italian wars of independence, and was home to anti-Nazi resistance groups in WWII.

The **tourist office** (☑0464 55 44 44; www.gardatrentino.it; Largo Medaglie d'Oro; ☺9am-7pm May-Sep, to 6pm Oct-Apr) advises on everything from climbing and paragliding to wine tasting and markets.

☉ Sights & Activities

Riva makes a natural starting point for walks and bike rides, including trails around **Monte Rocchetta** (1575m), which looms over the northern end of the lake. Immediately south of the town is the shingle beach. Like its neighbours Malcesine and Torbole, Riva is well known for windsurfing and has several schools, such as **Surfsegnana** (see p272) on Porfina Beach, that hire out equipment.

Cascata del Varone   WATERFALL
(www.cascata-varone.com; admission €5.50; ☺9am-7pm May-Aug, to 6pm Apr & Sep, to 5pm Mar & Oct) This 100m waterfall thunders down sheer limestone cliffs to an immense, dripping cave-like gorge. Walkways snake 50m into the mountain beside the torrent. You'll find it 3km northwest of Riva's centre.

Museo Civico   MUSEUM
(☑0464 57 38 69; Piazza Cesare Battisti 3; admission €2; ☺10.30am-12.30pm & 1.30-6pm Tue-Sun Apr-Nov) Riva's city museum reflects its turbulent past, both in terms of the exhibits and the 12th-century castle they are housed in. The most revealing exhibits are the antique maps dating from the 1579, 1667 and 1774 *Atlas Tyrolensis,* which show the area's shifting boundaries.

You can scale the adjoining 34m-tall **Torre Apponale** (adult/child €1/free) for a panorama of the lake and mountains.

🛏 Sleeping & Eating

TOP CHOICE **Restel de Fer**   INN €
(☑0464 55 34 81; www.resteldefer.com; Via Restel de Fer 10; s/d €68/90; ℗) The Meneghelli family's been running this charming *locanda* (inn) since 1400 and its rustic rooms are full of old oak dressers and brass bedsteads. The multi-course dinner at its downstairs restaurant, which includes specialities such as lake char with crayfish, Monte Baldo truffles and the best Trentino cheeses, is truly memorable (four-/six-courses €35/50).

Campeggio Bavaria   CAMPGROUND €
(☑0464 55 25 24; www.bavarianet.it; Viale Rovereto 100; camping 2 people, car & tent €36; ℗) Part of the Marco Segnana Surf Centre in Nago-Torbole.

LAKE GARDA'S BEST BEACHES

Lake Garda is not blessed with many good beaches. If you're looking for a nice spot to plunge in, here are some of the best:

» **Rocca di Manerba** This craggy promontory 10km south of Salò has a ruined castle and is designated a nature reserve.

» **Parco la Fontanella** A gleaming white pebble beach 300m north of Gargnano, backed by olive groves and Monte Baldo.

» **Campione del Garda** A ciff-backed beach north of Gargnano where fleets of windsurfers skim across the lake.

» **Riva del Garda** Encircled by towering rock faces on three sides, it's like swimming in a fjord.

» **Punta San Vigilio** A bewitching cypress-lined headland that curls out into the lake 3km north of Garda.

LAKE LEDRO

From Riva, first the SP37 and then the SS240 wind their way west up the mountains, past olive groves and vine-lined terraces. Around 11km from Riva the road flattens and Lake Ledro (www.valledildro.com) comes into view. Only 2.5km long and 2km wide, this diminutive lake sits at an altitude of 650m, set in a gorgeous valley beneath tree-covered mountains. Molina di Ledro is at the lake's eastern end, where tiny thatched huts line up beside a string of beaches and boat-hire pontoons.

Stay at the glass-and-timber ecolodge Hotel Elda (☑0464 59 10 40; www.hotelelda.com; Via 3 Giugno 3, Lenzumo; d €100-160; ℗⚡♿) set among apple trees in the Concei valley. Once a traditional inn, it has been converted by the family's prodigal son, who invited a team of architect-designers to reinvent the old building with five-star eco-credentials. The result is a happy combination of thermo-insulation and solar energy with space-age bathrooms and Philippe Starck chairs. Do the eco-thing and immerse yourself in the landscape. You'll find bikes at reception and a full-fledged bio spa, which comes in handy after mountain walks.

NAGO-TORBOLE
POP 2740

Lake Garda has an unusual meteorological quirk – the winds that blow over its surface are almost as regular as clockwork. The Pelèr gust from the north lasts 12 hours and is normally done by 10am, while the Ora blows from the south between noon and sunset. The predictability has ensured that the little fishing harbour of Torbole (along with Riva del Garda and Malcesine) is a magnet for windsurfers and sailors.

Fleets of operators provide tuition. Surf-segnana (☑0464 50 59 63; www.surfsegnana.it; Foci del Sarca) operates out of the Lido di Torbole.

Torbole's tourist office (☑0464 50 51 77; www.gardatrentino.it; Via Lungolago Verona 19; ⊙9am-7pm Mon-Sat, 9am-1pm & 3-7pm Sun May-Sep, 10am-1pm & 2-5.30pm Mon & Wed-Sat Apr, Oct & Nov) has a list of windsurfing schools and various windsurfing and sailing competitions. It also distributes free mountain-bike and walking maps.

MALCESINE
POP 3710

With the lake lapping right up to the tables of its harbourside restaurants and the vast ridge of Monte Baldo looming behind, Malcesine is another Garda hot spot. Like Riva del Garda and Torbole, it's a windsurfing centre and its streets are cobbled with thousands of lake pebbles. The whole affair is crowned by the chalky-white Castello Scaligero, where Goethe was temporarily imprisoned after being mistaken for a spy.

Malcesine's cable car, Funivia Malcesine-Monte Baldo (☑045 740 02 06; www.funiviedelbaldo.it; adult/reduced return €18/14.50; ⊙8am-7pm Apr-Sep, to 5pm Oct-Mar), whisks you 1760m above the lake in rotating, glass cabins. The mountain is actually part of a 40km-long chain, and the ridges are the starting point for mountain-biking tours and paragliding, as well as skiing in winter. Getting off the cable car at the intermediate station of San Michele (€5) is the starting point for some excellent hikes. The hour-long walk back to Malcesine along quiet roads and rocky mountain paths reveals a rural world far from the throngs at the lake. Hire bikes at Bikextreme (☑045 740 0105; Via Navene Vecchia 10; bikes €20 per day).

Olives harvested around Malcesine are milled into extra-virgin olive oil by Consorzio Olivicoltori di Malcesine (☑045 740 12 86; www.oliomalcesine.com; Via Navene; ⊙9am-1pm & 4.30-7pm). The 550 members all come from Malcesine's hills and produce 75,000L of oil annually – only half of that goes on sale. The oil is renowned for its light, fruity taste with traces of almonds. Prices of the cold-pressed extra virgin DOP oil range start at €11 for 0.5L.

The tourist office (☑045 740 00 44; www.malcesinepiu.it; Via Capitanato 6; ⊙9.30am-12.30pm & 3-6pm Mon-Sat 9.30am-12.30pm Sun) has information on windsurfing, sailing, walking and winter skiing.

BARDOLINO

More than 70 vineyards and wine cellars (many within DOC and even DOCG boundaries) grace the gentle hills that roll east from Bardolino on the east shore of Garda. They produce an impressive array of pink Chiaretto, ruby Classico, dry Superiore and young Novello.

One of the most atmospheric ways to savour their flavours is a tutored tasting at **Guerrieri Rizzardi** (☑045 721 00 28; www.guerrieri-rizzardi.com; Via Verdi 4; tastings €15; ⊙5pm Wed May-Oct). After a tour of wine cellars full of cobweb-laced bottles, relaxed tastings take place in the walled kitchen garden, with tables laid out beside salad crops, an orangery and a vineyard labyrinth. You get to sample local olive oil, cheeses and ham, too. Booking is required.

Bardolino is at its most Bacchic during the **Festa dell'Uva e del Vino** in early October, when the town's waterfront fills with food and wine stands.

THE PO PLAIN

The Lombard Plains, otherwise known as the Po or Padan Plain, spread out east and west of Milan, extending some 650km from Turin and Cuneo in the west to Mantua and Modena in the east. To the north the western Alps and the great lakes drain into the valley via the Ticino, Adda, Oglio and Mincio rivers.

Sitting on the Milan–Aquileia trade route, between the western Alps and the Gulf of Trieste, the region has been politically and economically significant since the Roman era, when Julius Caesar granted citizenship to the people of the valley and recruited many of his most loyal troops from the area. When Napoleon conquered northern Italy in the late 18th century he found the valley dotted with prosperous towns such as Bergamo, Brescia and Mantua, which continue to power a great deal of Italy's agriculture and light industry.

This is also where Lombardy's risotto rice comes from. The most well-known variety grown on the plain is arborio, although other high-quality risotto rices include Carnaroli, Baldo and Vialone Nano. In late May and early June many towns around Mantua hold risotto festivals.

Bergamo

POP 118,000

Split into a more modern lower town (*città bassa*) and a captivating hill town (*città alta*) that incorporates an attractive ensemble of medieval, Renaissance and baroque architecture, Bergamo is one of northern Italy's most attractive and interesting cities. With its privileged position at the foot of the pre-Alps between the Brembo and Serio river valleys, Bergamo has long been appreciated not only as a key trade centre (textiles and metals in particular) but a handy lookout over the Lombard plains.

Although Milan's skyscrapers to the southwest are visible on a clear day, historically Bergamo was more closely associated with Venice, which controlled the city for 350 years (1428–1797) until Napoleon arrived.

☉ Sights

The ancient *città alta* is a tangle of medieval streets, protected by 5km of Venetian walls. The main street is full of well-stocked wine bars and delicatessens. A funicular carries you from the western edge of the upper town up to the quaint quarter of San Vigilio, which offers some stunning views. On the plains below sprawls the modern *città bassa,* where you'll find the better dining options.

Piazza Vecchia   PIAZZA

The upper town's beating heart is this cafe-clad piazza, lined by elegant architecture that is a testament in stone to Bergamo's history. Le Corbusier apparently found it 'the most beautiful square in Europe'.

The white porticoed building on Via Bartolomeo Colleoni, which forms the northern side of the piazza, is the 17th-century **Palazzo Nuovo**, now a library. Turn south and you face the imposing arches and columns of the **Palazzo della Ragione**, built in the 12th century, and the seat of medieval city governance. The lion of St Mark is a reminder of Venice's long reign here. At the time of writing the palace was hosting a temporary exhibition of art work from the Accademia Carrara in its Sala delle Capriate. Works will be rotated every three months until the academy is reopened (same hours as the academy).

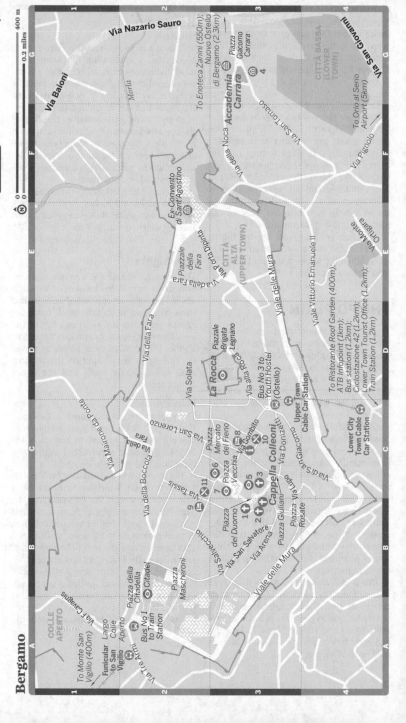

Bergamo

0 ─── 400 m
0 ─── 0.2 miles

Via Nazario Sauro

Via Baioni

COLLE APERTO

To Monte San Vigilio (400m);

Via F Cavagnis

Funicular to San Vigilio

Largo Colle Aperto

Via Tre Armi

Bus No 1 to Train Station

Piazza della Citadella

Citadel

Piazza Mascheroni

Via Mura della Ponte

Via della Fara

Morla

Via della Fara

Piazzale della Fara

Ex-Convento di Sant'Agostino

CITTÀ ALTA (UPPER TOWN)

Accademia Carrara

Piazza Giacomo Carrara

4

To Enoteca Zanini (550m); Nuovo Ostello di Bergamo (2.3km);

CITTÀ BASSA (LOWER TOWN)

To Orio al Serio Airport (5km);

Via San Giovanni

Via San Tomaso

Via della Noca

Via Solata

Via della Boccola

Via San Lorenzo

Via alta Rocca

La Rocca

Piazzale Brigata Legnano

Via alta Rocca

Bus No 3 to Youth Hostel (Ostello)

Upper Town Cable Car Station

Via della Mura

Viale delle Mura

Viale Vittorio Emanuele II

Via Monte Ortigara

Via Pignolo

To Ristorante Roof Garden (400m);
ATB Infopoint (1km);
Bus station (1.2km);
Ciclostazione 42 (1.2km);
Lower Town Tourist Office (1.2km);
Train Station (1.2km):

Via Tassis

Via Salvecchio

Piazza Vecchia

Piazza del Duomo

Piazza Mercato del Fieno

Via Colleoni

Via Gombito

6

7

11

9

8

5

1

3

2

10

Cappella Colleoni

Via Donizetti

Via di S.Giacomo

Lower City Town Cable Car Station

Piazza San Salvatore

Via San Salvatore

Via Arena

Piazza Arena

Piazza Giuliani

Via Porta Dipinta

Via Rosate

Viale delle Mura

Bergamo

Across the square from the palace, the 52m-high **Torre del Campanone** (adult/child €5/free; ⊙9.30am-7pm Tue-Fri, 9.30am-9.30pm Sat & Sun Mar-Oct, 9.30am-5.30pm Tue-Sun Nov-Feb) tolls the old 10pm curfew when the gates of the city were closed. There's a wheelchair-accessible lift.

Piazza del Duomo   PIAZZA

Tucked in behind these secular buildings is the core of Bergamo's spiritual life, the Piazza del Duomo. Roman remains were discovered here during renovations of the modest baroque **Duomo** (⊙7.30-11.45am & 3-6.30pm), a rather squat maroon building with a brilliant-white facade.

A great deal more interesting is the Romanesque **Basilica di Santa Maria Maggiore** (⊙9am-12.30pm & 2.30-6pm Apr-Oct, shorter hr Nov-Mar) next door. To its whirl of frescoed, Romanesque apses, begun in 1137, Gothic additions were added. Influences come from afar, with dual-colour banding typical of Tuscany and an interesting trompe l'œil pattern on part of the facade. What stands out most strikingly, however, is the Renaissance **Cappella Colleoni** (⊙9am-12.30pm & 2-6.30pm Mar-Oct, 9am-12.30pm & 2-4.30pm Tue-Sun Nov-Feb), the mausoleum-cum-chapel of the famous mercenary commander Bartolomeo Colleoni (1696–1770). Demolishing an entire apse of the basilica, he commissioned Giovanni Antonio Amadeo

to create a tomb that is now considered a masterpiece of Lombard art and architecture with its exuberant polychromatic marble exterior and Venetian rococo frescoes by Giambattista Tiepolo.

Detached from the church is the octagonal **baptistry**, built in 1340 but moved to its present spot in 1898.

⟨TOP CHOICE⟩ Accademia Carrara   ART GALLERY

(☑035 39 96 40; www.accademiacarrara.bergamo.it; Piazza Carrara 82a; adult/reduced €5/3; ⊙10am-9pm Tue-Sun Jun-Sep, 9.30am-5.30pm Mon-Fri, 10am-6pm Sat & Sun Oct-Apr) Just east of the old city walls is the enormous neoclassical edifice of the Accademia Carrara, one of Italy's great art repositories. Established in 1796 following the legacy of Count Giacomo Carrara, a wealthy collector and patron of the arts, its collection amounts to nearly 2000 paintings dating from the 15th to the 19th century, including a roster of star-studded names such as Botticelli, Bellini, Pisanello, Mantegna, Raphael, Moroni, Tiepolo and Canaletto. The most famous piece in the collection is Raphael's serene *San Sebastiano*, but there are many stunning works of art here.

To get here on foot from the *città alta*, pass through Porta di Sant'Agostino and down Via della Noca.

At the time of writing the Academy was closed for restoration work (until 2013), but a selection of its masterpieces was on show in the Palazzo della Ragione.

Galleria d'Arte Moderna e Contemporanea   ART GALLERY

(GAMeC; ☑035 27 02 72; www.gamec.it; Via San Tomaso 53; adult/reduced €4/2.50; ⊙3-8pm Tue-Wed & Fri, to 10pm Thu, 10am-8pm Sat & Sun) On the opposite side of the square from the Accademia is Bergamo's modern art gallery, which displays a small collection of modern works by Italian artists such as Giacomo Balla, Giorgio Morandi, Giorgio de Chirico and Filippo de Pisis.

La Rocca   FORTRESS

The defensive hulk of Bergamo's citadel, in the western corner of the *città alta* on Piazza Cittadella, is balanced by La Rocca, at the eastern corner. Located on the hill of Santa Eufemia, it was the Roman capital and was subsequently fortified and strengthened by the Viscontis and the Venetians. Now it houses a **museum** (adult/child €5/free; ⊙9.30am-1pm & 2-5.30pm) of minor interest detailing Bergamo's history during the 19th century. More interesting are the **gardens**, which have been transformed into a garden of rememberance commemorating the two world wars. From the battlements you can enjoy views over the medieval towers of the *città alta*.

🛏 Sleeping

Bergamo's proximity to the airport means hotels tend to fill up quickly – advance bookings are recommended, especially on weekends. The most charming accommodation is in the *città alta*.

Agnello d'Oro   INN €
(☎035 24 98 83; www.agnellodoro.it; Via Gombito 22; s/d €63/100; 🔊) Located on the corner of Piazza St Pancrazio, the Agnello d'Oro has 20 retro rooms and a heart-warming restaurant hung with copper pots. The building dates back to the 17th century and some of the rooms have small balconies overlooking Via Gombito. In summer, dinner is served outside around the piazza fountain.

Da Vittorio   RURAL INN €€€
(☎035 68 10 24; www.davittorio.com; Via Cantalupa 17; s €200-250, d €300-350; ☉Sep-Jul; P🔊🛜) Not only is Da Vittorio a noteworthy gourmet destination, it also offers 10 luxurious suites in its low-slung country estate. Each of the generous rooms enjoys its own sumptuous decor, with beautifully woven fabrics and marble bathrooms. The villa looks over a park and vineyard.

Hotel Piazza Vecchia   HOTEL €€
(☎035 428 42 11; www.hotelpiazzavecchia.it; Via Colleoni 3; s €140-180, d €160-200; 🔅@) Carved out of a 13th-century building a few steps off Piazza Vecchia, this hotel's 13 rooms are all quite different: some have exposed beams while others have a balcony or a king-sized bed. The owners' art works, amusing takes on the works of great artists, are hung throughout the hotel.

Nuovo Ostello di Bergamo   HOSTEL €
(☎035 369 23 76; www.ostellodibergamo.it; Via Galileo Ferraris 1, Monterosso; dm/s/d €18/35/50; P@) Bergamo's HI hostel is 4km north of the train station. Take bus 6 from Largo Porta Nuova near the train station.

🍴 Eating

The Bergamaschi like their polenta and even named a classic sweet after it: *polenta e osei* are pudding-shaped cakes filled with jam

and cream, topped with icing and chocolate birds. The final product looks like, but isn't, polenta. Bergamo's other famous dish is *casonsèi,* aka *casoncelli* (a kind of ravioli stuffed with spicy sausage meat), and the area is noted for its fine red wines, including Valcalepio.

🔝 Ristorante Roof Garden   MODERN ITALIAN €€€
(☎035 36 61 59; www.roofgardenrestaurant.it; Piazza della Repubblica 6, Città Bassa; meals €45-80) The fabulous new rooftop restaurant of the Hotel San Marco is both sexy and accomplished. Chef Fabrizio Ferrari has already garnered a Michelin star for his cooking, which he describes as *cucina metropolitana* (urban cooking). Dine on creamed beans and sausage, aged beef wrapped in mountain herbs or delicate veal with *cardoncelli* mushrooms and try not to be distracted by the wrap-around views of the *città alta*.

Enoteca Zanini   WINE BAR, RESTAURANT €€
(☎035 22 50 49; www.aisantibergamo.com; Via Santa Caterina 90a, Città Bassa; meals €30-35; ☉Mon-Fri, dinner Sat) Run by two accredited wine sommeliers who have worked for Gualtiero Marchesi in Erbusco, this is a great place to sample regional wine by the glass. The red-brick interior makes for a cosy atmosphere and the menu features original dishes such as ravioli stuffed with Taleggio and creamed rocket with toasted pine nuts.

Da Vittorio   GASTRONOMIC €€€
(☎035 68 10 24; Via Cantalupa 17, Brusaporto; set menus €70-140; ☉Thu-Tue Sep-Jul) Bergamo's acclaimed Vittorio, 9km east of town, is up there with the best restaurants in Italy, not the least on account of its truffle dishes (a special truffle menu can cost €280). Why not succumb to a *maialata* (literally a 'pig out'), with six courses of porcine-inspired pleasure. The estate also runs an expert cookery school (lessons €80).

Al Donizetti   RESTAURANT, WINE BAR €€
(☎035 24 26 61; www.donizetti.it; Via Gombito 17a, Città Alta; meals €20-35) Enjoy a late-morning coffee with pear and muscat cake under the Renaissance loggia of Donizetti, then come back for an evening *aperitivo*.

Il Fornaio   BAKERY €
(Via Bartolomeo Colleoni 1, Città Alta; pizza slices €1.50; ☉9am-6pm Mon-Sat; 🔊) Bergamo's best coffee and steaming-hot pizza slices.

ℹ️ Information

OspedaliRiuniti (☎035 26 91 11; www.ospedaliriuniti.bergamo.it; Largo Barozzi 1) Hospital.

Police station (☎035 27 61 11; Via Alessandro Noli 26)

Tourist office, upper town (☎035 24 22 26; Via Gombito 13; ⊙9am-12.30pm & 2-5.30pm)

Tourist office, lower town (☎035 21 02 04; www.turismo.bergamo.it; Piazza Gugliemo Marconi; ⊙9am-12.30pm & 2-5.30pm Mon-Fri) Province-wide information, including Alpine activities. Check out www.apt.bergamo.it too.

ℹ️ Getting There & Away

Air

Orio al Serio (☎035 32 63 23; www.sacbo.it) Bergamo's airport is 5km southeast of the train station.

Bus

Bus station (☎800 139392, 035 28 90 00; www.bergamotrasporti.it) Located just off Piazza Gugliemo Marconi. **SAB** (☎035 28 90 00; www.sab-autoservizi.it, in Italian) operates services to Brescia, Mantua and the lakes.

Train

Train station (☎035 24 79 50; Piazza Gug-lielmo Marconi) Services to Milan (€4.70, one hour), Lecco (€3.10, 40 minutes) and Brescia (€4.05, one hour, with connections for Lake Garda and Venice).

ℹ️ Getting Around

To/From the Airport

ATB (☎035 23 60 26; www.atb.bergamo.it) Every 20 minutes from Bergamo bus and train stations (€2 to €4.50, 15 minutes). Direct buses also connect the airport with Milan (adult/child €7/5, one hour).

Bicycle

ATB Infopoint (☎800 910658; Porta Nuova 16; www.bicincitta.com) For information on Bergamo's bike-sharing scheme.

Ciclostazione 42 (☎389 513 73 13; www.pedalopolis.org; Piazza Gugliemo Marconi; bikes per day €10; ⊙7.30-11.30am & 4-7.30pm Mon-Fri) Bike rental.

Public Transport

ATB bus 1 connects the train station with the funicular to the upper town. From Colle Aperto, bus 21 or a funicular continues uphill to San Vigilio. Buy tickets (€1), valid for 75 minutes' travel, from machines at the train and funicular stations or at newspaper stands. Funicular tickets cost €1.50.

Brescia

POP 191,600

Urban sprawl, a seedy bus and train station, and the odd 1960s skyscraper don't hint at Brescia's fascinating old town, which serves as a reminder of its substantial history. Its narrow streets are home to some of the most important Roman ruins in Lombardy and an extraordinary circular Romanesque church.

◉ Sights

Monastero di Santa Giulia CONVENT, MUSEUM
(☎030 297 78 34; www.bresciamusei.com; Via dei Musei 81b; adult/reduced €8/6, temporary exhibitions extra; ⊙10am-6pm Tue-Sun May-Sep, to 5.30pm Oct-Apr) The rambling Monastero di Santa Giulia and Basilica di San Salvatore is Brescia's single-most interesting sight. It houses the **Museo della Città**, the city museum, with collections that run the gamut from prehistory to the age of Venetian dominance.

The building of the monastery, which was begun as early as the 8th century, absorbed two *domus* (villas), which were left standing in what would become the monk's garden (Ortaglia) near the north cloister. The remains are known as the Domus dell'Ortaglia and have been protected by the monastery walls through the centuries. Their beautiful floor mosaics and colourful frescoes are the highlight of the museum.

The other star piece is the 8th-century Croce di Desiderio, a Lombard cross encrusted with hundreds of jewels.

Piazza Paolo VI PIAZZA
The most compelling of Brescia's religious monuments is the 11th-century **Duomo Vecchio** (Old Cathedral; Piazza Paolo VI; ⊙9am-noon & 3-7pm Tue-Sun), a rare example of a circular-plan Romanesque basilica, built over a 6th-century church. Interesting features include fragmentary floor mosaics and the elaborate 14th-century sarcophagus of Bishop Berado Maggi.

Next door, the **Duomo Nuovo** (New Cathedral; Piazza Paolo VI; ⊙7.30am-noon & 4-7pm Mon-Sat, 8am-1pm & 4-7pm Sun), dating from 1604, dwarfs its ancient neighbour but is of less interest.

Museo Mille Miglia MUSEUM
(☎030 33 65 31; www.museomillemiglia.it; Viale della Rimembranza 3; adult/reduced €10/8; ⊙10am-6pm Tue-Sun) The Mille Miglia was a classic

1000-mile (1600km) Italian car race that ran between 1927 and 1957. It started and ended in Brescia and was finally cancelled in 1957 after 11 spectators died. Nowadays a nostalgia race featuring vintage cars is held annually in May (www.1000miglia.eu).

The colourful museum, loaded with some great cars to cross the finish line, is housed outside central Brescia in the 11th-century Monastero di Sant'Eufemia della Fonte. As well as admiring the selection of racing cars, old-style petrol pumps and other paraphernalia, you can listen to audio material and watch race films.

Sleeping & Eating

Albergo Orologio   BOUTIQUE HOTEL €€
(☑030 375 54 11; www.albergoorologio.it; Via Beccaria 17; s €90-115, d €125-130; P❄@) Fine art and art works alongside soft-hued gold and olive-green furnishings and terracotta floors make this boutique hotel a gem. It's right by its namesake clock tower in the pedestrianised old town.

TOP CHOICE **Osteria al Bianchi**   OSTERIA €€
(☑030 29 23 28; www.osteriaalbianchi.it; Via Gasparo da Salò 32; meals €20; ☺Thu-Mon) Crowd inside this classic old bar – in business since 1880 – and try for a seat at one of a handful of marble tables. Or head out back for a plate of *pappardelle al Taleggio e zucca* (broad ribbon pasta with Taleggio cheese and pumpkin), followed by house specialities such as *pestöm* (minced pork meat served with polenta).

Information

Info Point (☑030 240 03 57; www.bresciatourism.it; Largo Formentone; ☺9.30am-6.30pm Mon-Sat, 10am-6pm Sun)

Getting There & Around

Bus station (☑030 4 49 15; Via Solferino) Buses operated by **SAIA Trasporti** (☑800 88 39 99; www.saiatrasporti.it, in Italian) serve destinations throughout the province including Desenzano del Garda and Mantua. Some leave from another station off Via della Stazione.

Train station (☑030 4 41 08; Viale della Stazione 7) Situated on the Milan–Venice line, with regular services to Milan (€6.25 to €18, 45 minutes to 1¼ hours) and Verona (€4.85, 40 minutes). There are also secondary lines to Cremona, Bergamo and Parma.

Mantua

POP 48,325

As serene as the three lakes it sits beside, Mantua (Mantova) is home to sumptuous ducal palaces and a string of atmospheric, cobbled squares. Settled by the Etruscans in the 10th century, Mantua and its surrounding farmland has long been prosperous. The Latin poet Virgil was born just outside the modern town in 70 BC, and the city preserves its long and illustrious antique timeline in its art and architecture, from austere medieval frescoes and soaring Gothic facades to Renaissance paintings and ornate baroque interiors. In 1328 the city fell to the Gonzaga dynasty, under whose rule it flourished until the Austrians seized control in 1708.

But despite its Unesco World Heritage credentials, Mantua is also a city in which to experience an unchanging slice of Lombard life. Relaxed, cultured and charming, its vibrant streets are home to daily markets and some of the region's best restaurants.

Sights

Palazzo Ducale   PALAZZO
(☑0376 224 832; www.mantovaducale.benicultura.it; Piazza Sordello 40; adult/reduced €6.50/3.25; ☺8.15am-7.15pm Tue-Sun) The 32,000-sq-metre ducal palace of the Gonzaga family has over 500 rooms, three squares and 15 courtyards occupying a huge area of the city's northeastern corner. In an orgy of self-aggrandisement, the Gonzagas commissioned the cream of the era's artists to decorate the palace – the result is some 40 display rooms featuring works by Pisanello, Giulio Romano, Andrea Mantegna and Giulio Rubens. During busy periods you may have to book to see the biggest draw – the wonderful mid-15th-century frescoes by Mantegna in the **Camera degli Sposi** (Bridal Chamber). Other rooms worth pausing over include the **Sala del Pisanello**, decorated with unfinished 15th-century frescoes of Arthurian legends by Pisanello, and the **Camera dello Zodiaco**, with its magnificent deep-blue ceiling festooned with figures from the zodiac. Equally bizarre is the 18th-century **Sala dei Fiumi**, a Habsburg-era folly with artificial grottoes covered in shells and mosaic. No photography is allowed.

Palazzo Te   PALAZZO
(☑0376 32 32 66; www.palazzote.it; Viale Te; adult/reduced €8/5; ☺1-6pm Mon, 9am-6pm Tue-Sun) Hardly more modest in scale, the Gonza-

gas' suburban villa where Duke Federico II could meet his mistress, Isabella Boschetti, is decorated in playboy style with stunning frescoes, playful motifs and encoded symbols. Look out for Federico's device, a salamander, in the **Camera delle Imprese**. It bears the inscription *quod hic deest, me torquet* ('what you lack, torments me'), playing on the conceit of Federico's notoriously passionate nature compared with the cold-blooded salamander.

Some of the best frescoes can be found in the **Camera di Amore e Psiche** (Chamber of Cupid and Psyche), where the palace's amorous theme is far from subtle. The most impressive room, though, is the overwhelming **Camera dei Giganti** (Chamber of the Giants). Here the towering figures of the rebel Titans cover every inch of wall, collapsing under the weight of huge celestial pillars in punishment for their assault against Mount Olympus.

Teatro Bibiena   THEATRE
(☑0376 32 76 53; www.societadellamusica.it; Via dell'Accademia 47; adult/child €2/1.20; ⊙9.30am-12.30pm & 3-6pm Tue-Sun) If ever a theatre was set to upstage the actors, it's the 18th-century Teatro Bibiena. Its design is highly unusual: a bell-shaped four storeys of intimate, gilded balconies interspersed with tiny candelabra-lined curving walls. The theatre's shape was intended to allow its patrons to be seen – balconies even fill the wall behind the stage. Just a few weeks after it opened in 1769, the theatre hosted a concert by the 14-year-old Wolfgang Amadeus Mozart. It's undoubtedly one of Mantua's hidden gems.

Basilica di Sant'Andrea   BASILICA
(☑0376 32 85 04; Piazza Andrea Mantegna; admission free; ⊙8am-noon & 3-7pm Mon-Fri, 10.30am-noon & 3-6pm Sat, 11.45am-12.15pm & 3-6pm Sun) The elaborate baroque cupola of Basilica di Sant'Andrea lords it over the city. Designed by Leon Battista Alberti in 1472, it safeguards golden vessels said to hold earth soaked by the blood of Christ. Longinus, the Roman soldier who speared Christ on the cross, is said to have scooped up the earth and buried it in Mantua after leaving Palestine. Today, these containers rest beneath a marble octagon in front of the altar and are paraded around the town in a grand procession on Good Friday.

The first **chapel** on the left as you enter contains the tomb of the celebrated fresco artist Andrea Mantegna.

 **Activities**

On a sunny day the people of Mantua head for the waterfront. The compact shore of Lago Mezzo, complete with the child-friendly Parco della Scienza (outdoor science park), is the most crowded; the quieter path beside Lago Superiore meanders amid reed beds and wading birds before petering out, while the shore of Lago Inferiore brings broad views. At all three you'll find waterside snack bars.

Boat Tours

Motonavi Andes (☑0376 36 08 70; www. motonaviandes.it; Via San Giorgio 2) organises a variety of boat tours of the lakes (from €8 for 1½ hours), including a five-hour excursion to the Benedictine abbey of San Benedetto Po (€14-16 one way) and day trips to Venice (€77-84). Boats arrive/depart from the Imbarco Motonavi Andes, behind Castello di San Giorgio on Lago di Mezzo's shore.

Cycling

The tourist office stocks a booklet in English detailing cycling itineraries along the Po river in the Parco del Mincio (☑0376 22 83 20; www.parcodelmincio.it; Piazza Porta Giulia 10, Cittadella) and around the lakes. Rent bikes from La Rigola (☑0376 36 66 77; Via Trieste 7; per day from €10).

Festivals & Events

Festivaletteratura   CULTURAL
(www.festivaletteratura.it) For five days each September Mantua is taken over by this literature festival, featuring bookstalls and readings.

Mantova Jazz   MUSIC
(www.mantovajazz.it) This annual jazz fest runs from late March to early May with performances at a variety of venues

Sleeping

C'A Delle Erbe   B&B €€
(☑0376 22 61 61; www.cadelleerbe.it; Via Broletto 24; r €60-180; ❄⊛⊜⋓) With an unbeatable location in the heart of old Mantua, this 16th-century town house offers fantastic value accommodation. The sensitive conversion teams ancient, exposed-brick walls and beams with modern art and frosted-glass bathroom cubicles fitted with huge rain showers. Ask for the room with the balcony overlooking Piazza delle Erbe.

MILAN & THE LAKES THE PO PLAIN

Mantua

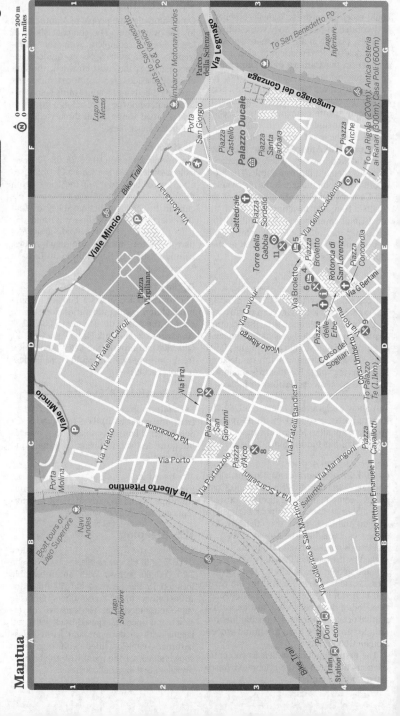

Mantua

Casa Poli   BOUTIQUE HOTEL €€€
(✆0376 288 170; www.hotelcasapoli.it; Corso Garibaldi 32; d €170-240; ✳@⊛) Housed in an elegant town house on Corso Garibaldi, Casa Poli is a boutique hotel with a modern bent. Rooms and public areas are styled in a soothing colour scheme of dove-grey, cream and beige with the occasional splash of colour. Imaginative touches are everywhere, from tucked-away TVs to room numbers projected onto the floor.

Hotel Broletto   HOTEL €€
(✆0376 22 36 78; www.hotelbroletto.com; Via dell'Accademia 1; s €60-90, d €95-130, tr €130-190; ✳⊛✦) A comfortable, well-priced hotel just off Piazza Broletto, 100m from the lake.

✗ Eating

Mantua and the surrounding region is a gastronomic destination. Mantua's most famous dish is *tortelli di zucca* (melt-in-your-mouth pumpkin-stuffed cushions of pasta). Pork also features heavily on the menu; look out for *salumi* (salt port), *prosciutto crudo* (salt-cured ham) and *risotto alla pilota* (risotto with minced pork). Many dishes are accompanied by a sweet mustard, *mostarda di mele* or *mantovana* (made with apples or pears). Sweet specialities include *torta di tagliatelle* (crunchy tagliatelle baked with sugar and almonds) and *torta sbrisolona* (a hard biscuit with almonds).

Pick up sweet local treats from **Caravatti** (Piazza delle Erbe 18) or **La Ducale** (Via Pier Fortunato Calvi 25), both dating from 1865, or the friendly **Pavesi** (cnr Via dell'Accademia & Via Broletto).

TOP CHOICE Il Cigno   MANTUAN €€€
(✆0376 32 71 01; Piazza d'Arco 1; meals €55-65; ⊙Wed-Sun) The building is as beautiful as the food is elegant: a lemon-yellow facade with shutters, and dining rooms adorned with antiques and Venetian glassware. Order the delicately steamed risotto with spring greens, the poached cod with polenta or the gamey guinea fowl with spicy Mantuan mustard. The extensive wine list includes fine Bardolino vintages.

Fragoletta Antica   TRATTORIA €€
(✆0376 32 33 00; www.fragoletta.it; Piazza Arche 5; meals €35; ⊙Tue-Sun; ✦) Wooden chairs scrape against the tiled floor as diners eagerly tuck into Slow Food–accredited *culatello di zibello* (prosciutto) at this friendly trattoria. Other Mantuan specials such as *risotto alla pilota* and perfectly seasoned steaks feature on the menu. Dine in the back room with its bright homemade art amid stacks of wine cases.

Antica Osteria ai Ranari   OSTERIA €€
(✆0376 32 84 31; www.ranari.it; Via Trieste 11; meals €30-35; ⊙Tue-Sun) Situated on the river at the mouth of Lago Superiore, Ranari used to be a local laundry. The menu is strictly seasonal and local, featuring dishes such as duck ravioli, donkey stew, steamed snails and *risotto alla pilota*. Wash it all down with a cheerful Lambrusco or a more sophisticated Soave.

L'Ochina Bianca   OSTERIA €€
(✆0376 323 700; www.ochinabianca.it; Via Finzi 2; meals €35-40; ⊙Tue-Sat, lunch Sun) Stone floors scattered with rugs and walls hung with antique plates give an indication of the warm atmosphere inside. Quality ingredients help create memorable dishes, with an emphasis on seafood. Try the scallops on spinach with butter and cinnamon or the tuna with peppers and tomatoes.

❶ Information

Ospedale Carlo Pola (✆0376 20 11; Via Albertoni 1) Hospital.

Police station (✆0376 32 70 22; Piazza Sordello 46)

Tourist office (✆0376 43 24 32; www.turismo.mantova.it; Piazza Mantegna 6; ⊙9am-6pm)

❶ Getting There & Around

Bus station (📞0376 23 03 46; www.apam. it; Piazza Don Leoni) Buses to Sabbioneta, San Benedetto Po and Brescia are run by **APAM**. Most leave from Piazza Don Leoni, but some leave from Viale Risorgimento.

Train station (Piazza Don Leoni) Regular services to Cremona (€5.20, 40 to 60 minutes), Milan (€9.85, two hours) and Verona (€2.60, 50 minutes).

Cremona

POP 72,250

A wealthy, independent city-state for centuries, Cremona boasts some fine architecture. The city is best known around the world, however, for its violin-making traditions.

◉ Sights

Piazza del Comune   PIAZZA

This beautiful pedestrianised square is considered one of the best-preserved medieval squares in Italy. To maintain the difference between the secular and spiritual, buildings connected with the Church were erected on the eastern side of the Piazza del Comune, and those concerned with secular affairs were constructed on the opposite side. On Sundays, the piazza is filled with antique stalls.

The business of city government was and still is carried out in the **Palazzo Comunale**. Begun in the 13th century, the arcaded walkways and courtyards were gradually extended. On the central pillar of the main facade, a marble **Arengario** (balcony from which decrees were issued and speeches given) was added in 1507. South across the lane, the **Loggia di Militi** is a Gothic gem built in 1292, where the captains of the citizen militia would meet.

Cattedrale   CATHEDRAL

(📞0372 2 73 86; www.cattedraledicremona.it, in Italian; Piazza del Comune; ⊙7.30am-noon & 3.30-7pm) Cremona's stately cathedral started out as a Romanesque basilica, but by the time it was finished in 1190 it was heavily overtaken by Gothic modishness. The interior is adorned with rich frescoes and paintings.

CREMONA'S VIOLINS

It was in Cremona that master craftsman Antonio Stradivari lovingly put together his first Stradivarius violins, helping establish a tradition that continues today. The Stradivarius violin is typically made from spruce (the top), willow (the internal blocks and linings) and maple (the back, ribs and neck) and is prized the world over for its unique sound quality, attributed to the peculiar density of the wood used and possibly the unique treatment and varnish Stradivari applied.

The 500 instruments that still survive command staggering prices, running from the hundreds of thousands to millions of dollars. Following the devastating Japanese earthquake and tsunami in 2011 the Nippon Music Foundation sold the 1721 'Lady Blunt' violin (so called as it was owned by Byron's granddaughter Lady Anne Blunt) at a fundraising auction for $15.9 million.

But Stradivari was by no means the only master craftsman in Cremona. Other great violin-making dynasties that started here include the Amati and Guarneri families, and even today some 100 violin-making workshops cluster in the streets around the Piazza del Comune. Stop by the tourist office or check out www.cremonaliuteria.it for more information and a list of addresses.

Various events dedicated to violin-making take place each year, while the **Triennale Internazionale degli Strumenti ad Arco** (International Stringed Instrument Expo; www. entetriennale.com) is held in Cremona every third year in September or October; the next will be in 2012.

Year-round you can visit the **Collezione gli Archi di Palazzo Comunale** (📞0372 40 70 33; http://musei.comune.cremona.it; Piazza del Comune 8; adult/reduced €6/4; ⊙9am-6pm Tue-Sat, 10am-6pm Sun), featuring instruments from the Stradivari workshop. The **Museo Civico** (📞0372 3 12 22; Via Ugolani Dati 4; adult/reduced €7/5; ⊙9am-6pm Tue-Sat, 10am-6pm Sun) displays drawings and tools as well as instruments by Amati and Guarneri.

To hear Cremona's violins in action, head to the 19th-century **Teatro Amilcare Ponchielli** (📞0372 02 20 01; www.teatroponchielli.it; Corso Vittorio Emanuele II 52), whose season runs from October to June.

The central nave and apse, in particular, flaunt a series of scenes dedicated to the lives of the Virgin Mary and Christ. The local Ferrara-born Renaissance master Boccaccio Boccaccino carried out many of them. Elegant though his compositions are, it is the *Storie di Cristo* (Stories of Christ) by Pordenone that stand out.

The cathedral's most prized possession is the 'Holy Thorn', allegedly from the Crown of Thorns worn by Jesus Christ, which was donated to the church by Cremona-born Pope Gregory XIV in 1591. It's kept behind bars in the **Capella delle Reliquie**. In the **crypt**, the robed and masked body of Cremona's 12th-century patron saint, Sant'Omobono Tucenghi, is on show in a glass casket.

✦ Festivals & Events

Festival di Cremona Claudio Monteverdi MUSIC
(www.teatroponchielli.it) A month-long series of concerts centred on Claudio Monteverdi and other baroque-era composers held in early May.

Festa del Torrone FOOD
(www.festadeltorronecremona.it) In late November the city centre is given over to various exhibitions and tastings of Cremona's *torrone* (nougat).

🍴 Sleeping & Eating

Dellearti Design Hotel DESIGN HOTEL €€
(✆0372 2 31 31; www.dellearti.com; Via Bonomelli 8; s/d €119/169; P✱@) This rather self-consciously hi-tech vision of glass, concrete and steel has rotating displays of contemporary paintings and photographs, a Turkish bath, gym and suitably chic rooms with clean lines, bold colours and artistic lighting. For those who want to feel like they never left the fashion crowd in Milan, this could be the place.

TOP CHOICE Hosteria 700 TRADITIONAL ITALIAN €€
(✆0372 3 61 75; www.hosteria700.it; Piazza Gallina 1; meals €25-30; Wed-Sun, lunch Mon) Behind the dilapidated facade lurks a series of vaulted rooms, some with ceiling frescoes. It sets a romantic scene for hearty Lombard cooking. Try the *marubini al brodo o al burro fuso* (meat- and cheese-stuffed discs of pasta in broth or melted butter), a Cremona speciality.

La Sosta OSTERIA €€
(✆0372 45 66 56; Via Vescovo Sicardo 9; meals €30-35; Tue-Sat, lunch Sun Sep-Jun) Surrounded by violin-makers' workshops, this is a beautiful place to feast on regional delicacies, such as *bollito* (boiled meats) and *cotechino* (boiled pork sausage) with polenta and Cremona's sweet mustard. Snail lovers might also be tempted by a plate prepared with spinach.

ℹ Information

Tourist office (✆0372 2 32 33; http://turismo.comune.cremona.it; Piazza del Comune 5; 9am-noon & 3-6pm)

ℹ Getting There & Away

Train station (Via Dante) Cremona is connected to Pavia, Mantua, Brescia and Piacenza. Trains to Milan (€7.80, one hour 10 minutes) and Mantua (€5.20, 40 to 60 minutes) run regularly.

Trento & the Dolomites

POP: 1.03 MILLION / AREA 13,613 SQ KM

Best Places to Eat

» Kallmünz (p308)

» Scrigno del Duomo (p292)

» Stüa de Michil (p313)

» El Molin (p300)

» Acherer Patisserie & Blumen (p315)

Best Places to Stay

» Lagacio Mountain Residence (p313)

» Hotel Terme Merano (p308)

» Hotel Greif (p303)

» Park Hotel Azalea (p299)

Why Go?

While they're not Italy's tallest mountains, the Dolomites' red-hued pinnacles are the country's most spectacular, drawing a faithful fan club of hikers, skiers, poets and fresh-air fanciers for at least the last few centuries. Protected by seven natural parks, the two semi-autonomous provinces of Trentino and Alto Adige offer up a number of stunning wilderness areas, where adventure and comfort can be found in equal measure. Wooden farmhouses dot vine- and orchard-covered valleys and the region's cities – the southerly Italian enclave of Trento, the Austro-Italian Bolzano and the very Viennese Merano – are easy to navigate, cultured and fun.

From five-star spa resorts to the humblest mountain hut, multi-generational hoteliers combine genuine warmth with extreme professionalism. Nowhere are the oft-muddled borders of Italy's extreme north reflected more strongly than on the plate: don't miss out on tasting one of Europe's most fascinating cultural juxtapositions.

When to Go
Bolzano

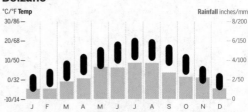

Jan Grab a bargain on the slopes in early winter.

Jul Hit the high-altitude trails and mountain huts of the Alta Vie.

Dec Get festive at Tyrolean Christmas markets in Bolzano, Merano and Bressanone.

Planning Your Trip

The ski season runs from early December to early April, with the high season taking in mid-December to early January and the last two weeks of February (then count on a gobsmackingly ultrahigh season between Christmas and New Year). Summer rates fall considerably, with the exception of August. Most Alpine resorts shut up shop in April/May and October/November, though making a base in the town during these times can mean some splendidly uncrowded trails or touring. *Rifugi* (mountain huts) open from the end of June to September, offering meals and accommodation for walkers and mountain bikers.

WINTER WONDERLAND, SUMMER LOVE

The jagged peaks of the Dolomites, or Dolomiti, span the provinces of Trentino and Alto Adige, jutting into neighbouring Veneto. Europeans flock here for highly hospitable resorts that can't be beaten for their sublime natural settings and for their extensive, well-coordinated ski networks. Come for downhill, cross-country and snowboarding or get ready for *sci alpinismo,* an adrenalin-spiking mix of skiing and mountaineering, freeride and a range of other winter adventure sports. You'll also never be far from a bolstering plate of dumplings, gulasch or pasta and a glass of excellent local wine (you are in Italy after all).

The region's two flexible passes are Dolomiti Superski (www.dolomitisuperski.com; 1-/3-/6-day pass €42/116/205), covering the east, with access to 450 lifts and some 1200km of ski runs spread over 12 resorts, and Superskirama (www.skirama.it; 3-/6-day pass €106/192), covering the western Brenta Dolomites, with 150 lifts, 380km of slopes and eight resorts.

In summer, come for rafting, mountain biking, Nordic walking and rock climbing (and look forward to pit stops at the region's famously hospitable *rifugi* – mountain huts). Road cycling is also big: Trentino has 400km of paved cycling paths and Bolzano is not far behind.

Sella's Circle

The Sella Ronda, a 40km circumnavigation of the Gruppo di Sella range (3151m, at Piz Boé) – linked by various cable cars and chairlifts – is one of the Alps' iconic ski routes. The tour takes in four passes and the four surrounding valleys – the Val Gardena, Val Badia, Arabba (in the Veneto) and Val di Fassa – all of them definitely, delightfully, Ladin. Kicking off from Selva (1565m), experienced skiers can complete the clockwise (orange) or anticlockwise (green) route in a day. In summer, the same trails are utilised by mountain bikers and there's a hop-on, hop-off bus for walkers.

KNOW YOUR LADIN

- » **Bun dé** Good morning
- » **Prëibel** Please
- » **Dilan** Thank you
- » **Bëgnodüs!** You're welcome

Fluent & Fluid

Trentino's first language is Italian but head north to Alto Adige (Südtirol) and you'll find 75% of the population are German speakers, a legacy of the region's Austro-Hungarian past. The Ladin language is spoken in both provinces, across five eastern Dolomiti valleys; it's a direct descendant of provincial Latin.

Hiking Highs

- » Alpe di Siusi, Sciliar and Catinaccio group
- » Brenta Dolomites
- » Gruppo del Sella
- » Pale di San Martino
- » Sesto Dolomites
- » Val di Genova/Adamello group

Resources

- » Find a mountain guide at www.bergfuehrer-suedtirol.it.
- » Lonely Planet's *Hiking in Italy* details five classic Dolomites hikes.
- » Cicerone (www.cicerone.co.uk) publishes specialist guides.

Trento & the Dolomites Highlights

1 Work up a high-altitude appetite on the slopes, then hit the fine-dining hot spot of **Alta Badia** (p313)

2 Be enchanted by the endless green pastures of the **Alpe di Siusi** (p311)

3 Test your mettle on a vertiginous **via ferrata** (p295) in the Brenta Dolomites

4 Sip a Veneziana spritzer on a frescoed piazza in **Trento** (p290)

5 Float away beneath palm trees and snowy peaks at **Terme Merano** (p307)

6 Uncover excellent contemporary art collections in **Rovereto** (p294), **Bolzano** (p301) and **Merano** (p306)

7 Discover Italy's most elegant white wines along the **Weinstrasse** (p306)

8 Get high above Bolzano's pretty streets on one of its three **cable cars** (p303)

9 Feast your way through schnitzel and *spätzle*, strudel and *knödel* in the **Val Pusteria** (p314)

10 Mountain bike the apple-clad hills of the **Val di Sole** (p298)

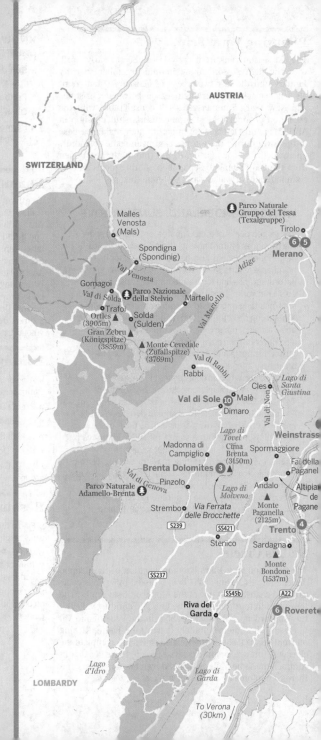

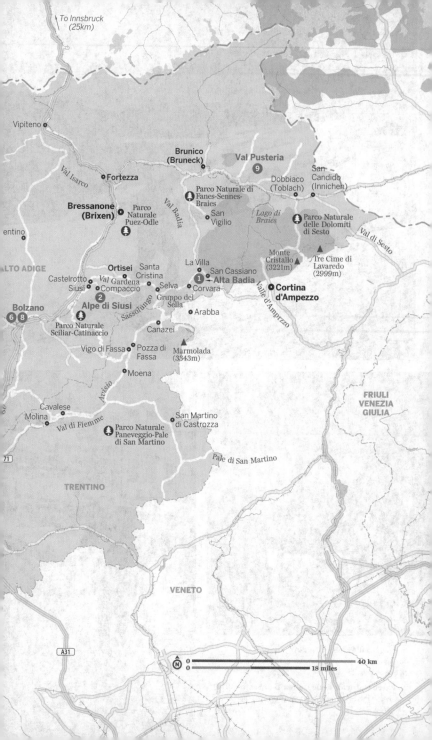

1. Cortina d'Ampezzo (p383)
Adventurers hit Cortina for climbing, hiking, skiing and snowboarding.

2. Parco Naturale delle Dolomiti di Sesto (p314)
Cyclists in the Sesto Dolomites, with Corvara visible in the background.

3. *Vie ferrate* (p295)
These spectacular fixed-protection climbing paths are known as *vie ferrate* (iron ways).

4. Bolzano (p301)
A market in Bolzano, the provincial capital of Alto Adige (Südtirol).

5. Alpe di Siusi (p311)
Cows graze in the pastures of Europe's largest plateau.

TRENTINO

Trento

POP 115,511 / ELEV 194M

Trento rarely makes the news these days, but that wasn't the case in the mid-16th century. During the tumultuous years of the Counter-Reformation, the Council of Trent convened here, dishing out far-reaching condemnations to uppity Protestants. Modern Trento is less preachy: quietly confident, liberal and easy to like. Bicycles glide along spotless streets fanning out from the atmospheric, intimate Piazza del Duomo, sporty students clink spritzers by Renaissance fountains and a dozen historical eras intermingle seamlessly amid stone castles, shady porticoes and the city's signature medieval frescoes. While not as Teutonic as Bolzano or Merano, Trentino has its share of Austrian influence: apple strudel is ubiquitous and beer halls not uncommon. Set in a wide glacial valley guarded by the crenulated peaks of the Brenta Dolomites, amid a patchwork of vineyards and apple orchards, it's a perfect jumping-off point for hiking, biking, skiing or wine tasting.

☉ Sights

Look out for helpful plaques that indicate the historical era that various buildings belong to (often several at once in this many-layered city).

Funivia Trento-Sardagna   CABLE CAR
(☎0461 23 21 54; Via Montegrappa 1; one way €1; ☉7am-10pm, 15min/half-hourly) A brief but spectacular cable-car ride from Trento's valley floor delivers you to a pretty village – admire the vista over a grappa or two.

Castello del Buonconsiglio   MUSEUM
(☎0461 23 37 70; www.buonconsiglio.it; Via Clesio 5; adult/reduced €8/5; ☉10am-5pm Wed-Mon) Guarded by hulking fortifications, Trento's bishop-princes holed up here until Napoleon's arrival in 1801. Behind the walls are the original 13th-century castle, the Castelvecchio, and the Renaissance residence Magno Palazzo, which provides an atmospheric backdrop for a varied collection of artefacts and hosts temporary exhibitions.

Duomo   CATHEDRAL
(☉6.30am-noon & 2-8pm) Once host to the Council of Trent, this dimly lit Romanesque cathedral displays fragments of medieval frescoes inside its transepts. Two colonnaded stairways flank its nave, leading, it seems, to heaven. Built over a 6th-century temple devoted to San Vigilio, patron saint of Trento, the foundations form part of a palaeo-Christian archaeological area (admission €1.50).

Museo Diocesano Tridentino   MUSEUM
(☎0461 23 44 19; Piazza del Duomo 18; incl Duomo's archaeological area adult/reduced €4/2.50; ☉9.30am-12.30pm & 2.30-6pm Wed-Mon) Sitting across the square from the *duomo* is Palazzo Pretorio, the former bishop's residence, dating from the 11th century. It now houses one of Italy's most important ecclesiastical collections, with enormous documentary paintings of the Council of Trent, along with Flemish tapestries, illustrated manuscripts, vestments and some particularly opulent reliquaries.

Piazza del Duomo   PIAZZA
Trento's heart is this busy yet intimate piazza, dominated, of course, by the *duomo*, but also host to the Fontana di Nettuno, a flashy late-baroque fountain rather whimsically dedicated to Neptune. Don't miss the intricate, allegorical frescoes that fill the 16th-century facades of the Casa Cazuffi-Rella, on the piazza's northern side.

Tridentum La Città Sotterranea   ARCHAEOLOGICAL SITE
(☎0461 23 01 71; Piazza Battisti; adult/reduced €2/1; ☉9am-noon & 2-5.30pm Oct-May, 9.30am-1pm & 2-6pm Jun-Sep, Tue-Sun) Explore Roman Tridentum's city walls, paved streets, a tower, domestic mosaics, and a workshop. The site was discovered less than two decades ago, during restoration works on the nearby theatre.

Museo di Arte Moderna e Contemporanea Trento   ART GALLERY
(MART; ☎0424 60 04 35; Via Sanseverino 45; adult/reduced €6/4; ☉10am-6pm Tue-Sun) MART's Trento outpost in the Palazzo delle Albere – due to reopen in late 2012 after extensive refurbishment – specialises in 19th- and early 20th-century Impressionist and symbolist paintings by Trentino artists. Look out for the colourful fragmentary frescoes on the walls.

Badia di San Lorenzo   CHURCH
(Via Andrea Pozzo 2; ☉6.30am-noon & 3-7pm) This 12th-century church epitomises the calm simplicity and harmonious proportions of its Bergameschi Benedictine builders. Look up to the cross-vaulting, touchingly festooned with rust-red stars.

FREE Palazzo Trentini ART GALLERY
(0461 49 51 11; via Manci 27; ⊙10am-6pm
Mon-Sat) This recently renovated *palazzo*
(mansion) houses the city council's gallery
and stages excellent, often internationally
significant shows.

🏃 Activities

The small ski station of **Vaneze di Monte**
(1350m) is a 17km winding drive from
Trento and is connected by cable car to its
higher counterpart, **Vasòn**, and the gentle
slopes of **Monte Bondone** (1537m; www.monte
bondone.it). Criss-crossed by 37km of cross-
country ski trails and nine downhill runs in
winter, Monte Bondone's pristine slopes are
also home to the **Giardino Alpine Botanico**
(Botanical Alpine Gardens; ☑0461 94 80 50; Viote
de Monte Bondone; adult/reduced €3.50/2.50;
⊙9am-noon & 2-5pm Jun & Sep, 9am-noon &
2-6pm Jul-Aug), with a collection of Alpine
plants from across Europe, as well as an indigenous nature trail. On weekends between
December and March, Skibus Monte Bondone, run by Trentino Trasporti, wends its
way from Trento to Vaneze (€1.50 one way).

For walking information, including suggested itineraries, *vie ferrate* (trails with
permanent cables and ladders) and *rifugi*
(mountain huts) in Trentino, visit the local
Società degli Alpinisti Tridentini (SAT;
☑0461 98 18 71; www.sat.tn.it; Via Manci 57; ⊙9am-
noon & 3-10pm Mon-Fri), staffed by friendly
mountaineers.

☞ Tours

The tourist office runs two-hour guided
walking tours of the city centre and Castello
del Buonconsiglio (€4) every Saturday morning and on Thursdays in July and August.

🛏 Sleeping

TOP CHOICE Elisa B&B B&B €
(☑0461 92 21 33; www.bbelisa.com; Viale Rovereto
17; s/d €60/90; ❄🛜) This is a true B&B in an
architect's family home, with three private
and stylish rooms and a charming host who
dispenses organic breakfasts (home-baked
cakes, freshly squeezed juice, artisanal
cheese), along with invaluable local tips.
There's a mini-kitchen for guests' use and
the bathrooms are large. It's located in a
quiet residential neighbourhood, a pleasant
stroll from the city centre, with lots of eating, shopping and drinking options along
the way.

HINTERLAND SLEEPS 291

Central hotels book out in early June,
when the **Festival Economia** (2012.fes-
tivaleconomia.eu) comes to town, and for
other occasional conferences. **Trentino
Agritur** (☑0461 23 53 23; www.agrituris-
motrentino.com, in Italian; Via Aconcio 13,
Trento; ⊙9am-noon Mon-Fri) can put you
in touch with rural B&Bs and *agriturismi*
(farm stay accommodation), often only
a short drive from the city.

Albergo Accademia HOTEL €€
(☑0461 23 36 00; www.accademiahotel.it; Vicolo
Colico 4/6; s €82-105, d €145-165; P❄@) Elegant small hotel in a historic medieval house
with rooms that are modern and airy (if a little on the staid side). Suites are luxuriously
spacious and there's a great roof terrace that
can be booked for private dinner parties.

Hotel Venezia HOTEL €
(☑0461 23 41 14; www.hotelveneziatn.it; Piazza del
Duomo 45; s €55, d with/without bathroom €76/59)
Friendly Venezia's rooms overlook either the
Piazza del Duomo or pretty Via Belanzani. It's
basic, but parquetry floors and dark-timber
furniture lend it a cosy, atmospheric feel.

Ostello Giovane Europa HOSTEL €
(☑0461 26 34 84; www.gayaproject.org; Via Torre
Vanga 9; dm/s/d €16/26/43; ⊙reception 5am-
10pm) This squeaky-clean place is bang in the
middle of town and just a few minutes' walk
from the main train station (convenient, yes,
but also noisy). Rooms are comfortable and
some have balconies and mountain views.

🍴 Eating & Drinking

Trento's table is a hearty one and draws many
of its ingredients – beef, game, fresh cheeses,
mushrooms – from its fertile hinterland.
There's a lot of cross-cultural traffic too: *co-
toletta* (schnitzel) and *canederli* (dumplings)
are decidedly northern, while polenta and
asparagus speak of the Veneto and Garda's
olive oil of the Mediterranean. Bakeries brim
with apple strudel, but don't overlook the
local carrot cake – *sans* the cinnamon of its
Anglo-American cousin. Wines to look out for
include Trento DOC, a sparkling wine made
from chardonnay grapes, the white Nosiola
and the extremely drinkable red, Teroldego
Rotaliano DOC. Trentino's smartly bottled
Surgiva mineral water is considered one of
Italy's best, for taste and purity.

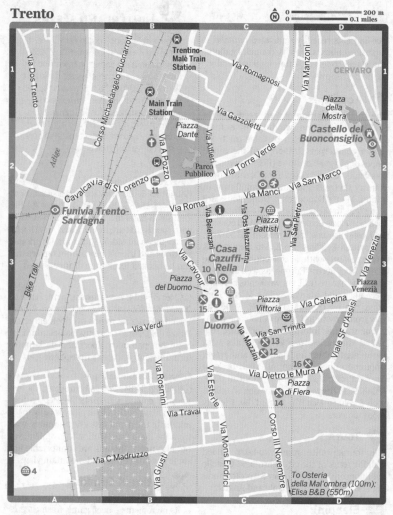

There are plenty of supermarkets and delis in the centre and along **Corso III Novembre** for self-catering.

Ai Tre Garofani MODERN TRENTINI €€
(☑0461 23 75 43; Via Mazzini 33; meals €35-50; ☺Tue-Sat) While the dining room vibes are traditional – a low-beamed ceiling and deep drapery – the staff here are far from it. Young, creative and unpretentious, they deliver a dining experience full of life and local colour. Diners are welcomed with a glass of *prosecco* (a type of sparkling wine), an *amuse-bouche* (perhaps a little cup of potato cream with Gar-

da olive oil) and house-made breads – local milk, potato, and dark grained. Alpine mugo pine scents a *tagliatelle* (ribbon pasta), rabbit is served with chestnut honey and an impossibly tender venison fillet sits on celeriac mash. Wines are well chosen and, of course, local.

Scrigno del Duomo GASTRONOMIC €€€
(☑0461 22 00 30; www.scrignodelduomo.com; Piazza del Duomo 29; meals €35, degustations from €50; ☺upstairs lunch & dinner daily, downstairs lunch Tue-Fri & Sun, dinner Tue-Sun) Trento's culinary epicentre is discreetly housed behind a solid wall in a building dating back

to the 1200s. Take the stairs down to the formal diner, with its glassed-in Roman-era cellar. Or stay upstairs underneath the beautiful painted wooden ceiling. Here it's a stylish turn on local specialities – organic beef carpaccio, lake fish, asparagus lasagne with *puzzone* cheese from Moena, thyme-scented crème brûlée – many made with '0km'-sourced produce. A wine at the bar, with Scrigno's baton-like *grissini* (Turin-style breadstick) for amusement, is always an option too, and staff wine recommendations are spot on.

Uva et Mente
PIZZERIA €

(☑0461 190 31 62; Via Dietro le Mura A 35; pizzas €7, meals €15-30; ☺to midnight Tue-Sun) A bustling basement with fresh, interesting mains, pastas and risottos, good pizzas and a dedicated beer menu. Pizzas can be ordered whole-meal or gluten-free (try to book ahead for these), and there's an €8 lunch deal.

Pedavena
BREWERY €

(☑0461 98 62 55; Piazza di Fiera 13; meals €18-30; ☺Wed-Mon) Proudly crowd-pleasing and perennially popular, this sprawling 1920s beer hall (complete with fermenting brew in the corner) serves up the comfort food you'd expect: bratwurst, schnitzel and steaming plates of polenta with mushroom stew and slabs of melty white *tosella* cheese.

Al Tino
TRENTINI €

(☑0461 98 41 09; Via San Trinita 10; meals €18-25) Al Tino has a sweet old-fashioned dining room and service to match, with a menu

dedicated to traditional dishes such as barley soup, *canederli in brodo* (dumplings in broth) and pork chops. Opens early – 6.45pm – for dinner.

Casa del Caffe
CAFE

(Via San Pietro 38; ☺Mon-Sat) Follow your nose to this wonderful coffee bar and provedore for Trento's best espresso. Beans are roasted on the premises and the crowded shelves feature some of the country's best boutique chocolate.

Osteria della Mal'Ombra
BAR

(www.osteriadellamalombra.com; Corso III Novembre 43; ☺8am-1am Mon-Sat) Join the locals for good wines and grappas, possibly more spirited political debate and, on Tuesdays, music.

❶ Information

Hospital (☑0461 90 31 11; Largo Medaglie d'Oro 9)

Police station (☑0461 89 95 11; Piazza della Mostra 3)

Tourist office (☑0461 21 60 00; www.apt.trento.it; Via Manci 2; ☺9am-7pm)

❶ Getting There & Away

Trento is well connected. Regular trains leave the main train station (Piazza Dante) for the following destinations:

Bologna (€11.30, 3¼ hours, every two hours)

Bolzano (€3.35, 30 minutes, four per hour)

Venice (€8.40, 2½ hours, hourly)

Verona (€5.40, one hour, every 30 minutes)

TRENTO CARD

Available from the tourist office and museums, this card (adult plus one child 24/48 hours €10/15) gets you free entry to city museums and the Botanical Alpine Gardens, free public transport – including the Trento – Sardagna cable car – wine tastings and cellar tours, bike hire and a raft of discounts. The 48-hour card also includes free entrance to MART Rovereto, Castel Thun and other regional museums.

Next door to the main station, the Trento–Malè train line connects the city with Cles in the Val di Non.

From the InterCity bus station (Via Andrea Pozzo), local bus company **Trentino Trasporti** (☑0461 82 10 00; www.ttspa.it, in Italian) runs buses to and from Madonna di Campiglio, San Martino di Castrozza, Molveno, Canazei and Rovereto.

Rovereto

POP 37,566

In the winter of 1769, Leopold Mozart and his soon-to-be-famous musical son visited Rovereto and found it to be 'rich in diligent people engaged in viticulture and the weaving of silk'. The area is no longer known for silk, but still produces some outstanding wines, including the inky, cherry-scented Marzemino (the wine's scene-stealing appearance in *Don Giovanni* suggests it may have been a Mozart family favourite). Those on a musical pilgrimage come to visit the Church of San Marco (Piazza San Marco; ☉8.30am-noon & 2-7pm), where the 13-year-old Wolfgang wowed the Roveretini, and for the annual Mozart Festival (www.festival mozartrovereto.com) in August. The town that Mozart knew still has its haunting, tightly coiled streets, but it's the shock of the new that lures most – one of Italy's best contemporary and 20th-century art museums.

Sights

TOP CHOICE **Museo di Arte Moderna e Contemporanea Rovereto**   ART GALLERY

(MART; ☑0464 43 88 87; english.mart.trento.it; Corso Bettini 43; adult/reduced €10/7, incl Casa del Depero €12/9; ☉10am-6pm Tue-Thu, Sat & Sun, 10am-9pm Fri) A four-floor, 12,000-sq-m steel, glass and marble behemoth, care of the

Ticinese architect Mario Botta, is both imposing but human, with mountain light gently filling a central atrium via a soaring cupola. It's home to some huge 20th-century works, including Warhol's *Four Marilyns* (1962), several Picassos and a clutch of contemporary art stars, including Bill Viola, Kara Walker, Arnuf Rainer and a whopping-great Anslem Keifer. Italian work is, naturally, well represented, with excellent pieces from Balla, Morandi, De Chirico, Fontana and Manzoni. Temporary exhibitions cast a broad net, from easygoing shows of Monet or Modigliani to cutting-edge contemporary surveys.

Casa del Depero   MUSEUM

(☑0424 60 04 35; Via Portici 38; adult/reduced €6/4, incl MART admission €13; ☉10am-6pm Tue-Sun) The futurists were never afraid of a spot of self-aggrandisement and local lad Fortunato Depero was no exception. This self-designed museum was launched shortly before his death in 1960. After recent restoration work by MART, it's again open to the public. The obsessions of early-20th-century Italy mix nostalgically, somewhat unnervingly, with a historic past – bold tapestries and machine-age-meets-troubadour-era furniture decorate a made-over medieval town house. Fascinating toys, books and ephemera also line three floors.

Eating & Drinking

Osteria del Pettirosso   WINE BAR

(www.osteriadelpettirosso.com; Corso Bettini 24; ☉Mon-Sat) There's a moody downstairs dining room but most people come here for the blackboard menu of wines by the glass, many from small producers, a plate of cheese (€7) or a couple of *crostone all lardo* (toasts with cured pork fat; €2.50).

Stappomatto   WINE BAR

(www.stappomatto.com; Corso Bettini 56; ☉7.30am-8.30pm Tue-Sat, 10.30am-4.30pm Sun) Cute wood-clad wine bar with an attached dining room serving hearty homestyle cooking.

Information

The **tourist office** (☑0464 43 03 63; www. apt.rovereto.tn.it; Corso Rosmini 6; ☉9am-1pm & 2-6pm Mon-Sat) has town maps, details of cycling trails and can help you out with free bike hire from **C'entro in bici**.

Rovereto is around 15 minutes by train from Trento on the Bologna–Brennero line.

Brenta Dolomites

The Brenta group lies like a rocky island to the west of the main Dolomite range. Protected by the Parco Naturale Adamello-Brenta, these sharp, majestic peaks are well known among mountaineers for their sheer cliffs and tricky ascents and are home to some of the world's most famous *vie ferrate* routes. Harnesses and ropes are essential for most of these high-altitude trails, including one of the group's most famous, the Via Ferrata delle Bocchette pioneered by British climber trailblazer Francis Fox Tuckett in the 1860s.

On the eastern side of the Brenta group is the Altipiano della Paganella, a high plateau offering some skiing and a range of outdoors adventures. On the densely forested western side is the glitzy resort of Madonna di Campiglio. The wiggly S421, S237 and S239 linking the two make a scenic, if perilous, drive. Regular bus connections with Trento are plentiful in the high seasons.

While the Superskirama pass covers all of the Brenta, separate passes are available. The 1-/3-/6-day passes for Madonna di Campiglio are €35/101/178, while those for Altipiano della Paganella cost €36/101/179.

ALTIPIANO DELLA PAGANELLA
POP 5000 / ELEV 2098M

Less than an hour's drive northwest of Trento, this dress-circle plateau looks out onto the towering Brenta Dolomites. The Altipiano incorporates five small villages: ski resort Fai della Paganella, touristy Andalo, lakeside Molveno and little Cavedago and Spormaggiore.

🏃 Activities

Alpine guide Dolomiti di Brenta-Paganella (☎329 5824146; guidealpine@esperienzatrentino.it) organises rock climbing and guided walks in summer and ski-mountaineering, ice climbing and snowshoeing excursions in the Parco Naturale Adamello-Brenta in winter. You can also organise private expeditions with the association's guides.

The Paganella ski area is accessible from Andalo by cable car and Fai della Paganella by chairlift. It has two cross-country skiing trails and 50km of downhill ski slopes, ranging from beginner-friendly green runs to the heart-lurching black.

From the top of Molveno village, a two-seater cable car (☎0461 58 69 81; one way/return €6/9.50) transports you in two stages up to Pradel (1400m) from where trail No 340, a pleasant and easy one-hour walk, leads to the Rifugio Croz dell'Altissimo (☎0461 58 61 95; ☺Jun-Sep) at 1430m. Several other trails, of varying difficulty, start from there.

🛏 Sleeping & Eating

The plateau's five villages have over 100 hotels; alternatively, check with the tourist offices for details of the numerous *agriturismo* (farm stay accommodation) and self-catering apartments.

CLOUD BURSTING

During WWI, while the British, French and Germans were drowning in the mud of Flanders, their Italian allies were engaged in an equally terrifying conflict against their Austrian foes on a battlefront that sliced across the Dolomites.

The scars of this brutal and lengthy WWI campaign are etched indelibly over the Alpine landscape. While scores of sculpted tunnels, trenches and emplacements remain, it's the high-altitude trails that have left the most lasting legacy.

In order to maximise ease of movement up in the rugged, perilous peaks, the two armies attached ropes and ladders across seemingly impregnable crags in a series of fixed-protection climbing paths known as *vie ferrate* (iron ways). Renovated with steel rungs, bridges and heavy-duty wires after the war, the *vie ferrate* evolved into a cross between standard hiking and full-blown rock climbing, allowing non-mountaineers access to what would normally be too challenging a terrain.

Vie ferrate exist all over the Dolomites and routes are graded one to five according to difficulty. You do need to don basic climbing gear (helmet, pads and gloves) and carry some special equipment, including a Y-shaped harness fitted with two karabiners to lock onto metal supports.

Madonna di Campiglio and Cortina d'Ampezzo are the gateways to the most spectacular routes.

Camping Spiaggia
CAMPGROUND €

(☎0461 58 69 78; www.campingmolveno.it; Via Lungolago 25; camping 2 people, car & tent €20-46; ☼reception 9am-noon & 2-7pm year-round; P@☎) These pleasant sites on the shores of Lago di Molveno come with free use of the neighbouring outdoor pool, tennis court and table tennis. It's an easy stroll into Molveno's bustling little village centre, and entertainment and water sports are on tap in high summer.

Alp & Wellness Sport Hotel Panorama
HOTEL €€

(☎0461 58 31 34; www.sporthotelpanorama.it; Via Carletti 6, Fai della Paganella; d €120-200; P✻ @☎⚘) With namesake panoramic views, rooms in this multicoloured modern edifice have clean lines and pared-down furnishings, and some have lofts. Wellness facilities are numerous, including indoor and outdoor pools.

Al Penny
TRENTINI €

(☎0461 58 52 51; Viale Trento 23, Andalo; meals €22-25; ☼11am-3pm & 5pm-2am) First impressions may clock the decor as a little too out of the box, but in fact it's a genuinely cosy spot. A glass of warming Marzemino sets the scene, then out come authentic and tasty Trentino specialities – venison *ragù* (meat and tomato sauce) with pine nuts, *taiadele smalzade* (pan-fried fat noodles) or mushroom *canederli*, served with homemade bread.

❶ Information

All tourist offices share a website (www.visit dolomitipaganella.it).

Andalo Tourist Office (☎0461 58 58 36; Piazza Dolomiti 1; ☼9am-12.30pm & 3-6.30pm Mon-Sat, 9.30am-12.30pm Sun) The main office, with good information for both winter and summer activities.

Fai della Paganella Tourist Office (☎0461 58 31 30; Via Villa; ☼9am-12.30pm & 3-6.30pm Mon-Sat, 9.30am-12.30pm Sun)

Guardia Medica (☎0461 58 56 37; ☼8pm-8am) After-hours medical call-out service.

Molveno Tourist Office (☎0461 58 69 24; Piazza Marconi 5; ☼9am-12.30pm & 3-6.30pm Mon, Wed, Fri & Sat, 9am-12.30pm Tue, Thu & Sun)

Tourist medical service (☎0461 58 60 45) Daytime medical aid.

❶ Getting There & Around

Trentino Trasporti (☎0461 82 10 00; www. ttspa.it, in Italian) runs buses between all five

villages and Trento (€2.90 to €3.30, 3½ hours, up to nine daily) and services to Madonna di Campiglio (€8.60) and Riva del Garda (€5.60) on Lago di Garda; tourist offices have timetables. Free ski buses serve the area in winter.

MADONNA DI CAMPIGLIO & PINZOLO

Oh, Madonna (population 700, elevation 1522m). Let there be no doubt, this is the Dolomites' glamour destination, where ankle-length furs are standard après-ski wear and the formidable downhill runs often a secondary concern. Austrian royalty, in particular Franz Joseph and wife Elisabeth, aka Sissi, set the tone in the 19th century; this early celeb patronage is commemorated in late February, when fireworks blaze and costumed pageants waltz through town for the annual **Habsburg Carnival**. Despite the traffic jams and mall-like hotel complexes, the central village square has retained something of its essence, overlooked by a pretty stone church and the jutting battlements of the Brenta Dolomites beyond. In summer this is an ideal base for hikers and *vie ferrate* enthusiasts.

Pinzolo (population 2000, elevation 800m), in a lovely valley 16km south, has a lively historic centre and quite a few less tickets on itself.

◉ Sights & Activities

A network of chairlifts and several cable cars (☎0465 44 77 44) take skiers and boarders from Madonna to its numerous ski runs and a snowboarding park (with half-pipe, slide park and boarder cross) in winter and to walking and mountain-biking trails in summer. In Pinzolo there is just one cable car (☎0465 50 12 56; www.funiviepinzolo.it, in Italian; Via Nepomuceno Bolognini 84; ☼8.30am-12.30pm & 2-6pm mid-Dec–Apr & Jun–mid-Sep), which climbs the mountain to 2100m-high Doss del Sabion (one way/return €5/8, 20min), stopping at mid-station Pra Rodont (1530m; one way/return €5/6, 10min) en route. **Mountain bikes** can be hired at this cable-car station in summer.

Madonna's tourist office teams up with the Parco Naturale Adamello-Brenta to run particularly scenic **guided walks** to a traditional Alpine pasture hut in the national park from mid-July to September, as well as others that focus on the area's unique geology.

In Campo Carlo Magno, 2km north of Madonna, the Cabinovia Grostè cable car (one way/return €11/16; ☼8.30am-12.30pm & 2-5pm mid-Dec–Apr & Jun–mid-Sep) takes walkers to the Passo Grostè (2440m). The **Via**

Parco Naturale Adamello Brenta – a wild and beautiful park encompassing more than 80 lakes and the vast Adamello glacier – was once home to the Alps' only brown bears. Although it became a protected area in 1967, bear numbers at one point dwindled to just three.

Beginning in 1999, park authorities set about reintroducing the bears, bringing in 10 Alpine brown bears from Slovenia. The first cubs were born in the park in 2002 and there have been cubs born every winter since, with a total of 20 bears inhabiting the park at the time of writing.

The brown bears measure 1.2m high when on all four paws and over 2m when standing; they weigh anywhere from 100kg to 250kg, depending on the season. They're closely monitored by park authorities via radio collars, and some can be viewed at the Casa dell'orso Spormaggiore (☏0461 65 36 22; Via Alt Spaur 6; adult/reduced €6/5, incl park admission; ◷10am-1pm & 2-6.30pm Tue-Sun Jun-Sep, book for other periods) in Spormaggiore, 15km northeast of Molveno. The centre has excellent exhibits about the bears' reintroduction, including some cute displays for kids, and you can book to see the bears in winter dormancy via infrared camera. It's hoped that in 50 to 100 years there will once again be bears all over the Alps. Of course, happy bears often mean unhappy farmers, but Trentino's provincial government pays for farmers to install electric fences and for any damage the bears cause.

Bears aside, the 620-sq-km park – Trentino's largest protected area – is home to ibexes, red deer, marmots, chamois and 82 bird species, along with 1200 different mountain flowers, including two (*Nigritella luschmannie* and *Eryshimum auranthiacum*) that are unique to the area.

Wildlife thrives around the banks of Lago di Tovel, set deep in a forest some 30km north of Spormaggiore in the park's heart. An easy one-hour walking trail encircles the once red lake. The lakeside visitors centre (☏0463 45 10 33; ◷10am-1pm & 2-6pm summer) has extensive information on other walks in the park.

For information on mountain huts, alpine guides, maps and itineraries, as well as eco-friendly accommodation, contact the park headquarters (☏0465 80 66 66; www.pnab.it, in Italian; Via Nazionale 12, Strembo; ◷10am-1pm & 2-6pm summer) a few kilometres south.

Bocchetta di Tuckett (trail No 305) – the *via ferrata* for which the Brenta group is most famous – also leaves from the cable-car station. Only the experienced should attempt it. Otherwise, check with the tourist office for details of a number of pre-glacial trails and mountain huts.

Pinzolo's beautifully sited 16th-century Chiesa di San Vigilio merits a visit for its *danza macabra* (dance of death) decor. North of Pinzolo is the entrance to the Val di Genova, often described as one of the Alps' most beautiful valleys. It's lined with a series of spectacular waterfalls: great walking country. Four mountain huts strung out along the valley floor make overnight stays an option – Pinzolo's tourist office has details.

🛏 Sleeping & Eating

Budget beds in Madonna are non-existent in winter, and most midrange hotels insist on full- or half-board and minimum stays during peak times. Commuting to the ski fields from the Val di Sole is a doable option.

Camping Parco Adamello   CAMPGROUND €
(☏0465 50 17 93; www.campingparcoadamello.it; Carisolo; camping 2 people, car & tent €28-36; ◷year-round; 🅿) Beautifully situated within the national park 1km north of Pinzolo, this camp ground is a natural starting point for outdoor adventures such as skiing, snowshoeing, walking and biking. There's also weekly apartment rentals.

Hermitage Biohotel   HOTEL €€€
(☏0465 44 15 58; www.biohotelhermitage.it; half-board d €170-350; 🅿❄🛜♨👫) Traditional European family-run hotel, with streamlined modern rooms and eco-principles. The low-key (though Michelin-starred) restaurant is gorgeous and there are fairy-tale views from the lounge bar and pool.

Chalet La Dolce Vita   DESIGN HOTEL €€
(☏0465 44 31 91; www.chaletdolcevita.it; d €130-250; 🅿❄♨🛜) This is the latest entry in the Madonna ultraluxe hotel stakes, with friendly staff and a quiet wooded setting. The bar

keeps the Milanese fashion set happy come *aperitivo* hour, and upstairs guests are co-cooned in beautiful, earthy rooms.

Hotel Bellavista
HOTEL €

(☑0465 50 11 64; www.bellavistanet.com, in Italian; Pinzolo; half-board per person per week €300-500; ☺year-round; ℗) About as no-frills as this region gets: a traditional, family-run place, mid-sized with 57 comfortable modern rooms and hearty Alpine food.

❶ Information

Guardia Medica (☑0465 44 05 38, 0465 80 16 00) Emergency doctor.

Madonna Tourist Office (☑0465 44 75 01; www.campiglio.to; Via Pradalago 4; ☺9am-12.30pm & 3-7pm Mon-Sat, 10am-1pm Sun)

Pinzolo Tourist Office (☑0465 50 10 07; www.pinzolo.to; Piazzale Ciciamimo; ☺9am-12.30pm & 3-6.30pm Mon-Sat, 9am-12.30pm Sun)

Tourist medical service (☑0465 44 30 73; ☺early Dec–Easter & mid-Jun–mid-Sep)

❶ Getting There & Away

Madonna di Campiglio and Pinzolo are accessible year-round by bus from Trento (€9, 1½ hours, five daily) and Milan (€27, 3¾ hours, one daily).

From mid-December to mid-April ski-shuttle buses run to and from Madonna and Pinzolo once a week from Milan's Malpensa and Linate airports via Bergamo's airport (one way €36), and Verona's Villafranca airport via Brescia's airport (one way €30).

Val di Non, Val di Sole & Val di Rabbi

Sandwiched between the Brenta group and Parco Nazionale dello Stelvio, these Italian-speaking farming valleys are an easy train ride from Trento.

VAL DI NON

The first thing you notice about Val di Non is the apple trees – their gnarly, tressellated branches stretch for miles (and are at their fragrant best in spring). Craggy castles dot the surrounding rises, including the stunning Castel Thun (☑0461 49 28 29; Vigo di Ton; adult/reduced €6/4; ☺10am-5pm Tue-Sun). The valley is centred on its main settlement, Cles, whose tourist office (☑0463 422 88 83; Corso Dante 30; ☺9am-12.30pm & 3-6pm Mon-Sat, 9am-noon Sun Jul & Aug) is just off the main road through town.

Italy's apple giant Melinda is a valley girl. Melinda Mondo (☑0463 46 92 99; www.melinda.it; Via della Cooperazione 21, Segno; tours by appointment ☺8.30am-12.30pm & 3-7pm Mon-Sat Oct-Jul, 9am-noon Sun Jul), near Mollaro, a couple of villages on from Cles, conducts tours of the orchards and processing plants and has a cheery shop selling apples and all sorts of apple-related products. Look out for the big cheese next door, the home of **Trentingrana**, Trentino's sweet, subtle 'Parmesan-style' Grana.

VAL DI SOLE

Leaving Cles in the rear-view mirror, the apple orchards draw you west into the aptly named Val di Sole (Valley of the Sun) tracing the course of the foaming river Noce, with its main town of Malè.

This valley is renowned for outdoor pursuits aside from the usual skiing and hiking, and is popular with young Trentini. The Noce makes for great rafting. Centro Rafting Val di Sole (☑0463 97 32 78; www.raftingcenter.it; Via Gole 105, Dimaro; ☺Jun-Sep) runs rafting trips (from €67), as well as kayaking, canyoning and Nordic walking. Sole also guards a flattish 35km section of the Brenta Dolomite Bike Loop and runs a special bike train from June to September, allowing cyclists to catch a ride when they get tired.

Kaiserkrone (☑0463 97 33 26; www.kaiserkrone.it; Piazza Serra 3, Dimaro; d €64-96; ✿❀☎🖥) has large comfortable blond-wood rooms in the centre of workaday but charming Dimaro; it's a great location for Sole pursuits and an easy, economical base for the Brenta ski fields. Dolomiti Camping Village (☑0463 97 43 32; www.campingdolomiti.com; Via Gole 105, Comezzadure; camping 2 people, car & tent €26-34, d bungalow €49-75; ☺mid-May–mid-Oct & Dec-Easter; ℗@✿🖥), riverside and adjacent to the rafting centre, has well-kept campsites and bungalows with access to a wellness centre, indoor and outdoor pools, volleyball courts and trampolines.

Cicli Andreis (www.cicliandreis.it; Via Conci 19/27, Malè) is handily located just off Malè's main street. Daily rental costs from €18 (less for kids' bikes).

The helpful Malè tourist office (☑0463 90 12 80; www.valdisole.net; Piazza Regina Elena 19, Malè; ☺9am-noon & 2.30-6.30pm Mon-Sat, 10am-noon Sun) has good information on the entire valley and can advise you on ski facilities and walking trails in nearby Stelvio.

VAL DI RABBI

Val di Rabbi is a refreshingly tranquil Alpine valley that provides the best southern entry into Parco Nazionale dello Stelvio. It is also

PALE DI SAN MARTINO

Pink blends seamlessly with green in the Pale di San Martino (elevation 1467m), where the luminous Dolomite mountains rise like ghosts above the ancient forest of Paneveggio, whose wood is made into prized violins. The mountains are embraced by the **Parco Naturale Paneveggio-Pale di San Martino**, home to roe deer, chamois, marmots, wild fowl and birds of prey such as the golden eagle. At the park's impressive headquarters in the 1853-built **Villa Welsperg** (☑0439 6 48 54; www.parcopan.org; Via Castelpietra 2, Val Canali; ☺9.30am-12.30pm, 3-6pm summer, 2-5pm winter), suspended aquariums illustrate the park's water life and its flora and fauna are also explored. The park website has detailed driving directions.

At the park's feet huddles **San Martino di Castrozza**, a small but popular ski resort and walking spot, accessible via bus from Trento. In summer, a chairlift and cable car whisk walkers to the **Rifugio Rosetta** (2600m) and a number of trails (some easy, some requiring mountaineering skills).

The **San Martino tourist office** (☑0439 76 88 67; www.sanmartino.com; Via Passo Rolle 165; ☺9am-noon & 3-6pm Mon-Sat, 9.30am-12.30pm Sun) has more information.

known for its supposedly curative Antica Fonte spring waters. The **Terme di Rabbi** (☺8am-noon & 4.30-8.30pm Mon-Fri, to 7pm Sat May-Sep) in the eponymous village offers a wide range of recuperative treatments and is administered by the businesslike **Grand Hotel Rabbi** (☑0463 98 30 50; www.grandhotelrabbi.it; Fonti di Rabbi 153; half-board d €90-140; ☺May-Sep; P⛱). Next door is a small **visitors centre** (☑0463 98 51 90; ☺8am-1pm & 3-7pm Jun-Sep, 8am-noon & 2-6pm Oct-May) and the starting point for a network of paths into Stelvio, some of which connect to Val Martello in Alto Adige. Regular buses head up the valley from outside Malè train station.

❶ Getting There & Around

Ferrovia Trento-Malè (☑0463 90 11 50) buses connect Rabbi, Madonna di Campiglio and Malè. Cles (€2.90, 45 minutes) and Malè (€5, 1½ hours, eight daily) are on the Trento–Comezzadure train line. A **cable car** (one way €5) ferries skiers and walkers up the mountainside from the train station.

Free ski buses loop around the area in winter; tourist offices have schedules.

Val di Fiemme

In a region where few valleys speak the same dialect (let alone agree on the same cheese recipe), the Val di Fiemme stands out. In the 12th century, independently minded local noblemen set up their own quasi-republic here, the Magnificent Community of Fiemme, and the ethos and spirit of the founders lives on.

Today the slightly less bolshie 'Community' is headquartered in the wonderfully frescoed **Palazzo Vescovile** (Piazza Battisti) in the valley's main town of **Cavalese** (population 3600, elevation 1000m). A few doors down and a few centuries on is the **Centro Arte Contemporanea Cavalese** (☑0462 23 54 16; www.artecavalese.it; Palazzo Firmian, Piazzetta Rizzoli 1; admission free; ☺3.30-7.30pm Fri-Sun).

From Cavalese, skiers can take a cable car up to the **Cermis ski area** (2229m), part of the extensive Superski Dolomiti region. Cavalese's **tourist office** (☑0462 24 11 11; www.visitfiemme.it; Via Bronzetti 60; ☺9am-noon & 3.30-7pm Mon-Sat) acts as a contact point for local Alpine guide groups who organise, among other things, mountaineering ascents on Pale di San Martino, Cima della Madonna and Sass Maor, a 120km-long high-altitude skiing excursion.

⛺ Sleeping & Eating

Park Hotel Azalea HOTEL €€
(☑0462 34 01 09; www.parkhotelazalea.it; Via delle Cesure 1, Cavalese; half-board d €90-180; P🛜👪) This forward-thinking hotel has a variety of light, relaxing rooms. Some have mountain views, others look out over the village's pretty vegetable garden, and all make use of ecologically sourced woods and natural fibres. Food, including a groaning afternoon tea spread, is organic, and there are beautiful children's facilities.

Hotel Garni Laurino HOTEL €€
(☑0462 34 01 51; www.hotelgarnilaurino.it; Via Antoniazzi 14, Cavalese; d €80-130; P@) A tumble

DON'T MISS

SAUSAGES!

In Canazei, look out for the fork-wielding Ladin sausage cook; his roadside stall, just off Piazza Marconi, draws queues of ravenous skiers for beer and wurst all winter long.

of floral fabrics and timber furniture in a 17th-century building right in the centre of town. Large rooms are even sweeter with a garden and mountain bikes thrown in.

El Molin GASTRONOMIC €€€
(☎0462 34 00 74; Piazza Battisti 11, Cavalese; upstairs meals €15-25, downstairs degustations €65-90; ⊙lunch & dinner Wed-Mon) A legend in the valley, and Michelin starred, this old mill sits at the historic heart of Cavalese. Downstairs, next to the old waterwheels, Alessandro Gilmozzi does playful gastronomic dishes featuring local, seasonal ingredients. Streetside, the casual (though rather stuffy) wine bar does baked-to-order eggs with Trentingrana or truffles, burgers, hearty mains and creative desserts. **Excelsior** (⊙7am-11pm Wed-Mon), a cosy nook on the same site, turns out excellent pizzas – don't pass up the one with local *puzzone* cheese. Attention to detail at all price points is high.

Val di Fassa

Val di Fassa is Trentino's only Ladin-speaking valley (there are four more in Alto Adige), framed by the stirring peaks of the Gruppo del Sella to the north, the Catinaccio to the west and the Marmolada (3342m) to the southeast. The valley spins on two hubs: **Canazei** (population 1866, elevation 1465m), beautifully sited but verging on overdevelopment, and the pretty riverside village of **Moena** (population 2690, elevation 1114m), more down to earth and increasingly environmentally conscious. Fassa is the nexus of Italy's cross-country skiing scene. Italian cross-country champ Christian Zorzi hails from Moena and the town also plays host to the sport's most illustrious mass-participation race, the annual Marcialonga (www.marcialonga.it), a 70km march through the snow.

Dolomiti Superski passes are valid here; alternatively there are three-/six-day passes for the Val di Fassa (€92/161) or the Tre Valli

(€88/157) covering the Fassa, Biois and San Pellegrino valleys.

⊙ Sights & Activities

Variety is the spice of life for skiers here, with 120km of downhill and cross-country runs, as well as challenging Alpine tours and the Sella Ronda ski circuit. In summer, you can ski down the Marmolada glacier.

The Gruppo del Sella is approached from **Passo Pordoi**, where a cable car travels to almost 3000m. The best approach to the Catinaccio group is from **Vigo di Fassa**, 11km southwest of Canazei near Pozza di Fassa; a cable car climbs to an elevation of 2000m, dropping you off near the cheerful mountain hut **Baita Checco** (☎0462 76 35 81; www.baitachecco.com; Vigo di Fassa; mains €7-12; ⊙8am-4.30pm Dec-Mar & Jul–mid-Sep).

For gentler summertime rambles, ask at the tourist office for a *Low-level Walks in the Fassa Valley* brochure, which outlines 29 walks (1.5km to 8km long), including visits to historic Ladin landmarks.

🛏 Sleeping, Eating & Drinking

Villa Kofler DESIGN HOTEL €€
(☎0462 75 04 44; www.villakofler.it; Via Dolomiti 63, Campitello; d €145-180; P 🛜) An intimate hotel in a valley of giants; choose from rooms that range across various current design trends and tastes. There's a little gym, a library and, bliss, in-room infrared saunas.

Garni Stella Alpina B&B €
(☎0462 60 11 27; www.stella-alpina.net; Via Antermont 6, Canazei; d €68-128; P) Like nowhere else you'll ever stay (unless you happen to have a Ladin aunt), with cosy rooms, a sauna-jacuzzi and a downstairs shop and wine cellar.

Central Hotel HOTEL €€
(☎0462 57 32 28; www.centralhotel.it; Strada Heilmann 4, Moena; s €75-100, d €110-160; P @) Rooms are small but have nice touches, like window seats, and the elegant, rambling building has lots of comfortable public areas.

El Paél TRENTINI €€
(☎0462 60 14 33; www.elpael.com; Via Roma 58, Canazei; meals €25-35; ⊙Tue-Sun) This *osteria tipica trentina* has a traditional Ladin kitchen cooking up specialities of the valley – nettle dumplings, asparagus with liquorice sauce, and venison with steamed pumpkin.

Malga Panna GASTRONOMIC €€€
(☎0462 57 34 89; www.malgapanna.it; Via Costa-
lunga 29, Moena; degustations from €65) Fine-
dining interpretations of mountain food stay
true to their culinary roots and are served
in an evocatively simple setting. Expect to
encounter the flavours of Alpine herbs and
flowers, and lots of game.

Kusk La Locanda BAR
(Via dei Colli 7; dishes from €7; ⊙8am-2am Wed-
Mon) Legendary throughout the Val di Fassa
for après-ski. This four-way split between a
pizzeria, American bar, trash disco and Italian restaurant still manages to maintain a
Ladin cosiness.

ⓘ Information

Val di Fassa's tourist offices have a coordinated
website (www.fassa.com) and share opening
hours (8.30am to 5pm Mondya to Saturday,
10am to 12.30pm Sunday, with rotating lunch
hours and late openings).
Canazei Tourist Office (☎0462 60 11 13;
Piazza Marconi 5)
Moena Tourist Office (☎0462 60 97 70;
Piazza del Navalge 4)

ⓘ Getting There & Away

The Val di Fassa can be reached by Trentino
Trasporti buses from Trento year-round (€5.25,
1½ to 2½ hours), and by local **SAD** (www.sad.it)
bus from Bolzano and the Val Gardena from June
to mid-September, with free ski buses also serving the region in winter.

ALTO ADIGE (SÜDTIROL)

Bolzano (Bozen)

POP 97,300 / ELEV 265M

The provincial capital of Alto Adige (Südtirol, or South Tyrol) is anything but provincial. Once a stop on the coach route between
Italy and the flourishing Austro-Hungarian
Empire, this small city is worldly and engaged, a long-time conduit between cultures. Its quality of life – one of the highest
in Italy – is reflected in its openness and
youthful energy and an all-pervading green-
ness. A stage-set-pretty backdrop of rotund
green hills sets off rows of pastel-painted
town houses. Bicycles ply riverside paths
and the aroma of Middle Europe lingers
around the wooden market stalls laid out
with cheese and speck (cured ham). German

may be the first language of 95% of the rest
of the region, but Bolzano is an anomaly. Its
Italian-speaking majority – a legacy of Mussolini's Italianisation program of the 1920s
and a more recent siren call of education
and employment opportunities – embraces
a history linked intrinsically with the Austrian Tyrol and today looks both north and
south for inspiration.

⊙ Sights

Messner Mountain Museum TOP CHOICE MUSEUM
(MMM; ☎0471 63 31 45; www.messner-mountain-
museum.it, in Italian; Via Castel Firmiano 53; adult/
reduced €9/7; ⊙10am-6pm Tue-Sun Mar-Nov) The
imposing Castel Firmiano, dating back to
AD 945, is home to the centrepiece of mountaineer Reinhold Messner's five museums.
Based around humankind's relationship
with the mountains across all cultures, it's
inspiringly designed so visitors climb literally hundreds of stairs, suggesting the experience of shifting altitudes. Wear sturdy shoes
to best traverse the uneven terrain and mesh
walkways.

The tourist office has details of summer
shuttle services to the castles, otherwise
catch a regional train to Ponte Adige (Sig-
mundskron) and be prepared for a long uphill and treacherous (for the wrong reasons)
walk along a busy road. Messner's other
museums are scattered across Alto Adige,
including Ortles.

Museion ART GALLERY
(☎0471 22 34 13; www.museion.it; Via Dante 2; adult/
reduced €6/3.50, Thu evening free; ⊙10am-6pm
Tue-Sun, to 10pm Thu) The city's contemporary
art space is housed in a huge multifaceted
glass cube, a surprising architectural asser-
tion that beautifully vignettes the old-town
rooftops and surrounding mountains from
within. There's an impressive permanent collection of international art work; temporary
shows are a testament to the local art scene's

ⓘ BOLZANO BOZEN CARD

This card (adult/child €28/16) grants
you entry to most city museums and
a number throughout the region as
well. Transport on local buses, regional
trains, bike hire and Bolzano's three
cable cars is also thrown in. It's available from the tourist office.

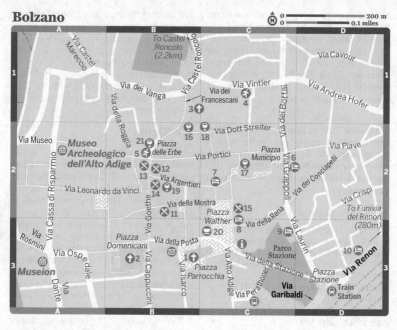

Bolzano

vibrancy, often highlighting an ongoing dialogue with Austria and Germany. The cafe faces the river and has a terrace perfect for a post-gallery spritzer.

Castel Roncolo   CASTLE
(Schloss Runkelstein; ☎0471 32 98 08; roncolo@comune.bolzano.it; Via Castel Ried; adult/child €8/5.50; ☺10am-6pm Tue-Sun) This stunningly located castle was built in 1237 and is re-

nowned for its rare 14th-century frescoes depicting scenes from secular literature, including the tale of Tristan and Isolde. The tourist office runs shuttles in summer; otherwise, catch suburban bus 12 or 14 from outside the regional bus terminal.

Chiesa dei Domenicani   CHURCH
(Piazza Domenicani; ☺9.30am-6pm Mon-Sat) The cloisters and chapel here feature light

and lovely 14th-century frescoes by the Giotto school.

Cathedral
CATHEDRAL

(Piazza Parrocchia; ⊗9.30am-5.30pm Mon-Sat) This splendid Gothic cathedral is Bolzano's most emblematic building, its imposing spires backed by the equally Gothic peaks of the not-so-distant Dolomites.

Activities

Bolzano's three cable cars include the world's longest running along one track – the **Funivia del Renon** (Via Renon; one way/return €2.50/3.50), which stretches for 4556m – and the world's oldest, the 1908-built **Funivia del Colle** (Via Campiglio; one way/return €3/4). The third is **Funivia San Genesio** (Via Sarentino; one way/return €2/3.20). A **narrow-gauge railroad** runs from the upper station of the Renon cable car in Oberbozen to **Klobenstein** (Soprabolzano-Collalbo; departures half-hourly to hourly; one way/return €2.50/3.50), a 15-minute trip that is awe-inspiringly scenic today but revolutionised life here in 1907; two of the original tram cars are still in use, joined by 'modern' cars from 1958 and 1977.

Bolzano is up there with Amsterdam in terms of bike love. You can exit the city without touching a road on countless willow-lined paths, which parallel the Adige river on its course west and south. They offer tantalising gateways into the surrounding mountains and a stunning 20km-long stretch connects Bolzano's castles. Grab a bicycle at the open-air **bike-rental stall** (☑0471 99 75 78; Via della Stazione 2; ⊗7.30am-7.45pm Easter-Oct). Bikes cost €1 for six hours; a deposit and ID are required. The tourist office also rents bikes for €10 per day (supplies are limited, so get in early) and has a list of recommended rental shops.

Tours

The tourist office organises seasonal guided walks and gentle treks (in Italian and German). For information on more-serious hikes in the surrounding area, contact local walking association **Club Alpino Italiano** (☑0471 97 81 72; Piazza delle Erbe 46; ⊗11am-1pm & 5-7pm Wed, 1-5pm Tue, Thu & Fri) or contact the **Alpine Information Office** (Alpenverein Südtirol; www.alpenverein.it; Galleria Vintler 16; ☑0471 81 41 55).

Sleeping

Alto Adige's wealth of appealing *agriturismi* (as well as farm restaurants) can be found on www.redrooster.it.

Hotel Greif
DESIGN HOTEL €€

(☑0471 31 80 00; www.greif.it; Piazza Walther; s €106-118, d €173-270; ❄️🛜) Tumbling golden text courtesy of the troubled poet Ezra Pound greets you in the stairwell (this was, it

---

THE ICEMAN COMETH

When Austrian hikers stumbled upon a human corpse wedged into a melting glacier on Hauslabjoch Pass in 1991, they assumed they'd found the remains of an unfortunate mountaineer caught in a winter storm. But when the mummified body was removed and taken to a morgue, it was discovered to be over 5300 years old. The male corpse – subsequently nicknamed Ötzi, or the Iceman – is the oldest mummified remains ever found in Europe, dating from an ancient Copper Age civilisation that lived in the Dolomites around the same time as ancient Egypt's founding.

Though initially claimed by the Austrian government, it was later ascertained that Ötzi had been unearthed 100m inside the Italian border on the Schnalstal glacier. After a brief diplomatic impasse and stabilisation work in Innsbruck, the mummy was returned to Italy, where it has been on display in Bolzano since 1998.

What Ötzi was actually doing 3200m up a glaciated mountainside, 52 centuries before alpinism became a serious sport, is still a matter of some debate. The museum explores the many mooted scenarios, as well as the events leading to his lonely death.

His clothing – a wonderful get-up of patchwork leggings, rush-matting cloak and fur cap – and other belongings are on display, while his still-frozen body, touchingly marked with faintly visible tattoos, is kept in a temperature-controlled 'igloo' room and can be viewed through a tiny window.

Visit Ötzi at the **Museo Archeologico dell'Alto Adige** (☑0471 32 01 00; www.iceman. it; Via Museo 43; adult/reduced €9/7; ⊗10am-6pm Tue-Sun); the museum has an important collection of other archaeological finds too.

seems, an 'art hotel' long before the modern makeover). Rooms here, even the singles, are generously proportioned, full of light and richly draped; all include a bath. Guests can use the garden at parent hotel Laurin, just down the lane, for cocktails or a swim.

Parkhotel Laurin
HOTEL €€€

(☑0471 31 10 00; www.laurin.it; Via Laurin 4; s €95-125, d €130-250; ⓟ❈ ⓢ⊛) Set in its own lush gardens in the centre of town, this five-star hotel has large rooms endowed with a weighty, old-fashioned opulence. There's a distinct individual style throughout though, with an idiosyncratic mix of original art works, Tyrolean antiques and 1980s Memphis pieces. The splendid ground floor is home to what's considered one of Bolzano's best restaurants and a bar that bustles from early morning to late at night.

Youth Hostel Bolzano
HOSTEL €

(☑0471 30 08 65 www.youthhostel.bz; Via Renon 23; dm/s €20.50/24; ⓢ) Close to the train station, the three- and four-bed dorms in this airy, comfortable and friendly hostel are configured for privacy. Rooms at the back have balconies and views, and they'll squeeze a foldout into the singles if needed. And, best of all, there's no daytime lockout.

Hotel Feichter
HOTEL €

(☑0471 97 87 68; www.hotelfeichter.it; Via Grappoli 15; s/d €60/90) A central, friendly family-run (and totally Tyrolean) hotel. Many of the cosy rooms have balconies or little breakfast nooks, bathrooms are renovated and some have baths.

Hotel Figl
HOTEL €€

(☑0471 97 84 12; www.figl.net; Piazza del Grano 9; s €87-92, d €120-125; ❈⊚) Mod-Euro rooms with geometric furniture, glass and wood are comfortable and look out over a pretty square.

✖ Eating

Redolent of rural mountain life one minute, Habsburg splendour the next, Bolzano's restaurants are a profound reminder of how far north you've come. Goat or rabbit are roasted, bone-warming soups hide *canederli*, venison finds its way into gulasch, and speck (the region's IGP cured ham, cold-smoked and juniper- and pepper-scented) turns up in everything bar dessert. Window displays in the city's many *konditorei* (pastry shops) brim with Sachertorte, cheese strudels, *krapfen* (doughnuts) and earthy buckwheat-and-berry cakes. Bakers turn out dark, dense seed-studded breads, including *schüttelbrot,* a crispy spiced rye and wheat flat bread.

Gasthaus Fink
SÜDTIROLEAN €€

(☑0471 97 50 47; Via della Mostra 9; meals €25-30; ⊙lunch & dinner Thu-Mon, lunch only Wed) Fink's dining room is a calm, contemporary take on *stube* style, with elegant box lights and fresh wildflowers on the tables. Young staff are relaxed and attentive and dishes – say, trout and almonds, buckwheat dumplings with cumin-scented butter or *gröstel* (a bubble-and-squeak type fry) – are as tasty as they are unfussy. A great lunch choice, with pastas well under €10.

Walthers'
MODERN ITALIAN €€

(☑0471 98 25 48; www.walthers.it; Piazza Walther 6; meals €20-25; ⊙8am-1am Mon-Sat, to 7pm Sun) Take your spritzer out onto the piazza terrace, then head inside to the low-lit back room to dine on bold-flavoured, appetite-appeasing dishes that roam from Sicily to Bolzano's backyard. Great service, a lively crowd and the management's penchant for Prince and Blondie can see a quick dinner become a big night out.

Hopfen & Co
SÜDTIROLEAN, PUB €

(☑0471 30 07 88; Piazza delle Erbe 17; meals €15-20; ⊙9.30am-1am Mon-Sat) A venerable 800-year-old inn that serves up hearty portions of traditional dishes, including sauerkraut and sausages cooked in ale. The dark bar is perfect for sampling the cloudy, unfiltered beer that's brewed on the premises.

Vögele
SÜDTIROLEAN €€

(☑0471 97 39 38; Via Goethe 3; meals €19-24; ⊙9am-1am) Dating back to 1277 and owned by the same family since 1840, this multi-level antique-stuffed restaurant is well loved for its schnitzels, steaks and suckling pig. The attached bar is pleasantly rowdy and a surprise favourite of the town's cool kids.

Market
MARKET

(Piazza delle Erbe; ⊙Mon-Sat) Pick up fruit, vegetables, bread, cheese and meats from this gorgeous street market.

🍷 Drinking

Bolzano after dark will come as a surprise after sophisticated but snoozy Trento. The pristine city centre may be hushed at 8pm, but it's a different story around midnight. Follow the locals heading for Piazza delle

While Germans make up the lion's share of hikers in the Dolomites, the man invariably venerated as the greatest hiker of them all, Reinhold Messner, was actually an Italian (albeit a German-speaking one) from the Alto Adige town of Bressanone (Brixen).

Messner grew up surrounded by the sharp, seductive peaks of the Dolomites. Scaling his first Alpine summit at the age of five, by his early 20s he was recognised as a rising star in the tough world of mountaineering. Derisive of the siege tactics employed by traditional Himalayan expeditions in the 1960s, Messner advocated a simpler Alpine-style approach to climbing that emphasised fast ascents with minimal equipment. By the '70s he had set his sights on Everest, confidently announcing his ambition to climb the mountain 'by fair means', without the use of supplementary oxygen.

The prophecy was heroically fulfilled in 1978 when Messner and Austrian Peter Habeler became the first men to summit the world's tallest peak without oxygen – a feat that was considered physically impossible, if not suicidal, at the time. Unsatisfied with his team effort, Messner returned two years later and hacked his way up the mountain's north face to the summit, alone – a superhuman achievement.

Messner's abilities have long intrigued his fellow climbers. Not only is his aerobic capacity relatively average for a man of his age, but he also spent the bulk of his climbing career hampered by the loss of three fingers and seven toes following an ill-fated Himalayan expedition in 1970 (one that also tragically claimed the life of his younger brother, Günter).

Undaunted by the ageing process, the iron-willed Messner logged another record in 1986 when, at 42, he became the first person to scale all eight-thousanders (the 14 mountains in the world over 8000m). Shunning a well-earned retirement, he also partook in the first unassisted crossing of Antarctica.

These days Messner treks at a gentler pace, mainly in the Dolomites. A retired Euro MP for the Italian Green Party, he now tends to his quintet of museums that explore mountain life across the world.

Erbe or the beer halls – including local Forst and the Bavarian Paulaner – along Via Argentieri and Via Goethe.

Enovit
WINE BAR

(Via Dott Streiter 30; ⊗to late Mon-Fri, 10am-1.30pm Sat) An older, well-dressed crowd frequents this warm, woody corner bar for expertly recommended, generously poured local wine by the glass. Many often stay for a few more rounds in the moody side room.

Il Baccaro
WINE BAR

(Via Argentieri 17; ⊗9am-9pm Mon-Fri, 9am-6pm Sat) Scurry down the cobbled passageway and poke your nose into this wonderful burrow of a wine bar, with a good blackboard selection of regional or Friulian wines and delightful hosts. *Stuzzichini* (snacks) are a euro or two and made to order.

Fischbänke
WINE BAR

(Via Dott Streiter 26; ⊗9am-7pm Mon-Fri, 9am-12.30pm Sat) Local wines and bruschetta (€6 to €13) care of artist bon vivant Cobo at the old fish market; pull up a streetside stool at one of the original marble-slab counters.

Loacker Moccaria
CAFE

(Piazza Walther 11) Global biscuit king Loacker is the local kid made good (it's based in Renon); come for espresso and Tyrolean cake in the signature red cafe or pick up tins of the cream-filled wafers.

Nadamas
BAR

(Piazza delle Erbe 43; ⊗Tue-Sun) Bolzano's party reputation got started at this Piazza delle Erbe veteran. If you can make it through the animated front-bar crowd, there's tables and a tapas menu (€3 to €6) out back.

Exil Café
CAFE, BAR

(Piazza del Grano 2; ⊗Tue-Sat) Everything in good time at this student favourite: smoothies and juice first thing, coffee all day, *aperitivo* come the afternoon, then late-night beers and grappa.

❶ Information

Hospital (☎0471 90 81 11; Via Böhler)
Police station (☎0471 94 76 11/80; Via Marconi 33)

TASTING TRAIL

Follow Alto Adige's Weinstrasse – wine road – far enough south from Bolzano and you'll hit **Paradeis** (☎0471 809 580; www.aloislageder.eu; Piazza Geltrude 5, Magrè; ☺10am-8pm, dining room noon-4pm Mon-Sat, to 11pm Thu). Take a seat at the long communal table, crafted from the wood of a 250-year-old oak tree, at fourth-generation winemaker Alois Lageder's biodynamic *weinschenke/vineria* (winery) for lunch or tasting. Whites – highly finessed, almost German in style, but shot through with the warmth and verve of an Italian summer – are the money here; over 70% of production is devoted to Pinot Grigio, chardonnay and Gewürztraminer. Even so, Lageder's Pinot noir and local Lagrein are also highly regarded.

If you're up for more tasting, or just a pleasant day's cycling, the Weinstrasse begins (or ends) north of Bolzano in Nals, meanders past Terlano (Terlan) through Upper Adige (Überetsch) and Lower Adige (Unterland) until it reaches Salorno (Salurn). Native grape varieties line the route: Lagrein, Vernatsch and Gewürztraminer, along with well-adapted imports Pinot blanc, sauvignon, merlot and cabernet. For cellar doors, accommodation and bike trails see www.weinstrasse.com.

Tourist office (☎0471 30 70 00; www.bolzano-bozen.it; Piazza Walther 8; ☺9am-7pm Mon-Fri, 9.30am-6pm Sat)

❶ Getting There & Around

Bolzano's **airport** (Aeroporto di Bolzano; ☎0471 25 52 55; www.abd-airport.it) is served by flights from Rome, Olbia and Cagliari.

Local buses run by **SAD** (www.sad.it) leave from the **bus station** (☎840 00 04 71; Via Perathoner) for destinations throughout the province, including Val Gardena (up to 12 daily), Brunico (up to 20 connections daily) and Merano (every 55 minutes, hourly). SAD buses also head for resorts outside the province, including Cortina d'Ampezzo. Updated timetables are on the SAD website.

Bolzano **train station** (Piazza Stazione) is connected by hourly trains with Merano (€2.40, 40 minutes), Trento (€3.35, 30 minutes) and Verona (€8, 2½ hours), with less-frequent connections to Brunico (1½ hours, six daily) in the Val Pusteria. Trains also run to Innsbruck and Munich via Brennero.

Merano (Meran)

POP 37,673 / ELEV 325M

With its leafy boulevards, birdsong, oleander and cactus, Merano feels like you've stumbled into a valley Shangri La. Long lauded for its sunny microclimate, this poignantly pretty town (and one-time Tyrolean capital) is where 19th-century Mitteleuropeans came to soothe their weary bones, do a 'grape' cure, and, perhaps, embark on a dalliance or two. The Habsburg-era spa was the hot destination of its day, favoured by the Austrian royals, Freud, Kafka and Pound. The Jugendstil (art nouveau) villas, recuperative walks and the grand riverside Kurhaus of this era fan out from its beautifully intact medieval core. The city's therapeutic traditions have served it well in the new millennium, with spa hotels drawing a new generation of health-conscious visitors and a booming organics movement in the surrounding valleys.

German is widely used here, sausage and beer stalls dot the streets and an annual open-air play celebrates Napoleonic-era Tyrolean freedom fighter Andreas Hofer; despite the palm trees, you're closer to Vienna than Rome.

◉ Sights

Castel Trauttmansdorff BOTANICAL GARDEN MUSEUM
(www.trauttmansdorff.it; Via San Valentino 51a; garden & museum adult/child €10.80/7.90; ☺9am-6pm Apr-Nov, to 11pm Fri summer) You could give over an entire day to these beautiful botanical gardens a little outside Merano. Exotic cacti and palms, fruit trees and vines, beds of lilies, iris and tulips all cascade down the hillside surrounding a mid-19th-century castle where Sissi – Empress Elisabeth – spent the odd summer. Inside, **Touriseum** (Tourism Museum; ☎0473 27 01 72; www.touriseum.it) charts two centuries of travel in the region, exploring the changing nature of our yearning for the mountains. There's a restaurant and a cafe by the lily pond.

Kunst Meran ART GALLERY
(☎0473 21 26 43; www.kunstmeranoarte.org; Via Portici 16; adult/reduced €5/4; ☺10am-6pm

Tue-Sun, 11am-7pm summer) Shows of high-profile international and regional artists are installed in this contemporary gallery, a thoughtful refiguring of a skinny medieval town house. Look out for monthly talks over *aperitivo*.

Castel Tirolo   MUSEUM
(Schlosstirol; ☎0473 22 02 21; www.schlosstirol.it; admission €6; ☺10am-5pm Tue-Sun mid-Mar–Dec, to 6pm Aug) The ancestral seat of the counts of Tyrol is home to a dynamically curated museum of Tyrolean history, including, in the keep, the turbulent years of the 20th century. The castle can be reached by taking the chairlift from Merano to Tirolo (Dorf Tirol). Book ahead for tours in English.

FREE Museo Ebraico   MUSEUM
(☎0473 23 61 27; Via Schiller 14; ☺3-6pm Tue & Wed, 9am-noon Thu, 3-5pm Fri) Housed in Merano's synagogue, built in 1901, this small but intriguing museum recounts the history of the town's Jewish community from the early 19th century through to WWII.

Activities

Some 6km east of town, the **Funivia Naif** (adult/child one way €12/6.50, return €17/10; ☺8.30am-5pm, to 7pm summer) cable car carries winter-sports enthusiasts up to **Piffling** in **Merano 2000** (www.meran2000.com; adult half-/full-day ski pass €25/34), with 30km of (mostly beginner) slopes. Bus 1B links Merano train station with the cable car. A **chairlift** (Via Galilei; one way/return €2.70/4; ☺9am-6pm Apr-Nov, to 7pm summer) runs to the village of **Tirolo** (Dorf Tirol). The tourist office has details of the many other cable cars and lifts that ring the town.

The promenade or *passeggiata* (evening stroll) has long been a Merano institution. Fin-de-siècle-era walks trace the river, traverse pretty parks and skirt **Monte Benedetto** (514m). A winter and summer pair follow opposing sides of the river, one shady, one sunny. The **Gilfpromenade** follows 24 poems carved on wooden benches (also handy for a breather). The **Tappeiner** meanders above the town for 4km. The tourist office has guides in summer, or can give you a detailed map; all routes have helpful signage.

Terme Merano   THERMAL BATHS
(Therme Meran; ☎0473 25 20 00; www.therme meran.it; Piazza Terme 1; bathing pass 2hr adult/child €12/8, all day €18/11; ☺9am-10pm) Bolzano-born Matteo Thun's dream commission –

a modern redevelopment of the town's thermal baths – was reopened in 2005. It houses 13 indoor pools and various saunas within a massive glass cube; there's another 12 outdoor pools open in summer. Swim through the sluice and be met by a vision of palm-studded gardens and snow-topped mountains beyond. First-timers might want to get the helpful front desk to give them a rundown on the potentially baffling change-room routine; on weekends get there early, or late, to avoid the crowds. See Hotel Terme Merano for details of spa facilities.

Sleeping

Hotel Aurora   HOTEL €€
(☎0473 21 18 00; www.hotelaurora.bz; Passeggiata lungo Passirio 38; s €85-110, d €136-190; ❄☎) This traditional family hotel is working some fresh ideas. 'New' rooms are Italian designed, bright and slick, but the parquetry-floored '60s originals do have their own charm (and balconies). The corridors are littered with mid-century pieces that would do a Williamsburg loft proud. A splendid breakfast spread includes *prosecco* and *kuglehof*; luckily, Terme Merano is just across the bridge (fluffy towels and robes are available for loan).

Imperial Art Hotel   HOTEL €€€
(☎0473 23 71 72; www.imperialart.it; Corso della Libertà 110; d €200-350; ❄☎) Upstairs in what was once a belle époque coffee palace, this inconspicuous hotel has 11 distinct artist-designed rooms – Tyrolean furniture morphs into neo-geo abstraction; velvet covers and dark-hued walls pay homage to the former Hotel Bristol; an armoire and walls emit an aluminium sheen. Comfort isn't sacrificed for quirk, however: huge bathrooms and/or monster free-standing baths are just the start.

Youth Hostel Merano   HOSTEL €
(☎0473 20 14 75; meran.jugendherberge.it; Via Carducci 77; dm/s €21/24; ℗@☎❄) An easy stroll from the train station and the riverside promenade, this hostel is a find: bright and modern, with a sunny terrace and other down-time extras. There's 59 beds, either singles or en suite dorms for four.

Eating & Drinking

As befits a town now dedicated to bodily pleasure, Merano has an excellent fine-dining scene, including the Michelin-starred

Sissi and Castel Fragsburg. Via Portici brims with speck-dealing delis, *konditorei* line Corso della Libertà, and there's more late-night imbibing options, often squirreled down lanes, than you'd imagine.

TOP CHOICE **Pur Südtirol** ARTISAN, WINE BAR €
(www.pursuedtirol.com; Corso della Libertà 35; plates from €7; 📶) This stylish regional showcase has an amazing selection of farm produce: wine, cider, cheese (some 80 varieties), speck and sausage, pastries and breads, tisanes and body care. Everything is hyper-local: Anton Oberhöller's chocolate is flavoured with apple, lemon balm or dark bread crisps. Specially commissioned wood, glass and textiles fill one corner of the shop. Stay for a coffee, glass of wine or the *bretteljause* – a plate of cured meat – at one of the communal tables.

Kallmünz GASTRONOMIC €€
(📞0473 21 29 17; www.kallmuenz.it; Piazza della Rena 12; degustations €40-50; ⊙Tue-Sun) With rough rendered walls and a dark-beamed ceiling, the dining room here is theatrically simple, and the food too strikes a balance between flirtatious experimentation and letting great ingredients shine. A venison tartare comes with baby herbs, pine nuts and a spritz of beet juice, there's fettucine, but it's made with rye, and a pea-and-lettuce risotto is as fresh and vibrantly green as the valley itself. Wine is from surrounding vineyards and very reasonably priced. Follow the recommendations of the quad- and quin-lingual black-clad staff; they don't disappoint.

Forsterbräu BREWERY €
(📞0473 23 65 35; Corso della Libertà 90; meals €25; ⊙Wed-Mon) This brewery restaurant has a huge beer garden and a number of cosy,

MOUNTAIN MAGIC

The culture of the 'cure' is no passing fad in Alto Adige. Spas have done a roaring trade here for over two hundred years and wellness continues to be been taken very seriously. Therapists often possess paramedical qualifications and many Europeans can claim spa visits on national health insurance. Massage and skincare aren't seen as 'pampering', but as part of a healthy lifestyle.

Local spa treatments use ingredients from field and forest – pine, honey, apples, grapes and whey – stirred, pounded or powered into packs, scrubs, massage oils or topping up soaking tubs. The most curious, and intrinsically Tyrolean, is the hay bath. Inspired by farm labourers' penchant for restorative naps on mounds of freshly threshed hay, today spa-goers are cocooned in aromatic Alpine grasses, flowers and herbs. The mulch slowly heats the body while releasing a potent mix of medicinal oils. Curative? Hmm... Relaxing? Absolutely.

Boutique manufacturers of body-care products and herbal tisanes, based around folk traditions and incorporating Alpine botanicals, are also a booming local industry – try natural pharmacies throughout the region if you don't make it to a spa.

Most mountain hotels will have a sauna and offer spa treatments of some kind. Some super-luxurious options in and around Merano:

Hotel Terme Merano (📞0473 25 90 00; www.hoteltermemerano.it; Viale delle Terme 1, Merano; s €117-137, d €160-320; 🅿@🌊) A private tunnel leads to the Terme complex from the serene, refreshingly simple rooms. Baths, packs and scrubs are as delicious as they sound, with chestnut, apples and red wine all making an appearance. An ornate brass tub is employed for the 'Sissi' – a milk bath.

Vigilius (📞0473 55 66 00; www.vigilius.it; Lana; s €190-225, d €310-360; 🅿@🌊) If splendid isolation appeals – access is by cable car only – come for pine-cone reflexology, polenta peels, a glassed-in jacuzzi overlooking the peaks, yoga and Nordic walking.

Arosea (📞0473 78 50 51; www.arosea.it; Santa Valburga, Val d'Ultimo; half-board per person €129-168; 🅿@🌊📶) Alternate lakeside horse riding and hikes with yoga and serious spa time; treatments include mineral-water therapy, scrubs or sand from mountain streams, and lambswool wraps.

Bad Schörgau (📞0471 62 30 48; www.bad-schoergau.com; Sarentino; d €185; ❄🌊) A cosy, modern bolt-hole on the edge of woodland, the spa here specialises in baths, using its own mineral-rich waters, along with Sarner pine, hay, honey and local raw milk.

atmospheric dining rooms. Come for a pint or heaped plates of *gulaschsuppe* (gulasch soup), trout and roast boar.

Café Kunsthaus
BAR, CAFE

(Via Portici 16, evening access from the back lane on Via Risparmio; ☺9am-midnight Tue-Sat, 9am-7pm Sun) You can while away the hours in this relaxed gallery cafe, then find yourself still here when the DJs begin and the beer and pizzas are doing the rounds.

ℹ Information

Ospedale Civile Tappeiner (☑0473 26 33 33; Via Rossini 5) For medical emergencies.

Post office (Via Roma 2) On the other side of the Passirio river from the old town.

Tourist office (☑0473 23 52 23; www.meraninfo.it; Corso Libertà 35; ☺9am-12.30pm & 2-6pm Mon-Fri, 9.30am-12.30pm Sat)

ℹ Getting There & Around

SAD buses connect Merano **bus station** (Piazza Stazione) with Monte Santa Caterina and other villages that give access to the Gruppo del Tessa, as well as to Silandro and the valleys leading into the Parco Nazionale dello Stelvio and the Ortles range.

Bolzano (€2.40, almost hourly) is an easy 40-minute ride from Merano train station (Piazza Stazione). Next door to the **train station**, hire a bike and helmet; the **bikemobil card** (☑0473 20 15 00; adult/child €24/12; ☺8am-8pm Apr-Nov) also gives you unlimited local train travel. Bike trails track the 65km route between Bolzano, Merano and Malles.

Parco Nazionale dello Stelvio

It's not quite Yellowstone, but 1346-sq-km Parco Nazionale dello Stelvio (☑0469 0 30 46; www.parks.it/parco.nazionale.stelvio) is northern Italy's (and the Alps') largest national park, spilling into the next-door region of Lombardy and bordering with Switzerland's Parco Nazionale Svizzero.

It's primarily the preserve of walkers who come for the extensive network of well-organised mountain huts and marked trails which, while often challenging, don't require the mountaineering know-how necessary elsewhere in the Dolomites. Stelvio's central massif is guarded over by Monte Cevedale (3769m) and Ortles (3905m), protecting glaciers, forests and numerous wildlife species, not to mention many mountain traditions and histories.

Ski facilities are rare, but Stelvio has a couple of well-serviced runs at Solda and the Passo dello Stelvio (2757m), both of which offer the novelty of year-round skiing. The latter is the second-highest pass in the Alps and is approached from the north from the hamlet of Trafoi (1543m) on one of Europe's most spectacular roads, a series of tight switchbacks covering 15km, with some very steep gradients. The road is also famous among cyclists, who train all winter to prepare for its gut-wrenching ascent (it has often featured in the Giro d'Italia). This high and hair-raising pass is only open from June to September, and always subject to closures dependent on early or late snowfalls.

Lying immediately south of Passo dello Stelvio, Bormio (1125m) is actually in Lombardy, but acts as an unofficial HQ for the park. It's a popular ski resort due to its proximity to some of Italy's highest runs. From October through May, Bormio is best approached from Sondalo in Lombardy, or via Tubre into Switzerland to take the Munt la Schera tunnel to Livigno. Cima Bianca rises just above the town, while nearby the year-round Pista Stelvio drops 1800m over 8km. The town's thermal springs have been famous since Roman times (Leonardo da Vinci liked a soak). The luxurious Bagni di Bormio Spa Resort (☑0342 91 01 31; www.bagnidibormio.it; Via Statale Stelvio), sits on the original Roman site, with 30 hot springs, 11 outdoor pools and a host of Euro-style treatments, and night bathing on Fridays and Saturdays. Hotel stays include unlimited spa access, but day passes are also available (passes €41-45; ☺10am-8pm, Bagni Nuovi to 11pm Fri & Sat). Bormio Terme (☑0342 90 13 25; www.bormioterme.it; Via Stelvio 10; admission half-day €10-14; ☺seasonal) also does treatments. Visit Bormio tourist office (☑0342 90 22 22; www.bormioonline.com; Via Roma 131b, Bormio; ☺seasonal) or the park headquarters (☑0342 90 16 54; Via Roma 24, Bormio) for maps, weather forecasts and trekking advice.

VAL DI SOLDA

The village of Solda (Sulden; 1906m), at the head of the Val di Solda, is a low-key ski resort that acts as a base for walkers and climbers in summer. Challenging trails lead quickly to high altitudes, including trail No 28, which crosses the Passo di Madriccio (3123m) into the Val Martello.

Located – literally – inside a hill, the Messner Mountain Museum – Ortles (☑0473 61 32 66; adult/reduced €6/5; ☺2-6pm

Wed-Mon, 1-7pm summer, closed May & Nov) articulates the theme of 'ice'. Messner's Yak & Yeti (Località Solda 55) restaurant, in a 17th-century farmhouse, is nearby.

The family-run Hotel Post (☎0473 61 30 24; www.hotelpost.it; Via Principale 24; d €160-190; P❄@), friendly if far from glam, has big, comfy rooms and a full quota of wellness facilities.

Solda's tourist office (☎0473 61 30 15; Solda; ☺seasonal) has information on activities.

SAD buses connect Solda with Merano (via Spondigna), summer weekdays only.

VAL MARTELLO

Every Alto Adige valley has its speciality: here it's strawberries. Berries aside, Martello is a convenient gateway to Stelvio, with both gentle rambles and hard-core hiking adventures available. Trail No 20 up into the Val di Peder is an easy walk, with picnic spots along the way where chamois and deer might say hello.

Unspoiled by ski lifts and downhill runs, Martello specialises in cross-country skiing in the winter. Ice climbers attempt the valley's frozen waterfalls from January to March.

Edelweiss (☎0473 74 45 26; www.gasthof-edelweiss.net; Dorf 98; s/d €35/70) has simple rooms and a sunny terrace bar. Or ask about hiring a small house (d €60) at Hotel Martell (☎0473 74 45 28; www.martellerhof.com; Gand 39).

The road into the valley is open year-round and SAD bus 107 runs to Martello village from Silandro.

Val Gardena (Gröden/ Gherdëina)

Despite its proximity to Bolzano, Val Gardena's historical isolation amid the turrets of Gruppo del Sella and Sassolungo has ensured the survival of many pre-mass-tourism traditions. This is one of only five valleys in the Dolomites where Ladin is a majority tongue and this linguistic heritage is carefully maintained. The pretty and bustling villages are full of reminders of this distinct culture too, with folksy vernacular architecture and a profusion of woodcarving shops (Ortisei's Museum de Gherdëina has a particularly exquisite collection of wooden toys and sculptures).

In recent times, the valley has become an 'everyman' ski area, with the emphasis firmly on classic runs and fine powder. The valley's main trilingual towns, Ortisei (St Ulrich; population 5700, elevation 1236m), Santa Cristina (population 1840, elevation 1428m) and Selva (Wolkenstein; population 2580, elevation 1563m) all have good facilities.

Activities

In addition to its own good runs, the valley forms part of the Sella Ronda and the Dolomiti Superski area. Passes for Val Gardena and Alpe di Siusi alone cost €38/108/190 for one/three/six days.

Vallunga, near Selva, is one of the region's best spots for cross-country skiing. There are stunning trails around Forcella Pordoi and Val Lasties in the Gruppo del Sella, and on the Sassolungo.

This is also a walkers' paradise with endless possibilities, from the challenging Alte Vie of the Gruppo del Sella and the magnificent Parco Naturale Puez-Odle, to picturesque strolls including the Naturonda, a signposted nature-and-geology trail beginning at Passo di Sella (2244m).

In summer cable cars operate from all three towns. From Ortisei you can ascend to Seceda, which, at 2518m, offers an unforgettable view of the Gruppo di Odle, a cathedral-like series of mountain spires. From Seceda, trail No 2A passes through a typical Alpine environment – impossibly green, sloping pastures dotted with wooden *malghe* (shepherds' huts).

Both the Sella and Sassolungo walking trails can be reached from Val Gardena resorts (or Canazei) by bus to Passo di Sella or Passo di Pordoi (steel yourself for some hairpin bends). From Passo di Pordoi (2239m), a cable car takes you to Sasso Pordoi (2950m).

🍴 Sleeping & Eating

If you're looking to spend a week in the mountains, the Val Gardena's hotels offer great half-board deals and are often more affordable than those in Alta Badia or Val di Fassa.

Chalet Gerard   HOTEL €€€

(☎0471 79 52 74; www.chalet-gerard.com; Plan de Gralba, Selva Val Gardena; half-board s €105-145, d €180-240; ☎🐾) Stunning and remote modern chalet with panoramic views, lots of cosy lolling by the (architect-designed) fire spots, a steam room and the option to ski in. The restaurant is both romantic – all pine, felt and candlelight – and highly regarded by local chefs.

Charme Hotel Uridl
HOTEL €€

(☎0471 79 32 15; www.uridl.it; Via Chemun 43, Santa Cristina; half-board s €65-100, d €110-190; P@❋) Nestled behind the church in the original 'high' village, this is a friendly character-filled hotel with bright, simple rooms, a heritage *stube*, and beautiful views back over the valley from its sunny garden.

Hotel am Stetteneck
HOTEL €€

(☎0471 79 65 63; www.stetteneck.com; Via Rezia 14, Ortisei; d €88-190, weekly stays only in winter; P@≋) This elegant, warm hotel dates from 1913 (during WWI Italian troops were bivouacked here) and is right in the middle of town. Come for graceful service, and lovely village and mountain views from big bay windows.

Saslong Smart Hotel
HOTEL €

(☎0471 77 44 44; www.saslong.eu; Strada Palua, Santa Cristina; d €58-90) Rooms are small but slick (Antonio Citterio had a hand in the design) and comfortable; the 'smart' concept keeps rates low by making room cleaning, wi-fi and breakfast optional, though far from exorbitant, extras.

Ristorante Concordia
SÜDTIROLEAN €€

(☎0471 79 62 76; Via Roma 41, Ortisei; meals €20-30) Pasta here is made by hand, as are the breads. The ham, too, is smoked on the premises.

❶ Information

The valley's tourist offices are online at www.valgardena.it.

Ortisei tourist office (☎0471 77 76 00; Via Rezia 1; ☺8.30am-12.30pm & 2.30-6.30pm Mon-Sat, 9am-noon & 5-6.30pm Sun)

Santa Cristina tourist office (☎0471 77 78 00; Via Chemun 9; ☺8am-noon & 2.30-6.30pm Mon-Sat, 9am-noon Sun)

Scuola di Alpinismo Catores (☎0471 79 82 23; www.catores.com; Piazza Stettenect 1, Ortisei; ☺5.30-7pm) Offers botanical walks, climbing courses, glacier excursions and treks.

Selva tourist office (☎0471 77 79 00; Via Mëisules 213; ☺8am-noon & 3-6.30pm Mon-Sat, 9am-noon & 5-6.30pm Sun)

Tourist medical (Ortisei ☎0471 79 77 85; Selva ☎0471 79 42 66)

❶ Getting There & Around

The Val Gardena is accessible from Bolzano and Bressanone by SAD buses year-round, and the neighbouring valleys in summer.

In summer the hop-on, hop-off **Sella Ronda bus** (€11/6 per adult/child) travels the circuit; the **Val Gardena card** gets you a week's unlimited transport (3/6 days €59/76). Regular buses connect the towns along the valley and you can reach the Alpe di Siusi by either bus or cable car. Timetables are available at tourist offices.

In winter the Val Gardena Ski Express shuttle bus service links the various villages and lifts in the valley; a €5 ticket covers a week's unlimited travel.

Alpe di Siusi & Parco Naturale Sciliar-Catinaccio

There are few more jarring or beautiful juxtapositions than the undulating green pastures of the Alpe di Siusi – Europe's largest plateau – ending dramatically at the base of the towering Sciliar Mountains. To the southeast lies the jagged Catinaccio range, its German name 'Rosengarten' an apt description of the eerie pink hue given off by

---

HIT THE HIGHWAYS

The Dolomite's Alta Vie – literally high ways – are high-altitude paths, designed for experienced walkers, but most not requiring true mountaineering skills or equipment. During mid-June to mid-September, a network of mountain huts offering food and accommodation line the route. The various tourist offices can provide maps and details of skill level required, Tourism Südtirol (www.trekking.suedtirol.info) maintains a comprehensive list of mountain huts. Descriptions of each route can be found at www.dolomiti-altevie.it.

» **Alta Via No1** Lago di Braies to Belluno, north to south

» **Alta Via No2** Bressanone to Feltre, passing through Odle, the mythical Ladin kingdom

» **Alta Via No3** Villabassa to Longarone

» **Alta Via No4** San Candido to Pieve di Cadore

the mountains' dolomite rock at sunset. The two areas are protected in the Parco Naturale Sciliar-Catinaccio. Signposted by their onion-domed churches, the villages that dot the gentle valleys – including **Castelrotto** (Kastelruth), **Fiè allo Sciliar** (Völs am Schlern) and **Siusi** – are lovingly maintained and unexpectedly sophisticated.

🏃 Activities

The region is part of the Dolomiti Superski network, with downhill skiing, ski-mountaineering, cross-country skiing and snowshoe trails all possible.

The gentle slopes of the Alpe di Siusi are perfect hiking terrain for families with kids; average stamina will get you to the **Rifugio Bolzano** (🕿0471 61 20 24; www.schlernhaus.it; ☺Jun–Oct), one of the Alps' oldest mountain huts, which rests at 2457m, just under **Monte Pez** (2564m), the Sciliar's summit. Take the **Panorama chairlift** (one way/return €3.50/5) from Compaccio to the Alpenhotel, followed by paths S, No 5 and No 1 to the *rifugio;* from here it's an easy walk to Monte Pez (three hours total). The more jagged peaks of the Catinaccio group and the Sassolungo are nearby. These mountains are revered among climbers worldwide, and harbour several *vie ferrate* and loads of good bike trails. They're usually accessed from Vigo in Val di Fiemme.

Horses are a big part of local life and culture and there's nothing more picturesque than a local chestnut Haflinger pony galloping across these endless pastures. Riding stables can be found throughout the area; **Gstatschhof Ponyhof** (🕿0471 727814; www.gstatschhof.com; Via Alpe di Siusi 39) offers accommodation and summer programs.

The Seiser Alm **cableway** (www.seiseralmbahn.it; one way/return €9/13.50; ☺8am–6pm mid-Dec–Mar & mid-May–Oct) is a dizzying 15-minute, 4300m trip (800m ascent) from Siusi to Compaccio. The road linking the two is closed to normal traffic when the cableway is open. Regular buses operated by **Silbernagl** (🕿0471 70 74 00; www.silbernagl.it) serve the area from Castelrotto and Siusi.

🛏 Sleeping & Eating

TOP CHOICE **Hotel Heubad** HOTEL €€
(🕿0471 72 50 20; www.hotelheubad.com, in Italian; Via Sciliar 12, Fiè allo Sciliar; half-board d €132-198; P❄@≋🐾) As if the pretty garden and spacious lounge areas here weren't relaxing enough, the spa is known for its typically Tyrolean hay baths, which have been on offer since 1903 and give the hotel its name. Delightful service is courtesy of the founder's great- and great-great-grandchildren. The upstairs rooms are modern, light and spacious, with balconies for taking in the Alpe di Siusi.

Schagaguler HOTEL €€€
(🕿0471 71 21 00; www.schgaguler.com; Via Dolomiti 2, Castelrotto; half-board per person €99-170; P❄🛜) Streamlined blond-wood rooms offer views from the bathroom, the bedroom, the living room…Downstairs Vinbar Rubin is an urbane spot with rustic views.

Gasthof Zum Turm HOTEL €€
(🕿0471 70 63 49; www.zumturm.com; Kofelgasse 8, Castelrotto; d €94-158; P) Nestled by Castelrotto's onion-domed church, with neat rooms and a strudel-scoffing-friendly garden.

ℹ Information

All tourist offices have coordinated hours (8am to noon and 2pm to 6pm Monday to Friday, 8am to noon Saturday) and a common website (www.alpedisiusi.info).
Castelrotto tourist office (🕿0471 70 63 33; Piazza Kraus 1)
Fiè allo Sciliar tourist office (🕿0471 72 50 27; Via Bologna 4)
Siusi tourist office (🕿0471 70 70 24; Via Sciliar 16)
The Alpe di Siusi is accessible by SAD bus from Bolzano, the Val Gardena and Bressanone.

Val Badia & Alpe di Fanes

For centuries potent Ladin legends have resonated across this mystical landscape, which inspired the latterly fantasies of JRR Tolkien. Not surprisingly, the valley and the adjoining high plains of Fanes are often touted as one of the most evocative places in the Dolomites. Since 1980 they have been protected as part of the Parco Naturale di Fanes-Sennes-Braies. Villages in the valley – **Colfosco** (1645m), **Pedraces** (1324m), **La Villa** (1433m), **San Cassiano** (St Kassian; 1537m) and **Corvara** (1568m) – form the Alta Badia ski area. While undoubtedly upmarket, they remain calm and filled with character.

🏃 Activities

The Alta Badia is located on the Sella Ronda, with the best access from Corvara, and forms part of the Dolomiti Superski network.

GOURMET HEIGHTS

While lashings of speck, schnitzel and dumplings do make perfect post-piste dinners, Alta Badia ups the Alpine ante with a disproportionate number of fine-dining (and often Michelin-starred) restaurants. This gastronomic hot spot also hosts the Chef's Cup food festival (www.chefscup.it) in January and from July to September organic farmers markets take over village squares. Current Michelin darlings include St Hubertus (Rosa Alpina Hotel; ☏0471 84 95 00; www.rosalpina.it; Strada Micurá de Rü 20, San Cassiano; meals €90-120; ⊘dinner Wed-Mon), part of the luxurious Rosa Alpina Hotel & Spa. This two-Michelin-starred restaurant is cosy and quietly elegant; the mountain beef cooked in salt and hay is a menu stalwart, as is suckling pig, though dishes also take a creative, delicate turn. Strewn with Alpine antiques and built entirely from wood, Stüa de Michil (Hotel La Perla; ☏0471 83 10 00; www.hotel-laperla.it; Col Alt 105, Corvara; meals €100; ⊘7-9.30pm Mon-Sat) is intimate and ridiculously atmospheric. Beautifully presented dishes rework Ladin or Tyrolean traditions and use biodynamic ingredients. Rare wines are also a speciality.

Alta Badia passes for 1/3/6 days cost from €37/107/188. Of the Alta Badia's 130km of slopes, the Gran Risa, 4.5km north of Corvara in La Villa, is undoubtedly the most legendary.

In summer a cable car ascends into the Parco Naturale di Fanes-Sennes-Braies from the Passo Falzarego (2105m). Alternatively, pick up trail No 12, near La Villa, or trail No 11, which joins Alta Via No 1 at the Capanna Alpina, a few kilometres off the main road between Passo Valparola and San Cassiano. Either trail takes you up to the Alpe di Fanes and the two *rifugi*, Lavarella and Fanes.

Horse riding, mountain biking and hang-gliding are other popular valley activities. Tourist offices have a list of places where you can hire mountain bikes and hotels often have bikes for guests' use.

▭ Sleeping & Eating

These resorts are known for their discreet, luxurious hotels. Budget options are scarce; residence apartments and mountain huts can be a good deal, but need to be booked well in advance.

Lagacio Mountain Residence   APARTMENT €€
(☏0471 84 95 03; www.lagacio.com; Strada Micurá de Rü 48; apt €146-290; P✳🛜🐾) A residence hotel with young friendly staff and contemporary, casual vibe. Stylishly pared-back apartments have heated floors, big baths and balconies. Attention to detail is keen: kitchens come with WMF gear, espresso machines and filtered mountain water. The breakfast buffet includes local meats and cheeses, Tyrolean and Italian cakes, DIY

vegetable juices and local herb tisanes, or they'll do you a fry-up.

Hotel La Villa   HOTEL €
(☏0471 84 70 35; www.hotel-lavilla.it; Boscda-plan 176, La Villa; d €70-130, half-board d €86-152; P@♒🐾) La Villa is in a lovely quiet village cul-de-sac and filled with larch-wood furniture and cosy Ladin ambience. There's a wellness centre and traditional restaurant.

Boconara 1927   RESTAURANT
(www.boconara.com; Strada Arlara, Corvara; 🐾) Most ski-in here but you can make it up on foot with a bit of boot traction. Beers and Italian-style snacks come with complimentary views and a petting farm for the kids.

Winebar & Grill   MODERN ITALIAN, SÜDTIROLEAN €€€
(Rosa Alpina Hotel; ☏0471 84 95 00; www.rosalpina.it; Strada Micurá de Rü 20, San Cassiano; meals €55; ⊘11am-11pm) This village hub is a lot more easygoing than its decor and old-style service (and prices) suggest; hoodie-clad teenagers slop in, and tables of littlies merrily munch on pizza. Ultra-local dishes are the business (hand-cut pasta with venison *ragù*, gelato of caramelised pumpkin seeds, pumpkin oil and cinnamon), though looking south is also tempting (creamy *burrata* with pesto and gazpacho, *vitello tonnato*).

Rifugio Scotoni   SÜDTIROLEAN €
(☏0471 84 73 30; www.scotoni.it; Alpe Lagazuoi 2, La Villa; meals €20-30; ⊘year-round) At 1985m there's stunning views, and the traditional food and mountain hospitality make this a quintessential Badia experience. The cosy, blond-wood bunkrooms are also worth considering for an overnight stay but need to be booked well ahead.

Delizius   DELI
(www.delizius.it; San Cassiano; daily) Specialist cheese and speck counters, well-priced local wine and grappa, plus an excellent selection of prepared meals – *canederli*, gulasch, lasagne – perfect for self-catering dinners.

ⓘ Information

Full ski-pass prices, lift information and the location of ski-pass sales points can be found online (www.altabadia.org) or at tourist offices.

Associazione Guide Alpine Val Badia (☑0471 83 68 98; guide.valbadia@rolmail.net; Via Burje, Corvara) Advice on skiing, heli-skiing, ice climbing and advanced walking trails. Phone lines are only staffed between 6pm and 7pm.

Corvara tourist office (☑0471 83 61 76; Via Col Alt 36; ◷8am-noon & 2-6pm Mon-Fri, 8.30am-noon & 3-6pm Sat, 10am-noon & 4-6pm Sun)

Helicopter mountain rescue (☑0471 79 71 71)

La Villa tourist office (☑0471 84 70 37; Via Colz 75; ◷8.30am-noon & 3-7pm Mon-Sat, 10am-noon & 4-6pm Sun)

San Cassiano tourist office (☑0471 84 94 22; Strada Micurá de Rü 24; ◷8.30am-noon & 3-7pm Mon-Sat, 10am-noon & 4-6pm Sun)

ⓘ Getting There & Away

Hourly **SAD** (☑800 84 60 47; www.sad.it) busses link Alta Badia's villages with Bolzano (2½ hours) and Brunico (1¼ hours) in winter and summer, with fewer in spring and autumn.

Less-frequent services link Corvara with the Val Gardena, Passo di Sella and Passo di Pordoi, Canazei and the Passo Falzarego. Buses re-route in winter to avoid crossing the higher mountain passes.

Val Pusteria (Pustertal)

The narrow, verdant Val Pusteria appears more pastoral and less crowded than its southern counterparts. Running from Bressanone (Brixen) to San Candido (Innichen) in the east, the region is profoundly Tyrolean and almost entirely German-speaking.

Bressanone is a picture-postcard historic town, known for its gardens and wonderful culinary heritage. Dobbiaco (Toblach) is the gateway to the ethereal Parco Naturale delle Dolomiti di Sesto, home of the much-photographed Tre Cime di Lavaredo, and has a beautifully located and well-tended Youth Hostel Dobbiaco (Via Dolomiten 29; toblach.jugendherberge.it; per person €22-24, with bathroom €30-34; P@).

Easy to reach from the Val Pusteria, Lago di Braies is a peaceful spot for a lakeside stroll. More-serious walkers might like to tackle part of the Alta Via No 1, which starts here. The Plan de Corones (Kronplaz) ski area – covered by Dolomiti Superski – is 4km to the south of Brunico and can be reached by cable car. Ample green and blue runs are a treat for beginners.

LADIN LANDS

Ladin is definitely not a dying language. According to one Val Gardena local in her 20s, to be Ladin is 'just a way of feeling...I've grown up speaking the language; I don't feel Italian, or South Tyrolean, I feel Ladin.' She is but one of 20,000 first-language Ladin speakers, with almost half from the Val Gardena, the others are spread across valleys in the neighbouring Val Badia and Val di Fassa, and the Arabba and Ampezzo near Cortina in the Veneto. Children in these valleys are taught in Ladin, alongside German and Italian, and the Ladin cultural and linguistic identity is enshrined in EU law. Contemporary media includes the newspaper *La Usc di Ladins* (The Voice; www.lauscdiladins.com, in Ladin and Italian) and the radio station Radio Gherdëina (94.2 FM), broadcast from the Val Gardena.

The culture is underpinned by vibrant poetry and legends peopled by the good-natured *salvan* and a host of fairies, giants and heroes. Encounter these and Ladin crafts and artefacts at the following places:

Museo Ladin (☑0474 52 40 20; www.museumladin.it; Tor 65, San Martino, Val Badia; adult/reduced €6/4.50; ◷10am-6pm Tue-Sat, 2-6pm Sun mid-Mar–Oct, 2-6pm Wed-Fri winter)

Museo Ladin de Fascia (☑0462 76 01 82; www.istladin.net; Via Milano 5, San Giovanni, Val di Fassa; adult/reduced €5-3; ◷10am-noon & 3-7pm daily Jun–mid-Sep, 3-7pm Tue-Sat mid-Sep–May)

Museum de Gherdëina (☑0471 79 75 54; www.museumgherdeina.it; Via Rezia 83, Ortisei, Val Gardena; adult/reduced €6/4; ◷10am-noon & 2-6pm Tue-Fri, Mon in summer)

Brunico's **tourist office** (☎0474 55 57 22; www.bruneck.com; Piazza Municipio 7; ☺9am-12.30pm & 3-6pm Mon-Fri, 9am-noon Sat) is helpful for resort information, as is the Val Pusteria website (www.kronplatz.com).

Regional Val Pusteria trains connect with the main Bolzano–Innsbruck line at Fortezza (Franzensfeste), and run down the valley as far as San Candido. SAD buses travel to Brunico (45 minutes, hourly) and Cortina (one hour, four daily) from San Candido. From either town sporadic buses and trains go to Dobbiaco, from where buses run to Lago di Braies.

BRUNICO (BRUNECK)

Val Pusteria's big smoke, Brunico (population 13,700; elevation 835m) gets a bad wrap by those who've only driven through its unremarkable main drag. The quintessentially Tyrolean historic centre is, however, a delightful detour.

Right by the town gate, head to **Acherer Patisserie & Blumen** (☎0474 41 00 30; www.acherer.com; Via Centrale; ☺8am-7pm Mon-Fri, 8am-5pm Sat & Sun), for apple strudel, cheesecakes and Sachertorte that may just be the region's best; the young owner reopened his grandfather's former bakery after apprenticing in Vienna. His inventive chocolates and seasonal preserves now grace many of the region's five-starred pillows and breakfast buffets. If you'd like your cake with coffee, they'll happily plate it and you can waltz next door to **Wörtz Bäck** (Via Centrale 12; ☺8am-late Wed-Fri, 8am-7pm Mon, Tue & Sat), a friendly bar where locals gather for jugs of beer and great wine by the glass.

Enoteque Bernardi (www.bernardi-karl.it, Via Stuck 6; ☺closed Sun) has bar stools looking over the river to the old town walls. It's the very picture of a smart Italian wine bar, but shelves are stacked with local specialities: speck, smoked salami and cans of venison gulasch. On the town's outskirts, visit local wool manufacturer **Moessmer** (Via Vogelweide) for cashmere and Tyrolean tweeds from its outlet shop, or just for an interesting slice of early-20th-century industrial architecture.

Hotel Blitzburg (☎0474 55 57 23; www.blitzburg.it; Via Europa 10; half-board d €90-148; ℗), in the new town, is a rambling old place with big, bright rooms and a nice mountain orientation.

SESTO DOLOMITES

At the far end of the Val Pusteria are the Dolomites' Austrian and Veneto borders; the Sesto Dolomites are a vast, mostly wild, territory. The Valle Campo di Dentro, near San Candido, and the Val Fiscalina, near Sesto, are criss-crossed with spectacular walking and cross-country skiing trails; most trails around the Tre Cime are suitable for inexperienced walkers and families. From the Val Fiscalina it's a long but easy walk along trail No 102 to **Rifugio Locatelli** (2405m), from where you can see the Tre Cime di Lavaredo in all its glory.

Venice & the Veneto

Includes »

Best Places to Eat

» Venissa (p358)

» All'Arco (p354)

» Corte Sconta (p356)

» Anice Stellato (p355)

» Locanda Lo Scudo (p380)

Best Places to Stay

» Novecento (p350)

» Oltre Il Giardino (p352)

» Palazzo Abadessa (p352)

» Relais Ca' Muse (p374)

» Bauer Palladio & Spa (p353)

Why Go?

Pinch yourself, and you might expect to awaken from this dreamscape of pink palaces, teal waters and golden domes. Instead you're in Venice, and all five senses never felt so alert. Gondoliers call 'Oooooooeeee!' round canal bends, nostrils flare at fresh espresso wafting from 250-year-old cafes, mouths water at cascades of purple artichokes on Rialto market stalls, and everywhere – constantly – water gently laps at your feet.

Scan the Veneto coastline, and you might spot signs of modern life: beach resorts, malls and traffic. But look closer and you'll discover Brenta Riviera villas opening to the public, and newly restored masterpieces being unveiled: Titians and Veroneses in Venice, Palladios and Tiepolos in Vicenza, and Giottos in Padua.

This calls for a toast with bubbly local *prosecco* (type of sparkling wine) or cult wines from Valpolicella and Soave. Elsewhere in Italy, *cin-cin* (cheers) will do – but in Veneto, raise your glass to *la bea vita* (the good life).

When to Go
Venice

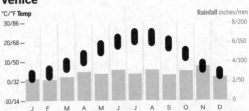

Jan & Feb Snow-covered gondolas, skiers on the Dolomites slopes and Carnevale partiers in Venice.

Apr–Jun Canalside dining, Vin-Italy toasts and Biennale openings (skip pricey Easter holidays).

Sep–Nov Venice Film Festival red carpets, wild duck pasta specials and palatial accommodation for less.

Navigating Venice

Although you can take a train or bus to the western edge of Venice, the only ways to navigate this city are on foot or by boat. Since 1171, the 117 islands that make up Venice have been loosely organised into six *sestieri* (districts): Cannaregio, Castello, San Marco, San Polo, Dorsoduro and Santa Croce. As you cross canals by footbridge, you may notice white signs informing you which *sestiere* you're entering. Directions to Piazza San Marco, the Rialto and Accademia are found on yellow signs – but the best adventures begin by ignoring those signs and wandering Venice's *calli* lanes.

VENETO MYTHS...& REALITIES

Verona is the home of Romeo and Juliet...never mind that they're fictional characters. Lovelorn visitors still leave notes to Juliet on the door of a Renaissance house with a balcony.

There's nothing to see in Padua...except pivotal Giotto frescoes that are the missing link between medieval and Renaissance art, rare botanical gardens planted in 1545 where the Italian Resistance was plotted in WWII, and Galileo's anatomy theatre that revolutionised scientific methods.

Everyone drinks prosecco in the Veneto...when they're not wine tasting in Valpollicella or Soave, or sampling rarely exported IGT blends at Venetian *enoteche* (wine bars) or Verona's annual VinItaly expo.

See one Palladian building and you've seen them all...other than Palladio's 24 Unesco-protected, soaring Veneto villas that raise spirits to the skies, three blinding-white Istrian stone churches with double the dazzle along Venice's Giudecca Canal, and the entire Greek metropolis inside Vicenza's Teatro Olimpico.

There's nowhere to stay the night in Venice...except for all those palaces converted to B&Bs and apartments that have become available in the decade since Venice loosened laws allowing families to open their homes to visitors.

Veneto's Best Freebies

» **Basilica di San Marco** (p321) Where East meets West under shimmering gold mosaic domes.

» **Verona's wine country** (p380) Free and fabulous tastings by appointment at area wineries.

» **Burano** (p347) Surely the most colourful fishing village in the Mediterranean.

» **Historical Vicenza** (p372) A Unesco-protected urban centre with Palladios at every turn.

» **Venice's Ghetto** (p343) The world's original ghetto – a centre of refuge, commerce and culture.

Fast Facts

» Population: 4.91 million

» Area: 18,378 sq km

» Unesco World Heritage Sites: 30, including three cities (Vicenza, Venice and Verona), Venice's lagoon and the Dolomites

» Number of union-certified artisans in Venice alone: 2000

High-Season Hints

Don't miss Venice's Biennale and Verona's open-air opera – if only to dodge summer crowds. Broaden your accommodation and restaurant options by visiting cities on weekdays and Veneto countryside on weekends.

Resources

» Veneto Regional Tourism (www.veneto.to) has information on what's happening around the Veneto, from dancing on the beaches to biking through the Dolomites.

Venice & the Veneto Highlights

1 Join the collective gasp at the golden mosaic domes of Venice's **Basilica di San Marco** (p321)

2 Compare Titian's radiant reds and Tintoretto's lightning-strike brushstrokes at Venice's **I Frari** (p338) and **Scuola Grande di San Rocco** (p339)

3 Shout 'Brava!' for opera diva encores at Verona's outdoor **Roman Arena** (p377)

4 Let the spirits move you from classic whites to cult reds to grappa in **Verona's wine country** (p380)

5 Villa-hop like a 1600s Venetian socialite along the **Brenta Riviera** (p364)

6 See the Renaissance coming through the tears in Giotto's moving frescoes for **Scrovegni Chapel** (p366)

7 Bike through Alpine wildflower meadows and ski craggy peaks in the Dolomites, using **Belluno** (p382) as a base

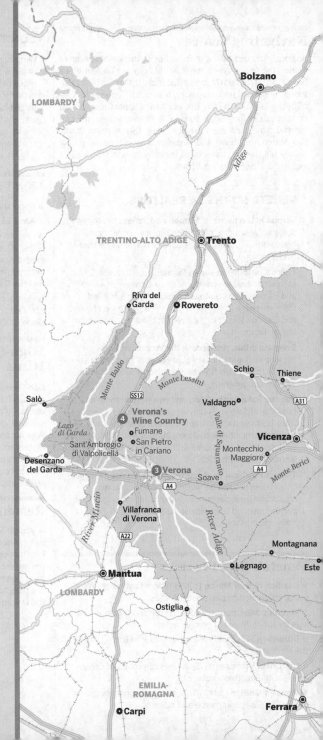

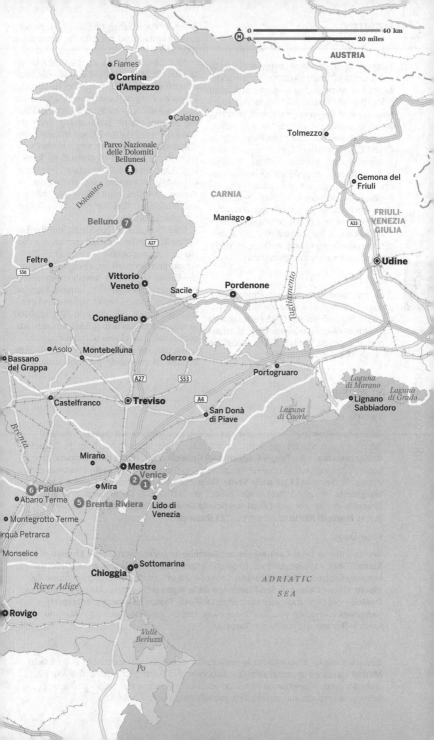

VENICE

POP 61,500 (CITY), 270,800 (TOTAL INCLUDING MAINLAND)

Imagine the audacity of people deciding to build a city of marble palaces on a lagoon. Instead of surrendering to *acque alte* (high tide) like reasonable folk might do, Venetians flooded the world with vivid painting, baroque music, modern opera, spice-route cuisine, bohemian-chic fashions and a Grand Canal's worth of Spritz: the signature *prosecco*/Aperol cocktail. Today cutting-edge architects and billionaire benefactors are spicing up the art scene, musicians are rocking out 18th-century instruments and backstreet *osterie* (casual taverns or eateries presided over by a host) are winning a Slow Food following. Your timing couldn't be better: the people who made walking on water look easy are well into their next act.

History

A malarial swamp seems like a strange place to found an empire, unless you consider the circumstances: from the 5th to 8th century AD, Huns, Goths and sundry barbarians repeatedly sacked Roman towns along the Veneto's Adriatic coast. In AD 726 the people of Venice elected their first doge, whose successors would lead the city for more than 1000 years.

Next Venice shored up its business interests. The city accepted a Frankish commission of 84,000 silver marks to join the Crusades, even as it continued trading with Muslim leaders from Syria to Spain. When the balance wasn't forthcoming from the Franks, Venice claimed Constantinople 'for Christendom' – but sent ships loaded with booty home, instead of onward to Jerusalem. After Venice was decimated by plague, Genoa tried to take over the city in 1380. But Venice prevailed, controlling the Adriatic and a backyard that stretched from Dalmatia to Bergamo.

Like its signature landmark, the Basilica di San Marco, the Venetian empire was dazzlingly cosmopolitan. Armenians, Turks, Greeks and Germans were neighbours along the Grand Canal, and Jewish communities persecuted elsewhere in Europe founded publishing houses, banks and medical practices in Venice. By the mid-15th century, Venice was swathed in golden mosaics, imported silks and clouds of incense.

As the Age of Exploration began, Venice lost its monopoly over seafaring trade

---

VENICE IN...

Two Days

Take detours from our 'Venice Labyrinth' walking tour' to check out **cicheti** (Venetian tapas), artisans' studios and Gothic architectural details. Museum-hop from the **Gallerie dell'Accademia** to the **Peggy Guggenheim Collection** and **Punta della Dogana**, then hop onto the *vaporetto* (small passenger ferry) to **Giudecca** for **Palladio churches** and a romantic dinner at **I Figli delle Stelle**. On day two, follow espresso in **Campo Santa Margherita** with glimpses of heaven in the Tiepolo ceilings at **Ca' Rezzonico**, Titian and Tintoretto masterpieces at **I Frari** and **Scuola Grande di San Rocco**, and shopping across **Ponte di Rialto** to happy hour at **I Rusteghi**.

Four Days

Devote a day to divine **Cannaregio** and **Castello**, beginning with **Museo Ebraico di Roma**'s Ghetto synagogue tour, Tintoretto's home church of **Madonna dell'Orto** and heavenly seafood at **Anice Stellato**. Cross canals to Castello's many-splendoured **Zanipolo**, serene **Chiesa di San Francesco della Vigna** and sunset cocktails at **Terrazza Danieli** – but don't miss your concert at **La Pietà**, **Teatro La Fenice** or **Interpreti Veneziani**. Island-hop your fourth day away, with blown-glass shopping in **Murano**, lunch in **Burano** and mosaics in **Torcello**.

A Week

Become a regular at your favourite restaurants, recognise local specialities at the **Rialto Market** and strike up conversations in sociable cafes. Sign up for a class, plan your days around themes – Venetian fashion, Lido beaches or Veronese paintings with dogs – or follow your instincts and camera lens through Venice's *calli* (lanes).

routes. The fall of Constantinople in 1453 and the Venetian territory of Morea (in Greece) in 1499 gave the Turks control over Adriatic Sea access. The Genovese opened transatlantic trade routes following Columbus' 1492 discovery of the Americas, and Portuguese explorer Vasco da Gama rounded Africa's Cape of Good Hope in 1498.

Once it could no longer rule the seas, Venice changed tack and began conquering Europe by charm. Venetian art was incredibly daring, bringing sensuous colour and sly social commentary even to religious subjects. Venetian nobles' illegitimate daughters were trained as musicians in *ospedaletti* (orphanages) by the likes of Vivaldi, and Venetian courtesans started trends for platform shoes and poetry. By the end of the 16th century, Venice was known across Europe for its painting, catchy music and 12,000 registered prostitutes.

Venetian reputations did nothing to prevent Napoleon from claiming the city in 1797 and looting it of its art. By 1817 one-quarter of Venice's population was destitute. When Venice rallied to resist the Austrian occupation in 1848–49, a blockade left it wracked by cholera and short on food. Venetian rebels lost the fight but not the war: they became early martyrs to the cause of Italian independence, and in 1866 Venice joined the independent kingdom of Italy.

The once-glamorous empire gradually took on an industrious workaday aspect, with factories springing up on Giudecca and a roadway from the mainland built by Mussolini. Italian partisans joined Allied troops to wrest Veneto from Fascist control, but the tragedy of war and mass deportation of Venice's historical Jewish population in 1942–44 shook Venice to its moorings. Postwar, many Venetians left for Milan and other centres of industry.

On 4 November 1966, disaster struck: record floods poured into 16,000 Venetian homes, stranding residents in the wreckage of 1200 years of civilisation. But Venice's cosmopolitan charm was a saving grace: assistance from admirers poured in (from Mexico to Australia, millionaires to pensioners) and Unesco coordinated some 27 international charities to redress the ravages of the flood.

Defying centuries of dire predictions, Venice has not yet become a Carnevale-masked parody of itself or a lost Atlantis. The city remains relevant and realistic, a global launch pad for daring art and film, ingenious craftsmanship, opera premieres and music reviv-

als, even as it seeks sustainable solutions to rising water levels.

⊙ Sights

PIAZZA SAN MARCO & AROUND

TOP CHOICE Basilica di San Marco   CHURCH
(St Mark's Basilica; Map p330; ☑041 241 38 17; www.basilicasanmarco.it; Piazza San Marco; basilica entry free; ⊙9.45am-5pm Mon-Sat, 2-4pm Sun & holidays) Creating Venice's signature architectural wonder took nearly 800 years of painstaking labour and one saintly barrel of lard. Legend has it that in AD 828, wily Venetian merchants smuggled St Mark's corpse out of Egypt in a barrel of pork fat to avoid inspection by Muslim customs authorities. Church authorities in Rome took a dim view of Venice's tendency to glorify itself and God in the same breath, but Venice defiantly created the basilica in its own cosmopolitan image, with Byzantine onion-bulb domes, a Greek cross layout, a Gothic rosette window and Egyptian marble walls. The roped-off circuit of the church is free and takes about 15 minutes. For entry, dress modestly (ie knees and shoulders covered) and leave large bags round the corner at Ateneo di San Basso's free one-hour baggage storage (⊙9.30am-5.30pm).

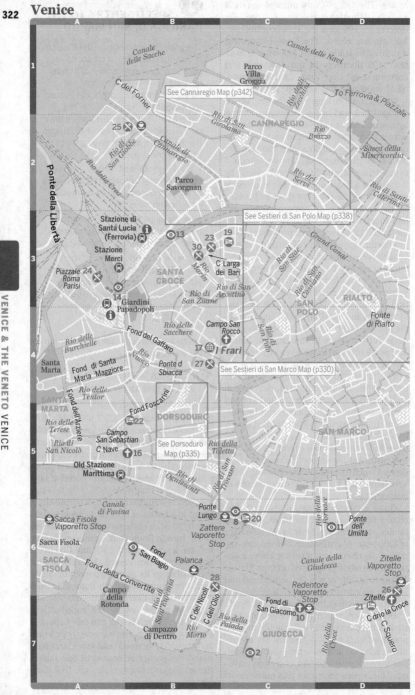

VENICE & THE VENETO VENICE

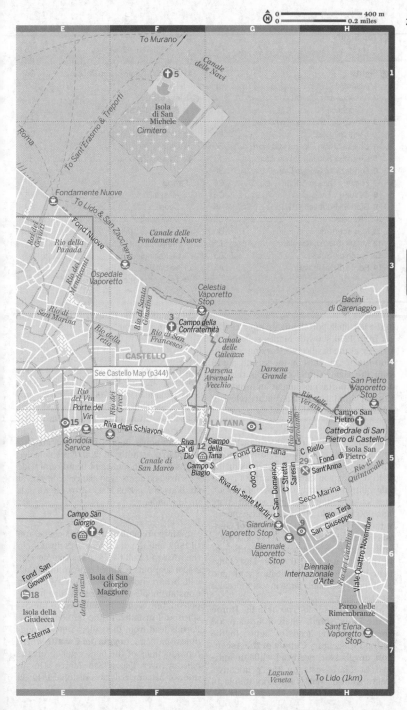

323

VENICE & THE VENETO SIGHTS

0 400 m
0 0.2 miles

To Murano

Canale delle Navi

5

Isola di San Michele
Cimitero

Roma

To Sant'Erasmo & Treporti

Fondamente Nuove

Fond Nuove

To Lido & San Zaccaria

Rio dei Gesuiti

Rio della Panada

Rio dei Mendicanti

Ospedale Vaporetto

Canale delle Fondamente Nuove

Rio di San Marina

Rio della Teta

Rio di Santa Giustina

Rio di San Francesco

Celestia Vaporetto Stop

Campo della Confraternità

3

CASTELLO

See Castello Map (p344)

Canale delle Galeazze

Bacini di Carenaggio

Darsena Arsenale Vecchio

Darsena Grande

Rio del Vin

Porte del Vin

Rio dei Greci

Riva degli Schiavoni

Rio di San Gerolamo

San Pietro Vaporetto Stop

Campo San Pietro

15

Gondola Service

Canale di San Marco

Riva Ca' di Dio

Riva dei Sette Martiri

Campo della Tana

12

Campo S Biagio

Fond della Tana

LA TANA

1

Rio delle Vergini

Cattedrale di San Pietro di Castello

Isola San Pietro

Rio di Quintavalle

C Copo

C San Domenico

C Stretta Saresin

C Riello

Fond di Pietro

29

Sant'Anna

Seco Marina

Campo San Giorgio

6

4

Giardini Vaporetto Stop

9

Rio Tera San Giuseppe

Biennale Vaporetto Stop

Biennale Internazionale d'Arte

Rio dei Giardini

Viale Quattro Novembre

Fond San Giovanni

18

Canale della Grazia

Isola di San Giorgio Maggiore

Isola della Giudecca

C Esterna

Parco delle Rimembranze

Sant'Elena Vaporetto Stop

Laguna Veneta

To Lido (1km)

Exterior

In the left-most portal, lunette mosaics dating from 1270 show St Mark's stolen body arriving at the basilica – a story repeated in 1660 lunette mosaics on the second portal from the right. Grand entrances through the central portal pass under an ornate triple arch with 13th- to 14th-century reliefs of vines, virtues and astrological signs.

Dome Mosaics

Inside the basilica are 8500 sq metres of mosaics, many made with 24-carat gold to represent divine light. In niches flanking the main door as you enter the narthex (vestibule) glitters *Apostles with the Madonna*, who looks stunning for her age: at more than 950 years old, this is the oldest mosaic in the basilica. The atrium's **Dome of Genesis** depicts the separation of sky and water with surprisingly abstract motifs, anticipating modern art by 650 years. Last Judgment mosaics cover the atrium vault and the Apocalypse looms large in vault mosaics over the gallery.

Mystical transfusions occur in the **Dome of the Holy Spirit**, where a dove's blood streams onto the heads of saints. In the central 13th-century **Cupola of the Ascension**, angels swirl overhead while dreamy-eyed St Mark rests on the pendentive. Scenes from St Mark's life story unfold in vaults flanking the **Dome of the Prophets** over the main altar.

Pala d'Oro

Tucked behind the main altar containing **St Mark's sarcophagus** is the Pala d'Oro (admission €2; ⊙9.45am-4pm Mon-Sat, 2-4pm Sun), studded with 2000 emeralds, amethysts, sapphires, rubies, pearls and other gemstones. Even more precious are biblical figures in vibrant cloisonné, begun in Constantinople in 976 and elaborated by Venetian goldsmiths in 1209. The enamelled saints have wild, unkempt beards and wide eyes fixed on Jesus, who glances sideways at studious St Mark as Mary throws her hands up in wonder.

Museum

San Marco remained the doge's chapel until 1807, and the ducal treasures upstairs in the Museo (adult €4; ⊙9.45am-4pm Mon-Sat, 2-4pm Sun) puts a king's ransom to shame. Gilt bronze horses taken by Venice from Constantinople were stolen in turn by Napoleon, but eventually returned to the basilica and installed in the 1st-floor gallery. Portals lead from the gallery onto the giddiness-inducing **Loggia dei Cavalli**, where reproductions of the horses gallop off the balcony over Piazza San Marco. On an interior balcony, Salviati's restored 1542–52 mosaic of the Virgin's family tree shows Mary's ancestors perched on branches, alternately chatting and ignoring one another, as families often do. Hidden over the altar is the **banquet hall**, where doges wined and dined among lithe stucco figures of Music, Poetry and Peace.

Treasury

Crusades loot fills the Tesoro (Treasury; admission €3; ☉9.45am-4pm Mon-Sat, 2-4pm Sun), including a 10th-century rock-crystal ewer with gazelle-shaped handle and winged feet made for Fatimid Caliph al-'Aziz-bi-llah. Velvet-padded boxes preserve doges' remains alongside alleged saints' relics, including St Roch's femur, St Mark's thumb, the arm St George used to slay the dragon and even a lock of the Madonna's hair.

TOP CHOICE **Palazzo Ducale** PALAZZO
(Ducal Palace; Map p330; ☑041 271 59 11; www.mus eicivicieneziani.it; Piazzetta San Marco 52; adult/reduced incl Museo Correr €14/8 or Museum Pass; ☉8.30am-7pm Apr-Oct, to 5.30pm Nov-Mar) Don't be fooled by its genteel Gothic elegance: underneath all that lacy pink cladding, the doges' palace flexes serious muscle. The seat of Venice's government for nearly seven centuries, this powerhouse survived wars, conspiracies and economic crashes, and was cleverly restored by Antonio da Ponte (who also designed Ponte di Rialto) after a 1577 fire.

Exterior

Outside, the *palazzo* (mansion) mixes business with pleasure, capping a graceful colonnade with medieval capitals depicting key Venetian guilds. Facing the piazza, Zane and Bartolomeo Bon's 1443 **Porta della Carta** (Paper Door) served as a bulletin board for government decrees.

Courtyard

Sansovino's brawny statues of Apollo and Neptune flank Antonio Rizzo's recently restored **Scala dei Giganti** (Giants' Staircase). Under the eastern arcade were the dread **Pozzi** (wells), where prisoners shivered below water level – now a baggage deposit is installed here.

1st Floor

Climb the **Scala dei Censori** (Stairs of the Censors) to the **Doges' Apartments**, where the doge lived under 24-hour guard with a short commute to work up a secret

staircase capped with Titian's *St Christopher*. **Sala del Scudo** (Shield Room) is covered with world maps that reveal the extents of Venetian power (and the limits of its cartographers) c 1483 and 1762. The upside-down New World map places Canada above Virginia and Florida near Asia, while the British Isles are essentially Scotland plus Newcastle.

2nd Floor

Head up Sansovino's 24-carat gilt stuccowork **Scala d'Oro** (Golden Staircase), and emerge into rooms covered with gorgeous propaganda. In **Sala delle Quattro Porte** (Hall of the Four Doors), ambassadors arrived under a Palladio-designed ceiling fresco by Tintoretto showing Justice presenting sword and scales to Doge Girolamo Priuli, near Titian's 1576 *Doge Antonio Grimani Kneeling before Faith* amid a bevy of approving *putti* (cherubs).

Delegations waited in the **Anticollegio** (College Antechamber), where Tintoretto drew parallels between Roman gods and Venetian government: *Mercury and the Three Graces* reward Venice's industriousness with beauty, and *Minerva Dismissing Mars* is a Venetian triumph of savvy over brute force. The recently restored ceiling is Veronese's 1577 *Venice Distributing Honours*, while on the walls is a vivid reminder of diplomatic behaviour to avoid: Veronese's *Rape of Europe.*

Few were granted audience in the Palladio-designed **Collegio** (Council Room), where Veronese's 1578–82 *Virtues of the Republic* ceiling shows Venice as a bewitching blonde waving her sceptre like a wand. Father–son team Jacopo and Domenico Tintoretto attempt similar flattery, showing Venice keeping company with Apollo, Mars and Mercury in their *Triumph of Venice* ceiling for **Sala del Senato** (Senate Hall), but frolicking lagoon sea monsters steal the scene.

Government cover-ups were never so appealing as in **Sala Consiglio dei Dieci** (Trial Chambers of the Council of 10; room 20), where Venice's star chamber plotted against political opponents under Veronese's *Juno Bestowing her Gifts on Venice,* a glowing goddess strewing gold ducats. Over the slot where anonymous accusations of treason were slipped in **Sala della Bussola** (Compass Room; room 21) is Veronese's *St Mark in Glory* ceiling.

Grand Canal

The 3.5km route of *vaporetto* (passenger ferry) No 1, which passes some 50 *palazzi* (mansions), six churches and scene-stealing backdrops featured in four James Bond films, is public transport at its most glamorous.

The Grand Canal starts with controversy: **Ponte di Calatrava** **1** a luminous glass-and-steel bridge that cost triple the original €4 million estimate. Ahead are castle-like **Fondaco dei Turchi** **2**, the historic Turkish trading-house; Renaissance **Palazzo Vendramin** **3**, housing the city's casino; and double-arcaded **Ca' Pesaro** **4**. Don't miss **Ca' d'Oro** **5**, a 1430 filigree Gothic marvel.

Points of Venetian pride include the **Pescaria** **6**, built in 1907 on the site where fishmongers have been slinging lagoon crab for 600 years, and neighbouring **Rialto Market** **7** stalls, overflowing with island-grown produce. Cost overruns for 1592 **Ponte di Rialto** **8** rival Calatrava's, but its marble splendour stands the test of time.

The next two canal bends could cause architectural whiplash, with Sanmicheli-designed Renaissance **Palazzo Grimani** **9** and Mauro Codussi's **Palazzo Corner-Spinelli** **10** followed by Giorgio Masari-designed **Palazzo Grassi** **11** and Baldassare Longhena's baroque jewel box, **Ca' Rezzonico** **12**.

Wooden **Ponte dell'Accademia** **13**, was built in 1930 as a temporary bridge, but the beloved landmark was recently reinforced. Stone lions flank **Peggy Guggenheim Collection** **14**, where the American heiress collected ideas, lovers and art. You can't miss the dramatic dome of Longhena's **Chiesa di Santa Maria della Salute** **15**, or **Punta della Dogana** **16**, Venice's triangular customs warehouse reinvented as a contemporary art showcase. The Grand Canal's grand finale is pink Gothic **Palazzo Ducale** **17** and its adjoining **Ponte dei Sospiri** **18**, currently draped in advertising.

Palazzo Grassi
French magnate François Pinault scandalised Paris when he relocated his contemporary art collection here, with galleries designed by Gae Aulenti and Tadao Ando.

Ca' Rezzonico
See how Venice lived in baroque splendour at this 18th-century art museum with Tiepolo ceilings, silk-swagged boudoirs and even an in-house pharmacy.

13 Ponte dell'Accademia

14 Peggy Guggenheim Collection

Chiesa di Santa Maria delle Salute

Punta della Dogana
Minimalist architect Tadao Ando creatively repurposed abandoned warehouses as galleries, which now host contemporary art installations from François Pinault's collection.

KRZYSZTOF DYDYNSKI/LONELY PLANET IMAGES ©

ADAM EASTLAND ITALY / ALAMY

Ponte di Calatrava
With its starkly streamlined fish-fin shape, the 2008 bridge is the first to be built over the Grand Canal in 75 years.

Fondaco dei Turchi
Recognisable by its polychrome, marble double colonnade, topped by 13th-century Byzantine capitals and flanked by watchtowers.

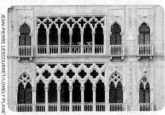

Ca' d'Oro
Behind the triple Gothic arcades are priceless masterpieces: Titians looted by Napoleon, a rare Mantegna and semi-precious stone mosaic floors.

2

3 Palazzo Vendramin

4

5

6 Pescaria

7 Rialto Market

10

Palazzo Grimani

9

Palazzo Corner-Spinelli

8 Ponte di Rialto

Ponte dei Sospiri

18

Palazzo Ducale 17

Ca' Pesaro
Originally designed by Baldassare Longhena, this palazzo was bequeathed to the city in 1898 to house the Galleria d'Arte Moderna and Museo d'Arte Orientale.

Ponte di Rialto
Antonio da Ponte beat out Palladio for the commission of this bridge, but construction costs spiralled to 250,000 Venetian ducats – about €19 million today.

Venice: Building the Dream City

Impossible though it seems, Venetians built their home on 117 small islands connected by some 400 bridges over 150 canals. But if floating marble palaces boggle, consider what's underneath them: an entire forest's worth of wood pylons, rammed through silty *barene* (shoals) into the clay lagoon floor.

While pylons do the heavy lifting, Venice's upkeep is constant and painstaking. Punta della Dogana's salt-corroded foundations were recently repaired by injecting specially formulated cement into thousands of holes. Venice's canals must be regularly dredged, by pumping water out of canals, removing pungent sludge and a technique Venetians call *scuci-cuci* (patching brickwork by hand).

When visitors marvel at their city, Venetians pass along the compliment to their extraordinary lagoon ecosystem. But deep channels dug to accommodate tankers and cruise ships allow more seawater into the lagoon, changing aquaculture and elevating *acque alte* (high tide). Mose, the multi-billion-euro mobile flood barrier, is intended to limit *acque alte,* but critics question its effectiveness, environmental impact and the diversion of funds critical for Venice's upkeep.

Solutions aren't easy, but simple gestures are. With 22 million visitors a year, minor adjustments in traveller behaviours will help keep Venice alive and dreaming.

HELP KEEP VENICE AFLOAT

» **Take the train to Venice** – instead of higher-impact cruise ships
» **Pick up litter** – to protect Venice's fragile ecosystem
» **Enjoy local products** – lagoon seafood, island-grown produce and Venetian handicrafts are Venice's pride, joy and livelihood
» **Go slowly on motor boats** – wakes expose and damage fragile foundations
» **Drink tap water** – to spare Venice recycling an annual 20–60 million water bottles

Clockwise from top left
1. Canal 2. View of Grand Canal from gondola 3. *Acqua alta*, Piazza San Marco 4. Grand Canal, San Marco district.

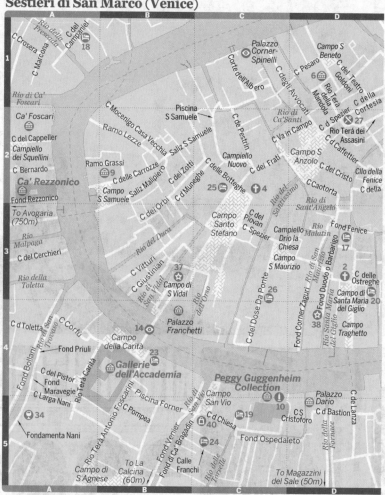

Behind the doge's throne in cavernous 1419 **Sala del Maggior Consiglio** (Grand Council Hall) is the 22m-by-7m *Paradise* by Domenico Tintoretto that's more politically correct than pretty: heaven is crammed with 500 prominent Venetians, including several Tintoretto patrons. Veronese's political posturing is more elegant in the oval *The Apotheosis of Venice* ceiling, where gods marvel at Venice's coronation by angels. In the frieze depicting the first 76 doges of Venice, note the black space: Doge Marin Falier would have appeared there, had he not lost his head for treason in 1355.

Prisons

Only visitors on the Itinerari Segreti tour (see the boxed text, p333) can access the Council of 10 headquarters and Piombi attic prison. For a shorter prison experience, pass through a chamber featuring apocalyptic visions by Hieronymus Bosch, then follow the footsteps of condemned prisoners across covered **Ponte dei Sospiri** (Bridge of Sighs) to Venice's 16th-century **Priggione Nove** (New Prisons). The dank cells are covered with graffitied protestations of innocence, and paved with marble stolen in a state-sanctioned heist: the sacking of Constantinople.

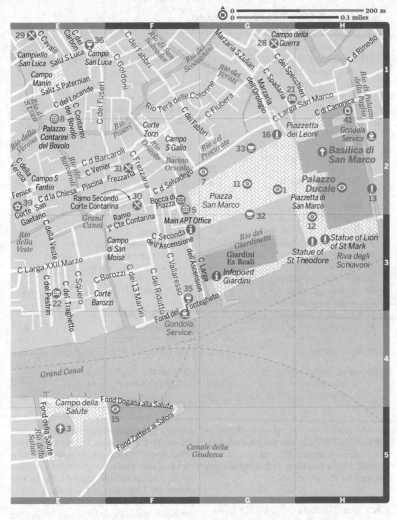

Museo Correr
MUSEUM

(Map p330; ☎041 240 52 11; www.museicivici
veneziani.it; Piazza San Marco 52; adult/reduced incl
Palazzo Ducale €14/8 or Museum Pass; ⏰10am-
7pm Apr-Oct, to 5pm Nov-Mar) Napoleon filled
his royal digs over Piazza San Marco with
the riches of the doges, and took some of
Venice's finest heirlooms to France as tro-
phies. But the biggest treasure here couldn't
be lifted: Jacopo Sansovino's 16th-century
Libreria Nazionale Marciana, covered
with larger-than-life philosophers by Veronese, Titian and Tintoretto and miniature
back-flipping sea creatures.

Venice successfully reclaimed many ancient maps, statues, cameos and weapons,
plus four centuries of artistic masterpieces
in the **Pinacoteca**. Not to be missed are
Paolo Veneziano's 14th-century sad-eyed
saints (room 25); Lo Schiavone's Madonna
with a bouncing baby Jesus, wearing a
coral good-luck charm (room 31); Jacopo
di Barbari's minutely detailed woodblock
perspective view of Venice (room 32); an
entire room of bright-eyed, peach-cheeked
Bellini saints (room 36); and a wonderful anonymous 1784 portrait of champion
rower Maria Boscola, five-time regatta

winner (room 47). Temporary shows in the neoclassical ballroom are hit-and-miss, but Antonio Canova's 1777 statues of star-crossed lovers Orpheus and Eurydice are permanent scene-stealers.

Torre dell'Orologio   LANDMARK
(Clock Tower; Map p330; ☑041 4273 0892; www.museiciviciveneziani.it; Piazza San Marco; adult/reduced €12/7 or Museum Pass; ☺tours in English 10am & 11am Mon-Wed, 2pm & 3pm Thu-Sat, in Italian noon & 4pm daily, in French 2pm & 3pm Mon-Wed, 10am & 11am Thu-Sun) Legend has it that the inventors of this gold-leafed timepiece (which tracks lunar phases) were assassinated so that no other city could boast a comparable engineering marvel. But the sinister plan backfired: the 1497 mechanism malfunctioned and bells rang randomly, because no one knew how to fix them.

A recent renovation has restored the clock to working order. Moving barrels indicate minutes and hour on the clock face; 132-stroke chimes keep the time; Do Mori (Two Moors) bronze statues strike the hour on a bell atop the tower; and wooden statues of Three Kings and the Angel emerge to wild cheers on Epiphany and the Feast of the Ascension. Tours climb the steep, claustrophobia-triggering spiral staircase behind the clock to the terrace for giddy, close-up views of the Moors in action.

Note that the only way to visit is on a tour, and that children must be at least six years old to enter.

Negozio Olivetti   NOTABLE BUILDING
(Olivetti Store; Map p330; ☑041 522 83 87; www.fondoambiente.it; Piazza San Marco 101, Procuratie Vecchie; audioguide adult/reduced €5/3; ☺10am-7pm Apr-Oct, to 5pm Nov-Mar) Like a revolver pulled from a petticoat, starkly modern Negozio Olivetti was an outright provocation when it first appeared under the frilly

arcades of Piazza San Marco in 1957. Hi-tech pioneer Olivetti commissioned Venetian architect Carlo Scarpa to transform a narrow, dim souvenir shop into a showcase for its sleek typewriters and 'computing machines' (several 1948–54 models are displayed).

Instead of fighting the elements, Scarpa slyly invited them indoors, slicing away walls to let light flood in, installing a huge planter, and adding a Belgian marble slab fountain as a wink at *acque alte*. Visitors cross floors of Murano glass tiles in appealing primary colours, scale a floating white marble stairway, pass satiny Venetian plaster walls, and stroll an indoor balcony sheathed in warm teak wood. Semicircular porthole windows resemble eyes that are opened wide to the piazza, but also to possibilities on more-distant horizons.

Campanile
LANDMARK

(Bell Tower; Map p330; Piazza San Marco; www.basilicasanmarco.it; admission €8; ⊙9am-9pm Jul-Sep, to 7pm Apr-Jun & Oct, 9.30am-3.45pm Nov-Mar) The basilica's 99m-tall bell tower has been rebuilt twice since its initial construction in 888. Critics called Bartolomeo Bon's 16th-century redesign ungainly, but when his version suddenly collapsed in 1902, Venetians rebuilt the tower as it had been, brick by brick.

Visits head to the top of the tower for 360-degree lagoon views and close encounters with the Marangona, a bronze bell echoing to Arsenale shipyards (bring earplugs). Due to ongoing stabilisation efforts and drainage works, the Sansovino-designed marble loggia is partially enclosed behind a safety barrier.

Teatro La Fenice
OPERA HOUSE

(Map p330; ☑041 78 65 11, reservations 041 24 24; www.teatrolafenice.it; Campo San Fantin 1965; audioguide adult/reduced €7/5; ⊙vary) Once its dominion over the high seas ended, Venice discovered the power of high Cs, hiring as San Marco choirmaster Claudio Monteverdi, the father of modern opera, and opening La Fenice ('The Phoenix') in 1792. Rossini and Bellini staged operas here, making La Fenice the envy of Europe – until it went up in flames in 1836.

Venice without opera was unthinkable, and within a year the opera house was rebuilt. Verdi premiered *Rigoletto* and *La Traviata* at La Fenice, and international greats Stravinsky, Prokofiev and Britten composed for the house. But La Fenice was again reduced to ashes in 1996; two electricians found guilty of arson were apparently behind on repairs. A €90-million replica of the 19th-century opera house reopened in late 2003, and though some critics had lobbied for Gae Aulenti's avant-garde design, the reprise performance of *La Traviata* was a sensation.

Museo Fortuny
MUSEUM

(Map p330; ☑041 4273 0892; www.museicivici veneziani.it; Campo San Beneto 3758; adult/reduced €9/6 or Museum Pass; ⊙10am-6pm Wed-Mon) Find design inspiration at the home studio of Venetian-Spanish designer Mariano Fortuny y Madrazo, whose shockingly uncorsetted Delphi goddess frocks for Isadora Duncan set global bohemian-chic standards. First-floor salon walls are vast moodboards, swagged with Fortuny art nouveau textiles and hung Fortunato Depero posters, Persian chain mail helmets and paintings of scantily clad muses.

STATE SECRETS REVEALED: ITINERARI SEGRETI

Discover state secrets in the Palazzo Ducale attic on a fascinating 75-minute guided tour: **Itinerari Segreti** (Secret Passages; ☑041 4273 0892; adult/reduced €18/12; ⊙tours in English 9.55am, 10.45am & 11.35am, in Italian 9.30am & 11.10am, in French 10.20am & noon). Head through a hidden passageway disguised as a filing cabinet in **Sala del Consiglio dei Dieci** (Chamber of the Council of 10), festooned with happy cherubim and Veronese's optimistic *Triumph of Virtue over Vice*. Suddenly you're in the cramped, unadorned **Council of 10 Secret Headquarters**, adjoining a **Trial Chamber** lined with top-secret file drawers.

Follow the path of the accused into the windowless **Interrogation Room** with a single rope, used in perversely imaginative ways to extract information until the 17th century. Next are the studded cells of the **Piombi**, Venice's notorious attic prison. In 1756, Casanova was condemned to five years' confinement here for corrupting nuns and spreading Freemasonry, but he escaped through the roof.

ⓘ MAKING THE MOST OF YOUR EURO

These passes can help you save admission costs on Venetian sights.

» **Museum Pass** (Musei Civici Pass; www.museicivicivenezia.it; adult/child €18/12) is valid for single entry to 10 civic museums for six months, or just the five museums around Piazza San Marco (adult/child €14/8). Purchase online or at participating museums, including Palazzo Ducale, Museo Correr, Museo Fortuny and Ca' Rezzonico.

» **Chorus Pass** (www.chorusvenezia.org; adult/reduced €10/7; ⊙visits Mon-Fri 10am-5pm) offers single entry to 16 Venice churches at any time within one year; on sale online or at church ticket booths.

» **Venice Card** (☑041 2424; www.hellovenezia.com; adult/reduced €40/30; ⊙call centre 8am-7.30pm) combines the Museum Pass and Chorus Pass and reduced entry to the Biennale, two public bathroom entries and discounts on concerts, temporary exhibits and parking. Purchase at tourist offices and at HelloVenezia booths at *vaporetto* (small passenger ferry) stops.

» **Rolling Venice** (14-29 yr €4) entitles young visitors to discounted access to monuments and cultural events, plus eligibility for a 72-hour public transport pass for just €18 rather than the regular price of €33. Identification is required for purchase at tourism offices or HelloVenezia booths (found near key *vaporetto* stops).

The salons showcase original Fortuny dresses alongside more-recent avant-garde fashion, such as Roberta di Camerino's trompe l'œil maxidresses. Large-scale art installations in the attic warehouse are often overshadowed by the striking architecture, but the downstairs gallery hosts fascinating rotating shows on Venetian themes, such as Paolo Venturi's moving photos of hand-built dioramas representing the Venice Ghetto c 1942.

Palazzo Grassi   ART GALLERY
(Map p330; ☑044 535 70 99; www.palazzograssi. it; Campo San Samuele 3231; adult/reduced €15/10, incl Punta della Dogana €20/15; ⊙10am-7pm Wed-Mon) Rounding a Grand Canal bend, gondola riders gasp with the shock of the new: installations by contemporary artists like Richard Prince and Jeff Koons docked at Giorgio Masari's 1749 neoclassical palace. French billionaire François Pinault installed his provocative contemporary art collection at the Palazzo Grassi in 2005, providing Venice with sensation and scandal between Biennales. Postmodern architect Gae Aulenti peeled back twee rococo decor to reveal Masari's muscular classicism in 1985–86, and minimalist Tadao Ando heightened the palace's stage-set drama with backlit scrims and spotlighting in 2003–05. Don't miss the cafe overlooking the Grand Canal, with interiors redesigned by artists for each show.

Chiesa di Santo Stefano   CHURCH
(Map p330; www.chorusvenezia.org; Campo Santo Stefano; admission €3 or Chorus Pass; ⊙10am-5pm Mon-Sat) The free-standing bell tower behind it leans disconcertingly, but this soaring brick Gothic church has stayed shipshape since 1325, even though a subterranean canal runs under the wood choir stalls. Credit is shared by architect Bartolomeo Bon for marble entry portals and Venetian shipbuilders, who constructed the vast wooden *carena di nave* (ship's keel) ceiling that looks like an upturned Noah's Ark.

Enter the **cloisters museum** to see Canova's 1808 funerary stelae featuring gorgeous women dabbing their eyes with cloaks, Tullio Lombardo's wide-eyed 1505 saint (which Titian is said to have referenced for his Madonna at I Frari) and three brooding Tintoretto canvases: *Last Supper,* with a ghostly dog begging for bread; the gathering gloom of *Agony in the Garden;* and the abstract, mostly black *Washing of the Feet.*

Chiesa di Santa Maria del Giglio   CHURCH
(Map p330; www.chorusvenezia.org; Campo di Santa Maria del Giglio; admission €3 or Chorus Pass; ⊙10am-5pm Mon-Sat) Experience awe through the ages in this compact church with a 10th-century Byzantine layout, baroque facade featuring charmingly mistaken maps of European cities c 1678 and three masterpieces. Veronese's *Madonna with Child* hides behind the altar, Tintoretto's four evangelists

flank the organ, and Northern Renaissance painter Peter Paul Rubens makes a cameo appearance in the Molin Chapel with Mary, St John and a Rubenesque baby Jesus.

FREE Palazzo Contarini del Bovolo   NOTABLE BUILDING

(Map p330; ☑041 532 29 20; Calle Contarini del Bovolo 4299; entry to open courtyard free; ⏰10am-6pm) There's no need to wait for San Marco sunsets to inspire a snog: this romantic Renaissance 15th-century *palazzo* with an external spiral *bovolo* (snail-shell) stairwell is closed for restoration, but its shady courtyard offers stirring staircase views and privacy for smooches.

DORSODURO

TOP CHOICE Gallerie dell'Accademia   ART GALLERY

(Map p330; ☑041 520 03 45; www.gallerie accademia.org; Campo della Carità 1050; adult/reduced €6.50/3.25; ⏰8.15am-2pm Mon, to 7.15pm Tue-Sun, last admission 1hr before close) Don't be fooled by Palladio's serene expansions for the former Santa Maria della Carità convent: these galleries contain more murderous intrigue, forbidden romance, shameless politicking and near-riots than the most outrageous Venetian parties. To guide you through the ocular onslaught, visits are loosely organised by style, theme and painter from the 14th to the 18th centuries, though recent restorations have temporarily shuffled round some of the masterpieces.

Rooms 1–5
Early collection highlights include Paolo Veneziano's c 1350 *Coronation of Mary* (room 1), which shows Jesus bestowing the crown on his mother with a gentle pat on the head. For sheer, shimmering gore, there's no topping Carpaccio's *Crucifixion and Glorification of the Ten Thousand Martyrs of Mount Ararat* (room 2) – Harry's Bar was correct naming its raw-beef dish after this painter. In rooms 3 to 5, Andrea Mantegna's 1466 haughtily handsome *St George* and Giovanni Bellini's *Madonna and Child* amid neon-red cherubs highlight Venice's twin artistic tendencies: high drama and glowing colour.

Rooms 6–10
Visits advance rapidly through the Renaissance, including Tintoretto's *Creation of the Animals,* a fantastical bestiary that suggests that God put forth his best efforts inventing Venetian seafood (no arguments here).

Dorsoduro (Venice)

◎ Sights
1 Scuola Grande dei Carmini................A2

✪ Eating
2 Enoteca ai Artisti..............................B3
3 Grom...B3
4 Pizza al Volo.....................................A2
5 Ristoteca Oniga...............................B2
6 Trattoria La Bitta.............................A3

◎ Drinking
7 Il Caffè Rosso....................................A1
8 Osteria alla Bifora............................A1

✪ Entertainment
9 Venice Jazz Club...............................B2

◎ Shopping
10 Lauretta Vistosi...............................B2

Recent restoration brings new light to one of Titian's last efforts, possibly finished posthumously by Palma il Giovane: a 1576 *Pietà* with smears of paint Titian applied with bare hands.

Artistic triumph over censorship dominates room 10. Paolo Veronese's controversial *Feast in the House of Levi* was originally called *Last Supper* until church Inquisition

ⓘ OUTSMARTING ACCADEMIA QUEUES

To skip ahead of Accademia ticket-booth queues, book ahead online or by phone (booking fee €1). Otherwise, queues tend to be shorter in the afternoon. But don't wait too long: the last entry to the Accademia is one hour before closing. Leave any large items behind, or you'll have to drop them off at the baggage depot (€0.50). Also available at the baggage depot is an audioguide (€5) that is mostly descriptive and largely unnecessary – it's better to avoid the wait and just follow your nose and the explanatory wall tags.

leaders condemned Veronese for showing dogs, drunkards, dwarfs and even Reformation-minded Germans cavorting amid the apostles. Veronese refused to change a thing about his painting besides the title, and Venice stood by this act of artistic defiance against Rome.

Rooms 11–19

Baroque portrait galleries scarcely contain larger-than-life Venetian personalities: Giorgione's decidedly un-Botoxed *Old Woman*, Lorenzo Lotto's 1525 soul-searching *Portrait of a Young Scholar;* Rosalba Carriera's brutally honest self-portrait (c 1730); Pietro Longhi's stern chaperone in *The Dance Lesson;* and Giambattista Piazzetta's saucy socialite in his 1740 *Fortune-Teller*.

Rooms 20–24

Gentile Bellini and Vittore Carpaccio pack room 20 with multicultural crowds of Venetian merchants embedded in their versions of *Miracles of the True Cross*. The newly restored Sala dell'Albergo is fronted by Antonio Vivarini's giant 1446 triptych and Titian's 1534–39 *Presentation of the Virgin,* with the young Madonna trudging up an intimidating staircase as onlookers point to her example.

TOP CHOICE Peggy Guggenheim Collection
ART GALLERY

(Map p330; ☎041 240 54 11; www.guggenheim-venice.it; Palazzo Venier dei Leoni 704; adult/reduced €12/7; ◷10am-6pm Wed-Mon) After tragically losing her father on the *Titanic,* heiress Peggy Guggenheim befriended Dadaists, dodged Nazis and amassed avant-garde works by 200 modern artists at her palatial home on the Grand Canal. Peggy's **Palazzo Venier dei Leoni** became a modernist shrine, chronicling surrealism, Italian futurism and abstract expressionism, with a subtext of Peggy's romantic pursuits – the collection includes key works by Peggy's ex-husband Max Ernst as well as Jackson Pollock, who was among Peggy's many rumoured lovers. Peggy collected according to her own convictions rather than for prestige or style, so her collection includes folk art and lesser-known artists alongside Kandinsky, Picasso, Man Ray, Calder, Joseph Cornell and Dalí.

Garden & Pavilion

Wander past bronzes by Moore, Giacometti and Brancusci, Yoko Ono's *Wish Tree* and a shiny black granite lump by Anish Kapoor in the sculpture garden, where the city of Venice granted Peggy honorary dispensation to be buried alongside her pet dogs in 1979. Through the gardens is a pavilion housing a sunny cafe, bookshop, toilets and temporary exhibits highlighting underappreciated modernist rebels.

TOP CHOICE Ca' Rezzonico
MUSEUM

(Museum of the 18th Century; Map p330; ☎041 241 01 00; www.museiciviciveneziani.it; Fondamenta Rezzonico 3136; adult/reduced €8/5.50 or Museum Pass; ◷10am-6pm Wed-Mon Apr-Oct, to 5pm Nov-Mar) Baldassare Longhena's luminous baroque palace on the Grand Canal celebrates 18th-century decadence in lavish music salons, sumptuous boudoirs and even an attic pharmacy with medicinal scorpions. Giambattista Tiepolo's Throne Room ceiling is a masterpiece of elegant social climbing, showing gorgeous Merit ascending to the Temple of Glory clutching the Golden Book of Venetian nobles' names – including Tiepolo's patrons, the Rezzonico family.

Collection highlights include the Pietro Longhi Salon of socialite satires, Rosalba Carriera's wry society portraits, Giandomenico Tiepolo's swinging court jesters in reassembled Zianigo Villa bedroom frescoes, and Emma Ciardi's moody Venice views on the top floor. Last entry is an hour before closing; check the schedule downstairs for concerts in the trompe l'œil frescoed ballroom.

Punta della Dogana
MUSEUM

(Map p330; ☎199 13 91 39; www.palazzograssi.it; adult/reduced 15/10, incl Palazzo Grassi €20/15; ◷10am-7pm Wed-Mon) Fortuna, the weathervane atop Punta della Dogana, swung Venice's way in 2005, when bureaucratic hassles in Paris convinced billionaire art collector François Pinault to showcase his art works at Palazzo Grassi and create an installation art gallery in long-abandoned customs warehouses at Punta della Dogana. Architect Tadao Ando opened interiors to the elements outside, flooding exposed-brick galleries with light through windows in water gates and polished-concrete channels – astute homages to Carlo Scarpa's designs for Negozio Olivetti.

Rotating installations here invade personal space and address personal fixations: Chen Zhen's landscape made from pure crystal versions of his own diseased internal organs, Edward Keinholz's full-scale recreation of a Vegas brothel parlour, and Abdel Abdessemed's drawings of Molotov cocktail throwers propped up on concert stands to create orchestrated violence. Not all works are intended for younger viewers, while other pieces (ie Jeff Koons' steel pool toys) may speak to them exclusively.

Chiesa di Santa Maria della Salute
CHURCH

(Map p330; www.seminariovenezia.it, in Italian; Campo della Salute 1b; ⊙9am-noon & 3-5.30pm) The equivalent of a monumental sigh of relief, this church was built in 1631 by survivors of Venice's 1630 plague as thanks for their salvation. Baldassare Longhena's unusual octagonal church is an inspired design that architectural scholars have compared to Graeco-Roman temples and Jewish Cabbala diagrams, and it remains the site of Festa della Madonna della Salute (Venetians' annual pilgrimage to pray for health; see p350). Extensive interior restorations may limit access to Tintoretto's surprisingly upbeat *The Wedding Feast of Cana* and 12 key works by Titian in the sacristy (admission €2), including a vivid self-portrait in the guise of St Matthew and his earliest known work, *Saint Mark on the Throne* from 1510.

Gesuati
CHURCH

(Church of Santa Maria del Rosario; Map p322; www.chorusvenezia.org; Fondamenta delle Zattere 918; admission €3 or Chorus Pass; ⊙10am-5pm Mon-Sat) No matter the weather outside, the outlook is decidedly sunny inside this high-baroque church designed by Giorgio Massari. Luminous late-afternoon skies surrounding St Dominic in Tiepolo's 1737–39 ceiling frescoes are so convincing that you'll wonder whether

SAN SEBASTIANO

337

Over three decades, the modest parish church of San Sebastiano (Map p322; www.chorusvenezia.org; Campo San Sebastiano 1687; admission €3 or Chorus Pass; ⊙10am-5pm Mon-Sat) was covered by Paolo Veronese with floor-to-ceiling masterpieces. Veronese's horses rear over the frames of the coffered ceiling; the organ doors are covered with vivid Veronese masterworks; and in Veronese's *Martyrdom of Saint Sebastian* near the altar, the bound saint defiantly stares down his tormentors amid a Venetian crowd of socialites, turbaned traders and Veronese's signature frisky spaniel. Pay respects to Veronese, who chose to be buried here among his masterpieces, but don't miss Titian's *San Niccolo* and the Tintorettos in the sacristy. Ongoing restoration may limit access to art works, but even so, San Sebastiano offers glimpses of greatness.

you're wearing enough sunscreen. Striking a sombre note on the left side of the nave, Tintoretto's 1565 *Crucifixion* shows Mary fainting with grief, but in the 1730–33 *Saints Peter and Thomas with Pope Pius V*, Sebastiano Ricci's chubby cherubs provide heavenly comic relief with celestial tumbling routines.

Scuola Grande dei Carmini
NOTABLE BUILDING

(Map p335; ☑041 528 94 20; www.scuolagrandecarmini.it; Campo Santa Margherita 2617; adult/reduced €5/4; ⊙11am-5pm) If a time machine could return you to Venice 300 years ago, you could stay in this refuge run by Carmelite nuns and lavishly appointed by Giambattista Tiepolo and Baldessare Longhena. Longhena designed the stucco-frosted and gold-leafed stairway to heaven, which is glimpsed upstairs in in Tiepolo's nine-panel ceiling of a resplendent *Virgin in Glory*. Ask downstairs about occasional concerts by Musica in Maschera (Musical Masquerade; www.musicainmaschera.it), performed here in 1700s costume.

FREE Magazzini del Sale
ART GALLERY

(Map p322; www.fondazionevedova.org; Zattere 266; donation suggested; ⊙10.30am-6pm Wed-Mon during shows) A recent retrofit designed by Pritzker Prize–winning architect Renzo Piano has transformed Venice's historical salt warehouses into city art galleries. Alongside a public art gallery and performance space is **Fondazione Vedova** (www.fondazionevedova.org), dedicated to pioneering Venetian abstract painter Emilio Vedova. At the Fondazione, shows are often literally moving and rotating: powered by renewable energy sources, 10 robotic arms designed by Vedova and Piano move art works in and out of storage slots.

SAN POLO & SANTA CROCE

TOP CHOICE I Frari CHURCH
(Basilica di Santa Maria Gloriosa dei Frari; Map p322; www.chorusvenezia.org; Campo dei Frari 3004; admission €3 or Chorus Pass; ⊙9am-6pm Mon-Sat, 1-6pm Sun) This soaring Italian-brick Gothic church features marquetry choir stalls, Canova's pyramid mausoleum, Bellini's achingly sweet *Madonna with Child* triptych in the sacristy, and Longhena's creepy Doge Pesaro funereal monument hoisted by burly slaves bursting from ragged clothes like Invisible Hulks – yet visitors are inevitably drawn to the small altarpiece.

This is Titian's 1518 *Assumption,* in which a radiant Madonna in a Titian-red cloak reaches heavenward, steps onto a cloud and escapes this mortal coil. Both inside and outside the painting, onlookers gasp and

Sestieri di San Polo (Venice)

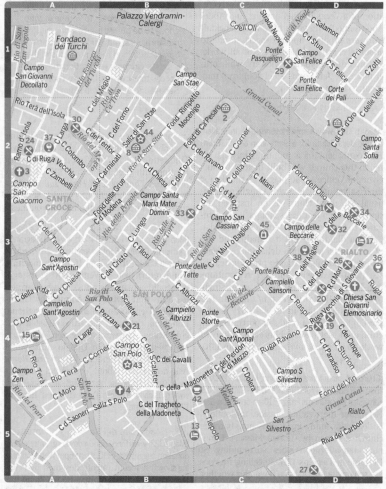

point out at the sight; Titian outdid himself here, upstaging his own 1526 Pesaro Altarpiece near the entry. Titian was lost to the plague in 1576, but legend has it that strict rules of quarantine were bent to allow his burial near his masterpiece.

TOP CHOICE Scuola Grande di San Rocco

MUSEUM

(Map p322; ☎ 041 523 48 64; www.scuolagrande sanrocco.it; Campo San Rocco 3052; adult/reduced €7/5; ⊙9.30am-5.30pm) Everyone wanted the commission to paint this building dedicated to the patron saint of the plaguestricken, so Tintoretto cheated: instead of producing sketches like rival Veronese, he gifted a splendid ceiling panel of patron St Roch, knowing it couldn't be refused or matched by other artists.

Upstairs

Old Testament scenes Tintoretto painted from 1575 to 1587 for the Sala Grande Superiore ceiling upstairs read like a modern graphic novel: you can almost hear the *swoop!* overhead as an angel dives down to feed ailing Elijah. Against the shadowy backdrop of the Black Death, eerie lightning-bolt illumination strikes Tintoretto's subjects in New Testament wall scenes.

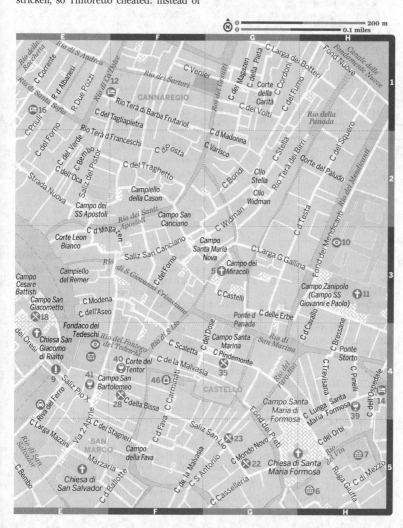

VENICE & THE VENETO SIGHTS

Downstairs

In the assembly hall, Tintoretto tells Mary's life story, starting on the left wall with *Annunciation* and ending with dark and cataclysmic *Ascension* opposite. Gregorian chant concerts are occasionally performed here (ask at the counter), and you can practically hear their echoes in Tintoretto's haunting paintings.

Ca' Pesaro   ART GALLERY
(Map p338; ☑041 72 11 27; www.museiciviciveneziani. it; Fondamenta de Ca' Pesaro 2070; adult/reduced €8/5 or Museum Pass; ☉10am-6pm Tue-Sun Apr-Oct, to 5pm Nov-Mar) Like a couple of Venetian eccentrics in Carnevale costume, the stately exterior of this Longhena-designed 1710 palazzo hides two quirky museums: the Galleria d'Arte Moderna and Museo d'Arte Orientale.

Galleria d'Arte Moderna

Three storeys of Venetian modern art history begin with flag-waving early Biennales, showcasing Venetian landscapes and Venetian socialites by Venetian painters (notably Giacomo Favretto and Guglielmo Ciardi). The savvy Biennale organisers soon diversified, showcasing Gustav Klimt's 1909 *Judith II (Salome)* and Marc Chagall's *Rabbi of Vitebsk* (1914–22). The 1st-floor 1961 De Lisi Bequest added Kandinskys and Morandis to the modernist mix of De Chiricos, Mirós and Moores, plus radical abstracts by postwar Venetian artists Santomaso and Vedova.

Museo d'Arte Orientale

Climb the creaky attic stairs past a phalanx of samurai warriors, girded for battle: this marks the beginning of an epic 1887–89 souvenir-shopping spree across Asia that Prince Enrico di Borbone preserved for posterity. Edo-era netsukes, screens and a lacquerware palanquin are standouts in his collection of 30,000 objets d'art.

GIANANTONIO DE VINCENZO: MUSICIAN

Surround Sound

To enjoy concerts, first you have to find them, but our idea with Venezia Suona is to have wonderful concerts find people wherever they are. We've invited international musicians to play inside boats, at deserted island army barracks, even on top of the Tronchetto parking garage. That's the ugliest place in Venice, but for one afternoon it was glorious.

Beyond Baroque

Vivaldi is like masquerade masks in Venice: it's everywhere, you can't miss it. When you encounter different music, stop and listen: this is how culture evolves, by paying attention to unexpected sensations. Otherwise we're stuck with whatever's on TV.

Dinner & a Show

Restaurants close early, but you can find *cicheti* (Venetian tapas) before and after concerts. I'll grab *panini* and natural-process *prosecco* (type of sparkling wine) at Al Mercà before shows, or hit the *cicheti* bar at Al Pesador afterwards.

Venetian Jazz

The creak of a gondola oar in the oarlock, followed by the rush of swirling water: those are the quiet, rhythmic sounds you can actually hear in Venice, because there is no aggressive traffic noise. Saturdays at Rialto Market, you'll hear an improvised call-and-response between vendors and shoppers – it's Venice's own jazz.

Gianantonio De Vincenzo is director of the Venezia Suona music festival.

VENICE & THE VENETO SIGHTS

Palazzo Mocenigo MUSEUM
(Map p338; ☎041 72 17 98; www.museicivici
veneziani.it; Salizada di San Stae 1992; adult/
reduced €5/3.30 or Museum Pass; ☺10am-5pm
Tue-Sun Apr-Oct, to 4pm Nov-Mar) Costume dramas unfold in this costume museum inside a baroque Grand Canal palace. Necklines plunge in the Red Living Room, lethal corsets come undone in the Contessa's Bedroom and men's paisley silk knee-breeches show some leg in the Dining Room. Even at the most risqué parties in the Green Living Room under Jacopo Guarana's 1787 *Allegory of Nuptial Bliss ceiling*, guests had to mind their tongues: the Mocenigo family once reported philosopher and sometime house guest Giordano Bruno to the Inquisition for heresy.

Chiesa di San Giacomo dell'Orio CHURCH
(Map p338; Campo San Giacomo dell'Orio 1457; admission €3 or Chorus Pass; ☺10am-5pm Mon-Sat) Early Venetian maritime conquests explain the hotchpotch, multiculti decor in this chilly yet charming medieval church, with its Latin cross layout, Lombard pulpit perched atop a 6th-century Byzantine column, and recently restored 14th-century *carena di nave* ceiling. Standout art works include luminous sacristy paintings by Palma Il Giovane, a rare Lorenzo Lotto *Madonna with Child and Saints* and an exceptional Veronese wooden crucifix (currently undergoing restoration).

Chiesa di San Polo CHURCH
(Map p338; Campo San Polo 2118; admission €3 or Chorus Pass; ☺10am-5pm Mon-Sat) Travellers often speed past this modest 9th-century Byzantine brick church between I Frari and the Rialto without suspecting that major dramas are unfolding behind these modest portals. Under the medieval wooden *carena di nave* ceiling, Tintoretto's *Last Supper* shows apostles alarmed and outraged by Jesus' announcement that one of them will betray him. Giandominico Tiepolo's disturbing *Stations of the Cross* sacristy cycle shows Jesus tormented by jeering onlookers, only to leap triumphantly from his tomb in a ceiling panel.

CANNAREGIO

TOP CHOICE **Chiesa della Madonna dell'Orto** CHURCH
(Map p342; Campo della Madonna dell'Orto 3520; admission €3 or Chorus Pass; ☺10am-5pm Mon-Sat) This elegantly spare 1365 brick Gothic cathedral dedicated to the patron saint of travellers remains one of Venice's best-kept secrets.

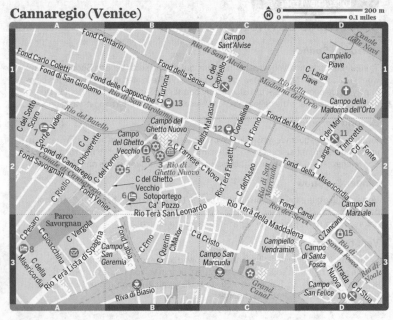

Cannaregio (Venice)

This was the parish church of Venetian Renaissance master Tintoretto, who is buried here in the corner chapel and saved two of his finest works for the apse: *Presentation of the Virgin in the Temple,* with throngs of star-struck angels and mortals vying for a glimpse of Mary, and his 1546 *Last Judgment,* where lost souls attempt to hold back a teal tidal wave while an angel rescues one last person from the ultimate *acque alte.*

Museo Ebraico   MUSEUM
(Map p342; 📞041 71 53 59; www.museoebraico. it; Campo del Ghetto Nuovo 2902b; adult/reduced €3/2; ⊙10am-7pm Sun-Fri except Jewish holidays Jun-Sep, to 6pm Oct-May) At the heart of the Ghetto, this museum explores the history of Venice's Jewish community and its pivotal contributions to the worlds of science, literature, fashion, religion, philosophy and commerce.

Synagogue Tour

(tours incl admission adult/reduced €8.50/7; ☺4 tours daily from 10.30am) Hour-long English-language tours leave from the museum, and lead inside three of the Ghetto's seven tiny synagogues: the 1528 Schola Tedescha (German Synagogue), with a gilded, elliptical women's gallery modelled after an opera balcony; the 1531 Schola Canton (French Synagogue), with eight charming landscapes taken from biblical parables; and either the simple, dark-wood Schola Italiana (Italian Synagogue) or the still-active Schola Spagnola (Spanish Synagogue), with interiors attributed to Baldassare Longhena.

Ca' d'Oro   MUSEUM

(House of Gold; Map p342; ☎041 520 03 45; www.cadoro.org; Calle di Ca' d'Oro 3932; adult/reduced €6/3; ☺8.15am-2pm Mon, to 7.15pm Tue-Sun) Even without original gold-leaf details that gave the palace its name, this splendid 15th-century Gothic palace is rivalled only by its own shimmering reflection in the Grand Canal. The lacy Gothic arcade framing the two-tier balcony makes for Venice's most irresistible photo-ops, and the intricate semiprecious stone mosaics paving the water door entry make a grander entrance than any red carpet.

Collection

Ca' d'Oro was donated to the city to house Galleria Franchetti, Baron Franchetti's art collection, plus a jackpot of bronzes, tapestries and paintings plundered from Veneto churches by Napoleon and reclaimed by Venice. Collection highlights include Andrea Mantegna's teeth-baring, arrow-riddled *Saint Sebastian,* Pietro Lombardo's tender *Madonna and Child* in glistening Carrara marble, and Titian fresco fragments rescued after Venice's 1966 flood.

CASTELLO

Zanipolo   CHURCH

(Chiesa dei SS Giovanni e Paolo; Map p338; ☎041 523 59 13; Campo SS Giovanni e Paolo; admission €2.50; ☺9am-6pm Mon-Sat, noon-6pm Sun) Built by Dominicans to rival the Franciscans' I Frari, this 14th-century church lacks I Frari's soaring grace but makes up the difference with the sheer scale and variety of its masterpieces. In the Cappella del Rosario, Paolo Veronese's ceiling depicts a rosy Virgin ascending a staggering staircase. The chapel dome on the southwest end of the nave boasts Giambattista Lorenzetti's *Jesus the Navigator,* with Jesus scanning the heavens like a Venetian sea captain. The church is also a kind of pantheon, with 25 doges' tombs by such notable sculptors as Nicola

---

THE ORIGINAL GHETTO

In medieval times, this Cannaregio outpost housed a *getto* (foundry). But it was as the designated Jewish quarter from the 16th to 18th centuries that this area gave the word a whole new meaning. In accordance with the Venetian Republic's 1516 decree, Jewish lenders, doctors and clothing merchants were allowed to attend to Venice's commercial interests by day, while at night and on Christian holidays most were restricted to the gated island of Ghetto Nuovo. Unlike most European cities at the time, pragmatic Venice granted Jewish doctors dispensation for consultations. In fact, Venice's Jewish and Muslim physicians are credited with helping establish the quarantine on incoming ships that spared Venice the worst ravages of plague.

When Jewish merchants fled the Spanish Inquisition for Venice in 1541, there was no place to go in the Ghetto but up. Around Campo del Ghetto Nuovo, upper storeys housed new arrivals, synagogues and publishing houses. Despite a 10-year censorship order issued by the church in Rome in 1553, Jewish Venetian publishers contributed hundreds of titles popularising new Renaissance ideas on religion, humanist philosophy and medicine. By the 17th century, Ghetto literary salons organised by philosopher Sara Copio Sullam, Rabbi Leon da Modena and others brought leading thinkers of all faiths to the Ghetto.

After Napoleon lifted restrictions in 1797, some 1626 Ghetto residents gained standing as Venetian citizens. However, Mussolini's 1938 race laws were throwbacks to the 16th century, and in 1943 most Jewish Venetians were rounded up and sent to concentration camps; only 37 returned. Today few of Venice's 400-strong Jewish community actually live in the Ghetto, but their children come to Campo del Ghetto Nuovo to play, surrounded by the Ghetto's living legacy of bookshops, art galleries and religious institutions.

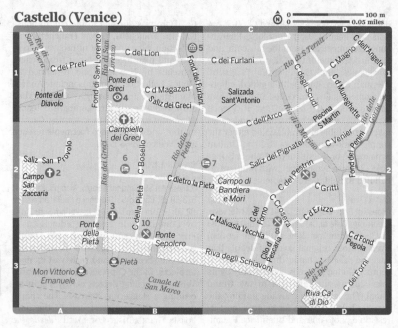

Castello (Venice)

Pisano and Tullio Lombardo. A 15th-century Murano stained-glass window in the south transept has been gorgeously restored.

Zanipolo's austere facade is nearly overwhelmed by the lavish Renaissance polychrome trompe l'œil facade by Pietro Lombardo for the adjacent **Scuola Grande di San Marco**, now Venice's main hospital (patient visits only).

Scuola di San Giorgio degli Schiavoni
CHURCH

(Map p344; ☑041 522 88 28; Calle dei Furlani 3259a; adult/reduced €4/2; ◎2.45-6pm Mon, 9.15am-1pm & 2.45-6pm Tue-Sat, 9.15am-1pm Sun) Venice's cosmopolitan nature is evident in Castello, where Turkish merchants, Armenian clerics and Balkan and Slavic labourers were considered essential to Venetian commerce and society. This 15th-century religious confraternity headquarters is dedicated to favourite Slavic saints George, Tryphone and Jerome of Dalmatia, whose lives are captured with precision and glowing, early-Renaissance grace by 15th-century master Vittore Carpaccio.

Palazzo Grimani
MUSEUM

(Map p338; ☑041 520 03 45; www.palazzogrimani. org; Ramo Grimani 4858; adult/reduced €9/7; ◎9am-7pm) Just south of Campo Santa Maria Formosa, this light-filled *palazzo* has finally reopened to the public after nearly three decades. Built in the 1500s by Doge Antonio Grimani to house his remarkable collection of Graeco-Roman antiquities (most of which are now in Museo Correr), the lovingly restored *palazzo* houses high-calibre temporary exhibitions.

Palazzo Querini Stampalia   MUSEUM

(Map p338; ☑041 271 14 11; www.querinistampalia.it, in Italian; Campiello Querini Stampalia 5252) Hidden behind the rambling facade of this 16th-century *palazzo* lies a series of unexpected attractions. Savvy tipplers take their *aperitivi* with a twist of high modernism in the Carlo Scarpa–designed garden (☺10am-9.30pm Tue-Sat, to 7pm Sun). The more sober of mind can wind their way through the Mario Botta–designed bookshop for a ticket to the upstairs Museo della Fondazione Querini Stampalia (adult/reduced €8/6; ☺10am-8pm Tue-Thu, to 10pm Fri & Sat, to 7pm Sun). The museum's temporary contemporary shows add an element of the unexpected to silk-draped salons preserved in period splendour since 1868.

Chiesa di San Francesco della Vigna   CHURCH

(Map p322; ☑041 520 61 02; Campo San Francesco della Vigna 2786; ☺9.30am-12.30pm & 3-6pm Mon-Sat, 3-6pm Sun) East of Campo SS Giovanni e Paolo you'll spot the bell tower of this enchanting church. Designed and built by Jacopo Sansovino with a facade by Palladio, it is one of Venice's most underrated attractions. The Madonna positively glows in Bellini's 1507 *Madonna and Saints* in the Capella Santa off the cloisters; swimming angels and strutting birds steal the scene in Antonio da Negroponte's c 1460–70 *Virgin Enthroned;* and Pietro Lombardo's lifelike lions seem ready to pounce right out of the 15th-century marble reliefs in the Capella Giustiniani, to the left of the altar.

Chiesa di San Giorgio dei Greci   CHURCH

(Map p344; ☑041 522 65 81; Campiello dei Greci 3412; admission free; ☺9am-12.30pm & 2.30-4.30pm Mon & Wed-Sat, 9am-1pm Sun) Greek Orthodox refugees fleeing conquering Turks built this church in 1536, with the aid of a special dispensation from Venice to collect taxes on Greek ships. Its distinctive bell tower, completed in 1603, has leaned precariously since shortly after its completion.

Just next to the church is the extraordinary Museo delle Icone (www.istitutoellenico.org; adult/student €4/2; ☺10am-5pm), a treasure

CHIESA DI SANTA MARIA DEI MIRACOLI

A minor *miracolo* (miracle) of early-Renaissance architecture, Pietro Lombardo's little marble chapel, Chiesa di Santa Maria dei Miracoli (Map p338; Campo dei Miracoli 6074; admission €3 or Chorus Pass; ☺10am-5pm Mon-Sat), was ahead of its time, dropping Gothic grandiosity for human-scale classical architecture. By pooling resources and scavenging multicoloured marble from San Marco slag heaps, the neighbourhood commissioned this church to house Niccolò di Pietro's Madonna icon when it miraculously started weeping in c 1480. Completing this monument to community spirit, Pier Maria Pennacchi filled 50 ceiling panels with portraits of prophets dressed as Venetians.

box of some 80 Greek icons from the 14th to the 17th century.

Arsenale   HISTORICAL BUILDING

(Map p322) Founded in 1104, the Arsenale soon became the greatest medieval shipyard in Europe, home to 300 shipping companies employing up to 16,000 people. Capable of turning out a new galley in a day, it is considered a forerunner of mass industrial production. Though it's closed to the public most of the year, arty types invade the shipyard during Venice's art and architecture Biennales, when it hosts exhibitions and special events.

Chiesa di San Zaccaria   CHURCH

(Map p344; ☑041 522 12 57; Campo San Zaccaria 4693; ☺10am-noon & 4-6pm Mon-Sat, 4-6pm Sun) When 15th-century Venetian girls preferred sailors to saints, they often had to do a penitential stint at the convent adjoining this remarkable church. A hotchpotch of Romanesque, Gothic, Renaissance and baroque, it represents centuries of the wealth of disgruntled parents. Don't miss Bellini's melancholy *Virgin* or Tiepolo's version of the flight into Egypt via Venetian-style boat. For €1, you can also visit hidden chapels and the waterlogged, 10th-century foundations.

Giardini Pubblici   PARK

(Map p322) Begun under Napoleon as the city's first green space, a large portion of these leafy public gardens serve as the main home of the Biennale, with curators and curiosity-seekers swarming the pavilions, from Carlo Scarpa's daring 1954 raw-concrete-and-glass Venezuelan Pavilion to Peter Cox's awkward 1988 Australian Pavilion, which is frequently mistaken for a shed. Part of the gardens is open to the public all year round; sometimes during off years you can wander among the pavilions and admire the facades.

La Pietà
CHURCH

(Map p344; ☎041 522 21 71; Riva degli Schiavoni; admission €3; ☺10am-5pm Thu-Sun, also for concerts) This light-filled, harmonious church designed by Giorgio Massari is famous for its association with the composer Vivaldi, who was concertmaster here in the early 18th century. Built shortly after Vivaldi's death, the acoustic-friendly oval shape honours his memory and is still regularly used as a concert hall. Note the ceiling that seems to float off its hinges, thanks to Giambattista Tiepolo's gravity-defying *Coronation of the Virgin*.

Museo Storico Navale
MUSEUM

(Map p322; ☎041 244 13 99; Riva San Biagio 2148; adult/reduced €1.55/0.77; ☺8.45am-1.30pm Mon-Fri, to 1pm Sat) This 42-room monument to Venice's maritime history is mostly of interest to specialists, with its miniature versions of ocean liners, seaside fortifications and WWII battleships. However, landlubbers will gawk at the sumptuous model of the *bucintoro* – the doge's gilded ceremonial barge, destroyed by Napoleonic troops – as well as Peggy Guggenheim's lavish gondola.

GIUDECCA

Originally known as the *spina longa* (long fishbone) because of its shape, Giudecca has survived many trials without losing its spirit. Venice's Jewish community lived here prior to the creation of the Ghetto, but Giudecca isn't related to the word 'Jewish' (*ebraico* in Italian). Giudecca is probably derived from *zudega* (from *giudicato*, or 'the judged'), the name given to rebellious Venetian nobles banished to Giudecca. The banishments backfired: Giudecca became fashionable and Venetians built weekend garden villas on the island. However, many were abandoned during times of plague and war, and were eventually displaced by 19th-century industry.

Today Giudecca is entering its third act, with brick factories converted into artists' lofts, galleries taking over the Fondamenta

San Biagio, and some of Venice's most reasonably priced restaurants. *Vaporetti* 41, 42, 82 and N (night) make Giudecca an easy stop between San Marco and Dorsoduro.

Il Redentore
CHURCH

(Chiesa del SS Redentore; Map p322; Campo del SS Redentore 194; admission €3 or Chorus Pass; ☺10am-5pm Mon-Sat) You can't miss Palladio's 1577 Il Redentore church, a triumph of white marble along the Giudecca Canal celebrating the city's deliverance from the Black Death. Inside above the portal, Paolo Piazza's strikingly modern 1619 *Gratitude of Venice for Liberation from the Plague* shows the city held aloft by angels in sobering shades of grey. Survival is never taken for granted by Venetians, who walk across the Giudecca Canal on a shaky pontoon bridge from the Zattere during Festa del Redentore.

Fortuny Tessuti Artistici
LANDMARK

(Map p322; ☎041 522 40 78; www.fortuny.com; Fondamenta San Biagio 805; ☺9am-noon & 2-5pm Mon-Fri) Marcel Proust waxed poetic over the creations of Spanish-born textile master Mariano Fortuny, who relocated permanently to Venice in 1889. Visitors can still browse Fortuny creations in the showroom, though fabrication methods remain a jealously guarded secret.

ISOLA DI SAN GIORGIO MAGGIORE

Chiesa di San Giorgio Maggiore
CHURCH

(Map p322; ☎041 522 78 27; Isola di San Giorgio Maggiore; ☺9.30am-12.30pm & 2.30-6.30pm Mon-Sat May-Sep, 9.30am-12.30pm & 2.30-4.30pm Oct-Apr) Solar eclipses are only marginally more dazzling than Palladio's white Istrian marble facade. Begun in the 1560s, it owes more to ancient Roman temples than the bombastic baroque of Palladio's day. Inside, ceilings billow over a generous nave, with high windows distributing filtered sunshine and easy grace. Two of Tintoretto's masterworks flank the altar, and a lift whisks visitors up the 60m-high bell tower (€3) for stirring Ventian panoramas – a great alternative to long lines at San Marco's *campanile*.

Behind the church, a defunct naval academy has been converted into a shipshape gallery by the Fondazione Giorgio Cini (☎041 220 12 15; www.cini.it; Isola di San Giorgio Maggiore; adult/reduced €12/10; ☺guided tours in English & French 11am, 1pm, 3pm & 5pm Sat & Sun, in Italian 10am, noon, 2pm & 4pm Sat & Sun). After escaping the Dachau internment camp with his son Giorgio, Vittorio Cini returned to Venice on a mission to save San Giorgio

Maggiore, which was a ramshackle mess in 1949. Cini's foundation restored the island into a cultural centre. In addition to its permanent collection of Old Masters and modern art, the gallery hosts important contemporary works, from Peter Greenaway to Anish Kapoor.

THE LIDO

When Karl Lagerfeld was looking for an appropriate location for Chanel's 2009 resort couture collection, the choice was obvious: the Lido (off Map p322). Only 15 minutes by *vaporetti* 1, 51, 52, 61, 62, 82 and N from San Marco, this barrier island has brought glamour to beach-going since the late 19th century, when Venetians began to flee muggy Venetian summers for the Lido's breezy, Liberty-style villas. Thomas Mann's novel *Death in Venice* was set here, and you'll spot wrought-iron balconies and seaside hotels that date from those elegantly decadent days. However, the most famous of all – Hotel des Bains – was closed for major restoration at the time of writing.

Lido beaches (deposit/chair/hut €5/6/11, umbrella & chair €17; ☺9.30am-7pm May-Sep) remain a major draw. But to avoid the crowds, rent a bicycle by the *vaporetto* stop at Lido on Bike (☑041 526 80 19; www.lidoonbike.it; Gran Viale 21b; bikes per 90min/day €5/9; ☺9am-7pm Apr-Sep) and head south to Alberoni and other pristine, windswept beaches.

The biggest event on the Lido social calendar is September's Venice Film Festival, when starlets and socialites attempt to blind paparazzi with Italian couture. Major events are held at the 1930s Palazzo del Cinema, which looks like a Fascist airport when stripped of its red carpet.

ISOLA DI SAN MICHELE

Shuttling between Murano from the Fondamente Nuove, *vaporetti* 41 and 42 stop at Venice's city cemetery, established on Isola di San Michele under Napoleon. Until then, Venetians were buried in parish plots across town – not the most salubrious solution, as Napoleon's inspectors soon realised. Today, goths, incorrigible romantics and music lovers pause here to pay respects to Ezra Pound, Sergei Diaghilev and Igor Stravinsky. Architecture aficionados stop here to see Renaissance Chiesa di San Michele in Isola (Map p322), begun by Codussi in 1469, as well as the ongoing cemetery extension scheduled for 2013 completion by David Chipperfield Architects. It includes the Courtyard of the

Four Evangelists, a rather gloomy bunker with a concrete colonnade and basalt-clad walls engraved with the Gospels.

MURANO

Venetians have been working in crystal and glass since the 10th century, but due to fire hazards all glass-blowing was moved to the island of Murano (off Map p322) in the 13th century. Woe betide the glass-blower with wanderlust: trade secrets were so jealously guarded that any glass-worker who left the city was accused of treason and subject to assassination. Today glass artisans ply their trade at workshops along Murano's Fondamenta dei Vetrai marked by 'Fornace' (Furnace) signs. To ensure glass you buy is handmade in Murano and not factory-fabricated elsewhere, look for the heart-shaped seal guarantee.

Museum of Glass   MUSEUM
(Museo del Vetro; ☑041 73 95 86; www.musei civiciveneziani.it; Fondamenta Giustinian 8; adult/reduced €8/5.50 or Museum Pass; ☺10am-6pm Apr-Oct, to 5pm Nov-Mar) Since 1861, this palace has showcased Murano's glass-making prowess. Downstairs displays exhibit surprisingly intact 1500-year-old iridescent Roman glass, but upstairs Murano shows off with displays ranging from 17th-century winged aventurine goblets to a whimsical 1930s glass cactus. Geek out in the gallery explaining glass-making techniques innovated on Murano, from mosaic miniatures to Venetian trade beads.

Chiesa dei SS Maria e Donato   CHURCH
(☑041 73 90 56; Campo San Donato; ☺9am-noon & 3.30-7pm Mon-Sat, 3.30-7pm Sun) Fire-breathing is the unifying theme of Murano's medieval church, with its 12-century gilded glass Madonna apse mosaic made in Murano's red-hot *fornace* (furnaces) and the legendary bones of a dragon hanging behind the altar. According to local lore, this beast was slain by San Donato, whose mortal remains were also brought here from Cephalonia as relics.

BURANO

If Venice's Gothic architecture is making you feel slightly loopy, Burano (off Map p322) will bring you down to earth and back to your senses with a reviving shock of colour. The 50-minute Laguna Nord (LN) ferry ride from the Fondamente Nuove is packed with photographers vying for the best shot of pea-green stockings hung to dry between hot-pink and royal-blue houses.

Besides its colourful character, Burano is famed for lemon-scented, S-shaped *buranelli* biscuits and handmade lace. At the time of writing, Museo del Merletto (Lace Museum; www.museicivicieveneziani.it) remained closed for expansion, and much of the lace for sale in Burano boutiques was imported – be sure to ask for a guarantee of authenticity.

TORCELLO

On the pastoral island of Torcello (off Map p322), a three-minute T-line ferry-hop from Burano, sheep outnumber the 14 or so human residents. This bucolic backwater was once a Byzantine metropolis of 20,000, but of its original nine churches and two abbeys, only the striking brick Chiesa di Santa Fosca and splendid mosaic-filled Santa Maria Assunta remain.

On leisurely walks around the island, you'll spot a few relics, including a worn stone throne Attila the Hun is said to have occupied in the 5th century where lagoon birds now perch – it's been a while since Ernest Hemingway's hunting parties gave them cause for fear. Time permitting before the last ferry departure, peek at early mosaics painstakingly assembled from half-centimetre tesserae and miniature bronzes collected from Torcello's Byzantine heyday inside the small Torcello museum (Piazza Torcello; admission incl cathedral €8; ⊙10.30am-5pm Tue-Sun Apr-Oct).

Santa Maria Assunta   CATHEDRAL
(Piazza Torcello; admission & audioguide cathedral €6, incl museum €8; ⊙10.30am-6pm Mar-Oct, 10am-5pm Nov-Feb) Don't let its restrained exteriors and advanced age fool you: this Byzantine cathedral built in 639 and rebuilt around 1008 is bursting with colourful stories in interior mosaics. The soaring bell tower offers commanding lagoon views, but is currently undergoing restoration. Last entry is half an hour before closing.

Mosaics

A beatific Madonna rises above corn poppies in the golden eastern apse mosaic, while on the western wall a mosaic Last Judgment shows the Adriatic as a sea nymph ushering souls lost at sea towards St Peter, who's jangling the keys to Paradise like God's own bouncer. A sneaky devil tips the scales of justice, while his minions drag sinners into a hell populated with bloated gluttons, greedy bejewelled merchants, and envious cadavers with snakes coming out of their eyes. In the centre, Jesus offers reassuring words: 'I am God and Man; I am not far from the guilty, but close to the repentant.'

Activities

A gondola ride is anything but pedestrian, with glimpses into *palazzi* courtyards and hidden canals otherwise invisible by foot. Official daytime rates are €80 for 40 minutes (six passengers maximum) or €100 from 7pm to 8am, not including songs (negotiated separately) or tips. Additional time is charged in 20-minute increments (day/night €40/50). You may negotiate a price break in low season, overcast weather or around midday, when other travellers get hot and hungry. Agree on a price, time limit and singing in advance to avoid surcharges. Gondole cluster at *stazi* (stops) along the Grand Canal, at the train station (☎041 71 85 43), the Rialto (☎041 522 49 04) and near major monuments (eg I Frari, Ponte Sospiri and Accademia), but you can also book a pick-up at a canal near you (☎041 528 50 75).

☞ Tours

From April to October, APT tourist offices (see p362) offer guided tours ranging from the classic gondola circuit (€40 per person) to a penetrating look at Basilica di San Marco (€18 per person).

Laguna Eco Adventures   BOAT
(☎329 722 62 89; www.lagunaecoadventures.com; 2½-8hr trips per person €40-150) Explore the far reaches of the lagoon by day or hidden Venetian canals by night in a traditional *sampierota*, a narrow twin-sailed boat. Reserve ahead and note that trips are subject to weather conditions.

Row Venice   BOAT
(☎345 241 52 66; www.rowvenice.com; 2hr lessons from €40) The next best thing to walking on water: rowing a *sandolo* (Venetian boat) standing up like gondoliers do, with Australian-Venetian rowing coach Jane Caporal.

Terra e Acqua   BOAT
(☎347 420 50 04; www.terraeacqua.com; day trips per person incl lunch from €70) Spot rare lagoon wildlife, admire architectural gems of Burano and Torcello, and moor for a tasty fish-stew lunch, all via *bragosso* (Venetian barge).

Venicescapes   WALKING
(www.venicescapes.org; 4-6hr tours incl book 2 adults US$150-275, additional adult/under 18yr US$50/25) Run by a nonprofit historical society, these intriguing walking tours explore

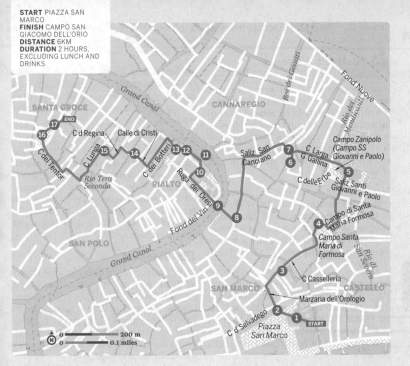

Walking Tour
Venice Labyrinth

> This adventure, which explores Venice's crooked *calli* (lanes) and charming hidden *campi* (squares), begins with the obligatory salute to ① **Basilica di San Marco**. Duck under the ② **Torre dell'Orlogio** and follow the *calle* veering right into narrow ③ **Campo della Guerra**, where you'll hear Venetian gossip whispered over Spritz and gondoliers singing. Pass over the bridge along Calle Casselleria into sunny ④ **Campo Santa Maria Formosa**. Straight ahead is Calle Santa Maria della Formosa; follow it to the left across two bridges to Salizada Santi Giovanni e Paolo, which leads left to the massive Gothic cathedral, ⑤ **Zanipolo**.

Calle Larga Gallina leads over a bridge, and before you cross a second bridge turn left for a glimpse of heaven at Venice's small wonder, the marble-clad ⑥ **Chiesa di Santa Maria dei Miracoli**. Backtrack to the bridge, and cross it to browse through ⑦ **Campo Santa Maria Nova** to Salizada San Canciano, which you'll follow down to skinny ⑧ **Campo San Bartolomeo**, lined with designer showrooms

and souvenir stalls. To the right is ⑨ **Ponte di Rialto**; stay on the right as you cross and duck away from the crowds towards happy-hour central, ⑩ **Campo Cesare Battisti**, and continue along the ⑪ **Grand Canal** to Venice's tastiest *campi*: produce-piled ⑫ **Campo Rialto Mercato** and the covered seafood market, ⑬ **Pescaria**.

Turning left along Calle dei Botteri and another on boutique-lined Calle di Cristi, you'll come to oddly shaped ⑭ **Campo San Cassian**, the site of the world's first public opera house. Cross the bridge to Calle della Regina, then head right to cross another bridge to sociable ⑮ **Campo Santa Maria Mater Domini**, with its cafes and ancient neighbourhood well. Turn left down Calle Lunga and over a bridge until it dead-ends, then jog left to Rio Tera Seconda and right again onto Calle del Tentor. Straight ahead, you'll see its namesake medieval church, ⑯ **San Giacomo dell'Orio**, and your pick of Italy's best natural-process wines at ⑰ **Al Prosecco**. *Cin-cin!*

themes like Venice's multi-ethnic roots or the Venetian art of espionage.

✨ Festivals & Events

Carnevale
CULTURAL
(www.carnevale.venezia.it) Masquerade madness stretches over two weeks in February before Lent. Tickets to La Fenice's masked balls start at €200, but there's a free-flowing wine fountain to commence Carnevale, public costume parties in every *campo* (square), and a Grand Canal flotilla marking the end of festivities.

Festa di San Marco
RELIGIOUS
(www.comune.venezia.it) Join the celebration of Venice's patron saint on 25 April, when Venetian men carry roses in processions through Piazza San Marco, then bestow them on women they love.

Vogalonga
CULTURAL
(www.vogalonga.it) A show of endurance each May or June, this 32km 'long row' starts with 1000 boats launching outside the Palazzo Ducale, loops past Burano and Murano, and ends with cheers, sweat and enough *prosecco* to numb blisters at Punta della Dogana.

La Biennale di Venezia
CULTURAL
(www.labiennale.org) In odd years the Art Biennale runs from June to October, while in even years the Architecture Biennale runs from September to November. The main venues are Giardini Pubblici pavilions and the Arsenale. Every summer, the Biennale hosts avant-garde dance, theatre, cinema and music programs throughout the city.

Festa del Redentore
CULTURAL
(www.turismovenezia.it) Walk on water across the Giudecca Canal to Il Redentore via a wobbly pontoon bridge on the third Saturday and Sunday in July, then watch the fireworks from the Zattere.

Venice Film Festival
FILM
(www.labiennale.org/en/cinema) The only thing hotter than a Lido beach in August is the Film Festival's star-studded red carpet, usually rolled out from the last weekend in August through the first week of September.

Regata Storica
CULTURAL
(www.comune.venezia.it) Never mind who's winning, just check out all the cool gear: 16th-century costumes, eight-oared gondolas and ceremonial barques feature in a historical procession (usually held in September), which re-enacts the arrival of the Queen of Cyprus.

Venezia Suona
MUSIC
(www.veneziasuona.it) Hear medieval *campi* and baroque palaces echo with music from around the world over a glorious September weekend.

Festa della Madonna della Salute
CULTURAL
(www.turismovenezia.it) If you'd survived plague, floods and Austrian invasion, you'd throw a party too. Every year since the 17th century, on 21 November Venetians cross a pontoon bridge across the Grand Canal to give thanks at Chiesa di Santa Maria della Salute and splurge on sweets.

🛏 Sleeping

Many Venetians open their historical homes as B&Bs; **APT tourist board** (www.turismo venezia.it) lists 270 B&Bs, 288 *affittacamere* (rooms for rent) and 944 apartments to rent in Venice proper. More can be found at **Craigslist Venice** (http://venice.it.craigslist.it), www.guestinitaly.com and www.veniceapart ment.com; see also p908.

The best hotel rates are in Venice's low season, typically November, early December, January and the period between Carnevale and Easter, but you might swing deals in July and August. For 400 options, see www. lonelyplanet.com, and for still more choices, try **A Guest in Venice** (www.unospitedivenezia. it) or **Venice Hoteliers Association** (www. veneziasi.it).

PIAZZA SAN MARCO & AROUND

TOP CHOICE Novecento
BOUTIQUE HOTEL €€
(Map p330; ☑041 241 37 65; www.novecento. biz; Calle del Dose 2683/84; d €130-260; ❋ 🐾 🛜) World travellers put down roots in nine bohemian-chic rooms with Turkish kilim pillows, Fortuny draperies and 19th-century scallop-shell carved bedsteads. Linger over breakfast in the garden under an Indian sun parasol, meet the artists at hotel-organised art exhibitions, go for a massage at sister property Hotel Flora or mingle around the honesty bar.

Gio' & Gio'
B&B €€
(Map p330; ☑347 366 50 16; www.giogiovenice. com; Calle delle Ostreghe 2439; d €90-150; ❋ 🛜) Restrained baroque sounds like an oxymoron, but here you have it: polished wood

floors, pearl-grey walls, bronze silk curtains, burl-wood dressers and spotlit art. It's ideally located near Piazza San Marco along a side canal; angle for rooms overlooking the gondola stop, and wake to choruses of *Volare, oh-oh-oooooh!*

Hotel Flora   HOTEL €€
(Map p330; ☑041 520 58 44; www.hotelflora.it; Calle Bergamaschi 2283a; d €150-290; ☀️🛜🚶) Down a lane from glitzy Calle Larga XXII Marzo, this ivy-covered garden retreat quietly outclasses brash top-end neighbours with its plush rooms, delightful tearoom and gym offering shiatsu massage. Guestrooms feature antique carved beds piled with soft mattresses and fluffy duvets; ask for opulent gilded No 3 or No 32, which opens onto the garden.

AD Place Venice   DESIGN HOTEL €€€
(Map p330; ☑041 241 23 24; www.adplacevenice. com; Fondamenta della Fenice 2557a; d incl breakfast €125-290; ☀️🛜) Taking its cue from Teatro La Fenice across the canal, AD Place goes for romantic high drama, from the lobby's patchwork curtains and candlelit lanterns to patent leather bedsteads and gilded mirrors upstairs. Let savvy staff arrange gondola pick-ups and custom art tours, and don't skip the buffet breakfasts on the cushion-strewn terrace.

Hotel Ai Do Mori   HOTEL €
(Map p330; ☑041 520 48 17; www.hotelaidomori. com; Calle Larga San Marco 658; d €50-110; ☀️🛜) These are cosy artists' garrets just off Piazza San Marco; book ahead to score an upper-floor room with wood-beamed ceilings, parquet floors and views over the basilica. Ask for No 11, with a private terrace (pack light as there is no lift here).

Locanda Art Deco   B&B €€
(Map p330; ☑041 277 05 58; www.locandaartdeco. com; Calle delle Botteghe 2966; d incl breakfast €80-170; ☀️) Rakishly handsome, cream-coloured guestrooms have parquet floors and comfy beds in custom wrought-iron bedsteads. Helpful hotel staff arrange in-room massages and boat tours with Venice's pioneering woman gondolier.

DORSODURO
Charming House DD.724   B&B €€€
(Map p330; ☑041 277 02 62; www.thecharming house.com; Ramo de Mula 724; d incl breakfast €99-400; ☀️@🛜) Hole up in your own modern art–filled Venetian bolthole, with lavish breakfast buffets in the library and a multimedia room. Guestrooms are designer-sleek yet cosy, and the superior double has a bathtub and balcony overlooking Peggy Guggenheim's garden. Babysitting, massages and guided tours available on request.

La Calcina   INN €€
(Map p322; ☑041 520 64 66; www.lacalcina.com; Fondamenta Zattere ai Gesuati 780; s €80-150, d €110-310; ☀️🛜) An idyllic seaside getaway, it has breakfasts on the roof terrace, an elegant canalside restaurant and 29 airy, parquet-floored guestrooms, several facing the Giudecca Canal and Palladio's Redentore church. Book ahead for rooms with en suite bathrooms and/or views, especially No 2, where John Ruskin stayed while he wrote his classic (if inexplicably Palladio-bashing) 1876 *The Stones of Venice*.

La Chicca   B&B €€
(Map p330; ☑041 552 55 35; www.lachicca-venezia. com; Calle Franchi 644; d incl breakfast €50-200; ☀️🛜) It's neatly wedged among Dorsoduro's trifecta of museums – Accademia, Peggy Guggenheim, Punta della Dogana – yet all you'll hear at night in this new family-run B&B is the lapping of the canal at the end of the *calle*. Venetian damask-clad guestrooms are spacious and blessedly uncluttered; book ahead to nab one with a tub.

Hotel Galleria   INN €€
(Map p330; ☑041 523 24 89; www.hotelgalleria. it; Campo della Carità 878a; s incl breakfast €70-120, d incl breakfast €100-200) Smack on the Grand Canal at the Ponte dell'Accademia, this converted 17th-century mansion offers small doubles overlooking the Grand Canal (Nos 7, 8 and 9). Most rooms share updated bathrooms; two rooms accommodate larger families.

Palazzo Zenobio   HOSTEL €
(Map p322; ☑041 522 87 70; www.collegioarmeno. com; Palazzo Zenobio; s €30-65, d €56-100, s/d/tr/q without bathroom €30/56/80/100) Formerly a school for Venice's Armenian community, this gilded 1690 palace recently opened its doors to guests. Accommodation is monastic and chilly, lower-priced rooms have shared bathrooms, and there's a 1.30am curfew. The overgrown formal garden is among Venice's largest and loveliest, and guests are invited to on-site art events.

SAN POLO & SANTA CROCE

TOP CHOICE Oltre il Giardino B&B €€€

(Map p338; ☎041 275 00 15; www.oltreilgiardino -venezia.com; Fondamenta Contarini 2542; d €150- 350; ❄@) Live the designer dream in six guestrooms brimming with historical charm and modern comforts: marquetry composer's desks, flat-screen TVs, candelabra, Bulgari bath products, 19th-century poker chairs and babysitting services. Though 'Turquoise' is sprawling and 'Green' occupies a private corner of the walled garden, 'Grey' has a sexy wrought-iron bed frame under a cathedral ceiling.

Pensione Guerrato PENSIONE €€

(Map p338; ☎041 528 59 27; www.pensione guerrato.it; Ruga due Mori 240a; d incl breakfast €95-140; ❄) In a 1227 landmark that once sheltered knights heading off on the Third Crusade, updated guestrooms haven't lost their sense of history – ask for one with frescoes or glimpses of the Grand Canal, or the newly restored apartment. Its prime Rialto Market location and reliable dining recommendations make Pensione Guerrato the Holy Grail for visiting foodies.

Ca' Angeli B&B €€

(Map p338; ☎041 523 24 80; www.caangeli.it; Calle del Traghetto della Madonnetta 1434; d €80-250; ❄@) Brothers Giorgio and Matteo inherited this Grand Canal mansion and converted it into an antique showplace, with original Murano glass chandeliers, namesake angels from the 16th century and a restored Louis XIV sofa in the canalside reading room. Organic breakfasts are served on antique plates in the dining room, overlooking the Grand Canal.

Domina Home Ca' Zusto BOUTIQUE HOTEL €€

(Map p322; www.dominavacanze.it; Campo Rielo 1358; d incl breakfast €118-225; ❄🖥) With a wink at the nearby Fondaco dei Turchi, the historical Turkish trading house, strikingly modern guestrooms are named after Turkish women and decked out in harem stripes and silk brocade, with plush beds fit for pashas.

Al Campaniel B&B €

(Map p330; ☎041 275 07 49; www.alcampaniel. com; Calle del Campaniel 2889; d incl breakfast €55-105; ❄🖥) A real find off quiet Campo San Tomá, it's steps from the *vaporetto* stop and I Frari, handy to action-packed Campo Santa Margherita and overlooks a chocolate shop. In tasteful shades of cream

and crimson, rooms are surprisingly spacious and inviting; standard doubles have en suite toilets but shared showers.

CANNAREGIO

TOP CHOICE Palazzo Abadessa BOUTIQUE HOTEL €€€

(Map p338; ☎041 241 37 84; www.abadessa.com; Calle Priuli 4011; d €125-345; ❄🖥) Evenings seem enchanted in this opulent 1540 Venetian *palazzo*, with staff fluffing pillows, plying guests with *prosecco*, arranging water taxis to the opera and plotting romantic wedding proposals. Sumptuous guestrooms feature plush beds, silk-damask walls and 18th-century vanities; go baroque and request a larger room with ceiling frescoes, Murano chandeliers and canal or garden views.

Domus Orsoni B&B €€

(Map p342; ☎041 275 95 38; www.domusorsoni. it; Corte Vedei 1045; s incl breakfast €80-150, d €100-250; ❄@) Surprise: along a tranquil back lane near the Ghetto are five of Venice's most stylish guestrooms. In summer breakfast is served in the garden by Orsoni mosaic works, located here since 1885 – hence the mosaic fantasias glittering across walls, headboards and bathrooms.

Ca' Pozzo INN €€

(Map p342; ☎041 524 05 04; www.capozzoven ice.com; Sotoportego Ca' Pozzo 1279; d €80-170; ❄🖥) Biennale-bound travellers find a home away from home in this minimalist-chic hotel near the Ghetto. Several guestrooms have balconies, two accommodate guests with disabilities and spacious No 208 could house a Damien Hirst entourage.

Alla Vite Dorata B&B €€

(Map p338; ☎041 241 30 18; www.allavitedorata. com; Rio Terà Barba Frutariol 4690b; d incl breakfast €90-150; ❄🖥) *Venexiarse* (become Venetian) at this family home recently converted to a B&B in a quiet, untouristed neighbourhood. Romantics can upgrade to rooms with brocade-curtained beds overlooking a canal, but all rooms have high wood-beamed ceilings, wrought-iron furnishings and colourful drapery.

Hotel Villa Rosa INN €€

(Map p342; ☎041 716 569; www.villarosahotel. com; Calle della Misericordia 389; d incl breakfast €70-140; ❄🖥) Blooming window boxes and cheery staff make arrivals feel at home round the corner from the train station. Guestrooms are compact but high ceilinged, with damask wallpaper, tapestry bedspreads and modern bathrooms.

CASTELLO

Ca' Dei Dogi
BOUTIQUE HOTEL €€

(Map p322; ✆041 241 37 51; www.cadeidogi.it; Corte Santa Scolastica 4242; d €100-140; ✳️🛜) Even the neighbouring Bridge of Sighs can't dampen the spirits of the sunny yellow Ca' Dei Dogi. Streamlined modern rooms look like ships' cabins, with wood-beamed ceilings, dressers resembling steamer trunks, and compact mosaic-covered bathrooms.

Foresteria Valdese
RELIGIOUS ACCOMMODATION €

(Map p338; ✆041 528 67 97; http://foresteria venezia.it; Palazzo Cavagnis, Castello 5170; dm €25-30, d from €82) Holy hostel, Batman: many of the digs in this rambling palace retreat, owned by the Waldensian church, boast 18th-century frescoes and canal views. Dorm beds are available only for families or groups; book well ahead.

Palazzo Soderini
B&B €€

(Map p322; ✆041 296 08 23; www.palazzosoderini. it; Campo di Bandiera e Mori 3611; d €150-200; ✳️🛜) This tranquil, all-white retreat with a lily pond in the garden offers a welcome reprieve from Venice's visual onslaught. Minimalist decor emphasises spare shapes and clean lines. There are only three rooms; book ahead.

GIUDECCA

Bauer Palladio & Spa
LUXURY HOTEL €€€

(Map p322; ✆041 520 70 22; www.palladiohotel spa.com; Fondamenta della Croce 33; d from €590; ✳️🛜) Splash out in a serene, Palladio-designed former cloister with San Marco views, private solar-powered boat service and a superb spa. Once home to nuns and orphans, this converted monastery now offers heavenly comfort in rosy, serenely demure guestrooms, many with garden terraces or water views.

Ostello Venezia
HOSTEL €

(Map p322; ✆041 523 82 11; www.ostellovenezia.it; Fondamenta delle Zitelli 86; dm €22-27; ✆check-in 1.30-11.30pm, check-out 9.30am) Serene canal views make hostel bunks seem miles away from the madding crowds of San Marco, yet they're just a *vaporetto* ride away. Arrive promptly after 1.30pm opening time to claim a bunk by the window; reserve ahead for one of two viewless private rooms.

For basic grocery needs, Billa Supermarket (Map p342; Strada Nova 3660; ✆8.30am-9pm Mon-Sat, 9am-9pm Sun) fits the bill, but the deli selection is better at the regional agricultural cooperative retailer Coop (✆9am-1pm & 4-7.30pm Mon-Sat) San Lio 5989 (Map p338); Campo San Giacomo dell'Orio 1492 (Map p338); Piazzale Roma (Map p322).

PIAZZA SAN MARCO & AROUND

TOP CHOICE Enoteca al Volto
VENETIAN €

(Map p330; ✆041 522 89 45; Calle Cavalli 4081; cicheti €2-4, mains €7-18; ✆9.30am-3pm & 5.30-10pm Mon-Sat) Join the bar crowd working its way through the vast selection of wine and *cicheti* (Venetian tapas), or come early for a table outdoors (in summer) or inside the snug back room and seaworthy bowls of pasta with *bottarga* (dried fish roe) or house-made ravioli. Cash only.

Osteria San Marco
MODERN ITALIAN €€

(Map p330; ✆041 528 52 42; www.osteriasan marco.it; Frezzeria 1610; mains €20-30; ✆12.30-11pm Mon-Sat) Romance is in the air here – but the top-notch wines lining the exposed-brick walls surely help. Under strategic spotlights, dishes seem to arrive with a halo, especially heavenly lagoon clams with squid-ink linguine. Wine selections by the glass are limited and meat dishes are modestly sized, but all is forgiven over *passito* (dessert) wine with artisan cheeses.

Osteria da Carla
OSTERIA €

(Map p330; ✆041 523 78 55; Frezzeria 1535; mains €8-13; ✆10am-9pm Mon-Sat) For the price of a Piazza San Marco hot chocolate, diners in the know duck into this hidden courtyard to feast on ravioli with poppy seed, pear and sheep's-milk cheese. Expect to wait at lunch and happy hour, when gondoliers abandon ship for DOC Soave and *sopressa crostini* (soft salami on toast).

Cavatappi
OSTERIA €

(Map p330; ✆041 296 02 52; Campo della Guerra 525/526; cicheti €2-4, mains €8-13; ✆10am-9pm Tue-Thu & Sun, 10am-11pm Fri & Sat) This casual charmer offers *cicheti,* DOC bubbly by the glass and that rarest of San Marco finds: a tasty sit-down meal under €20. Get the risotto of the day and sheep's-milk cheese drizzled with wildflower honey for dessert.

VENICE'S TOP GELATERIE

» **Alaska** (Map p322; ☑041 71 52 11; Calle Larga dei Bari 1159; gelati €1.50-2; ☺noon-8pm) Outlandish organic gelato: enjoy a Slow Food scoop of house-roasted local pistachio, or two of tangy Sicilian lemon with vaguely minty *carciofi* (artichoke).

» **Gelateria Suso** (Map p338; ☑Calle della Bissa 5453; gelati €2-3; ☺10am-10pm) Indulge in Suso's ostentatiously rich 'Doge' gelato: fig sauce and walnuts swirled into mascarpone cream. All Suso's gelati are locally made and extra-creamy, but a waffle cone with hazelnut and extra-dark chocolate passes as dinner.

» **Grom** (Map p335; ☑041 099 17 51; www.grom.it; Campo San Barnaba 2461; gelati €2.50-4; ☺noon-11pm) Lick the landscape at Grom, which features Slow Food ingredients from across Italy (lemon from the Amalfi Coast, strawberries from Sicily and hazelnuts from Piedmont), plus Fair Trade–certified chocolate and coffee.

Caffè Mandola   SANDWICH SHOP €

(Map p330; ☑041 523 76 24; Calle della Mandola 3630; panini €3-7; ☺9am-7pm Mon-Sat) Carbload before the opera or between museums with fresh focaccia loaded with tangy tuna and capers or lean *bresaola* (air-cured beef), rocket and seasoned Grana Padano cheese.

DORSODURO

Trattoria La Bitta   TRATTORIA €€

(Map p335; ☑041 523 05 31; Calle Lunga San Barnaba 2753a; meals €35-40; ☺7-10pm Mon-Sat) The daily menu is presented on a miniature artists' easel, while the rustic fare looks like a still life and tastes like a dream: gnocchi is graced with pumpkin and herbs, and roast rabbit arrives on a bed of marinated rocket. Non-pescatarians pack this meat-focused restaurant; book ahead.

Enoteca ai Artisti   TRADITIONAL ITALIAN €

(Map p335; ☑041 523 89 44; www.enotecaartisti. com; Fondamenta della Toletta 1169a; mains €9-23; ☺noon-4pm & 6.30-10pm Mon-Sat) Heartwarming pasta and inspired cheeses are paired with exceptional wines (by the glass) by your oenophile hosts. Pavement tables for two make for great people-watching, but book indoor tables for groups.

Ristoteca Oniga   VENETIAN €€

(Map p335; ☑041 522 44 10; www.oniga.it; Campo San Barnaba 2852; meals €18-30; ☺noon-3pm & 7-10pm Wed-Mon) Purists come for chef Annika's Venetian seafood platter with exemplary *sarde in soar* (sardines in a sweet and sour sauce), vegetarians are spoiled for choice with seasonal pasta – try broccoli rabe, *pecorino* (sheep's-milk cheese) and breadcrumbs – and everyone appreciates the selection of 150 wines and fixed-price menus starting at €17.

Avogaria   MODERN ITALIAN €

(☑041 296 04 91; Calle dell'Avogaria 1629; cicheti €1.5-4; mains €10-22; ☺noon-3pm & 6-11pm Wed-Sun) Dates begin casually enough in this exposed-brick, wood-beamed restaurant, with happy-hour *cicheti* and Spritz at the sleek glass bar, but a few bites of Venetian *crudi* (sushi) laced with fresh herbs leads to seafood risotto for two – and once the tiramisu arrives, you'll be swooning.

Impronta Café   TRADITIONAL ITALIAN €

(Map p322; ☑041 275 03 86; Calle Crosera 3815; meals €8-15; ☺11am-1am Mon-Sat) Join Venice's value-minded jet set for *prosecco* and bargain polenta–salami combos, surrounded by witty architectural diagrams of cooking pots. Arrive by 6.30pm to take advantage of Milan-style *aperitivi*, where access to an appetiser buffet is free with drink purchases.

Pizza al Volo   PIZZERIA €

(Map p335; ☑041 522 54 30; Campo Santa Margherita 2944; pizza slices €2-4; ☺noon-1am) Peckish night owls run out of options fast in Venice once restaurants start to close at 10pm – but slices here are cheap and tasty, with a thin yet sturdy crust that won't collapse on your bar-hopping outfit.

SAN POLO & SANTA CROCE

TOP CHOICE All'Arco   VENETIAN €

(Map p338; ☑041 520 56 66; Calle dell'Arco 436; cicheti €1.50-4; ☺noon-8.30pm Mon-Sat Apr-Jun & Sep, to 3.30pm Oct-Mar, closed Jul & Aug) Maestro Francesco and his son Matteo invent Venice's best *cicheti* daily with Rialto Market finds, and if you ask nicely and wait patiently, they'll invent a seasonal speciality for you. On Mondays when the Pescaria is closed, Francesco might wrap wild asparagus in rare roast beef with grainy mustard; when

Saturday's seafood haul arrives, Matteo might create Sicilian tuna tartare with mint, Dolomite strawberries and aged balsamic. Even with copious *prosecco,* hardly any meal here tops €20 or falls short of five stars.

TOP CHOICE **Al Pesador** MODERN ITALIAN €€
(Map p338; ✆041 523 94 92; www.alpesador.it; Campo San Giacometo; mains €15-30; ⊗noon-3pm & 7-11pm Mon-Sat) Watch the world drift down the Grand Canal outside, or canoodle in the vaulted dining room – but once the food comes, you'll sit up and pay attention. Just when you thought you knew Venetian cuisine, Pesador reinvents it with culinary finesse: *cicheti* feature a terrine of tiny lagoon clams topped with lemon *gelée,* while *primi* (first courses) include red-footed scallops kicking wild herbs across squid-ink gnocchi.

Pronto Pesce Pronto SEAFOOD €
(Map p338; ✆041 822 02 98; Rialto Pescheria 319; cicheti €3-8; ⊗noon-2.45pm Tue-Sat) Alongside Venice's fish market, this designer deli specialises in artfully composed *crudi* and seafood salads. Grab a stool and a (unfortunately) plastic glass of DOC Soave with *folpetti* (baby octopus) salad and plump prawn *crudi*, or enjoy yours dockside along the Grand Canal.

Dai Zemei VENETIAN €
(Map p338; ✆041 520 8546; www.osteriadaizemei.it; Ruga Vecchia San Giovanni 1045; cicheti €2-5; ⊗9am-8pm Wed-Mon) Small meals with outsized imagination: octopus salad with marinated rocket, duck breast drizzled with truffle oil, or crostini loaded with velvety tuna mousse. Arrive early and consult twin gourmet masterminds Giovanni and Franco (*zamei* is Venetian for twins, hence the photos above the bar) for ideal DOC/IGT wine pairings.

Tearoom Caffé Orientale VEGETARIAN €
(Map p322; ✆041 520 17 89; Rio Marin 888; meals €6-12; ⊗noon-9pm Fri-Wed) Detour from tourist-trail espresso bars and seafood restaurants to this art-filled canalside tearoom; it offers vegetarian delights from asparagus-studded quiches to hearty bean soups. Baked goods are made in-house with extra-fluffy, high-protein Italian '00' flour – so after that whisper-light apple crumble, you'll be raring to tackle museums.

Osteria La Zucca MODERN ITALIAN €
(Map p338; ✆041 524 15 70; www.lazucca.it; Calle del Tentor 1762; small plates €5-12; ⊗12.30-2.30pm

& 7-10.30pm Mon-Sat) Vego-centric seasonal small plates bring spice-trade influences to local produce: zucchini with ginger zing, cinnamon-tinged pumpkin flan and raspberry spice cake. Herbed roast lamb is respectable here too, but the vegies have star quality. The snug wood-panelled interior gets toasty, so reserve canalside seats in summer.

Antica Birreria della Corte PIZZERIA €
(Map p338; ✆041 275 05 70; Campo San Polo 2168; pizzas €8-13; ⊗noon-11pm Mon-Fri) An outpost of pizza and beer in a city of wine and fish seems like a deliberate provocation, but it's hard to protest with your mouth full. Standouts include wood-fired *bresaola*, and rocket and buffalo mozzarella, washed down with beer – German on tap, Italian artisan in bottles.

CANNAREGIO

TOP CHOICE **Anice Stellato** VENETIAN €€
(Map p342; ✆041 72 07 44; Fondamenta della Sensa 3272; meals €25-40; ⊗noon-2pm & 7.30-11pm Wed-Sun) If finding this obscure corner of Cannaregio seems like an adventure, wait until dinner arrives: herb-encrusted lamb chops, house-made ravioli and lightly fried *moeche* (soft-shelled crab) gobbled whole. Tin lamps and recycled paper place-mats on communal tables keep the focus on local food and local company – all memorable. Book ahead.

CICHETI: VENICE'S BEST MEAL DEALS

Even in unpretentious Venetian *osterie* (casual taverns of eateries), most dishes cost a couple of euros more than elsewhere in Italy – not a bad mark-up, given fresh seafood and local produce brought in by boat. But *cicheti*, Venetian bar snacks, are some of the best foodie finds in the country, served at the bar in Venetian *osterie* at lunch and about 6pm to 8pm. *Cicheti* range from basic €1 to €2 bar snacks (spicy meatballs, fresh tomato bruschetta) to wildly inventive small plates for €2 to €5: think white Bassano asparagus and plump lagoon shrimp wrapped with pancetta at All'Arco (p354), Bronte pistachio spread and mortadella stuffed into fresh-baked sesame croissants at Zenzero (p356) or crostini piled with *sopressata* (soft local salami) and truffled *pecorino* at I Rusteghi (p358).

TOP CHOICE Dalla Marisa   VENETIAN €€

(Map p322; ☑041 720 211; Fondamenta San Giobbe 652b; set menus €30-35; ⏱11am-3pm & 7-11pm Tue & Thu-Sat) Like a friend of the family, you'll be seated where there's room and get no menu. You'll have whatever Marisa's cooking, but you will be informed that the menu is meat- or fish-based when you book, and house wine is included in the price. Venetian regulars confess Marisa's *fegato alla veneziana* (Venetian calf's liver) is better than their grandmothers', while fish nights bring hauls of lagoon seafood grilled, fried and perched atop pasta and rocket.

Osteria L'Orto dei Mori   MODERN ITALIAN €€

(Map p342; ☑041 524 36 77; Campo dei Mori 3386; meals €20-40; ⏱12.30-3.30pm & 7.30-midnight Wed-Mon) Not since Tintoretto lived next door has this sleepy neighbourhood stayed up so late, thanks to this smart new *osteria*. Sicilian chef Lorenzo makes fresh pasta daily, including squid atop spinach *tagliolini* and bow-tie pasta with sausage and *raddichio di Treviso* (red, bitter chicory). Upbeat staff and fish-shaped lamps add a playful air to evenings here, and you'll be handed *prosecco* to endure the wait for tables (book ahead).

La Cantina   VENETIAN €€

(Map p338; ☑041 522 82 58; Campo San Felice 3689; cicheti €3-6, mains €15-30; ⏱11am-11pm Mon-Sat) Talk about Slow Food: grab a stool and local Morgana beer while you await seasonal bruschetta made to order and hearty bean soups. Seafood platters require larger appetites and deeper pockets – market price varies, so ask today's rate – but mullet with roast potatoes and *scampi crudi* (sweet prawn sushi) are worthy investments.

CASTELLO

TOP CHOICE Corte Sconta   MODERN ITALIAN €€€

(Map p344; ☑041 522 70 24; Calle del Pestrin 3886; meals €45-65; ⏱12.30-2.30pm & 7-9.30pm Tue-Sat, closed Jan & Aug) Seek out this vine-covered *corte sconta* (hidden courtyard) for imaginative house-made pasta and ultrafresh, visually striking seafood: imagine crustaceans arranged on a platter like paint on an artist's palette, or black squid-ink pasta topped with bright-orange squash and tender scallops. Reservations essential.

TOP CHOICE Zenzero   SANDWICH SHOP €

(Map p338; ☑041 241 28 28; Campo Santa Marina 5902; panini €2-4.50; ⏱9am-8pm Mon-Sat) Two *panini* on house-baked croissants make a feast that deserves a DOCG *prosecco* toast. Seasonal speciality combos include truffle-topped prosciutto, mortadella with pistachio purée, or organic buffalo mozzarella and sun-dried tomatoes.

Met   GASTRONOMIC €€€

(Map p344; ☑041 520 50 44; www.hotelmetropole. com; Hotel Metropole, Riva degli Schiavoni 4149; meals from €100; ⏱dinner Tue-Sun) Chef Corrado Fasolato earns his two Michelin stars with wildly inventive takes on local game and seafood, including savoury pheasant cannelloni and eel-stuffed pasta. Expect the unexpected, like red wine and horseradish transformed into savoury sorbets.

Al Covo   OSTERIA €€€

(Map p344; ☑041 522 38 12; www.ristorante alcovo.com; Campiello della Pescaria 3968; meals €55-75; ⏱lunch & dinner Fri-Sun, lunch Mon-Tue) This place has all the markings of a classic Venetian trattoria – low-beamed ceilings, regulars installed in the corners – but adds sophisticated twists to typical dishes. Trademark dishes include Caprese salad served with a cherry tomato *gelée*, squid-ink pasta with clams and squash blossoms, and Adriatic tuna with five sauces. Prices are understandable given lagoon-fresh ingredients, and offset by reasonably priced wine.

🌿 Le Spighe   VEGETARIAN €

(Map p322; ☑041 523 81 73; Via Garibaldi 1341; meals €10-15; ⏱9.30am-2pm & 5.30-7.30pm Mon-Sat) All vegetarian, all organic and vegan-friendly, this little spot offers quick, delicious eats based on seasonal produce, from crunchy fennel salads to delicious potato-and-squash pies.

GIUDECCA

TOP CHOICE I Figli delle Stelle   MODERN ITALIAN €€

(Map p322; ☑041 523 00 04; www.ifiglidellestelle.it; Zitelle 70; meals €25-40; ⏱12.30-2.30pm & 7-10pm Tue-Sun, closed mid-Nov–mid-Mar) A creamy fava bean soup with chicory and fresh tomatoes coats the tongue in a naughty way, and the mixed grill for two with langoustine, sole and fresh sardines is a commitment – though given the cuisine and waterfront views of San Marco, this is a surprisingly cheap date.

La Palanca   VENETIAN €

(Map p322; ☑041 528 77 19; Fondamenta al Ponte Piccolo 448; meals €20-30; ⏱8am-8.30pm Mon-Sat) Lunchtime competition for canalside

GOURMET CENTRAL: THE RIALTO DISTRICT

Rialto Market (Map p338) offers superb local produce next to the legendary **Pescaria** (Map p338), Venice's 600-year-old fish market. Nearby backstreets are lined with bakeries, *bacari* (bars) and two notable gourmet shops: **Aliani** (Map p338; ☑041 522 49 13; Ruga Vecchia di San Giovanni 654), with cheeses, cured meats and gourmet specialities from balsamic vinegar aged 40 years to *bottarga* (dried fish-roe paste); and **Drogheria Mascari** (Map p338; ☑041 522 97 62; Ruga degli Spezieri 381; ⊙8am-1pm & 4-7.30pm Mon-Tue & Thu-Sat, 8am-1pm Wed), an emporium lined with copper-topped jars, spices and truffles galore, plus an entire back room of speciality Italian wines. For organic edibles and sustainably produced wines, visit **Rialto Biocenter** (Map p338; ☑041 523 95 15; www.rialtobiocenter.it; Calle della Regina 2264; ⊙8.30am-1pm & 4.30-8pm Mon-Thu, 8.30am-8pm Fri & Sat).

tables is stiff, but views make *tagliolini ai calamaretti* (narrow ribbon pasta with tiny calamari) and tuna steak with sesame taste even better. A bargain at €7 to €9 for full plates of pasta, and the bar is open for *cicheti* all day.

THE LIDO

Trattoria La Favorita   SEAFOOD €€€
(☑041 526 16 26; Via Francesco Duodo 33; meals €35-50; ⊙noon-3.30pm & 7.30-11pm Wed-Sun, 6-10pm Tue, closed Jan–mid-Feb) Spider crab *gnochetti*, fish risotto and *crudi* at non-celebrity prices make La Favorita earn its name. Book ahead for the wisteria-filled garden.

Pizzeria alla Botte   PIZZERIA €
(☑041 526 06 81; Gran Viale 57/A; pizzas €6-10; ⊙11.30am-3.30pm & 6-10.30pm, closed Nov-Jan) With one of the only wood-burning ovens in Venice, this touristy-looking place offers quality pizza with a thickish crust and just the right amount of chewiness.

🍷 Drinking

In prime tourist zones, the price of coffee at a table seems more like rent, so take your coffee standing or splash out for architecturally splendid cafes in the Museo Correr, Palazzo Querini Stampalia or Piazza San Marco. An orchestra surcharge is often added to bills in Piazza San Marco – you might as well get your money's worth and do the tango.

PIAZZA SAN MARCO & AROUND

Caffè Florian   CAFE
(Map p330; ☑041 520 56 41; www.caffe florian.com; Piazza San Marco 56/59; drinks €8-12; ⊙10am-midnight Thu-Tue) Florian adheres to rituals established c 1720: uniformed waiters serve hot chocolate on silver trays, lovers canoodle in plush banquettes indoors,

and the orchestra strikes up a tango as fading sunlight illuminates San Marco's portal mosaics. Ever forward-thinking, this cafe was among the first to admit women, served as a clubhouse for Italy's independence movement, and still hosts contemporary art and design events.

Caffè Lavena   CAFE
(Map p330; ☑041 522 40 70; www.lavena.it; Piazza San Marco 133/4; drinks €1-12; ⊙9.30am-11pm) Opera composer Richard Wagner had the right idea: when Venice leaves you weak in the knees, get a pick-me-up at Lavena. The €1 espresso at this mirrored 18th-century bar is the sweetest deal in Piazza San Marco, but get a table for *caffè corretto* (coffee 'corrected' with liquor) and live music. Florian's orchestra provides friendly competition across the square, but Lavena's lightning-speed tarantella usually wins by crowd roars.

Harry's Bar   BAR
(Map p330; ☑041 528 57 77; www.cipriano.com; Calle Vallaresso 1323; ⊙10.30am-11pm) Aspiring auteurs throng the bar frequented by Ernest Hemingway, Charlie Chaplin, Truman Capote, Orson Welles and others, enjoying a signature €15 Bellini (fresh peach juice and *prosecco*) with a side of reflected glory. Despite the basic bistro decor and minuscule tables, this is one of Italy's most expensive restaurants – stick to top-shelf cocktails.

Torino@Night   PUB
(Map p330; ☑041 522 39 14; Campo San Luca 4592; ⊙7pm-1am Tue-Sat) Eclectic, loud, funky Torino livens up staid San Marco with €2 to €5 drinks and live jazz most Saturdays, plus occasional marathon DJ sessions of vintage reggae on vinyl.

WORTH A TRIP

VENISSA

A scallop daintily dips its red foot into a black espresso reduction: starting with her highly amusing *amuse bouche*, chef Paola Budel treats local ingredients with the evident delight of an Italian chef returned home from restaurants abroad. The stars (including the Michelin variety) are aligning over **Venissa** (☎041 527 22 81; www.venissa.it; Fondamenta Santa Caterina 3; ☸noon-3pm & 7-9.30pm Tue-Sun) in Mazzorbo, the garden island over the bridge from Burano where anything grows. You can practically eat the island landscape in Budel's breadcrumb gnocchi that bob in a fragrant broth of wild fennel, asparagus shoots, young mint and basil. A dish of 63 minuscule lagoon octopi served on a *barene* (shoal) of garlicky fava bean purée gives an inkling what it's like to be a ravenous Venetian sea monster that's satisfied at last. Book ahead, budget at least €60 per person, and bring sunblock to enjoy the outdoor patio alongside Venissa's vineyard.

DORSODURO

Cantinone 'Già Schiavi' BAR
(Map p330; ☎041 523 00 34; Fondamenta Nani 992; ☸8.30am-8.30pm Mon-Sat) Good lungs and steady hands are instrumental to make your order heard and transport *cicheti* (try creamy tuna with leeks), *ombre* (wine by the glass) and *pallottoline* (small bottles of beer) outside to the canal without spilling on architecture students and gondola builders.

Osteria alla Bifora WINE BAR
(Map p335; ☎041 523 61 19; Campo Santa Margherita 2930; ☸noon-3pm & 6pm-midnight) Other bars around this campo cater to Spritz-pounding students, but this converted medieval wine cellar caters to dreamers who flirt over glasses of big-hearted Veneto merlot and shareable plates of cold cuts in the flattering glow of five chandeliers.

Il Caffè Rosso BAR
(Map p335; ☎041 528 79 98; Campo Santa Margherita 2963; ☸7am-1am Mon-Sat) Sunny piazza seating is the place to recover from last night's revelry and today's newspaper headlines, until the cycle begins again at 6pm with Spritz cocktails and standing-room-only student crowds.

SAN POLO & SANTA CROCE

Al Prosecco WINE BAR
(Map p338; ☎041 524 02 22; Campo San Giacomo da l'Orio 1503; www.alprosecco.com; ☸9am-9pm Mon-Sat) The urge to toast sunsets in Venice's loveliest *campo* is only natural – and so is the wine at Al Prosecco. This forward-thinking bar specialises in *vini naturi* (natural-process wines) – organic, biodynamic and wild-yeast-fermented – and memorable *ombre,* from signature €3.50 unfiltered 'cloudy' *prosecco* to silky, €5 Veneto Ven-

egazzú that trails across the tongue and lingers in the imagination.

Al Mercà WINE BAR
(Map p338; ☎393 992 47 81; Campo Bella Vienna 213; ☸9-3pm & 4-9pm Mon-Sat) Discerning drinkers throng this cupboard-sized bar crammed with *cicheti* and 60 different wines, including top-notch *prosecco* and DOC wines by the glass (€2 to €3.50). Arrive early for meatballs and mini-*panini* (€1 to €2) and easy bar access, or mingle with crowds stretching to Grand Canal docks.

Cantina Do Spade BAR
(Map p338; ☎041 521 05 83; www.cantinadospade.it; Calle delle Do Spade 860; ☸10am-3pm & 6-10pm Mon-Sat) Since 1488 this bar has kept Venice in good spirits, and friendly young management extends warm welcomes to Spritz-sipping Venetian regulars and visiting connoisseurs here for double-malt Dolomite beer and bargain Venetian DOC Cab Franc. Come early for market-fresh *fritture* (batter-fried seafood; €2 to €6) and stick around for local gossip (free).

Pasticceria Rizzardini CAFE
(Map p338; ☎041 522 38 35; Campiello dei Meloni 1415; ☸7.30am-8pm Wed-Mon) 'From 1742' reads the shopfront sign of this standing-room-only cafe-bakery serving historical Venetian specialities: killer *krapfen* (doughnuts), wagging *lingue di suocere* (mother-in-law's tongues) and sugar-sprinkled *pallone di Casanova* (Casanova's balls).

CASTELLO

TOP CHOICE I Rusteghi WINE BAR
(Map p338; ☎041 523 22 05; Corte del Tentor 5513; mini-panini €2-5; ☸10.30am-3pm & 6-9pm Mon-Sat) Honouring centuries of Venetian *enoteca*

(wine bar) tradition, 4th-generation sommelier Giovanni will open any wine bottles on his shelves just to pour you an *ombra* (half-glass of wine) – including near-mythic collector's wines like 1996 Quintarelli Amarone. Request *'qualcosa di particolare'* and Giovanni will reward you with a sensual Tocai or heady Refosco you won't find elsewhere. Pair yours with 30 types of *cicheti,* including rolls packed with boar salami and truffle.

Enoteca Mascareta   WINE BAR

(Map p338; ☎041 523 07 44; Calle Lunga Santa Maria Formosa 5138; meals €30-45; ☺7pm-2am Fri-Tue) Oenophiles keep this atmospheric place packed year-round, thanks to brilliantly curated local meats, cheeses and above all wines – including cloudily organic *prosecco.*

Osteria All'Alba   WINE BAR

(Map p338; ☎340 124 56 34; Ramo del Fontego dei Tedeschi 5370; ☺7-1pm) That roar behind the Rialto means the DJ's funk set is kicking in at All'Alba. Squeeze inside to order salami sandwiches (€1 to €2.50) and DOC Veneto wines (€5 to €6), and check out walls festooned with vintage LPs and thanks scrawled in 12 languages.

CANNAREGIO

Al Timon   WINE BAR

(Map p342; ☎041 524 60 66; Fondamenta degli Ormesini 2754; ☺11am-1am Thu-Tue & 6pm-1am Wed) Pull up your director's chair along the canal and watch the motley parade of drinkers and dreamers arrive for crostini (open-faced sandwiches) and quality wines by the *ombra* or carafe. Folk singers sometimes play sets, which turn to singalongs as the evening unfolds.

Agli Ormesini   PUB

(Da Aldo; Map p342; ☎041 71 58 34; Fondamenta degli Ormesini 2710; ☺8pm-1am Mon-Sat) While the rest of Venice is awash in wine, Ormesini offers 120 brews, including local Birra Venezia. The cheery, beery scene often spills into the street – but keep it down, or the neighbours get testy.

☆ Entertainment

To find out what's on the calendar in Venice during your visit, drop by the APT tourist office (p362), click on the Calendar button at www.comune.venezia or visit these sites:

A Guest in Venice (www.aguestinvenice. com) Hotelier association that provides information on upcoming exhibits, events and lectures.

Venezia da Vivere (www.veneziadavivere.com) The creative guide to Venice, featuring music performances, art openings, nightlife and design events.

Venezia Si (www.veneziasi.it) Online booking service with calendar listings for Venice venues and festivals.

Casinos

Casinò di Venezia   CASINO

(Map p342; ☎041 529 71 11; www.casinovenezia.it; Palazzo Vendramin 2040; admission €5 or free with €10 gaming token purchase; ☺11am-2.30am Sun-Thu, to 3am Fri & Sat) No opera can match the dramas at Venice's palatial gambling house

---

TOP FIVE VENETIAN HAPPY HOUR ORDERS

» **Prosecco** Veneto's signature sparkling wine is enjoyed by dandies and fishermen alike, from €1.50 nonvintage to €3.50 DOCG Conegliano Prosecco Superiore.

» **Spritz** This *prosecco* cocktail made with Campari bitters or bittersweet Aperol is a stiff drink at an easy price (€1 to €2.50). It's a cross-generational hit with students and pensioners at bars and cafes across Venice, except for speciality *enoteche* (wine bars).

» **Amarone** The deep red wine blended from Valpollicella Corvina grapes is a stormy love affair in a bottle – complex and costly (€6 to €18 per glass), but utterly captivating while it lasts.

» **Soave** This white wine made with Veneto garganega grapes is ideal with seafood in refreshing young versions (€2 to €5) or as a conversation piece in complex Classico versions (€2.50 to €6).

» **'Qualcosa di particolare'** 'Something interesting' is a challenge to Venetian sommeliers to reach behind the bar for one of Veneto's obscure varietals or innovative winemakers. Ask for an *ombra* (taste) or you might end up with a very interesting bill.

PURCHASING EVENT TICKETS

For blockbuster events like the Biennale or La Fenice operas, you'll need to book ahead online at the appropriate website or www.veniceconnected.com. However, you might luck into last-minute discounts at **Weekend a Venezia** (http://en.venezia.waf.it). Otherwise, event tickets are sold at **HelloVenezia ticket outlets** (☏041 24 24; www.hellovenezia.com), located near key *vaporetto* (small passenger ferry) stops.

since the 16th century: Richard Wagner survived the 20-year effort of composing his stormy *Ring* cycle only to expire here in 1883. Slots open at 11am; to take on the gaming tables, arrive after 3.30pm wearing your best jacket and poker face.

Cinemas

Arena di Campo San Polo   CINEMA

(Map p338; www.comune.venezia.it, in Italian; Campo San Polo; ⊙Jul & Aug) Where bullfights were once held by rowdy Austrians, the city now hosts free open-air films, and concerts and theatre performances in July and September – but watch this space year-round for kiddie carousels, political rallies and street musicians.

Casa del Cinema   CINEMA

(Map p338; ☏041 524 13 20; Salizada San Stae 1990; adult/reduced €6/5; ⊙shows Mon-Sat afternoon) Venice's public film archive shows art films in a new 50-seat, wood-beamed screening room inside Palazzo Mocenigo. Original-language classics are shown Mondays and first-run independent films on Friday nights and Saturday afternoons; check online for screenings with introductions by directors, actors and scholars.

Opera & Classical Music

TOP CHOICE Teatro La Fenice   OPERA HOUSE

(Map p330; ☏041 78 66 11; www.teatrolafenice.it; Campo San Fantin 1965; tickets €40-120) Tours are possible with advance booking (☏041 24 24), but the best way to see La Fenice is with the *loggione* – opera buffs who pass judgment from the top-tier cheap seats. When the opera is in recess, look for symphonies and chamber music concerts.

TOP CHOICE Interpreti Veneziani   LIVE MUSIC

(Map p330; ☏041 277 05 61; www.interpretiveneziani.com; Chiesa San Vidal 2862; adult/reduced €25/20; ⊙doors open 8.30pm) Everything you knew of Vivaldi from lift music and mobile-phone ringtones is proved fantastically wrong by Interpreti Veneziani, who play Vivaldi on 18th-century instruments as a dramatic soundtrack for Venice – you'll never listen to *The Four Seasons* again without hearing summer storms erupting over the lagoon, or muffled footsteps hurrying across footbridges in winter night's intrigue.

La Pietà   LIVE MUSIC

(Map p344; ☏041 522 21 71; Riva degli Schiavoni) With fine acoustics, soaring Tiepolo ceilings and a long association with Vivaldi, this church makes an ideal venue for live baroque music.

Musica a Palazzo   LIVE MUSIC

(Map p330; ☏340 971 72 72; www.musicapalazzo.com; Palazzo Barbarigo-Minotto, Fondamenta Barbarigo o Duodo 2504; tickets €50; ⊙doors open 8pm) In salons overlooking the Grand Canal with splendid Tiepolo ceilings, the soprano's high notes might make you fear for your wine glass. During 1½ to two hours of selected arias, 70 guests trail singers in modern dress from receiving-room overtures to heartbreaking finales in the bedroom.

Jazz

Venice Jazz Club   LIVE MUSIC

(Map p335; ☏041 523 20 56; www.venicejazzclub.com; Ponte dei Pugni 3102; tickets incl drink €20; ⊙doors open 7pm) Resident Venice Jazz Club Quartet swings to Miles Davis and Charles Mingus and grooves on Italian jazz standards. Drink prices are steep, so starving musicians booze beforehand and arrive early for cold-cut platters before the 9pm show.

Nightclubs

B.each   NIGHTCLUB

(☏041 526 80 13; Lungomare D'Annunzio 20x; ⊙9am-2am May-Sep) Days flow into nights at this Lido beach venue with four-poster sunbeds, sports and chill-out zones for daytime use, plus cocktails, occasional live music and DJs after dark.

Shopping

Retail therapy approaches delirium in Venice, but the city's ultimate shopping triumphs are unique finds at surprisingly reasonable prices, handmade by artisans in

Murano and backstreet studios. By bringing home avant-garde originals, you will *fa la bella figura* (cut a fine figure) while showing your support for Venice's cutting-edge craftsmanship.

Cartè
ARTISANAL, GIFTS

(Map p338; ✉320 024 87 76; www.cartevenezia.it; Calle di Cristi 1731; ⏱10am-6.30pm Mon-Sat) This is the cupboard-sized studio of Rosanna Corró, a former book restorer who learned the ancient art of *carta marmorizzata* (marbled paper) and began creating bookish beauties: marbled cocktail rings, mesmerising statement necklaces and surreal bookbound handbags in woodgrain patterns.

Marina e Susanna Sent
ARTISANAL, GLASS

(Map p330; ✉041 520 81 36; www.marinaesusanna sent.com; Campo San Vio 669; ⏱10am-1pm & 3-6.30pm Tue-Sat, 3-6.30pm Mon) Having trained as an architect and a jeweller, respectively, these sisters from Murano were told that women couldn't handle working in molten glass. They have gone on to create Murano's best-selling line of colourfully minimalist, hand-blown glass jewellery.

Malefatte
ARTISANAL, GIFTS

(Map p342; ✉041 521 02 72; www.rioteradeipens ieri.org; Calle Zancani 2433; ⏱10am-1pm & 3-6pm Tue-Sat) Make up for any past gift-giving *malefatte* (misdeeds) while giving a second chance to Giudecca prison inmates, who run this nonprofit vocational training project and craft one-of-a-kind wallets and man-bags from recycled Venice museum vinyl banners. Also organic botanical skincare products.

Giovanna Zanella
ARTISANAL, SHOES

(Map p338; ✉041 523 55 00; Calle Carminati 5641; ⏱9.30am-1pm & 3-7pm) Don extraordinary custom-designed sculpted heels, high-button boots and spats in punk-rock colours to treat your feet kindly as you storm the red carpets of the Venice Film Festival.

Lauretta Vistosi
ARTISANAL, ACCESSORIES

(Map p330; ✉041 528 65 30; www.laurettavistosi. org; Calle Lunga San Barnaba 2866b; ⏱10am-1pm & 3-7pm Tue-Sat) A Murano-born Renaissance artisan, Lauretta Vistosi hand-crafted shoes, stationery and dresses before inventing an entirely new craft: ultramodern hand-stitched handbags, totes and journals, emblazoned with Murano-glass bullseye buttons.

Old World Books
BOOKSTORE

(Map p342; ✉041 275 94 56; Punto del Ghetto Vecchio 282; ⏱10am-1pm & 4-7pm Mon Fri) Rare books, local histories, poetry chapbooks and speciality titles (such as *Chimney Pots of Venice*) for Venice obsessives.

Studium
BOOKSTORE

(Map p342; ✉041 522 23 82; Calle della Canonica 337a; ⏱9am-7.30pm Mon-Sat, 9.30am-1.30pm Sun) Consult bibliophile staff for worthy holiday reads, page-turning history, guidebooks and phrasebooks in English, Italian and French.

ℹ Information

Emergency

Ambulance (✉118)

Police station (✉112/113) Castello (Fondamenta di San Lorenzo 5053); Piazza San Marco (Piazza San Marco 67)

Internet Access

Wi-fi access is widely available and internet cafes are dispersed throughout the city. There is also a city-wide **wi-fi service** (www.venice connected.com; 1hr/72hr/week €5/8/15).

World House (✉041 528 48 71; Calle della Chiesa 4502; per hr €8; ⏱10am-11pm)

Medical Services

Information on rotating late-night pharmacies is posted in pharmacy windows and listed in the free magazine *Un Ospite di Venezia*, available at the tourist office.

Ospedale Civile (✉041 529 41 11; Campo SS Giovanni e Paolo 6777) Venice's main hospital; for emergency care and dental treatment, ask for *pronto soccorso* (casualty).

Money

There are ATMs spread throughout the city, with clusters near the Rialto and Piazza San Marco.

Travelex Piazza San Marco (✉041 528 73 58; Piazza San Marco 142; ⏱9am-6pm Mon-Sat, 9.30am-5pm Sun); Rialto (✉041 528 73 58; Riva del Ferro 5126; ⏱9am-6pm Mon-Sat, 9.30am-5pm Sun); Marco Polo airport (✉041 269 8107; ⏱6am-8.30pm).

Post

There are post offices in every *sestiere*, with addresses and hours searchable at www.poste. it (in Italian).

Post office Rialto (Map p338; Calle San Salvador 5106; ⏱8.30am-6.30pm Mon-Fri, to 1pm Sat); Stazione di Santa Lucia (Map p342; Lista di Spagna 233, Cannaregio; ⏱8.30am-2pm Mon-Fri, to 1pm Sat).

Tourist Information

Azienda di Promozione Turistica (APT; info line 041 529 87 11; www.turismovenezia.it) Marco Polo airport (arrivals hall; ⊕9.30am-7.30pm); Piazzale Roma (Map p322; ⊕9.30am-4.30pm); Piazza San Marco (Map p330; Piazza San Marco 71f; ⊕9am-3.30pm Mon-Sat); Stazione di Santa Lucia (Map p322; ⊕8am-6.30pm)

❶ Getting There & Away

Air

Most flights arrive and depart from **Marco Polo airport** (🖉041 260 92 60; www.veniceairport.it), 12km outside Venice, east of Mestre. Ryanair also uses **San Giuseppe airport** (🖉0422 31 51 11; www.trevisoairport.it), about 5km southwest of Treviso and a 30km, one-hour drive from Venice.

Boat

Minoan Lines (www.minoan.gr) and **Anek** (www.anekitalia.com) run regular ferries between Venice and Greece. **Venezia Lines** (www.venezialines.com) runs high-speed boats to and from Croatia and Slovenia in summer. However, consider big-ship transport carefully – long-haul ferries and cruise ships have an outsized environmental impact on tiny Venice and its fragile lagoon aquaculture. Take the lower-impact train instead, and Venice will be most grateful. Boats leave from the ferry terminal, near Piazzale Roma.

Bus

All buses leave from the bus station (Map p322) on Piazzale Roma.

ACTV (Azienda del Consorzio Trasporti Veneziano; 🖉041 24 24; www.actv.it) Has buses to Mestre and surrounding areas.

ATVO (Azienda Trasporti Veneto Orientale; 🖉041 520 55 30) Has services to destinations all over the eastern Veneto, including airport connections.

CHEAP THRILLS ON THE GRAND CANAL: TRAGHETTI

A *traghetto* is the gondola service locals use to cross the Grand Canal between its widely spaced bridges. *Traghetti* rides cost just €0.50 and typically operate from 9am to 6pm, although some routes finish by noon; for major *traghetto* crossings, consult maps on p330 and p342, though note that service can be spotty at times for all crossings.

Eurolines (www.eurolines.com; 🖉041 538 2118) Operates a wide range of international routes.

Car & Motorcycle

The congested Trieste–Turin A4 passes through Mestre. From Mestre, take the Venezia exit. From the south, take the A13 from Bologna, which connects with the A4 at Padua.

Once over the Ponte della Libertà bridge from Mestre, cars must be left at the car park at Piazzale Roma or Tronchetto; expect to pay €20 or more for every 24 hours. Parking stations in Mestre are cheaper. Car ferry 17 transports vehicles from Tronchetto to the Lido.

The car-rental companies listed here all have offices on Piazzale Roma and at Marco Polo airport. Several companies operate in or near Mestre train station, too.

Avis (🖉041 523 73 77)
Europcar (🖉041 523 86 16)
Hertz (🖉041 528 40 91)

Train

Prompt, affordable, scenic and environmentally savvy, trains are the preferred transport option to and from Venice. Trains run frequently to Venice's Stazione Santa Lucia (signed as Ferrovia within Venice).

Local trains that link Venice to the Veneto are frequent, reliable and remarkably inexpensive (faster trains also serve Veneto destinations, but the time saved may not be worth the 200% surcharge). In addition, there are direct InterCity services to most major Italian cities, plus major points in France, Germany, Austria, Switzerland, Slovenia and Croatia.

TO	FARE (€)	DURATION (HR)	FREQUENCY
Florence	24-43	2-3	1-2 per hour
Milan	15-32	2½-3½	2-3 per hour
Naples	49-121	5½-9	1 per hour
Padua	3	½-1	3-4 per hour
Rome	45-75	3½-6	1-2 per hour
Verona	6.35	1¾	3-4 per hour

❶ Getting Around

To/From the Airport

BOAT Alilaguna (🖉041 240 17 01; www.alilaguna.com) operates several lines that link the airport with various parts of Venice, including the Linea Blu (Blue Line, with stops at Lido, San Marco, Stazione Marittima and points in between), the Linea Rossa (Red Line, with stops at Murano and Lido) and Linea Arancio (Orange

Here are key *vaporetto* (small passenger ferry) lines and major stops, subject to seasonal change:

1 Piazzale Roma–Ferrovia–Grand Canal (all stops)–Lido and return

2 San Zaccaria–Redentore–Zattere–Tronchetto–Ferrovia–Rialto–Accademia–San Marco

5 San Zaccaria–Murano and return

13 Fondamente Nuove–Murano–Vignole–Sant'Erasmo–Treporti and return

20 San Zaccaria–San Servolo–San Lazzaro and return

41 Murano–Fondamente Nuove–Ferrovia–Piazzale Roma–Redentore–San Zaccaria–Fondamente Nuove–San Michele–Murano

42 Reverse direction to line 41

51 Lido–Fondamente Nuove–Ferrovia–Piazzale Roma–Zattere–San Zaccaria–Giardini–Lido

52 Reverse direction to line 51

N (all-stops night circuit, 11.30pm to 5am) Lido–Giardini–San Zaccaria–Grand Canal (all stops)–Ferrovia–Piazzale Roma–Tronchetto–Zattere–Redentore–San Giorgio–San Zaccaria

DM (Diretto Murano) Tronchetto–Piazzale Roma–Ferrovia–Murano and return

T Torcello–Burano (half-hourly service) and return (7am to 8.30pm)

Line, with stops at Stazione Santa Lucia, Rialto and San Marco via the Canal Grande). Boats to Venice cost €13 and leave from the airport ferry dock (an eight-minute walk from the terminal).

BUS ATVO (☏041 520 55 30; www.atvo.it) buses run to the airport from Piazzale Roma (€5, one hour, every 30 minutes 8am to midnight).

Vaporetto

The city's main mode of public transport is *vaporetto* – Venice's distinctive water buses. Tickets can be purchased from the **HelloVenezia ticket booths** (www.hellovenezia.com) at most landing stations. You can also buy tickets when boarding; you may be charged double with luggage, though this is not always enforced.

Instead of spending €7 for a one-way ticket, consider a Tourist Travel Card (www.actv.it; available from Hellovenezia booths and ticket machines at major stops). This timed pass allows unlimited travel within a set period (beginning at first validation). Passes for 12/24/36/48/72 hours cost €18/20/25/30/35. A week pass costs €50. Swipe your card every time you board, even if you have already validated it upon initial boarding.

Vaporetto stops can be confusing, so check the signs at the landing dock to make sure you're at the right stop for the *vaporetto* line and direction you want. At major stops like Ferrovia and around San Marco, there are often two separate docks for the same *vaporetto* line,

headed in opposite directions. Some lines make only limited stops, so check boat signage. Note that San Zaccaria is the main stop for Piazza San Marco.

Water Taxis

The standard **water taxi** (☏041 522 23 03, 041 240 67 11; www.venicewatertaxi.com) between Marco Polo airport and Venice costs €90 to €100 for up to four people. Official rates start at €8.90 plus €1.80 per minute, plus €6 if they're called to your hotel and more for night trips, luggage and large groups. Prices can be metered or negotiated in advance.

AROUND THE VENETO

Most visitors to the Veneto devote all their precious time to Venice itself, which is perfectly understandable – until you discover the rich variety of sensations that await just an hour or two away.

First, there are the city-states Venice annexed in the 15th century: Padua (Padova) with its animated university crowds and pre-Renaissance fresco cycles; Vicenza with its lion's share of Palladio's peerless architecture; and Verona with its sophisticated bustle atop ancient Roman foundations. All are easily reached by train from Venice; the hardy could see two in a single day.

Then there are the wines. Near Verona, Valpolicella was long known for quaffable reds and Soave for inoffensive whites. Now, both regions are undergoing a renaissance. In particular, Valpolicella's bold Amarones are wooing experts and amateurs alike. In a party mood? The hills around Conegliano produce Italy's finest bubbly: Prosecco Superiore. For harder stuff, charming Bassano del Grappa obliges with its own eponymous firewater.

For sober minds, nothing can rival the humane order of Palladio's country villas, which set the pattern for European architecture for centuries. Scattered across the region and with odd hours set by private owners, they require patience and a set of wheels, but that's part of the adventure. In the meantime, you get to see the Veneto's rich alluvial plains as they give way to the first hints of the Alps.

On the rare day when the Adriatic wipes Venice clean of its mists, you can catch glimpses of the snowcapped Dolomites from the lagoon itself. It's hard to believe, but in less than two hours you can go from murky canals to the crisp Alpine clarity of Belluno and Cortina d'Ampezzo – land of idyllic hikes, razor-sharp peaks and the world's most fashion-conscious skiing.

Brenta Riviera

Every 13 June for 300 years, summer officially kicked off with a traffic jam along the Grand Canal, as a flotilla of fashionable Venetians headed to their villas along the banks of the Brenta. Every last ball gown and poker chair was loaded onto barges for dalliances that stretched until November. The party ended when Napoleon arrived in 1797, but 80 villas still strike elegant poses along the Brenta. Private ownership and privacy hedges leave much to the imagination, but four historical villas are now open as museums.

⊙ Sights

Villa Foscari　　　　　HISTORICAL BUILDING
(☑041 520 39 66; www.lamalcontenta.com; Via dei Turisti 9, Malcontenta; adult/reduced €10/8; ☺9am-noon Tue & Sat, closed Nov-Apr) The most romantic Brenta Riviera villa is the Palladio-designed 1555–60 villa known as 'La Malcontenta' after a grand dame of the Foscari clan was allegedly exiled here for adultery. But these effortlessly light, sociable salons

hardly constituted a punishment. The villa was abandoned for years, but Giovanni Zelotti's frescoes have recently been restored to daydream-inducing splendour.

Villa Widmann Rezzonico Foscari　　　HISTORICAL BUILDING
(☑041 560 06 90; www.riviera-brenta.it; Via Nazionale 420, Mira; adult/reduced €5.50/4.50; ☺10am-5pm Tue-Sun Mar-Oct, 10am-5pm Sat & Sun Nov-Feb) Originally owned by Persian-Venetian nobility, this 18th-century villa captures the Brenta's last days of rococo decadence, with Murano sea-monster chandeliers, a frescoed grand salon and an upstairs ladies' gambling parlour.

Villa Pisani Nazionale　　　　MUSEUM
(☑049 50 22 70; www.villapisani.beniculturali.it; Via Doge Pisani 7, Stra; adult/reduced €10/7.50, grounds only €7.50/5; ☺9am-5pm Tue-Sun, to 8pm Apr-Sep, last admission 1hr before close) Doge Alvise Pisani provided a Versailles-like reminder of who was in charge with this 1770s villa and vast gardens, complete with labyrinthine hedge-maze and reflecting pools. The villa's 114 rooms have seen their share of history: the grand bathroom with a tiny wooden throne used by Napoleon; a sagging bed where Vittorio Emanuele II apparently tossed and turned as the new head of independent Italy; and the reception hall where Mussolini and Hitler met for the first time in 1934, ironically under Tiepolo's ceiling masterpiece depicting the *Geniuses of Peace*.

Villa Foscarini Rossi　　　　MUSEUM
(☑049 980 03 35; www.villafoscarini.it; Via Doge Pisani 1/2, Stra; admission €7; ☺9am-1pm & 2.30-6pm Mon-Fri, 2.30-6pm Sat & Sun Apr-Oct, 9am-1pm Mon-Fri Nov-Mar) Back in the day, well-heeled Venetians wouldn't dream of decamping to the Brenta without their favourite cobblers, sparking an enduring tradition of high-end shoemaking. Today 950 companies in the region produce 20 million pairs of shoes annually. The art of Brenta cobblers is commemorated with a **Shoemakers' Museum** in this 18th-century villa, with a dream collection that ranges from 18th-century slippers to contemporary works by Yves Saint Laurent, Pucci and more.

⊂⊃ Tours

Seeing the Brenta by boat reveals an engineering marvel: the ingenious hydraulic locks system developed in the 15th century to prevent river silt from dumping into the lagoon.

Il Burchiello
BOAT

(☎049 820 69 10; www.ilburchiello.it; day cruise adult €71-84, reduced €56, half-day €51/40) This modern luxury barge lets you watch 50 villas drift by from cushy velvet couches with a glass of *prosecco* in hand. Day cruises stop at Malcontenta, Widmann and Pisani villas; half-day tours (about €50) cover two villas. Full-day cruises leave from Venice's ferry terminal (Tuesday, Thursday and Saturday) or Padua (Wednesday, Friday and Sunday), with bus transfers to train stations included in both half- and full-day trips.

I Batelli del Brenta
BOAT

(☎049 876 02 33; www.battellidelbrenta.it; full-day tours adult €85-89, reduced €40-56, half-day tours adult €47-51, reduced €39-41; ☺by reservation Tue-Sun Mar-Nov) Offers a range of half-day and full-day excursions, with departures from both Venice and Padua.

Rental Bike Venice
BICYCLE

(☎346 847114; www.rentalbikevenice.blogspot. com; Via Gramsci 85, Mira; bicycle per day €10, foldable €14; ☺8am-8pm) Speed past tour boats on 150km of cycling routes along the Brenta plains. This operator is accessible by bus from Venice, Mestre or Padua (see website for directions) and offers city bikes with baskets, mountain bikes and handy foldable bikes to take on buses, plus roadside assistance, itinerary advice in English and pick-up/drop-off of bikes at Mestre train station.

Festivals & Events

Dolo Mercatino dell'Antiquariato   MARKET
(Antiques Market; Isola Bassa, Dolo) The region's largest antiques market is held (weather permitting) on the 4th Sunday of the month from April to October.

StraOrganic   FOOD, ARTS
(www.comune.stra.ve.it) Held on the last weekend in April and first weekend in May, the Brenta claims bragging rights to local, organic foods and handicrafts in Stra.

Riviera Fiorita   CULTURAL
(www.rivierafiorita.it) Party like it's 1527 with baroque costume parties at the Villa Pisani and Villa Widmann, historically correct country fairs and even gelati in baroque-era flavours. Held on the 1st or 2nd weekend in September.

Venice Marathon   SPORT
(www.venicemarathon.it) Run like Casanova caught in the act from Villa Pisani along the Brenta to Venice, with the final legs crossing pontoon bridges. Usually held in October, with proceeds funding clean-water projects in Africa.

Sleeping & Eating

Villa Tron Mioni   INN €€
(☎041 41 01 77; www.villatron.it; Via Ca' Tron 23, Dolo; d €92-140; ❄🐾) Surrounded by gardens, this 19th-century villa provides aristocratic flourishes at middle-class prices. Rooms in the main villa are done up in simple good taste, and a few new apartments are handsomely decorated in rustic-chic style. However, the ramblingly romantic gardens are the real draw. Best to have your own car.

Da Conte   MODERN ITALIAN €
(☎041 47 95 71; Via Caltana 133, Mira; meals €10-15; ☺dinner Tue-Sat) An unlikely bastion of sophistication lodged practically underneath an overpass, Da Conte has one of the best wine lists in the region and creative takes on classic lagoon cuisine, from roasted quail to ginger-infused langoustines.

❶ Getting There & Around

ACTV's Venezia–Padova Extraurbane bus 53 leaves from Venice's Piazzale Roma about every half-hour, stopping at key Brenta villages en route to Padua. Local Venice–Padua train services stop at Dolo (€2.40, 25 minutes, one or two hour) en route to Padua. By car, take SS11 from Mestre-Venezia towards Padua and take the Autostrada A4 towards Dolo/Padua.

Padua
POP 213,000

Though just 37km west of Venice, Padua looks more like Milan, with oddly shaped medieval piazzas, a vibrant student population and broad boulevards that lump together elegant Liberty edifices, sinister Fascist facades and postwar cereal-box architecture.

Padua has certainly been through the wringer since its founding in the late 12th century BC, and restless reinvention has long been its trademark. Romans took over the town from Veneti tribes and renamed it Patavium, but Goths and Lombards had wiped it out by AD 602. A fire destroyed a growing medieval core in 1164, but the

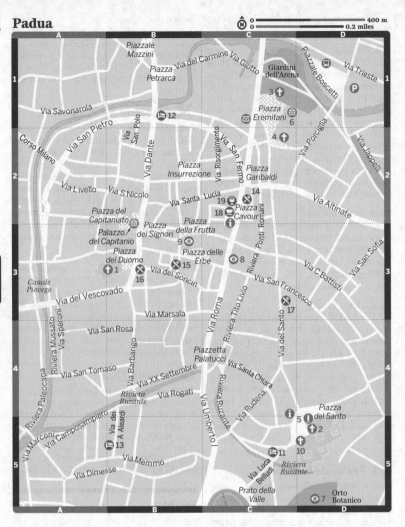

city-state soon made a comeback to conquer Vicenza and surrounding territories. Padua established Italy's third university in 1222, becoming the magnet for thinkers and artists. For the next few centuries Padua and Verona challenged each other for dominance over the Veneto plains. But Venice finally settled the matter by occupying Padua permanently in 1405.

As a strategic military-industrial centre, Padua became a parade ground for Mussolini speeches, an Allied bombing target and a secret Italian Resistance hub based at the university. Once Padua was wrested from

Fascist control in 1945, there was a new industrial zone east of the city within a year, the university was back in session and the puzzlework that is Padua began anew.

◉ Sights

CAPPELLA DEGLI SCROVEGNI & AROUND

TOP CHOICE **Cappella degli Scrovegni** CHURCH (☎049 201 00 20; www.cappelladegliscrovegni. it; Giardini dell'Arena; adult/reduced €13/8 or PadovaCard; ◷9am-7pm by reservation, call centre 9am-7pm Mon-Fri & 9am-6pm Sat) Almost 200 years before Michelangelo's

Padua

Sistine Chapel came Padua's Renaissance breakthrough: Giotto's moving, modern 1304–06 frescoes in the Scrovegni Chapel. Medieval churchgoers were accustomed to blank stares from two-dimensional saints, but Giotto depicted biblical figures as human beings in recognisable settings caught up in extraordinary circumstances. Onlookers gossip as middle-aged Anne tenderly kisses Joachim; exhausted new dad Joseph falls asleep in the manger as sheep and angels watch over baby Jesus; and Jesus stares down Judas as the traitor puckers up for the kiss that sealed his master's fate.

Booking is required online or by phone, possibly weeks ahead between April and October. Chapel visits last 15 minutes, preceded by a mandatory, 15-minute video about the frescoes' history and renovation. During summer, hours are extended with night sessions from 7pm to 10pm, with visits lasting 20 minutes.

Musei Civici agli Eremitani   MUSEUM
(☑049 820 45 51; Piazza Eremitani 8; adult/reduced €10/8 or PadovaCard, free with Capella degli Scrovegni; ◷9am-7pm Tue-Sun) This converted monastery houses artefacts dating from Padua's pre-Roman history on the ground floor, plus notable 14th- to 18th-century works from Veneto artists, from Bellini to Canova, upstairs. The show-stopper is a crucifix by Giotto, showing a heartbroken Mary wringing her hands as Jesus' blood drips onto the rocky earth.

Chiesa degli Eremitani   CHURCH
(☑049 875 64 10; Piazza Eremitani; ◷7.30am-12.30pm & 3.30-7pm Mon-Fri, 9am-12.30pm & 4-8pm Sat & Sun) In 1944 a bombing raid demolished the extraordinary 1448–57 frescoes by Andrea Mantegna in the Capella Overtari of this church. After a half-century of painstaking reconstruction, the shattered, humidity-damaged stories of SS James and Christopher have been puzzled together, revealing extreme perspectives that make Mantegna's saints look like superheroes.

HISTORICAL CENTRE

Ancient Padua can be glimpsed in twin squares framed by arcades, the **Piazza delle Erbe** and **Piazza della Frutta**, which are separated by the triple-decker Gothic tribunal known as the Palazzo della Ragione. The *palazzo's* arcades still serve as a food market, where you can stock up on horse meat – a local speciality since before Roman times.

Palazzo del Bó   HISTORICAL BUILDING
(☑049 827 30 47; Via VIII Febbraio; adult/reduced €5/3.50; ◷tours 9.15am, 10.15am & 11.15pm Tue, Thu & Sat, 3.15pm, 4.15pm & 5.15pm Mon, Wed & Fri) This 16th-century palace is the seat of Padua's illustrious university, which was founded by renegade Bolognese scholars in the 1220s. Some of Italy's greatest and most controversial thinkers taught here, including Copernicus, Galileo, Casanova and the world's first woman doctor of philosophy, Elena Cornaro Piscopia. Guided tours cover Galileo's lecture hall and the world's first anatomy theatre. Note there are fewer tours November to March.

Villas, Vino & Vertigo

While the allures of Venice are renowned, those who manage to escape the misty lagoon city will find a remarkable variety of experiences – from savouring the wines of Valpolicella to hiking the slopes of the Dolomites – awaiting just an hour or two away.

Brenta Riviera

1 For centuries, fashionable Venetians packed up each June and headed to villas along the banks of the Brenta (p364). Today you can retrace their steps, and visit their old haunts, via bike or barge.

Wine Country

2 Veneto vineyards produce some of Italy's most thrilling *vino*, including crisp *prosecco* (sparkling wine) from Conegliano (p381), Valpolicella's heady Amarone (p381) and the increasingly complex whites of Soave (p380).

Dolomites

3 Considering the humid confines of Venice, it's hard to believe the Alpine crispness of the Dolomites (p381) lies just 100km away. This Unesco-protected landscape provides wildflowers in spring, hiking in summer and some of Italy's best skiing in winter.

City-states

4 Before Venice established its hegemony over the Veneto, Vicenza (p372), Padua (p365) and Verona (p375) vied for medieval supremacy. Today each preserves its own unique heritage, from Padua's medieval frescoes, Vicenza's Palladian *palazzi* (mansions) and Verona's Roman-era arena.

Palladian Villas

5 Before transforming European architecture, Palladio first redefined the fabric of his adoptive Vicenza (p372). However, many of his most influential works are scattered across the Veneto countryside, from iconic La Rotonda (p374) to masterful Villa Maser (p377).

Clockwise from top left
1. Villa Foscari 2. Vineyards, Soave 3. Lago d'Antorno, Dolomites 4. Palazzo della Ragione, Padua.

GLENN VAN DER KNIJFF / LONELY PLANET IMAGES ©

3

MAKING THE MOST OF YOUR EURO

A **PadovaCard** (per 48/72hr €16/21) gives one adult and one child under 14 free use of city public transport and access to almost all of Padua's major attractions, including the Cappella degli Scrovegni (plus €1 booking fee; reservations essential). PadovaCards are available at Padua tourist offices and monuments covered by the pass.

Basilica del Duomo CHURCH

(☑049 66 28 14; Piazza del Duomo; ☉7.30am-noon & 4-7.30pm Mon-Sat, 8am-1pm & 4-8.45pm Sun & holidays) South of the *palazzo* is the city's cathedral, built from a much-altered design by Michelangelo. Its luminous restraint is upstaged by the adjoining 13th-century **baptistry** (adult/reduced €2.80/1.80 or PadovaCard; ☉10am-6pm), a Romanesque gem completely covered in Giusto de' Menabuoi's luminous frescoes, including a cupola depicting hundreds of saints posed as though for a school graduation photo.

Palazzo della Ragione HISTORICAL BUILDING

(☑049 820 50 06; Piazza delle Erbe; adult/reduced €4/2; ☉9am-7pm Tue-Sun, to 6pm Nov-Jan) The city's Gothic tribunal dates from the 13th century, and its vast main hall is awash in frescoes by Giotto acolytes Giusto de' Menabuoi and Nicolò Mireto. Much restored in wake of flood and fire, they depict the medieval astrological theories of Pietro d'Abano.

PIAZZA DEL SANTO & AROUND

Basilica di Sant'Antonio CHURCH

(www.basilicadelsanto.org; Piazza del Santo; ☉6.30am-7.45pm Apr-Oct, to 6.45pm Nov-Mar) The soul of the city, this vast basilica serves as the final resting place of the town's patron saint, St Anthony of Padua (1193–1231). Along the left transept, the saint's tomb is covered with requests and thanks for miracle cures and the recovery of lost objects. Under vaulted Gothic ceilings you'll find notable works like the lifelike 1360s crucifix by Veronese master Altichiero da Zevio, a 1528 sacristy fresco of St Anthony preaching to spellbound fish, and 1444–50 high altar reliefs by Florentine Renaissance master Donatello (ask guards for access).

Outside, Donatello's 1453 equestrian statue, which commemorates 15th-century Venetian mercenary leader Gattamelata ('Honeyed Cat'), is considered the first great Italian Renaissance bronze.

Oratorio di San Giorgio & Scoletta del Santo CHURCH

(Piazza del Santo; admission €4; ☉9am-12.30pm & 2.30-5pm Oct-Mar, to 7pm Apr-Sep) Two of Padua's greatest treasures hide in plain sight across the square from Saint Anthony's basilica. The Oratorio di San Giorgio is awash in jewel-like frescoes by Altichiero da Zevio and Jacopo Avanzi in 1378. Upstairs, the Scoletta del Santo proffers Titian paintings that include a 1511 portrait of St Anthony calmly reattaching his own foot.

Orto Botanico HISTORIC PARK

(☑049 827 21 19; www.ortobotanico.unipd.it; Via dell'Orto Botanico; adult/reduced €4/1; ☉9am-1pm & 3-7pm Apr-Oct, 9am-1pm Mon-Sat Nov-Mar) South of Piazza del Santo, a Unesco World Heritage Site is growing. Padua's botanical gardens were planted in 1545 by Padua University's medical faculty in order to study the medicinal properties of rare plants. It also served as a clandestine Resistance meeting headquarters in WWII.

🛏 Sleeping

The tourist office publishes accommodation brochures and lists dozens of B&Bs and hotels online.

TOP CHOICE Belludi37 BOUTIQUE HOTEL €€

(☑049 66 56 33; www.belludi37.it; Via Luca Belludi 37; s €80, d €120-150; ❋@⛟) A sleek boutique hotel with soul: expect generous beds, modern yet serene rooms, and a helpful staff quick with savvy advice for making the best of Padua.

Hotel Sant'Antonio GUESTHOUSE €

(☑049 875 13 93; www.hotelsantantonio.it; Via San Fermo 118; s €63-69, d €82-94; ❋) This is a calm, canalside hotel with unfussy, airy rooms, most with new bathrooms and a few with canal views. There are also some cheaper singles with a shared bathroom (€39 to €42).

Ostello Città di Padova HOSTEL €

(☑049 875 22 19; www.ostellopadova.it; Via dei A Aleardi 30; dm €19; ☉reception 7-9.30am & 3.30-11.30pm) This central hostel on a quiet side street has decent dorm rooms with four to six beds. Sheets and wi-fi are free, but there's no kitchen. Take bus 3, 8 or 12 or the city's new tram from the train station.

COLLI EUGANEI (EUGANEAN HILLS)

Southwest of Padua, the Colli Euganei (Euganean Hills) feel a world away from the urban sophistication of Venice and the surrounding plains. To explore the walled hilltop towns, misty vineyards and bubbling hot springs, the Padua tourist office offers area maps, accommodation, hiking and transport information online (www.turismotermeeuganee.it). Trains serve all towns except Arquà Petrarca.

Just south of Padua lie the natural hot spring resorts of **Abano Terme** and **Montegrotto Terme**. The towns are uninspired, but the waters do cure aches and pains.

In the medieval village of **Arquà Petrarca**, look for the elegant little **house** (☑0429 71 82 94; Via Valleselle 4; adult/reduced €4/2; ⊙9am-12.30pm & 3-7pm Tue-Sun Mar-Oct, 9am-12.30pm & 2.30-5.30pm Tue-Sun Nov-Feb) where great Italian poet Petrarch spent his final years in the 1370s.

At the southern reaches of the Euganei, you'll find three walled medieval towns: **Monselice**, with its remarkable **medieval castle** (www.castellodimonselice.it; adult/reduced €5.50/4.50; ⊙1hr guided tours 9am, 10am, 11am, 3pm & 4pm Tue-Sun Apr-Nov); **Este**, whose **archaeological museum** (Via Guido Negri 9c; adult/reduced €3/1.50; ⊙8.30am-7.30pm) has an important collection of artefacts from the pre-Roman Veneti tribes; and **Montagnana**, with its magnificent 2km defensive perimeter. Just outside Montagnana's east gate, look for Palladio's small but important Villa Pisani, still a private residence.

Eating

Godenda
TOP CHOICE

MODERN ITALIAN €€

(☑049 877 41 92; www.godenda.it; Via Squarcione 4/6; meals €30-50; ⊙10am-3pm & 7pm-1am Mon-Sat, closed Aug) Though hidden under an ancient portico, this foodie favourite manages to be airy and modern. The menu changes with the seasons, with creative takes on old Venetian classics like a sublime monkfish with fava beans and house made pasta sprinkled with jerked horse meat. The wine list is long and excellent. Reservations recommended.

Caffè Cavour
CAFE €

(☑049 875 12 24; www.caffecavour.com; Piazza Cavour 10; pastries €1.50-4; ⊙7.30am-8pm Wed-Sun, to midnight May-Sep) Pistachio macaroons, wild-berry tarts and other two-bite indulgences sweeten the expressions of traffic cops bolting espresso at the curved granite bar.

Osteria Dal Capo
OSTERIA €€

(☑049 66 31 05; Via degli Obizzi 2; meals €25-35; ⊙lunch & dinner Tue-Sat) Rub elbows with locals – literally – at tiny tables precariously piled with traditional Venetian seafood and a few inspired novelties, such as *caviale di melanzane con bufala* (eggplant caviar with buffalo mozzarella atop crispy wafer bread). Reservations and a sociable nature advised.

Piadineria Italiana
SANDWICH SHOP €

(☑340 294 64 80; Via del Santo 7; meals €5-10; ⊙10am-5pm Mon-Sat) Students from the nearby university head hear for a cheap and delicious variation on pizza known as the *piadina*, a classic quick eat from the region around Ravenna.

Drinking & Entertainment

Sundown isn't official until you've joined the crowds for a Spritz in Piazza delle Erbe or Piazza dei Signori. Also note that Padua is the region's unofficial capital of gay and lesbian life.

Enoteca Santa Lucia
WINE BAR

(☑049 8759483; Piazza Cavour 15; ⊙7pm-midnight Mon-Sat) Santa Lucia offers upmarket wines by the glass for €5 to €10 with a free buffet of local specialities and cheeses from 7pm to 10pm nightly. Occupy your battle station at the glassed-in bar for buffet forays, or head inside for serious boozing.

Caffetteria Manin
CAFE

(☑049 876 16 09; Via Manin 56; ⊙7am-7pm Mon-Fri, 7am-12.30pm Sat) Top-flight coffee is still toasted on the premises at this old-fashioned cafe, where locals pop in all day for a frothy jolt at the bar – there are no tables.

Caffè Pedrocchi
CAFE

(☑049 878 12 31; www.caffepedrocchi.it, in Italian; Via VIII Febbraio 15; ⊙9am-10pm Sun-Wed, to 1am

Thu-Sat) Since 1831, this neoclassical landmark has been a favourite of Stendhal and other pillars of cafe society for heart-poundingly powerful coffee and elaborate *caffè correto* (coffee cocktails).

Flexoclub
NIGHTCLUB

(☎049 807 47 07; www.flexoclub.it, in Italian; Via Turazza 19; ⊗from 10pm Wed-Sun) This sprawling gay venue about 2km east of the train station features a bar/disco, with occasional live music and drag shows, plus an adjacent sauna.

❶ Information

Hospital (☎049 821 11 11; Via Giustiniani 1) Main public hospital.

Police station (☎049 83 31 11; Piazzetta Palatucci 5)

Tourist Office (www.turismopadova.it) train station (☎049 875 20 77; ⊗9am-7pm Mon-Sat, 9am-12.30pm Sun); Galleria Pedrocchi (☎049 876 79 27; ⊗9am-1.30pm & 3-7pm Mon-Sat); Piazza del Santo (☎049 875 30 87; ⊗9am-1.30pm & 3-6pm Mon-Sat, 10am-1pm & 3-6pm Sun Apr-Oct).

❶ Getting There & Around

BUS SITA buses (☎049 820 68 34; www.sitabus.it, in Italian) from Venice's Piazzale Roma (€3.70, 45 to 60 minutes, hourly) arrive at Piazzale Boschetti, 500m southeast of the train station. Check online for buses to Colli Euganei towns (see p371).

TRAIN The easiest way to reach Padua from Venice (€3 to €15, 25 to 50 minutes, three or four per hour), Verona (€5.10 to €16, 40 to 90 minutes, two or three per hour), Vicenza (€3 to €13, 15 to 30 minutes, two or three per hour) and most other Italian destinations; the station is about 500m north of Cappella degli Scrovegni.

TRAM It is easy to get to all the sites by foot from the train and bus stations, but a new single-branch tram runs from the train station passes within 100m of all the main sites. Tickets (€1.20) are available at tobacconists and newsstands.

Vicenza

POP 115,500

When Palladio escaped an oppressive employer in his native Padua, few would have guessed the humble stonecutter would, within a few decades, transform not only his adoptive city but also the history of European architecture. By luck, a local count recognised his talents in the 1520s and sent him to study the ruins in Rome. When he returned to Vicenza, the autodidact began producing his extraordinary buildings that marry sophistication and rustic simplicity, reverent classicism and bold innovation. It's no wonder Vicenza and surrounding villas have been declared one grand Unesco World Heritage Site.

Despite its outsized heritage, this charming town remains quietly unpretentious – a fine place to join locals lingering over simple lunches of local *salumi* (cured meats), game and handmade pasta. Centrally located and with good-value accommodation, Vicenza makes an ideal base for the rest of the Veneto.

◉ Sights

Teatro Olimpico
THEATRE

(☎0444 22 28 00; www.olimpico.vicenza.it; Palazzo Matteotti 11; incl Museo Civico adult/reduced €8/6; ⊗9am-5pm Tue-Sun) Behind a charming walled garden lies a Renaissance marvel – a theatre that Palladio began in 1580 with inspiration from Roman amphitheatres. Vincenzo Scamozzi finished the elliptical theatre after Palladio's death, adding a stage set modelled on the ancient Greek city of Thebes. Since its restoration in 1934, Italian performers have vied to make an entrance on this stage; check online for opera, jazz and classical performances.

Piazza dei Signori & Around
HISTORICAL BUILDING

The heart of historical Vicenza is Piazza dei Signori, where Palladio lightens the mood of government buildings with his trademark play of light and shadow. Dazzling white Piovene stone arches frame shady double arcades in the **Basilica Palladiana**. Across the piazza, white stone and stucco grace the exposed red-brick colonnade of the 1571-designed **Loggia del Capitaniato**. Palladio fans will find more of his *palazzi* north of the piazza along Contrà Porti. You cannot visit any of the interiors of these buildings, but the facades are a feast to behold.

Museo Civico
MUSEUM

(☎0444 22 28 11; www.museicivicivicenza.it; Palazzo Chiericati, Piazza Matteotti 37/39; incl Teatro Olimpico adult/reduced €8/6; ⊗9am-5pm Tue-Sun) Vicenza's Museo Civico occupies the 1550 Palazzo Chiericati, one of Palladio's finest buildings. The lavishly frescoed ground floor includes the Sala dal Firmamento (Salon of the Skies), with Domenico Brusasorci's ceiling fresco of Diana galloping across the sky to meet the sun. Upstairs

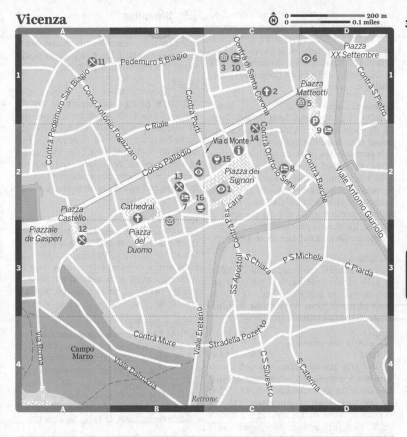

Vicenza

galleries present works by Vicenza masters in the context of major works by Venetian masters (Veronese, Tiepolo and Tintoretto), plus works by Hans Memling, Jacopo Bassano, Elisabetta Marchioni and Giambattista Piazzetta.

Gallerie di Palazzo Leoni Montanari MUSEUM
(☎800 57 88 75; www.palazzomontanari.com; Contrà di Santa Corona 25; adult/reduced €5/4; ☺10am-6pm Tue-Sun) Outside it looks like a bank, but a treasure beyond accountants'

imagining awaits inside. Grand salons are adorned with Canaletto's lagoon landscapes and Pietro Longhi 18th-century society satires. Up another flight hides a superb collection of 400 Russian icons, gorgeously spotlit in darkened galleries with Gregorian chants setting the scene.

Chiesa di Santa Corona
CHURCH

(☎0444 22 28 11; Contrá Santa Corona) Built by the Dominicans in 1261 to house a supposed relic from Christ's crown of thorns, this Romanesque brick church also houses three light-filled masterpieces: Palladio's 1576 Valmarana Chapel in the crypt, Paolo Veronese's *Adoration of the Magi* (much praised by Goethe) and Giovanni Bellini's radiant *Baptism of Christ*. At the time of writing, the church was closed for major restoration, with no fixed date for reopening.

VICENZA SOUTH

Two of Palladio's most extraordinary villas lie a 20-minute walk south of the train station, or you can catch local bus 8 (€1.50) in front of the station. A charming footpath connects the two villas.

TOP CHOICE Villa Valmarana 'ai Nani'
HISTORICAL BUILDING

(☎0444 32 18 03; www.villavalmarana.com; Stradella dei Nani 8; admission €8; ◷10am-noon & 3-6pm Tue-Sun Apr-Oct, 10am-noon & 2-.30-5pm Sat & Sun Nov-Mar) Nicknamed 'ai Nani' (dwarfs) for the 17 garden-gnome statues around the garden walls, this 18th-century neoclassical villa has charming grounds, but the real draw is the sublime 1757 frescoes by Giambattista Tiepolo and his son Giandomenico. Giambattista painted the Palazzina wing with his signature mythological epics, while Giandomenico painted the Foresteria with fanciful rural, carnival and Chinese themes.

TOP CHOICE La Rotonda
HISTORICAL BUILDING

(☎049 879 13 80; www.villalarotonda.it; Via della Rotonda 45; admission villa/gardens €10/5; ◷gardens 10am-noon & 3-6pm Tue-Sun, villa Wed & Sat only, closed mid-Nov–mid-Mar) La Rotonda is a showstopper no matter how you look at it, with its namesake dome and identical colonnaded facades on all four sides. It has inspired imitators across Europe and the USA, including Thomas Jefferson's Monticello (the late owner, Mario di Valmarana, was coincidentally a retired University of Virginia architecture professor). Inside, the central hall soars up into a cupola with trompe l'œil frescoes.

🛏 Sleeping

Dozens of hotels in greater Vicenza are listed on the tourism board website (www.vicenzae.org) and a dozen or so B&Bs can be found at www.vitourism.it (in Italian).

TOP CHOICE Relais Ca' Muse
DESIGN HOTEL €€

(☎0444 37 64 43; www.camuse.it; Via Valle 62, Sovizzo; d from €140; P🌂❄@🛜♨) Impossible to categorise, this gallery/hotel/social experiment in an old stone farmhouse is well worth the 15-minute drive from Vicenza for its serene rooms, remarkable and racy collection of contemporary art, well-tended grounds, and breakfasts of the freshest, best local ingredients.

Hotel Palladio
BOUTIQUE HOTEL €€

(☎0444 32 53 47; www.hotel-palladio.it; Contrà Oratorio Servi 25; s/d €110/170; P🌂@🛜) The top choice in central Vicenza, this four-star hotel boasts well-appointed rooms done up with minimalist good taste, while preserving key details of the Renaissance *palazzo* it occupies.

Albergo Due Mori
INN €

(☎0444 32 18 86; www.hotelduemori.it; Contrà do Rode 26; s/d without bathroom €40/60, d/tr with bathroom €85/100; @🛜) This central, historical 1854 hotel has been restored to its period charm, with Liberty-style bedsteads and antique armoires. Rooms don't have TV or air-con, but nods to modernity include disabled access and wi-fi. No breakfast.

Relais Santa Corona
BOUTIQUE HOTEL €€

(☎0444 32 46 78; www.relaissantacorona.it; Contrà di Santa Corona 19; s/d €100-150; P🌂@🛜) This boutique bargain offers soothingly stylish, soundproofed rooms in an 18th-century palace.

Ostello Olimpico
HOSTEL €

(☎0444 54 02 22; www.ostellovicenza.com; Via Antonio Giuriolo 9; dm/s/d €20/28/48; ◷reception 7.30-9.30am & 3.30-11.30pm) A good HI youth hostel near the Teatro Olimpico, with free internet access, shared kitchen facilities and laundry.

🍴 Eating

TOP CHOICE Antico Ristorante agli Schioppi
OSTERIA €€

(☎0444 54 37 01; www.ristoranteaglischioppi. com; Contrà Piazza del Castello 26; meals €30-40; ◷lunch Tue-Sat, dinner Mon-Sat) Tucked discreetly under an ancient arcade is one of the city's simplest and best restaurants. The owners are devotees of locally sourced products, from wild forest greens to baby river trout. The menu changes with the season, but think quail stuffed with dandelion greens in spring and pasta with musky mushrooms in the fall.

Antico Guelfo
OSTERIA €€

(0444 54 78 97; www.anticoguelfo.it; Contrà Pedemuro San Biagio 90; meals €30-40; ⊙dinner Mon-Sat) This culinary hideaway is a hit with Slow Foodies for its inventive daily market menu, making the most of local specialities in such dishes as Amarone risotto or buckwheat crêpes with Bastardo di Grappa cheese.

Ristorante Il Castello
TRADITIONAL ITALIAN €€

(0444 37 90 32; www.ristoranteilcastellosovizzo. it; Via Castello 2, Montemezzo di Sovizzo; meals €35-45; ⊙lunch Sat & Sun, dinner Tue-Sun) You won't regret the 20-minute drive to this extraordinary hilltop restaurant, which occupies a 15th-century villa of thick stone walls and nobly proportioned rooms. The menu, too, is both noble and rustic, based on local ingredients like perfectly grilled meats and homemade pasta confected with seasonal vegetables.

Dai Nodari
MODERN ITALIAN €

(0444 54 40 85; Contrà do Rode 20; meals €20-30; ⊙noon-3.30pm & 7-11pm) Rustic fare gets hip in the heart of historical Vicenza, attracting both young and old with hearty yet reasonably priced dishes like duck in beer sauce or a thick soup of orzo, beans and radicchio.

Gastronomia Il Ceppo
DELI €

(0444 54 44 14; www.gastronomiailceppo.com; 196 Corso Palladio; prepared dishes per 100g €3-5; ⊙8am-1pm & 3.30-7.45pm Mon-Tue & Thu-Sat, 8am-1pm Wed) San Daniele hams dangle over a 9m shop counter filled with fresh seafood salads, house-made pasta and speciality cheese – perfect picnic provisions.

 Drinking

Sorarù
CAFE

(0444 32 09 15; Piazzetta Palladio; ⊙7.30am-12.30pm & 3.30pm-7.30pm Thu-Tue) Drink in history at this marble-topped bar serving bracing espresso and homemade pastries, with jars of sweets stashed on carved and gilded shelving.

Antica Casa della Malvasia
WINE BAR

(0444 54 37 04; Contrà delle Morette 5; meals from €35; ⊙11am-12.30pm Mon-Thu & Sat, 5.30pm-2am Fri) Purveyor of wines since 1200, when Malvasia wine was imported from Greece by Venetian merchants, this *enoteca* offers full meals as well as 80-plus wines and hundreds of grappas from nearby Bassano del Grappa. Next door, the wine bar offers quick bites and quality pours by the glass.

 Information

Ospedale Civile (0444 75 31 11; Viale F Rodolfi 37) Hospital.

Police station (0444 33 75 11; Viale G Mazzini 213)

Post office (Contrà Garibaldi 1; ⊙8.30am-6.30pm Mon-Fri, 8.30am-1pm Sat)

Tourist office (0444 32 08 54; www.vicenzae.org; Piazza Matteotti 12; ⊙9am-1pm & 2-6pm) Especially knowledgeable and helpful.

Getting There & Away

Large car parks are located near Piazza Castello and the train station.

BUS FTV (0444 22 31 15; www.ftv.vi.it) buses leave for outlying areas from the bus station, located next to the train station.

TRAIN Three to four trains arrive hourly from Venice (€4.40 to €14, 30 minutes to 1¼ hours), Padua (€3 to €18, 15 to 40 minutes) and Verona (€4 to €14, 30 minutes to 60 minutes), and twice-hourly from Milan (€11 to €24, 1½ to two hours).

Verona
POP 264,500

Shakespeare placed star-crossed Romeo Montague and Juliet Capulet in Verona for good reason: romance, drama and fatal family feuds have been the city's hallmark for centuries.

From the third century BC, Verona was a Roman trade centre, with ancient gates and a grand amphitheatre to prove it – but Shakespearean tragedy came with the territory. Lombard king Alboin, who conquered Verona in AD 569, was murdered by his wife three years later. After Mastino della Scala (aka Scaligeri) lost re-election to Verona's commune in 1262, he claimed absolute control, until murdered by his rivals. Mastino's son Cangrande I (1308–28) went on to conquer Padua and Vicenza, with Dante, Petrarch and Giotto benefitting from the city's patronage. But the fratricidal rage of

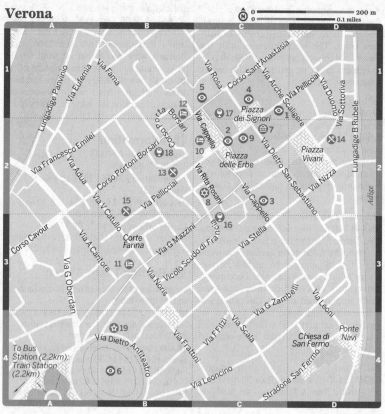

Verona

◎ Sights
1 Arche Scaligere	C1
2 Arco della Costa	C2
3 Casa di Giulietta	C2
4 Loggia del Consiglio	C1
5 Palazzo Maffei	C1
6 Roman Arena	B4
7 Scavi Scaligeri	C2
8 Synagogue	C2
9 Torre dei Lamberti	C2

🛏 Sleeping
10 Albergo Aurora	C2
11 Anfitheatro B&B	B3
12 Hotel Gabbia d'Oro	B1

✖ Eating
13 Café Noir	B2
14 Pintxos Bistrot	D2
15 Pizzeria Du de Cope	B2

◎ Drinking
16 Antica Bottega del Vino	C3
17 Caffè Filippini	C1
18 Osteria del Bugiardo	B2

✪ Entertainment
Ente Lirico Arena di Verona	(see 19)
Roman Arena	(see 6)
19 Roman Arena Ticket Office	B4

Cangrande II (1351–59) complicated matters, and the Scaligeri were run out of town in 1387. Venice took definitive control in 1404, ruling until Napoleon's arrival in 1797.

The city became a Fascist control centre from 1938 to 1945, a key location for Resistance interrogation and transit point for Italian Jews sent to Nazi concentration camps. Today, as the city grapples with its changing identity as an Italian, European and international commercial centre, it has become a Lega Nord (Northern League) stronghold. Yet the city is a Unesco World Heritage Site and a cosmopolitan crossroads, especially in summer when the 2000-year-old arena hosts opera's biggest names.

◉ Sights

Roman Arena HISTORICAL BUILDING
(☎045 800 32 04; www.arena.it; Piazza Brà; adult/reduced €6/4.50 or Verona Card; ☺8.30am-7.30pm Tue-Sun, 1.30-7.30pm Mon, last admission 6.30pm) Symbol of Verona, this pink marble amphitheatre was built by Romans in the 1st century AD and survived a 12th-century earthquake to become Verona's legendary open-air opera house, with seating for 30,000 people. It's still at its most spectacular during live performances (see p377).

Castelvecchio MUSEUM
(☎045 806 26 11; Corso Castelvecchio 2; adult/reduced €6/4.50 or Verona Card; ☺8.30am-7.30pm Tue-Sun, 1.30-7.30pm Mon) Built by tyrannical Cangrande II to guard the Adige river, this 1350s fortress was severely damaged by Napoleon's troops and WWII bombings. Architect Carlo Scarpa reinvented the building in the 1960s, placing bridges over exposed foundations, covering bomb blasts with glass panels, and balancing a statue of Cangrande I above the courtyard on a concrete gangplank. Now Verona's main museum, it houses a collection ranging from medieval artefacts to works by Giovanni Bellini, Tiepolo, Carpaccio and Veronese, plus often-excellent temporary shows.

Basilica di San Zeno Maggiore CHURCH
(www.chieseverona.it; Piazza San Zeno; admission €2.50, combined Verona church ticket €6 or Verona Card; ☺8.30am-6pm Tue-Sat, 12.30-6pm Sun Mar-Oct, 10am-1pm & 1.30-5pm Tue-Sat, 12.30-5pm Sun

---

WORTH A TRIP

BASSANO DEL GRAPPA, ASOLO & PALLADIO'S VILLA MASER

A road trip north from Vicenza takes you through one of Italy's most sophisticated stretches of countryside. You can visit all the key sites, even with a latish start and leisurely lunch.

Head first to **Bassano del Grappa**, which sits with charming simplicity on the banks of the Brenta river as it winds its way free from Alpine foothills. Located 35km northeast of Vicenza, the town is famous above all for its namesake spirit, a fiery distillation of leftovers from winemaking: skins, pulp, seeds and stems. The town's most important structure is the **Ponte degli Alpini** (aka Ponte Vecchio), the covered bridge designed by Palladio. At the **Poli Museo della Grappa** (☎0424 52 44 26; www.poligrappa.com; Via Gamba 6; admission free; ☺9am-7.30pm), you can drink in four centuries' history of Bassano's signature grappa (including a free tasting). Before heading out of time, have lunch at the brightly contemporary **Ristorante Al Ponte** (☎0424 21 92 74; www.alpontedibassano. com; Via Volpato 60; meals €35-50; ☺lunch Wed-Sun, dinner Tue-Sun), with its seasonal menu, long wine list, garden seating and perfect river views.

About 17km east of Bassano rises **Asolo**, known as the 'town of 100 vistas' for its panoramic hillside location, once the haunt of Romans and Veneti and a personal gift from Venice to Caterina, 15th-century queen of Cyprus, in exchange for her abdication. An historical hit with writers, including Pietro Bembo, Gabriele d'Annunzio and Robert Browning, its highbrow heritage outstrips its small size.

Another 5km east lies Villa **Villa Maser** (☎423 92 30 04; www.villadimaser.it; adult/reduced €6/5; ☺10am-6pm Tue-Sat, 11am-6pm Sun Apr-Jun & Sep-Oct, 10.30am-6pm Tue, Thu & Sat, 11am-6pm Sun Mar & Jul-Aug, 11am-5pm Sat-Sun Nov-Feb), where Palladio and Paolo Veronese conspired to create the Veneto countryside's finest monument to *la bella vita*. Palladio set the arcaded yellow villa into a verdant hillside with a fanciful grotto out the back. Inside Paolo Veronese nearly upstages his collaborator with wildly imaginative trompe l'œil architecture of his own. Vines climb the walls of the Stanza di Baccho; an alert watchdog keeps one eye on the painted door of the Stanza di Canuccio (Little Dog Room); and in a corner of the frescoed grand salon, the painter has apparently forgotten his spattered shoes and broom.

Nov-Feb) This masterpiece of Romanesque architecture was begun in the 12th century to honour the city's patron saint. Its vast nave is lined with 12th- to 15th-century frescoes, including Mary Magdalene modestly covered in a curtain of her own hair and St George casually slaying a dragon atop a startled horse. Mantegna's 1457–59 altarpiece proffers such convincing perspective and textures that you'd swear there were real garlands behind the Virgin's throne. And don't miss the 12-century bronze doors depicting the Wheel of Fortune in meticulous detail. Below the altar, St Zeno's corpse is harboured in a crypt with eerily carved medieval capitals.

Duomo
CHURCH

(www.chieseverona.it; Piazza del Duomo; admission €2.50, combined Verona church ticket €6 or Verona Card; ⊙10am-5.30pm Mon-Sat, 1.30-5.30pm Sun Mar-Oct, 10am-1pm & 1.30-5pm Tue-Sat, 1.30-5pm Sun Nov-Feb) Verona's 12th-century cathedral is a strikingly striped Romanesque building, with polychrome reliefs and bug-eyed statues of Charlemagne's paladins Roland and Oliver by medieval master Nicoló on the west porch. The extravagant interior was frescoed during the 16th to 17th centuries. Near the front door, a chapel by Jacopo Sansovino boasts a vibrant Titian *Ascension*.

Casa di Giulietta
MUSEUM

(Juliet's House; ☑045 803 43 03; Via Cappello 23; adult/reduced €6/4.50 or Verona Card; ⊙8.30am-7.30pm Tue-Sun, 1.30-7.30pm Mon) Never mind that Romeo and Juliet were completely fictional characters, and that there's hardly room for two on the narrow stone balcony: romantics flock to this 14th-century house to add their lovelorn pleas to the graffiti on the courtyard causeway.

Piazza delle Erbe & Piazza dei Signori
HISTORICAL BUILDING

Originally a Roman forum, Piazza delle Erbe is ringed with buzzing cafes and some of Verona's most sumptuous buildings, including the baroque Palazzo Maffei (now a corporate headquarters) at the north end.

Separating Piazza delle Erbe from Piazza dei Signori is the monumental gate known as Arco della Costa, hung with a whale's rib that, according to legend, will fall on the first just person to walk beneath it. So far, it remains intact, despite visits by popes and kings. On the north side of Piazza dei Signori stands Verona's early-Renaissance Loggia del Consiglio, the 15th-century city council building (not open to visitors). Through the archway at the far end of the piazza are the open-air Arche Scaligere – elaborate Gothic tombs of the Scaligeri family where murderers are interred next to the relatives they killed.

Between the two piazzas, the striped Torre dei Lamberti (☑045 927 30 27; adult/reduced €6/4.50 or Verona Card; ⊙8.30am-7.30pm Oct-May, to 8.30pm Jun-Sep) rises a neck-craning 85m. Begun in the 12th century and finished in 1463 – too late to notice Venetians invading – this watchtower still offers panoramic views.

Scavi Scaligeri
MUSEUM

(☑045 800 74 90; Cortile del Tribunale; adult/reduced €6/4.50 or Verona Card; ⊙vary) Below the Piazza dei Signori lies these labyrinthine Roman ruins excavated in the 1980s. They now house well-curated contemporary photography exhibitions. Galleries close between exhibitions, and opening times vary.

Jewish Ghetto
LANDMARK

Southwest of Piazza delle Erbe lies Verona's historical Jewish district. On the southeast side of Via Rosani is Verona's newly restored synagogue, where you might find the doors open to Jewish visitors and others who express a sincere interest.

⭐ Festivals & Events

VinItaly
WINE

(www.vinitaly.com) Held in March, the country's largest wine expo is open only to food and wine professionals. The event includes tastings, presentations about winemaking and unmatched insight into the breadth and depth of Italian wines.

🛏 Sleeping

Cooperativa Albergatori Veronesi
(☑045 800 98 44; www.veronapass.com) offers a no-fee booking service for two-star hotels. For homestyle stays outside the city centre, check Verona Bed & Breakfast (www.bedandbreakfastverona.com).

Anfitheatro B&B
B&B €€

(☑347 248 84 62; www.anfiteatro-bedandbreakfast.com; Via Alberto Mario 5; s €60-90, d €80-130, tr €100-150) This recently restored 19th-century town house offers spacious guestrooms with high wood-beamed ceilings, antique armoires and divans for swooning after shows at the nearby Roman Arena.

Albergo Aurora
B&B €€

(☎045 59 47 17; www.hotelaurora.biz; Piazza XIV Novembre 2; s €90-135, d €100-160; ❄) Right off bustling Piazza Erbe, this hotel has spacious, unfussy doubles, some with city views. There are cheaper single rooms without bathroom (€58 to €80).

Hotel Gabbia d'Oro
HOTEL €€€

(☎045 59 02 93; www.hotelgabbiadoro.it; Corso Porta Borsari 4a; d from €220; P❄@⊕) One of the city's top addresses and one of its most romantic, the Gabbia d'Oro features luxe rooms inside an 18th-century *palazzo* that manages to be both elegant and cosy. The rooftop terrace and central location are icing on this wedding cake.

Villa Francescati
HOSTEL €

(☎045 59 03 60; www.ostelloverona.it; Salita Fontana del Ferro 15; dm €18-20; ⊙7am-midnight) This HI youth hostel is housed in a 16th-century villa on a garden estate a 20-minute walk from central Verona. Catch bus 73 (weekdays) or bus 90 (Sunday and holidays) from the train station. Rooms must be vacated between 9am and 5pm. Reserve ahead during summer opera season.

Camping Castel San Pietro
CAMPGROUND €

(☎045 59 20 37; www.campingcastelsanpietro.com; Via Castel San Pietro 2; camping adult/reduced/tent €7/4.50/7; ⊙May-Sep) This leafy campground is a stone's throw from town, with a minimarket, washing machines and other mod cons. Catch bus H or 95 from the train station.

🍴 Eating

🍦 Gelateria Ponte Pietra
GELATERIA €

(☎340 471 72 94; Via Ponte Pietra 23; ⊙2.30-7.30pm, to 10pm Jun-Aug, closed Nov-Feb) Impeccable gelato made on premises includes *bacio bianco* (white chocolate and hazelnut) and *mille fiori* (cream with honey and bits of pollen gathered from local hillsides).

Pintxos Bistrot
GASTRONOMIC €€€

(☎045 59 42 87; www.ristorantealcristo.it; Piazzetta Pescheria 6; meals €40-60; ⊙lunch & dinner Tue-Sun) Inspired by Catalan tapas, this airy bistro offers an excitingly eclectic menu mixing Italian pasta, Catalan cheeses and hams, and small-plate dishes perfumed with exotic ingredients like lemon grass and tamarind. A local foodie favourite, it gets packed during the summer opera season. Look for the sign for Ristorante al Cristo, which shares the premises.

VeronaCard (2/5 days €15/20), available at tourist sights as well as tobacconists, grants access to most major monuments and churches (including all listed in this book), plus unlimited use of town buses.

Pizzeria Du de Cope
PIZZERIA €

(☎045 59 55 62; www.pizzeriadudecope.it; Galleria Pellicciai 10; pizzas €6-12; ⊙noon-2pm & 7-11pm) This fashion-forward pizzeria manages to blend refinement with a relaxed ease in its airy and vividly coloured dining space. Wood-fired pizzas from the wood-burning oven are excellent.

Café Noir
CAFE €

(☎045 803 05 00; Via Pellicciai 12; meals €10-15; ⊙7.30am-7.30pm Mon-Sat) In addition to excellent coffee, teas and wickedly thick hot chocolate, this trim little cafe serves up economical two-course lunches for under €12. No dinner.

🍷 Drinking

Antica Bottega del Vino
WINE BAR

(☎045 800 45 35; www.bottegavini.it; Vicolo Scudo di Francia 3; ⊙lunch & dinner Wed-Mon) Wine is the primary consideration at this historical *enoteca* with beautiful wood panelling, backlit bottles of Valpolicella and fine spirits.

Osteria del Bugiardo
WINE BAR

(☎045 59 18 69; Corso Portoni Borsari 17a; ⊙11am-11pm, to midnight Fri & Sat) On busy Corso Portoni Borsari, traffic converges at Bugiardo for glasses of upstanding Valpolicella bottled specifically for the *osteria*. Polenta and *sopressa* make worthy bar snacks for the powerhouse Amarone.

Caffè Filippini
BAR

(☎045 800 45 49; Piazza delle Erbe 26; ⊙4pm-2am Thu-Tue) On the town's most bustling square, the hippest joint in town has been here since 1901, perfecting the house speciality Filippini, a killer cocktail of vermouth, gin, lemon and ice. Open daily June to August.

⭐ Entertainment

Roman Arena (☎045 800 51 51; www.arena.it; Piazza Brà, ticket office Ente Lirico Arena di Verona, Via Dietro Anfiteatro 6b; tickets €15-150; ⊙opera season

Jun–Aug) This is where Placido Domingo made his debut, and the annual June–August opera season includes 50 performances by the world's top names. In winter months, classical concerts are held across the way at the 18th-century Ente Lirico Arena di Verona.

ℹ Information

Ospedale Borgo Trento (🕿045 807 11 11; Piazza A Stefani) Hospital northwest of Ponte Vittoria.

Police (🕿113; Lungadige Galtarossa 11) Near Ponte Navi.

Tourist office (www.tourism.verona.it) Verona-Villafranca airport (🕿045 861 91 63; ⏲10am-3pm Mon-Sat); Via degli Alpini (🕿045 806 86 80; Via degli Alpini 9; ⏲10am-1pm & 2-6pm Mon-Tue, 9am-6pm Wed-Sat, 10am-4pm Sun, shorter hr Jan & Feb)

ℹ Getting There & Around

AIR **Verona-Villafranca airport** (🕿045 809 56 66; www.aeroportoverona.it) is 12km outside town and accessible by ATV Aerobus to/from the train station (€5, 15 minutes, every 20 minutes 6.30am to 11.30pm). Flights arrive from all over Italy and some European cities, including Amsterdam, Barcelona, Berlin, Brussels, Dusseldorf, London and Paris.

BUS The main intercity bus station is in front of the train station in the Porta Nuova area. Buses run to Padua, Vicenza and Venice.

AVT (www.atv.verona.it) city buses 11, 12, 13 and 14 (bus 91 or 92 on Sunday and holidays) connect the train station with Piazza Brà. Buy tickets from newsagents and tobacconists before you board the bus (tickets one hour/day €1.20/3.50).

TRAIN There are at least three trains hourly to Venice (€6.35 to €20, 1¼ to 2½ hours), Padua (€5.10 to €16, 40 to 90 minutes) and Vicenza (€4 to €14, 30 minutes to one hour). There are also services at least hourly to Milan (€9.50 to €19, 1½ to two hours), and regular services to Florence (€21 to €35, 1½ to three hours) and points south, as well as direct international services to Austria, Switzerland and Germany.

Verona's Wine Country

A drive through Verona's hinterland is a lesson in fine wine. To the north and northwest are Valpolicella vineyards, which pre-date the arrival of the Romans, and east on the road to Vicenza lie the white-winemakers of Soave.

SOAVE

Southeast of Verona, Soave serves its namesake DOC white in a storybook setting. The town may be entirely encircled by medieval fortifications, including 24 bristling watchtowers, but these days strangers are more than welcome to taste the good stuff. To get here, hop onto the Milan–Venice train to San Bonifacio (€2.35 to €3.55, 20 minutes) and catch the local ATV bus 30 (€1.50, 10 minutes, about two hourly), or exit the A4 autostrada at San Bonifacio and follow the Viale della Vittoria 2km north into town.

◎ Sights

Castello di Soave   HISTORICAL BUILDING
(🕿045 768 00 36; www.castellodisoave.it; admission €6; ⏲9am-noon & 3-6pm Tue-Sun Apr–mid-Oct, to 5pm mid-Oct–Mar) Built on a medieval base by Verona's fratricidal Scaligeri family, the **castello** complex encompasses an early-Renaissance villa, grassy courtyards, the remnants of a Romanesque church and the Mastio – a defensive tower apparently used as a dungeon (during restoration, a mound of human bones was unearthed here).

Azienda Agricola Coffele   WINERY
(🕿045 768 00 07; www.coffele.it; Via Roma 5; ⏲9am-12.30pm & 2-7pm Mon-Sat & by appointment) Across from the church in the old town, this family-run winery offers tastings of lemon-zesty DOC Soave Classico and nutty, faintly sweet bubbly DOCG (guaranteed-quality) Recioto di Soave. The family also rent rooms among vineyards a few kilometres from town.

Suavia   WINERY
(🕿045 767 50 89; www.suavia.it; Via Centro 14, Fitta; ⏲9am-1pm & 2.30-6pm Mon-Fri, 9am-1pm Sat & by appointment) Soave is not known as a complex white wine, but this trailblazing winery, 8km outside Soave via SP39, is changing the equation. Don't miss DOC Monte Carbonare Soave Classico, with its mineral, ocean-breeze finish.

🛏 Sleeping & Eating

TOP
CHOICE **Locanda Lo Scudo**   MODERN ITALIAN €€
(🕿045 768 07 66; www.loscudo.vr.it; Via Covergnino 9; meals €35-45; ⏲lunch & dinner Tue-Sat) Just outside the medieval walls, Lo Scudo is half country inn and half high-powered gastronomy. Arrive early and order quickly – or miss out on daily fish specials or risotto made with Verona's zesty Monte Veronese cheese. Above the restaurant, the owners rent out four bright, lovely rooms (singles/doubles €75/110) that continue the theme of countrified sophistication. Both restaurant and hotel close in August.

Trattoria Dal Moro TRADITIONAL ITALIAN €
(☎045 768 0204; Viale della Vittoria 3; meals €12-
25; ⊗lunch & dinner Tue-Sat, closed Aug) Head
here for honest home cooking just outside
the city's main gates. The lunchtime menu
nets you an honest plate of pasta, a meat
course and a drink for just €12.

Caffé Cremeria Mattielli GELATERIA €
(☎340 1449038; http://cremeriamattielli.com; Via
Roma 16; ⊗7.30am-12.30pm & 2.30-7.30pm Thu-
Tue, to 11pm Jun-Aug) Top-notch gelati, including ambitious daily specials like celery and
goat cheese.

VALPOLICELLA
Just a dozen kilometres northwest of Verona, you'll find some of Italy's most celebrated vineyards just as the Veneto plains
give way to the foothills of the Alps. Most
famous for Amarone – an intense red made
from partially dried grapes – the best of
Valpolicella's terroirs in 2009 won DOCG
status, Italy's highest mark of oenological
distinction. Note that many wineries are
open only by appointment, and most close
on Sunday. Points of interest are spread
out, so it's best to visit with wheels, whether car or bike.

By car, follow the SS12 highway northwest
out of Verona, veer north onto SP4 and follow the route west towards San Pietro in
Cariano, the region's main hub. Alternatively, APT bus 3 departs Verona's Porta Nuova
for San Pietro about every half-hour (www.
apt.verona.it, in Italian; €2.40, 40 minutes).
For tourist information, visit the Pro Loco
Valpolicella tourist office (☎045 770 19 20;
www.valpolicellaweb.it; Via Ingelheim 7; ⊗9am-1pm
Mon-Fri, 9am-noon Sat) for information about
visiting wineries, as well as information
about biking and hiking.

In San Pietro in Cariano, you can swing
by Montecariano Cellars (☎045 683 83
35; www.montecariano.it; Via Valena 3; ⊗by appointment Mon-Sat) off central Piazza San Giuseppe to sample award-winning Amarone.

Foodies head north to the little town of
Fumane, where Enoteca della Valpolicella (☎045 683 91 46; Via Osan 47; meals €25-35;
⊗lunch & dinner Tue-Sat, lunch Sun) keeps flavours pure (eg risotto with wild herbs, and
game with polenta) so as not to compete
with 700 Italian wines on the menu. If Bacchus leaves you wobbly, it's a short crawl
to the delightful La Meridiana B&B (☎045
683 91 46; www.lameridiana-valpolicella.it, in Italian; Via Osan 16c; s/d €70/90), a 1600s stable

converted into simple but elegant guestrooms by the owners of the *enoteca*. Bonuses include tasty breakfasts and a swimming
pool 1km away.

A few kilometres west of San Pietro,
Gargagnago is known for Amarone, and if
you call ahead, you can taste excellent DOC
Amarone and lighter DOC Valpolicella reds
outside Gargagnano at Corte Leardi Winery (☎045 770 13 79; www.cortealeardi.com; Via
Giare 15; ⊗by appointment).

A short ride (or well-marked 5km, two-
hour hike) west takes you through the hillside town of Sant'Ambrogio di Valpolicella and onward to the picturesque, hilltop
village of San Giorgio, with its fresco-filled,
cloistered 8th-century Romanesque Pieve
di San Giorgio (⊗7am-6pm), on a little
square littered with remnants of a Roman
settlement.

Dolomites
Whether you get high on skiing, Alpine hiking or premium *prosecco*, head for Veneto's
mountain border with Trentino-Alto Adige.

CONEGLIANO
POP 35,700
At the foothills of the Alps, Conegliano is
the toast of the Veneto. Its hillsides produce
prosecco, a dry, crisp white wine made from
prosecco grapes in *spumante* (bubbly), *friz-
zante* (sparkling) or still varieties. Conegliano's *prosecco* was promoted to DOCG
status in 2009, Italy's highest oenological
distinction. Plot a tasting detour along
the Strada di Prosecco (Prosecco Rd) from
Conegliano to the Valdobbiadene at www.
coneglianovaldobbiadene.it, or head to
Conegliano's APT tourist office (☎0438 212
30; Via XX Settembre 61; ⊗9am-12.30pm Tue-Sun,
3-6pm Thu-Sun).

Along Via XX Settembre in the centre
of town, you can't miss the eye-catching
Scuola dei Battuti, covered inside and out
with 16th-century frescoes by Ludovico Poz-
zoserrato. This building was once home to a
religious lay group known as *battuti* (beat-
ers) for their enthusiastic self-flagellation.
Enter the Duomo through the Scuola to discover early works by Veneto artists, notably
a 1492–93 altarpiece by local master Cima
da Conegliano.

If you decide to spend the night, Hotel Canon d'Oro (☎0438 342 46; www.hotel
canondoro.it; Via XX Settembre 131; d from €130;
⊗7am-midnight) provides classic elegance and

VENICE & THE VENETO DOLOMITES

modern comforts in a 15th-century *palazzo*. **La Tartare dell'Hotel Cristallo** (☎0438 354 45; www.hotelcristallo.tv.it; Corso Mazzini 45; meals around €50; ☺lunch & dinner Tue-Sun) is beloved by locals for its rustic elegance in both menu and decor, with a fusion of ingredients from the rich Veneto plains and the nearby Alps.

BELLUNO
POP 36,600 / ELEV 390M

Perched on high bluffs above the Piave river and backed majestically by snowcapped Dolomites, Belluno makes a scenic and strategic base to explore the surrounding mountains. The historical old town is its own attraction, with easy walks past Renaissance-era buildings in the long shadow of the Dolomites. And you'll be happy to fuel up for tramps in the nearby mountains with the city's mountain-based cuisine (think hearty polenta, wild game and mushrooms), and some of Italy's most remarkable cheeses, including Schiz (semi-soft cow's milk cheese, usually fried in butter) and the flaky, butter-yellow Malga Bellunense.

◉ Sights & Activities

Belluno's main pedestrian square is the **Piazza dei Martiri** (Martyrs' Square), named after the four partisans hanged here in WWII. Nearby, the **Piazza del Duomo** is framed by the early-16th-century Renaissance **Cattedrale di San Martino**, the 16th-century **Palazzo Rosso** and the **Palazzo dei Vescovi**, with a striking 12th-century tower.

Parco Nazionale delle Dolomiti Bellunesi   NATIONAL PARK
(www.dolomitipark.it) Northwest of Belluno, this is a splendid national park that offers trails, wildflowers and crisp mountain air. As a result of the beauty of the region and the uniqueness of its ecosystem, vast swaths of it have been granted Unesco World Heritage status. Between late June and early September, hikers test their strength on the six different *alte vie delle Dolomiti* (high-altitude walking trails).

🛏 Sleeping & Eating

To explore hotel, B&B, camping and *agriturismo* (farm stay accommodation) options in Belluno, the Parco Nazionale and beyond, check www.infodolomiti.it.

TOP CHOICE Azienda Agrituristica Sant'Anna   AGRITURISMO €
(☎0437 274 91; www.aziendasantanna.it; Via Pedecastello 27, Castion; d per night €50-80, per week €330-460) This idyllic stone farmhouse 4km outside Belluno proffers mod cons without losing rustic charms: think iron bedsteads, timber floors and beamed ceilings, all with shared or private kitchens. Enthusiastic, English-speaking hosts happily point visitors towards hiking and eating options, and also offer hands-on classes in agricultural practices on the adjacent farm. No breakfast.

Ostello Imperina   HOSTEL €
(☎0437 624 51; www.parks.it/ost/imperina; Località Le Miniere; dm/half-/full board €20/37/50; ☺7.20am-10pm Apr-Oct) The area's only youth hostel lies inside the Parco Nazionale delle Dolomiti Bellunesi, 35km northwest of Belluno at Rivamonte Agordino. Book ahead in summer. To get there, take the Agordo bus (50 minutes) from Belluno.

Albergo Cappello e Cadore   HOTEL €
(☎0437 94 02 46; www.albergocappello.com; Via Ricci 8; s €45-75, d €90-103; P🖳) At this rose-coloured, 19th-century inn just off Piazza dei Martiri, guestrooms are small and monastery-modest, with plain pine bedsteads. A few top-floor rooms have views. Reserve ahead, as this is the only affordable option in town.

TOP CHOICE Al Borgo   TRADITIONAL ITALIAN €€
(☎0437 92 67 55; www.alborgo.to; Via Anconetta 8; meals around €35; ☺lunch Wed-Mon, dinner Wed-Sun) If you have wheels or strong legs, seek out this delightful restaurant in an 18th-century villa in the hills about 3km south of Belluno. Considered Belluno's best, the kitchen produces everything from homemade salamis and roast lamb to artisanal gelato.

La Taverna   ITALIAN €€
(☎0437 251 92; Via Cipro 7; meals €25-30; ☺lunch & dinner Mon-Sat) Taverna's bar serves top-notch seasonal bruschetta with *prosecco* or other local wines. In the dining room, carb-load for your hike with fresh porcini *tagliolini*, or try Taverna's seasonal specialities like wintertime eel with snails or springtime rabbit with zucchini flowers.

❶ Information

Tourist office (☎0437 94 00 83; www.info dolomiti.it; Piazza del Duomo 2; ☺9am-12.30pm & 3.30-6.30pm Mon-Sat) Information on skiing, hiking and other sporting activities, plus weather conditions and advisories.

❶ Getting There & Away

By car, take the A27 from Venice (Mestre) – it's not the most scenic route, but avoids traffic around Treviso.

BUS In front of the train station, **Dolomiti Bus** (☑0437 21 71 11; www.dolomitibus.it) offers regular service to Cortina d'Ampezzo, Conegliano and smaller mountain towns.

TRAIN Services from Venice (€6, two to 2½ hours, five to 10 daily) run here via Treviso and/ or Conegliano. Some require a change, which can add another hour.

CORTINA D'AMPEZZO
POP 6100 / ELEV 1224M

The Italian supermodel of ski resorts, Cortina d'Ampezzo is fashionable, pricey, icy and undeniably beautiful. The town's stone church spires and pleasant piazzas are framed by magnificent Alps. It doubles as a slightly less glamorous but still stunning summertime base for hiking, biking and rock-climbing.

🏃 Activities

Winter crowds arrive in December for top-notch downhill and cross-country skiing facilities and stay until late March or April. Summertime adventurers hit Cortina for climbing and hiking from June until October. Two cable cars whisk skiers and walkers from Cortina's town centre to a central departure point for chairlifts, cable cars and trails. Lifts usually run from 9am to 5pm daily mid-December to April and resume June to September or October.

Ski and snowboard runs range from bunny slopes to the legendary Staunies black mogul run, which starts at 3000m. The Dolomiti Superski pass (see the boxed text, p285) provides access to 12 runs in the area, and are sold at Cortina's **ski pass office** (☑0436 86 21 71; Via G Marconi 15; 1-/2-/3-day €46/91/132, week pass €247; ⊙vary). Passes with more limited access starting at €28 per day.

Other winter adventures in Cortina include dogsledding, ice-climbing and skating at the **Olympic Ice Stadium** (☑0436 88 18 11; Via dello Stadio 1; adult/child incl skate rental €10/9; ⊙vary), built for the 1956 Winter Olympics.

Gruppo Guide Alpine Cortina (☑0436 86 85 05; www.guidecortina.com; Corso Italia 69a) runs rock-climbing courses (three-day climbing course including gear rental €260), mountain-climbing and guided nature hikes (prices vary). In winter it also offers courses in off-trail skiing, snowshoeing and more.

🛏 Sleeping & Eating

Cortina's pedestrian centre is ringed with pizzerias and cafes, which are your best bets for reasonable eats. For additional sleep options, consult www.infodolomiti.it. Note that prices vary widely with the seasons, and

spike wildly at the Christmas holidays. Many places close in April, May and/or November.

TOP CHOICE Baita Fraina INN €€
(☑0436 36 34; www.baitafraina.it; d summer/ winter €50/65, Jan-Nov €60-100, Dec €100-140; P) Reserve ahead in high season at this beloved, Swiss-style inn with simple but spotless rooms of knotty pine. The fine restaurant has a menu inspired by local ingredients, from mountain herbs to wild game.

Hotel Montana HOTEL €
(☑0436 86 21 26; www.cortina-hotel.com; s €52-65, d €88-97; @ 🕙) Right in the heart of Cortina, this friendly, vintage 1920s Alpine hotel offers simple but well-maintained rooms. In winter, there's a seven-night minimum (€310 to €580 per person), but call for last-minute cancellations. Reception areas double as gallery space for local artists.

International Camping Olympia CAMPGROUND €
(☑0436 50 57; www.campingolympiacortina.it; camping adult €6-10, tent & car €9-10; P) Sleep beneath towering pines 4km north of Cortina in Fiames, with free shuttles to town and on-site pizzeria, market, laundry and sauna.

Il Meloncino TRADITIONAL ITALIAN €€
(☑0436 44 32; www.ilmeloncino.it; Locale Rumerlo 1; meals €50-60; ⊙lunch & dinner Wed-Mon) With a rustically elegant dining room and spectacular terrace seating when weather permits, Il Meloncino proffers local specialities that are as jaw-dropping as the Alpine views, including roasted boar and venison-stuffed ravioli in a hazelnut sauce. Note that it is a short ride or 15-minute hike uphill from central Cortina.

❶ Information

Tourist office (☑0436 32 31; www.info dolomiti.it; Piazzetta San Francesco 8; ⊙9am-12.30pm & 3.30-6.30pm Mon-Sat)

❶ Getting There & Away

The following companies operate out of Cortina's **bus station** (Via G Marconi).

Cortina Express (☑0437 86 73 50; www. cortinaexpress.it) Daily direct services to Mestre train station (2¼ hours) and Venice airport (two hours).

Dolomiti Bus (☑0437 21 71 11; www.dolomiti bus.it) For smaller mountain towns, Belluno and other Veneto locales.

SAD buses (☑0471 45 01 11; www.sad.it) Services to nearby towns, Bolzano and other Alto Adige destinations.

Friuli Venezia Giulia

POP 1.23 MILLION / AREA 7845 SQ KM

Includes »

Best Places to Eat

» La Frasca p398)
» Pirona (p391)
» Salumare (p391)

Best Places to Stay

» L'Albero Nascosto (p390)
» Palazzo Lantieri (p397)
» Hotel Clocchiatti Next (p404)

Why Go?

With its triple-barrelled moniker, Friuli Venezia Giulia's multifaceted nature should come as no surprise. Cultural complexity is cherished in this small, little-visited region, tucked away on Italy's far northeastern borders with Austria and Slovenia. Friuli Venezia Giulia's landscapes offer profound contrasts too, with the foreboding, perpetually snowy Giulie and Carnic Alps in the north, idyllic grapevine-filled plains in the centre, the south's Venetian-like lagoons and beaches and the curious, craggy karst encircling Trieste.

While there's an amazing reserve of often uncrowded historical sights, from Roman ruins to Austro-Hungarian palaces, this is also a fine destination for simply kicking back with the locals, tasting the region's world-famous wines and discovering a culinary heritage that will broaden your notions of Italian cuisine. Serene, intriguing Trieste and friendly, feisty Udine make for great city time – they're so easy and welcoming you'll feel as if you're Friulian, Venezian or Giulian too.

When to Go

Trieste

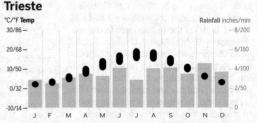

Feb Discover the uncrowded slopes and low-key ski resorts of the Giulie Alps.

Jun Fill up on prosciutto at San Daniele's Aria di Festa.

Oct Watch sails fill the horizon at Trieste's Barcolana Regatta.

History

The semi-autonomous region of Friuli Venezia Giulia came into being as recently as 1954; its new capital, Trieste, had already traded national allegiances five times since the beginning of the century. Such is the region's history, a rollicking, often blood-stained one of boom, bust and conquest that began with the Romans in Aquileia, saw Cividale rise to prominence under the Lombards, and witnessed the Venetians do their splendid thing in Pordenone and Udine. It was Austria, however, that established the most lasting foothold, with Trieste as its main seaport. While the region today is a picture of quiet prosperity, much of the 20th century was another story. War, poverty and political uncertainty saw Friulians become the north's largest migrant population, most bound for Australia and Argentina.

Friuli Venezia Giulia Highlights

❶ Commune with the literary ghosts in **Trieste's grand cafes** (boxed text, p394)

❷ Spot lynx and marmot in the wilds of the **Carnic Alps** (p407)

❸ Picture a 4th-century-AD Roman port as you wander **Aquileia's ruins** (p399)

❹ Sip Friulano and scoff a *frico* (thick cheese-and-potato omelette) in one of Udine's friendly **wine bars** (p404)

❺ Marvel at an 8th-century Lombard chapel in **Cividale del Friuli** (p406)

❻ Stroll the lively old town of sun-drenched beach resort **Grado** (p399)

❼ Straddle the cold war border and discover a glorious (and sometimes gory) past in **Gorizia** (p396)

❽ Ski across borders at **Sella Nevea** (p408)

ⓘ FVG CARD

This discount card (48hr/72hr/7 days €15/20/29) gives free admission to all civic museums; free transport in Udine, Lignano and on the Udine–Cividale del Friuli train; free audio tours; and numerous discounts in the region's shops, spas, beaches and parks. The cards are available from all FVG tourist offices, online and at many hotels (see the website for the full list).

ⓘ Getting There & Around

Most of the region's major destinations can be reached by train or road from Venice in around two hours. **Friuli Venezia Giulia airport** (www. aeroporto.fvg.it; Via Aquileia 46), aka Ronchi dei Legionari or Trieste Regional Airport, is 33km northwest of Trieste, near Monfalcone, with daily flights from Rome, London, Munich and Frankfurt, and less-frequent services to and from Belgrade and Tirana. The Austrian cities of Salzburg and Graz are around four hours' drive from Udine.

Trieste

POP 205,523

Trieste, as travel writer Jan Morris once opined, 'offers no unforgettable landmark, no universally familiar melody, no unmistakable cuisine', yet it's a city that enchants many, its 'prickly grace' inspiring a cult-like roll-call of writers, travellers, exiles and misfits. Devotees come to think of its glistening belle époque cafes, dark congenial bars and even its maddening bora wind as their own; its lack of intensive tourism can make this often feel like it's true.

Tumbling down to the Adriatic from a karstic plateau and almost entirely surrounded by Slovenia, the city is physically isolated from the rest of the Italian peninsula. Its historical singularity is also no accident. From as long ago as the 1300s, Trieste has faced east, becoming a free port under Austrian rule. The city blossomed under the 18th- and 19th-century Habsburgs; Vienna's seaside salon was also a fluid borderland where Italian, Slavic, Jewish, Germanic and even Greek culture intermingled.

◉ Sights

Most of Trieste's sights are within walking distance of the city's centre, the vast Piazza dell'Unità d'Italia, or can be accessed by Trieste's efficient bus network.

Piazza dell'Unità d'Italia   PIAZZA

This vast public domain – said to be the biggest square opening onto a waterfront in Italy – is an elegant triumph of Austro-Hungarian town planning and contemporary civil pride. Pristine but perpetually peopled, it's not only a place for a drink or a chat, but also for a quiet moment staring out at ships on the horizon.

Borgo Teresiano   NEIGHBOURHOOD

Much of the graceful city-centre area north of Corso Italia dates to the 18th-century reign of Empress Maria Theresa, including the photogenic Canal Grande. Reflecting centuries of religious tolerance, it's here you'll also find the mosaic-laden Serbian Orthodox Chiesa di Santo Spiridione (1868) juxtaposed with the neoclassical Catholic Chiesa di Sant'Antonio Taumaturgo (1842). On the Via Roma bridge stands a life-sized statue of James Joyce (Piazza Hortis is home to a similar bronze of Italo Svevo).

Castello di San Giusto   MUSEUM

(☑040 30 93 62; Piazza della Cattedrale 3; adult/reduced €4/3; ◷summer 9am-7pm, winter to 1pm) Once a Roman fort, this sturdy 15th-century castle was begun by Frederick of Habsburg and finished off by blow-in Venetians. The city museum is housed here, with temporary exhibitions and a well-stocked armoury. Wander around the walls for magnificent views.

Basilica di San Giusto   CHURCH

(◷8am-5pm) Completed in 1400, this Ravennan-Byzantine hybrid is the synthesis of two earlier palaeo-Christian basilicas. The interior contains 13th-century frescoes and wonderfully preserved 12th- and 13th-century mosaics, including one of St Justus, the town's patron saint.

Synagogue   SYNAGOGUE

(☑040 672 67 36; www.triestebraica.it; Via San Francesco d'Assisi 19; admission €3.50; ◷guided tours 10am, 11am & noon Sun) Testament to the strength of Trieste's Jewish community is this imposing and richly decorated neoclassical synagogue, built in 1912. Heavily damaged during WWII, it has been meticulously restored and remains one of the most important synagogues in Italy.

Roman Trieste   HISTORICAL SITE

Behind Piazza dell'Unità d'Italia rise remains of the **Roman theatre** (Via del Teatro Romano), built between the 1st and 2nd centuries AD, but only uncovered in 1938. The **Arco di Riccardo** (Via del Trionfo) is an earlier Roman remnant, one of the old town gateways, dating from 33 BC; it's named for the English King Richard, who was supposed to have passed through en route from the Crusades.

Museo Revoltella   MUSEUM

(☑040 675 43 50; www.museorevoltella.it; Via Diaz 27; adult/reduced €6.50/4.50; ☺10am-7pm Wed-Mon) This city museum was founded in 1872 and now spills into two neighbouring buildings. Baron Revoltella's original mid-19th-century house throbs with conspicuous consumption; his cup runneth over with chandeliers, ornate gilded plasterwork and flamboyant silk wallpaper. The modern Palazzo Brunner has an interesting collection of 19th- and 20th-century works by Triestine artists, including some arresting early-20th-century portraiture and busts. There's also a pretty rooftop cafe and good bookshop.

Civico Museo Sartorio   MUSEUM

(☑040 30 14 79; Largo Papa Giovanni XXIII 1; adult/child €5/3; ☺9am-1pm Tue-Sun) Another significant city villa, stuffed with art, applied arts and jewellery, and featuring beautiful ceiling frescoes, some dating to the late 18th century, and a basement Roman mosaic. Don't miss the room of superb **Tiepolo drawings**, virtuosic and intimate in turns.

Civico Museo di Storia ed Arte ed Orto Lapidario   MUSEUM

(History & Art Museum & Stone Garden; ☑040 31 05 00; Piazza della Cattedrale 1; adult/reduced €4/3; ☺9am-1pm Tue-Sun) This creaky old museum houses Roman antiquities unearthed in and around Trieste and Aquileia, including the impressive iron horde of the Necropolis of Reka from the Slovenian border. The Orto Lapidario (Stone Garden) has a potluck assembly of weather-resistant stone finds scattered among flowers and fruit trees.

FREE Museo Joyce & Svevo   MUSEUM

(☑040 359 36 06; 2nd fl, Via Madonna del Mare 13; admission free; ☺9am-1pm Mon-Sat, also 3-7pm Thu) Joyce would enjoy the irony: his museum really belongs to friend and fellow literary great, Italo Svevo, housing a significant collection of the Triestini's documents, photos and other memorabilia. Joyce is dealt with ephemerally, with a wall map of his haunts and homes, an English-language film and a Bloomsday bash in June (Svevo's birthday is also celebrated, on December 19).

THE DUBLINER

'Think you're escaping and run into yourself. Longest way round is the shortest way home.'

James Joyce, Ulysses

Stifled by the gloom and obligations of Dublin, James Joyce escaped to Trieste in 1905 with a contract to teach English at the local Berlitz language school. Along with lover (and soon wife) Nora Barnacle, the precocious but still unpublished 22-year-old arrived in a city that epitomised the twilight years of the Austro-Hungarian empire.

Trieste was a booming, brilliantly cosmopolitan place, with a polyglot creative class and no shortage of dissolute aristocrats. The gregarious Irishman wasted no time getting involved in this fertile scene and quickly picked up the floral Triestini dialect. In between his teaching commitments, various failed business ventures, family life and all-night benders, he slowly set about drafting the text of his first two ground-breaking novels, *Dubliners* and *Portrait of the Artist as a Young Man*. Perennially poor, he spent the bulk of his writing hours in the city's fin de siècle cafes, Trieste life all about him.

The Joyces remained in the city until 1915, when the outbreak of WWI forced them to relocate to neutral Zurich. Joyce returned after the war, but he was unimpressed by the brash new order and quickly made tracks for Paris. *Ulysses* may have been given form in the City of Light, but its genesis was undoubtedly in the multilingual melting pot that was pre-WWI Trieste.

Trieste

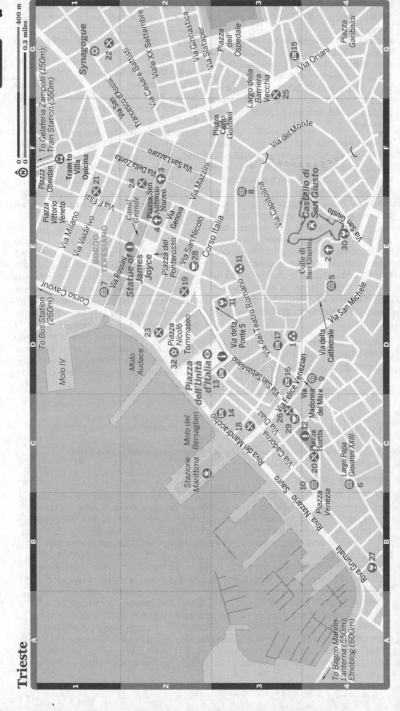

400 m
0.2 miles

To Gelateria Zampolli (150m);
Train Station (550m)

Synagogue

Piazza
dell'
Ospedale

Piazza
Garibaldi

Via Oriani

Via Ginnastica
Viale XX Settembre
Via Cesare Battisti
Via Slataper

Via San Francesco d'Assisi

Largo della
Barriera
Vecchia

Piazza
Oberdan
Tram to
Villa
Opicina

Piazza
Vittorio
Veneto

Piazza
Carlo
Goldoni

Via Della Zonta
Via San Lazzaro

Via del Monte

Via Milano
Via Valdirivo

Via F Filzi

Piazza San
Antonio Nuovo

Canal Grande

Via Mazzini

BORGO
TERESIANO

Via Genova

Via Rossini

Castello di
San Giusto

Via Capitolina

Statue of
James Joyce

Piazza del
Ponterosso

Corso Italia

Colle di
San Giusto

Via San Giusto

Corso Cavour

To Bus Station
(260m)

Via San Nicolò

Via della
Ponte

Via del Teatro Romano

Via San Michele

Via della
Cattedrale

Molo IV

Molo
Audace

Piazza
Nicolò
Tommaseo

Piazza
dell'Unità
d'Italia

Via San Sebastiano

Via San Michele

Molo del
Bersaglieri

Riva del Mandracchio

Madonna
del Mare

Via Felice Venezian

Via
Diaz

Via Cadorna

Stazione
Marittima

Riva Nazario Sauro

Piazza
Hortis

Largo Papa
Giovanni XXIII

Piazza
Venezia

Riva Grimana

To Bagno Marino
Lanterna (550m);
Etnoblog (600m)

No 2 Tram TRAM

(departs from Piazza Oberdan; hourly/daily €1.10/3.60 Trieste Trasporti tickets are valid; ⊘departs half-hourly 7am-8pm) For wonderful sea and city views, jump on the vintage Villa Opicina tram. It's a regular tram for most of the 5km journey, but a funicular section tackles the steep gradient as it heads up into the Carso. It's a short but significant trip; **Villa Opicina** was once almost entirely Slovenian-speaking and today retains a decidedly un-Italian feel. Before you descend, visit **Saint Honore** (Via di Prosecco 2) for its *carsolina,* a walnut-and-almond cake, or a stash of little chocolate trams.

Museo della Comunità Ebraica Carlo e Vera Wagner MUSEUM

(☑040 63 38 19; Via del Monte 5; adult/reduced €5/3; ⊘4-7pm Tue, 10am-1pm & 4-7pm Wed, Thu & Sun) Small, highly prized collection of liturgical items, textiles, documents and photographs, including a touching number of personal items stolen by Nazi troops in 1945.

Civico Museo Teatrale Carlo Schmidl MUSEUM

(☑040 675 40 72; Via Rossini 4; adult/child €3.50/2.50; ⊘9am-7pm Tue-Sun) Trieste's long-standing cultural cred is documented in the grand Palazzo Gopcevich, with a collection that traces the city's rich musical and theatrical heritage from the 18th century onwards.

Activities

Any hint of sun will see the Triestini flock to the concrete platforms along the waterfront **Viale Miramare** (a lot more pleasant than it sounds). For sun-worshipping closer to town, and a dip, head to **Bagno Marino Lanterna** (☑040 30 59 22; Molo Fratelli Bandiera 3; adult €1; ⊘7.30am-7.30pm May-Sep), tucked away behind the city's disused 19th-century lighthouse. It's a living piece of Austro-Hungarian history, its pebbly beach still genteelly gender-segregated.

🛏 Sleeping

Trieste's mid- to high-end places often slash rates on weekends and can be astonishingly

WORTH A TRIP

RISIERA DI SAN SABBA

This former rice-husking plant became Italy's only extermination camp in 1943 and has been a **national monument and museum** (☎040 82 62 02; Via Palatucci 5; admission free; ⊗9am-7pm) since the 1960s.

The site commemorates the 5000 people who perished here and the many thousands more that passed through on the way to Nazi forced labour and death camps. These included a great many of the city's Jewish population along with Triestine and Slovenian Resistance fighters.

Although the death cells remain, most of the camp's horrific wartime structures were destroyed by the retreating German forces in 1945. The monument solemnly traces their outlines in metal and stone, their absence creating areas of reflection. A collection of prisoners' photographs, letters and other artefacts are deeply personal and vividly alive.

Take bus 8 from the train station, or bus 10 from stops along the Riva; from the last bus stop walk past the stadium, turning left into Via Palatucci.

good value, especially compared with other Italian cities.

TOP CHOICE **L'Albero Nascosto** HOTEL €€
(☎040 30 01 88; www.alberonascosto.it; Via Felice Venezian 18; s €70, d €100-125; ❋🛜🖫) A friendly little hotel hidden smack in the middle of the old town, Nascosto exemplifies Trieste's discreet, no-fuss style. Rooms are generously sized and decorated with a vintage piece or two; all except the single have a small kitchen. Breakfasts are similarly simple but thoughtful, with local cheese, top-quality preserves and Illy coffee on tap.

Hotel Savoia Excelsior Palace LUXURY HOTEL €€
(☎040 7 79 41; savoiaexcelsiorpalace.starhotels. com; Riva del Mandracchio 4; d €130-200; ❋🛜) This glamorous 'newcomer' to Trieste's hotel scene, a classic but contemporary (and ever so slightly camp) refit of the great-boned Habsburg-era Grand Hotel, is giving the Duchi a run for its money. Grand it still is, with over 100 light-filled luxurious rooms, first-rate public areas, superb service, sea views and (for the moment at least) unbeatable prices.

Hotel Victoria HOTEL €€
(☎040 36 24 15; www.hotelvictoriatrieste.com; Via Oriani 2; d €100-150; ❋🛜) This is a far-from-bland business-oriented place: there's a crisp Upper East Side aesthetic in the rooms, a guest-only sauna and Turkish bath, and a reading room. James Joyce was once a resident and there are small homages to him throughout the hotel, including a dedicated suite and contemporary art works.

Residence Sara APARTMENT €
(☎327 4475405; www.residencesara.it; Via dei Capitelli 4; s/d/tr/q €50/70/90/100; ❋@) Spread over two quiet but super-central old-town buildings, these apartments are comfortable and great value, with new, if basic, furniture, as well as washing machines, dishwashers and full-sized fridges in the larger ones.

Hotel Miramare HOTEL €€
(☎040 224 70 85; www.hotelmiramaretrieste. it; Viale Miramare 325/1; d €120-140; ℗❋🛜) Beautiful sea views from all rooms, simple beachy design and a well-priced but stylish – love the Cassina leather chairs – restaurant and summery bar.

Grand Hotel Duchi d'Aosta LUXURY HOTEL €€€
(☎040 760 00 11; www.grandhotelduchidaosta. com; Piazza dell'Unità d'Italia 2; €140-259; ❋🛜🏊) There's been a hotel of sorts on this prime site since Roman times and the 'Duchi' remains Trieste's grand dame. Public spaces are hushed and intimate, and the rooms are opulently traditional – the way repeat visitors like them. The bathrooms might be a tad frumpy for some five-star tastes, but the moody basement swimming pool is a good trade-off (the modern Vis a Vis wing is also worth considering).

Ostello Tergeste HOSTEL €
(☎040 22 41 02; www.ostello-trieste.191.it; Viale Miramare 331; dm/d €16/22; ⊗reception 7am-noon & 3.30-11.30pm; 🛜) This HI hostel is 7km northwest of town along the waterfront from Castello di Miramare. The views from the dorm rooms and the terrace bar are fabulous (and almost make up for the

care-worn fittings and noncommittal staff). There's doubles and quads with ensuites as well. From town take bus 36, or, at night, bus 6.

Eating

Trieste's long years as one of Europe's busiest ports, along with its Austrian and Slavic ties, are nowhere clearer than in the kitchen. Seafood is fantastic, with dishes often reminiscent of those in Venice, but the real Trieste memories will come from the *jota* (bean-and-cabbage soup) and boiled meat and *kren* (horseradish), the *putizza* (a nut-filled brioche) and excellently made Illy coffee.

TOP CHOICE Salumare
SEAFOOD €

(www.salumare.it; Via Cavana 13a; meals €18-22; ⊙10.30am-2pm & 5.30-9pm Tue-Sat) This is a bright, buzzing reinvention of the Triestine buffet, featuring fish and seafood. Order at the bar from a menu of small dishes: white polenta and *baccalá mantecato* (salt-cod purée), prawn ceviche, smoked eel and green apple tartines. Wash it down with a Friulian or Veneto wine, or the signature Bellini, made with white peach purée. There's plenty of reasons to linger, starting with the huge library of cookbooks and restaurant guides, and a daily delivery of international newspapers.

Al Bagotto
SEAFOOD €€€

(☑040 30 17 71; www.albagatto.it; Via Cadorna 7; degustations from €50; ⊙dinner Mon-Sat) This old-timer, with its dark, brooding dining room, could be stuffy, but it's far from it, with young, engaging staff and fresh bold flavours on the plate. The seafood *degustazione – fritto misto* (fried seafood) and something involving squid ink will invariably play a part – is daunting but delicious, or order like the suited regulars: the freshest of fish by the *etto* (100g), weighed and filleted at the table.

Buffet da Siora Rosa
BUFFET €€

(☑040 30 14 60; Piazza Hortis 3; meals €25-28; ⊙Mon-Fri) Opened before WWII by Mrs Rosa Caltaruzza – a portrait of whom still graces the wall – the family-run Siora Rosa is still one of the most traditional of Trieste's buffets, set in a wonderfully retro room. Sample sausages, sauerkraut and other Germanic and Hungarian offerings, or go for the ravioli or dumplings.

Buffet Da Pepi
BUFFET €

(Via Cassa di Risparmio 3; meals €15-20; ⊙Mon-Sat) Da Pepi has been concocting traditional boiled meats, cold cuts and beer since – oh – 1897. Come for the pork joints, served up with the house sauerkraut.

Buffet Rudy
BUFFET €

(Via Valdirivo 32; meals €18-22; ⊙10am-midnight Mon-Sat) The counter here is a site of porcine carnage: legs, necks, bellies, tongues and testicles, all awaiting a slap of relish from the huge ceramic jars of mustard, or a grate of *kren*.

Pirona
PASTRIES & CAKES €

(Largo Barriera Vecchia 12; ⊙Tue-Sat) This jewel-box pastry shop and cafe was once one of Joyce's favourites. Its nutty, spicy, boozy Triestine speciality cakes *putizza* and *presnitz* are particularly good.

La Bomboniera
PASTRIES & CAKES €

(Via XXX Ottobre 3a; ⊙closed Sun afternoon & Mon) Viennese-style macaroons and Sachertorte share historic counter space here with the famed *fave dei morti* sweets – broadbean-shaped marzipan.

Gelateria Zampolli
GELATERIA €

(Via Carlo Ghega 10; ⊙9.30am-midnight Thu-Tue) Be prepared for the crowds if you want to sample the city's best gelati: the Sachertorte flavour is a must, and its mousse-style range can't be beaten.

BUFFET BOUNTY

While you'll be sure to eat well, perhaps *extremely* well, at a Triestine buffet, banish any thought of all-you-can-eat meal deals. These rowdy bar-restaurants are yet another legacy of the city's Austro-Hungarian past; if Trieste's bakeries conjure up Vienna, its buffets are Budapest all over. Usually all-day, and night, affairs, small snacks – cod or zucchini fritters, topped toasts and *panini* – are available from early morning and gobbled over lunch or at *aperitivo* time. But no one comes just for zucchini. While beef brisket is a standard, pork – baked, boiled, cured, stuffed into a sausage or fried – is the star attraction. Fresh grated *kren* (horseradish), *capuzi* (sauerkraut) and *patate in tecia* (mashed potatoes) are traditional accompaniments.

Coffee Culture

From Trapani to Tarvisio, every day in Italy begins with coffee. While a quick cup from a stove-top moka pot might be the first, the second (and third and fourth) will inevitably be from a neighbourhood bar. Italians don't linger over coffee – it's a stand-up sniff, swirl and gulp, and a *'Buon proseguimento!'* (have a great day) from the barista.

Coffee first arrived in the mid-16th century in Venice, and a few years later in Trieste, care of the Viennese, who were switched on to the brew after retreating Ottoman armies left their beans behind. While basic espresso technology appeared in the early 19th century, it wasn't until 1948 that Gaggia launched the first commercial machines that produced full-bodied espresso shots with the characteristic *crema:* Italy was hooked.

Best-of lists will only get you so far here. There's as much chance of getting a perfect coffee in a small-town bar as there is in Rome's famed Caffè Sant'Eustachio or Florence's Caffè Gilli. Knowing your bean brands can be a helpful navigation tool. Global giants like Trieste's Illy and Turin's Lavazza, rarely disappoint or seek out local roasters like Verona's Giamaica, Parma's Lady, Turin's Coffee Lab and Pascucci from Le Marche. And while the rest of the world innovates with single-origin beans, latte art and new brewing technologies, tradition holds sway in Italy. Italians wouldn't have it any other way.

BARISTA BASICS

- » **Caffè, espresso** short shot of black coffee
- » **Ristretto** shorter espresso shot
- » **Macchiato** espresso 'stained' with a splash of milk
- » **Cappuccino** espresso with frothed milk
- » **Cappuccino scuro** strong cappuccino
- » **Marochino** small cappuccino with powdered chocolate
- » **Americano** long black coffee
- » **Latte macchiato** small dash of coffee in frothed milk

Clockwise from top left
1. Espresso being made 2. Caffè Sant'Eustachio, Rome
3. Waiter, Perugia 4. Cafe, Rome.

DON'T MISS

BITTER SWEET

Trieste's cafes have never been gulp-and-run affairs. While these grand palaces evoke times past, they're still a thriving, and deeply satisfying, part of daily city life.

Caffè Tommaseo (☎040 36 26 66; www.caffetommaseo.com; Riva III Novembre; meals €22; ⏰8am-12.30am) Virtually unchanged since its 1830 opening, the richly moulded ceilings, primrose-yellow wall and Viennese mirrors here couldn't be any more evocative. Take coffee at the bar, but return for a schnitzel and a chance to linger among the ghosts.

Caffè Torinese (Largo della Barriera Vecchia 12; ⏰Tue-Sun) The most central and, dare we say, friendliest of the historic bunch, this is an exquisite little room that's just as nice for wine as a morning *capo un' b* (macchiato in a glass).

Caffè San Marco (Via Battisti 18; ⏰Tue-Sun) Opening just before WWI, this melancholy giant is spectacularly decorated with odd mask paintings, dark chocolate-coloured walls and miles of marble tables.

Drinking

Cafes, bars and buffets blur in Trieste, as does what constitutes *aperitivo*. Evenings out are a refined, relaxed mix of young and old, though early-evening drinks often stretch well into the night with the help of hearty buffet snacks. Via San Nicolo's bars cater to a smart after-work set, while the old town's cluster of bars are of a more boho bent. In summer, there's come-and-go outdoor places along the Viale Miramare.

Chocolat   CAFE
(Via Cavana 15b; ⏰Tue-Sat) This lovely cafe and chocolate shop makes everything in-house, including the hot chocolate slowly simmering in a great pot behind the counter and, in summer, gelato. Bonus: there's no surcharge for sitting at the big communal table on the square.

Osteria da Marino   WINE BAR
(Via della Ponte 5; ⏰ from 12.30pm Mon-Fri, from 6pm Sat & Sun) They know their wine at this bottle- and barrel-lined place. If you can't make it to the Carso, get the owner to ply you with indigenous grape varieties (its Vitovska selection is encyclopedic). Or just settle in with a Franciacorte sparkling or a Tuscan red and wait for the little meatballs or tomato and *pecorino* (sheep's-milk cheese) toasts to appear.

Grip Wunderbar   BAR
(Via San Giusto 22; ⏰ 7pm-2am Wed-Thu, 7pm-3am Fri & Sat) Booths, beer on tap and vinyl! Yes, Trieste goes indie at this great little corner bar beneath Castello di San Giusto.

Buffet Al Spaceto   BUFFET
(Via Belpoggio 3a; snacks €1.80-3; ⏰8am-8.30pm Mon-Fri, 8am-2pm Sat) An eccentric and convivial grab bag of locals gathers here for glasses of local wine and a few rounds of what's on offer in the snack counter.

☆ Entertainment

Teatro Verdi   OPERA HOUSE
(☎040 672 21 11; www.teatroverdi-trieste.com; Riva III Novembre 1) Trieste's opera house is a little bit Scala and a little bit Fenice (thanks to a pair of duelling architects), but wears the mix well. Don't miss a chance to see a performance here; the Triestini are passionate opera lovers and make a great audience.

Etnoblog   LIVE MUSIC
(www.etnoblog.org; Riva Traiana 1) Check the website for this portside warehouse's calendar of upcoming bands, sometimes international, and not-to-be-sniffed-at DJ sets.

Tours

The tourist office offers two-hour walking tours (⏰10.30am daily Apr-Oct, 10.30am Sat Nov-Mar; €5/free with FVG card; bookings advised) of the city, themed seasonally.

❶ Information

Hospital (☎040 399 11 11; Piazza dell'Ospedale 2)

Police station (☎040 379 01 11; Via Tor Bandena 6)

Tourist office (☎040 347 83 12; Via dell'Orologio 1; ⏰9.30am-7pm Mon-Sat, 9am-1pm Sun)

❶ Getting There & Away

Air
Friuli Venezia Giulia airport (www.aeroporto. fvg.it; Via Aquileia 46), aka Ronchi dei Legionari or Trieste Regional Airport, is 33km northwest of Trieste, near Monfalcone. There are direct daily flights to and from Rome, London, Munich and Frankfurt, and less-frequent services for Belgrade and Tirana. Venice's Marco Polo airport is around two hours away.

Boat
Ferries use the **Stazione Marittima** (ferry terminal; Molo dei Bersaglieri 3) in town. **Agemar** (☏040 36 37 37; Nuova Stazione Marittima – Molo IV) sells tickets for the twice-weekly car ferry to and from Durres in Albania (deck seat one way low/high season €65/80).

From mid-June to late September there are motor-boat services to and from Grado, Lignano and points along the Istrian coast in Slovenia and Croatia; check with the tourist office for the most current seasonal operator.

Bus
National and international services operate from the **bus station** (☏040 42 50 20; Via Fabio Severo 24). Runs include to Udine (€5.70, 1¼ hours, at least hourly) and destinations in Slovenia and Croatia such as Ljubljana (€10, 2¾ hours, once daily Monday to Saturday), Zagreb (€15, five hours, once daily Monday to Saturday) and Dubrovnik (€61.50, 15 hours, once daily). Bus services to Belgrade in Serbia (€55, 10 hours, two days a week) and Sofia in Bulgaria (€54, 16½ hours, daily) are operated by **Florentia Bus** (☏040 42 50 20; www.florentiabus.it).

Train
The **train station** (Piazza della Libertà 8) serves Gorizia (€3.90, 50 minutes, hourly), Udine (€7.25, one to 1½ hours, at least hourly), Venice (€9.40 to €14.85, two hours, at least hourly) and Rome (€85.70, 6½ to 7½ hours; most require a change at Mestre).

❶ Getting Around

Boat
Shuttle boats operated by **Trieste Trasporti** (☏800 016675; www.triestetrasporti.it, in Italian) link the **Stazione Marittima** with Muggia year-round (one way/return €3.50/6.50, 30 minutes, six to 10 times daily). Check for other seasonal services with the tourist office.

Bus
Bus 30 connects the train station with Via Roma and the waterfront; bus 24 runs from the station to Castello di San Giusto; bus 36 links Trieste bus station with Miramare. A one-hour ticket costs €1.10, an all-day ticket €3.60.

---

❶ COFFEE, TRIESTE-STYLE

This `capital has its own, often confounding, naming conventions. For an espresso ask for *un nero*, for a cappuccino, order a caffe latte, for a macchiato order a *capo* – a cappuccino – and, for either in a glass, specify '*un b*' – the 'b' short for *bicchiere*, a glass.

Bus 51 runs to the airport approximately every 30 minutes between 4.30am and 10.35pm from Trieste **bus station** (€5, one hour). Buses are operated by the Gorizia-based **APT** (Azienda Provinciale Trasporti Gorizia; ☏800 955957; www.aptgorizia.it, in Italian).

Taxi
☏040 30 77 30; www.radiotaxitrieste.it; €3 flag fall, €2 surcharge between 10pm and 6am.

Around Trieste

MUGGIA
POP 13,410

The fishing village of Muggia, five kilometres south of Trieste, is the only Italian settlement on the historic Istrian peninsula. Slovenia is just 4km south and Croatia (the peninsula's main occupant) a score more. With its 14th-century castle and semi-ruined walls, the port has a Venetian feel and its steep hills make for lovely views back towards Trieste.

Locals gather over jugs of wine and groaning platters of deer or boar salami at **Pane, Vine e San Daniele** (Piazza Marconi 5; ⊙8am-2pm & 8pm-2am Mon-Sat) on the main square behind the port, or there are a number of seafood restaurants along the waterfront. Boats sail between Muggia and Trieste.

IL CARSO

If Trieste is known for its cultural idiosyncrasy, its hinterland is also fittingly distinct. Dramatically shoehorned between Slovenia and the Adriatic, the Carso (*Karst* in German, *kras* in Slovenian) is a windswept calcareous tableland riddled with caves and sinkholes. This wild landscape has long inspired myths, legends and those of a romantic inclination, while its geology has lent its name – karst – to terrain around the world characterised by soluble limestone or dolomite rock. It's a compelling place to visit in any season but is particularly pretty in spring, when the grey-green hills are speckled with blossom, or in autumn, when the vines and *ruje* – smoke trees – turn crimson and rust, and rural villages sell their wares at *osmize* (roadside shacks).

◉ Sights

Grotta Gigante
CAVE

(☏040 32 73 12; www.grottagigante.it; adult/reduced/child €11/9/8; ☺50min guided tours half-hourly 10am-6pm daily summer, 10-6pm Tue-Sat Apr & Sep, hourly 10am-4pm Oct-Mar) The area's big-ticket attraction is the near Villa Opicina, 5km northeast of Trieste. At 120m high, 280m long and 65m wide, it's one of the largest and most spectacular caves that's accessible on the continent. It's easily reached from Trieste by tram 2 or bus 42.

FREE Casa Carsica
MUSEUM

(☏040 32 71 24; Rupingrande 31; ☺10-11.30am & 3-7pm Sun Apr-Nov) This house museum in Rupingrande recreates a pre-modern Slovenian-speaking Carso. It also organises the plateau's most important folk festival, Nozze Carsiche (*Kraška ohcet;* Karstic Wedding), held every two years for four days at the end of August in a 16th-century fortress in Monrupino.

Castello di Duino
CASTLE

(☏040 20 81 20; www.castellodiduino.it; adult/reduced €7/5; ☺9.30am-5.30pm Wed-Mon Apr-Sep, reduced hours Mar & Oct-Nov) Fourteen kilometres northwest along the coast from Miramare stands this 14th- and 15th-century bastion tumbling picturesquely down the cliff and surrounded by a verdant garden. The Czech poet Rainer Maria Rilke was a guest here from 1911, a melancholy windswept, winter stay which produced the *Duino Elegies*. To get here, take bus 41 from Piazza Oberdan (in Trieste).

Gorizia

POP 35,980 / ELEV 86M

To view its serene modern incarnation, you'd never guess the turmoil of Gorizia's past. An often contested border zone throughout much of its history and the scene of some of the most bitter fighting of WWI's eastern front, it was, most recently, an Iron Curtain checkpoint. The town's name is unmistakably Slovenian in origin and before the outbreak of WWI it was not uncommon to hear conversations in several different languages

– German, Slovenian, Friulian, Italian and Venetian – in the main square.

Gorizia's appeal today lies in its aristocratic ambience, its unique Friulian-Slovenian cooking and its easy access to surrounding countryside, famed for its winemakers and country restaurants.

◉ Sights

Borgo Castello
MUSEUM

(☏0481 53 51 46; Borgo Castello 36; adult/child €3/free, exhibitions €4-9/free; ☺9.30am-1pm & 3-7.30pm Tue-Sun Apr-Oct, 9.30am-6pm Tue-Sun Nov-Mar) Gorizia's main sight is its *castello* (castle) perched atop a knoll-like hill. It has some convincing recreations and a fine wood-panelled great hall. Beneath the main fortress huddle two oddly paired museums. The tragic and often gory history of the WWI Italian-Austrian front is explored at the Museo della Grande Guerra (☏0481 53 39 26; Borgo Castello 13-15; adult/child €3.50/free; ☺9am-7pm Tue-Sun) including a to-scale recreation of a local trench. Then there's fashion: 19th-and early-20th-century finery at the Museo della Moda e delle Arti Applicate (☏0481 53 39 26; Borgo Castello 13-15; admission with Museo della Grande Guerra ticket; ☺9am-7pm Tue-Sun).

Piazza Transalpina
HISTORICAL SITE

One for cold war kids. The Slovenian border – a mere formality since December 2007 – bisects the edge of Gorizia, and you can celebrate Schengen with a bit of border hopscotch at this piazza's centre, while pondering the now crumbling fences, border posts and watchtowers.

Palazzo Coronini Cronberg
PALAZZO

(☏0481 53 34 85; www.coronini.it; Viale XX Settembre 14; adult/reduced €5/3; ☺10am-1pm & 2-7pm Tue-Sun) This 16th-century residence is jammed with antiquities and is surrounded by lush gardens, which are free to visit on their own.

Chiesa di Sant'Ignazio
CHURCH

(Piazza della Vittoria; ☺8am-noon & 3-7pm) Constructed from 1654 to 1724, the onion-shaped domes of this high-baroque church watch over Gorizia's old town square.

🍴 Sleeping & Eating

Cafes and bars can be found on Corso Italia and Via Terza Armata, while the old-town streets below the castle and around the covered food market (Via Verdi 30) are the best places to find casual restaurants.

DON'T MISS

CASTELLO DI MIRAMARE

Sitting on a rocky outcrop 7km from the city, Castello di Miramare (☎040 22 41 43; www.castello-miramare.it; adult/reduced €6/4; ⊙9am-6:30pm) is Trieste's elegiac bookend, the fanciful neo-Gothic home of the hapless Archduke Maximilian of Austria.

Maximilian came to Trieste in the 1850s as the commander-in-chief of Austria's imperial navy, an ambitious young aristocrat known for his liberal ideas. After chancing upon Miramare's site while sailing, he decided to build a home there. In 1864, while work was still in progress, Maximilian was talked into taking up the obsolete crown of Mexico, a reactionary folly that was to end badly. When Benito Juárez re-established republican rule in 1867, Maximilian was shot by a firing squad. His wife, Princess Charlotte of Belgium, was so stricken with grief that she spent the rest of her life believing Maximilian was still alive, and only briefly returned to Miramare.

The house has remained essentially as the couple left it, a reflection of Maximilian's eccentric wanderlust along with the obsessions of the imperial age. A bedroom is modelled to look like a frigate's cabin, there's ornate orientalist salons and a red-lined throne room.

Upstairs, a suite of rooms used by the Anglophile military hero Duke Amadeo of Aosta in the 1930s is also intact; it's interestingly furnished in the Italian rationalist style. Amadeo was to be as ill-fated as Maximilian: appointed viceroy of Ethiopia in 1937, he died five years later in a British POW camp in Kenya.

Maximilian was a keen botanist and the castle is set in 22 hectares of gardens (⊙8am-7pm Apr-Sep, shorter hr rest of year), which burst with the colour and scent of rare and exotic trees.

TOP CHOICE **Palazzo Lantieri**   B&B €€

(☎0481 53 32 84; www.palazzo-lantieri.com; Piazza Sant'Antonio 6; s/d €80/140, apt €200-220; P🅿️🌐🐾) This palazzo stay offers light, spacious antiques-strewn rooms in the main house or self-catering apartments in former farm buildings, all overlooking a glorious Persian-styled garden. Goethe, Kant and Empress Maria Theresa were repeat guests back in the day, but the charming Lantieri family are far from stuck in the past. Their contemporary art commissions mean there's a Michelangelo Pistoletto on the ceiling and a Jannis Kounellis in the attic. Nonguests can arrange guided tours.

Grand Hotel Entourage   HOTEL €€€

(☎0481 55 02 35; www.entouragegorizia.com; Piazza Sant'Antonio 2; s/d €105/200; P✳️@) Well-mannered traditional hotel that's every inch the Mitteleuropean, with sunny yellow walls, Biedermeier-style furniture and oak floors. The hotel's Michelin-starred Avenanti (dinner Tue-Sat, lunch Sun) is the town's best restaurant.

Flumen B&B   B&B €

(☎0481 39 18 77; www.bbflumen.it; Via Brigata Cuneo 20; s €35-50, d €60-95; P🖥️) Solid, simple and cosy, this quintessentially Friulian riverside house has three pleasant, spacious rooms with modern bathrooms. It's a little out of the centre but makes a good base if you're driving.

Majda   GORIZIAN €€

(☎0481 3 08 71; Via Duca D'Aosta 71; meals €20-30; ⊙Mon-Sat) With a courtyard bar, friendly staff and enthusiastic decor, Majda is a happy place to sample local specialities such as ravioli with beetroot and local herbs or Slovenian-style with potato; wild boar on polenta; and interesting sides like steamed wild dandelion.

Pasticeria Centrale   PASTRIES & CAKES

(Via Garibaldi 4a; ⊙7.30am-7.30pm Mon-Sun) No visit to Gorizia would be complete without tasting the town's signature pastry, *gubana*, a fat snail of shortcrust filled with nuts, sultanas and spices.

ℹ️ Information

Tourist office (☎0481 53 57 64; Corso Italia 9; ⊙9.30am-6.30pm)

ℹ️ Getting There & Away

The **train station** (Piazzale Martiri Libertà d'Italia), 2km southwest of the centre, has regular connections to and from Udine (€3.30, 25 to 40 minutes, at least hourly) and Trieste (€3.90, 50 minutes, hourly). **APT** (☎800 955957; www.aptgorizia.it, in Italian) runs buses from the train station across to Slovenia's **Nova Gorica bus station** (€1, 25 minutes).

RUSTIC TABLES

Friulian food is essentially rural food. Its bold flavours and earthy ingredients make the most of the seasons and of traditional *miseria* (poverty) techniques, even when it's taken way upmarket.

La Frasca (☏0432 67 51 50; Viale Grado, Lauzacco, Pavia di Udine; meals €24-40; ☉closed Wed) The *frasca* tradition is similar to that of the *osmize*, a rustic place serving *salumi* (cured meats), prosciutto and wine. Scarbolo vineyard's smart dining room has retained the *frasca* experience with its own artisan cured meats and, naturally, wines at the heart of the menu.

La Subida (☏0481 6 05 31; www.lasubida.it; Località Monte, Cormons; meals €30-50; ☉lunch & dinner Sat & Sun, dinner Mon, Thu, Fri) A famous family-run inn, with border-crossing dishes and ingredients – rabbit, boar, flowers and berries – that bring the landscape to the plate.

Terre e Vini (☏0481 6 00 28; www.terraevini.it; meals €28-55; Via XXIV Maggio, Brazzano di Cormons; ☉dinner Tue-Sat, lunch Tue-Sun) The Felluga family are Friulian wine royalty (their wines are often the first Friulians that non-Italians discover) and their 19th-century *osteria* looks out over the plantings. Feast on tripe on Thursdays, salt cod on Fridays and Gorizia asparagus, goose stew or herbed frittata any day of the week.

Palmanova

POP 5340

Shaped like a nine-pointed star – although you'd need an aeroplane to check – Palmanova is a defensively designed town-within-a-fortress built by the Venetians in 1593. Once common throughout Europe, these urban monoliths were known as 'star forts' or *trace italienne*. So impregnable were the town's defences that Napoleon used and extended them in the late 1700s, as did the Austrians during WWI. To this day the Italian army maintains a garrison here.

From hexagonal Piazza Grande, at the star's centre, six roads radiate through the old town to the defensive walls. An inviting grassy path connects the bastions and three main *porte* (gates): Udine, Cividale and Aquileia. Weaponry from the Venetian and Napoleonic eras stars at the Civico Museo Storico (☏0432 92 91 06; Borgo Udine 4; adult/reduced €3/2; ☉9.30am-12.30pm Thu-Tue), inside Palazzo Trevisan. The museum also acts as a tourist office (☏0432 92 48 15); ask for information on secret-tunnel tours.

The Museo Storico Militare (☏0432 92 35 35; Borgo Cividale Dongione di Porta Cividale; admission free; ☉9am-noon & 2-4pm Mon-Thu, 9am-noon Fri & Sat) is inside hulking Porta Cividale. The military museum traces the history of troops stationed in Palmanova from 1593 to WWII.

Cafes stud central Piazza Grande, or head to Le Zagare (Borgo Udine 21; ☉Mon-Sat)

for blackboard wines, great *stuzzichini* (snacks), salads and a spot of postprandial Friulian song.

Regular buses link Palmanova with Udine (€2.20, 25 to 30 minutes) and Aquileia (€2.20, 30 to 40 minutes), leaving from Via Rota, just inside the walls.

Aquileia

POP 3519

Friuli, peripheral? Not 2000 years ago. Colonised in 181 BC, Aquileia was once one of the largest and richest cities of the Roman Empire, at times second only to Rome, with a population of at least 100,000 at its peak. After the city was levelled by Attila's Huns in AD 452, its inhabitants fled south and west where they founded Grado and then Venice. A smaller town rose in Aquileia's place in the early Middle Ages with the construction of the present basilica, though it still went on to become the largest Christian diocese in Europe. Conferred with a Unesco World Heritage listing in 1998, this charmingly rural town/living museum still guards one of the most complete, unexcavated Roman sites in Europe.

◉ Sights

Basilica   CHURCH
(Piazza Capitolo; ☉9am-6pm Mon-Sat, 10-11.15am Sun) The entire floor of the Latin cross-shaped basilica, rebuilt after an earthquake in 1348, is covered with one of the largest and most spectacular Roman-era mosaics in

the world. The 760-sq-metre floor of the basilica's 4th-century predecessor is protected by glass walkways, allowing visitors to wander above the long-hidden tile work, which includes astonishingly vivid episodes from the story of Jonah and the whale, the Good Shepherd, exacting depictions of various lagoon wildlife, and portraits of, presumably, the wealthy Roman patrons and their quotidian business interests.

Treasures also fill the basilica's two crypts (adult/reduced €3/2.50). The 9th-century **Cripta degli Affreschi** (Crypt of Frescoes) is adorned with faded 12th-century frescoes depicting the trials and tribulations of saints, while the **Cripta degli Scavi** (Excavations Crypt) reveals more mosaic floors in varying states of preservation. Some images were destroyed or badly damaged by the erection of the basilica's 73m-high bell tower (adult €1.20; ⊙9.30am-1.30pm & 3.30-6.30pm), built in 1030 with stones from the Roman amphitheatre.

Roman Ruins RUINS
Scattered remnants of the Roman town include extensive ruins of the Porto Fluviale (River Port; Via Sacra; ⊙8.30am-1hr before sunset), the old port, which once linked the settlement to the sea. It's also possible to wander among the partially restored remains of houses, roads and the standing columns of the ancient Forum on Via Giulia Augusta.

Guided tours of the extraordinary Roman sights are organised by the tourist office (☑0431 91 94 91; ⊙9am-1pm & 2-6pm, 9am-7pm summer); otherwise, wander at will.

Museo Archeologico Nazionale MUSEUM
(☑0431 910 16; Via Roma 1; adult/reduced €4/2; ⊙8.30am-7.30pm Tue-Sun) Locally excavated statues, pottery, glassware and jewellery are displayed in this museum, representing one of northern Italy's most important collections of Roman-era treasures.

FREE Museo Paleocristiano MUSEUM
(☑0431 9 11 31; Piazza Pirano; ⊙8.30am-1.45pm Tue-Sun) Part of the Museo Archeologico Nazionale, this muesum houses early-Christian-era mosaics and funerary monuments gathered from the surrounding ruins.

🛏 Sleeping & Eating

Ostello Domus Augusta HOSTEL €
(☑0431 9 10 24; www.ostelloaquileia.it; Via Roma 25; €20 per person; P🖩) Spotless if rather institutional hostel with two- to six-bed rooms and private bathrooms down the hall. Friendly, relaxed staff are helpful and happy to dole out maps and timetables.

Hotel Restaurant Patriarchi HOTEL €
(☑0431 91 95 95; www.hotelpatriarchi.it; Via Giulia Augusta 12; s €44, d €88; P❄) On the town's main road and a stone's throw from the main sights, this is a sizeable place with a well-regarded restaurant and busy bar. Folksy rooms are spacious and some have views of the basilica.

Taberna Marciani Aquileia WINE BAR
(www.tabernamarciani.com; Via Roma 10; ⊙daily) The bearded and slightly dishevelled crew holding up the bar at this gently 2nd-century-AD themed place might look like, and act, like they are in an a touring band, but they're more likely to be Austrian archaeologists on a dig. Popular for plates of local meats and cheese (€3 to €4), and good wines by the glass, not to mention late opening hours.

Grado
POP 8614

Another Friulian surprise is the tasteful beach resort of Grado, 14km south of Aquileia, spread along a narrow island backed by lagoons and linked to the mainland by a causeway. Behind the less-than-spectacular beaches you'll find a maze-like medieval centre, criss-crossed by narrow *calli* (lanes) and dominated by the Romanesque Basilica di Sant'Eufemia (Campo dei Parriarchi) and the nearby remains of a 4th- to 5th-century church mosaic (Piazza Biagio Marin). Belle époque mansions, beach huts and thermal baths line the cheerful seafront (the greyish local sand is used in treatments). Grado comes alive from May to September, but is also prime *passeggiata* (evening stroll) territory on any sunny Sunday.

Small *casoni* (reed huts) used by fishermen dot the tiny lagoon islands. In summer some can be visited by boat; many of the islands are, however, protected nature reserves and off limits. The tourist office (☑0431 87 71 11; Viale Dante Alighieri 72; ⊙9am-10pm summer) has details.

On the first Sunday in July, a votive procession sails to the Santuario di Barbana, an 8th-century church on a lagoon island. Fishermen have done this since 1237 when the Madonna of Barbana was claimed to have miraculously saved the town from the

DON'T MISS

POP-UP WINE SHOPS

Osmize pre-date the trendy retail pop-up phenomena by a few centuries, care of an 18th-century Austrian law that gave Carso farmers the right to sell surplus from their barns or cellars once a year (the term *osmiza* comes from the Slovenian word for eight, the number of days of the original licence). It's mainly vineyards who hold *osmiza* today, though farm cheeses and cured meats are always on offer too. While the Carso is known for its gutsy, innovative winemakers, *osmize* traditions still hold sway. Don't try asking for a list: finding an *osmiza* is part of the fun. Look first, along Carso roads, for the red arrows. Then look up, to gates or lintels bearing a *frasca* – a leafy branch hung ceremoniously upside down announcing that the *osmiza* is open for business. Don't forgo the chance to try the Carso's native wines, the complex, often cloudy, sometimes fierce, white Vitovska and Terrano, or Teran, a berry-scented red. Zidarich wines (☑040 20 12 23; www.zidarich. it; Prepotto 23, Duino Aurisina) does, in fact, announce its *osmiza* dates, usually November and April, on its website, and cellar visits can be arranged at other times.

plague. Boats link the sanctuary with Grado; contact Motoscafisti Gradesi (☑0431 8 01 15; Riva Scaramuzza; ⊙daily Apr-Oct, Sun only winter) for specific departures and prices.

🛏 Sleeping & Eating

The town has a huge number of hotels and vacation rentals, but rooms are still scarce in summer. The old town's streets are known for their boisterous wine bars, casual *fritterias* and seafood restaurants.

TOP CHOICE Albergo Alla Spiaggia HOTEL €€

(☑0431 8 48 41; www.albergoallaspiaggia.it; Via Mazzini 2; s €62-80, d €108/144; ⊙Apr-Oct; P🅿✸@) The Spiaggia sports a South Beach meets Santa Monica look, with an original pre-war modernist building and beachy '60s extension. The fitout is fresh and it's in a great position wedged between the pedestrian zone, old town and the beach.

Stralonga SEAFOOD €

(Piazza Duca d'Aosta 55; meals €15-18; ⊙Thu-Tue) Pizza and seafood shack, Grado-style (yes, you can order polenta by the slice to go with your fish). Plates of crumbed sardines, grilled octopus and excellent pizzas can be eaten inside or out on cheerful wooden benches.

L'Osteria da Sandra WINE BAR

(Camp San Niceta 16; ⊙Tue-Sun) Cute hole-in-the-wall bar that attracts a local crew for early-evening spritzers on an old-town corner. Has an excellent chilled white selection for taking away too.

❶ Getting There & Away

Buses run between Grado and Udine (€3.55, 1¼ hours, 12 daily) via Aquileia. Regular SAF buses

link Aquileia with Grado (€1.60, 15 minutes), Palmanova (€2.20, 30 minutes, up to eight daily) and Udine (€3, 1¼ hours). There are trains to Venice.

Around Grado

Riserva Naturale Regionale della Valle Cavanata NATURE RESERVE

(☑0431 8 82 72; www.vallecavanata.it, in Italian; ⊙9am-12.30pm Mon, Wed & Fri, 2-6pm Sat, 10am-6pm Sun Apr-Sep, 9am-12.30pm Tue & Thu, 10am-4pm Sun winter) This reserve protects a 1920s fish-farming area and extraordinary birdlife in the east of the lagoon. More than 230 bird species have been observed, including the greylag goose and many wading birds.

Riserva Naturale Regionale Foce dell'Isonzo NATURE RESERVE

(☑0432 99 81 33; Isola della Cona; adult/child €2/1; ⊙9am-5pm Fri-Wed) Further east, the final 15km stretch of the Isonzo river's journey into the Adriatic flows through the Riserva Naturale Regionale Foce dell'Isonzo, a 23.5-sq-km nature reserve where visitors can birdwatch, horse ride, cycle or walk around salt marshes and mudflats.

Laguna di Marano

At the head of the Adriatic, sandwiched between the beach resorts of Grado and Lignano, Italy succumbs to nature – in particular birdlife – in the Laguna di Marano.

Marano Lagunare, a Roman fishing port that was later fortified, is the only settlement on the lagoon shore. Beyond the workaday docks, peace and quiet is ensured by two nature reserves – the 13.77-sq-km Riserva Naturale della Foci dello Stella, protecting the marshy mouth of the Stella river and reached by boat, and the Riserva Naturale della Valle Canal Novo, a 121-hect-are reserve in a former fishing valley. The visitor centre (☑0431 6 75 51; Via delle Valli 2; park admission adult/reduced €3.50/2.50; ☉9am-5pm Tue-Sun), in a characteristic reed hut, is shared by the two reserves.

Lignano

Modern Lignano is one of northern Italy's premier beach destinations, with sweeping stretches of sand set against a backdrop of dark pines in Lignano Pineta and Lignano Riviera, and theme parks and multi-story car parks in brash, but never boring, Lignano Sabbiadoro.

Three camping grounds, including Pino Mare (☑0431 42 44 24; www.campingpinomare. it; Lungomare Riva 15; camping 2 people, car & tent €60), a tree-shaded cabin village at the mouth of the Tagliamento river, supplement the 100-plus hotels. At the other end of the scale, Mitteleuropean luxe is heaped on at Hotel Greif (☑0431 42 22 61; www.greifhotel. it; Arco del Grecale 25; d €160, full board only from May-Sep d from €300), with wood-floored rooms, big bathrooms, views, and jaunty guest bicycles.

The tourist office (☑0431 42 21 69; Via dei Pini 53, Lignano Pineta; ☉May-Sep) can help with holiday rentals. Lignano Sabbiadoro is linked by bus to Udine (€5.10, 1½ hours, many daily).

Pordenone & Around

PORDENONE
POP 51,404

Pordenone may not be on anyone's travel hot list this year, but it's the kind of place you wouldn't mind calling home. Pedestri-anised Corso Vittorio Emanuele II draws in an elegant curve between Piazza Cavour and the duomo (cathedral). Lined with an almost unbroken chain of covered portici (porches), the historic streetscape buzzes with smart shops and busy cafes – this is a young and social town.

The bare Romanesque-Gothic facade of the Duomo di San Marco (Piazza San Marco; ☉7.30am-noon & 3-7pm) betrays signs of frequent alteration down the centuries. Inside, among the frescoes and other art works, is the Madonna della misericordia, by the Renaissance master Il Pordenone (1484–1539). In defiance of the other-worldly, the Palazzo del Comune (Town Hall) stands facing away from the duomo. The 13th-century brick structure has three Gothic arches and some extravagant Renaissance additions. Opposite the Palazzo del Comune is the medieval Palazzo Ricchieri, in whose richly decorated upper rooms is the city's fascinating Museo d'Arte (☑0434 39 23 11; Corso Vittorio Emanuele II 51; adult/child €3/2; ☉3-7pm Tue-Sat, 10am-1pm & 3-7pm Sun). Its collection of Friulian and Veneto artists ranges from the 15th to the 18th centuries. The building is in itself a treasure, with timber ceilings and remains of 14th-century frescoes suddenly appearing throughout.

The streetside barrels at Enoteca al Campanile (Vicolo del Campanile; ☉Mon-Sat) make an atmospheric spot for a glass or two, or head to La Vecia Osteria del Moro (☑0431 2 86 58; Via Castello 2; meals €30-40; ☉Mon-Sat), just off the Corso, a vaulted den offering snacks, grills and Venetian-style baccalá (cod).

Grab detailed maps from the tourist office (☑0434 52 03 81; Piazza XX Settembre 11; ☉9am-1pm & 2.30-6.30pm Mon-Fri, 9am-1pm Sat) on the way from the train station.

Pordenone is on the Venice–Udine train line. Frequent services run to and from Udine (€3.80, 30 to 40 minutes). From Venice (Mestre) trains run every half-hour (€4.95, 1¼ to 1½ hours). ATAP (☑800 101040; www.atap.pn.it) runs buses to the surrounding towns.

SACILE
POP 20,302

The so-named Giardino della Serenissima (Garden of Serenity) is formed by two islands standing amid the willow-lined Livenza river and a network of canals. Sacile indeed took much of its early architectural inspiration from the Most Serene Republic of Venice, which is reflected in the typically Venetian town houses and palaces that, despite various earthquakes and WWII bombings, still line the tranquil little waterways. Of the many, the impressively frescoed Palazzo Ragazzoni-Flangini-Billia is worth a peek.

Friendly La Piola (☑0434 78 18 93; www. lapiolasacile.it; meals €25-30; Piazza del Popolo 9; ☉lunch & dinner Tue-Sat, lunch only Sun) has windows and a terrace backing on to the canal. Its menu of traditional dishes – lots

ℹ FRIULI VENEZIA GIULIA TOURISM ONLINE

Tourist offices throughout the region fall under the regional FVG tourism organisation and share the same website (www.turismofvg.it). The offices are helpful and stock excellent maps and information for the whole region.

of Serenissima-style seafood – are delivered with a fresh eye, and the wine selection is impressive. If a riverside stroll calls for gelato, **Il Gelatone** (Viale Pietro Zancanaro 1; ⊙Tue-Sun) will help you out.

The annual August **Sagra dei Osei** (bird festival) has been held since 1274 and is one of the oldest festivals in Italy. Look out for exhibitions, a market and a (bird) song contest.

Sacile is on the main train line between Venice (€4.60, one hour) and Udine (€5.50, 45 minutes).

Udine

POP 99.439 / ELEV 114M

While reluctantly ceding its premier status to Trieste in the 1950s, this confident, wealthy provincial city remains the spiritual and gastronomic capital of Friuli. Udine gives little away in its sprawling semi-rural suburbs, but encased inside the peripheral ring road lies an infinitely grander medieval centre: a dramatic melange of Venetian arches, Grecian statues and Roman columns. The old town is pristine, but also lively; bars here are not just for posing – kicking on is the norm.

⊙ Sights

Piazza della Libertà   PIAZZA
A shimmering Renaissance epiphany materialising from the surrounding maze of medieval streets, Piazza della Libertà is dubbed the most beautiful Venetian square on the mainland. The graciously arched **Palazzo del Comune** (Town Hall), also known as the Loggia del Lionello after its goldsmithing architect, Nicolò Lionello, is another clear Venetian keepsake, as is the **Loggia di San Giovanni** opposite (its clock tower modelled on the one gracing Venice's Piazza San Marco). The **Arco Bollani** (Bollani Arch), next to the Loggia di San Giovanni, an Andrea Palladio work from 1556, leads up to the castle used by the Venetian governors.

FREE Cathedral   CATHEDRAL
(Piazza Duomo) A couple of chapels of Udine's 13th-century Romanesque-Gothic cathedral house the **Museo del Duomo** (☑0432 50 68 30; admission free; ⊙9am-noon & 4-6pm Tue-Sat, 4 6pm Sun), among whose most interesting elements are the 13th- to 17th-century frescoes in the **Cappella di San Nicolò**. Across the street, the cathedral's 17th-century **Oratorio della Purità** (Piazza del Duomo; guided tours only) was originally a theatre; its beautiful ceiling painting of the Assumption by Giambattista Tiepolo and eight biblical scenes in chiaroscuro by Giandomenico Tiepolo on the walls are exquisite.

Castello   MUSEUM
The castle, rebuilt in the mid-16th century after an earthquake in 1511, affords rare views of the city and the Alps beyond. It houses the **Galleria d'Arte Antica** (☑0432 27 15 91; adult/child €3/1.50, Sun morning free; ⊙9.30am-12.30pm & 3-6pm Tue-Sun), with a handful of works by Caravaggio (a portrait of St Francis in room 7) and Tiepolo (several works in room 10). The bulk of the collection is dedicated to lesser-known Friulian painters and religious sculpture.

Museo Etnografico del Friuli   MUSEUM
(☑0432 27 19 20; Via Grazzano 1; adult/reduced €5/2.50; ⊙10.30am-5pm Tue-Sun, to 7pm summer) A small but engaging museum of daily life, with various exhibitions devoted to the Friulian hearth, spiritual practices, folk medicine and dress. The building itself features intricate 19th-century woodwork, with carved Friulian forest scenes, and its own little canal gurgling by the entrance.

Galleria d'Arte Moderna   ART GALLERY
(☑0432 29 58 91; Via Ampezzo 2; adult/reduced €3/2; ⊙10.30am-5pm Wed-Mon, to 7pm summer) Formed from a number of bequests, this gallery has a number of works by well-known 20th-century Italian artists, such as De Chirico, Morandi, Campigli and Severini.

Chiesa di San Francesco   CHURCH
(Largo Ospedale Vecchio; adult/reduced €5/3.50; ⊙exhibitions 9am-noon & 3.30-7pm Tue-Sun) This striking 13th-century church now hosts an interesting rota of cultural events and high-profile art shows.

🛏 Sleeping

Central Udine has a number of small, smart midrange hotels, but a dearth of budget places. If you're driving, consider a B&B or

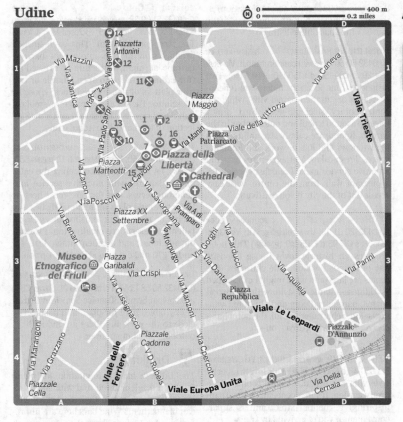

Udine

◉ Top Sights

◉ Sights

◉ Sleeping

◉ Eating

◉ Drinking

agriturismo (farm stay accommodation) in the surrounding suburbs or countryside (the tourist office has online listings).

Hotel Clocchiatti Next DESIGN HOTEL €€

(☑0432 50 50 47; www.hotelclocchiatti.it; Via Cividale 29; s €99-150, d €150-190; P✳🛜🏊) Two properties, one location: older-style (cheaper) rooms are in the original villa, while the contemporary steel-and-glass Next annex lines up around a pool and outdoor bar in the garden. Rooms are calmly streamlined with big windows and lots of work and lounging spaces. Fresh cakes, Mariage Frères teas and attentive service make breakfast special. It's a pleasant walk from the centre, with easy access out of the city if you're driving.

Hotel Allegria BOUTIQUE HOTEL €€

(☑0432 20 11 16; www.hotelallegria.it; Via Grazzano 18; s €77-95, d €105-140; P✳@) This hotel occupies an historic town house opposite one of Udine's loveliest little churches. The rooms are large and what might be described as Udinese-organic in style, with lightwood beams, parquetry floors and shuttered windows. Most charmingly of all, the hotel has a *bocciofila* – bowling area – on-site.

Casa Stucky B&B €

(☑0432 52 16 49; www.casastucky.it; Via Calatafimi 9; s €30-42, d €60-70; P@) This lovely Liberty-style villa has bright, modern rooms and a pretty garden. It's in a peaceful (if less-than-inspiring) residential street and is super-convenient if you're arriving by train.

✖ Eating

Udine's flavours are as intriguing as the city itself. Look out for country-style cheeses – smoked ricotta, Montasio – game, San Daniele prosciutto (ham) and delicious gnocchi and dumplings. Open-air cafes and restaurants are dotted around Piazza Matteotti and the surrounding pedestrian streets. Via Paolo Sarpi and its surrounding streets are lined with lively restaurants and bars.

Trattoria ai Frati FRIULIAN €€

(☑0432 50 69 26; Piazzetta Antonini 5; meals €25-30; ⊙Mon-Sat) A popular old-style eatery on a cobbled cul-de-sac where you can expect such local specialities as *frico* (thick cheese-and-potato omelette), pumpkin gnocchi with smoked ricotta, or, in season, white asparagus and fish stew. It's loved by locals for its whopper steaks and its raucous front bar.

Jolanda de Colo WINE BAR €

(☑0432 51 09 38; www.jolandadecolo.it; Via Paolo Sarpi 18a; meals from €15; ⊙closed Mon & lunch Tue, shop from 10.30am) This well-stocked produce store morphs into a wine bar/restaurant at night, attracting a dressed-up (for Udine) crowd who open a bottle or two over platters of house-cured duck, goose or prosciutto. There's also a range of smoked, cured and raw fish, big salads and a nice selection of local and Alto Adige wines.

Matteotti MODERN ITALIAN €€

(☑0432 174 41 50; Piazza Matteoti 17; meals €30; ⊙daily;) A slick little place among the cafes on the square, with attentive service and generous serves. Opt for rare roast beef or the interesting plays on regional dishes, say rabbit in mustard or mushroom *ragù* on polenta; desserts are creative too. Pleasant outside tables and excellent lunch deals for under €10 make it a good daytime option.

Pizzeria Concordia PIZZERIA €

(☑0432 50 58 13; Via Porta Nuova 21; pizzas €5-7; ⊙9am-4pm, 6pm-12.30am Tue-Sun) Join huge happy tables here for pizza and pasta. It's close to the park and there are indoor/outdoor tables in summer.

🍷 Drinking

The Udinese have a reputation for being fond of a drink or three, and with such stellar wines produced in their backyard, who can blame them? Wine bars here are unpretentious but serious about their wares, with blackboards full of local drops to help you familiarise yourself. *Stuzzichini* (snacks, usually in the form of toasts with various toppings) are plentiful at most bars and, if not complimentary, can be had for pocket change.

Osteria delle Mortadele WINE BAR

(Riva Bartolini 8; ⊙Mon-Sat) Yes, there's a popular restaurant out back, but it's the spill-onto-the-road front bar that will hold your interest. A real rock-and-roll soundtrack, excellent wine by the glass and a great company make this a one-drink-or-many destination.

Caffè Caucigh BAR

(www.caucigh.com; Via Gemona 36) This ornate dark-wooded bar is a perfect Udinese compass point – it feels far more like Prague than Rome. Regulars take glasses of red to the pavement for a chat with passing strangers. A calendar of jazz acts – Friuli's

WAYNE YOUNG: COMMUNICATIONS & MARKETING (& FORMER CELLAR-HAND), BASTIANICH WINES

Friulians are proud, hard-working, tight-knit people – they often describe themselves as cold but I disagree. They love to socialise, especially with visitors. Friuli isn't touristy, so getting attention from the outside world is a pleasure. Prepare to stop and chat and have a glass of wine or an espresso.

World-Class Whites

There's no other place in the world where the combination of soil, climate and the interplay between sea and mountain comes together to create whites like these. Local grape Friulano is fresh and aromatic. The sauvignon blancs are special too, and don't overlook the outstanding white blends (*uvaggi*). Reds to try: Refosco, merlot and the interesting Schioppettino.

Tasting Tips

Look out for wines from Ronchi di Cialla, Moschioni, Venica & Venica and Vie di Romans. And Bastianich, of course!

Stomach Liners

Frico! It's a melted Montasio cheese pancake made with potatoes and, sometimes, bacon and onions...*awesome*.

Night Out

Udine is a great little city and deserves respect. There's a fantastic old bar called Caffè Caucigh (p404): go for wine, coffee or live jazz. Or head to the countryside, to upscale La Frasca (boxed text, p398) for salumi and prosciutto.

finest and some international surprises – play from 10pm on Friday nights.

Al Cappello   WINE BAR
(Via Paolo Sarpi 5; ⊘closed Sun night) If you're overwhelmed by the hundreds of wines scribbled on the giant blackboard at this bustling bar, just follow the locals' lead and order what may be Italy's most reasonably priced spritzer (€1) through the window. *Stuzzichini* here are generous enough to constitute dinner, but there's also a restaurant within.

Caffè Contarena   CAFE
(Via Cavour 11; ⊘closed Sun) Beneath the arcades of Palazzo d'Aronco, Contarena's soaring domed ceilings glitter with gold leaf and other Liberty fancy. Designed by a master of the genre and one-time local, Raimondo d'Aronco, it's a glamorous espresso stop; come late for cocktails.

I Piombi   PUB
(Via Manin 12) Head downstairs into a labyrinth of vaulted brick rooms with long timber benches (no mere styling, this was the city's prison). It's open late for jugs of beer and suitably hearty pub food.

ℹ Information

Hospital (☎0432 55 21; Piazza Santa Maria della Misericordia 15) About 2km north of the centre.

Tourist office (☎0432 29 59 72; Piazza I Maggio 7; ⊘9am-7pm Mon-Sat, 9am-1pm Sun)

ℹ Getting There & Away

From the **bus station** (☎0432 50 69 41; Viale Europa Unita 31), services operated by **SAF** (☎800 915303, 0432 60 81 11; www.saf.ud.it) go to and from Trieste (€5.10, 1¼ hours, hourly), Aquileia (€3, one to 1¼ hours, up to eight daily), Lignano Sabbiadoro (€5.10, 1½ hours, eight to 11 daily) and Grado (€3.55, 1¼ hours, 12 daily). Buses also link Udine and Friuli Venezia Giulia airport (€3.55, one hour, hourly).

From Udine's **train station** (Viale Europa Unita) services run to Trieste (€6 to €7, one to 1½ hours), Venice (€8, 1¾ to 2½ hours, several daily) and Gorizia (€3.25, 25 to 40 minutes, hourly).

WORTH A TRIP

VILLA MANIN

Home to the noble Venetian Manin family from the 1600s until the last century (including the last of Venice's doges), **Villa Manin** (☎0422 42 99 99; www.villamanin-eventi.it; Piazza Manin 10, Passariano; adult/reduced €10/8; ☺9am-6pm during exhibition periods) is 30km southwest of Udine. The mansion is itself a treat – gobsmackingly grand and set in 19 hectares of manicured garden – but it's the villa's art blockbusters that draw the crowds. Shows are themed to illuminate the relationship between modernism and European geography and identity; both Courbet and Munch have recently featured.

Regional trains between Venice and Udine stop at Codroipo; from there, take a taxi (or, if you have the patience, an often elusive SAF bus) for the 3km ride.

Cividale del Friuli

POP 11,600 / ELEV 138M

Cividale del Friuli (15km east of Udine) is a small town these days but it's hugely significant in terms of Friulian history and identity. Founded by Julius Caesar in 50 BC as Forum de Lulii (ultimately condensed into 'Friuli'), the settlement reached its apex under the Lombards who first arrived in AD 568 and by the 8th century had usurped Roman Aquileia. Though it has long since passed the big-town baton onto Udine, Cividale is hauntingly picturesque and well worth a morning's quiet contemplation as you ramble around its dark stone streets.

◉ Sights

Ponte del Diavolo BRIDGE
Splitting the town in two is the symbolic Devil's Bridge that crosses the emerald-green Natisone river. Rebuilt post-WWI after being blown up by retreating Italian troops, the 22m-high bridge was first constructed in the 15th century with its central arch supported by a huge rock said to have been thrown into the river by the devil.

Tempietto Longobardo CHAPEL
(☎0432 70 08 67; Borgo Brossano; combined ticket incl Museo Cristiano adult/reduced €6/4; ☺9.30am-12.30pm & 3-5pm, to 6.30pm summer) Cividale's most important sight is this cha-

pel, also known as the Oratorio di Santa Maria in Valle. The stunning complex houses the only surviving example of Lombard architecture and art work in Europe. Dating from the 8th century AD, its frescoes and ancient woodwork are both unusual and extremely moving.

Cathedral CATHEDRAL
(Piazza del Duomo) This 16th-century cathedral houses the **Museo Cristiano** (☎0432 73 04 03; adult €4; ☺10am-1pm & 3-6pm Wed-Sun). Its 8th-century stone Altar of Ratchis is a stunning early-Christian relic. Sharp-etched carvings, including a be-quiffed Jesus with one piercing stare, dramatically pop against the smooth white background.

✘ Eating & Drinking

Al Monastero FRIULIAN €€
(☎0432 70 08 08; www.almonastero.com; Via Ristori 9; meals €25-30; ☺lunch & dinner Tue-Sat, lunch Sun) Feast on *cjalcions* (dumplings), duck with carrot pudding and *gubana* with plum brandy at this posh, undeniably touristy but well-regarded restaurant.

Central Caffè del Corso CAFE
(Corso Mazzini 38) The place for a spritzer or coffee (lovingly made with Verona's Giamaica beans).

Al Campanile FRIULIAN
(☎0432 73 24 67; Via Candotti 4; plates from €6; ☺9am-3pm & 6pm-11pm Tue-Sun) For beers, herbed frittata, *frico* or cured meats at its pavement wooden benches.

❶ Information

The **tourist office** (☎0432 71 04 60; Piazza Paolo Diacono 10; ☺9.30am-noon & 3.30-6pm) has information on walks around the medieval core. Look to the 'lodging and eating' section of the city's website (www.cividale.com) for a comprehensive listing of *agriturismo* and farm restaurants.

❶ Getting There & Away

Private (and cute) trains run by **Ferrovie Udine Cividale** (☎0432 58 18 44; www.ferrovie udinecividale.it) connect Cividale with Udine (€2.30, 20 minutes), at least hourly.

San Daniele del Friuli

POP 8222

Hilltop San Daniele sits in an undulating landscape that comes as a relief after the Venetian plains, with the Carnic Alps jutting

DON'T MISS

CIVIDALE CERAMICS

Working with ancient Roman and Middle Eastern techniques, local ceramic artist Stefania Zurchi creates sculptures, reliefs and beautifully decorated utilitarian objects that are both vividly contemporary and totally timeless. Her palette evokes the Friulian landscape, an evocative mix of moody deep blues and olives with flashes of bright oxide yellow and dusty pink. Her girl figures representing the seasons are highly sought after, as are her touching Madonna-and-child reliefs. The work can be found at her central Cividale del Friuli shop, **Tirare** (Via Ristori 12; ⊙Tue-Sat).

up suddenly on the horizon. While ham is undoubtedly the town's raison d'être, it also has a general gastronomic bent, with excellent local trout – farmed sustainably and available hot or smoked – and many good *alimentari* (grocery stores) dotted throughout the town. Buy all the ham your heart and stomach desire at **Bottega di Prosciutto** (Via Umberto I; ⊙closed Mon & Wed afternoon) then visit **Adelia di Fant** (Via Garibaldi 26; ⊙Tue-Sun) for chocolates, syrups, jellies and biscuits.

Frescoes are another of San Daniele's fortes and you'll find some colourful examples etched by Pellegrino da San Daniele, aka Martino da Urbino (1467–1547), in the small Romanesque **Chiesa di San Antonio Abate** (Via Garibaldi). Next to the church, the **Biblioteca Guarneriana** (☑0432 95 79 30; www.guarneriana.it, in Italian; Via Roma 1; guided tours €3; ⊙Wed-Sat, by appointment only) is one of Italy's oldest and most venerated libraries. Founded in 1466, it contains 12,000 antique books, including a priceless manuscript of Dante's *Inferno*.

Osteria Tancredi (☑0432 94 15 94; Via Sabotino 10; plates €8, meals €25-30; ⊙lunch & dinner Thu-Tue) serves up crowd-pleasing platters of prosciutto and the Friulian classics: *cjalcions*, *frico* and apple gnocchi.

If you want to get out into the countryside, three **cycling itineraries**, each 22km, take you past pristine lakes and through the castle-dotted hills around the village; ask at the tourist office.

Regular buses run to San Daniele from Udine (€4, 40 to 60 minutes), 25km to the southeast.

North of Udine

Hit the hard north of Italy's most northeasterly region and you'll find yourself surrounded by the Carnic and Giulie Alps. Of the two, the former is the less foreboding, with hills that stretch as far west as the Dolomites and as far north as the border with Austria. The loftier Giulie, named after Julius Caesar, meanwhile, are rugged, frigid peaks shared with Slovenia – the Triglavski Narodni Park lies just across the border. Both areas are excellent hiking terrain and deliver some of the loneliest, most scenic trails in Italy. Standing at the meeting point of three different cultures, multilingual skills can come in handy in these parts. Hikers should be ready to swap their congenial *salve* (Italian) for a *grüss gott* (German) or *dober dan* (Slovenian).

Tolmezzo & Carnia

The region known as Carnia is intrinsically Friulian (the language is widely spoken here) and named after its original Celtic inhabitants – the Carnics. Geographically, it contains the western and central parts of the Carnic Alps and presents wild and beautiful walking country flecked with curious villages.

Stunningly sited Tolmezzo (population 10,725; elevation 323m) is the region's capital and gateway. The **Museo Carnico delle Arti e Tradizioni Popolari** (☑0433 4 32 33; www.carniamusei.org, in Italian; Via della Vittoria 2; adult/reduced €5/3; ⊙9am-1pm & 3-6pm Tue-Sun) has a rich display on mountain life and folklore. Pleasant rooms at **Albergo Roma** (☑0433 46 80 31; www.albergoromatolmezzo.it; Piazza XX Settembre 14; s/d €50/100; ℙ@) overlook the main piazza or one of the town's many hills. An interesting detour, 6km northeast of the town, is the hill village of **Illegio**, with buildings dating back to the 4th century and a still-operating 16th-century mill and dairy. Tolmezzo's **tourist office** (☑0433 4 48 98; Piazza XX Settembre 9; ⊙9am-1pm daily & 2-6pm Mon-Sat) is helpful for information on surrounding hiking trails and *agriturismi*.

SAF buses run to Udine approximately every hour (€3.90, 50 minutes) from Via Carnia Libera.

To the northwest, a minor road passes the plunging Lumiei Gorge to emerge at the cobalt-blue Lago di Sauris, an artificial lake about 4km east of Sauris di Sotto. Another 4km on (up eight switchbacks) is the prettier Sauris di Sopra. This twin hamlet is an island of timber houses and German-speakers. The area (in German, Zahre) is known for its fine hams, sausages and locally brewed beer. There are lots of good walking trails. The Albergo Ristorante Riglarhaus (☎0433 8 60 13; alberghi.carnia.org/riglar; Fraz Lateis 3; s €44, d €74; P) brims with rustic charm; if a mountain immersion experience is what you're after, look to the region's alberghi diffusi – literally 'scattered' hotels – small village B&Bs or farm stays in remote villages (details can be found at www.albergodiffusosauris.com).

Close to the border with Veneto, Forni di Sopra is a popular ski resort that receives a heavy dump of winter snow and offers sledging, skating and ice-climbing as well as downhill skiing. Forni is equally revered for its carpet of summer wildflowers and herbs; the latter are utilised in the local cuisine and are the central theme of the annual spring Festa delle Erbe di Primavera. There are numerous hotels in the town, including Hotel Edelweiss (☎0433 8 80 16; www.edelweiss-forni.it; Via Nazionale 19; s/d €65/105; P@♨), a family-friendly vista-laden place with gratis

mountain bikes. The tourist office (☎0433 88 66 86; Via Cadore 1) has information on activities, lifts and the like.

Regular SAF buses from Tolmezzo service this region and stop in Ampezzo (€2.75, 35 minutes) and Forni de Sopra (€3.90, one hour and 20 minutes).

Tarvisio & the Giulie Alps

POP 8222 / ELEVATION 754M

The Giulie Alps are dramatic limestone monoliths that bear more than a passing resemblance to their more famous Dolomites cousins. Though undergoing some recent development, including a cross-border ski lift, the area is still relatively pristine and retains a wildness often lacking further west.

Tarvisio is 7km short of the Austrian border and 11km from Slovenia. Down to earth and prettily wedged into the Val Canale between the Giulie and eastern Carnic Alps, it's a good base for both winter and summer activities.

The area is increasingly touted for its uncrowded skiing; despite its relatively modest elevations, this is the snowiest (and coldest) pocket in the whole Alpine region, with heavy snowfalls not uncommon into May. The main ski centres are at Tarvisio – with a good open 4km run that promises breathtaking views and 60km of cross-country tracks – and at Sella Nevea. The Sella Nevea (www.sellanevea.net) resort is linked to Bovec in Slovenia, making for

HAMMING IT UP

There are two world-revered prosciuttos manufactured in Italy: the lean, deliciously nutty (and more famous) ham from Parma, and the dark, exquisitely sweet Prosciutto di San Daniele. It might come as a surprise to find that the latter – Friuli Venezia Giulia's greatest culinary gift to the world – comes from a village of only 8000 people, where it is salted and cured in 27 prosciuttifici (ham-curing plants) safeguarded by EU regulations.

Standards are strict. San Daniele's prosciutto is made only from the thighs of pigs who were raised in a small number of northern Italian regions. Salt is the only method of preservation allowed – no freezing, chemicals or other preservatives can be used. The X factor is, of course, terroir, the land itself. Some prosciuttifici claim it's the cool, resinous Alpine air meeting the Adriatic's humid, brackish breezes that define their product, others argue that it's about San Daniele's fast-draining soil: such effective ventilation makes for perfect curing conditions.

In August the town holds the Aria di Festa, a four-day annual ham festival when prosciuttifici do mass open house tours and tastings, musicians entertain and everyone tucks in. San Daniele's friendly tourist office (☎0432 94 07 65; Piazza Pellegrino 4; ◉9am-1pm & 2-6pm Mon-Fri, 11am-1pm & 4.30-6.30pm Sat & Sun) has a list of prosciuttifici that welcome visitors year-round; call ahead to book.

around 30km of slopes, with a number of satisfying red runs and good freeride and backcountry skiing. In summer the hiking, caving, canoeing and windsurfing are all good.

The **Laghi di Fusine** (Fusine Lakes) lie within mirror-signalling distance of the Slovenian border and are perennially popular with hikers (in summer) and cross-country skiers and snowshoers (in winter). The two lakes – Lago Superiore and Lago Inferiore – are ringed by paths and encased in the **Parco Naturale di Fusine**. For more-adventurous walkers, there's a moderately challenging 11km hike up to **Rifugio Zacchi** (☏0419 63 79 33; dm €10-20; ☺mid-Jun–mid-Sep) and across the face of Monte Mangart. In summer, buses run up to four times daily from Tarvisio (€1.50, 15 minutes).

Tarvisio has a number of well-priced hotels, including **Hotel Edelhof** (☏0428 4 00 81; www.hoteledelhof.com; Via Armando Diaz 13; s €45-55, d €90-100; P☏) situated right by the lifts with large, airy folk-art furnished rooms and a basement spa. **Ristorante Adriatico** (☏0428 26 37; Via Roma 59; meals €15-20), typical of Tarvisio's economical eating joints, has set two-course meat or fish menus. The town is also famous for its

CROSS-BORDER SKIING

Multi-day passes (2/4/6 days from €44/80/114) enable you to ski Italy, Slovenia and Austria on the slopes of Sella Nevea, Tarvisio, Zoncolan, Bovec, Kranjska Gora and Arnoldstein. Both day and multi-day passes can also be used at the Friulian resorts of Piancavallo and Forni di Sopra. The Monte Canin ski lift is free to FVG Card holders, and they receive discounts on multi-day passes and equipment hire. **Promotur** (☏0428 65 39 15; www. promotur.org; Camporosso, Tarvisio) sell passes at each of the resorts.

historic Saturday market; it's long attracted day trippers from Austria and Slovenia and has a definite border-town buzz, though these days it's mostly dubious-looking leather jackets for sale.

The helpful **tourist office** (☏0428 21 35; Via Roma 14; ☺9am-1pm & 3-7pm) has trekking maps and details on Alpine conditions.

Trains connect Tarvisio with Udine (€7.60, 1½ hours, up to seven daily).

Emilia-Romagna & San Marino

POP 4.43 MILLION

Includes »

Best Places to Eat

» Hosteria Giusti (p425)

» La Greppia (p433)

» Drogheria della Rosa (p420)

» Osteria La Mariola (p446)

Best Places to Stay

» Prendiparte B&B (p419)

» Hotel Centrale Byron (p446)

» Century Hotel (p432)

» Grand Hotel (p449)

Why Go?

The secret's in the mud. The roots of Emilia-Romagna's supersonic economy lie not in the mechanics of its famous Ferraris, but in its exceptionally fertile soil. Since antiquity, the verdant plains of the region's Po river valley have sown enough agricultural riches to feed a nation and finance an unending production line of lavish products: luxury cars, regal *palazzi* (mansions), fine Romanesque churches, prosperous towns, a sturdy industrial infrastructure, a gigantic operatic legacy (Verdi and Pavarotti, no less), and food. Ah yes, did anyone mention the food?

You can eat like a Roman emperor here, and, if you have any appetite left, dip your toe tentatively into the places that time-poor Rome-o-philes serially miss. There's Bolshie Bologna with its *ragù* (meat and tomato sauce) and porticoes, posh Parma with its opera and cheese, Modena and its balsamic vinegar, the wealthy micro-nation of San Marino, and Ravenna with its mosaics. Come to Emilia-Romagna *ragazzi* (guys). Just don't forget the mud that made it.

When to Go

Bologna

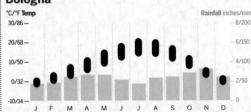

Mar-Apr Avoid the heat on the Po plains and the crowds on Rimini's beaches.

Jun-Aug Summer festivals galore in Bologna, Modena, Ravenna and Rimini.

Sep Ideal hiking conditions in Parco Nazionale dell'Appennino Tosco-Emiliano.

Don't Leave Without Trying

» **Ferrara** *Cappellacci di zucca* (hat-shaped pasta stuffed with squash, herbs and nutmeg, sautéed with butter and sage)

» **Bologna** *Tagliatelle al ragù* (pasta served with a dry meat-based sauce)

» **Parma** *Pesto di cavallo* (raw minced horsemeat seasoned with herbs, olive oil and Parmesan)

» **Modena** *Cotechino Modena* (fresh stuffed pork sausage served with lentils)

» **Rimini** *Piadina* (flat bread wrap with various fillings)

VIA EMILIA

Built by the Romans between their axis cities of Placentia (Piacenza) and Ariminum (Rimini), the ruler-straight Via Emilia quickly came to define the character of the Emilia-Romagna region, and led to the birth of its four most significant towns: Bononia (Bologna), Regium (Reggio Emilia), Mutina (Modena) and Parma. The road was completed in 187 BC following the subjugation of hostile Celtic tribes by the Romans, and ran for 260km through the Po river valley. Within decades it had opened up Italy's fertile northern hinterland to colonisation and economic expansion, and had converted the rich river plain into the empire's proverbial breadbasket – a position it still enjoys today.

The remarkable Ponte Tiberio on the Marecchia river in Rimini is one of the few original features of the Via Emilia still intact.

Know Your Romanesque

Like all Italian regions, Emilia-Romagna exhibits a wide range of architectural genres; yet it is the early-medieval style of Romanesque that defines it the best. Romanesque emerged in the late 10th century and was in vogue for about 200 years until usurped by the appearance of 'Gothic' in the early 1200s. Its defining feature was the rounded 'Roman' arch (as opposed to the pointed Gothic arch that followed), but it had a number of other recognisable trademarks, including thick walls, dramatic scale, decorative 'blind' arcades, and simple, yet symmetrical sculpture and ornamentation. Another adaptation in Italy was a free-standing ecclesial bell tower that stood apart from the main body of the church.

Pure Romanesque isn't always visible today in its original incarnation due to later additions by overzealous Gothic and Renaissance architects, but it can be thrillingly glimpsed in a trio of magnificent Emilia-Romagna cathedrals: Parma, Piacenza and Unesco-listed Modena.

EMILIA-ROMAGNA EXPANDS

In August 2009 Emilia-Romagna was officially expanded when, following a popular referendum, seven communes formerly part of Le Marche region were transferred across and merged with the province of Rimini.

Internationally Acclaimed Natives

» Giuseppe Verdi (composer) – born Le Roncole 1813

» Arturo Toscanini (conductor) – born Parma 1867

» Enzo Ferrari (car manufacturer) – born Modena 1898

» Federico Fellini (film director) – born Rimini 1920

» Luciano Pavarotti (opera singer) – born Modena 1935

Resources

» Official tourist site (www.emiliaromagnaturismo.it)

» Visit Emilia-Romagna (www.visitemiliaromagna.com)

» San Marino tourist site (www.visitsanmarino.com)

Emilia-Romagna & San Marino Highlights

1 Take a very long, very slow, and very delicious lunch in that well-known bastion of good taste, **Parma** (p429)

2 Reawaken your enthusiasm for dark Italian churches amid the lucid mosaics of the Basilica di San Vitale in **Ravenna** (p443)

3 Interpret the intricacies of Lombard-Romanesque in all its medieval purity inside Modena's **cathedral** (p423)

4 Hire a bike and circumnavigate the muscular medieval walls of Renaissance **Ferrara** (p437)

5 Leave the flatlands behind and take a bus out to the **Pietra di Bismantova** (boxed text, p432) for a day of hiking

6 Follow the undergraduates and discover cheap bars and restaurants in **Bologna's university quarter** (p421)

7 Swap high culture for high decibels in Rimini's famous **clubbing scene** (p452)

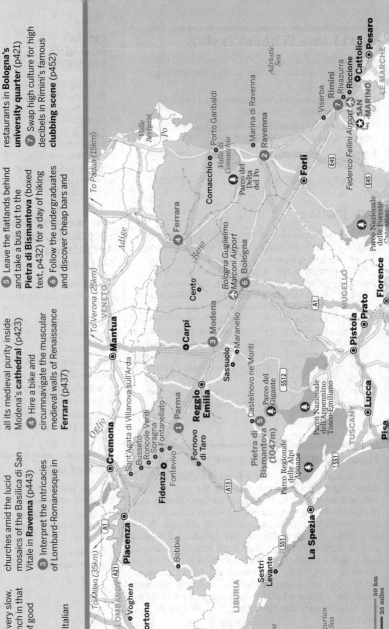

EMILIA-ROMAGNA

Bologna

POP 372,000

If you've ever puzzled over how to combine haughty elegance with down-to-earth urban grit, come to Emilia-Romagna's fat, red, learned city where suave opera-goers waltz out of regal theatres into graffiti-embellished piazzas full of boozing students. Sometimes stylish, often scruffy, Bologna is a place of many monikers. Its nickname La Grassa (the fat one) celebrates a rich food legacy (*ragù* or bolognese sauce was first concocted here). La Dotta (the learned one) doffs a cap to the city university; the world's oldest, founded in 1088. La Rossa (the red one) alludes to the ubiquity of terracotta medieval buildings as well as the city's longstanding penchant for left-wing politics. All three names still ring true. Bologna is the kind of city where you can be conversing with a Bolshie student one minute, and be eating like a king the next. Sure, there are plenty of zealous churches and musty museums to contemplate, but save some time to uncover the real highlight – the city's intriguing split personality.

◉ Sights

PIAZZA MAGGIORE & AROUND

Flanked by the world's fifth-largest basilica and a series of impressive Renaissance *palazzi* (mansions), all roads lead to pivotal Piazza Maggiore.

Fontana del Nettuno   FOUNTAIN

(Neptune's Fountain; Piazza del Nettuno) Adjacent to Piazza Maggiore, Piazza del Nettuno owes its name to this explicit bronze statue sculpted by Giambologna in 1566. Beneath the muscled sea god, four cherubs represent the winds, and four buxom sirens, water spouting from every nipple, symbolise the four known continents of the pre-Oceania world.

FREE Palazzo Comunale   ART GALLERY

(Piazza Maggiore) The palace that forms the western flank of Piazza Maggiore (known also as Palazzo D'Accursio after its original resident, Francesco D'Accursio) has been home to Bologna city council since 1336. A salad of architectural styles, it owes much of its current look to makeovers in the 15th and 16th centuries. The statue of Pope Gregory XIII, the Bolognese prelate responsible for the Gregorian calendar, was placed above the main portal in 1580, while inside, Donato Bramante's 16th-century staircase was designed to allow horse-drawn carriages to ride directly up to the 1st floor.

On the 2nd floor you'll find the *palazzo's* two art galleries (◉9am-6.30pm Tue-Fri, 10am-6.30pm Sat & Sun): the Collezioni Comunali d'Arte with its interesting collection of 13th- to 19th-century paintings, sculpture and furniture, and the Museo Morandi, dedicated to the trademark still-life paintings of Bolognese artist Giorgio Morandi.

Outside the *palazzo*, three large panels bear photos of hundreds of partisans killed in the resistance to German occupation, many on this very spot.

Palazzo del Re Enzo   PALAZZO

(Piazza del Nettuno) This 13th-century palace is named after King Enzo, the illegitimate son of Holy Roman Emperor Frederick II, who was held here by papal forces between 1249 and 1272. Dating to the same period, the neighbouring Palazzo del Podestà was the original residence of Bologna's chief magistrate. Beneath the *palazzo*, there's a whispering gallery where two perpendicular passages intersect. Stand diagonally opposite someone and whisper: the acoustics are amazing. Both *palazzi* are off limits to the public unless there's a temporary exhibition on (check with the tourist office found in the same square).

Basilica di San Petronio   CHURCH

(Piazza Maggiore; ◉7.45am-12.30pm & 3.30-6pm) The world's fifth-largest church, measuring 132m by 66m by 47m, hides some interesting oddities. 1) Though construction started in 1390, the church wasn't consecrated (officially blessed) until 1954. 2) It has been the target of two thwarted terrorist attacks, in 2002 and 2006. 3) The church exhibits an unusual scientific intrusion into a religious setting; inside, a huge sundial stretches 67.7m down the eastern aisle. Designed in 1656 by Gian Cassini and Domenico Guglielmi, it was instrumental in discovering the anomalies of the Julian calendar and led to the creation of the leap year. 4) One look at the incomplete front facade and you'll quickly deduce that the church was never finished. Originally it was intended to be larger than St Peter's in Rome, but in 1561, some 169 years after building had started, Pope Pius IV blocked construction by commissioning a new university on the

Bologna

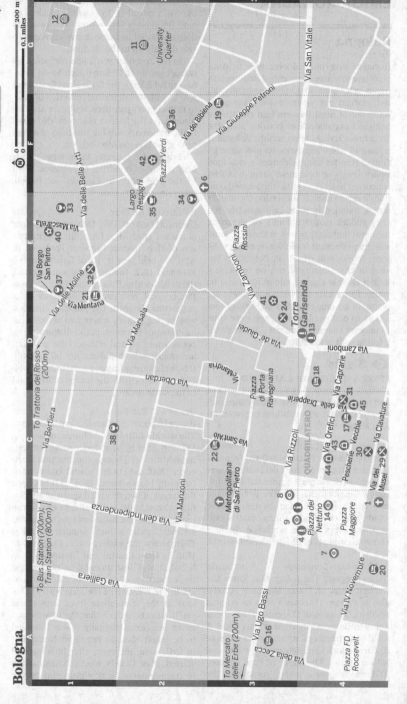

200 m
0.1 miles

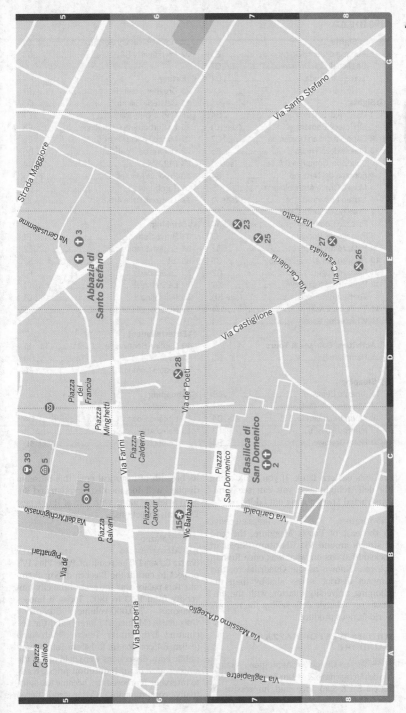

basilica's eastern flank. If you walk along Via dell'Archiginnasio you can see semi-constructed apses poking out oddly.

Quadrilatero   HISTORICAL CENTRE
To the east of Piazza Maggiore, the grid of streets around Via Clavature (Street of Locksmiths) sits on what was once Roman Bologna. Known as the Quadrilatero, this compact district is less shabby than the adjoining university quarter, with the emphasis on old-style delis selling the region's world-famous produce.

SOUTH & WEST OF PIAZZA MAGGIORE

FREE Museo Civico Archeologico   MUSEUM
(Via dell'Archiginnasio 2; ☺9am-3pm Tue-Fri, 10am-6.30pm Sat & Sun) Free and impressive in

its breadth of historical eras, this museum displays well-documented Egyptian and Roman artefacts along with one of Italy's best Etruscan collections.

FREE Palazzo
dell'Archiginnasio   PALAZZO, MUSEUM
(Piazza Galvani 1) The result of Pope Pius IV's project to curtail the Basilica di San Petronio, this palace was the seat of the city university from 1563 to 1805. Today it houses Bologna's 700,000-volume Biblioteca Comunale (Municipal Library) and the fascinating 17th-century Teatro Anatomico (☺9am-6.45pm Mon-Fri, to 1.45pm Sat), where public body dissections were held under the sinister gaze of an Inquisition priest, ready to intervene if proceedings became too spiritually compromising. Cedar-wood tiered

seats surround a central marble-topped table while a sculptured Apollo looks down from the ceiling. The canopy above the lecturer's chair is supported by two skinless figures carved into the wood.

Basilica di San Domenico   CHURCH
(Piazza San Domenico 13; ☉9.30am-12.30pm & 3.30-6.30pm Mon-Fri, to 5.30pm Sat & Sun) Part of Italy's attraction and myth is its hallowed ground. Every chapel in every church tells a slightly different story. Luring you towards this basilica built in 1238 is the legend of San Domenico, founder of the Dominican order, who died in 1221. His remains lie in an elaborate sarcophagus in the Cappella di San Domenico, which was designed by Nicola Pisano and later added to by a host of artists. Other famous ghosts present in the church include Michelangelo, who carved the angel on the right of the altar when he was only 19, and Mozart, who spent a month at the city's music academy and occasionally played the church's organ.

Chiesa di San Francesco   CHURCH
(Piazza San Francesco; ☉6.30am-noon & 3-7pm) Think Gothic. This dark mysterious church was one of the first in Italy to be built in the French Gothic style. Inside check out the tomb of Pope Alexander V and the remarkable 14th-century marble altarpiece depicting sundry saints and scenes from the life of St Francis.

UNIVERSITY QUARTER
Bolshie graffiti, communist newspaper-sellers, and the whiff of last night's beer (and urine) characterise the scruffy but strangely contagious streets of the university quarter, the site of Bologna's former Jewish ghetto.

TOP CHOICE Le Due Torri   TOWER
Standing sentinel over Piazza di Porta Ravegnana, Bologna's two leaning towers are the city's main symbol. The taller of the two, the 97.6m-high Torre degli Asinelli (admission €3; ☉9am-6pm, to 5pm Oct-May) is open to the public, although it's not advisable for vertigo-sufferers or owners of arthritic knees (there are 498 steps up a semi-exposed wooden staircase). Superstitious students also boycott it: local lore says if you climb the tower you'll never graduate. Built by the Asinelli family between 1109 and 1119, today the tower leans 1.3m off vertical. The neighbouring 48m Torre Garisenda is sensibly out of bounds given its drunken 3.2m tilt.

Abbazia di Santo Stefano   CHURCH
(Via Santo Stefano 24; ☉9am-12.30pm & 3.30-6.30pm) Not just another church, the Santo Stefano is a rather unique (and atmospheric) medieval religious complex. Originally there were seven churches – hence the basilica's nickname Sette Chiese – but only four remain. Entry is via the 11th-century Chiesa del Crocefisso, which houses the bones of San Petronio and leads through to the Chiesa del Santo Sepolcro. This austere octagonal structure probably started life as a baptistry. Next door, the Cortile di Pilato is named after the central basin in which Pontius Pilate is said to have washed his hands after condemning Christ to death. In fact, it's an 8th-century Lombard artefact. Beyond the courtyard, the Chiesa della Trinità connects to a modest cloister and a small museum. The fourth church, the Santi Vitale e Agricola, is the city's oldest. Incorporating recycled Roman masonry and carvings, the bulk of the building dates from the 11th century. The considerably older tombs of two saints in the side aisles once served as altars.

Oratorio di Santa Cecilia   CHURCH
(Via Zamboni 15; ☉10am-1pm & 2-6pm) This is one of Bologna's unsung gems. Inside, the magnificent 16th-century frescoes by Lorenzo Costa depicting the life and Technicolor death of St Cecilia and her husband Valeriano are in remarkably good nick, their colours vibrant and their imagery bold and unabashed. The Oratorio hosts regular free chamber music recitals. Check the board outside for upcoming details.

FREE University Museums   MUSEUM
The world's oldest university has a slew of free museums that make a break from the ecclesiastical art/dark church alternation. Most are in the Palazzo Poggi (www.museopalazzopoggi.unibo.it; Via Zamboni 33; ☉10am-1pm & 2-4pm Tue-Fri, 10.30am-1.30pm & 2.30-5.30pm Sat & Sun), where you can peruse waxwork uteri in the Obstetrics Museum and giant tortoise shells in the Museum of Natural Sciences. There are further surprises (and stuffed exhibits) over at the Museo di Zoologia and the Museo di Antropologia on nearby Via Selma 3.

Pinacoteca Nazionale   ART GALLERY
(Via delle Belle Arti 56; admission €4; ☉9am-7pm Tue-Sun) The city's main art gallery has a powerful collection of works by Bolognese

DON'T MISS

THE CHURCH ON THE HILL

About 3.5km southwest of the city centre, the hilltop Basilica Santuario della Madonna di San Luca (Via di San Luca 36; ⊙7am-12.30pm & 2.30-7pm Apr-Sep, to 5pm Oct-Feb, to 6pm Mar) prompts memories of Turin's 'Superga'. The church houses a representation of the Virgin Mary, supposedly painted by St Luke and transported from the Middle East to Bologna in the 12th century. The 18th-century sanctuary is connected to the city walls by the world's longest portico, held aloft by 666 arches, beginning at Piazza di Porta Saragozza. Take bus 20 from the city centre to Villa Spada, from where you can continue by minibus to the sanctuary. Alternatively, continue one more stop on bus 20 to the Meloncello arch and walk the remaining 2km under the arches.

artists from the 14th century onwards, including a number of important canvases by the late-16th-century Carracci cousins Ludovico, Agostino and Annibale. Among the founding fathers of Italian baroque art, the Carraccis were deeply influenced by the Counter-Reformation sweeping through Italy in the latter half of the 16th century. Much of their work is religious and their imagery is often highly charged and emotional, designed to appeal to the piety of the viewing public. Works to look out for include Ludovico's *Madonna Bargellini,* the *Comunione di San Girolamo* (Communion of St Jerome) by Agostino and the *Madonna di San Ludovico* by Annibale. Elsewhere in the gallery you'll find several works by Giotto, as well as Raphael's *Estasi di Santa Cecilia* (Ecstasy of St Cecilia). El Greco and Titian are also represented, but by comparatively little-known works.

NORTH OF PIAZZA MAGGIORE

MAMbo   ART GALLERY

(Museo d'Arte Moderna di Bologna; Via Don Minzoni 14; adult/reduced €6/4; ⊙noon-6pm Tue, Wed & Fri, to 10pm Thu, to 8pm Sat & Sun) Avant-gardes, atheists, and people who've had their fill of dark religious art can seek solace in Bologna's newest museum (opened 2007) housed in a cavernous former municipal bakery. Its permanent and rotating exhibits showcase the work of up-and-coming Italian artists. Entrance to the permanent collection is free on Wednesday.

🏃 Activities

Hammam Bleu   SPA

(☑051 58 01 62; www.hammam.it; Vicolo Barbazzi 4; ⊙noon-10pm Mon-Fri, 11am-7pm Sat & Sun) If the tranquillity of all those churches hasn't calmed you down, try this Turkish bath in the historic centre. Prices start at €50 for a

half-hour rub-down or €40 for just the spa facilities (steam room, sauna, jacuzzi).

📖 Courses

La Vecchia Scuola Bolognese   COOKING

(www.lavecchiascuola.com; Via Malvasia 49) It stands to reason; Bologna is also a good place to learn to cook and this is one of several schools that offer courses for English speakers. Prices range from €80 for a single four-hour course to €210 for three days.

☞ Tours

Various outfits offer guided, two-hour walking tours in English (€13). Groups assemble outside the main tourist office on Piazza Maggiore (no booking required).

La Chiocciola   WALKING

(☑051 22 09 64; www.lachiocciolasnc.com) Meets 10.15am Wednesday, Saturday and Sunday.

Trambus Open   BUS

(www.trambusopen.com) Runs an hour-long, hop-on, hop-off bus tour of the city departing from the train station several times daily. Tickets (€10) can be bought on board.

🎆 Festivals & Events

Bologna has an eclectic events calendar, mainly centred on music. Performances – or in rock-and-roll parlance, 'gigs' – range from street raves to jazz concerts, ballet performances and religious processions. Summer is generally the best time. Big events include the following.

Bologna Estate   ARTS

A three-month (mid-June to mid-September) program of concerts, film projections, dance performances and much more. Held in open-air venues throughout the city, many events are free. Tourist offices carry details.

Salotto del Jazz   MUSIC

(July to August) A small-scale jazz fest organised by four venues in and around Via Mascarella in the university quarter northwest of Via Zamboni.

🛏 Sleeping

Accommodation in Bologna is geared to the business market, with a glut of midrange to top-end hotels and precious few budget options. If possible, avoid the busy spring and autumn trade-fair seasons, when prices skyrocket, hotels get heavily booked and advance reservations are essential. Outside of fair season, some hotels offer discounts of up to 50% and attractive weekend rates.

TOP CHOICE Prendiparte B&B   B&B €€€

(✆051 58 90 23; www.prendiparte.it; Via Sant'Alò 7; r €250-300) You will never – repeat, *never* – stay anywhere else like this. Forget the B&B tag: you don't just get a room here, you get an entire 900-year-old tower (Bologna's second tallest). The living area (bedroom, kitchen and lounge) is spread over three floors and there are nine more levels to explore, with a 17th-century prison halfway up and outstanding views from the terrace up top. Find a millionaire to shack up with and pretend you're an errant medieval prince(ss) for the night.

Il Convento dei Fiori di Seta   BOUTIQUE HOTEL €€€

(✆051 27 20 39; www.silkflowersnunnery.com; Via Orfeo 34; r €130-270, ste €280-440; ❋) Before you get to Bologna's budget options, you have to gawp at all the pricey places, including this chic boutique hotel housed in a 14th-century convent. Religious-inspired frescoes sit alongside Mapplethorpe-style flower photos and snazzy modern light fixtures; beds come with linen sheets and bathrooms feature cool mosaic tiles.

Hotel University Bologna   HOTEL €€

(✆051 22 97 13; www.hoteluniversitybologna.com; Via Mentana 7; d €70-95, tr €90-110; ❋@🛜) Remember student digs? Well, heave a sigh of relief, they were nothing like this. It's good to see that the world's oldest university town can still muster up a hotel that's not a million miles beyond the price range of its large undergraduate population. The HU Bologna is billed as a three-star, but it's recently renovated and punches well above its weight.

Albergo Rossini   HOTEL €

(✆051 23 77 16; www.albergorossini.com; Via dei Bibiena 11; s €40-75, d €70-100; ⊘closed mid-Jul–mid-Aug; ❋) The approach isn't promising; a short walk off Piazza Verdi along an alley that tipsy drinkers use as an alfresco pee-spot. But, once inside, the journeyman Rossini is warm, friendly and eager to please. Try to bag a room on the top floor, where strategically placed skylights let the sun pour in.

Hotel Orologio   DESIGN HOTEL €€€

(✆051 745 74 11; www.bolognarthotels.it; Via IV Novembre 10; s €100-325, d €170-350; P❋@🛜) One of four upmarket hotels run by Bologna Arts Hotels, this refined pile just off Piazza Maggiore seduces guests with its slick service, smart rooms furnished in elegant gold, blue and burgundy, swirling grey and white marble bathrooms, complimentary chocs and an unbeatable downtown location.

Albergo Garisenda   HOTEL €

(✆051 22 43 69; www.albergogarisenda.com; 3rd fl, Galleria del Leone, Via Rizzoli 9; d without bathroom €65-85, d with bathroom €85-110; P🛜) In the shadow of Bologna's leaning towers, the Garisenda has seven no-nonsense rooms with comfy beds and modest furniture. The entrance is in a covered shopping gallery off Via Rizzoli. Parking is €7, breakfast €5.

Albergo delle Drapperie   HOTEL €

(✆051 22 39 55; www.albergodrapperie.com; Via delle Drapperie 5; s €60-70, d €75-85; ❋) Right in the heart of the atmospheric Quadrilatero district, the Drapperie is one of those 'hidden' hotels encased in the upper floors of a larger building. Buzz in at ground level and climb the stairs to discover 21 attractive rooms with wood-beamed ceilings, the occasional brick arch and colourful ceiling frescoes. Breakfast is €5 extra.

Ostello Due Torri-San Sisto   HOSTEL €

(✆051 50 18 10; bologna@aighostels.com; Via Viadagola 5 & 14; dm/s/d €16/25/42; P@🛜) Some 6km north of the centre, Bologna's two HI hostels, barely 100m apart, are modern, functional and cheap. Take bus 93 (Monday to Saturday, until 8.20pm) from Via Irnerio, bus 301 (Sunday) from the bus station or bus 21B (evenings, hourly from 8.40pm to 12.40am) opposite the train station.

Albergo Centrale   HOTEL €€

(✆051 22 51 14; www.albergocentralebologna.it; Via della Zecca 2; s €45-60, d €75-120 incl breakfast; ❋) Offering comfort and a central location, the large old-fashioned rooms at Albergo Centrale come with parquet floors, modern furniture and an ample buffet breakfast.

Centro Turistico Città di Bologna
CAMPGROUND €

(☎051 32 50 16; www.hotelcamping.com; Via Romita 12; camping per adult/child €8.50/5 & tent €13, 2-person bungalows €49-90; @⛵) A large, well-equipped campground 6km from the train station. On-site facilities include a bar, minimarket and newsagent. Take bus 68 from the main bus station.

✕ Eating

Gastronomic tip No 1: learn the local lingo and ask for *tagliatelle al ragù*. Calling the city's signature meat sauce 'spag bol' is like calling champagne 'fizzy wine'. Two meals into your Bologna stay and you'll start to understand why the city's known as La Grassa. Food is second only to Catholicism here. *Mortadella* is baloney or Bologna sausage. Tortellini is another speciality, often served stuffed with pumpkin and herbs and cooked with butter and sage. The hills nearby produce the light, fizzy Lambrusco red and a full, dry sauvignon blanc.

The university district northeast of Via Rizzoli harbours hundreds of restaurants, trattorias, takeaways and cafes catering to hard-up students and gourmet diners alike. If you're cooking your own, head to the historic delis in the Quadrilatero.

TOP CHOICE **Drogheria della Rosa**
TRATTORIA €€

(☎051 22 25 29; www.drogheriadellarosa.it; Via Cartoleria 10; meals €35-40; ☉lunch & dinner) With its wooden shelves, apothecaries' jars and bottles, it's not difficult to picture this place as the pharmacy that it once was. Nowadays it's a charming, high-end trattoria, run by a congenial owner who seems to find time to get round every table and explain the day's short, sweet menu. Expect superbly prepared versions of Bolognese classics such as tortellini or steak with balsamic vinegar.

Trattoria del Rosso
TRATTORIA €

(www.trattoriadelrosso.com; Via A Righi 30; meals €16-18; ☉lunch & dinner) You don't have to pay big euros to eat well in Bologna. Doubters should step inside the Rosso, where unfancy decor and quick service attract plenty of hard-up single diners enjoying pop-by lunches. They say that the trattoria is the

oldest in the city, further proof that ancient formulas work best.

Tamburini
BUFFET €

(www.tamburini.com; Via Caprarie 1; meals €10-20; ☉lunch Mon-Sat) Fast food done fresh and imaginatively is no oxymoron in Tamburini, a traditional delicatessen full of swinging hams and pungent cheeses that also runs a popular grab-a-tray buffet. Fill up on alluringly decorated cheese and meat boards, colourful salad bowls, and a choice of three to four daily pasta dishes. Prepare for queues.

Osteria de' Poeti
OSTERIA €€

(www.osteriadepoeti.com; Via de' Poeti 1b; meals €30-40; ☉closed Mon Oct-May, Sun Jun-Aug) In the wine cellar of a 14th-century *palazzo*, this historic eatery is an atmospheric place to enjoy hearty local fare. Take a table by the impressive stone fireplace and order from a selection of staples such as *tagliolone con fiori di zucca, zucchini e prosciutto di Parma* (pasta with pumpkin flowers, zucchini and Parma ham). Evenings feature frequent live music.

Marco Fadiga Bistrot
SEAFOOD €€

(☎051 22 01 18; www.marcofadigabistrot.com; Via Rialto 23; meals €35-40; ☉dinner Tue-Sat) Specialising in fine wine and seafood, from its oyster bar to its let-out-all-the-stops Grand Plateau Royal (an extravagant combo platter that includes just about every sea creature imaginable), this elegant yet relaxed eatery is ideal for a romantic dinner.

Godot Wine Bar
MODERN ITALIAN €€€

(☎051 22 63 15; Via Cartoleria 12; meals €40-50; ☉Mon-Sat) Don't let the name fool you! Yes, there's a great wine selection, with daily specials chalked up on the board and an emphasis on Italian vintages, but Godot has also emerged as one of Bologna's premier restaurants, whipping up some truly extravagant concoctions.

TOP CHOICE **La Sorbetteria Castiglione**
GELATERIA €

(Via Castiglione 44; ☉8.30am-11pm) Everyone has a wondrous Italian ice-cream story and more than a few (including one of a recent *New York Times* reviewer) were made here in this temple to gelati. It's a bit peripheral to the centre but worthy of the walk.

Gelateria Gianni
GELATERIA €

(www.gelateriagianni.com; Via San Vitale 2; ☉noon-10pm) Edging Torinese import 'Grom' into third place is this new contender where generous dollops of flavours such as white chocolate and cherry have brought a sweet ending to many an undergraduate date night. There are two other branches.

Trattoria Fantoni
TRATTORIA €

(Via del Pratello 11a; meals €15; ⊘closed Sun & dinner Mon) A much-loved eatery dishing up classic Italian food at welcome prices. The atmosphere's jovial and the decor is an agreeable clash of clutter and modern art.

P122@s
PIZZERIA €

(Via dei Musei 2-4; pizzas €6-9) This trendy spot attracts a fashionable local crowd with its wood-fired pizzas. Set under the porticoes near Piazza Maggiore.

Trattoria Belle Arti
TRATTORIA €

(Via Belle Arti 14; meals €20) Kiss goodbye to touchy-feely table service. Belle Arti is noisy, crowded and sometimes chaotic; but it knocks out 'real' food starring numerous undone Bolognese classics.

Self-Catering

Stock up on victuals at the **Mercato delle Erbe** (Via U Bassi 27; ⊘7am-1.15pm Mon-Sat, 5-7.30pm Mon-Wed & Fri), Bologna's main covered market. Alternatively, the Quadrilatero area east of Piazza Maggiore harbours a daily **produce market** (Via Clavature; ⊘7am-1pm Mon-Sat, 4.15-7.30pm Mon-Wed, Fri & Sat) and some of the city's best-known delis.

Drinking

Hit the graffiti-strewn streets of the university district after sunset and the electrifying energy is enough to make a jaded 40-year-old feel 20 again. Clamorous bars spill out into the street, groups of earnest drinkers sit down in circles on the hard pavement, and talented musicians jam old Thelonius Monk numbers. Piazza Verdi is the nexus for thirsty students; for a more upmarket, dressier scene head to the Quadrilatero.

TOP CHOICE Le Stanze
WINE BAR

(www.lestanzecafe.com; Via Borgo San Pietro 1; ⊘11am-3am Mon-Sat) If La Scuderia reeks of undergraduate days you'd rather forget, hit the more chic Le Stanze, a former chapel where each of the four interior rooms has its own design concept. The *aperitivo* buffet is top-notch here, with paellas, pastas and chicken drumsticks to accompany your wine/cocktail.

La Scuderia
BAR, CAFE

(www.lascuderia.bo.it; Piazza Verdi 2; ⊘8am-1am Mon-Sat; ☎) On Piazza Verdi, the shabby-chic Scuderia envelops the whole square on a good night. This being Bologna, the clientele is made up of a socialist republic of pavement loungers, hairy Goths, down-but-not-quite-out students, and the odd stray opera-goer swept up in the nostalgia of their undergraduate days. The bar occupies the Bentivoglio family's former stables and features towering columns, vaulted ceilings, and arty photos.

English Empire
BAR

(Via Zamboni 24a; ⊘7pm-3am) Despite the fact that Bologna never was part of any English Empire, this pungent pub does a roaring trade in both Guinness and Bass (on tap), spilling its patrons halfway up the colonnaded sidewalks. Early-morning joggers glide past the remnants.

ITIT
CAFE

(Largo dei Respighi 2; ☎) A new trend in coffee consumption? This new student-quarter cafe is a haven of wi-fi geeks, hung-over revellers and lunch-breakers choosing pre-packed sandwiches. It offers coffee in takeaway cups, double shots, low-fat, and numerous other 'Americanisms'.

Nu-Lounge Bar
BAR

(Via de' Musei 6f) A swish bar in the Quadrilatero quarter, Nu-Lounge's well-groomed Italian crowd quaffs pre-dinner *aperitivi* while checking their reflections in the large glass windows of the porticoed terrace.

Bravo Caffè
BAR

(Via Mascarella 1; ⊘8pm-late) Across from Cantina Bentivoglio, Bravo is a sexy wine bar with red walls, black furniture and soft, subtle lighting. It also features regular live jazz and a full food menu.

Marsalino
CAFE, BAR

(Via Marsala 13d; ⊘lunch & dinner Tue-Sat, dinner Sun, lunch Mon) Tiny, laid-back and chameleonic, Marsalino is a laid-back watering hole that opens as a tearoom at 4pm, morphs into a wine bar at 6pm, and becomes a restaurant at 8pm.

Entertainment

Bologna, courtesy of its large student population, knows how to rock; but it also knows how to clap politely at the opera. The most comprehensive listings guide is *Bologna*

Spettacolo (€1.50, in Italian), available at newsstands.

Cantina Bentivoglio
LIVE MUSIC

(www.cantinabentivoglio.it; Via Mascarella 4b; 8pm-2am) Bologna's top jazz joint, the Bentivoglio is a jack of all trades. Part wine bar (choose from over 500 labels), part restaurant (the daily prix-fixe menu costs €28) and part jazz club (there's live music nightly), this much-loved institution oozes cosy charm with its ancient brick floors, arched ceilings and shelves full of wine bottles.

Kinki
NIGHTCLUB

(www.kinkidisco.com; Via Zamboni 1a; 11pm-late Sep-May) Forget the medieval *palazzi*. Kinki is over 50 years old, ancient history by nightclub standards. It took on its current moniker in 1975 and remains a crucial fount for Bologna's club scene, with art exhibitions, video projections, house music and a Sunday gay night.

Cassero
NIGHTCLUB

(www.cassero.it; Via Don Minzoni 18; 9.30pm-5am Sat, to 2am Wed-Fri, to midnight Sun-Tue) Saturday and Wednesday are the big nights at this legendary gay and lesbian (but not exclusively) club, home of Italy's Arcigay organisation.

Villa Serena
LIVE MUSIC

(Via della Barca 1; 9.30pm-3am Fri & Sat) Three floors of film screenings and music, live and canned, plus a garden for outdoor chilling.

Cinema Chaplin
CINEMA

(www.cinemachaplin.it; Piazza di Porta Saragozza 5; admission €5) Screens films in English every Monday from September through May.

Teatro Comunale
THEATRE

(www.tcbo.it; Largo Respighi 1) Wagner's works were heard for the first time in Italy in Bologna's main opera and classical music venue.

🛍 Shopping

If you came for the food, head for the Quadrilatero, a haven of family-run delis and speciality food shops. Leaders in the field are Paolo Atti (Via Drapperie 6; 7.30am-1.30pm & 4-7.15pm Mon-Sat) and La Baita (Via Pescheria Vecchie 3; 8am-8pm, closed Sun Jun-Aug)

📷 Librerie Coop
BOOKSTORE

(Via Orefici 19; 9am-midnight Mon-Sat, to 8pm Sun) A dream for hungry bookworms (or erudite gourmands), this three-level bookshop coop is a joint project with ethical Turin supermarket chain, Eataly. There are two eating options and thousands of books inside.

ℹ Information

Internet Access

Iperbole (www.comune.bologna.it/wireless; Palazzo D'Accursio. Piazza Maggiore 6; internet & wi-fi free; 9.30am-6.30pm Mon-Sat) The municipal government's free internet service, allowing one hour daily on six public computers, or three hours of wi-fi access. Register at the Iperbole desk inside Palazzo D'Accursio.

Medical Services

Ospedale Maggiore (☎051 647 81 11; Largo Nigrisoli 2) West of the city centre; take bus 19 from Via Bassi.

Post

Post office (Piazza Minghetti 4)

Tourist Information

Tourist office (www.bolognaturismo.info; Piazza Maggiore 1e; 9am-7pm) Also offices in the airport and train station.

ℹ Getting There & Away

Air

Bologna's Guglielmo Marconi airport (www.bologna-airport.it) is 8km northwest of the city. It's served by over two dozen airlines including British Airways (daily flights to Gatwick) and Ryanair (one daily flight to Stansted).

Bus

Intercity buses leave from the main bus station (www.autostazionebo.it) off Piazza XX Settembre, just southeast of the train station. However, for nearly all destinations, the train's a better option.

Car & Motorcycle

Bologna is linked to Milan, Florence and Rome by the A1 Autostrada del Sole. The A13 heads directly to Ferrara, Padua and Venice, and the A14 to Rimini and Ravenna. Bologna is also on the SS9 (Via Emilia), which connects Milan to the Adriatic coast. The SS64 goes to Ferrara.

Major car-hire companies are represented at Guglielmo Marconi airport and outside the train station. City offices include Budget (Via G Amendola 12f) and Hertz (Via G Amendola 16a).

Train

Bologna is a major transport junction for northern Italy. The new high-speed train to Florence (€25) opened in December 2009 and takes only 37 minutes. Rome (regional €25.50, five hours;

Eurostar €59, two hours 20 minutes) and Milan (regional €13.60, 2¼ hours; Eurostar €42, one hour) also offer quick links.

Frequent trains from Bologna serve cities throughout Emilia-Romagna; for details, see Getting There & Away listings under individual cities in this chapter.

ⓘ Getting Around

To/From the Airport

Aerobus shuttles (www.atc.bo.it) depart from the main train station for Guglielmo Marconi airport every 15 to 30 minutes between 5.30am and 11.10pm. The 20-minute journey costs €5 (tickets can be bought on board).

Car & Motorcycle

Much of the city centre is off limits to vehicles. If you're staying downtown, your hotel can provide a ticket (€7 per day) that entitles you to enter the ZTL (Zona a Traffico Limitato), park in designated spaces and make unlimited trips on city buses for 24 hours.

You can hire a bike at **Autorimessa Pincio** (Via dell'Indipendenza 71z; per 12/24hr €13/18; ⊘7am-midnight Mon-Sat), located near the bus station.

Public Transport

Bologna has an efficient bus system, run by **ATC** (www.atc.bo.it). It has information booths at the main train station, the bus station and on Via Marconi. Buses 25 and 30 are among several that connect the train station with the city centre.

West of Bologna

MODENA
POP 179,900

If Italy were a meal, Modena would be on the main course. Here, on the flat plains of the slow-flowing Po, lies one of the nation's great gastronomic centres, the creative force behind *real* balsamic vinegar, giant tortellini stuffed with tantalising fillings, sparkling Lambrusco wine, and backstreets crammed with some of the best restaurants no one's ever heard of. For those with bleached taste buds, the city has another equally lauded legacy: cars. The famous Ferrari museum is situated in the nearby village of Maranello. Modena is also notable for its haunting Romanesque cathedral, and as the birthplace of the late Italian opera singer, Pavarotti.

◉ Sights

TOP
CHOICE **Cathedral**   CATHEDRAL
(Corso Duomo; ⊘7am-12.30pm & 3.30-7pm) Modena's celebrated cathedral combines the austerity of the Dark Ages with throwback traditions from the Romans in a style known in Europe as Romanesque. The church stands out among Emilia-Romagna's many other ecclesial relics for its remarkable architectural purity. It is, by popular consensus, the finest Romanesque church in Italy, and in 1997 was listed as a Unesco World Heritage Site. While not as large or spectacular as other Italian churches, the cathedral – dedicated to the city's patron saint, St Geminianus – has a number of striking features. The dark interior is dominated by the huge Gothic 'rose window' (actually a 13th-century addition) that shoots rays of light down the grand central apse. To the sides, a series of vivid bas-reliefs depicting scenes from Genesis are the work of the 12th-century sculptor Wiligelmo. Interior highlights include an elaborate rood screen decorated by Anselmo da Campione and, in the crypt, Guido Mazzoni's *Madonna della pappa*, a group of five painted terracotta figures.

Opposite the entrance to the cathedral, the Musei del Duomo (Via Lanfranco 6; adult/child €3/2; ⊘9.30am-12.30pm & 3.30-6.30pm Tue-Sun) holds yet more of Wiligelmo's signature stonework.

Inseparable from the cathedral is the early-13th-century Torre Ghirlandina (closed for renovation at the time of research), an 87m tower topped with a Gothic spire that was named after Seville's famous 'Giralda' in the early 16th century by exiled Spanish Jews. Facing it across Piazza Grande is the elegant facade of the Palazzo Comunale.

Palazzo dei Musei   MUSEUM
(Piazzale Sant'Agostino 337) Modena's main museums and galleries are all conveniently housed in the Palazzo dei Musei on the western fringes of the historic centre.

The most interesting, the Galleria Estense (admission €4; ⊘8.30am-7.30pm Tue-Sun) features the Este family's collection of northern Italian paintings from late medieval times to the 18th century. There are also some fine Flemish works and a canvas or two by Velázquez, Correggio and El Greco. Downstairs, the Biblioteca Estense (admission free; ⊘9am-1pm Mon-Sat) holds one of Italy's most valuable collections of books, letters and manuscripts, including the celebrated *Bibbia di Borso d'Este*, a masterpiece of medieval illustration.

A combined ticket (€4) gives entry to the Museo Archeologico Etnologico (⊘9am-noon Tue-Fri, 10am-7pm Sat & Sun) and the

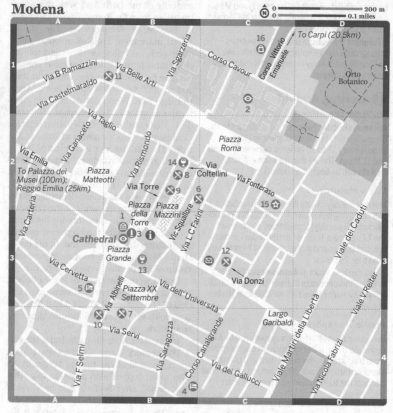

Modena

◎ Top Sights

Museo Civico d'Arte (⊙9am-noon Tue-Fri, 10am-1pm & 3-6pm Sat & Sun). The former has some well-displayed local finds from Palaeolithic to medieval eras, as well as exhibits from Africa, Asia, Peru and New Guinea. Most interesting among the Museo Civico d'Arte's eclectic collection are the sections devoted to traditional paper-making, textiles and musical instruments.

Palazzo Ducale   LANDMARK
Dominating Piazza Roma, this heavy baroque edifice is home to one of Italy's top military academies. It was started in 1634 and was the Este family residence for two centuries. Admission is only by guided tour (tour €6; ⊙tours Sun). Contact ModenaTur (p426) to book.

🎇 Festivals & Events
Modena Terra di Motori   CAR
(www.modenaterradimotori.com, in Italian) Between late March and early May, vintage cars and snazzy Ferraris take to Modena's historic streets in this annual car fest.

Serate Estensi   MEDIEVAL
(www.comune.modena.it/seratestensi, in Italian) In late June and early July, this festival is a celebration of all things medieval, involving banquets, jousts and plenty of dressing up.

🛏 Sleeping
Hotel Cervetta 5   HOTEL €€
(☎059 23 84 47; www.hotelcervetta5.com; Via Cervetta 5; s/d/tr €80/120/155; ❄️🛜) Cervetta is about as posh as Modena gets without pampering to the convention crowd. A location adjacent to intimate Piazza Grande is complemented by quasi-boutique facilities, clean, modern bathrooms and the latest in TV technology. Fruity breakfasts and wi-fi are included; garage parking (€12) isn't.

Canalgrande Hotel   HOTEL €€
(☎059 21 71 60; www.canalgrande hotel.it; Corso Canalgrande 6; s €114-132, d €154-180; ❄️@🛜) A venerable Modenese institution, the Canalgrande exudes old-school elegance with its acres of marble, gilt-framed paintings, sparkling chandeliers and a spacious terrace overlooking the garden out back. Parking costs €12.

Ostello San Filippo Neri   HOSTEL €
(☎059 23 45 98; modena@aighostels.com; Via Santa Orsola 48-52; dm/s/d €16/20/35; @🛜) Modena's businesslike HI hostel has 80 beds in single-sex dorms and family units. Pluses include disabled access, capacious lockers, uncrowded rooms (maximum three beds per dorm) and a bike-storage area. Drawbacks are the 10am to 2pm lockout and the lack of breakfast (though you can bring takeaway food into the hostel's dining area).

Hotel San Geminiano   HOTEL €
(☎059 21 03 03; www.hotelsangeminiano.it; Viale Moreali 41; s/d €60/80; [P]🛜) Geminiano's slightly off-centre location and dark, unspectacular rooms are saved by down-to-earth service and the salt-of-the-earth restaurant next door, which serves shockingly economical pizzas (€4.50), and pesto sauce that tastes like it's been dug straight out of the Emiliano soil.

🍴 Eating
Modena would easily make a top-10 list of best Italian culinary towns. The beauty lies not just in the food, but in the way in which it is unpretentiously presented in unfancy, nondescript restaurants shoehorned up blind alleys or hidden inside faceless office blocks, often without signage. Its most famous product is *aceto balsamico di Modena,* aged between four and 12 years depending on whether you're having it with cheese or on your ice cream. The city also produces excellent *prosciutto crudo* (cured ham, aka Parma ham) and *zampone* (stuffed pig's trotters), along with Lambrusco wine, a lively, sparkling red, drunk chilled and paired with everything.

TOP CHOICE **Hosteria Giusti**   GASTRONOMIC €€€
(☎059 22 25 33; www.hosteriagiusti.it; Vicolo Squallore 46; meals €70; ⊙12.30-2pm Tue-Sat) With only four tables, a narrow back-alley location, no real signage and a 90-minute daily opening window, this perplexingly unassuming *osteria* isn't really setting itself up for legendary status. But tentative whispers turn to exuberant shouts when regional specialities like *cotechino fritto con zabaglione al lambrusco* (fried Modena sausage with wine-flavoured egg custard) arrive at your table. The plaudits are growing, including from hard-to-impress Italian-American Iron Chef Mario Batelli, who lists it as one of his favourite hang-outs in Italy.

Trattoria Aldina   TRATTORIA €
(Via Albinelli 40; meals €17; ⊙lunch Mon-Sat) Upstairs in a utilitarian apartment block, Aldina feels like a precious secret guarded loyally by local shoppers, who roll in from the adjacent produce market. The lunch-only menu

is spearheaded by the kind of no-nonsense homemade food that only a 50-plus Italian mamma raised on handmade pasta is capable of concocting. There's no written menu; take what's in the pot and revel in the people-watching potential.

Ristorante da Danilo TRADITIONAL ITALIAN €€
(Via Coltellini 29-31; meals €25-30; ⊙Mon-Sat) Speedy waiters glide around balancing bread baskets, wine bottles and pasta dishes in this deliciously traditional dining room where first dates mingle with animated families and office groups on a birthday jaunt. What would pass as outstanding in any other country passes as normal in Danilo: antipastos of salami, *pecorino* (sheep's-milk cheese) and fig marmalade; secondos of *bollito misto* (mixed boiled meats), and a vegetarian risotto *al radicchio trevigiano* (with red chicory).

Ristorante da Enzo TRADITIONAL ITALIAN €€
(⌨059 22 51 77; Via Coltellini 17; meals €25-30; ⊙closed Sun dinner & Mon) Get in early! This restaurant is highly regarded for its classic, regional cooking, not least its signature *scaloppina all'aceto balsamico* (cutlets in balsamic vinegar). You enter innocuously through the kitchen prep area where charismatic chefs are up to their elbows in floury pasta dough. The decor is no frills – the star treatment is reserved entirely (and rightly) for the food.

Trattoria Ermes TRATTORIA €
(Via Ganaceto 89; meals €20; ⊙lunch Mon-Sat) Here's yet another fabulous, affordable little lunch spot, tucked into a single wood-panelled room at the northern edge of downtown Modena. An older couple runs the place – she cooks, he juggles plates and orders while keeping up a nonstop stream of banter with the customers. The menu changes daily depending on what's fresh at the market.

Trattoria Il Fantino TRATTORIA €€
(⌨059 22 36 46; www.gustamodena.it/ilfantino; Via Donzi 7; meals €15; ⊙closed Mon) More homemade Modenese miracles forged in a hole-in-the-wall-sized dining room that can't have changed much since the Risorgimento (reunification period). Arrive early and squeeze into one of 45 narrow pews.

SELF-CATERING
Modena's fresh-produce market (⊙6.30am-2.30pm Mon-Sat year-round, 4.30-7pm Sat Oct-May) has its main entrance on Via Albinelli.

⚑ Drinking
A youthful bar-hopping crowd congregates along Via dei Gallucci. There's also a cluster of bars along Via Emilia near the cathedral. Another stand out place is Compagnia del Taglio (Via Taglio 12).

Cafe-Ristorante Concerto CAFE, BAR
(www.cafeconcertomodena.com; Piazza Grande 26; ⊙8am-3am) This Piazza Grande establishment manages a delicate juxtaposition between trendy (ubercontemporary decor) and old (cobbled central-square location) without appearing out of place. Inside any 19-hour window it wears three hats: all-day cafe, (pricey) restaurant, and evening bar/club. The latter is its best incarnation, primarily because of the free bar snacks (minimum consumption €5), chilled Lambrusco and footloose party atmosphere so often lacking in Italy's Renaissance cities.

☆ Entertainment
During July and August, outdoor concerts and ballet are staged on Piazza Grande.

Teatro Comunale Luciano Pavarotti THEATRE
(www.teatrocomunalemodena.it; Corso Canal-grande 85) It will come as no surprise that the birthplace of Pavarotti has a decent opera house. The Comunale opened in 1841 and has 900 seats and 112 boxes. Following the death of its exalted native son in September 2007, it was renamed in his honour.

⚐ Shopping
Enoteca Ducale FOOD, WINE
(Corso Vittorio Emanuele 15; ⊙9am-7pm Tue-Sun) Do your friends back home a favour by loading up on balsamic vinegar presents here – aged anywhere from three to 100 years (tasting is allowed). They'll never buy the supermarket stuff again!

ⓘ Information
ModenaTur (www.modenatur.it, in Italian; Via Scudari 8; ⊙2.30-6.30pm Mon, 9am-1pm & 2.30-6.30pm Tue-Sat) A private agency that organises tours to balsamic-vinegar producers and *parmigiano reggiano* (Parmesan) dairies.

Post office (Via Emilia 86)

Tourist office (http://turismo.comune. modena.it; Piazza Grande 14; ⊙3-6pm Mon, 9am-1pm & 3-6pm Tue-Sat, 9.30am-12.30pm Sun) Provides city maps and the useful *Welcome to Modena* brochure.

Ufficio Relazioni con il Pubblico (Piazza Grande 17; per hr €2.50; ⊙9am-1pm & 3-6pm Mon, Tue & Thu, 9am-1pm Wed & Fri) Municipal

FERRARI FANTASY

It's not every day that you get to tune out of *Top Gear* and tune in (briefly) to the motoring fantasy that is Maranello. The metaphoric haj for all petrolheads is the Galleria Ferrari (www.galleria.ferrari.com; Via Ferrari 43; adult/reduced €13/9; ⊙9.30am-7pm May-Sep, to 6pm Oct-Apr); they come here to obsess over the world's largest collection of Ferraris, including Formula 1 exhibits, a trajectory of the cars' mechanical evolution, and a revolving feature of 40 of the landmark models. Just down the road, the company factory is off limits to the 99.99% of the world's population who don't own a Ferrari.

The town of Maranello is 17km south of Modena. From Modena's bus station take bus 800 (€2.30, 30 minutes).

internet service with initial €2 registration fee, plus hourly rate thereafter.

❶ Getting There & Around

The bus station is on Via Molza, northwest of the centre. **ATCM** (www.atcm.mo.it, in Italian) buses connect Modena with most towns in the region.

By car, take the A1 Autostrada del Sole if coming from Rome or Milan, or the A22 from Mantua and Verona.

The train station is north of the historic centre, fronting Piazza Dante. Destinations include Bologna (€3.30, 30 minutes, half-hourly), Parma (€4.60, 30 minutes, half-hourly) and Milan (regional/express train €12.50/26.50, two hours, hourly).

ATCM's bus 7 links the train station with the bus station and city centre.

CARPI
POP 65,800

A small town with a giant square, Carpi is defined by humungous Piazza del Martini, fringed by 50 porticoes and big enough to mark out an aeroplane landing strip. It's only 15 minutes on the train from Modena and well worth an afternoon's detour.

⊙ Sights

Piazza dei Martiri   PIAZZA

Measuring 270m by 60m, the Piazza dei Martiri is Italy's third largest after Piazza San Pietro in Rome and Venice's Piazza San Marco. Over 50 columns holding up an equitable number of porticoes run down the western side.

Palazzo Pio   MUSEUM

(⊙10am-1pm & 3-7pm Fri-Sun) Flanking the east side of the square, this muscular palace houses two museums. The Museo Civico (adult/reduced €5/3) has archaeological exhibits and a recently opened art gallery with paintings from the 15th to 20th centuries. More poignant is the Museo Monumento

al Deportato Politico e Razziale (adult/reduced €3/2), which documents the experience of prisoners in the nearby Fossoli Concentration Camp in 13 simple but haunting rooms. Ask at the entrance for translated versions (in English, French and German) of the profoundly moving quotes that cover the museum's walls, extracted from letters written home by prisoners.

Cattedrale Dell'Assunta   CATHEDRAL

(Piazza dei Martiri) Begun in 1515 and finished in the 19th century, the cathedral is an architectural cocktail of styles, sporting a baroque facade and a neoclassical interior. The initial plan was based, rather ambitiously, on St Peter's in Rome.

✗ Eating

Caffè-Ristorante del Teatro   CAFE €

(Piazza dei Martiri 72; snacks €6-13; ⊙closed Tue) Square-gazers hog the tables outside the bright-orange neoclassical facade of the Municipal Theatre, where a small cafe has been grafted into the right-hand wing. The fish-themed antipasto plate is a great accompaniment to the unfolding theatre below.

❶ Information

Tourist office (www.turismo.carpidiem.it; Via Berengario 2; ⊙9.30am-1pm & 3-6pm Tue-Sat, 9.30am-12.30pm Sun, 2.30-6pm Mon) Just off the vast main square.

❶ Getting There & Away

Trains run between Carpi and Modena (€1.80, 15 minutes) every 30 to 60 minutes.

REGGIO EMILIA
POP 162,300

Often written off as an emergency pit stop on the Via Emilia, Reggio Emilia states its case as birthplace of the Italian flag – the famous red, white and green tricolour – and a convenient base for sorties south into the region's best natural attraction – the Parco Nazionale dell'Appennino Tosco-Emiliano. Those savvy enough to get out of their train/ car/bus will find a city of attractive squares, grand public buildings and a leafy park. In 2010, Reggio Emilia was named Italy's most cycle-friendly city.

Known also as Reggio nell'Emilia, the town started life in the 2nd century BC as a Roman colony along the Via Emilia. Much of Reggio was built by the Este family during the 400 years it controlled the town, beginning in 1406.

Sights

Reggio's pedestrianised city centre is an agreeable place to wander or cycle. The main sights are centred on Piazza Prampolini and adjacent Piazza San Prospero.

Duomo

DUOMO

(Piazza Prampolini; ⊙8am-noon & 4-7pm) Reggio's 13th-century cathedral was first built in the Romanesque style but was given a comprehensive makeover 300 years later. Nowadays, virtually all that remains of the original is the upper half of the facade and, inside, the crypt.

FREE Museo del Tricolore

MUSEUM

(Piazza Prampolini; ⊙9am-noon Tue-Fri, 10am-1pm & 3-7pm Sat-Sun) A small exhibition that attempts to cover a large subject, this proud memorial to the Italian tricolour flag is in the main square. Next door in the 14th-century Palazzo del Comune is where the flag was actually conceived. At a meeting in the multi-tiered Sala del Tricolore in 1797, Napoleon's short-lived Cispadane Republic was proclaimed and the green, white and red tricolour was adopted for the first time.

Basilica della Beata Vergine della Ghiara

CHURCH

(Corso Garibaldi) Reggio's most important church is associated with a miracle involving a deaf and dumb boy called Marchino, who found his voice (and ears) after an apparition of the virgin in front of a painting of the Blessed Virgin of Ghiara (by G Bianchi) in 1569. The church was built in 1597 as a sanctuary to honour this miracle and the virgin has been faithfully reproduced in a chapel inside. Architecturally the church is classic baroque with notable painting and frescoes by the top Emiliano artists of the period.

FREE Musei Civici

MUSEUM

(www.musei.re.it; ⊙9am-noon Tue-Fri, 10am-1pm & 4-7pm Sat & Sun) Reggio Emilia has five city museum sites, but the best artefacts are located inside the Palazzo San Francesco (Via Spallanzani). Thematic collections here include Roman archaeological finds (look out for the mosaics), 18th-century art, natural history exhibits and a precis of the town's history.

FREE Galleria Parmeggiani

ART GALLERY

(Corso Cairoli 1; ⊙9am-noon Tue-Fri, 10am-1pm & 4-7pm Sat & Sun) The town's main art gallery hails some worthwhile Italian, Flemish and Spanish paintings, as well as a heterogeneous collection of costumes, arms, jewellery and cutlery.

Sleeping

Ostello Basilica della Ghiara

HOSTEL €

(☏0522 45 23 23; Via Guasco 6; dm/s/d €15/20/36) There's no shortage of space at Reggio's memorable HI hostel, housed in a former convent. The two to six-bed guestrooms line vast, echoing corridors, and in summer breakfast is served under the porticoes in the internal garden. The hostel was temporary closed at the time of writing and was scheduled to open under new management in summer 2011. Check ahead.

Albergo Morandi

HOTEL €

(☏0522 45 43 97; www.albergomorandi.com; Via Emilia San Pietro 64; s €60-65, d €85-105; P❉@) Halfway between the train station and historic centre, the Morandi features spruce rooms with big beds, gleaming bathrooms and satellite TV. There's free parking, and the service is unfailingly courteous.

Hotel Posta

HOTEL €€

(☏0522 43 29 44; www.hotelposta.re.it; Piazza del Monte 2; s/d/ste €140/190/280; ❉@) Elegant inside and out, the grand four-star Posta is housed in the 13th-century Palazzo del Capitano del Popolo, one-time residence of Reggio's governor. Rooms are individually decorated, with plenty of heavy floral fabrics, gilt-framed mirrors and antique furniture. Parking costs €12. Just around the corner, you'll find the hotel's less expensive, 16-room annexe, Albergo Reggio (☏0522 45 15 33; www.albergoreggio.it; Via San Giuseppe 7; s/d €75/105).

Eating

Reggio's central squares host a **produce market** (⊙7am-1pm Tue & Fri). Typical local snacks include *erbazzone* (herb pie with cheese or bacon) and *gnocco fritto* (fried salted dough). Parmesan is also produced locally.

La Taverna dell'Aquila TRADITIONAL ITALIAN €
(Via dell'Aquila 6a; meals €20-25; ⊙Tue-Sat) With its colourful, funky decor, jazzy soundtrack and tasty, homemade food, this bright eatery is a bit different from your classic wood-and-wine-bottle trattoria. The fixed-price lunch menus (€6 to €12) are exceptionally good value.

La Bottega dei Briganti OSTERIA €€
(www.bottegadeibriganti.it; Via San Carlo 14b; meals €25-35; ⊙dinner Mon-Sat) Duck under the porticoes to this cosy *osteria* (wine bar serving food) with its conspiratorial atmosphere and small leafy courtyard. The food is excellent, particularly the pasta and risottos.

☆ Entertainment

Teatro Municipale Valli THEATRE
(www.iteatri.re.it, in Italian; Piazza Martiri VII Luglio) Reggio's splendid neoclassical theatre with 12 Tuscan columns stages a full season of dance, opera and theatre. It's named after local-born actor Romolo Valli, who starred alongside Burt Lancaster in *The Leopard* (1963).

❶ Information

Tourist office (www.municipio.re.it/turismo; Via Farini 1a; ⊙8.30am-1pm & 2.30-6pm Mon-Sat, 9am-noon Sun)

❶ Getting There & Around

Bus operator **ACT** (www.actre.it) serves the city and region from its brand-new bus station, just behind Reggio's train station. Destinations include Carpi (€3.50, one hour, 10 daily) and Castelnovo ne' Monti (€4.30, 1¼ hours, seven to 14 daily).

Reggio is on the Via Emilia (SS9) and A1 autostrada. The SS63 is a tortuous but scenic route that takes you southwest across the Parma Apennines to La Spezia on the Ligurian coast.

The train station is east of the town centre. Frequent trains serve all stops on the Milan–Bologna line including Milan (regional/express €10.30/23.50, 1½ to 2½ hours, hourly), Parma (€2.50, 15 minutes, half-hourly), Modena (€2.50, 15 minutes, half-hourly) and Bologna (€5.10, 45 minutes, half-hourly).

If reincarnation ever becomes an option, pray you come back as a Parmesan. Where else do you get to cycle to work through traffic-light cobbled streets in uncrinkled Prada, lunch on fresh-from-the-attic prosciutto and aged *parmigiano reggiano* cheese, quaff full-bodied Sangiovese wine in regal art nouveau cafes, and spend sultry summer evenings listening to classical music in architecturally dramatic opera houses? Smarting from its position as one of Italy's most prosperous cities, Parma has every right to feel smug. More metropolitan than Modena, yet less clamorous than Bologna, this is the city that gave the world Lamborghinis, a composer called Verdi, and enough ham and cheese to start a deli-chain. Stopping here isn't an option, it's a duty.

◉ Sights

Duomo DUOMO
(Piazza del Duomo; ⊙9am-12.30pm & 3-7pm) Another daring Romanesque beauty? Well, yes and no. Consecrated in 1106, Parma cathedral's facade is classic Lombard-Romanesque, but inside, the gilded pulpit and ornate lamp-holders scream baroque. Take note, there are some genuine treasures here: up in the dome, Antonio Correggio's *Assunzione della Vergine* (Assumption of the Virgin) is a kaleidoscopic swirl of cherubims and whirling angels, while down in the southern transept, Benedetto Antelami's *Deposizione* (Descent from the Cross; 1178) relief is considered a masterpiece of its type.

Battistero BAPTISTERY
(Piazza del Duomo; adult/reduced €5/3; ⊙9am-12.30pm & 3-6.45pm) Overshadowing even the cathedral, the octagonal pink-marble baptistry on the south side of the piazza is one of the most important such structures in Italy. Its architecture is a hybrid of Romanesque and Gothic and its construction started in 1196 on the cusp of the two great architectural eras. Architect and sculptor Benedetto Antelami oversaw the project and it contains his best work, including a celebrated set of figures representing the months, seasons and signs of the zodiac. The baptistry wasn't completed until 1307 thanks to several interruptions, most notably when the supply of pink Verona marble ran out.

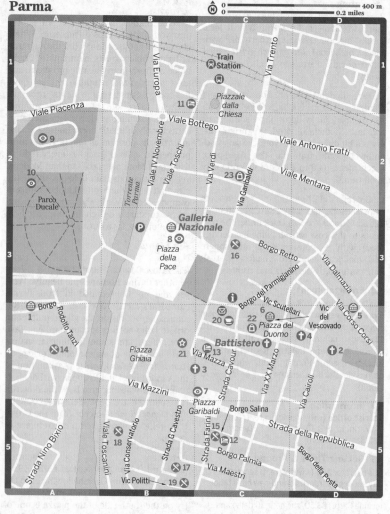

Museo Diocesano MUSEUM
(Vicolo del Vescovado 3a; admission €4; ☉9am-12.30pm & 3-6.30pm) On the other side of the square, in the cellars of the former bishop's palace, this museum displays yet more statuary. Highlights include a finely sculpted Solomon and Sheba and a 5th-century early-Christian mosaic, which was discovered under Piazza del Duomo.

A combined ticket (€6) allows entry into the baptistry and Museo Diocesano.

**Chiesa di San Giovanni
Evangelista** CHURCH
(Piazzale San Giovanni; ☉8-11.45am & 3-7.45pm) This abbey church rises directly behind the Duomo and is attached to a monastery. Its 16th-century facade is mannerist (the less harmonious, rational style that followed the high Renaissance) and is noted for its magnificent frescoed dome, the work of Correggio which was highly influential for its time (and inspired many later works). The adjoining monastery (☉8.30am-noon & 3-6pm) is known as much for the oils and unguents that its monks produce as for its

Parma

Renaissance cloisters. Upstairs, a library is adorned with huge old maps that hang from the walls of a musty reading room.

Palazzo della Pilotta   MUSEUM

Looming over Piazza della Pace's manicured lawns and modern fountains, this monumental palace is hard to miss. Supposedly named after the Spanish ball game of pelota that was once played within its walls, it was originally built for the Farnese family between 1583 and 1622. Heavily bombed in WWII, it has since been largely rebuilt and today houses several museums.

The most important of these, the Galleria Nazionale (adult/child incl Teatro Farnese €6/free; ⏲8.30am-1.30pm Tue-Sun), displays Parma's main art collection. Alongside works by local artists Correggio and Parmigianino, you'll find paintings by Fra Angelico, El Greco and a piece attributed to da Vinci. Before you get to the gallery, you'll pass through the Teatro Farnese, a copy of Andrea Palladio's Teatro Olimpico in Vicenza. Constructed entirely out of wood, it was almost completely rebuilt after being bombed in WWII.

For a change of period, the Museo Archeologico Nazionale (☎0521 23 37 18; admission €2; ⏲9am-2pm Tue-Sun) exhibits Roman artefacts discovered around Parma and Etruscan finds from the Po valley.

Piazza Garibaldi   PIAZZA

On the site of the ancient Roman forum, Piazza Garibaldi is Parma's cobbled hub bisected by the city's main east–west artery, Via Mazzini, and its continuation, Strada della Repubblica. On the square's north side, the facade of the 17th-century Palazzo del Governatore, these days municipal offices, sports a giant sundial, added in 1829. Behind the palace in the Chiesa di Santa Maria della Steccata (Piazza Steccata 9; ⏲9am-noon & 3-6pm), you'll find some of Parmigianino's most extraordinary work, notably the stunning, if rather faded, frescoes on the arches above the altar. Many members of the ruling Farnese and Bourbon families lie buried here.

Parco Ducale   PARK

(⏲6am-midnight Apr-Oct, 7am-8pm Nov-Mar) Stretching along the west bank of the Parma river, these formal gardens seem like Parma personified – refined, peaceful and with barely a blade of grass out of place. They were laid out in 1560 around the Farnese family's Palazzo Ducale, which now serves as headquarters of the provincial carabinieri (military police).

Casa Natale di Toscanini   MUSEUM

(www.museotoscanini.it, in Italian; Borgo R Tanzi 13; admission €2; ⏲9am-1pm & 2-6pm Tue-Sat,

PARCO NAZIONALE DELL'APPENNINO TOSCO-EMILIANO

In the late 1980s Italy had half a dozen national parks. Today it has 24. One of the newest additions is Parco Nazionale dell'Appennino Tosco-Emiliano (www.appennino reggiano.it), a 260-sq-km hectare parcel of land that straddles the border between Tuscany and Emilia-Romagna. Running along the spine of the Apennines mountains, the park is notable for its hiking potential, extensive beech forests, and small population of wolves. Of its many majestic peaks, the highest is 2121m Monte Cusna, easily scale-able from the village of Civago near the Tuscan border on a path (sentiero No 605) that passes the region's best mountain hut, the Rifugio Cesare Battisti (☎0522 89 74 97; www.rifugio-battisti.it). The *rifugio* sits aside one of Italy's great long-distance walking trails, the three-week, 375km-long **Grande Escursione Appennenica (GEA)**, which bisects the park in five stages from Passo della Forbici near the Rifugio Cesare Battisti up to its termination point just outside the park's northwest corner in Montelungo. Sections of the GEA can be done as day walks. *Trekking in the Apennines* by Gillian Price (published by Cicerone) provides an excellent detailed guide of the whole route.

One of the best gateways to the park is the village of Castelnovo ne' Monti about 40km south of Reggio Emilia, along the winding SS63 on a delightfully scenic ACT bus route. The large village has an ultra-helpful tourist office (www.reappennino.com, in Italian; Via Roma 15b; ⏰9am-1pm & 3-6pm Mon-Sat) that stocks bags of free information and sells cheap maps of the region for hikers, cyclists and equestrians.

If you've arrived by bus, you can walk 3km from the village centre up to one of the national park's defining landmarks, the surreal Pietra di Bismantova (1047m), a stark limestone outcrop visible for miles around that's popular with climbers and weekend walkers. In its shadow lies the Rifugio della Pietra, open for food and drinks in summer, and the tiny Eremo di Bismantova monastery, which dates from 1400. From here various paths fan out to the rock's summit (25 minutes). You can also circumnavigate the rock on the lovely 5km **Anella delle Pietra** or even tackle it on a difficult *via ferrata* (trail with permanent cables and ladders) with the proper equipment.

Castelnovo ne' Monti offers a variety of overnight accommodation, including Albergo Bismantova (☎0522 81 22 18; www.albergobismantova.com; Via Roma 73; s/d €47/75), which has an attached restaurant, Le Mormoraie (meals from €25).

Getting to the park on public transport is possible by bus with ACT (www.actre.it) from Reggio Emilia or TEP (www.tep.pr.it) from Parma. Several buses run every day.

2-6pm Sun) At the park's southeast corner the birthplace of Italy's greatest modern conductor, Arturo Toscanini (1867–1957), retraces his life and travels through relics and records. Of interest is his collaborations with acclaimed Italian tenor Aureliano Pertile.

La Casa del Suono
MUSEUM

(Piazzale Salvo D'Acquisto; admission €2; ⏰9am-6pm Thu-Sat, 2-6pm Sun) Oh no, not another church, you groan, until you realise that this one (the 17th-century Chiesa di Santa Elisabetta) has been converted into a funky modern music museum that focuses on the history of music technology. Review the 'ancient' 1970s tape recorders, ponder over jazz age gramophones and stop to listen under a hi-tech 'sonic chandelier'.

🛏 Sleeping

TOP CHOICE / Century Hotel
HOTEL $$

(☎0521 03 98 00; www.centuryhotel.it; Piazzale dalla Chiesa 5a; s/d/ste €80/120/200; 🅿@🛜) Hotels next to train stations are often scruffy little abodes designed for economically minded fly-by-nighters, but the trussed-up Century, still smarting from a modern makeover, offers slick four-star fixtures and amenities at three-star prices.

Hotel Button
HOTEL €€

(☎0521 20 80 39; www.hotelbutton.it; Borgo Salina 7; s €70-84, d €90-118; 🅿@🛜) The spare, hospital-green decor leaves a lot to be desired, but it's hard to argue with Hotel Button's spacious rooms and bathrooms, free wi-fi and convenient location in the heart of historic Parma. Parking costs €10.

Hotel Torino
HOTEL €€

(☎0521 28 10 46; www.hotel-torino.it; Via Mazza 7; s/d €90/130; ❄@) Despite its popularity with performers from the nearby Teatro Regio, there's nothing particularly theatrical about the Torino's rooms; still, it's a reliable, centrally located midrange choice that periodically offers online discounts. Parking costs €12.

Ostello di Parma
HOSTEL €

(☎0521 191 75 47; www.ostelloparma.it; Via San Leonardo 86; dm/d €18.50/41; ☎) Near the autostrada on Parma's northern outskirts, this modern hostel has free wi-fi, inexpensive laundry facilities and a dining area (but no guest kitchen). Breakfast costs €2.50 extra. There's good bike-path access; otherwise take bus 13 or 2N (€1, five minutes) from the train station and get off at the Centro Torri stop.

✗ Eating

Parma specialities need no introduction to anyone familiar with the food of Planet Earth. Both *prosciutto di Parma* (Parma ham) and *parmigiano reggiano* (Parmesan) make excellent antipasto plates accompanied by a good Sangiovese red. Nab one of the following perches and dig in.

TOP
CHOICE **La Greppia**
GASTRONOMIC €€€

(☎0521 23 36 86; Via Garibaldi 39a; meals from €45) A legend in its own lunchtime (and dinnertime, come to that), La Greppia is hallowed ground for the kind of Emilia-Romagna gourmands who know their *ragù* from their bolognese. Sticking tradition and modernity in the same blender, it comes up with Parmesan mousse, pear poached in wine, and plenty more surprises. Service is impeccable.

Trattoria del Tribunale
TRATTORIA €

(www.trattoriadeltribunale.it; Vicolo Politti 5; meals €22) Walk through a gauntlet of ham slicers and waiters gouging lumps out of giant *parmigiano reggiano* cheeses in a pungent entrance vestibule, and you've arrived at one of about 25 contenders for Parma's best restaurant. Start with an elaborate plate of Parma ham, proceed to the *tortelli di Erbette* (pasta stuffed with spinach in butter and Parmesan), and finish, if you dare, with *trippa alla parmigiana* (tripe in Parmesan and breadcrumbs). Pure Parma!

Trattoria Corrieri
TRATTORIA €€

(☎0521 23 44 26; Via Conservatorio 1; meals €25) Eat on the patio under a leafy trellis, or in the labyrinth of rustically decorated interior rooms at this convivial trattoria, under the same ownership as Gallo d'Oro. Everything's top quality and homemade – from the *torta fritta* (warm fried bread) to the Parmesan risotto to the *torta di cioccolato e pere* (pear-and-chocolate cake) for dessert.

Gallo d'Oro
TRADITIONAL ITALIAN €€

(☎0521 20 88 46; www.gallodororistorante.it; Borgo Salina 3; meals €25; ⊘closed dinner Sun) Vintage magazine covers and artfully placed wine bottles lend the Gallo d'Oro a very agreeable bistro feel. But it's not all image: this is one of Parma's best trattorias, serving consistently good Emilian cuisine. For proof, try the cheese plates, rabbit, or – if you're brave – local favourite, *pesto di cavallo* (raw minced horse meat with herbs and Parmesan). Booking is recommended.

Dal Teo
PIZZERIA €

(☎0521 23 54 00; Piazzale Corridoni 15e; pizzas €5-9, meals €15-25; ⊘closed Sat lunch & Sun) Bored with his day job, the enterprising Teo convinced his mum to help him open a pizzeria, using the same recipe he adored as a child. Mum is up at 4am making dough, and Teo takes care of the rest. Just across the bridge from Parma's historic centre, it's a popular hang-out for evening beers and conversation, as well as for its incomparably delicious pizza crust – thick, light and crunchy all at once.

Osteria dei Mascalzoni
OSTERIA €€

(www.osteriadeimascalzoniparma.it; Vicolo delle Cinque Piaghe 1; meals €25-35; ⊘closed Sat lunch & Sun) Cosy inside and out, this restaurant features a beamed dining room and outdoor tables that take over the adjacent alleyway on warm summer evenings. The menu emphasises grilled meat, plus an excellent selection of Parma's famous cheeses and pork products, including *culatello, fiocchetto* and of course prosciutto.

● Drinking

Tabarro
BAR

(Strada Farini 5b; ⊘Tue-Sun) Most of the city's animated drinking scene is centred on Strada Farini, home to numerous wine bars, including this one where aficionados sip fine vintages at tables made from barrels.

Cavour Gran Caffè CAFE
(Strada Cavour 30b; ⊙7am-8pm) Echoes of
Turin are evident in the finely frescoed interior of this classic Parmesan cafe. You'll
pay extra for that cappuccino, of course.

☆ Entertainment
There are few better places in Italy to see
live opera, concerts and theatre. The season
runs from October to April and in summer
there are outdoor-music programs.

Teatro Regio THEATRE
(www.teatroregioparma.org, in Italian; Via Garibaldi
16a) Offers a particularly rich program of
music and opera, even by exacting Italian
standards.

Teatro Due THEATRE
(www.teatrodue.org, in Italian; Via Salnitrara 10)
Presents the city's top drama.

🛍 Shopping
Libreria Fiaccadori BOOKSTORE
(Strada Duomo 8a; ⊙9am-7.30pm Mon-Sat, 10am-
1pm & 3.30-7.30pm Sun) Good old-fashioned
bookshop with ladders to reach the high
shelves and plenty of titles in English.

Salumeria Garibaldi FOOD
(Via Garibaldi 42; ⊙8am-8pm Mon-Sat) Stock
up on the fat of the land at this bountiful delicatessen with dangling sausages,
shelves of Lambrusco wines, slabs of

Parma ham and wheel upon wheel of
parmigiano reggiano.

❶ Information
Police station (☎0521 21 94; Borgo della
Posta 16a)
Post office (Via Melloni)
Tourist office (http://turismo.comune.parma.
it/turismo; Via Melloni 1a; ⊙9am-1pm & 3-7pm
Mon, 9am-7pm Tue-Sat, 9am-1pm Sun)

❶ Getting There & Away
From Piazzale dalla Chiesa in front of Parma's
train station, **TEP** (www.tep.pr.it, in Italian) operates buses throughout the region, including six
daily (one on Sunday) to Busseto (€3.40, one
hour) via Soragna (€2.85, 45 minutes).

Parma is on the A1 connecting Bologna and
Milan and just east of the A15, which runs to La
Spezia. Via Emilia (SS9) passes right through
town.

There are frequent trains to Milan (regional/
express €8.70/21, 1¼ to 1¾ hours, hourly),
Bologna (€6.20, one hour, half-hourly), Modena
(€4.60, 30 minutes, half-hourly) and Piacenza
(€4.60, 40 minutes, half-hourly).

❶ Getting Around
Traffic is banned from the historic centre, so
leave your car at the underground car park
on Viale Toschi and grab a bike, available
for hire next door at **Parma Punto Bici** (www.
parmapuntobici.pr.it, in Italian; Viale Toschi 2a;

FOOD APPRECIATION

Understanding Emilia-Romagna means understanding its traditional food culture. Here
are four essential pit stops where you can get all the info you need straight from the
horse's mouth.

» **Museo del Balsamico Tradizionale** (www.museodelbalsamicotradizionale.org; Via
Roncati 28; adult/reduced €2/1; ⊙9.30am-1pm & 3-7pm Tue-Sun) In the town of Spilam-
berto 17km southwest of Modena, is this temple to balsamic vinegar offering movie
exhibits and guided tours.

» **Museo del Parmigiano Reggiano** (www.museidelcibo.it; Via Volta 5; admission &
tasting €5; ⊙10am-1pm & 3-6pm Sat & Sun Mar-Dec) A walk-through history lesson of one
of the world's most famous cheeses, this pungent museum is in Soragna, 30km northwest of Parma.

» **Museo del Prosciutto di Parma** (www.museidelcibo.it; Via Bocchialini 7; adult/
reduced €3/2; ⊙10am-6pm Sat & Sun Mar-Dec) Ponder swine breeds and the art of ham
preservation in the town of Langhirano, 20km south of Parma. There's a tasting room,
of course.

» **Museo del Pomodoro** (www.museidelcibo.it; Strada Giarola 11; adult/reduced €4/3;
⊙10am-6pm Sat & Sun Mar-Oct) This museum in Collecchio just south of Parma concentrates on the botany, cultivation and sub-products of that omnipresent Italian cooking
ingredient, the good ole' tomato.

per hr/day bicycles €0.70/10, electric bikes €0.90/20; ⏱9am-1pm & 3-7pm Mon-Sat, 10am-1pm & 2.30-7.30pm Sun).

VERDI COUNTRY

During the 'golden age of opera' in the second half of the 19th century, only Wagner came close to emulating Giuseppe Verdi, Italy's operatic genius who was born in the tiny village of Le Roncole in 1813. You can tour his gigantic legacy starting in the town of Busseto, 35km northwest of Parma.

⊙ Sights

TOP CHOICE **Museo Nazionale Giuseppe Verdi**   MUSEUM
(www.museogiuseppeverdi.it; Via Provesi 35, Busetto; adult/reduced €9/7; ⏱10am-6pm Tue-Sun) The latest and best dedication to the great composer is a 21-room museum – set in the lavish 16th-century Villa Pallavicino on the periphery of Busseto – that tracks his life and 27 operas in rich atmospheric detail. There are also gardens, a bookshop, a cafe and regular musical events.

Teatro Verdi   THEATRE
(Piazza Verdi; adult/reduced €4/3; ⏱9.30am-1pm & 3-6.30pm Tue-Sun) A stately theatre on Busseto's aptly named Piazza Verdi was built in 1868, although Verdi himself initially pooh-poohed the idea. It opened with a performance of his masterpiece *Rigoletto*.

Casa Natale di Giuseppe Verdi   MUSEUM
(Roncole Verdi; adult/child €4/3; ⏱9.30am-12.30pm & 2.30-6.30pm Tue-Sun) The humble cottage where Giuseppe Verdi was born in 1813 is now a small museum. It's in the hamlet of Roncole Verdi, 5km beyond Soragna.

Casa Barezzi   MUSEUM
(Via Roma 119; adult/child €4/3; ⏱10am-12.30pm & 3-6.30pm Tue-Sun) Another museum in the centre of Busseto is encased in the home of the composer's patron and the site of Verdi's first concert. It's lovingly curated and filled with Verdi memorabilia including papers, furnishings and valuable recordings.

Villa Verdi   MUSEUM
(www.villaverdi.org; Via Verdi 22; adult/reduced €8/6.50; ⏱9-11.45am & 2.30-6.45pm Tue-Sun, closed Dec & Jan) Verdi's villa, where he composed many of his major works, is in Sant'Agata di Villanova sull'Arda, 5km northwest of Busseto. Verdi lived and worked here from 1851 onwards. Guided visits through the furnishings and musical instruments should be booked in advance online.

ℹ Information

A combined ticket for the latter three Verdi venues costs €8.50. For more information, contact Busseto's **tourist office** (www.bussetolive.com, in Italian; Piazza Verdi 10; ⏱9.30am-1pm & 3-6.30pm Tue-Sun).

ℹ Getting There & Away

TEP (www.tep.pr.it) buses from Parma run along this route six times daily or you can catch a train from Parma to Busseto (€3.30, 45 minutes).

PIACENZA
POP 100,300

Named 'pleasant place' (Placentia) by the Romans, Piacenza soon proved itself to be an important strategic location as well. Just short of the regional border with Lombardy, the contemporary city is day-trip fodder, though there are some decent hotels if you've been priced out of Parma. Its picturesque centre reveals a beautiful Gothic town hall and a couple of august churches.

⊙ Sights

Piazza dei Cavalli   PIAZZA
Dominated by **Palazzo Gotico**, the impressive 13th-century town hall, Piacenza's main square is named after its two martial bronze horses. The two baroque statues, cast by the Tuscan sculptor Francesco Mochi between 1612 and 1625, depict the Farnese dukes Alessandro and Ranuccio.

Duomo   DUOMO
(Piazza del Duomo 33; ⏱7am-noon & 4-7pm) A close runner-up to Modena's immense Romanesque cathedral, Piacenza's 12th-century Lombard-Romanesque *duomo* (cathedral) harmoniously blends white and pink marble, mellow sandstone and red brick. Inside, there are some magnificent 17th-century dome frescoes by Morazzone and Guercino.

Palazzo Farnese   MUSEUM
(www.musei.piacenza.it; Piazza Citadella; combined admission €6; ⏱9am-1pm Tue-Thu, 9am-1pm & 3-6pm Fri-Sun) On the northern edge of the *centro storico* (historic centre), this vast palace was started in 1558 but never fully completed. It now houses the Pinacoteca, an art gallery, along with minor museums of archaeology, carriages, Italian unification and ceramics.

🛏 ✕Sleeping & Eating

Ostello Don Zermani
HOSTEL €

(📞0523 71 23 19; www.ostellodipiacenza.it; Via Zoni 38-40; dm/s/d €18/25/46; 🅿) In a quiet residential area 20 minutes' walk southwest of the city centre, this well-run private hostel offers bright, spotless rooms. Laundry facilities are available, and the building has access for guests with disabilities. Take bus 1, 16 or 17 from the train station.

Hotel Astor
HOTEL €

(📞0523 32 92 96; www.hotelastorpc.eu; Via Tibini 29-31; d €68-98; ✳) This rather worn three-star hotel near the train station offers modest accommodation at reasonable rates. The rooms make no great impression, but they're clean and comfortable enough.

Antica Trattoria Dell'Angelo
TRATTORIA €

(Via Tibini 14; meals €20-25; ⊘Thu-Tue) With its beamed ceiling, wood-fired heater and red-checked tablecloths, this laid-back trattoria is as traditional as they come. The food is hearty, homemade fare – think spinach-and-ricotta *tortelloni*, roast meat and fizzy local red wine. Weekday lunch specials are a steal, with pasta/main courses costing €4/5.

ℹ Information

You'll find the **tourist office** (www.comune. piacenza.it/english; Piazza dei Cavalli 7; ⊘9am-1pm & 3-6pm Tue-Sat, 9.30am-12.30pm Sun & Mon) handily placed in central Piazza dei Cavalli.

ℹ Getting There & Around

Piacenza's bus station is located on Piazza Citadella; however, the train is a more convenient way to reach most destinations. There are frequent trains to/from Milan (regular/Eurostar €5.75/13, one hour, hourly), Parma (€4.60, 40 minutes, half-hourly) and Bologna (regular/Eurostar €9.50/20.50, 1½ hours, hourly).

Piacenza is just off the A1 linking Milan and Bologna and the A21 joining Brescia and Turin. Via Emilia (SS9) also runs past on its way to Rimini and the Adriatic Sea.

Bus 2 (€1) runs between the train station and Piazza dei Cavalli.

East of Bologna

FERRARA
POP 133,600

Ferrara is a city for lingerers, treasure-seekers, or the overtly curious. Well off the tick list of a tourist demographic made up primarily of Rome-lovers and Venice-o-philes, it remains unexplored and deliciously tranquil. Considered one of Italy's great Renaissance cityscapes, the settlement is renowned for its walls (the longest complete defensive ring in Italy), its bicycle-friendliness, and its weighty stash of early-Renaissance palaces. Historically it was once the domain of the powerful Este clan, rivals to Florence's Medici in power and prestige, who endowed the city with its signature building – a huge castle complete with moat positioned slap-bang in the city centre. Ferrara suffered damage from bombing raids during WWII, but its historical core remains intact. Of particular interest is the former Jewish ghetto, the region's largest and oldest, which prevailed from 1627 until 1859.

◉ Sights

Renaissance palaces reborn as museums are Ferrara's tour de force. Also check out the intricate old town with its one-time Jewish ghetto. An entry card valid for all of Ferrara's museums costs €17/10 adult/reduced. Most museums are closed on Monday.

Castello Estense
CASTLE

(Viale Cavour; adult/reduced €8/6.50, tower extra €1; ⊘9.30am-5.30pm) Complete with moat and drawbridge, Ferrara's towering castle was commissioned by Nicolò II d'Este in 1385. Initially it was intended to protect him and his family from the town's irate citizenry, who were up in arms over tax increases, but in the late 15th century it became the family's permanent residence.

Although sections are now used as government offices, a few rooms, including the royal suites, are open for viewing. Highlights are the **Sala dei Giganti** (Giants' Room) and **Salone dei Giochi** (Games Salon), the **Cappella di Renée de France** and the claustrophobic **dungeon**. It was here in 1425 that Duke Nicolò III d'Este had his young second wife, Parisina Malatesta, and his son, Ugo, beheaded after discovering they were lovers, providing the inspiration for Robert Browning's *My Last Duchess*. Linked to the castle by an elevated passageway, the 13th-century crenellated **Palazzo Municipale** was the Este family home until they moved next door to the castle in the late 15th century. Nowadays, it's largely occupied by administrative offices but you can wander around its twin courtyards.

Duomo
DUOMO

(Piazza Cattedrale; ⊘7.30am-noon & 3-6.30pm Mon-Sat, 7.30am-12.30pm & 3.30-7.30pm Sun) The outstanding feature of the pink-and-white 12th-century cathedral is its three-tiered marble facade, combining Romanesque and Gothic styles on the lower and upper tiers respectively. Much of the upper level is a graphic representation of the Last Judgment and heaven and hell (notice the four figures clambering out of their coffins). Astride a pair of handsome lions at the base squats an oddly secular duo, mouths agape at the effort of holding it all up.

On the other side of Piazza Trento Trieste, the **Museo della Cattedrale** (Via San Romano; adult/reduced €6/3; ⊘9am-1pm & 3-6pm Tue-Sun) houses various artefacts from the cathedral, including a serene *Madonna* by Jacopo della Quercia, a couple of vigorous Cosimo Tura canvases, and some witty bas-reliefs illustrating the months of the year.

Palazzo dei Diamanti PALAZZO, MUSEUM
(Corso Ercole I d'Este 21) Named after the spiky diamond-shaped ashlar stones on its facade, the 'diamond palace' was built for Sigismondo d'Este late in the 15th century.

Pinacoteca Nazionale
(adult/reduced €4/2; ⊘9am-2pm Tue, Wed, Fri & Sat, to 7pm Thu, to 1pm Sun) Regarded as the Este family's grandest *palazzo*, Diamanti now hosts the Pinacoteca Nazionale; its interesting collection of paintings are from the Ferrarese and Bolognese schools.

Museo del Risorgimento e della Resistenza
(Corso Ercole I d'Este 19; adult/reduced €4/2; ⊘9am-1pm & 3-6pm Tue-Sun) Next door to Pinacoteca Nazionale, this small museum exhibits documents, proclamations and posters from the Italian unification movement and WWII, as well as numerous uniforms, guns and hand grenades.

Casa Romei PALAZZO, MUSEUM
(Via Savonarola 30; adult/reduced €3/1.50; ⊘8.30am-7.30pm Tue-Sun) This palace was once owned by Giovanni Romei, a top administrator to the Este clan – and his importance shows in the architecture. The austere brick exterior hides a peaceful inner patio (once part of an adjacent monastery). On the 1st floor is a 16th-century apartment preserved in its original state. There's plenty more art and frescoes dotted around.

Palazzo Schifanoia PALAZZO, MUSEUM
(Via Scandiana 23; adult/reduced €6/3; ⊘9am-6pm Tue-Sun) Ferrara's most famous frescoes are in the Este's 14th-century pleasure palace built in 1385. The museum is bitingly ordinary at first, but hold out until the **Salone dei Mesi** (Room of the Months), where frescoes executed by Francesco del Cossa in 1470 depict the months, seasons and signs of the zodiac. Some are badly faded, but they are unusually un-religious in tone and the only ones of their type in Italy.

Museo Lapidario
(Via Camposabbionario; ⊘9am-6pm Tue-Sun) Your ticket to Schifanoia also gives entry to this nearby museum, which has a small, undocumented collection of Roman and Etruscan stele, tombs and inscriptions.

TOP CHOICE Palazzo Massari PALAZZO, MUSEUM
(Corso Porta Mare 9) Another early-Renaissance palace, but this time the art inside is punchier and more modern. The best of the building's museums is the **Museo Giovanni Boldini** (adult/reduced €6/3; ⊘9am-1pm & 3-6pm Tue-Sun), dedicated solely to the works of Ferrara-born Giovanni Boldini, the so-called *Master of Swish* (check out the brush technique). His portraits of women from Victorian rigidity to 1920s chic are amazing. The entrance fee also gets you into the **Museo dell'Ottocento** with its 19th-century art and a pleasant sculpture garden. You must pay extra for the **Museo d'Arte Moderna e Contemporanea Filippo de Pisis** (adult/reduced €4/2), half of which is devoted to the said modern Ferraranese painter famous for his cityscapes and still life.

City Walls CITY WALLS
Only Lucca in Tuscany can claim a more complete set of walls than Ferrara, though with a total circumference of 9km, Ferrara's are longer. Adorned with a well-marked set of paths, unbroken on the northern and eastern sections, the walls make an idyllic walking or cycling loop.

☆☆ Festivals & Events

Il Palio HORSE RACING
(www.paliodiferrara.it) On the last Sunday of May each year, the eight *contrade* (districts) of Ferrara compete in a horse race that momentarily turns Piazza Ariostea into medieval bedlam. Claimed to be the oldest race of its kind in Italy, the first official competition was held in 1279.

Buskers' Festival MUSIC
(www.ferrarabuskers.com) Ferrara's streets are filled with musicians in late August during this music festival.

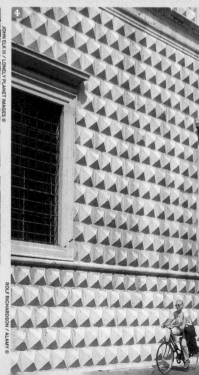

1. **Piazza Maggiore (p413), Bologna**
Palazzo del Podestà (pictured, left) and Palazzo dei Banchi (pictured, right) both flank this square.

2. **Palazzo Comunale (p413), Bologna**
This palace is also known also as Palazzo D'Accursio after its original resident, Francesco D'Accursio.